POLITICAL PARTIES AND NATIONAL
INTEGRATION IN TROPICAL AFRICA

Published under the auspices of the African Studies Center
University of California, Los Angeles

POLITICAL PARTIES
AND
NATIONAL INTEGRATION
IN
TROPICAL AFRICA

EDITED BY JAMES S. COLEMAN
AND CARL G. ROSBERG, JR.

University of California Press
BERKELEY, LOS ANGELES, AND LONDON

1970

University of California Press
Berkeley and Los Angeles
University of California Press, Ltd.
London, England
© 1964 by The Regents of the University of California
Third Printing, 1970
Standard Book Number 520-00253-9
Library of Congress Catalog Card No. 64-19636
Designed by Ward Ritchie
Printed in the United States of America

PREFACE

The purpose of this symposium is to further our understanding of politics and political development in contemporary Tropical Africa. Our focus is upon political parties and their role in national integration. It has been and remains our assumption that political parties are the most crucial political structures shaping the new African polities, and that the crisis of national integration is the major hurdle in nation building. For enhanced understanding of both the unique and the generic aspects of these phenomena and problems we need not only studies in depth of party development in individual countries, but also comparisons among representative samples of different patterns of party development. It is our hope that this symposium makes a modest contribution to these goals.

All books on the African political scene are plagued by the problem of comprehensiveness. Although we were much tempted by the suggestion of one of the contributors that we entitle the symposium "African Parties: Apter to Zolberg," we felt—and we believe our colleagues concur—that this would be a bit too pretentious. We particularly regret the omission of studies of party development in the sixteen other states of Tropical Africa not specifically covered herein. It has not been our intention, however, to be exhaustive. We believe that the twelve studies of different countries which are included, coupled with the four analytical studies of selected groups, illuminate the main patterns of party development as well as the essential aspects of the relationship between political groups and the nation-building process in contemporary Tropical Africa.

A collaborative volume inevitably raises the question of collective responsibility. As editors, we alone are responsible for soliciting the individual articles that make up the symposium; our only criterion in choosing contributors was a genuine respect for their intellectual honesty and scholarly integrity. We do not necessarily agree with all that they have written, nor does each of them necessarily find himself in agreement with our concluding essay or with other contributors. Each author is solely responsible for his own essay, and for his own essay alone; we alone are accountable for the conclusions. Once this fact is emphasized, we personally welcome a diversity of interpretations regarding African political development.

Because the political scene in Africa changes so rapidly, several contributors have added postscripts to their essays to cover recent events.

We acknowledge, with much gratitude, support received from the Human Environments in Middle Africa Project of the National Academy of Sciences, and from the Carnegie Corporation of New York. We also appreciate the assistance we have received from the African Studies Center, University of California, Los Angeles; the Institute of International Studies, University of California, Berkeley; and the Center for Advanced Study in the Behavioral Sciences, Stanford. Needless to say, none of these institutions is responsible for the views expressed or the judgments made in the symposium.

We are particularly grateful to several persons who have contributed so much to the completion and the publication of this volume. Thanks are owing to Professor Paul J. Bohannan, former director of the Human Environments in Middle Africa Project of the National Academy of Sciences, and to Robert Zachary of the University of California Press, for their encouragement and patience. We are greatly indebted to Dr. Gulgun Karal for her splendid assistance in the final stages of editing, and for reading the proofs and preparing the index, and to Mrs. Ailene Benson for her expert final typing of the manuscript. Above all we wish to express our very special thanks to Dr. Grace Stimson of the editorial staff of the University of California Press, not only for her meticulous final editing of the entire work, but also for her forbearance and superb coöperation.

J. S. C.
C. G. R., Jr.

CONTRIBUTORS

DAVID E. APTER, born in New York City in 1924, is professor of political science at the University of California, Berkeley, where he is also associate director of the Institute of International Studies. He was formerly associate professor of political science and executive secretary for the Committee for the Comparative Study of New Nations at the University of Chicago. He has done extensive research in Africa and Europe and has lectured at the Universities of Warsaw, Ghana, and Elisabethville. He was a Fellow of the Center for Advanced Study in the Behavioral Sciences in 1958–59. Among his publications are *The Gold Coast in Transition* (revised in April, 1963, as *Ghana in Transition*); *The Political Kingdom in Uganda; Comparative Politics: A Reader* (with Harry Eckstein); and the forthcoming *Ideology and Discontent* and *The Politics of Modernization.*

ELLIOT J. BERG, born in New York City in 1927, is assistant professor of economics at Harvard University and research associate at the Harvard Center for International Affairs. He was a Fellow of the Ford Foundation in Africa in 1957–1959. His major research interests are comparative industrial relations and problems of African economic development. Among his publications are "French West Africa," in W. Galenson, ed., *Labor and Economic Development;* "Backward Sloping Labor Supply Functions in Dual Economies: The Africa Case," in *Quarterly Journal of Economics;* and "Real Income Trends in West Africa, 1939–1960," in M. J. Herskovits and M. Harwitz, eds., *Economic Transition in Africa.*

JEFFREY BUTLER, born in Cradock, Cape Province, South Africa, in 1922, has been a research associate in government and history in the African Studies Program at Boston University since 1957. After teaching in South Africa, he went to Oxford in 1950, where he stayed as student and tutor until 1957, when he moved to Boston. He has written on contemporary South African politics and on British policy. At present he is engaged on a study of the debate among British Liberals on South African issues at the end of the nineteenth century.

A. A. CASTAGNO, JR., born in Hartford, Connecticut, in 1920, is associate professor of political science at Queens College of the City University of

New York. He studied at the former Colonial Institute of the University of Florence (on a Fulbright grant) in 1949–50. His field work in Africa stressed Somalia with some attention to Northeast and East African territories (Ford Foundation grant, 1956–1958, and Social Science Research Council grant, summer, 1962). He has been visiting associate professor at Columbia University and New York University. His works include *Somalia* (Carnegie Endowment for International Peace) and a number of articles and monographs on the Horn of Africa. His present research is concerned with ethnicity and politics in developing areas.

VICTOR D. DU BOIS was born in Chicago in 1932. He spent 1959–60 in Guinea doing field research for his doctorate in politics at Princeton University, which he received in 1962. He is currently African correspondent of the American Universities Field Staff and author of numerous articles on political development in the former French territories of sub-Saharan Africa.

WILLIAM J. FOLTZ, born in Mt. Vernon, New York, in 1936, is assistant professor of political science at Yale University. He spent 1960–61 in West Africa on a Ford Foundation grant. His major research interests have been the French-speaking areas of Africa and the problems of organizing large-scale political communities. He is coeditor of *Nation-Building*.

WILLIAM JOHN HANNA, born in Cleveland, Ohio, in 1931, is assistant professor in the Department of Political Science and the African Studies Center at Michigan State University. He has had research affiliations with the African Studies Center, University of California, Los Angeles, and the Institute of African Studies, University of Ibadan. He conducted research in Africa in 1960 and 1963. His primary teaching and research interests include political recruitment, the psychoanalytic interpretation of political behavior, urban African politics, and field research procedures in Africa. He is editor of a forthcoming volume, *Independent Black Africa: The Politics of Freedom*.

THOMAS HODGKIN, born in Oxford, England, in 1910, is at present director of the Institute of African Studies of the University of Ghana, and an Affiliate Fellow of the Institute of Islamic Studies, McGill University, Montreal. He has been traveling extensively in Africa since 1947. His main fields of interest are African history and politics, about which he has written extensively in a variety of journals, including, in particular, *West Africa*. In addition to many articles in scholarly publications, he has written three books: *Nationalism in Colonial Africa; Nigerian Perspectives;* and *African Political Parties*.

Martin Kilson, born in East Rutherford, New Jersey, in 1931, is lecturer on government at Harvard University and research associate at the Harvard Center for International Affairs. He spent 1959–1961 in West Africa on a Ford Foundation research fellowship, and did research in West Africa in the summer of 1962 under a grant from the Harvard Center for International Affairs. He teaches courses on African political institutions, and is the author of the forthcoming volume, *Political Change in a West African State.*

Rene Lemarchand, born in Nantes, France, in 1932, is assistant professor of political science at the University of Florida. He spent part of the year 1960–61 as a teaching assistant in the Faculty of Law at Lovanium University, Leopoldville. Subsequently he was on the research staff of the Institut de Sociologie Solvay in Brussels. His special area of interest is African studies, with particular reference to the former Belgian Congo and the former trust territory of Ruanda-Urundi. He is the author of numerous articles in various academic journals, including the *American Political Science Review, Africa,* and the *Revue de l'Institut de Sociologie.*

Victor T. Le Vine, born in Berlin in 1928, is assistant professor of political science at Washington University, St. Louis. He has held fellowships from the Ford Foundation and the Haynes Foundation, and has traveled extensively and done field research in West Africa. His primary interest, in research and teaching, has been comparative and international politics. He was book review editor of the *American Political Science Review,* and he has published articles in several professional journals. He contributed chapters to *The Educated African* and *Five African States,* and is the author of *Cameroun: From Mandate to Independence.*

J. Gus Liebenow, born in Berwyn, Illinois, in 1925, is associate professor of government and director of the African Studies Program at Indiana University. He has traveled extensively in Europe, Asia, and Latin America, and has spent more than three years in East, West, and South Africa. He has received fellowships from the Ford Foundation, the Social Science Research Council, Harvard University, the University of Illinois, the University of Texas, and Indiana University. His primary fields of research are African politics and political theory. He has published widely in journals in political science and African studies, and is the contributor to six major volumes on African affairs and international politics.

Peter C. Lloyd, born in Bournemouth, England, in 1927, is senior lecturer in sociology at the University of Ibadan where he has been responsible for developing the teaching of sociology and social anthropology since 1959. The ten preceding years were spent in research, principally among the Yoruba people of western Nigeria. He has also traveled widely throughout Africa. His primary field of interest is the political systems of the traditional African kingdoms. He is the author of *Yoruba Land Law* and numerous articles on the Yoruba and the Itsekiri.

MICHAEL F. LOFCHIE, born in Boston, Massachusetts, in 1936, is assistant professor of political science at the University of California, Los Angeles. He has spent eighteen months in Zanzibar on a grant from the Foreign Area Fellowship Program and is currently preparing a dissertation on "Constitutional Change and Political Parties in Zanzibar." His article, "Party Conflict in Zanzibar," has been published in the *Journal of Modern African Studies.*

RUTH SCHACHTER MORGENTHAU, born in Vienna, Austria, in 1931, is associate professor of politics at Brandeis University, and former research associate, African Studies Program, Boston University. She has held a Fulbright scholarship, a studentship at Nuffield College, Oxford, and a Rockefeller Foundation grant (1963–64). In addition to various monographs and articles on West Africa and African political thought contributed to scholarly journals, she has written *Political Parties in French-speaking West Africa,* and (with Thomas Hodgkin)*French-speaking West Africa in Transition.*

RICHARD L. SKLAR, born in New York City in 1930, is assistant professor of politics at Brandeis University and temporary lecturer in government at the University of Ibadan, Nigeria. He has studied politics in Nigeria under the auspices of the Ford Foundation Foreign Area Fellowship Program, and he is the author of *Nigerian Political Parties: Power in an Emergent African Nation.*

IMMANUEL WALLERSTEIN, born in New York City in 1930, is associate professor of sociology, a member of the Program of Studies on Africa, and chairman of the University Seminar on Africa at Columbia University. In 1955–1957 he held a Ford Foundation African Training Fellowship. He has traveled widely in Africa. His primary fields of interest are social change and political sociology. His major publications are *Africa: The Politics of Independence* and *The Road to Independence: Ghana and the Ivory Coast.*

C. S. WHITAKER, JR., born in Pittsburgh, Pennsylvania, in 1935, is assistant professor of political science at the University of California, Los Angeles. He was formerly lecturer in politics at Princeton University.

In 1959–60 he was in Nigeria under a Social Science Research Council grant. His research has focused on the influence of traditional political systems on modern government and politics in Africa. He is the author of several articles on aspects of African politics and is presently preparing a book entitled *The Politics of Tradition: A Study of Continuity and Change in Northern Nigeria.*

ARISTIDE R. ZOLBERG, born in Brussels, Belgium, in 1931, is assistant professor of political science and a member of the Committee for the Comparative Study of New Nations at the University of Chicago. He has taught at the University of Wisconsin. In 1958–59 he held a Ford Foundation Foreign Area Training Fellowship. Since completing *One-Party Government in the Ivory Coast* (1963), he has been engaged in a comparative analysis of political regimes in West Africa and has begun research on the politics of modernization.

CONTENTS

INTRODUCTION

The major focus of this study is upon political parties. We are also concerned with other types of politically relevant aggregates and associations, particularly as they relate to political parties, that is, with political groups in general. We are not interested in political groups as such, although the systematic study and comparison of the internal structure and the dynamics of groups, as universes unto themselves, would be a worthy intellectual excercise. Rather, our particular interest, and one that we endeavor to emphasize in this symposium, is the role of political parties and other groups in the functioning and the development of the new African societies and the political systems of which they are a part. As already noted, it is our contention—emphatically confirmed, we believe, by the studies presented here—that at this stage of Africa's development political parties not only illuminate most clearly the nature of African politics, but also are important determinants of the unfolding African political scene.

In affirming the primacy and the centrality of parties in African politics, we are at once confronted with the issue of the group approach to politics. We are not seeking to prove, with data drawn from a new and exotic milieu, the proposition of Arthur Bentley and others that everywhere groups are the most relevant phenomena to study in politics. Whatever is valid in the group approach to politics elsewhere is also valid for African politics, and we do not here wish to encumber the argument with this particular issue.[1] Our contention, rather, is based essentially on the highly determinative role political groups have been allowed or compelled to assume in contemporary Africa because of the nature of the new societies in which they function.

In the relatively stabilized national societies of more highly developed countries, considerable attention and weight must be given to other factors in the political process, and, in particular, to the structure and the functioning of formal political institutions and to the socializing and constraining influence of national cultures. In the new states of Tropical

---

[1] See Arthur F. Bentley, *The Process of Government* (Chicago: University of Chicago Press, 1908); David B. Truman, *The Governmental Process* (New York: Knopf, 1951); Earl Latham, *The Group Basis of Politics* (Ithaca: Cornell University Press, 1952); and Robert T. Golembiewski, "The Group Basis of Politics: Notes on Analysis and Development," *American Political Science Review*, LIV (Dec., 1960), 962–971.

1

Africa with which we are concerned, however, there is an almost complete institutional vacuum at the central, national level. The "national" representative institutions set up hastily during the terminal colonial period have tended, after independence, to remain fragile and nonfunctional in the processes of government. Moreover, in the new states, the politically relevant cultures are not those of the new nations the state builders are seeking to create; rather, they are those of the hundreds of heterogeneous ethnic communities and tribal societies arbitrarily bunched together within the artificial boundaries imposed during the colonial period. Under these circumstances of institutional fragility and the absence of national cultural traditions, power within the new states has passed, by default, into the hands of the leaders of organized groups.

The study of the character and the development of African political groups also offers a particularly inviting opportunity for advancement in theory regarding the origin and evolution of groups. Over a brief time span one can study the birth and the developmental patterns of groups with special reference to their relationship to traditional social organization, ethnic patterns, social structure, stratification, colonial policies and institutions, and a variety of situational factors. In Tropical Africa the opportunity to discern regularities and general patterns is enormously enhanced because there is a large number of sovereign political entities which have shared a fairly common historical experience in terms of the character and the brevity of external influences and of the sequence and the timing of group formation and evolution. Indeed, it is this very multiplicity of geographically contiguous case studies which has led many social scientists to regard Tropical Africa as an ideal laboratory for developmental analysis.

The term "group" may be, and is, used in a multitude of ways; indeed, any aggregate of persons, whether formally associated or not, constitutes a group. For our purposes, however, only three general types of groups need be distinguished: (1) political parties, (2) interest associations, and (3) categoric groups. Political parties are associations formally organized with the explicit and declared purpose of acquiring and/or maintaining legal control, either singly or in coalition or electoral competition with other similar associations, over the personnel and the policy of the government of an actual or prospective sovereign state. Interest associations are formally organized associations that seek to protect or to further the consciously shared interests of their members—which may be specific (e.g., occupational or professional; ideal or material), or general (e.g., communal, tribal, racial, etc.)—by making demands through or upon the government or the political party or parties controlling the government. Categoric groups are demographic categories (chiefs, students, clerks, teachers, lawyers, and so forth) in which the persons con-

cerned may or may not share a common outlook or organize a formal association to assert and protect their presumptively common interests.[2] The
dividing line among these various types is not sharp and clear; indeed,
depending upon the circumstances and the phase of political development, some aggregates would quite properly fall into any one of or all
these categories. Although our central focus here is upon African political
parties, we do have a secondary concern with how such parties are related, or seek to relate themselves, to other formally organized aggregates
(i.e., interest associations), as well as to the various elements in the population (i.e., categoric groups), which exert an actual or potential influence
upon political life, or are otherwise politically relevant.

The variant patterns of genesis, birth, and evolution of political
parties in Tropical Africa have elsewhere been described and extensively
analyzed by Thomas Hodgkin,[3] and are further illuminated by the studies
on twelve countries and by Immanuel Wallerstein's essay on associations
in this symposium. In general it may be said that African parties are the
organizational end product of the massive social and economic changes
of the colonial era, including, in particular, the appearance of new assertive social groups and claimant elites; the provocations, frustrations, and
challenges of alien rule; and the formation of a variety of interest associations, protest groups, and nationalist movements directed first toward the
amelioration of specific grievances and later toward the displacement of
the colonial power by independent African governments. As noted elsewhere, however, formal political parties in the narrow sense defined
herein did not appear until constitutional reforms were introduced "providing for (1) the devolution by the imperial government of a sufficiently
meaningful and *attractive* measure of power to induce or to provoke nationalist leaders to convert their movements into political parties and (2)
the introduction or refinement of institutions and procedures, such as an
electoral system, which would make it technically possible for parties to
seek power constitutionally." [4] The governing party or parties in most
new states in Africa are the ones brought to power under institutional

---

[2] For a discussion of the concept "categoric group" see Truman, *op. cit.*, p. 23.

[3] *Nationalism in Colonial Africa* (London: Frederick Muller, 1956), and *African Political Parties* (Penguin Books, 1961).

[4] James S. Coleman, "The Emergence of African Political Parties," in C. Grove Haines ,ed *Africa Today* (Baltimore: Johns Hopkins Press, 1955), pp. 234–235. The definition of a party in terms of electoral competition, and the notion of a "one-party system," create a host of conceptual problems. By definition a party is a "part"; both competition and the concept of system imply the existence of more than one part. Because our main emphasis here is upon the genetic and developmental aspects of parties—that is, our focus is diachronic rather than synchronic—we will not attempt to resolve these admittedly serious conceptual ambiguities. The immediate point is that, with few exceptions, African political parties initially emerged through electoral competition. Their subsequent transformation from political parties in this more conventional sense is one of the main concerns of this book.

arrangements established during the terminal stages of colonial rule. Some of these were lineal descendants of already existent political organizations; others were called into being literally "from scratch," by competing elites confronting their first election and the prospect of power. In any event, whatever their origin, they are all products of the colonial period.

All but a few of Tropical Africa's new states have single-party political systems, or systems where one party is dominant, and everywhere the trend is toward the establishment of one or the other of these two types. So striking and uniformly manifest is this phenomenon that a considerable number of analytical studies have already appeared on the subject.[5] Although single-party regimes were fairly well established in several countries before independence (e.g., Mali, Guinea, the Ivory Coast, and Tanganyika), the usual pattern in Africa has been the progressive consolidation of one-party dominance after independence. The many factors helping to explain this general trend, as well as the character of the consolidation process, will be critically examined in the conclusions. Our immediate concern here is to identify the main differentiae by which the variant manifestations of the African one-party syndrome may be distinguished.

The development of a useful scheme of classification of African one-party systems is difficult, for a variety of reasons. One is their very brief existence, which suggests, indeed, that one may call them "systems" only in a tentative and qualified sense. Another reason is the extreme fluidity and the dynamic change characteristic of the African political scene; parties and party systems are still in the process of being consolidated and stabilized. A third reason is the presence of the same "inexhaustible mixture" of differentiating elements which the late Sigmund Neumann lamented in his own efforts to develop a typology in his classic *Modern Political Parties.* Parties that might cluster together on the basis of shared organizational features are found poles apart in terms of their ideology or of their relationship to traditionalism. Others that might fall into a common category in terms of the total monopoly they have established over nonparty associations may be widely separated on such important counts as the degree of mass participation or of involvement in the political process. As in all efforts to classify complex phenomena, one confronts

---

[5] See especially Hodgkin, *African Political Parties;* Madeira Keita, "Le Parti unique en Afrique," *Présence Africaine,* no. 30 (Feb.–March, 1960), 3–24; Martin L. Kilson, "Authoritarian and Single-Party Tendencies in African Politics," *World Politics,* XV (Jan., 1963), 262–294; C. H. Moore, "The National Party: A Tentative Model," in *Public Policy* (Cambridge: Harvard University Press, 1960); Ruth Schachter, "Single Party Systems in West Africa," *American Political Science Review,* LV (June, 1961), 294–307; Francis X. Sutton, "Authority and Authoritarianism in the New Africa," *Journal of International Affairs,* XV, no. 1 (1961), 7–17; and Rupert Emerson, *Political Modernization: The Single-Party System,* University of Denver Monograph Series in World Affairs, No. 1 (Denver, 1964).

the dilemma that the units to be classified either are ultimately *sui generis* or are not consistently and meaningfully distinguishable for analytical purposes. Here we will draw a distinction between two general tendencies in uniparty or one-party-dominant states, (1) the "pragmatic-pluralistic" pattern, and (2) the "revolutionary-centralizing" trend.

Table 1

TENDENCIES AMONG UNIPARTY AND ONE-PARTY-DOMINANT AFRICAN STATES

Differentiating factor	Pragmatic-pluralistic pattern	Revolutionary-centralizing trend
I. IDEOLOGY		
A. Degree of ideological preoccupation, declamation, and rationalization	Limited preoccupation	Heavy preoccupation; constant and compulsive
B. Scope, depth, and tempo of modernization objectives	Adaptive; aggregative of a tolerated but controlled pluralism	Revolutionary, transformative, antitraditional
C. Degree of insistence upon and commitment to consummation of African nationalist objectives		
1. Neutralism	Pragmatic; formally neutralist but tolerant regarding continued unbalanced dependence on West	"Positive neutralism"
2. Pan-African unity	Pragmatic, functional coöperation	Political unification
3. Tempo and degree of decolonization and "Africanization"	Pragmatic	Immediate and total
II. POPULAR PARTICIPATION		
A. Degree of political mobilization and expected popular commitment	Partial/intermittent	High/constant
B. Mode of individual participation	Direct and indirect	Direct only between individual and party-state
III. ORGANIZATIONAL ASPECTS		
A. Degree of intraparty hierarchism, centralism, and discipline	Variable; hierarchical and centralized by tolerated and controlled pluralism	High; monolithic; concentration; conformity sanction severe
B. Degree of associational monopoly and fusion	Variable; looser relationship	High/total monopoly and fusion
C. Degree of party-government assimilation	Limited assimilation	Total assimilation

The differentiae set forth in table 1 illuminate these two tendencies and the attributes of each. The dominant parties in African states representative of the revolutionary-centralizing trend are heavily and compulsively preoccupied with ideology, the content of which is programmatic and transformative regarding the socioeconomic modernization of contemporary African society, and militantly neutralist, Pan-Africanist, and nationalistic regarding relationships with other African states and with the external world. They tend also to be ultrapopulistic and egalitarian, with heavy stress upon direct commitment to and participation in the party and the state. Organizationally the parties tend to be monolithic and strongly centralized, achieving a monopoly over—frequently, indeed, a complete fusion with—all other associations, as well as an assimilation of party and governmental structures throughout the society. In contrast, leaders of the dominant parties of the pragmatic-pluralistic type place far less emphasis upon ideology; they are far less concerned over the persistence of traditional elites and structures within their societies and over continued dependence upon the former colonial power. The degree of popular mobilization and commitment is substantially less than in revolutionary-centralizing states, and although unitary and hierarchical, the pragmatic-pluralistic states permit a looser relationship between the party and other associations, in a climate of "tolerated but controlled pluralism." One or the other of the foregoing two tendencies is manifest in all African uniparty or one-party-dominant states.

The first seven papers in Part I of this symposium are intended to illuminate the one-party trend in contemporary Africa. We have selected Senegal, the Ivory Coast, Sierra Leone, and the Cameroun as case studies to illustrate the variant types of parties found within the pragmatic-pluralistic pattern, and Guinea and Mali on the one hand, and Ghana on the other, to represent two different strands in the revolutionary-centralizing trend. Although significant variations among these several party systems will be vividly evident to the reader, it is in point here to note that Senegal and the Ivory Coast, largely because of their historic link with France and their association in the former Federation of French West Africa, are distinguishable from Sierra Leone and the Cameroun. One reason for the distinction is that traditional forces, although existent and tolerated in varying degrees, have played a somewhat less crucial role in the one-party-dominant systems of government in Senegal and the Ivory Coast than they have in Sierra Leone and the Cameroun. It is important to make this distinction because of the fairly common belief that traditionalism in Africa is largely irrelevant in modern power structures, particularly in one-party-dominant modernizing states. Similarly, there are many significant differences between Guinea and Mali— the closest approximations to the pure party-state—and Ghana. One of the most striking contrasts has been between the puritanical, organization-centered collegial-leadership aspects of the ideology of the Parti Démocratique de Guinée and the Union Soudanaise of Mali, and the eclecticism and the personalism of leadership and symbols in the ideology of President Kwame Nkrumah and the Convention People's Party of Ghana. These and other differences will be discussed at greater length in the conclusions.

A problem confronted by one-party-dominant regimes of both tendencies is how to establish an effective party relationship with nonparty groups, that is, with interest associations and politically relevant categoric groups. The relationship desired is one that ensures that the activities of such groups are congruent with and supportive of the modernization objectives of the regime. The essence of the problem has been to define the degree and the form of control by the dominant party over all other types of group activity. In the revolutionary-centralizing states the tendency has been to make the entire associational infrastructure an integral part of the monolithic party structure; in the pragmatic-pluralistic states a somewhat looser type of relationship has been allowed to develop or to exist. The character of nonparty groups which are the objects of control is analyzed in papers 8 through 11. In the first of these Immanuel Wallerstein surveys the development of associations in Tropical Africa with special reference to their relationship to political parties and to politics. This is followed by the Berg and Butler paper on the political role of trade unions, which are perhaps the most visible and the most politically salient associations to emerge in the modern sector of the new African societies. Both essays point up the special character of interests in African societies, and the relationship of interest associations to political parties in the new states.

Knowledge regarding African interest associations and their relationship to parties is vital not only to an understanding of African politics, but also to meaningful comparisons of African political parties with parties elsewhere. In the developed industrial countries of the West, interest associations tend predominantly to be functionally specific in character; that is, they express, or articulate, the specific interests and demands of a particular professional, occupational, economic, or other single-purpose interest group. Thus they reflect the division of labor, the occupational specialization, the structural differentiation, the social mobility, and the weakening of ties of kinship and locality characteristic of the modern industrial syndrome. One of the major functions of political parties in a competitive democratic system is to aggregate the myriad interests that have been articulated and made politically manifest by interest associations. Given the facts that industrialization has hardly commenced in Africa, that ties of kinship and locality are still transcendent for the vast bulk of the population, and that competitive party systems have been displaced by uniparty and one-party-dominant states, the functions, and hence the performance, of interest associations and of political parties are bound to be markedly different.

There are, of course, many types of politically relevant aggregates or categories in a population which are not formally organized into associations. Some may have only presumptively common interests, as a result of a shared situation or status in society at a given phase of its development. Politically, they may have only latent or potential importance. Nevertheless, in every society there are some nonassociational aggregates which have more political relevance than others. In some societies, army officers may constitute such a group; in others, it may be religious leaders; in still others, an unorganized peasant class. For this symposium we have selected traditional rulers and university students (papers 10 and 11) as two of the more politically relevant categoric groups in the developing African states. This selection is based on the rationale that a not insignificant dimension of the problem of nation building and national integration confronted by the incumbent party elites is the dual challenge posed by traditional elites, who possess residual influence among the mass of the population, and by university students, who, in varying degrees, envisage themselves as the governing elites of the future. In the modernization and nation-building processes, the residual power of traditional elites, if obstructive and divisive, must be either neutralized or extinguished, or, if instrumentally supportive, must be coöpted and integrated. As key elements in the claimant third-generation "successor" elite, and as the most articulate and potentially powerful elements in the present political opposition, university students have yet to find their energies absorbed, and their career ambitions realized, in the national parties controlling the present political systems. The success with which the present party elites cope with this dual challenge will be a major factor in the political stabilization of the new states.

Just as the one-party trend is the most striking feature of the political structure of the new African states, so the problems of integration are the major issues and obstacles in the task of nation building, which is itself the primary preoccupation of the leadership of the new states. Parties are destined, because of their central importance, to play a determinative role in the resolution of, or in the failure to solve, the problems of integration. In Part II of this symposium we have endeavored to illuminate the role of parties within the context of two different problems of national integration.

The concept of "national integration" has a variety of meanings which are not always clearly identified. For our purposes *national* integration is regarded as a broad subsuming process, whose two major dimensions are (1) *political* integration, which refers to the progressive bridging of the elite-mass gap on the vertical plane in the course of developing an integrated political process and a participant political community, and (2) *territorial* integration, which refers to the progressive reduction of cultural and regional tensions and discontinuities on the horizontal plane in the process of creating a homogeneous territorial political community.[6] For both processes there is a wide range of empirical problem situations in contemporary Africa. The problem of political integration (that is, closure of the elite-mass gap) in new states whose political elite is of indigenous origin—however sharply differentiated from the mass in terms of education and life styles—is markedly different from the problem in states whose political elite is an alien ethnic or cultural minority. Following M. G. Smith, we will reserve the term "plural societies" for the latter.[7] Similarly, the problem of territorial integration in those states emerging from unitary colonial administrative systems is strikingly different in magnitude from the same problem in states where an effort is being made to create large-scale federations or supraterritorial unions transcending former colonial or administrative entities. In Part II of this symposium we endeavor to illuminate the role of parties in the two most difficult types of the foregoing problem situations: (1) the political integration of cultural communities long separated by a subordinate-superordinate relationship of minority domination in Africa's historic oligarchic states (i.e., plural societies); and (2) the territorial integration of diverse cultural groups and former political or administrative entities in the process of expansion in political scale incident to the creation of large-scale federations and unions.

The problem of political integration is widespread in contemporary Africa, because historically the majority of the population has been dominated by a culturally, and frequently racially, differentiated minority. Such situations are found at all levels in African societies: in cities (for example, the historically dominant position of the Creoles in Freetown, or of the coastal Swahili in Dar es Salaam), in sections or regions of a coun-

---

[6] These definitions differ from those used in other studies of integration and nation building. Cf. Ernst B. Haas, *The Uniting of Europe* (Stanford: Stanford University Press, 1958), p. 16: "Political integration is the process whereby political actors in several distinct national settings are persuaded to shift their loyalties, expectations and political activities toward a new centre, whose institutions possess or demand jurisdiction over the pre-existing national states." Also see Karl W. Deutsch and William J. Foltz, eds., *Nation-Building* (New York: Atherton Press, 1963), pp. 6 ff.

[7] M. G. Smith, "Social and Cultural Pluralism," *Annals of the New York Academy of Sciences*, vol. 83, art. 5 (Jan. 20, 1960), pp. 763–777. Smith argues for a much narrower definition of a plural society than does J. S. Furnivall, who coined the term. For Smith a plural society is not only culturally heterogeneous (in Furnivall's sense), but is also one in which incompatible institutional systems coexist, with one cultural section exercising a monopoly of power.

try (for example, in Fulani oligarchies in northern Nigeria and in Hima and Bito oligarchies in the interlacustrine kingdoms of East Africa), and in entire countries (for example, Ethiopia, Liberia, European-dominated Southern Rhodesia and South Africa, and, until recently, Zanzibar and Rwanda). European colonial policies operated to perpetuate such situations in many instances, most pronouncedly in northern Nigeria, in former Ruanda-Urundi, and in the territories of European settlement in southern Africa. In other instances the colonial power tolerated, or even assisted in, the destruction of these superordinate-subordinate relationships, or, at least, did not allow them to become generalized and institutionalized in the modern territorial political systems (for example, the status reversal that colonialism facilitated in the relationship between the once culturally dominant Creole minority and the protectorate peoples of Sierra Leone, between the minority of *citoyens* of the *quatre communes* of Dakar and its environs and the mass of Senegalese in the hinterland, and between the culturally dominant Baganda and the majority of the people in modern Uganda). The collapse of this form of domination was frequently initiated (most dramatically in respect to the dominant Batutsi and the Bahutu mass of Rwanda) by the simple innovation of universal suffrage in the terminal stages of colonialism as part of the frantic efforts of colonial governments to create a democratic order before the transfer of power to new governing elites. Such innovations were a response, in part at least, to the ultrademocratic demands of the leaders of popular nationalist movements. In balance, however, it has been and will be the fundamental egalitarianism, together with the inexorable leveling impact, of modernity itself which has challenged these situations and, ultimately, will probably ensure either their extinction or a revolutionary status reversal.

In this symposium we are particularly concerned with the role of political parties in those historic oligarchic situations of minority domination in Tropical Africa which embrace whole political systems. Such situations have usually given rise to communal parties, organized by the dominant minority seeking to maintain its position or by the dominated mass asserting the right to participate in, or itself to dominate, the system. Two contrasting studies, on Liberia and Zanzibar, are presented in papers 12 and 13 to illuminate the variant ways in which such situations have developed and are being altered, and the role of parties in this process. Although there are many interesting differences between these two countries, the most significant concerns colonial experience; Liberia has had none, whereas Zanzibar has been until recently a British dependency. Although these two studies shed much light on the problem of vertical integration in Tropical Africa, their relevance to the most acute manifestation of this problem in the modern world, in Southern Rhodesia and

South Africa, is, unfortunately, very limited. These last redoubts of un-assimilable white oligarchies, determined through superior might to preserve indefinitely their domination over colored majorities, must be considered as a separate and distinct phenomenon beyond both the scope and the area focus of this study.

The second major problem of integration we have selected for consideration is horizontal in character. It arises from the effort to form large-scale federations or unions embracing politico-administrative systems which previously had, or have since acquired, considerable autonomy, or, in some instances, even sovereignty, and it is, of course, but one aspect of the larger problem of territorial integration confronted by all the states of Tropical Africa. Distinctive of the particular segment of the problem upon which we focus are the largeness of or the expansion in scale, and the existence before federation or union of geographical entities which had acquired a sort of personality or a symbolism, vested interests, and their own set of political groups. It is a problem that lies at the heart of two of the most powerful but contradictory political forces at work in contemporary Africa: the drive to overcome the disabilities of fragmentation through larger union, and the even more powerful tendency toward preservation and consolidation of the independent sovereign statehood of each of the nearly fifty former colonial entities.

The most striking manifestations of this second problem of integration are illustrated by the final three studies in this volume, on the Somali Republic, the Congo (Leopoldville), and Nigeria. The Somali Republic was created through the union of the former Trust Territory of Somalia under Italian Administration and former British Somaliland. It is one of the few examples in Africa of an apparently successful voluntary integration of two previously separate colonial entities. The others are the union of former British Togoland and the Gold Coast to form modern Ghana, the federation of the former southern British Cameroons and the French Cameroun, and the integration of the former northern British Cameroons into the Northern Region of Nigeria. The unification of Ethiopia and Eritrea and the abortive Mali Federation are not in the same category. The former can hardly be called a voluntary union, and the Mali Federation (made up of the present republics of Senegal and Mali) collapsed, for reasons discussed in the papers on Senegal and Mali in Part I, after two months of turbulent and precarious existence. The Somali Republic and the Cameroun are the only examples of the integration of two colonial territories, each of which had been administered by a different European power. The former stands alone, however, in two respects: (1) the peoples of the two entities being integrated share a common (i.e., Somali) culture and language; (2) political groups have tended to be Pan-Somali, rather than territorial, in character.

The development of political groups in the Federation of the Congo (Leopoldville) and in the Federation of Nigeria, Tropical Africa's two most populous and complex countries, strikingly illuminates the problems of integration involved in the formation and the maintenance of large-scale federations. Although markedly different in ethnic composition and colonial experience, they both illustrate the difficulties of integration in federal systems where the center of gravity and the focus of political-group activity remain at the subsystem (i.e., regional or provincial) level, and where national governments are at best no more than loose coalitions.

PART 1

THE ONE-PARTY TENDENCY

The Pragmatic-Pluralistic Pattern

1. SENEGAL

By William J. Foltz

INTRODUCTION

Political life in Senegal * has long had a pluralistic character. In part this character is a result of the influence of European forms of political organization and of the long participation of Senegalese politicians in French national politics. Even more it stems from a changing Senegalese society, marked by antagonisms or conflicts between the old urbanized population and the rural and newly urbanized groups; between independent traders and advocates of centralized economic planning; between religious and ethnic groups; and, most important, between differing regional and local interests. In Senegal these conflicting interests are usually incarnated in leaders who either participate directly in politics or use their economic, religious, or social influence to sway political decisions. To hold power in Senegal, a political party must amalgamate these opposing interests by distributing rewards to groups or to group leaders, or by championing an issue on which many groups can unite.

One political party, the Union Progressiste Sénégalaise (UPS), today controls the Senegalese government. In recent elections the UPS won all posts in the National Assembly and in regional and municipal councils, and the large majority of Africans holding important positions in the civil service are UPS members. Under the leadership of Léopold Senghor and Mamadou Dia, the party has absorbed most of its early rivals, and is supported by a wide variety of interests. Under UPS direction the Senegalese government has maintained close economic and political relations with France and has begun a program of gradual, planned economic development.

The Parti du Regroupement Africain–Sénégal (PRA-Sénégal), while still technically a legal party, is subject to considerable governmental harassment. It has not presented electoral lists since 1959. None of its members hold political office. The PRA-Sénégal seeks to mobilize popular support behind a nationalist policy of rapid economic and social change at home and strong anticolonialism in foreign affairs.

* Field research for this paper was made possible by a Ford Foundation Foreign Area Training Fellowship. I wish to thank Immanuel Wallerstein for commenting on an earlier draft, but I alone am responsible for all statements of fact and interpretation.

This paper was completed before the elimination of Mamadou Dia, the Senegalese prime minister, in December, 1962. I have added a short analysis of the effects of this change at the end of the paper.

The Parti Africain de l'Indépendance (PAI), though outlawed since August, 1960, continues to operate clandestinely. The PAI is an avowedly revolutionary Marxist organization calling for the establishment, by violence if necessary, of a workers' and peasants' dictatorship, and for an alliance with the "forces of socialist revolution" throughout the world.

A fourth party, the Bloc des Masses Sénégalaises (BMS), was created in September, 1961, by several former UPS members who, for various reasons, were dissatisfied with the UPS leadership. Although its popular support has not been adequately tested, the BMS seems to represent primarily a traditionalist and conservative opposition.

HISTORICAL DEVELOPMENT OF POLITICAL PARTIES

Political life in Senegal before independence differed markedly from that in other French West African territories. As the first territory in Afrique Occidentale Française (AOF) to be conquered and administered as a colony, Senegal early gained political privileges not extended elsewhere until 1956. Beginning in 1872, the inhabitants of the principal coastal settlements—St. Louis, Rufisque, Gorée, and Dakar—chose their own municipal councils and, in 1875, sent a deputy to the Chamber of Deputies in Paris. The General Council established in 1879 gave the inhabitants of the self-governing municipalities, or *communes*, as they were called, a limited say in territorial affairs. In 1914 urban electors sent the first African, Blaise Diagne, to Paris as their deputy.[1]

Diagne quickly became the dominant force in Senegalese politics, and, by keeping intact an effective electoral coalition, held his post until his death in 1934. Though a member of the Serer tribe himself, he won the backing of the Lebous, native to the Dakar area, by espousing their grievances against the government; with their support he became Dakar's mayor in 1924. In St. Louis, the capital, he backed the complaints of the Muslim religious leaders, or Marabouts (an important group in a country 85 per cent Islamized), against governmental restrictions, and those of young African governmental employees seeking pay equal to that of Europeans. The organization of Diagne's followers, the "Young Senegalese,"[2] was a simple electoral grouping formed for the sole purpose of supporting his campaign, and was not a continuing body. In Paris, Diagne represented only the communes and obtained confirmation of special rights, including French citizenship and exemption from forced labor, for his constituents. This greatly widened the gulf between them and the

[1] Much of Senegal's political history is covered in Kenneth Robinson, "Senegal: The Elections to the Territorial Assembly, March 1957," in W. J. M. Mackenzie and Kenneth Robinson, eds., *Five Elections in Africa* (Oxford: Clarendon Press, 1960), pp. 306–334.

[2] Raymond L. Buell, *The Native Problem in Africa* (2 vols.; New York: Macmillan, 1928), I, 955.

"subjects" of the interior, whose only representation, prior to 1939, was through a few chiefs in the Colonial Council.

Blaise Diagne's death in 1934 brought no significant changes. His successor, Galandou Diouf, a Dakar métis, continued Diagne's policies and political style. Diouf was unsuccessfully opposed by Lamine Guèye, a former mayor of St. Louis and a lawyer in Dakar. Lamine Guèye campaigned with the backing of the Parti Socialiste Sénégalais, a local organization formed in 1929 or 1930 with the support of African intellectuals and a few French Socialists. The establishment of Léon Blum's Popular Front government in France gave new impetus to the socialist movement in Senegal, and in March, 1937, a regular Senegalese branch of the French Socialist Party (SFIO) was formed with Lamine Guèye as political director. Although it adopted the constitution of an SFIO section, and formed groups in a few interior towns, in actual functioning it differed little from Diagne's commune-based electoral organization. The major aim of political action was control over the municipalities, with their patronage and their resources for party coffers. This policy demanded close attention to local problems, and the advancement of people with strong local backing. The small representation afforded the subjects in the Colonial Council by the reform of 1939 did not perceptibly alter the dominance of the citizens.

World War II and AOF's submission to the Vichy government forced a halt in Senegalese political life. With the return of political activity in 1945, Lamine Guèye's Socialists, as the main holdovers from prewar politics, easily dominated the Senegalese scene. Under his direction, various recently organized Senegalese political groups united to form the Bloc Africain to send representatives to the First and Second Constituent Assemblies for the Fourth Republic. In an election held under a double-franchise system, Lamine Guèye was returned by the first or citizens' college, and his hand-picked candidate, Léopold Senghor, "the deputy of the bush," easily captured the support of the newly enfranchised subjects in the second college.

The postwar political context differed in that now other French Black African territories, too, had representation in Paris, and all West African territories sent representatives to the Grand Council of AOF to debate problems of federation-wide interest. Representatives from these other territories, along with some Senegalese, met in Bamako in October, 1946, to found an interterritorial political movement, the Rassemblement Démocratique Africain (RDA). At the request of the metropolitan SFIO, the Senegalese Socialists did not adhere. Thus, in the November, 1946, elections, in which Senegalese citizens and noncitizens voted for the first time on a common roll for their deputies to the National Assembly, the Socialists were opposed by the local section of the RDA, the Union

Démocratique Sénégalaise (UDS). The UDS, however, captured only 1,180 votes to Lamine Guèye's and Senghor's 128,000.

Despite its electoral success and territory-wide support, the Senegalese Socialist Party's structure and outlook had evolved but little since prewar days. Lamine Guèye's personality was the party's major asset with the electorate, and his web of personal associates constituted its effective decision-making and implementing structure. Party finances and membership were never put on a regular basis; at its height the party had a maximum of 6,000 regular dues-paying members. The Socialists did not maintain a permanent office, but conscripted municipal employees when needed for particular tasks, or relied on sympathetic nonpolitical organizations or on the personal influence of prestigious party supporters to mobilize particular groups for rallies or elections. Party finances came principally from contributions by wealthy supporters and candidates, and from salary kickbacks by the vast flock of municipal employees and hangers-on.

The effectiveness of this system in the context of the old communes should not be underestimated. The personal connections between influential members of these communities and the Socialist leaders were extensive and of long date. The SFIO received the near-total support of the St. Louis citizens and of the Dakar Lebous, whose perpetual quarrels with the administration Lamine Guèye, like Blaise Diagne before him, had found it politic to espouse.[3] The minor civil servants, too, flocked to Lamine Guèye's banner. If for many this was a simple acknowledgment that they owed their livelihood to a Socialist municipal administration, equally important was the air of gentility maintained by the party leaders, setting them and their ardent supporters apart from the rabble of the bush.

Party ideology and long-range political planning were among the weakest points in the Socialist structure. The African Socialists' activities in the French Parliament seemed to be dictated more by the metropolitan party's hierarchy than by purely African considerations.[4] Although such subtle distinctions were doubtless lost on the mass of the electorate, the lack of parliamentary initiative lent credence to later opposition charges that the Senegalese Socialists simply acquiesced in the plans of the colonial masters.

The continuation of prewar political habits was an insufficient response to a new political context most baldly evident in the increase in the electorate resulting from the extension of the franchise to the bush

---

[3] Lamine Guèye was mayor of St. Louis from 1925 to 1926, and mayor of Dakar from 1945 to 1961.

[4] "La Vie du parti" in the Socialist paper *AOF* (Dakar), Feb. 14, 1947, gives some idea of the close relations between Senegalese Socialists and the metropolitan hierarchy.

population. Whereas some 20,000 bush electors voted in the spring of 1946 for their representative at the Second Constituent Assembly (as against 32,000 citizens), by the November, 1946, elections, held for the first time on a common electoral roll, their number was above 100,000 (see table 1). Further, the communes themselves were changing. Beginning with the demobilization of the Tirailleurs Sénégalais, the West African troops, and increasing in pace as economic activity picked up after the war, an influx of new rural immigration swelled the cities' population.

These elements found their spokesman in Léopold Senghor, whom Lamine Guèye had so successfully presented to the new bush electors as *their* representative. Senghor and his followers attacked with increasing vehemence the clannishness and the lack of responsiveness of the party's leaders. After the party hierarchy had refused to accept a series of reforms he proposed, Senghor resigned from the SFIO on September 27, 1948,[5] and created a new party, the Bloc Démocratique Sénégalais (BDS), with Mamadou Dia, a primary school teacher, as secretary-general. The BDS was the bush population's instrument of revenge against the long domination of the old communes. The party's structure, as elaborated at its congress in Thiès in April, 1949, was designed to associate these populations newly active in politics with the party on terms they could easily grasp. The party was, in the words of its secretary-general, an "organic federation"[6] with which people could be associated either individually or through regional or other intermediary groupings, such as the powerful Tukulor Union Générale des Originaires de la Vallée du Fleuve and the Mouvement des Forces Démocratiques de la Casamance, as well as tiny local ethnic or craft groups. The party emphasized African values and interests, and advocated specific economic and social measures which had a direct appeal to the bush population. On the parliamentary level Senghor affiliated the BDS with the Indépendants d'Outre-Mer (IOM), a group of overseas deputies who, like Senghor, refused the SFIO label and could not accept the RDA's alliance with the Communist Party.

The first test of the new Senegalese party came in the National Assembly election on June 17, 1951. The BDS ran Senghor and the Dakar labor leader, Abbas Guèye, against the Socialists. While Lamine Guèye carried on his usual confident campaign in the larger towns, Senghor went on a grueling forty-day tour stumping the Senegalese bush. Party workers concentrated on building up strong sections in the important interior towns of Thiès, Kaolack, Diourbel, and Ziguinchor, while the affiliated organizations took care of organizing the rural masses. The BDS leaders quietly pushed contacts with local ethnic, religious, and economic leaders.

[5] See Senghor's letter of resignation, "Lettre à Guy Mollet," *Condition Humaine* (Dakar), Oct. 5, 1948.
[6] "Rapport Moral," *Condition Humaine,* April 26, 1949.

TABLE 1

ELECTIONS, 1945–1951

Election	Registered voters	Valid votes	SFIO	BDS	Others
Constituent Assembly, October 21 and November 4, 1945[a]					
First college	44,292	26,439	21,528		4,911
Second college	25,188	19,126	15,095		4,031
Constituent Assembly, June 2, 1946[a]					
First college	46,985	32,213	31,288		. . .
Second college	28,461	20,718	20,718		. . .
National Assembly, November 10, 1946	192,861	130,118	128,284		1,834
General Council,[b] December 15, 1946	196,696	103,566	87,215		16,351
National Assembly, June 17, 1951	665,281	314,207	95,353	213,916	4,938

[a] SOURCE: Kenneth Robinson, "Senegal: The Elections to the Territorial Assembly, March 1957," in W. J. M. Mackenzie and Kenneth Robinson, eds., *Five Elections in Africa* (Oxford: Clarendon Press, 1960), table 8, p. 311.

[b] Later called the Territorial Assembly.

TABLE 2

ELECTIONS TO THE TERRITORIAL ASSEMBLY, MARCH 30, 1952

Electoral district[a]	Registered voters	Valid votes	BDS	SFIO
1. Cap Vert (Dakar)	97,208	43,231	19,326	23,905
2. Thiès	104,281	54,103	40,045	14,058
3. Diourbel	108,782	52,894	35,748	17,146
4. Senegal River (St. Louis)	103,367	24,854	13,017	11,837
5. Eastern Senegal	21,402	7,976	6,602	1,374
6. Kaolack	128,542	67,655	51,490	16,165
7. Casamance	94,892	37,545	34,180	3,365
Total	658,474	288,258	200,408	87,850

[a] To permit comparison of regional voting strength, electoral results for this and later elections are here combined in the districts established in 1959. A few of the previous electoral units were divided among the new districts, but the actual number of votes affected is negligible.

Though himself a Catholic, Senghor paid particular attention to the Muslim religious leaders. Mamadou Dia, a Muslim, led the attack on a lower level by appealing to the local imams and attacking the traditional Socialist rallies, or *khawarés,* which blended Muslim prayers with political oratory and a carnival atmosphere in a way displeasing to local religious leaders.[7] Years later Senghor was to recall, "It was the imams in the mosques who made our triumph."

The greatest help to the BDS campaign was the enfranchisement of new groups of rural electors, more than tripling the size of the 1946 electorate. The final election results confirmed the wisdom of the party's strategy. The BDS rolled up overwhelming majorities in the interior for which the Socialist votes in the communes could not compensate (see table 1). The triumph was repeated the following spring in the Territorial Assembly elections, when the Socialists obtained only nine out of fifty seats and carried only Dakar and St. Louis (see table 2). In the National Assembly elections of January, 1956, the BDS increased its margin of victory (see table 3), though it was still unable to reduce the Socialist fortresses of Dakar and St. Louis.

TABLE 3

ELECTIONS TO THE NATIONAL ASSEMBLY, JANUARY 2, 1956

Electoral district	*Registered voters*	*Valid votes*	*BDS*	*SFIO*	*UDS*
1. Cap Vert (Dakar)	117,199	54,589	17,867	35,737	893
2. Thiès	125,984	67,767	57,318	10,104	345
3. Diourbel	146,740	72,195	59,248	11,860	1,029
4. Senegal River (St. Louis)	105,541	50,018	24,390	24,914	617
5. Eastern Senegal	34,866	13,854	10,290	2,195	1,389
6. Kaolack	194,015	133,601	122,038	10,585	968
7. Casamance	108,479	63,908	55,882	6,333	1,663
Total	832,824	455,932	347,033	101,728	6,904

By 1955 it had become apparent to BDS leaders that a new force was arising in Senegalese politics, a nationalist intelligentsia composed mainly of students recently returned from France and young labor leaders. For the most part these men joined the UDS,[8] or became asso-

---

[7] *Condition Humaine,* March 24, May 8, 24, 1951.

[8] The UDS, which had refused to follow the RDA Central Committee's decision to break its Communist ties, was expelled from the RDA at its July, 1955, congress. The congress also established an orthodox RDA section in Senegal, the Mouvement Populaire Sénégalais (MPS). The UDS contested the 1956 elections, but, severely hampered by BDS tactics and without RDA financial support, it polled less than 7,000 votes.

ciated with the independent newspaper *Réalités Africaines*. The BDS leaders, to increase their party's unity and effectiveness and to attract these younger men, disaffiliated the party from the regional and ethnic associations at its April, 1955, congress, and demanded that all members join the "regularly constituted party sections." [9] Virtually all groups accepted the decision except part of the Casamance movement, which, under the leadership of Assane Seck, formed the Mouvement Autonome Casamançais and contracted an electoral alliance with the Socialists.

A small but influential group of younger men, notably Abdoulaye Ly and Mokhtar M'Bow, were enough impressed by the BDS's continued success to conclude that it was indeed the "party of the Senegalese masses," and on January 25, 1956, announced that they would join the party.[10] Senghor and Dia used these young men to strengthen the party's organization in the interior and to complete its structural reforms. The new men rapidly attained positions of substantial influence, and at their urging the BDS called a general conference on regrouping Senegalese parties. After prolonged negotiations, the conference brought the UDS, the Mouvement Autonome Casamançais, some individual Socialists, and a few members of the Mouvement Populaire Sénégalais (the orthodox RDA section) into the BDS, rebaptized for the occasion Bloc Populaire Sénégalais (BPS).[11] The BPS ran candidates in the municipal elections in the fall of 1956; though generally successful, it still could not capture Dakar (see table 4).

TABLE 4

MUNICIPAL ELECTIONS, NOVEMBER 18, 1956

Town	Registered voters	Valid votes	BPS	SFIO	Others
Dakar	50,371	42,654	18,151	24,503	. . .
Gorée (Cap Vert)	372	262	. . .	. . .	262[a]
Thiès	13,150	9,544	6,611	2,933	. . .
Diourbel	7,138	5,335	3,281	2,054	. . .
Louga (Diourbel)	5,609	4,267	1,557	930	1,780[b]
Kaolack	11,097	8,270	5,993	2,277	. . .
Ziguinchor	4,905	4,131	2,932	1,199	. . .
Total	92,642	74,463	38,525	33,896	2,042

[a] Liste d'Union.
[b] Liste Démocratique de N'Diambour, a dissident BPS group.

[9] "Résolution sur la Politique générale," *Condition Humaine*, April 22, 1955.
[10] See their letter to *Paris-Dakar*, Jan. 25, 1956, and Senghor's response in the same paper the following day.
[11] *Unité* (Dakar), March 5, May 25, 1957.

Partly because of the party's new members, but even more in response to changes in the African political climate and to the play of political rivalries in Dakar and Paris, the ideological tenor of the BPS became more outspokenly radical. In Paris, Senghor denounced the 1956 Loi-Cadre reforms proposed by Guy Mollet's Socialist government (which included the RDA leader Félix Houphouet-Boigny) as not going far enough in granting internal autonomy and as threatening the future cohesiveness of AOF by a conscious program of Balkanization. This preoccupation with AOF-wide problems of unity led Senghor to try to improve on the loose IOM formula. He therefore called a conference, which met in Dakar in January, 1957, to set up an interterritorial party, the Convention Africaine, to capture the initiative from the RDA. At the same moment the different African Socialist parties met in Conakry under Lamine Guèye's guidance to form the Mouvement Socialiste Africain (MSA), with a directorate independent of the metropolitan party. The Senegalese section took the name of Parti Sénégalais d'Action Socialiste (PSAS).

The March, 1957, elections to the Territorial Assembly were won handily by the BPS (see table 5), but elsewhere in AOF there were major

TABLE 5

ELECTIONS TO THE TERRITORIAL ASSEMBLY, MARCH 31, 1957

Electoral district	Registered voters	Valid votes	BPS	PSAS	Others[a]
1. Cap Vert (Dakar)	74,744	61,974	29,926	32,048	. . .
2. Thiès	168,968	92,646	80,508	12,138[b]	. . .
3. Diourbel	193,062	102,883	85,888	10,626	6,369
4. Senegal River (St. Louis)	148,977	63,108	28,395	23,836	10,877
5. Eastern Senegal	63,703	24,961	19,831	2,072	3,058
6. Kaolack	222,147	140,218	120,481	18,820	917
7. Casamance	199,834	95,049	89,504	5,545	. . .
Total	1,071,435	580,839	454,533	105,085	21,221

[a] Most of these are dissident BPS groups which were reintegrated into the party immediately after the election.

[b] Union pour la Défense des Intérêts du Cercle de Thiès, allied with the PSAS.

RDA victories, leaving the Convention Africaine dominant only in Senegal and the MSA with a majority only in Niger. As this outcome meant abandoning the Grand Council to RDA leadership, there was a natural pressure for the Convention Africaine and the MSA to form some sort of coherent opposition. After Lamine Guèye was faced with the defection of several younger Socialists to the BPS, a general conference of Senegalese parties on February 1, 1958, succeeded in rallying the PSAS to the BPS on the basis of a "minimum political program" acceptable to all.[12] Aside from the MPS-RDA, the only party absent from the new formation, now called the UPS, was the Communist-influenced PAI, led principally by the left wing of the old UDS which had broken loose soon after that party's fusion with the BPS. The Senegalese leaders then fused the inter-territorial structures of the Convention Africaine and the MSA into a new party, the Parti du Regroupement Africain (PRA), which included virtually all non-RDA parties in AOF.

Before the PRA constitutive congress could take place, the dissolution of the Fourth French Republic presented the African territories with the possibility of attaining immediate independence. At the PRA congress at Cotonou in July, 1958, Senghor, in a long disquisition, stressed the primacy of economic problems for the African territories and played down the independence question. The younger element in the Senegalese delegation, led by Abdoulaye Ly, promptly let it be known that Senghor spoke only for himself. The congress adjourned with a final communiqué calling for internal autonomy and for negotiations for a federation of French Africa, and, despite Senghor's tacit disapproval, the delegates adopted the slogan of "immediate independence." [13]

Throughout the summer of 1958 the UPS and the other PRA sections debated whether they should press for immediate independence or accept the de Gaulle constitution, which offered continued association with France. With the younger elements in the party pressing for independence by a "Non" vote on the constitution, and the Muslim leaders and other conservative forces insisting on a "Oui" vote, the UPS leadership was in a delicate position. The leaders knew they ran a grave risk of defeat, and of permanent dislocation of the complex system of alliances on which their party rested, if they campaigned in the face of the opposition of the French administration, backed by the army, the Muslim leaders, and many of the conservative local leaders within the party. In two tumultuous meetings on September 11 and 20, the old BDS core of the party decided that the political dangers of a "Non" vote outweighed their desire for immediate independence. This promptly provoked the secession of some of the party's younger members under the leadership of Abdoulaye Ly, Assane Seck, and Diaraf Diouf, who formed the PRA-Sénégal, a party "faithful to the principles of the Cotonou Congress." [14] Senegal voted massively to accept the constitution (see table 6).

[12] *La Semaine Sénégalaise* (Dakar), no. 1 (Feb., 1958).

[13] On the Cotonou congress see Gil Dugué, *Vers les Etats-Unis d'Afrique* ([Dakar]: Lettres Africaines, 1960), pp. 91–104.

[14] For a defense of their position, see the first issue of their paper, *Indépendance Africaine* (Dakar), Jan. 10, 1959.

TABLE 6

REFERENDUM ON THE CONSTITUTION FOR THE FIFTH REPUBLIC,
SEPTEMBER 28, 1958

Electoral district	Registered voters	Valid votes	Yes	No
1. Cap Vert (Dakar)	92,643	68,516	62,783	5,732
2. Thiès	169,407	145,495	144,500	995
3. Diourbel	195,610	170,690	170,025	665
4. Senegal River (St. Louis)	148,495	109,065	107,563	1,504
5. Eastern Senegal	75,403	52,946	52,205	741
6. Kaolack	228,249	193,592	192,602	990
7. Casamance	190,916	151,959	140,684	11,275
Total	1,100,723	892,263	870,362	21,902

The UPS justified its vote by insisting that "real" independence required a larger base than that afforded by individual territorial units, which the party leaders considered too small either to permit effective economic development or to resist external political and economic pressures. Further, they argued, once the territories had tasted the heady wine of national sovereignty, it would be doubly difficult to bring them together. This reasoning was very close to that of the Union Soudanaise–RDA, the dominant party in neighboring Soudan, which met with PRA leaders in a conference of profederation representatives from Soudan, Senegal, Upper Volta, and Dahomey on December 29–30, 1958, in Bamako. The conference, meeting again two weeks later in Dakar, drew up a constitution for a West African federation to be known as the Mali Federation, which promised to seek independence in "association" with France.

All this was too much for the conservative forces in Senegal. In February, 1959, they formed a new right-wing party, the Parti de la Solidarité Sénégalaise (PSS), which sought to maintain Senegal's links with France, to combat the Mali Federation, and to base the principles of government on Muslim law. This was precisely the sort of group that Senghor and Dia had feared might oppose them in the September referendum. The PSS, however, did not have the advantage of overt French administration support nor, finally, did it receive the crucial support of the Mouride sect's Marabout, Falilou M'Backé. The UPS swept the March 29, 1959, territorial elections without losing a seat and a year later enticed the PSS leaders back into the fold.

Although Dahomey and Upper Volta soon dropped out of the federation, the common political party, the Parti de la Fédération Africaine

(PFA), set up by the pro-Mali forces at their March and July congresses in Dakar, included representation for minority federalist elements in the other territories as well as in Senegal and Soudan. In Senegal, a common interest in federalism brought the MPS into the UPS.

After considerable hesitation, France finally opened negotiations with the Mali representatives for the peaceful transferral of sovereignty to the federation. Things were not going smoothly, however, between the federation's two partners, who had fundamentally divergent views as to what form the federation ought to take. The Soudanese, solidly united behind their *parti unique,* sought a strong centralized government which they could expect to dominate, if not by their larger population, at least by their superior political discipline. The UPS leaders, realizing that Senegalese money would finance the activities of the federal government, sought to limit their commitments. Likewise, party discipline had never been a UPS strong point, and it was apparent that even a small defection from its ranks would give the Soudanese a permanent majority in the government, which was split evenly between the two partners. After the federation became officially independent on June 20, 1960, the situation rapidly deteriorated. At a congress of the UPS Youth Movement in July, Modibo Keita, the Soudanese leader who had been invited as an observer, invoked his role as PFA president to intervene in the debate on the side opposing Senghor and Dia. It furthermore became obvious that the Soudanese leaders were picking up converts in the UPS ranks by playing on old divisions within the party. They already had close personal relations with some of the former UDS and MPS members whom they had known as RDA companions,[15] and now they seemed to be making headway among the old Socialists. When Soudanese leaders also started on a round of visits with Senegalese Marabouts, the UPS leaders felt that their hold over their own back yard was threatened; on August 20, in response to some provocative Soudanese moves, the Senegalese abruptly broke up the federation and sent the Soudanese leaders back to Bamako.[16]

In the year following the federation's breakup and the adoption of the constitution of the independent Senegalese Republic, there was no outward change in the line-up of Senegalese parties. In the summer of 1961, however, a dispute over leadership of the UPS organization in Dakar led some of the defeated faction, mostly former members of the Socialist Party, to oppose the UPS candidates in elections for the municipal council and for a vacant National Assembly seat. Although expelled

[15] Chief among these was Doudou Guèye, PFA organization secretary and former MPS leader, who later became Modibo Keita's adviser on Senegalese affairs.
[16] The two sides of the story of the federation's breakup are set forth in *Livre Blanc sur le Coup d'Etat manqué du 19 août au 20 août 1960,* Republic of Senegal (Dakar, 1960), and in Modibo Keita's speech before the Soudanese Legislative Assembly on August 29, 1960.

from the UPS, they forced the government party to unusual lengths before the UPS candidates triumphed. In September this group, together with some of the old PSS elements who were dissatisfied with their role in the UPS and a few Dakar intellectuals, formed a new party, the Bloc des Masses Sénégalaises (BMS). Despite much initial activity, the BMS did not receive the popular support necessary to make it a serious threat to the UPS.

PARTY MEMBERSHIP

Measured by the size and the spread of its membership, the UPS is today the only national party in Senegal. The official count of dues-paying members at the time of the February, 1962, congress was 272,515, though this certainly underestimated the number of Senegalese who would consider themselves UPS members.[17] Party leaders calculate potential membership at some 600,000.

Unfortunately, there exists no detailed breakdown of social, regional, or occupational characteristics of the UPS membership, but it is certain that whatever the fruits of amalgamating other parties may have been, the core of UPS strength still lies in the central regions of Thiès and Kaolack which supported the rise of the BDS to power. As the only party known to peasants in all the rural areas, it unquestionably still holds their loyalty everywhere except in the Casamance. The old Socialists of the coastal cities, while nominally UPS, are not overly enthusiastic in their membership. Aside from the high percentage of intellectuals attracted to the opposition parties, there seems to be no occupational category not significantly represented in the UPS, though, as one would expect from the country's economy, peasants make up the largest part of the base membership. There is no evidence that the UPS base membership is drawn from any specific ethnic or religious groups.

More detailed information is available about the party's leadership, composed of the 302 members of the Executive Committee, including the 79 UPS National Assembly deputies and the 42 members of the Executive Bureau, the party's highest organ. The 223 nonparliamentary seats on the Executive Committee are apportioned by regions, roughly on the basis of population;[18] within each region the main population groups are represented approximately in proportion to their numerical strength. The deputies, though not required by law to be residents of the areas they represent, with few exceptions either were born in their respective areas,

---

[17] The number of party cards sold is at best an approximate measure of party strength. Many party faithful in the poorer rural areas do not have the 100 francs (about 40 cents) to spare at collection time. On the other hand, some local leaders try to increase their influence at party congresses, where representation is proportionate to paid membership, by buying large numbers of cards themselves.

[18] See p. 36.

now live there, or have spent considerable time there.[19] The Executive Bureau is less sensitive to the requirements of regional distribution (see table 7). It is not surprising that the first electoral district, comprising

TABLE 7

REGIONAL DISTRIBUTION OF UPS EXECUTIVE BUREAU MEMBERS

Electoral district	Electoral seats		Executive bureau members	
	Number	Per cent	Number	Per cent
1. Cap Vert (Dakar)	10	13	9	21.5
2. Thiès	11	14	7	16.5
3. Diourbel	13	16	7	16.5
4. Senegal River (St. Louis)	10	13	7	16.5
5. Eastern Senegal	5	6	1	2.5
6. Kaolack	17	21	7	16.5
7. Casamance	14	17	4	9.5
Total	80	100	42	99.5

NOTE: The criteria used for assigning each individual to a region are: (1) the place represented in the National Assembly, where applicable; and (2) the place of current or longest residence. Gabriel d'Arboussier and Alioune M'Bengue, both of whom live in the Cap Vert and were elected to seats from the Kaolack region, were scored as being from the Cap Vert.

Dakar and its suburbs, is overrepresented, for the business of government has long brought abler politicians there; more notable is the poor representation afforded Senegal's two "disinherited regions": the Casamance, where UPS control is weakest, and Eastern Senegal, the poorest and least developed part of the country. This was a subject of much discussion at the February, 1962, party congress, and the Executive Bureau subsequently increased the representation of the Casamance from two to four, and added one man from Eastern Senegal.

Table 8 lists the ethnic origins of deputies and of Executive Bureau members. The overrepresentation of the Lebous shows that the old inhabitants maintain their hold on political office in the Dakar region, eight of whose nine UPS deputies are Lebous. (As only nineteen of the thirty-four Dakar representatives on the Executive Committee, however, are Lebous, the newer urban populations seem finally to be coming into their own.) A few outstanding examples suggest that a man's regional ties are more important than his ethnic origin, and that his regional ties are determined more by his place of work or residence than by his place of birth. The new mayor of Dakar, Joseph Gomis, is from a Diola family of

[19] Robinson, *op. cit.*, pp. 343, 359–360.

TABLE 8

ETHNIC ORIGIN OF UPS DEPUTIES AND EXECUTIVE BUREAU MEMBERS

Ethnic group[a]	Per cent of population[b]	Deputies		Executive bureau members	
		Number	Per cent	Number	Per cent
Wolof	35	32	41	24	57
Serer	16	5	6	3	7
Lebou	2	10	13	2	5
Tukulor	9	10	13	5	12
Fulani	15	5	6	3	7
Diola	9	5	6	2	5
Mande, Bambara	7	3	4	1	2
European	2	3	4	0	0
Métis	1	5	6	2	5
Rest	4	1	1	0	0
Total	100	79	100	42	100

[a] A person of mixed ethnic parentage has been categorized in his father's group unless commonly considered to belong to his mother's group.

[b] SOURCE: SERESA, *Rapport Général* (Dakar, 1960), Part I, "Situation–Problèmes–Facteurs de développement," chap. i, p. 38, and my own calculations. The percentages of total population given for each ethnic group are approximations at best, and should be used only as general indications.

Casamance origin, though he has spent most of his life in Dakar. True, he is the candidate of the newer populations, but the Lebous' perennial favorite, Lamine Guèye, is a Wolof of St. Louisian parents, born in the Soudan. Similarly, the mayor of Tambacounda and political boss of Eastern Senegal is a native of the Cap Vert.

If ethnic group is of less political importance than it is in many other African countries, a person's caste is probably more so. With the exception of the Diolas and a few related tribes in the Casamance,[20] the Senegalese tribes all have similar and extremely strong caste systems with fine gradations of rank, which for our purposes may be divided into noble (*guer* in Wolof) and nonnoble, each representing about half the population.[21]

All but three of the seventy-nine UPS deputies are of noble caste, and two of these three are ministers and members of the UPS Executive Bureau.[22] This suggests that, in principle, public office is still reserved

[20] L. V. Thomas, *Les Diola* (2 vols.; Dakar: IFAN, 1958), I, 29–35, 228–232.

[21] Thiam Bodiel, "Hiérarchie de la Société Ouolove," *Notes Africaines*, no. 41 (Jan., 1949), p. 12; David P. Gamble, *The Wolof of Senegambia*, Ethnographic Survey of Africa, Western Africa, Part XIV (London, 1957), p. 44.

[22] In addition, it is widely contended that the Prime Minister is of lower-caste origin, though his partisans claim this is a politically motivated calumny.

for those of upper caste unless the person has some particular competence or extraordinary attribute. The two lower-caste ministers both have close ties with religious leaders, and one has done brilliant law studies in France. The only nonministerial deputy of lower caste is a wealthy trader who has played an important role in the marketing and transport of the Senegalese peanut crop. A much higher proportion of lower-caste people have advanced through the government administrative hierarchy, and it seems evident that caste discrimination in the party's nominations for political office is primarily a response to a still-unenlightened electorate. Data on the caste composition of the UPS Executive Committee, though incomplete, suggest that caste prejudice plays a lesser role within the party hierarchy itself, and is less important in the representation of the interior regions than in that of the coastal cities. The relatively high proportion of lower-caste persons among the Youth Movement representatives suggests that the caste problem will eventually become less important in party life.

The average age of UPS deputies on January 1, 1963, was forty-nine, and, of Executive Bureau members, forty-six. This does not differ notably from the ages of people in similar positions in other countries that formerly were part of AOF.[23] I have no information on the ages of other Executive Committee members.

As table 9 shows, most party leaders have a background of government employment. This is particularly true for the nonparliamentary members of the Executive Committee, and somewhat less so for the deputies. The 1962 Executive Bureau was the first to include more governmental employees than professionals. The predominance of governmental employees is explained in part by the distribution of political spoils, but it also results from the predominance of the public sector in the Senegalese employment market, where it takes up 37 per cent of the salaried work force. The low proportion of farmers among UPS leaders in a country where 80 per cent of the population are peasants is not so surprising if one takes into account the educational background required for party leadership and the tendency of those with a minimum of education to seek white-collar jobs. Furthermore, it is probable that many Executive Committee members who do not list a profession are in fact farmers.[24]

The commitment the average UPS member must make to the party, both intellectually and in terms of time spent in party work, is likely to be rather slight. The party statutes demand only that a member pay his dues regularly and belong to no "regional or ethnic group of a political nature." The party makes no rule as to the frequency with which local

---

[23] Jean-Louis Seurin, "Elites sociales et Partis politiques d'A.O.F.," *Annales Africaines* (1958), pp. 123–157. See also Robinson, *op. cit.*, p. 358.

[24] Cf. Seurin, *op. cit.*, pp. 138, 151–154.

TABLE 9

PROFESSIONS OF UPS POLITICAL LEADERS

Occupational group	Nonparliamentary members of Executive Committee[a]		Members of National Assembly		Members of Executive Bureau	
	Number	Per cent	Number	Per cent	Number	Per cent
Government employment						
Education	25	14.9	23	29.1	14	33.3
Administration	97	58.0	22	27.9	10	23.9
Railroad	11	6.6	5	6.3	3	7.2
Total	133	79.5	50	63.3	27	64.4
Professional employment						
Doctors, veterinarians, etc.	7	4.2	8	10.1	4	9.5
Lawyers	1	0.6	10	12.7	8	19.1
Total	8	4.8	18	22.8	12	28.6
Business, farming, etc.						
Commerce and industry	19	11.4	8	10.1	1	2.4
Agriculture	3	1.8	0	0.0	0	0.0
Other	4	2.4	3	3.8	2	4.8
Total	26	15.6	11	13.9	3	7.2
Grand total	167	99.9	79	100.0	42	100.2

[a] Data for fifty-six members were unavailable or unclear.

groups should meet, nor as to the regularity of attendance. Bush village committees may refrain from calling a general membership meeting for months at a time unless there is an election or some other special reason. Urban committees generally meet more often, and in Dakar the average is fifteen to twenty meetings a year. Nevertheless, party *militants* trying to rise through the party structure may, even at lower levels, put in one or more nights a week for party meetings and other activities. At the Executive Committee level, party work is a man's primary activity. Well above half of the working time of some government employees at this level may be devoted to party tasks, particularly in ministries like those of the interior and of youth and sports, where there is no easy dividing line between party and governmental work. It goes without saying that the members of the Executive Bureau are party men before all else.

Detailed information on the social characteristics of members and leaders of the opposition parties is more sparse, owing to the difficulties under which they must labor. Generally speaking, both the PRA-Sénégal and the PAI are parties of urban intellectuals and organized salaried workers, though the PRA-Sénégal also has a rural base in the Casamance. Neither party shows a particular religious or ethnic bias, aside from that dictated by its lack of support in rural areas.

PRA-Sénégal membership is probably between 3,000 and 4,000, exclusive of the Casamance where it claims the support, if not the actual membership, of more than half the population. St. Louis is the city most closely associated with the PRA-Sénégal's leadership; four of its thirteen Political Bureau members come from or have been associated with that area, and two others are from the nearby Fouta Toro region. The next best-represented area is the Casamance, with three members. In the March, 1959, elections, the PRA-Sénégal felt itself strong enough to present candidates in four of the seven electoral districts: Cap Vert (Dakar), Senegal River (St. Louis), Kaolack, and Casamance. Although the results of that election are not entirely reliable as indicators of a party's strength, only in Casamance did the official tally reveal any notable degree of support (see table 10). Only one member of the PRA-

TABLE 10

ELECTIONS TO THE TERRITORIAL ASSEMBLY, MARCH 22, 1959

Electoral district	Registered voters	Valid votes	UPS	PSS	PRA-Sénégal	Others
1. Cap Vert (Dakar)	92,366	66,049	59,394	5,248	1,318	89
2. Thiès	165,318	131,657	107,751	23,906	...	...
3. Diourbel	201,318	171,737	160,122	11,615	...	...
4. Senegal River (St. Louis)	149,104	94,736	73,008	17,913	3,815	...
5. Eastern Senegal	73,023	49,309	42,618	6,691	...	...
6. Kaolack	234,613	174,807	139,920	34,012	842	33
7. Casamance	193,730	134,225	99,904	...	34,321	...
Total	1,109,472	822,520	682,717	99,385	40,296	122

Sénégal Political Bureau is of lower caste. Five of the thirteen Political Bureau members have done advanced work in French universities, and one of them now teaches at the University of Dakar and another is assistant director of the Dakar Institut Français d'Afrique Noire. Three others are schoolteachers, one is a veterinary doctor, three are government employees, and one, who lists his profession as "publicist," was described by a colleague as "the nearest thing to a professional revolutionary we have." The average age of Political Bureau members is just above forty, making them, for African politics, a fairly mature group of "young radicals."

The PAI, as an outlawed revolutionary organization, divulges little accurate information about itself. One of its leaders has described the organization as composed predominately of *"petit bourgeois* intellectual revolutionaries with a base of worker and peasant support." Aside from a few former trade-union officials and their personal followings, the worker and peasant base is not apparent to an outside observer, though there can be no doubt that many members are zealously carrying the party's message into field and factory. The PAI, by capitalizing on the perennial dissatisfaction of the St. Louis population, has recently achieved some measure of popular following there, largely because it was the only party to present an opposition list in the July, 1960, elections to the regional assemblies (see table 11). The armed attack the PAI made on the gover-

TABLE 11

ELECTIONS TO THE REGIONAL ASSEMBLIES, JULY 31, 1960

Region	Registered voters	Valid votes	UPS	PRA-Sénégal
Thiès	135,516	126,803	126,803	...
Diourbel	175,256	166,930	166,930	...
Senegal River (St. Louis)[a]	131,069	114,482	114,482	...
Eastern Senegal	68,125	58,070	58,070	...
Kaolack	207,673	194,475	194,475	...
Casamance	186,274	139,419	116,065	23,354
Total	903,913	800,179	776,825	23,354

[a] The PAI presented candidates in St. Louis. As the party was outlawed immediately after the election, its vote was not reported.

nor's residence after their observers were expelled from the polls resulted both in their being outlawed and in their acquiring considerable local renown. The core of the PAI's membership, however, comes from students and recent graduates of the University of Dakar and the French universities. Although a few of the "old-timers" have now passed forty, most of the PAI members are between twenty and thirty years of age. Some spokesmen have claimed the support of up to 10,000 people, but my own estimate is that the number of current members and active supporters does not exceed 2,500. I have no information about ethnic groups, castes, or current occupations of PAI members or supporters, although the party, not being an electoral organization, clearly takes no particular account of the first two criteria. Membership in both the PRA-Sénégal and the PAI demands an intellectual commitment as well as one of time, energy, and, frequently, fortune. With the exception of members like the PAI's St.

Louisians or the PRA-Sénégal's Casamance peasants, who are regarded by the party as a potential electoral base, the main body of militants in both parties is expected to be truly *engagé*, both in the sense of accepting the party program and its discipline and of working constantly for party goals. The difficulties under which both the PAI and the PRA-Sénégal must operate considerably reduce the scope, if not the intensity, of the activities of their militants, and the need for gainful employment in turn reduces the amount of time party leaders can devote to political activities.

BMS membership is still an unknown quantity; its potential at this point can best be analyzed by looking at its leadership. The BMS slate of officers combines unsuccessful older politicians and younger political newcomers, all with important family or political connections. The president, Samba Diop, is an old Lebou Socialist who led the old-guard resistance when the ex-BDS faction took over the Dakar party leadership in the summer of 1961, and was expelled from the UPS when he brought the fight into the open. The first vice-president, Boubacar Guèye, is Lamine Guèye's nephew and law partner; an old Dakar Socialist, too, he was expelled from the UPS for siding with the Soudanese in the federation dispute.[25] The third vice-president, Ali Baïdi Mayé Kane, comes from an aristocratic Tukulor family of Eastern Senegal. Formerly a Socialist, he was in 1959 one of the main supporters of the PSS. The second vice-president, Abdou Rahmane Diop, and the secretary-general, Cheikh Anta Diop, are both Dakar intellectuals who have hitherto kept out of Senegalese politics, and are alike in coming from families of important Muslim religious leaders.[26]

The BMS could potentially rally a conservative rural-urban coalition, based on historical and current grievances against the UPS leadership. Whether it will succeed depends largely on the enticements it can offer conservative notables, and the ability of its leaders to attract dissatisfied local personages within the UPS. Without the financial and coercive resources of the government at its disposal, it is unlikely to be able to appeal to any but the urban masses, except through such intermediary powers.

PARTY STRUCTURE

In formal structure, as set out in party statutes, the three older Senegalese parties are similar, and presumably the BMS will be like them.

---

[25] Whether or not these two will succeed in rallying old-Socialist support behind the BMS depends in large part on Lamine Guèye's attitude. He has given the party no public endorsement, but the distant attitude he maintained toward UPS leaders after refusing reëlection as mayor of Dakar led some to suspect he did not entirely disapprove his nephew's initiative.

[26] Cheikh Anta Diop's descent from the M'Backé family could be especially important to the new party. He has been associated, in particular, with Cheikh M'Backé, nephew of the Mouride Grand Khalif.

This similarity results as much from the continued influence of a common European Marxist tradition as from a common response to Senegalese conditions.

Union Progressiste Sénégalaise

In the UPS the basic unit is the local committee, composed of from twenty to fifty members. Usually organized on the scale of the rural village or the urban *quartier* or neighborhood, the local committee is increasingly based on a government office or a commercial enterprise. When such a unit gets too large, it may be subdivided into smaller groups, or cells. Representatives of several village committees or of all committees in a city meet at the subsection[27] level in a group known as the administrative commission (C.A.), which elects a governing bureau of at least nine members. This bureau in turn sends representatives to the next-higher organ, the coördination commission for a *cercle* (one of the country's twenty-eight major administrative divisions). The bureau of each coördination commission sends representatives to a regional union which includes also the National Assembly deputies from that region; there are seven regional unions in the country. Similarly, each regional union elects a bureau in which all the coördination commissions are obligatorily represented. At the national level is the UPS Executive Committee, composed of the party's ministers and deputies, the members of the UPS Youth Movement Bureau, and a delegation from each cercle proportionate to its population. In addition, twenty seats are divided among the cercles that have the largest number of party members. The Executive Committee each year elects the Executive Bureau, the five-member Financial Control Commission chosen from outside the Executive Committee, and the Conflict Commission consisting of six older party militants.

The structure of the UPS Youth Movement (MJUPS) parallels that of the party itself. Membership is obligatory for party supporters between eighteen and twenty-five years of age, and optional for those between twenty-six and thirty-five. At the subsection level, a delegation from the party bureau sits with the Youth Movement Bureau, and fifteen members of the Youth Bureau have seats on the adult administrative commission and four members sit with the adult bureau. The fifteen members of the national MJUPS Bureau are automatically members of the UPS Executive Committee, and four of its members are on the UPS Executive Bureau.

Women may be organized into separate women's committees or may, if they are full party members, be members of the same local committees as the men. The women's committees in a given locality elect a women's

---

[27] In Dakar a unit called the sector is interposed between the local committee and subsection levels.

council, which is represented in the UPS subsection administrative commission.

Within this elaborate structure the actual distribution of power is determined by the two main focuses of political activity, the subsection and the Executive Bureau. The subsection, corresponding to the municipality, still dominates much of Senegalese politics, as it did in the days of Blaise Diagne. The original BDS alliances with local leaders, and a recent party policy of naming candidates for national office to seats from the areas where they actually live, have maintained the importance of this level. Local politics tend, by their intimate nature, to reflect conflicts of individual personalities and their followings, or "clans," as they are known in Senegal. Conflict between clans, whose continued prevalence is attested to by the regularity and the vehemence with which they are denounced in party councils,[28] has long been a serious aspect of Senegalese politics. The clans may be aligned on ethnic or religious grounds, on conflicts of generations, on fights between groups that once met in open popular contest but are now part of the same party, or occasionally on substantive or ideological issues. In the past, clan conflict has frequently led to the presentation of electoral lists by local opposition groups, which usually rejoin the parent party after the election. Conflict has occasionally been so intense among clans that remain within the party as to prevent the functioning of regular party subsections for prolonged periods of time. Although clans provide representation for local interests that might otherwise be overlooked, they have reduced the effectiveness of the UPS's response to national problems.[29]

Above the subsection level the Executive Bureau is sovereign, the effective powers of the intermediate structures being limited to regional or local housekeeping tasks. Though the whole Executive Committee meets every two weeks, and in principle shares with its Executive Bureau the responsibility of implementing the party line laid down at the annual congress, in fact it is never in a position to block the will of the bureau, and frequently it is bypassed altogether on urgent or delicate matters. Subsection reports are forwarded directly to the bureau, which may communicate directly with any level. The bureau oversees the publication of *Unité Africaine*, the party newspaper.

The Executive Bureau is formally chosen by the Executive Commit-

---

[28] For recent denunciations see Léopold Senghor, "Rapport sur la Politique générale" (mimeographed), presented at the July, 1960, UPS congress, pp. 48–49, and Thiam Mame Ciré, "Rapport sur l'Organisation" (mimeographed), presented at the July, 1961, MJUPS congress (unpaged). Robinson, *op. cit.*, pp. 344–345, gives an example of clan infighting.

[29] The effects of the 1955 structural reforms, in large part designed to eliminate clans, were greatly attenuated by the resignation of the men now leading PRA-Sénégal, who had earlier led the battle against clans.

tee after each annual congress. In fact, it is a self-perpetuating body coöpting into its membership those who its leaders feel are particularly qualified for political direction, who command strong local support in key areas, or who represent economic or religious interests within the country. The difficulty in choosing the Executive Bureau's members is attested to by the increase in its membership, first to thirty, and then, at the February, 1962, congress, to forty-two, from the twenty-one stipulated in the party statutes. The new Executive Bureau includes twenty-five officers charged with specific duties, and seventeen members, including four representatives of the party Youth Movement, with general responsibilities. Although the bureau's officers in general are more influential than those without specific responsibilities, the degree of power a man wields may bear little relationship to his title or rank in the formal party hierarchy. It is determined primarily by the strength of his personal following or by his relationship with top leaders. The real directive power is held by the secretary-general, Léopold Senghor, who frequently delegates it to his right-hand man, Ousmane N'Gom, the political secretary who is charged with making sure that the bureau's directives are understood and obeyed by the party's lower echelons. These two men, along with the assistant secretary-general, Prime Minister Mamadou Dia, and the organization secretary, Interior Minister Valdiodio N'Diaye, constitute the hard core of the bureau's leadership. Close behind come a dozen other members usually present in Dakar and currently in the good graces of at least part of the top leadership.

It is apparent that the influence of the old Socialists has been all but eliminated from the Executive Bureau. Only three of the thirty-eight adult members, Lamine Guèye, Babacar Sèye, and Makha Sarr, entered the UPS directly from the PSAS. Lamine Guèye, despite his title of political director, wields little real power in the bureau, and has been replaced as mayor of Dakar by an ex-BDS man. Sèye, who bears the title of organization secretary, was politely "exiled" as ambassador to Morocco after having been ousted as mayor of St. Louis, also by an ex-BDS man.

The reduction of old-Socialist influence does not mean the elimination of disputes within the UPS Executive Bureau. Aside from the strictly personal differences that exist in any group of party leaders, there is a cleavage, which, if not quite ideological, at least represents a difference in approach to a wide range of political problems, between the younger and the older members of the party, exemplified within the bureau by Valdiodio N'Diaye and Ousmane N'Gom, respectively. In addition, any specific issue is likely to provoke an *ad hoc* grouping of forces based on the impact the issue might have on different interests or sectors of the population. The ultimate decision in these disputes is usually made by two men, Mamadou Dia, upholding the point of view of governmental effectiveness and long-run planning, and Léopold Senghor, the master politician weighing the effects on the party's continued dominance within the country. In their party as well as in their governmental roles, these men make all major decisions, and the current pattern of leadership within both party and country is likely to prevail only so long as they continue to work together.[30]

The Executive Bureau's main problem has been its lack of consistent control over its own parliamentary party. Although held in fairly close check on major legislative matters, individual deputies retain considerable freedom of maneuver on the local level. Most of them owe their positions more to their local clans than to the support of the Executive Bureau. Further, by their presence in Dakar and their personal contacts in the government they are able to do favors for important local citizens or groups. Thus, on a few limited matters—but ones that may be of great personal importance to some individuals—they have the same, if not better, local contacts and executive power as the elaborate party structure itself. Such use of influence for local or individual gain frequently goes contrary to broad-gauge plans of the government and party leaders.[31]

At the risk of provoking local displeasure, the Executive Bureau has intervened vigorously in local disputes when its members were united on the issue. Thus, through a long series of maneuvers, it broke the troublesome Lebous' stranglehold over Dakar and installed a slate of officers more amenable to Executive Bureau direction.[32] The crucial test will come when it is time for renewal of the National Assembly, for the deputies will then have to seek the investiture of the Executive Bureau. If, as the top leaders clearly hope, there is no real challenge from opposition parties within the country, the Executive Bureau will be able to use its nominating power as a club to hold recalcitrant deputies in line.[33]

The UPS financial structure reinforces the Executive Bureau's dominance. The main source of funds is the sale of party cards. Of the 100 CFA francs (about 40 cents) collected for each card, 25 francs stay with the subsection and 75 are transmitted to the party's national treasury. The treasurer's report presented to the February, 1962, party congress listed the total amount collected from this source as 27,251,450 CFA

[30] See Senghor, *op. cit.*, p. 31, for his comments on his relationship with Dia.

[31] See Senghor's attack on this in *ibid.*, pp. 48–50.

[32] Indeed, four of Dakar's seven borough heads, including the mayor himself, are members of the Executive Bureau.

[33] The PSS and PRA-Sénégal opposition in 1959 was serious enough to force the party to rely on the active coöperation of local powers in many areas to ensure its victory; it therefore did not take the chance of ruffling the feathers of local leaders by insisting on candidates of its choice. For the two by-elections held since then, the Executive Bureau chose very loyal candidates.

francs, or about $90,000. The second major source of revenue is regular monthly contributions from the UPS deputies and ministers, each of whom donates 5,000 CFA francs a month from his salary, of which 2,000 go to support the party newspaper. According to the report, the total of such contributions was 4,289,000 CFA francs, or about $17,000, for the preceding year. The total national party budget for the two years 1962 and 1963 was estimated in advance at 61,000,000 CFA francs, or a little under $250,000, assuming a sale of 300,000 party cards each year.

In addition to the income from these regular sources, the party receives gifts from private groups and individuals, and takes up special collections among members and supporters for its campaign chest. Neither of these sources is covered in the regular party budget. There exist, further, two unofficial sources of revenue. The first is money raised independently by the local committees, which may amount to a fair proportion of the party's receipts in areas where the committees are particularly active. Second, the UPS benefits directly or indirectly from some governmental goods and services. These include official automobiles used for party functions; government trucks used to haul loyal voters to the polls in rural districts; the services of party functionaries who, though occupying positions in the administration, devote most of their time to party duties; and the use of the Prime Minister's secret political fund for party as well as governmental purposes.

These unofficial contributions to the party's budget make any estimate of total financial resources impossible. The total is quite elastic, however, and could doubtless be expanded to meet any emergency the party leadership thought sufficiently important to warrant special efforts. Certainly, to the extent that electoral expenses have a decisive effect, the UPS will continue to possess a significant advantage over any competitors in the electoral arena.

Parti du Regroupement Africain–Sénégal

The formal structure of the PRA-Sénégal does not differ markedly from that of the UPS. The basic unit is the local committee, which in turn may be broken down into smaller groups of about twenty members, where possible. The local committee is required to meet at least once a month, though once every two weeks is considered an optimum; its bureau must meet at least once every two weeks to consider or act on directives coming down from the top. The bureau of the local committee delegates its secretary-general, its treasurer, and one other member to the administrative commission, at a level corresponding to the subsection C.A. in the UPS. The C.A. also should meet at least once every two weeks. According to the statutes, an annual congress of C.A. representatives elects each year the party's supreme organ, the Political Bureau. In fact, the party has not yet held a congress, and the Political Bureau is composed of those leaders who broke with the UPS in 1958 and since then have remained in office. The leaders emphasize that the Political Bureau is a truly collegial body whose decisions are taken by majority vote, with no man's word counting more than that of any other member.

The outstanding feature of PRA-Sénégal's functioning is the constant intervention of the Political Bureau at the local and C.A. levels; the Political Bureau tries to hold as many of its meetings as possible outside Dakar and in conjunction with a local C.A., and from time to time the Political Bureau delegates one or more of its members to sit with a specific C.A. or local committee. This direct contact is designed to "avoid the creation of feudal fiefs," the reason given also for the party's refusal to create party structures at the cercle and regional levels, and to advance the political education of its militants. The leaders pride themselves on their ability to discuss complex issues and to analyze the more recondite aspects of party doctrine in the vernacular. As the party has been forced to cease publishing its newspaper, this direct contact is the major means of detailing the leadership's viewpoint to the members; it also permits the leadership to understand local problems, a difficult thing when communication through normal means might fall into unfriendly hands.

The Political Bureau's dominant role in party affairs is reinforced by the party's financial structure. Party cards cost 50 francs (about 20 cents) each, and revenues from their sale go directly to the Political Bureau for redistribution. In addition, each member is expected to give a voluntary monthly contribution proportional to his means, and it is understood that outstanding items of personal property, such as automobiles or typewriters, are to be kept constantly at the party's disposal. Each local committee is required to live by its own means, to make regular contributions to the party's national treasury over and above the individual contributions of its members, and, further, to be prepared to make extraordinary contributions for emergencies. Although most of this money pays for transportation, clerical costs, and other usual party expenses, a significant part is used to support the families of militants who have been imprisoned or have lost their jobs as a result of political activities.

It is extremely difficult for an outsider to estimate the extent and the effectiveness of the PRA-Sénégal's organization. In areas outside Dakar, where I have been able to check, there is little evidence of PRA-Sénégal activity. The leaders claim that this results from the organization's being forced underground and from instructions to its members not to reveal their allegiance. In the party's main electoral base, the Casamance, despite the expulsion and imprisonment of several local leaders,[34] even the UPS

___
[34] After a PRA-Sénégal demonstration in Ziguinchor on November 1, 1960, four Casamance leaders were expelled and were forbidden to return to the area. In October, 1961, Assane Seck, the PRA-Sénégal leader in the Casamance, was arrested on charges of being implicated in a plot to smuggle arms into the area. He was held for several months before being released without trial.

recognizes the continued effectiveness of the PRA-Sénégal's organization. It appears unlikely, though, that the party has been able to develop or to hold on with the same tenacity in other areas.

Parti Africain de l'Indépendance

The formal organization of the PAI, as befits a party of intellectuals inspired by Communist methods, calls for the most rigidly structured hierarchy of any Senegalese party. As the party is conceived on the scale of a Pan-African federation, the Senegalese party is technically only a territorial section, though in fact its federal machinery functions almost exclusively for Senegal's benefit. The basic unit of the PAI is the *noyau* or cell, composed of from seven to thirty members, drawn from a given workshop, street, or small village. Each noyau elects three secretaries—the first charged with general responsibilities, the second responsible for the press, and the third in charge of finances—who represent their noyau at the sector level covering an industrial enterprise, a section of a city, or a large village. Each sector is in turn represented at the section conference covering a city or a group of villages; the sections are similarly represented at the regional level and the regions at the level of the territory or nation. The territorial conference selects its three secretaries to represent it at the federation congress, and in addition chooses a nine-member central secretariat to take care of housekeeping tasks and a five-member secretariat of control charged with the political direction of the territorial party. A similar set of secretaries is elected at the federal level. The party works on the principle of democratic centralism, to which "all militants at all levels are equally subjected." [35]

The noyau constitutes the main functional division of the PAI, and so far as an outsider can tell, there are no permanently functioning bodies between the noyau and the territorial secretariat of control, although Dakar would seem to have some means of informal coördination among its noyaux. Party finances are based on contributions from members and sympathizers. There is no fixed scale for dues, each person contributing according to his station and means. It would further seem likely that the PAI receives some financial support, at least indirectly, from foreign sources.

PARTY RELATIONSHIPS

The Government

It is difficult to draw a distinction between the party role and the governmental role of UPS leaders. The higher the leaders go in the hierarchy, the more flexible their interchangeability. In theory the party

[35] *La Lutte* (Dakar), Oct. 12, 1957.

and the government coöperate closely, though each has a well-defined role to play. The party's Executive Committee and its bureau set the general political line to be followed, choosing goals and indicating the methods to be used to attain them. The government ministers then translate the political line into concrete legislative proposals, which are modified and then voted by the National Assembly. In its final form, legislation is applied by the administration in the field with the assistance of the local party, which is expected to ensure popular support for the government's activities on the local level. The UPS is not supposed to interfere once the governmental apparatus has been set in motion. Although a local committee or subsection may report to the party's higher organs on the popular success of a particular governmental campaign, it is not supposed to check constantly on governmental efficiency or loyalty. Such matters are left, both in principle and in fact, to the government itself.

At the highest level the coördination of party policy and governmental activity poses no problem. Eleven of the fifteen ministers are members of the Executive Bureau and are thus able to represent the governmental point of view and ensure the automatic agreement of the Council of Ministers with a party decision. Furthermore, the unusual "Gaullist" provision of the Senegalese constitution, which authorizes the president of the Republic to preside over the Council of Ministers, means that Senghor, the UPS secretary-general, will be beside Mamadou Dia at all important ministerial deliberations.

Liaison with the National Assembly is maintained through Ousmane N'Gom, second vice-president of the Assembly and political secretary of the UPS. He presides over Assembly sessions during the not infrequent absences of its president and, more important, over the private meetings of the UPS deputies, where most of the Assembly's real business is done. In legislative matters on which the Executive Bureau is itself divided, or on which its decision seems likely to encounter substantial opposition in the country at large or from lower party echelons, the Assembly may be given considerable freedom to work out a compromise. On any issue on which it is united, the Executive Bureau can almost certainly bring the Assembly round to its point of view.

Despite the overlap in membership, relations between the government administrators and the party are not always smooth. While the party, particularly at the local level, complains that the administrators are taking over everything and are insensitive to local interests, the administration frequently feels that the party more often hinders than helps its efforts. This has been particularly true in the application of some of the government's new economic and administrative reforms,[36] which

<hr>

[36] See Valdiodio N'Diaye, "Principes et Modalités de la réforme administrative au Sénégal," *Sénégal Magazine,* no. 3 (April–May, 1960), and the texts of the decrees on economic reforms in *Sénégal Documents,* no. 2 (June 15, 1960).

run counter to certain cherished local and individual interests. At a higher level, many party regulars resent the Prime Minister's appointment of apolitical technicians to posts of administrative responsibility, like the governorships of Senegal's seven regions. It should be noted, however, that these difficulties appear only on the operative level. The national party has officially given its support to the government's reform plans, and by opposing their implementation, local politicians risk losing credit with the national party hierarchy and possibly with their own local population.

Labor Unions

The role of labor unions in Senegal, as elsewhere in French West Africa, has always been a highly political one: "It is not as an economic institution, as a seller of labor, that the [French West] African trade union has its strength, but rather as a latent political agency, a potential rocker of the political boat." [37] Since the UPS government assumed power, its policy has been to restrict the unions' power to rock the boat, and to transform their latent political strength into a useful support for governmental plans.[38]

The UPS began its efforts to domesticate the labor movement after the 1958 referendum, in which most union leaders had campaigned for a "Non" vote. In a series of moves the UPS government broke the dominance of the PRA-Sénégal–oriented Union Générale des Travailleurs d'Afrique Noire, and set the stage for the unification of virtually all Senegal's unions in the Union Générale des Travailleurs Sénégalais (UGTS), which held its constitutive congress at Dakar on January 21 and 22, 1961, under the sympathetic but watchful eye of a UPS Executive Bureau delegation.

Although the new union, recently rebaptized the Union Nationale des Travailleurs Sénégalais (UNTS), has no legal ties with the UPS and is not recognized by statute as the "official" Senegalese labor union, its program is closely tied to that of the government and its action is coördinated with that of the party. Loyalty is to be shifted from a class to a national plane, and the role of the union is as much to educate and rally the workers behind a given governmental policy as to defend their particular interests. The union has specifically been charged with safe-

---

[37] Elliot Berg, "French West Africa," in Walter Galenson, ed., *Labor and Economic Development* (New York: John Wiley & Sons, 1959), p. 218.

[38] Mamadou Dia, *Déclaration d'Investiture . . . devant l'Assemblée Législative du Sénégal . . . 4 avril 1959* (Dakar, 1959), p. 6. The Prime Minister has been particularly critical of the pretensions of some labor leaders to political power and their dedication to rigid Marxism, arguing that "labor-union leaders must cease to dream of a proletarian dictatorship in a country where 80 per cent of the working population is nonsalaried" (*Déclaration . . . devant le Comité Exécutif de l'UPS à Rufisque le 4 octobre 1958* [Dakar, 1958], p. 11).

guarding the interests of the great mass of nonsalaried peasants, on the argument that "if we, their natural guides, do not aid them to organize, . . . it is against us that their action will be directed once they have found other guides." [39]

This "reconversion" does not mean that the labor movement has been smashed, as the opposition has charged, nor that its action has become less politically oriented. Rather, the arena of its political action has changed from the public forum to the inner councils of the party. Here, through personal contact with party leaders, the UNTS leaders may influence national policy when they can find support within the party Executive Bureau. This was true notably in the spring of 1961, when the union leaders protested the deputies' voting themselves a retroactive pay rise and forced the legislature to back down. Although recently personal vendettas among UNTS leaders have limited their influence, they usually support positions taken by Mamadou Dia and the party's younger elements interested in speeding up the rate of social and economic change.

The creation of the UNTS seems to have eliminated, at least for the moment, any direct PRA-Sénégal or PAI hold over the labor movement. Some of their leaders do, however, retain a measure of popularity among many elements in the union, and, should the UNTS seem ineffective, or should for any reason the stock of opposition parties rise, the UPS government's good relations with the labor movement might be jeopardized.

Youth Groups

Like the labor movement, organized youth groups play an important role in Senegalese politics. Both the Socialists and the BDS had their own youth organizations, which lived a precarious existence; their main function was to turn out for various party duties at election time. It was not until the PFA established a comprehensive all-Mali youth movement that the UPS put its own Youth Movement on an effective permanent basis. [40]

The MJUPS has an ambiguous formal relationship with the party. As its statutes specify:

The UPS Youth Movement adopts the doctrine and the course of action of the Union Progressiste Sénégalaise. It enjoys a large measure of autonomy of action, which cannot in any event be used to weaken the unity or the principles of the party. The UPS Youth Movement must contribute to strengthening Senegalese

---

[39] "Résolution sur la Doctrine et l'Orientation," UGTS Congrès Constitutif, reproduced in *Unité Africaine,* Feb. 7, 1961.

[40] The government helped the party youth to break the hold of the independent, but generally left-wing, Conseil de Jeunesse over most youth activities by ousting them and their supporters from direction of the various Maisons des Jeunes et de la Culture (*Afrique Nouvelle,* Jan. 15, 1960).

youth for the satisfaction of their demands, and for peace and brotherhood between the youth of Africa and the whole world.

In the eyes of party leaders, the youth group should serve two main functions. The first is to widen the base of support for the UPS and to train young leaders to replace their elders. The second is the much broader function of educating and integrating the country's youth into the new Senegal the UPS government hopes to build. While admitting the necessity and the utility of these functions, the MJUPS leadership itself emphasizes a third function, that of being the party's avant-garde. In internal politics the youths' avant-garde position leads them to push for more rapid replacement of Europeans by Africans in both the public and the private sector, a subject of obvious bread-and-butter interest for people just beginning their careers.[41] In foreign affairs the MJUPS leadership has favored a policy less closely tied to that of France and hence more "African" in character.

Not surprisingly, the young avant-garde has occasionally found itself at odds with the main body of UPS leadership. At the MJUPS congress held in July, 1961, the senior party delegation found it necessary to protest a formal report that severely took UPS leaders to task for allowing self-interest and clan politics to dictate too many decisions,[42] and to obtain the passage of a final resolution much milder in tone than that intended by the MJUPS leaders.

The greatest weakness of the MJUPS, as of the UPS itself, is its inability to win the allegiance of the young university elite. It was not until mid-1961 that the UPS was able to implant a modest local committee in the University of Dakar. The large majority of students reproach the UPS and the government for having "sold out to the imperialists," and the members of the MJUPS for forgetting their ideals for the sake of government jobs.[43] Although it may be true, as the government confidently expects, that these students will later come round to the party's point of view, at the present time lack of intellectual leadership keeps the MJUPS from playing a dynamic role within the party.

The main organs of expression for student opposition, aside from the PAI itself, which is almost as much youth movement as political party, are the associations of students at Dakar University and at the universities of France, the Union Générale des Etudiants d'Afrique Noire, and

---

[41] During the existence of the Mali Federation the Soudanese won a sizable audience among the Senegalese youth by berating the UPS leaders for their slowness in replacing Senegal's many European functionaries. The Senegalese leaders mention this as one of their specific grievances against the Soudanese in *Livre Blanc*, p. 28.

[42] Ciré, *op. cit.*

[43] The secretary-general of the MJUPS and many of his lieutenants broke with the UPS and entered PRA-Sénégal at the time of the 1958 referendum, but were subsequently enticed back into the government party.

the Fédération des Etudiants d'Afrique Noire en France. Though not exclusively Senegalese, these organizations are dominated by the PAI and seldom miss a chance to lambaste UPS policies. The government has so far taken a tolerant view of such activities, and has put no serious pressure on Senegalese students to change or withhold their political opinions.[44]

Religious Leaders

In a country where the traditional chieftainships crumbled soon after colonial occupation—and one that is 85 per cent Islamized—Muslim religious leaders represent the main traditional force in Senegalese politics. Their political power derives from two sources: (1) the great respect they command among their *talibés,* or followers; and (2) the important role most Marabouts play in the Senegalese economy, either directly through their own extensive holdings of peanut-producing land, or indirectly through their control of farmers' coöperatives.

The Marabouts have been greatly handicapped in exercising political influence by the division of Senegalese Islam into different sects,[45] and by the many personal rivalries, centering principally on questions of precedence, succession rights, or economic advantage, among Marabouts of different sects or of the same sect. Of the half-dozen Muslim sects in Senegal, the two most important are the Tijaniyya, numbering today well above a million, and the Mourides, numbering about 600,000. Despite the Tijaniyya's numerical advantage, the Mourides are considered by Senegalese politicians of all stripes to be the more potent political force because they are led by a single family of Marabouts, the M'Backés, whereas the Tijanis are split into three main groups, each with its own Maraboutic hierarchy. Furthermore, the true Mourides believe that entry into paradise depends on their following blindly their Marabouts' orders in all domains of life, whereas most Tijanis feel that their Marabouts' political advice, at least in principle, should count no more than that of any other wise man.

The Marabouts received both moral and financial support from the colonial administration, which relied on them to keep their talibés politically submissive to colonial authority.[46] The colonial power intervened frequently in religious questions with possible social, economic, or politi-

---

[44] Contra, see PAI, "Les Libertés universitaires menacées par le Gouvernement du Sénégal," *Momsarev* (Dakar), n.s., no. 5 (n.d.). The examples cited, however, do not make the menace seem very serious as yet.

[45] See Alphonse Gouilly, *L'Islam dans l'Afrique Occidentale Française* (Paris: Larose, 1952), esp. pp. 85–125.

[46] The Tijani leader, Malick Sy, adjured his faithful: "Give your total adherence to the French government. . . . God has chosen them to protect our persons and our property" (cited in Paul Marty, *Etudes sur l'Islam au Sénégal* [Paris, 1917], I, 208–209).

cal repercussions. In succession disputes, for example, the administration usually supported the more tractable candidate.[47] With few exceptions, the Marabouts have shown great personal loyalty to France. Their loyalty, coupled with their desire to protect their economic position, led them to oppose Senegal's march to independence. It has therefore been difficult at times for the UPS government to receive the unquestioned support accorded the French.

The Marabouts' disquiet over the country's political evolution was not allayed by Senegal's "Oui" vote in the 1958 referendum, and on November 13, 1958, they formed the Conseil Supérieur des Chefs Religieux du Sénégal in order to harmonize the country's political evolution with the precepts of Islam. The Conseil Supérieur backed the formation of the Parti de la Solidarité Sénégalaise to contest the March, 1959, elections under the leadership of the young Tijani Marabout, Cheikh Tidjane Sy. The PSS leaders, lacking the necessary executive talent to run a national campaign, were unable to present a coherent political program. The UPS successfully played on the Marabouts' personal rivalries and, through a combination of political pressures and economic promises, induced most of them to abandon the PSS before election time.[48]

This does not mean that the Marabouts are no longer a political force. As one of the Senegalese ministers said privately, "They are like women; we can't get along with them, and we can't get along without them." Their influence, however, is almost entirely negative. They can frequently block, hinder, or delay the application of governmental decisions which they feel directly menace their interests, but their divisions and their lack of abilities in the modern political arena deny them power of initiative. Their only positive power lies in supporting a point of view held by one or another faction within the dominant party.

The UPS government's policy toward the Marabouts has been one of conciliation and subtle pressure. The party has politely refused their extreme demands, but has allowed them some political privileges. Chief among these is the presence of four Mourides, who have close relations with the Grand Khalif, in the cabinet and the UPS Executive Bureau. More and more, however, these privileges are becoming symbolic; only one of the Mouride ministers is now actually in a position to act directly on Mouride interests. While easing them out on the political level, the UPS and the government continue to accord them many symbolic substi-

---

[47] In 1945, for example, the French governor blocked the candidacy of the former Mouride khalif's son, Cheikh M'Backé, thus ensuring the election of the khalif's oldest brother, Falilou M'Backé. The defeated candidate has since often been at odds with the new khalif.

[48] The party was unable to capture a single seat, and Cheikh Tidjane Sy himself was put in jail and kept there until he could be persuaded to rejoin the UPS. He was later named ambassador to Cairo.

tutes. Mamadou Dia and Senghor pay homage to the importance of the Marabouts' spiritual mission, and the government has kept up the colonial regime's practice of subsidizing the Marabouts. Thus, just before the 1960 elections, the government advanced 85,000,000 CFA francs ($340,000) to Falilou M'Backé for work on the great mosque in Touba. The Marabouts can usually commandeer government trucks and tractors to prepare their fields, and are assured of government guarantees for many of their involved financial enterprises. In the long run the Marabouts' dependence on government subsidy weakens their bargaining position, for the threat of withholding these advantages is a powerful coercive tool in the government's hands.

The Marabouts' participation in politics has resulted in an increasing politicization of all Muslim affairs. Religious festivals like the Gamou of Tivaouane or the Magal of Touba have become forums for important political pronouncements.[49] The government will surely also take an interest in succession disputes. The Mouride succession, in particular, is soon likely to become an important issue, as the current khalif is in his seventies.

Only if UPS rule were to be seriously challenged by a split within the party, or by the rise of a strong opposition party, could the Marabouts hope to increase their influence by making the political factions bid for their support. Neither the PRA-Sénégal nor the PAI seems well enough organized or close enough to the Marabouts in political philosophy to offer such an opportunity.[50] Unless an individual Marabout feels he has much to lose personally if the UPS continues in power—for instance, the government might oppose his claim in a succession dispute—the financial and other risks of opposing the government unsuccessfully and openly would seem too serious.

Alien Groups

The two principal alien groups in Senegal, the Libano-Syrians and the French, number about 5,000 and 40,000, respectively. As a group, neither has at any time since the war played a significant role in Senegalese politics. The Libano-Syrians, responsible for much of the petty commerce and the moneylending in the towns and in the bush, enjoy a position vis-à-vis the dominant population analogous to that of the Jews in medieval Europe and, like them, are often resented by the local population among whom they work and live. Although some Libano-Syrians

---

[49] It was at the August, 1960, Magal that the Senegalese leaders gave the first public hint that they were dissatisfied with the way the Mali Federation was evolving.

[50] PRA-Sénégal and the PSS did contract an electoral alliance before the 1959 elections, but it fell through at the last minute when it occurred to the PSS leaders that their partners would certainly dominate the coalition should it be victorious.

have contributed heavily to the campaign chests of political parties, they have done so mainly to avoid antagonizing any group likely to be in power. As the Libano-Syrian community is closely knit and has adequate financial resources, it might attempt to exert influence behind the scenes should the government consider discriminatory measures against it.

Overt participation by the French population in Senegalese politics is virtually nil. Even before the French were disenfranchised by the 1961 law on nationality, only a tiny minority showed any interest in Senegalese politics.[51] On an individual level some Frenchmen have played political roles, such as the old Socialist Jules Téty, Guy Etcheverry of the RDA, or Albert Touzard who, until his death in September, 1961, was questeur of the National Assembly. The political participation of such men, however, was occasioned primarily by political conviction or by defense of personal economic interests, and not by a desire to defend the French minority. Within the government itself, the French presence, in the form of technical advisers left over from the colonial era, is still evident. Their influence is unquestionably strong in the implementation of governmental decisions and in areas like economic planning, which require considerable expertise. Although the opposition parties vehemently reproach the government for its employment of European advisers, it seems unlikely that these men are in reality doing the work of France and not that of Senegal.

On the level of official governmental policy, the French unquestionably do exercise influence, but this influence comes directly from France, not from the French residing in Senegal. That the UPS government has elected to follow France's lead in many aspects of its foreign and, to a much lesser extent, its domestic policy, reflects Senegal's dependent economic position and the pro-French orientation of its leaders, rather than a surreptitious French domination of the UPS or of governmental machinery.

Economic Interests

The UPS government has managed to live on good terms with most of the country's major economic interests, which generally support the ruling party as the best means of exerting influence within the government. The economic interests of the modern sector of the economy are expressed through chambers of commerce, industry, and agriculture in the various regions, headed by the Chamber of Commerce in Dakar. This organization carries considerable weight in government councils on economic matters, but there is no indication that it has attempted to obstruct the government's plans for nationalizing some sectors of the Senegalese economy. Its policy has been to emphasize the extent to which private

---

[51] See André Peytavin, "Les Européens doivent voter," *Afrique Nouvelle,* March 5, 1957.

enterprise can work within the perspectives of the socialist economy foreseen by the economic planners.

On the local level, coöperatives in which important individuals have immediate interests, be they the Marabouts' peanut coöperatives or the Synjarmar truck-garden coöperative near Dakar, in which many deputies have holdings, are able to exercise substantial influence over governmental decisions directly affecting their interests. This influence has so far been directed chiefly toward achieving limited concessions and advantages from the government to satisfy immediate needs.

The African bush traders represent a largely unorganized economic interest group which has in the past played an important political role, but today finds its influence reduced. They were successfully courted by the BDS during its fight against the SFIO, and it was partly their local influence that enabled the BDS to build up support in the bush. The traders have maintained their influence on the party at the local level, and are still often at the bottom of clan squabbles, but at the national level and in major policy making their importance is slight. When they have stood in the way of the government's economic reforms, they have been politely but firmly pushed aside, or have been offered temporary palliatives which did not change the proposed reform. Thus, when a government-supervised peanut-buying program was instituted in the Thiès region, only 205 of 350 trading firms operating in 1959 were judged sufficiently reliable and efficient to continue under government control.[52] Occasionally a major trader or trucker with many personal clients may seek to advance upon the party's national scene, thanks to the local political base his economic power provides, but—and the distinction is important—it is his electoral base, his hold over the masses, and only indirectly his economic role which determine his advancement.

Neither the PRA-Sénégal nor the PAI has any significant relations with major economic groups, partly because of their publicized hostility to the existing economic system and to capitalism in general, but, even more, simply because they are not in power. Although people active in the coöperative movement might feel that the long-range interest of their coöperatives would best be served by a PRA-Sénégal or a PAI victory, it would certainly not serve the coöperatives' more immediate interests to publicize the fact. Should either party come to power, doubtless most economic interests would try to make their peace with the new government. The BMS has sought to establish closer ties with economic groups. One of its publicized goals is defense of the African bush trader against governmental encroachment. Should the BMS succeed in capturing the

---

[52] "Action de l'Office de Commercialisation Agricole," *Sénégal Documents*, no. 29 (Aug. 15, 1961). The government permitted some of the smaller traders to combine into larger, more efficient groups, but despite their protest to Dakar the others were eliminated.

support of the bush traders, it could use their connections in the interior to help form the base of local support necessary to challenge the UPS.

PARTY PROGRAMS

Union Progressiste Sénégalaise

In setting forth the UPS program, Léopold Senghor and Mamadou Dia have worked as a complementary team, as they do in other phases of party life. Senghor is the broad theorist who has expounded in terms of the whole culture the party's goals and values. Dia's role has been to translate these goals and values into a concrete program of governmental action. Their program, which they have called the "African Road to Socialism,"[53] seeks to adapt modern European technology and socialist theory to African realities and values, while affirming the worth of traditional African culture and its relevance to modern life.[54] As Senghor expresses it, Africa's main contribution to the African road to socialism is a new concern with man, not as a tiny part of a vast social force, as he is seen by Marx, nor yet as a totally discrete individual, as he is represented in orthodox capitalist theory, but as man living in a "communal" society, "a group of persons animated by the same faith, linked by mutual solidarity, and living in symbiosis." [55] Senghor disclaims any goal of narrow cultural exclusivity. He feels that the African nations, newly fortified with an appreciation of their particular cultural pattern expressed through a modern state, should accept the "historical necessity" of being thrust into the modern world by the colonial administration, and should go on to make their own contribution to what may someday be a true universal civilization.

In translating this general intellectual approach into a governmental program, Mamadou Dia emphasizes the role of economic development. For him, Senegal's economic problems are "the key to our future": "In fact, all problems may be summed up in one: Senegal is an underdeveloped country. To avoid catastrophe we must face up to this situation and

---

[53] This is explained most fully in Léopold Senghor's "La Voie africaine du Socialisme," in *Séminaire organisé à l'Occasion du Congrès de l'Union Nationale de la Jeunesse du Mali*, Parti de la Fédération Africaine (Dakar, 1960), pp. 56–96, and in his "Rapport sur la Doctrine et le programme du parti," *Congrès Constitutif du Parti de la Fédération Africaine* (Dakar, 1960), pp. 9–71.

[54] This affirmation is basic to the concept of *négritude*, first discussed by Aimé Césaire and Senghor in the 1930's and expressed through the publications of Présence Africaine and the activities of societies for African culture. For an appreciation of négritude in modern Senegal, see Michael Crowder, *Senegal: A Study in French Assimilation Policy* (London: Oxford University Press, 1962), pp. 35–48.

[55] Senghor, "Rapport sur la Politique générale," pp. 58–59. At this same UPS-PFA congress in 1960, Senghor changed the goal of the party, as set forth in Article 5 of the UPS statutes, from the creation of a "société collectiviste" to that of a "société communautaire" (*ibid.*, p. 28).

promote an integral and harmonious development. This is reality; we must understand it. All the rest is but literature." [56] This preoccupation with economic questions is pushed to the point where "the economic takes precedence over the political," or, more precisely, where economic development is the primary aim of political action.

To set the course of national development, the UPS government drew up a detailed plan for the years 1961–1964 based on the work of a group of experts who, under the direction of the French economist, Father L. J. Lebret, made a two-year study of Senegalese economic and social life and outlined a developmental program for the next twenty-five years. This planning operation is one of the most extensive undertaken by any African state. The Prime Minister and thus, officially at least, the UPS are totally committed to the plan, the embodiment of the African road to socialism. To mobilize all intellectual resources for the plan, the government maintains European technical advisers in every ministry, and, despite pressure from many elements within the UPS, nonparty and even opposition members are sometimes given jobs requiring technical competence.

The UPS leaders believe that their fundamental problem is to associate the people with the development plan by "creating a *mystique* of development" and by "mobilizing the masses." They refuse to use strong-arm methods, however, feeling that the mobilization must be the people's own response to a new understanding of their needs and of the potential for remedial action. The government hopes to stimulate this response through its program of rural promotion (*animation rurale*). This program takes young men from the villages and trains them for a few weeks in the basic techniques of modern agriculture, hygiene, and coöperative leadership. The men then return to their villages to put their training to work, at first under the supervision of government agents. Later, it is hoped, they themselves will become unofficial agents of change in the villages by demonstrating to their neighbors the concrete benefits of the new way of doing things, and by providing the political and social leadership of the villages in the years to come. Through their influence and that of the supervisory government personnel, it is hoped that the villages themselves will be stimulated to present their own projects for local development to the administration, and then coördinate their own voluntary labor on community projects with large-scale governmental efforts. The effects of animation rurale on local UPS committees have not been overlooked. If the local party coöperates, it can play an active role of propaganda; if it does not, it will risk being discredited in the eyes of the villagers. Indeed, the UPS leaders consider that one of the most important long-term bene-

---

[56] *Déclaration faite . . . à l'Assemblée Constituante du Sénégal à Saint-Louise le 17 décembre 1958* (St. Louis, 1958), p. 10.

fits of animation rurale will be to infuse new blood into local party leadership and, for the first time, to make the local party an active agent of national development.[57]

Working from the top down, the UPS government seeks to change the country's commercial structure, based until now on the practice followed by the large European trading companies of buying up peanuts from the farmers and selling them imported manufactured articles. This commerce satisfied the peasants' immediate desires and gave employment to a host of middlemen, but provided little opportunity for capital accumulation within the country and little security for the peasant. To remedy this, the government has backed the establishment of agricultural producers' coöperatives, which by October, 1961, numbered more than 800. Mamadou Dia has long advocated the expansion of the coöperative movement in Africa as being a natural adaptation of African communal traditions to a modern economy.[58] These coöperatives will be integrated into a national marketing system for agricultural produce through the Office de Commercialisation Agricole (OCA), which in a few years should handle marketing arrangements for all the major cash crops throughout the country. Two further organizations play crucial roles in the developmental program. The Centre Régional d'Assistance pour le Développement in each of the seven regions supervises and coördinates all development projects within its area, and controls the lending of seed and agricultural machinery to coöperatives and villages. The Development Bank, financed partly by the coöperatives, which turn over to it 25 per cent of their profits, provides the agency of capital accumulation for future investment in both agricultural and industrial projects.

Industrial development, the Senegalese planners realize, cannot be financed entirely out of the domestic budget. The government welcomes foreign capital, both private and public, for any industrial enterprise that fits in with the plan. The plan provides for tariff protection for Senegal's infant industry, and the government is disposed to give guarantees of tariff protection and of freedom from nationalization to industrial enterprises financed by foreign as well as by Senegalese capital. The first four-year plan foresees a slow sustained growth, with gross national product increasing at an average rate of 3.5 per cent and the raw rate of investment rising from 10 to 15 per cent by 1964. Most outside observers feel that these goals, though ambitious, can be attained if gov-

---

[57] Referring to the animation rurale program, Mamadou Dia observed: "The experiment . . . has surpassed all our expectations, breaking up the little cliques of local politics, the micropolitics of opposition, to orient the peasants in the direction of national duty" (*Sénégal Documents*, no. 22 [May 1, 1961]).

[58] Mamadou Dia, "Contribution a l'étude du mouvement coopératif en Afrique noire," in *Le Mouvement coopératif en territoires tropicaux arriérés*, Afrika-Institut, Rijkslandbouwhogeschool (Leiden, 1953), pp. 123–158.

ernment leadership stimulates support throughout all sectors of the society.[59]

Despite the government's ambitious goals and the sense of urgency,
the plan does not call for heavy sacrifices from the population. The actual
amount of voluntary labor foreseen for communal projects is insignificant
compared with that demanded in a country like China, though more than
that foreseen in India's planning.[60] Similarly, despite appeals for austerity
in government and a rise in capital expenditures, the level of noncapital
government expenditures (as well as the style of living of deputies and
top administrators) remains high. Nor does the plan impose a break with
tradition. In particular, the government has not yet dared attack directly
the traditional system of land tenure which works to the advantage of
the religious leaders and renders rational large-scale exploitation of communal fields difficult. Plans for a redistribution of village lands to the
peasants have been under study for some time, but opposition from traditional interests and the general inertia of the population make such a
break with tradition unlikely for a considerable time.

If the plan is to succeed without imposing heavier costs on the
Senegalese people and without eliminating privileges ingrained in the
country's social and political system, the government must rely on foreign financial support. Since independence, France has continued to grant
substantial assistance to Senegal, and the Senegalese leaders count on
the continuance of this aid. Although precise statistics are not available,
total French direct and indirect aid has been estimated unofficially at
about $40 million annually.[61] Although it is easy to exaggerate the degree
of influence this gives France over the Senegalese government, so heavy
an economic dependence on the former colonial master should be reckoned
among the chief indirect costs of the Senegalese development program.

The attachment of the UPS leaders to the ideal of democracy is real,
if severely tempered by their concern for popular unity behind those
charged with national development. Senghor has called the UPS regime
one of *la démocratie forte*, in which opposition parties are permitted to
exist so long as they have no links with a foreign power and work in the
same sense as the government for national progress, offering only "con-

---

[59] See, for example, the abstract of the observations made by René Dumont in
Sénégal Documents, no. 29 (Aug. 15, 1961), and the analysis of the plan by André
Fusi in *Industries et Travaux d'Outre-Mer*, no. 86 (Jan., 1961), pp. 6–23; no. 91
(June, 1961), pp. 437–453.

[60] Dumont, *op. cit.*

[61] In 1960 development aid from the French Fonds d'Aide et de Coopération
amounted to more than $6 million, and seems likely to remain at about that level.
In addition, France has continued to pay the salaries of many of the top administrative
personnel and to offer other indirect forms of financial support, such as buying
Senegalese peanuts at a price normally above the world price. About 70 per cent of
Senegal's foreign trade is with France.

structive" criticism of government actions.[62] Intraparty opposition is treated in the same manner. As the government is the judge of what criticism is constructive, and as the definition of a foreign power was modified as recently as August, 1960, by the rupture of the Mali Federation, this doctrine leaves the opposition little room for maneuvering. Although the UPS shows no disposition to permit a substantial electoral challenge to develop within the country, the very fact that it permits opposition parties to exist (and to be formed as recently as was the BMS) does point to a more serious interest in Western democratic forms than is evident in some of Senegal's neighboring states.

Traditionalism in the form of a return to tribal modes of government is not an issue in Senegal today. Against such manifestations of traditionalism as the secular power of the Marabouts, the caste problem, and the land tenure question, the UPS tries to avoid a frontal attack; instead, it seeks gradually to minimize the political influence of such traditions, and to keep them from hindering the nation's development. The Senegalese leaders emphasize that the incorporation of traditional African values in their socialism is to contribute to, not retard, modernization. As one UPS man said, "Traditions, yes; but not traditionalism."

Pan-Africanism has long concerned UPS leaders. From a philosophical point of view, Senghor, even when championing the cause of a West African federation, has always rejected much of the cultural exclusivity of Pan-Africanism, preferring a panhumanism that would embrace men of all cultures.[63] On a political plane, the UPS leaders have emphasized the desirability of maintaining Africa's old colonial boundaries, at least as a point of departure. They fear that otherwise certain African states might in their turn harbor imperialist designs on their neighbors.[64] Since its unfortunate experience with the Mali Federation, the UPS has drawn away from its earlier commitment to a political regrouping of African states. The UPS has, however, been active in establishing the loose accords of the Brazzaville and Monrovia groups, based on the principles of "noninterference in the internal affairs of other states," "economic and cultural coöperation on a basis of equality," and "concerted diplomacy."

Although the UPS government has maintained Senegal's membership in the French Community, and has accepted the continued presence of French bases in Dakar and Thiès, in Great Power affairs it has not joined any bloc and in the United Nations has occasionally taken positions contrary to those of its former colonial master. Senegal's neutrality, however, has a definite pro-Western leaning. Not until 1962 did Senegal open

[62] Senghor, "Rapport sur la Politique générale," p. 52.

[63] "La Voie africaine du Socialisme," p. 70.

[64] See particularly Senghor's speech before the United Nations on October 3, 1961, in which he invokes this principle in explaining Senegal's attitude in the Mauritania-Morocco dispute.

tentative negotiations with members of the Communist bloc over exchanging embassies, and although it has declared its willingness to accept any economic and technical aid offered with no strings attached, it has as yet accepted assistance only from Western countries. On "colonial" questions the UPS government has advocated applying its own experience of independence through negotiations. When this has been impossible, it has generally supported the anticolonialist point of view (e.g., its UN votes to condemn Portugal and the Union of South Africa) unless major French interests were directly involved. Thus, in the Algerian affair, Senegal, though supporting the principle of a free Algeria, refused to vote to censure France. The settlement of the Algerian war should free the UPS from an extremely delicate and often uncomfortable position.

Parti Africain de l'Indépendance

The ideas guiding the PAI program are expressed most fully in the writings of its founder, Majhemout Diop. In his *Contribution à l'Etude des problèmes politiques en Afrique Noire*[65] he combines a passionate African nationalism with a fundamental belief in the universal applicability of Marxist-Leninist theory and political techniques. Recently, the PAI has sought, by modifying somewhat the rigidity of orthodox Marxism-Leninism, to bring its doctrine into closer accord with local realities (e.g., the peasantry is now given greater stature as a potential revolutionary force alongside the urban proletariat), but the party retains its belief in scientific socialism as the only viable method of emancipating the African masses.

First on the list of priorities is the smashing of the "repressive capitalist system" which party leaders consider the prime cause of Africa's poverty and the instrument of continued domination of a nominally independent Africa by the "imperialist clique." All economic activity should be under the direction of the state, which should "socialize the economy, completely industrialize the country, and totally mechanize agriculture." [66] The government administration is to be Africanized immediately, although the PAI acknowledges that it might later accept technicians and financial aid from nations sympathetic to its aims.

In its role as opposition party, the PAI has protested violently against all suppression of democracy by the UPS government in power. It is not entirely clear what form democracy might take in the new state the PAI hopes to create, but the party's admiration for the institutions of the people's democracies suggests that privileges of expression would not be

---

[65] Published in Paris in 1959 by Présence Africaine. See also his article, "L'unique Issue: L'indépendance totale," *Présence Africaine,* no. 14 (1953), 145–184, and the PAI newspapers *La Lutte* and *Momsarev.*

[66] "Manifeste du Parti Africain de l'Indépendance," reproduced in part in *Présence Africaine,* no. 16 (Oct.-Nov., 1957), p. 198.

extended to those acting contrary to the interests of the masses, as represented by the group in power.

The PAI has strongly supported the ideals of Pan-African political union, as its interterritorial structure indicates. At the time of the referendum it supported the immediate establishment of an independent, centralized, French-speaking West African government, which could later fuse with other regional formations, and it subsequently criticized the Mali Federation for being an imperialist creation designed to combat, rather than to advance, African unity by encompassing only two territories and by not centralizing all governmental power. Recently the PAI has supported the Ghana-Guinea-Mali Union as a tentative step in the right direction, but regrets its refusal to form a unitary state.

In foreign affairs the PAI is resolutely on the side of all who combat Western capitalism, imperialism, and neocolonialism by whatever means, and, alone among the opposition parties, it reserves its most virulent attacks for the United States, "the principal bastion of modern colonialism." [67] In Great Power affairs the PAI consistently supports the Communist bloc, and on "colonial" questions it resolutely backs the extreme nationalist point of view.

Parti du Regroupement Africain–Sénégal

The PRA-Sénégal shares the PAI's commitment to African nationalism and to collectivism, but tempers its program with what one of its leaders has called "a more mature understanding of African realities." Like the UPS leaders, the PRA-Sénégal has tried to adapt Marxism to local conditions,[68] though its insistence on large-scale collectivization and on political agitation among the masses goes considerably further than the communalism and the animation rurale of the UPS. The PRA-Sénégal has criticized the UPS plan as a "mystification designed to fool the people," but, aside from a few pointed criticisms of the functioning of the OCA,[69] it has not presented a full critique of the UPS plan or suggested an alternative. Its major objections are (1) that the plan cannot possibly reflect "African realities," as it was drawn up and is in part administered by European experts, instead of coming forth from the people themselves; and (2) that the UPS, even though many of the objectives in its plan may be praiseworthy, cannot carry them out because of the reactionary elements within the party and the government's

---

[67] In "Lettre ouverte à notre Compatriote Gortilou N'Doye" (mimeographed), July 1, 1931, the party warns the head of the village of Kayar against Vice-President Lyndon Johnson's motives in presenting the village with a Johnson outboard motor.

[68] See particularly Abdoulaye Ly, *Les Masses africaines et l'actuelle Condition humaine* (Paris: Présence Africaine, 1956), and the party newspaper, *Indépendance Africaine*.

[69] *Indépendance Africaine*, Aug. 20, 1960.

links with foreign imperialist and capitalist groups. To remedy this, the PRA-Sénégal calls for the establishment of a national party like the Parti Démocratique de Guinée or the Union Soudanaise capable of substituting for "a class-based state under French and capitalist domination, a sovereign and socialist workers' and peasants' national state charged with promoting democracy . . . and building a democratic collectivism." [70] The development programs of Guinea and Mali have greatly impressed PRA-Sénégal leaders, and any concrete program they might present would doubtless bear a strong resemblance to those of Guinea and Mali, as would their interpretation of democracy.

The PRA-Sénégal's platform formally commits it to seek unity through "federation or fusion of territorial political organizations . . . [and] through federation or fusion of territorial states leading to the formation of a great West African national state (United States of West Africa) capable eventually of forming a confederation with other African national states." [71] The party has, however, been denounced as a partisan of "Senegalese micronationalism" by both the UPS (for refusing to support the Mali Federation) and the PAI (for refusing to join an interterritorial front in 1959). Actually, both positions were predicated on the PRA-Sénégal's support for the Ghana-Guinea Union (later including Mali), which the party considers to be the proper basis for a great independent West African national state. [72]

In foreign relations the PRA-Sénégal takes a strong nationalist and positive neutralist line, like that adopted by the African states of the Casablanca group, but avoids the automatic support of the Communist bloc implicit in the PAI's policy.

Bloc des Masses Sénégalaises

The BMS program, unlike those of the PAI and the PRA-Sénégal, is designed to have immediate emotional appeal to major sections of the Senegalese people, rather than to present a detailed plan of action. It comprises three main objectives: Pan-African political union, African cultural exclusivity, and rapid economic development. [73] Under the first heading the program calls for "the immediate federation of former French Africa, former British Africa, former Belgian Africa, etc.," and for support of all African national liberation movements. The future federation

---

[70] *Ibid.*, Sept. 17, 1960, p. 8.

[71] *Plate-forme du PRA-Sénégal* (Dakar, July 5, 1959), p. 12.

[72] See *Indépendance Africaine,* Jan. 10, 1959, and the speech of a PRA-Sénégal deputy to the Senegalese Constituent Assembly, Jan. 22, 1959, reproduced in *ibid.,* Feb. 2, 1959.

[73] Most of the ideas presented here reflect those expressed by Cheikh Anta Diop in *Les Fondements culturels, techniques, et industriels d'un futur Etat fédéral d'Afrique noire* (Paris: Présence Africaine, 1960).

is to be strengthened by restoring "consciousness of [Africa's] historical unity" and replacing European languages by African languages for official use and in primary and secondary education, leading to eventual "linguistic unification, simultaneously on the territorial and continental levels."

In the economic domain the BMS program emphasizes the creation of a state sector in both industry and agriculture, both of which should be "modernized and mechanized." It seeks the creation in Senegal of institutes of aeronautics, electronics, and nuclear physics and chemistry; the creation of an African monetary zone; and the "equitable distribution of national revenue." Like most electoral opposition parties, the BMS calls for a series of unspecified measures to help specific, politically important groups which are, for some reason, unhappy with the current regime. These include the "reorganization and defense of traditional commerce," the "rebuilding of African trade-unionism," and "effective Africanization" of all jobs. At this stage foreign affairs seem to play but a small part in the thinking of BMS leaders, who nevertheless favor "normal diplomatic relations with all nations" and seek a policy of "nondiscriminatory foreign trade," which might be taken to mean an end to the privileged position held by France and the West in Senegal's foreign relations.

The program here outlined reflects the thinking of the Dakar intellectuals in the BMS leadership, and it is not certain that the old Socialists and the former PSS elements are vitally interested in many of the more extreme proposals. It is difficult to see either of these conservative groups advocating expanding the state sector in agriculture or alienating Senegalese sovereignty to a Pan-African union, much as they might approve government support for traditional commerce and the "creation of social peace" promised in the program's preamble. Until the BMS has had a chance to prove itself further, one might best consider the party's importance to lie more in the different forces within the country its leaders represent than in its program.

PARTY STRATEGIES

The over-all political strategy of the UPS leaders must satisfy two aims: (1) it must maintain them in power; and (2) it must implement the party program, notably the economic and structural reforms inspired by the Prime Minister.

To maintain themselves in power, the UPS leaders must fight on two fronts: against dislocation of their hold over the party, and against any opposition formations outside the party. These two fights are related. The successful dispersal of extraparty opposition should reinforce the leaders' hold over the party itself, and uniting the party behind their unquestioned leadership should give them a more effective tool with which to withstand nonparty opposition. The leaders, moreover, have a resource that is not available to either their intra- or extraparty opponents, for they control the central government structure and the principal means of economic and physical coercion. Government employment is a standard means of rewarding the faithful and enticing dissidents into the fold, and public funds may be used indirectly, as they were with religious leaders, to advance the party's cause. When enticement has not had the desired effect, the government has used repression. The emergency powers voted to preserve public order after the breakup of the Mali Federation long remained in force, and in October, 1961, the government established special tribunals to try political offenses against the state. Using these special powers and courts, as well as preëxisting law and practices, the government has outlawed the PAI; has jailed leaders of the PAI, the PSS, and the PRA-Sénégal; and has maintained censorship which not only has effectively prevented the opposition from printing newspapers (though they do circulate clandestine tracts), but has also reduced the content of political news in the independent Dakar papers. Finally, the government's supervision of elections and its publication of definitive results make it unlikely that an opposition party with anything less than an overwhelming majority of the votes could officially win an election if the UPS leaders thought such a victory would constitute a serious threat to their position.

Nevertheless, the UPS leaders avoid such methods whenever possible. They prefer to stay in power by absorbing the opposition, as the BPS did the SFIO, and by reinforcing their control over the party and the party's control over the countryside. Here the UPS leaders run into a basic contradiction, for the local leaders and clans on whom their power rests are not enthusiastic supporters of the government's reform program. In one way or another they all have advantages under the current system, and most of them are not anxious to see any radical changes in the country's economic and social organization. The government cannot count on them to be agents of local reform; indeed, it risks their disaffection to a rival party if it pushes them too hard.

The strategy of the UPS leaders has two aspects. The first is to push ahead with their reforms—though temporizing and making occasional concessions to local interests where absolutely necessary—by using the government's administrative apparatus as the agent of change. They bypass local leaders and attempt to gain popular confidence in their reform measures, thus forcing the party to jump on the band wagon so that it will not be left behind. This further permits the party to associate some of the younger opposition intellectuals with the reform movement through an administrative role, and thus draw them into support of a UPS program and eventually, it is hoped, into the UPS itself.

To do this, the leaders must be sure of maintaining themselves in power while carrying out their program. If they cannot coerce a local party leader directly for fear of disrupting the party machinery and weakening their hold over his area, they can make the alternative of quitting the party and going into the opposition a very unattractive choice by reinforcing repressive measures against the hard-core opposition. At the same time they continue to entice amenable opposition members into the fold.

The opposition so far has helped by being notably ineffective. The PRA-Sénégal has long clung to the belief that it could build up enough strength to win an election—an outside chance, as it has developed. More recently, in the face of active government harassment, it has dropped this tactic, but has not yet countered with anything more dynamic for fear that more vigorous open action would result in its being outlawed. Thus, when its Casamance leader was arrested, the party did nothing, feeling that the government's action was just an attempt to provoke its members to open violence. The PAI, faced with a similar situation in 1960, concluded it would never be permitted to win an election, and allowed its members to be goaded into an open attack on polling officers and local administrators in St. Louis. It was outlawed two days later. In 1961 the PAI launched an appeal for a "national union" government in which it, and other "democratic forces," would be asked to participate. The UPS government showed no great interest in the prospect.[74] A more likely prospect would be fusion, or at least concerted action with the PRA-Sénégal. There have been various attempts at such a *rapprochement* in the past, notably in 1959 after the elections, but they have broken up over the question of the PAI's involvement in an international movement or over questions of precedence.[75]

Three possible strategies are open to the BMS. First, it can openly contest elections against the UPS, possibly in a tactical alliance with one or both of the other opposition parties. To succeed, however, it would first have to establish mass support and throw all the prestige of its leaders and any still-covert backers into the fight to make it difficult for the government to influence the elections, as it has done in the past. Second, the BMS may try to force a split within the UPS by attracting some of the local clan leaders and some of the old-Socialist national leaders to its program. Third, it may try to work out a compromise with UPS leaders and be taken back into the fold, hopefully with some attention to its leaders'

---

[74] A tactic commonly imputed to the left opposition is that of trying to split off some of the more dynamic elements within the UPS. This seems somewhat unlikely, however, as the UPS elements most likely to share some of the PRA-Sénégal and PAI perspectives, and to be most impatient with the current leadership, are those associated with the Minister of the Interior, the man who has in the past very effectively carried out the job of repressing the opposition.

[75] See *Momsarev*, no. 17 (n.d.), for a discussion of fusion problems.

major complaints and some consideration for their personal advancement. There are many within the UPS who, supported by party tradition, see this as the preferred outcome for all concerned.

POSTSCRIPT

The emphasis on the Prime Minister's development plan has both increased the rate of social and economic change and exacerbated the tensions already existing between the younger elements in the UPS leadership and the clan leaders and deputies. These tensions broke out in the open in December, 1962, when the National Assembly entertained a motion of censure against the Dia government. The Prime Minister, backed by Interior Minister Valdiodio N'Diaye, ordered the *gendarmerie* to lock the deputies out of the Assembly and so prevent a vote. This forced President Senghor to choose between, on the one hand, the party's old guard and clan leaders who had ensured his initial and continued success, and, on the other, the dynamic policies of his political associate of seventeen years. As he and Dia had done in September, 1958, and again in August, 1960, Senghor chose to maintain his personal power base rather than push a previously established course of action to its logical conclusion. The President, acting with Lamine Guèye's support, promptly called out the army which outmaneuvered the *gendarmerie* and arrested Dia and several of his close associates. These men were subsequently sentenced to long prison terms.

Senghor's choice seems to carry certain consequences. First, at least in the short run, the plan's impetus may be blunted, and several of its provisions opposed by clan interests may be dropped or altered. Second, also in the short run, the influence of local and clan interests should increase at the expense of the influence of administration and the UPS left wing. Senghor is a superb politician, however, and he is unlikely to let his hands be permanently tied by the more reactionary and immobilist forces of Senegal. He has emerged from the affair with undisputed power and formal recognition as head of the party and the nation. Furthermore, he is now in a position to offer reconciliation to both the BMS and the PRA-Sénégal, unhindered by the personal quarrels that exacerbated relations between leaders of both groups and the former Prime Minister. If Senghor can reintegrate the legal opposition into the UPS, he may realize Mamadou Dia's strategy of controlling the clans by removing all possibility of maneuver outside the party. At the same time he may acquire the younger and more dynamic talents necessary to modernize both party and nation.

Such an evolution is by no means assured, and far-reaching and more dramatic upheavals may be in the offing. The social and economic changes of the last few years have brought new people with an interest in continued change into the political arena. They may be young administrators, new graduates of the animation rurale program, or simply peasants who have profited from new ways of doing things. If the plan is to be shelved, if clan politics block the application of proposed reforms, if the masses are mobilized only to be disappointed, the UPS leaders will face strong challenges both from opposition parties and within their own party.

2. IVORY COAST

By Aristide R. Zolberg

INTRODUCTION

There is but one party in the Ivory Coast* and Félix Houphouet-Boigny is its leader. Although this statement has not been turned into an article of faith, it expresses the political reality of recent years. In the last election marked by a contest, held in 1957, candidates endorsed by the Parti Démocratique de la Côte d'Ivoire (PDCI) obtained 89 per cent of the votes cast and filled 58 of the 60 seats in the Territorial Assembly. Since then voters have been given no choice. In 1959 a union list sponsored by the PDCI provided the only candidates for the 100 seats in the Legislative Assembly and for the 160 seats in the regional councils. In 1960 the party newspaper announced that "on November 27 next the Ivory Coast people will unanimously elect M. Félix Houphouet-Boigny president of the Republic, and the seventy candidates of the PDCI deputies to the National Assembly." [1] The people did.

In the Ivory Coast, as in many other African countries, the current regime is the heritage of the recent nationalist past. The emergence of the PDCI as a dominant political organization built around a single individual will be briefly reviewed. The emphasis in this study will be placed on the PDCI as a government party. Within the political context of a continent where single-party governments seem to be the norm, the investigation of differentiations among them imposes itself as an important research task. Such undertakings require an intimate knowledge of internal processes within the party. But the observer meets serious obstacles which stem from the nature of the systems under consideration. In the Ivory Coast, for example, where there is no press other than the party organ and no public debate of issues, and where party proceedings are usually kept secret, intruders are sometimes viewed with suspicion. The academic researcher is deprived of many of the usual resources of his trade. Although the validity of his conclusions may suffer accordingly, the attempt to analyze the character of these new polities—however imperfectly realized—is a worthwhile task.

---

* Unless otherwise stated, I obtained the information on which this study is based in interviews with Ivory Coast politicians and through personal observation in 1959. Field work was made possible through a grant from the Ford Foundation and through the coöperation of Ivory Coast government and party officials.

[1] *Fraternité,* Nov. 18, 1960, p. 1.

HISTORICAL DEVELOPMENT

Origins of Parties

Political organizations were born in the Ivory Coast immediately after World War II, when voluntary associations coalesced into electoral alliances designed to elect their leaders to the offices made available to Africans as the result of reforms in the colonial system. These groups, similar to those found elsewhere in Africa, included tribal associations led mostly by white-collar workers, which rallied young men dissatisfied with various aspects of traditional society, especially with chiefly rule. Because of status competition among ethnic groups, some of these associations merged into federations that corresponded to major regional and cultural alignments: the southeast, which had the longest experience of Western contact and claimed leadership over the entire country; the center, including mostly Baoule tribesmen who challenged the peoples of the southeast; the west, considered by Europeans and by many Africans to be inhabited by primitive and savage peoples; and the north, which derived some distinctiveness and unity from its penetration by African Islam.

Other organizations followed lines of occupational differentiation. African businessmen, mostly traders and transporters, organized guilds to promote their economic interests. White-collar workers had begun to organize trade unions in the Popular Front period. Although several attempts had been made to organize African cocoa and coffee farmers in the 1930's, they met with little success. During World War II, however, these farmers, who had hitherto benefited from the system of recruited manpower instituted by the French administration,[2] were deprived of their quota of labor. Furthermore, discriminatory trade practices were instituted in favor of European planters. In 1944, under the leadership of Félix Houphouet-Boigny, a former auxiliary doctor who had been appointed county chief of his native Baoule tribe, and with the support of the new governor, who was concerned with eliminating pro-Vichy colonists from the economic leadership of the country, the farmers organized the Syndicat Agricole Africain (SAA) in order to secure a better deal for African cocoa and coffee growers. At the end of its first year, its membership numbered about 8,000, half of whom were Baoule. As the

---

[2] This system was known as "forced labor." Under the taxation system, Africans were liable to *prestations*, which required every adult male to contribute a number of workdays every year toward road maintenance; this system existed in France as well. When Europeans, encouraged to settle in the Ivory Coast during the interwar period, engaged in farming, while many Africans were also becoming producers of cash crops, a shortage of agricultural manpower developed. The French forcibly recruited northerners from the Ivory Coast and from Upper Volta, allocated them on a quota basis to European and African farmers, and supervised the enforcement of contracts.

system of recruited manpower continued to favor European planters, the SAA advocated its abolition. In the process the SAA's president became widely known as the champion of African emancipation.

In the first territorial elections, held in October, 1945, Houphouet-Boigny competed with thirteen other candidates from the Ivory Coast and Upper Volta for a single seat in the French Constituent Assembly.[3] He had the support of the SAA, whose members constituted an important segment of the electorate. In addition, he benefited from Baoule enthusiasm for one of their own tribesmen. He also had organized an alliance of former classmates and other civil servants who brought in support from the various organizations in which they were active. Most Ivory Coast voters rallied around him as the most likely man to stop the leading Upper Volta candidate. On the second ballot, Houphouet-Boigny obtained 50.7 per cent of the votes cast.

In succeeding months some of the defeated candidates in the Ivory Coast proper attempted to forge an alliance to challenge Houphouet-Boigny in the next election. Following the example set by the SAA, they sought to base their electoral organization on an association of farmers from the southeast, who had not joined the SAA because of ethnic opposition to the Baoule, and an organization of Muslim cattlemen from the north. When the Houphouet-Boigny alliance took the name of Parti Démocratique de la Côte d'Ivoire in April, 1946, its opponents called themselves the Parti Progressiste de la Côte d'Ivoire. Its leaders ran against Houphouet-Boigny in June, 1946. While in Paris, however, the president of the SAA had cosponsored a law abolishing all forms of forced labor in Overseas France. By June he not only benefited from the support discussed earlier, but he had also earned the overwhelming gratitude of his countrymen. In the election to the Second Constituent Assembly, he received 98 per cent of the votes cast in Ivory Coast districts. In November the triumvirate composed of Houphouet-Boigny, representing the Ivory Coast proper, and two Upper Volta men representing the Mossi and the non-Mossi areas, respectively, was unopposed. In the December elections to the newly created Territorial Assembly, candidates had no choice but to obtain Houphouet-Boigny's endorsement in order to be elected. At this time the Houphouet-Boigny organization had the support of almost every organized group in the country. It was a highly heterogeneous alliance which included a multiplicity of ethnic groups native to the Ivory Coast as well as foreign residents from other parts of French West Africa; chiefs as well as the young men who op-

---

[3] When Upper Volta was dismembered in 1932, the major part of the colony went to the Ivory Coast. Sentiment for administrative reunification was strong and provided unity among the electorate from Upper Volta districts, who made up more than half of the total electorate in this election.

posed them; Africans who were associated with the Socialist Party, or who had been subjected to Communist influence; and individuals active in Catholic associations.

The goals of the organization were reformist. In addition to the elimination of forced labor and other features of the prewar colonial system, its leaders advocated a single electoral college; the extension of full citizenship rights, including suffrage, to all Africans; and the creation of democratic institutions at the territorial level. They demanded the allocation of territorial resources, supplemented by French aid, to education, health, road construction, housing, and agricultural modernization. In keeping with the colonial doctrines of the French Left, their objective was to secure territorial autonomy within a federation of French-speaking states. These goals were to be attained through parliamentary action.

Militant Nationalism

The structure of the French union embodied in the 1946 Constitution fell short of African expectations. It was indeed much less liberal than the proposals advanced earlier by the French Left, owing in part to the efforts of colonial pressure groups in which European residents of the Ivory Coast actively participated. Although many of the demands of the PDCI and of other African parties had been met, this only whetted their appetite for further reforms. Immediately after adoption of the constitution, Houphouet-Boigny and other African representatives in Paris called a conference at Bamako to demand its revision. A superterritorial political organization, the Rassemblement Démocratique Africain (RDA), was launched in order to coördinate the efforts of the individual territorial parties.

From the very beginning, Houphouet-Boigny had established ties with the extreme Left in the French Parliament. Other French parties prevented their African allies from participating in the Bamako Conference. The RDA thus became identified with the French Communist Party. When the French regime waged its own battle of Prague during the next two years, it viewed the RDA as a Communist organizational weapon. The colonial administration was ordered to engage the movement in its major bastion, the Ivory Coast. At the same time the RDA pledged itself to participate in the "anti-imperialist struggle" and expressed solidarity with "working classes everywhere." In order to extend its activities outside the debate chambers, the PDCI decided to transform itself into a militant party with an organizational structure inspired by that of the French Communist Party, but adapted to African conditions. This decision was implemented at the first RDA territorial congress, held in Abidjan in October, 1947.

At first party activities were limited to urban areas. But after having been subjected to a critique formulated by French Communist officials, who feared the dangers of a "Titoist deviation," in the summer of 1948, the PDCI extended into the rural hinterland. There it became inextricably involved in local antagonisms which had long prevailed in many communities: dynastic struggles, disputes over the allocation of land among clans or between different tribes, conflicts between natives and immigrants, contests between traditionalists and modernizers. Usually, when one side was supported by the PDCI and became a party unit, the other responded to the call for support formulated by competing political entrepreneurs.

The latter were former members of the Houphouet-Boigny alliance who broke away from the party because of internal rivalries or disagreements over the organization's ideological orientation. These defections were sometimes stimulated by direct pressures from the colonial administration, in the form of rewards for those who left the party and of sanctions for those who remained faithful to the RDA. Several new parties emerged in this manner. Most of them were simply revived components of the original alliance: the Parti Progressiste, drawing most of its support from southeastern ethnic groups; the Entente Eburnéenne and a socialist group, centered in the west; and the Entente des Indépendants, based in the north. Their structure was rudimentary; some of them, however, inherited PDCI units which had defected wholesale. Most of these political organizations benefited from administrative aid in the form of preferential allocation of scarce commodities to their supporters, loans and gifts to their leaders, and other types of patronage.

Community conflicts among several competing groups might have been sufficient to create a climate of widespread unrest, characterized by the eruption of civil disorder in various parts of the country. The disorder was intensified by the desire of the PDCI to demonstrate its strength through constant harassment of the colonial administration, the actions of *agents provocateurs*, and the disastrous economic conditions that prevailed during this period. Prices for the Ivory Coast's commodities dropped on the world market, while the prices of imported goods rose substantially. At the beginning of 1949, when the RDA congress convened in Abidjan and decided to launch a campaign of positive action, many important PDCI leaders—except for those who benefited from parliamentary immunity—were jailed. Others were vacillating. After the PDCI marked its permanent opposition in the Territorial Assembly by refusing to vote for the 1950 budget, several representatives left its ranks. At the end of 1949 the party had lost its majority in the Assembly. Its leaders in jail staged a hunger strike; demonstrations were stepped up throughout the country.

The struggle was intensified at the beginning of 1950, and some bloodshed occurred. A committee of the French Parliament was dispatched to investigate the situation.

In the summer of 1950 Houphouet-Boigny announced that he had severed the ties that bound him to the Communist Party. The cost of militancy had proved to be very high; France might retaliate by reducing its contribution to the country's development. Furthermore, elections were approaching and the PDCI might lose its electoral monopoly. Party cadres were enjoined to stop all agitational activity and to engage in the work of reconciling antagonists. It is possible that this decision could be taken and implemented only because the more militant party leaders were in jail. In any event, economic conditions improved dramatically with the outbreak of the Korean War, which sent world prices for primary commodities soaring. Unrest rapidly subsided. Although the PDCI attempted to negotiate a new electoral alliance, other parties held off because they hoped for an electoral victory in 1951. In the elections to the second French National Assembly, notwithstanding the electoral manipulations of the colonial administration on behalf of anti-RDA parties, the PDCI obtained 61 per cent of the votes cast. On the basis of proportional representation, however, it retained only one of every two seats. With many leaders in jail and others in hiding to avoid judicial pursuits, Houphouet-Boigny stood alone at the helm of the party.

The Period of Diarchy

A third phase of political activity began when Houphouet-Boigny affiliated himself with the Union Démocratique et Socialiste de la Résistance, a small but crucial parliamentary group whose leader was twice prime minister during the life of the second legislature. Houphouet-Boigny, who was president of the RDA, thus established a good bargaining position within the French political system. Between 1951 and 1957, mostly through his personal activity in France, the Ivory Coast secured protected markets for its commodities and preferential allocation of French aid for development. At all levels, from Paris down to the lowest administrative districts, the PDCI was consulted by French officials in matters concerning the government of the Ivory Coast. Long before a system of diarchy was formally created through the reforms of the Loi-Cadre of 1956, it existed in fact in the Ivory Coast.

In 1952 Houphouet-Boigny created a new alliance, even more all-encompassing than the original one. It included not only most African political groups, but also the spokesmen for European business interests, who found it increasingly to their advantage to establish good relationships with the man who had the ear of the French government. The alliance was based on mutually compatible self-interest. To the extent that support for Houphouet-Boigny depended on his influence over the allocation of resources and on his control over access to political office, his organization exhibited many of the characteristics of American political machines. Leaders who had defected were given an opportunity to return to the fold. They were granted a place on the PDCI-sponsored electoral slates in exchange for a pledge of noninterference in decision making; when they returned, they often brought with them blocs of supporters. Social and economic pressure was exerted to bring about conformity, or at least consent, among party leaders. This process of amalgamation was nearly completed by 1956, when Houphouet-Boigny and his running mate, Ouezzin Coulibaly, were supported by 86 per cent of the voters. Immediately afterward Houphouet-Boigny became the first African to hold the rank of full-fledged minister in a French government.

Notwithstanding these major changes in organization and strategy, the basic goals of the party remained remarkably consistent. The Ivory Coast still hoped to become a member of some form of French-speaking international community based on equal rights and equal duties for all its members. The PDCI continued to press for universal suffrage and for the abolition of separate electoral colleges. It demanded in 1956, as it had in 1946, a territorial executive accountable to the local assembly. The party never relaxed its efforts to obtain more help from France in developing the Ivory Coast in all spheres.

On the issue of federalism in French West Africa, even while the PDCI was engaged in creating the RDA in 1947, its leaders sided with Europeans, other Africans, and even with the colonial administration in the Ivory Coast in opposing existing financial arrangements under which the Ivory Coast contributed a large share of its potential public revenue to the Dakar government. In 1947 and again in 1948, the party had subscribed to motions, formulated by the Territorial Assembly, demanding territorial autonomy and the removal of the intermediary level of government established between the Ivory Coast and France. Although this issue led to a serious split between the Ivory Coast and most of its RDA partners in 1957, it created unity within the country itself, where all groups agreed on an antifederal stand.

Most of these objectives were achieved through the implementation of the Loi-Cadre of 1956, which bore the stamp of Houphouet-Boigny, who had participated in its drafting. The final objective, membership in a Franco-African community, came into sight in 1958. Having voted "Yes" in the referendum of September, 1958, the Ivory Coast chose the status of autonomous republic, member of the community. From mid-1957 on, the PDCI controlled the territorial executive, and had thus become a government party.

Are the characteristics acquired by political organizations during the period of colonial rule compatible with the vastly different tasks that must be shouldered by the government of an underdeveloped country? In the Ivory Coast, party leaders derived from their role as government officials an increasing awareness of serious deficiencies in the instrument they had created during the twelve years preceding self-government. They felt that the party's inadequacies placed serious constraints upon their choice of solutions to problems of rapid social and economic development. Furthermore, the task of nation building was unfinished; in some instances the party had created obstacles to national integration. In order to enable the government to carry out needed programs, it would be necessary to reorganize the party. Thus the PDCI, as considered in the remainder of this essay, is in a period of transition. Although the process of transformation has barely begun, an examination of specific aspects of the party may clarify the possible directions of change and the consequences it may have for the future of Ivory Coast politics.

PARTY LEADERS, MEMBERS, AND SUPPORTERS

If nominal officeholders at all levels of party organization and in ancillary bodies are included, the PDCI cadres add up to 30,000 or more. Most of these individuals staff the bureaus of village and neighborhood committees distributed throughout the country. The party secretary at this level was often the leader of a faction that challenged the ruling headman during the militant nationalist phase. Although party regulations stipulate that all officials are to be elected by the membership for a limited period, in most instances regular elections have not been held. These committee leaders are only intermittently involved in party affairs. Although party directives have repeatedly emphasized that PDCI officials should not be considered as substitutes for the chiefs, local party leaders often settle family disputes and perform other chiefly functions. Transmission of party office has sometimes taken on dynastic connotations; at the death of the incumbent, his heir according to custom may become the new party secretary.

The next higher level in the party hierarchy is that of the *sous-section,* governed by a bureau headed by a general secretary who is the acknowledged party boss in each region. After many of the civil servants who organized the party branches withdrew under pressure around 1949, this office was filled by local traders and planters with little formal education. In many parts of the country, including the southern regions, the general secretary is a Dioula, a Muslim from the northwest, who acts as intermediary between African producers and Syrian or Lebanese merchants; in addition, the Dioula sometimes own farms and engage in transport as well.[4] Their economic influence, based on manipulative skills, was easily transformed into political power at the local level. As most of them are immigrants into the region, they have little support among the native population of the rural areas, but they wield a great deal of influence among the immigrant urban communities, economically more dynamic. The general secretary's position is thus based on control of local economic activity and on the backing of the national leadership, rather than on support of the local party community as expressed through elections. He is usually deeply involved in political and in governmental work. Where municipalities have been created, he is either the mayor or the first assistant to the official mayor.

According to the principle of democratic centralism, the party congress, made up of general secretaries and other delegates, should elect the territorial party executive on a yearly basis. In reality, however, no congress was convened between October, 1947, and March, 1959. The national leadership elected in 1947 governed the party during most of its existence. Most of the leaders were the self-appointed founders of the party who had responded to Houphouet-Boigny's call in 1945 and in 1946. With few exceptions, they were civil servants—teachers, clerks or secretaries in the colonial administration, auxiliary doctors and pharmacists—trained at the Ecole William Ponty, the apex of the prewar educational structure in French West Africa. Before the party was founded, they were active in professional and tribal associations; some had had contact with the French Left during the Popular Front period. This small educated elite, made up of young men about thirty years old or less in 1945, scattered throughout the country wherever administrative centers had been established, constituted an effective freemasonry. They included not only members of most Ivory Coast ethnic groups, but also Africans from other parts of French West Africa serving in the country. When gaps appeared in the original leadership group, comprising about thirty people, they were filled by coöpting general secretaries of important sous-sections and the leaders of voluntary associations. Immediately before the 1959 congress, the national executive numbered eighteen members, most of whom had become professional politicians.

In recent years the criteria defining support of and membership in the party have become so diluted that distinctions can be made only with difficulty. Support, defined in electoral terms, indicates that with no choice but to vote for party-sponsored candidates, more than 95 per cent of the

---

[4] Dioula, as used in the Ivory Coast, does not refer to a specific ethnic group; usually, however, these traders belong to the Mande groups such as the Malinke or the Mahou. The language has become a lingua franca throughout the country. The communication links among these traders and their control over much of the network of local transportation were very useful in the conduct of party activities.

electorate participated in the 1959 and 1960 elections (see table 1); to the extent that these were genuine plebiscites, they suggested that the party had the support of nearly the entire adult population.[5] In a sample survey carried out in the capital city, every respondent said that he belonged to the party. Even individuals who expressed opposition to Houphouet-Boigny's policies stated in interviews that they considered themselves of the party and even claimed that they alone had remained faithful to its spirit.

Membership may be defined as involving at least the payment of party dues. In Treichville (the largest African borough of Abidjan), for example, 32,000 dues were collected between 1949 and 1952; party leaders claim that there were at that time about 1 million members in the country, approximately the entire adult population of both sexes. Many individuals, encouraged by party organizers, viewed allegiance to the government and to the party as mutually exclusive. In the period of militant nationalism tax collectors often reported that many people refused to pay the annual head tax because they felt they had already fulfilled this obligation by "paying to the RDA."

The opposite has taken place since the PDCI became the government. When general secretaries attempt to collect party dues today, they find many people who feel that they have already demonstrated their loyalty by paying their annual taxes.[6] In the sous-sections investigated in 1959, general secretaries reported that from one-third to one-half of those who had at one time purchased membership cards continued to pay their annual dues of 100 CFA francs (about 40 cents). Nevertheless, party officials felt that the payment of dues was not the sole criterion of membership, and that anyone who did not actively oppose the party was in fact a member. In this sense, membership in the party was largely indistinguishable from membership in the body politic. Few demands were made upon members or supporters beyond acceptance of party and governmental decisions and turning out occasionally for public festivities. Their degree of involvement is represented by the mood of the country, described by the general secretary of the PDCI immediately before the 1960 elections as one of "apathie sympathique." [7]

In recent years there has been much dissatisfaction with the lack of change in leadership at all levels. In many sous-sections, individuals object

---

[5] It is impossible to determine what proportion of the electorate actually went to the polls. As there was only one slate of candidates, there were of course no poll watchers from other parties. Reports from many parts of the country indicated that there had been, in fact, mass abstentions which were not recorded. Several people proudly claimed that they had done their party duty by voting early and often to make up for those who did not.

[6] After a tour of the country, the general secretary of the PDCI reported that he had found a similar pattern in many communities (*Fraternité*, Feb. 26, 1960).

[7] *Ibid.*, Nov. 18, 1960.

TABLE 1

MAJOR IVORY COAST ELECTIONS, 1945–1960

Date	Registered electorate	Valid votes	PDCI[a]		Seats	
			Total	Per cent of valid votes	Total	PDCI[a]

ELECTIONS TO THE FRENCH NATIONAL ASSEMBLY

Date	Registered electorate	Valid votes	PDCI Total	Per cent of valid votes	Seats Total	Seats PDCI
October, 1945[b]	15,101	10,730	8,456	79	1	1
November, 1945[b]	14,971	10,869	9,067	83	1	1
June, 1946[b]	18,958	15,641	15,277	98	1	1
November, 1946	187,904	125,752	125,752	100	3	3
June, 1951	189,154	109,759	67,200	61	2	1
January, 1956	875,594	583,410	506,494	86	2	2

ELECTIONS TO THE IVORY COAST ASSEMBLY[c]

Date	Registered electorate	Valid votes	PDCI Total	Per cent of valid votes	Seats Total	Seats PDCI
1946[b]	128,525	76,911	71,916	94	15	15
1952[d]	203,174	92,947	67,876	74	32	28
1957	1,483,044	807,410	720,278	89	60	58
1959[e]	1,543,012	1,457,292	1,457,292	100	100	100
1960	1,661,833	1,586,518	1,586,518	100	70	70

ELECTIONS TO THE PRESIDENCY

Date	Registered electorate	Valid votes	PDCI Total	Per cent of valid votes	Seats Total	Seats PDCI
1960	1,661,833	1,641,352	1,641,352	100	1	1

[a] These are the results for all PDCI-sponsored candidates, some of whom have appeared on the tickets of such groups as the Rassemblement Démocratique Africain or the Union pour le Développement Economique et Social de la Côte d'Ivoire.

[b] Results for Ivory Coast districts, second college (Africans) only. Beginning in November, 1946, there was a single college for elections to the French National Assembly. Upper Volta was reconstituted as a separate territory in 1947.

[c] The Ivory Coast Assembly has been known by various names since its creation in 1946: Conseil Général, Assemblée Territoriale, Assemblée Constituante, Assemblée Législative, and finally, in 1960, Assemblée Nationale.

[d] Results for second college only.

[e] These figures include the results of the election of 160 members of newly created regional councils, all controlled by the PDCI.

to the boss rule of the Dioula; some of the general secretaries found it unsafe to venture outside the towns in 1959 because of widespread hostility toward them in rural areas. The new generation, composed not only of students but also of young men everywhere, has become impatient with the "old men," the incumbent leadership. From the point of view of the government, many party leaders who had demonstrated their ability to engage in agitational or in machine politics had outlived their

usefulness. If the party was to mobilize energies for agricultural modernization, for mass education, and for other high-priority government programs, it would be necessary to promote new cadres. Friendly apathy
among the members was perhaps genuinely welcomed by the leadership
during the last phase of colonialism, as it gave them a free hand in
negotiation, but it was not the mood in which the building of a modern
nation could begin.

Despite the resistance of some officials, the party authorized the
creation of a youth branch in 1958. Six slates of candidates competed in
the election of the first national executive of the Jeunesse RDA de la Côte
d'Ivoire (JRDACI) at its founding congress in March, 1959. Nine of the
nineteen members of the youth executive were elected immediately afterward to the PDCI executive, renewed for the first time in thirteen years.
Although electoral proceedings of the PDCI congress of March, 1959,
were kept secret, it is known that the outgoing executive submitted several
slates that were unacceptable to the delegates. The final outcome, announced after forty-eight hours of tough infighting, brought several
important changes in leadership.

The national executive (Comité Directeur) was enlarged to include
sixty members; of these, fifteen formed the ruling inner committee
(Bureau Politique). Although these bodies were duly elected, participants
reported that the "Old Man"—Houphouet-Boigny—had explained that
the congressional delegates could choose about half of the members,
while he and the inner committee would retain control over the appointment of the others. The organizational affiliations of the members reveal
that this was an accurate representation of the pattern of recruitment. Of
the sixty members, twenty-two were general secretaries of sous-sections
and three were women leaders of affiliated committees; these twenty-five
members represented the party cadres. Eighteen were outgoing members
of the party executive, some of whom lacked the support of the local
cadres. The remainder were relative newcomers; they included the nine
members of the youth executive, five representatives of voluntary associations, and three former leaders of opposition parties.

The most visible change occurred at the uppermost level of the party
hierarchy. The new Bureau Politique included only eight members of the
former national executive; the seven newcomers were youth and association leaders. Auguste Denise, who had been general secretary of the
PDCI since 1947, remained on the Bureau Politique but was replaced at
the helm of the organization by Jean-Baptiste Mockey. Although he too
was one of Houphouet-Boigny's top lieutenants, he was not a Baoule; in
addition, he was generally regarded as the leader of the left wing of the
party. The most important fact about leadership recruitment was revealed
only after the congress had adjourned. Although Mockey had been duly

elected, he was forced to resign a few months afterward at Houphouet-Boigny's demand. In the final analysis, then, party leaders are appointed by Houphouet-Boigny rather than elected.

Table 2 summarizes the educational and occupational background of the party leaders in 1959. Most of the general secretaries who were mem-

TABLE 2

BACKGROUND OF IVORY COAST PARTY LEADERS[a] IN 1959

Years of formal education	Occupation						
	Farming and business[b]	*Clerical and adminis- trative*	*Educa- tion*	*Health*	*Technical*	*Law*	*Total*
0–6	21	1	...	...	...	...	22
7–13	4	11	9	5	2	...	31
14 or more	...	3	2	2	5	2	14
Total	25	15	11	7	7	2	67

[a] This table includes the sixty members of the Comité Directeur elected in 1959 and the ten members of the Executive Committee of the Jeunesse RDA de la Côte d'Ivoire who were not also on the Comité Directeur, plus Houphouet-Boigny himself. Information was not available for four of this total of seventy-one individuals. Information on the rest was obtained from published biographical sketches and through interviews.

[b] Most large farmers also engage in some trading and transport; individuals in this category reported their occupation as "planteur, commerçant, transporteur."

bers of the Comité Directeur were in the category "Farming and business," with only a minimal amount of formal education. The members of the old party executive are for the most part included among those who had at least some secondary education. Almost all those who had some university training were JRDACI leaders. It is important to note that about half of the total were government employees, including those in education and in health as well as those in clerical and administrative positions. Most individuals, however, could be classified in more than one occupational category; most political leaders also have some interest in family agricultural enterprises or in business ventures. Finally, many of them could be called professional politicians whose income in recent years was derived mostly from elective or appointive offices.

The distribution of leaders among ethnic groups follows the over-all population distribution. The Baoule and the Mande groups, usually called "Dioula," accounted for twenty-four of the seventy-one leaders; these two ethnic groups make up approximately 35 per cent of the total population.

The remainder included members of most other ethnic groups in the country; seven were born in other French-speaking territories. Of the sixteen top leaders—members of the Bureau Politique and Houphouet-Boigny—six were Baoule, or twice as many as there would be if the distribution reflected the total population of the Ivory Coast. This gave some weight to complaints often voiced by other ethnic groups about Baoule domination.

Changes in the party were not limited to the upper strata alone. After the congress, when it became obvious that the Ivory Coast would soon be fully independent, roving teams of the JRDACI and of the PDCI toured the country to reorganize basic units; in many places elections were held for the first time since the units were founded. The party newspaper announced that the proper payment of dues was necessary in order to establish a census of those who were conscientious and active party militants, concerned with participating in the future of the country. Although the outcome of these efforts will not be visible for some time, the very fact that they were undertaken reveals the intent of the leaders to transform the party into a more efficient instrument of government rule.

INTERNAL PARTY ORGANIZATION

The formal structure of the PDCI, as created in 1947, has persisted to the present with only minor changes. It is based on village and neighborhood committees throughout the country, linked vertically to a sous-section at the level of the fifty or so administrative subdivisions into which the Ivory Coast was divided by the colonial administration. These larger units are further linked vertically to the Comité Directeur. The PDCI as a whole is a *section* of the RDA. The members of the basic units elect their own leaders; each level elects the next higher one, on the principle of democratic centralism. Formally, the PDCI is a direct party, strongly articulated vertically, based on branch-type basic units.[8] In reality, the structure, the pattern of communications, and the distribution of power within the party deviate considerably from this model.

In 1959 about one-half of the 8,000 villages in the Ivory Coast had, at least nominally, a PDCI committee. But many of these units existed on paper only. General Secretary Denise emphasized in his report to the congress that the village committees "must be awakened because, for the most part, they have fallen into some sort of lethargic state." [9] Since 1951 party activity has been limited essentially to urban areas; only during electoral periods has an effort been made to penetrate the hinter-

---

[8] This nomenclature follows the one used by Maurice Duverger, *Political Parties*, trans. Barbara and Robert North (New York: John Wiley & Sons, 1954), pp. 1–60.

[9] "Proceedings of the PDCI Congress of 1959," in "Rapport Moral" (mimeographed), p. 8.

land. The sous-section, instead of being the apex of a series of basic units, has become a caucus-type unit made up of local notabilities. In the towns the neighborhood committees are in fact ethnic units, simply because neighborhoods are usually homogeneous; each immigrant tribal group settles in a separate area of the town. In Treichville, a borough of the capital city, colonial regulations prevented this pattern from emerging. But when party organizers were faced with the task of creating highly solidary units in an environment where many different languages were spoken, they seized upon tribal associations as the nuclei for the organization of party committees. In 1959 there were more than 100 ethnic subcommittees in the Treichville sous-section. In this way the party, which might have provided new social units based on nontraditional affiliations, instead reinforced links based on ethnicity.

This structure was condemned by the party congress in 1959 as being incompatible with true nationalism. A task force was appointed to reorganize urban branches on a nonethnic basis. In the face of resistance on the part of party cadres who manned the existing units and who perceived reorganization as a threat to their own position in the party hierarchy, implementation of the party decision was postponed "until people learned to live together regardless of tribe."

Another important change in party structure took place when the JRDACI was organized. The national leadership sanctioned this development in response to the demands of the new generation, but also because of their own increasing awareness that young people, usually more educated and more modern-minded than their elders, must be directed to work for the party in order to enable the organization to carry out developmental tasks. The problem was, however, how to organize the youth so as to minimize antagonism between JRDACI and PDCI basic units without creating a parallel semiautonomous organization which could later develop into a competing political party.[10] As organized in 1959, the JRDACI was a parallel party; it had its own separate units at the local level, linked vertically to a hierarchy that culminated in the national executive discussed earlier. The units sold JRDACI rather than PDCI membership cards. In many local communities the youth committee became the rallying point not only for young people, but also for those who, regardless of age, were dissatisfied with the rule of the PDCI general secretary; sometimes the unit became a refuge for former adherents to opposition parties. In 1960 separate membership cards were eliminated, and general secretaries were given some control over the youth committees. Thus, after a short experiment leading toward an indirect organization, the PDCI has once more become a direct party.

---

[10] It must be remembered that demography in the Ivory Coast gives young adults (those between 18 and 30) a majority over their elders.

At the beginning the PDCI was heavily dependent upon member-ship dues and upon the personal wealth of some of its leaders, such as Houphouet-Boigny and Denise. In recent years the payment of dues has fallen off. But, while deprived of this revenue, the party has gained access to important new resources which more than made up for the loss. Since 1957 elected representatives have had the power to fix their own salaries; of the substantial sum they allocate to themselves, a share is contributed to the party. Some European businessmen, elected in 1957 and again in 1959, served without pay; their entire salary could thus be turned over to the party. Businessmen and traders, who paid tribute in the past to traditional chiefs and to colonial officials, have now shifted their gifts to the new men of power. The most important change in the party's finan-cial structure, however, stems from its status as the government party. Most party expenses can now be met out of public funds. Because party leaders are also government officials, expenses they incur while touring the country or attending meetings are drawn out of the budget: trans-portation is provided by the government; important meetings are held in public buildings; party rallies are regarded as public festivities. In this respect also, party and government have become one.

It is in the distribution of power and in the pattern of decision making that the PDCI in practice deviates most widely from the theoretical model of a party based on democratic centralism. Power resides almost exclusively in the hands of an individual who is outside the formal party structure, the PDCI's honorary president, Félix Houphouet-Boigny. Evi-dence to confirm this fact is abundant. Reference has already been made to his control of recruitment of party leadership. Another indication may be found in the process of selecting candidates to public office. In 1959, for example, the sous-sections were asked to draw up lists of candidates and submit them for final selection to the Bureau Politique. Many more names were thus suggested than there were seats available; estimates range up to 1,000 names for 100 seats in the Legislative Assembly. In making the final decision, the Bureau Politique had a wide choice, but some of its members reported that there was in fact little consultation within the party's highest organ; decisions were made by the Old Man alone. Although he explained the grounds for his selections to high party officials, recruitment to public office, like membership in the party execu-tive, was, in fact, tantamount to appointment by Houphouet-Boigny.

In this respect the general political mood of the Ivory Coast is more significant than any specific decision. Although communications within the party must in theory follow the chain of command provided by the hierarchy, often they skip all intermediary levels and reach Houphouet-Boigny directly. Final decisions are seldom made by anyone in the party or in the government, but are submitted to Houphouet-Boigny. During his many absences from the country, the work of government sometimes seemed to come to a halt. Even routine decisions had to await his return. This was the result of institutionalized insecurity among officials at all levels, including those of cabinet rank. After the first Ivory Coast government was formed in 1957, decrees issued by ministers who were also members of the party executive were repeatedly voided after they had been published in the *Journal Officiel* of the Ivory Coast while Houphouet-Boigny was absent. By 1959 many had learned their lesson and were refusing to commit themselves to specific action unless it had been cleared at the top. Decisions made by lesser officials were seldom considered authoritative unless approved by Houphouet-Boigny in person.

If the question of power is raised, however, it is necessary to ask to what extent Houphouet-Boigny—and, through him, the PDCI—can get the people of the Ivory Coast to do things they would not otherwise do. What demands are made upon individuals and groups? In 1958 and again in 1959 they were asked to pass up the opportunity to choose independence; there was little doubt, however, that the people and most leaders shared general African feelings on this subject. Yet many party officials who personally disagreed with Houphouet-Boigny's policy did not oppose him publicly and were willing to go along with his decision. When asked to explain, they referred to the need to maintain cohesion and discipline; open disagreement might jeopardize the country's future. And they insisted that their disagreement with the Old Man was after all only a matter of timing; as his judgment had been good in the past, why not accept it again?

In the matter of reorganizing the party to eliminate ethnic subcommittees, the entire party hierarchy, including Houphouet-Boigny, was powerless in the face of local resistance. The outcome was strategic retreat. In how many other instances did a similar pattern prevail? How many times were decisions that were considered necessary by Houphouet-Boigny and other party leaders not taken because of fear that they could not be carried out? The information necessary to answer these questions is unfortunately not available. In its absence, only tentative conclusions may be suggested. Houphouet-Boigny wields a great deal of authority in the Ivory Coast because few have seen the need to challenge him. Those who have—for example, Ivory Coast students in Paris—did not have much of a following and could easily be put in their place. With very few exceptions, the leader's decisions have been viewed as beneficial for the country as a whole. Perhaps most important of all, he has made few demands that entailed personal sacrifices by his followers.

PARTY RELATIONSHIPS WITH OTHER GROUPS AND INSTITUTIONS

The integration of party and government has become official policy in the Ivory Coast. As General Secretary P. Yace put it, "The PDCI is now the governmental party in the Ivory Coast. Government, assembly, and party therefore share the same single goal. This is why you find at the head of the government, a chief: Houphouet-Boigny; at the head of the elected bodies, a leader: Houphouet-Boigny; at the head of the party, a president: Houphouet-Boigny." [11] This relationship prevails at all levels. While Houphouet-Boigny was a minister in the French government, his three top lieutenants occupied the highest public offices in the country: A. Denise was prime minister, J.-B. Mockey was minister of the interior, and Yace was president of the Legislative Assembly. Of the sixty members of the Comité Directeur in 1959, thirty-three held office at the national level and twenty-one others at the regional or the municipal level. In the Ivory Coast, little or no debate occurs in the conciliar organs provided by the constitution for this purpose. All exchanges of views, all explanations, all compromises are made privately rather than publicly. In several instances, when disagreement came to light in the Legislative Assembly over the passage of an item of legislation, the sitting was interrupted to allow party leaders to iron out difficulties. Publicly, decisions are nearly always unanimous.

In the 1959 government several important cabinet positions in the sphere of economics—public works, finances, planning, economic affairs, and agriculture—were entrusted to European specialists rather than to party leaders. This reflected a form of division of labor in the regime; the business aspects of government were carried out by managers, whereas the party dealt with public relations. The party was concerned with the engineering of consent for decisions formulated by specialists accountable to Houphouet-Boigny alone. This arrangement was viewed as a temporary one, to last until party reorganization was completed.

Ever since 1951, when the PDCI began to reconstruct a territorial alliance, its relationships with other political parties and organized associations were based on negotiations and bargaining rather than on all-out contests. As the membership of the four territorial assemblies (1952–1957, 1957–1959, 1959–1960, 1960———) shows, opposition candidates defeated in earlier elections were later given a place on the PDCI ticket. A similar procedure was followed in respect to major trade unions, agricultural organizations, and youth associations. Room was made for the representation of foreign Africans residing in the Ivory Coast and for Frenchmen as well. Although the Ivory Coast has a single-party system, the party rules through an ever-shifting coalition. This enables it to adjust to pressures without giving up its political monopoly. Until recently, for example, Houphouet-Boigny had always been careful to include foreign Africans in the coalition, in part because they make up an important segment of the Ivory Coast population, and in part because this was a way to respond to criticisms of selfishness and of an anti-African

[11] Address to a party rally reported in *Fraternité*, Feb. 26, 1960, p. 10.

attitude formulated by other African countries. This policy led to some internal discontent among Ivory Coasters themselves, who complained of foreign domination. In 1960 all foreigners were dropped from the ticket; instead, several individuals who had been active in antiforeign movements were included.

As part of its current reorganization efforts, the party has attempted to nationalize major voluntary associations. Trade unions in the Ivory Coast were previously affiliated with superterritorial *centrales,* such as the Union Générale des Travailleurs d'Afrique Noire and the Confédération des Travailleurs Croyants de la Côte d'Ivoire. In 1959 a national federation of trade unions, the Union des Travailleurs de la Côte d'Ivoire, was created; its leaders were given membership in the Comité Directeur and in the 1959 Legislative Assembly. Some of the civil servants' unions resisted integration, however, and one of their leaders was exiled to Guinea. His lieutenants immediately launched a retaliatory strike which was condemned as "political" by the government; on this ground, strike leaders were arrested and several hundred civil servants were dismissed from their jobs or suspended. The aftermath too is important, because it reveals a significant aspect of the regime: one of the strike leaders was released a few months later and his name was placed on the 1960 party ticket. Coercion is thus used as a measure of last resort, when everything else fails; even then, it is only a temporary measure. Twice in recent years general amnesty laws brought the release of former political prisoners.

The party's relationship to traditional chiefs has always been ambiguous. Houphouet-Boigny is himself a *chef de canton* and has always insisted that he would not act against forward-looking traditional rulers. The institution of chieftaincy has long been politicized throughout the country. Many chiefs were agents of the SAA in 1944 and 1945; under administrative pressure, many of them later took sides against the PDCI; after 1951 reconciliation took place. More recently the chiefs have formed a kind of trade union, the Syndicat des Chefs Coutumiers, of which Houphouet-Boigny is honorary president. This organization serves as an informal representative body which presents grievances to Houphouet-Boigny; it is convoked by him to be told of decisions that affect its members. Like the Vicar of Bray, Ivory Coast chiefs have been flexible in their political loyalties; like him also, most of them have remained in office undisturbed throughout the postwar period of rapid political change. Although most party leaders who were interviewed regarded the chiefs as the representatives of a dying era who were of little use in the process of national construction, the party has avoided making a frontal attack upon the institution lest this lead to organized reaction wherever the chiefs retain some support. In only a few instances has it been necessary to take strong action against the chiefs. The traditional ruler of Sanwi State, who was involved in a separatist Agni movement, was brought to trial and heavily penalized. On that occasion Houphouet-Boigny publicly castigated narrow-minded chiefs and their even more narrow-minded intellectual followers who should know better.

The PDCI has remained a section of the RDA and Houphouet-Boigny has occupied the office of president since the superterritorial movement was founded. The relationship between the sections and the RDA organization has always been difficult to evaluate. Since 1956 the issues facing French West Africa have been vastly different from those that existed ten years earlier, when the RDA was created. After the Ivory Coast adopted an antifederalist stand, it found itself in opposition to the two other major RDA sections in Guinea and Soudan. Further disagreements arose within the RDA on the question of independence, and more recently on several international issues. It would be misleading to consider the RDA at the present time as a political party or even as a movement; much of its recent history would be more clearly understandable if it were viewed as an alliance of individual parties for specific purposes. Today the RDA is in fact a coalition of governments bound by common views; many of its adherents are paradoxically yesterday's enemies. At the same time, however, the personal ties developed between Ivory Coast leaders and their RDA associates in Guinea and in Mali have remained very strong; perhaps they will provide the sources of renewed relationships in the future.

GOALS AND VALUES

The ultimate objectives of the PDCI have been remarkably consistent throughout the party's existence. As stated in the campaign literature of 1945 and 1946, in RDA pamphlets of the militant years, and in recent public pronouncements, the goals include transformation of an agglomerate of traditional societies into a single national community; achievement of political equality and of democratic control over territorial government; emancipation of the Ivory Coast from its colonial status; economic development and social progress. These objectives are interdependent. The building of a national community requires broadening of the educated strata, which necessitates increased material resources; economic development in turn requires control over the country's own resources and external aid. Economic considerations have therefore been primordial; from them are derived political decisions. To Kwame Nkrumah's exhortation, "Seek ye first the political kingdom," Houphouet-Boigny opposed his own warning, "Freedom has never thrived and will never thrive in the midst of misery."

At the PDCI congress of 1959, Auguste Denise stated that the party, now that its political goals had been achieved, must devote itself to the new task of economic development. Although many thinkers had suggested that the socialist or the Communist approach alone was suitable, the Ivory Coast, Denise emphasized, would rely on "economic liberalism." This did not imply the laissez-faire variety, but "a liberalism that will benefit from the entire range of economic experimentation carried out by others," to which the Ivory Coast would contribute her own experience. It would include policies designed to attract capitalist investments from abroad, but would also be "a coöperative movement with a socialist orientation," inspired by European and Asian examples and characterized by a reliance on human investments, the mobilization of youth, and a will to succeed at all costs. In fact, Denise concluded, this was nothing but a return to the kind of collectivism which is rooted in African tradition.[12]

This eclectic approach is widely supported by other political leaders; in interviews, many of them expressed some admiration for the Chinese Communist example, but viewed it as unnecessarily harsh and probably unfeasible in the Ivory Coast. They usually preferred the Indian and the Israeli examples, based, as they saw it, on persuasion, coöperation, and substantial outside aid. A similar view was formulated by Denise's successor, General Secretary Yace. In an editorial in the party newspaper entitled "Concerning the Realistic Definition of an Economic Policy," he stated that the PDCI rejected "anarchic liberalism," "totalitarian *dirigisme*," and all other "doctrinaire formulas." Although the country followed with interest experiments in "African socialism" carried on elsewhere, "we refuse to offer the present generation as a holocaust for future ones in the name of any ideology whatsoever." [13]

This approach has been made possible so far because the Ivory Coast has several important advantages over some other underdeveloped countries. A large part of the population is basically self-sufficient in terms of the necessities of life; famine is unknown. By African standards, the Ivory Coast is a relatively rich country and has a sizable income from the sale abroad of its two major commodities, coffee and cocoa. Plans for economic development have included diversification, modernization of production, and quality improvement in the field of agriculture; the creation of a small number of transformation industries based on locally produced commodities; and continued search for valuable minerals.

Economic concerns have characterized the Ivory Coast's external relations as well. Its stand on the issue of federation has been reviewed earlier in this paper. As the result of the breakup of the former Federation of French West Africa, the country's budget grew threefold within

---

[12] "Proceedings of the PDCI Congress of 1959," in "Rapport Moral," p. 12.
[13] *Fraternité*, Dec. 25, 1959, pp. 1–2.

four years without an increase in tax rates. After the French Community came into being, Houphouet-Boigny was most outspoken concerning the economic advantages it would offer to the country. At a special RDA congress in September, 1959, he pointed out that "nominal independence" was meaningless in the face of economic underdevelopment. The twentieth century was the era of "interdependence." But why seek unity in misery with other underdeveloped African countries, as some of the advocates of Pan-Africanism would have it? Instead, the Ivory Coast preferred to become a member of some union in which the partners were complementary to one another. The union with France would be possible only if it embodied the twin principles of "equality and solidarity." This meant that the principal partner would give increased aid to the poorer partners. Although France had been helpful in the past, she must be willing to make greater sacrifices than ever.[14]

After the congress it became increasingly obvious that the senior partner did not share these views. An Ivory Coast spokesman warned of the song of the Baoule maidens: "I have given myself to you; now it is up to you to keep me." In June, 1960, the party newspaper announced that the community was "stillborn," and on the same day the Ivory Coast proclaimed its decision to become a sovereign state. France did not object. Because the Ivory Coast refused to reënter the community, however, negotiations for postindependence aid from the metropole encountered some difficulties and were not completed until mid-1961. Since then relationships between the two countries have remained very close, and France continues to assist the Ivory Coast in most fields concerned with social and economic development.

Besides the question of economic development, the party has become increasingly concerned with the problem of amalgamating the many groups that compose the country into a national community. Addressing the Constitutional Committee in 1959, Auguste Denise expressed his dismay at the fact that in recent years, contrary to the PDCI's hope, during its years of struggle, to transform the country into something like "a single tribe," ethnic groups had become increasingly vociferous.[15] There have been a few separatist movements among the border tribes: the Agni and the Nzima of the southeast have occasionally shown a desire to become part of Ghana; in the west there have been border incidents with Guinea and Liberia. The government has been greatly concerned over these evidences of centrifugal tendencies. Furthermore, about one-fourth of the Ivory Coast population is made up of immigrants; rela-

---

[14] *Rapport du Président Houphouet-Boigny au Congrès Extraordinaire du Rassemblement Démocratique Africain,* Sept. 4, 1959 (Abidjan, 1959).

[15] "Procès-Verbal des Travaux de la Commission Spéciale," Côte d'Ivoire, Assemblée Constituante, 1959 (mimeographed), p. 12.

tions between them and the natives are tense. In the fall of 1958 xeno-phobic outbursts led to the mass exodus of more than 20,000 Dahoman, Togolese, Ghanaian, and Nigerian residents. Outbreaks of violence be-tween Ivory Coast employers and agricultural workers from Upper Volta are very common. The abolition of "racism and ethnic particularism" has therefore been given a high priority in party and government pro-grams. This objective was invoked as the rationale for avoiding electoral competition.

Discussing the means to achieve these goals, Houphouet-Boigny de-clared: "We must get down to work on the basis of discipline, which I hope will be freely accepted; but I shall impose it if necessary, because our country must succeed." [16] The formal provisions of the Ivory Coast constitutions of 1959 and 1960 proclaim the country's attachment to democratic principles. Nevertheless, many political leaders feel that the Ivory Coast cannot afford a Western-type democracy; they point out that even France, a highly developed country, has had to transform its regime in order to meet twentieth-century problems. One of the members of the Constitutional Committee, who had exclaimed "You put too much trust in the people!" in the course of the debates, explained this remark in an interview:

Democracy is a system of government for virtuous people. In young countries such as our own, we need a chief who is all-powerful for a specified period of time. If he makes mistakes, we shall replace him later on. . . . The people are amorphous; they cannot study problems such as questions of economic development. We need a system in which alternatives are debated by an elite.

Asked how this could take place within a single-party system, he con-tinued:

The process of choice is not visible because the party does not think its dis-cussions should be public. Debate might get out of hand as it does in other countries more mature than our own. . . . But don't worry about autocracy because we rely on African tradition; a chief must always listen to a council made up of elders, clan leaders, young men. His orders are carried out without hesitation only because discussion has taken place beforehand and he has earned the approval of all concerned.

In the 1959 Constitution these views were translated into a modified parliamentary system in which the executive was dominant. Even then the founding fathers expressed their preference for a presidential system. Their wishes became fundamental law after independence and are em-bodied in the Constitution of 1960.

As an alternative to federation, the Ivory Coast has promoted the formation of an association of French-speaking African states based on

---

[16] *Fraternité,* Sept. 25, 1959, p. 1.

economic and administrative agreements, the Conseil de l'Entente. This organization avoids those features of the former French West African unit which the Ivory Coast considered objectionable, while it preserves many of the advantages. On the international scene, this bloc is currently committed to the support of Western positions in the United Nations. If past behavior offers any guidance for the future, the Ivory Coast may be expected to continue to act in the light of self-interest as she understands it. The country hopes to secure aid for economic development from the West, preferably through continued adherence to a European-African community. In pursuing these objectives, however, the country runs the risk of becoming increasingly isolated from its former RDA partners, Guinea and Mali. The discomfort arising from such a situation may well lead to a readjustment in the Ivory Coast's international outlook.

POLITICAL STRATEGY, TECHNIQUES, AND STYLE

Ever since it became a government party the PDCI has maintained itself through its distributive capacity. Many new political offices have been created to accommodate demands for representation; at the same time, the regime has gained complete control over the allocation of these offices and has reduced government accountability to representative organs. Some of the techniques used were (1) to enlarge constituencies until, in 1960, all seventy members of the National Assembly were elected at large; (2) to require challengers to make up a full slate in order to compete in the election; and (3) to announce the final make-up of the party ticket only a few minutes before the deadline for filing, so that by the time those who were not included found out about it, it was too late to organize a new slate. Thus nomination by the party caucus has been tantamount to election.

The government greatly increased its distributive capacity when it retained the budgetary resources that had earlier been earmarked for the Dakar government. These funds made possible a vast expansion of expenditures on such items as schools, roads, markets, and other tangible features of development, and also permitted the government to win control over bureaucratic offices formerly supervised by French West African authorities. The preferred treatment the Ivory Coast received from France was reflected in increased expenditures by the Fonds d'Investissement pour le Développement Economique et Social, and in market protection. By obtaining approximately 50 per cent more for its coffee than that commodity would fetch on the world market, the Ivory Coast secured an artificial prosperity for its farmers. The satisfactions created in this manner lessened the immediate burdens of government.

In 1960 two additional measures helped promote support. The head tax, considered to be the last vestige of colonialism, was abolished; a few months earlier, a member of the Legislative Assembly had said that "if the government sees its way clear to do this, we're good for another five years at least." Finally, the decision to become independent eliminated many pressures which, building up throughout the country, had made the regime hypersensitive to criticism.

Coercive techniques seem to be used only when all other means prove ineffective; they include warnings, arrests, and exile to other African countries. Ivory Coast practice resembles the technique of preventive detention, although it has not yet been formally institutionalized. Usually, when the emergency is over, or when the issue that led to opposition has been resolved, many of those who were arrested are released.

The most important source of support for the regime continues to be the relationship between the people of the Ivory Coast and Houphouet-Boigny. For many individuals, allegiance to the regime means simply allegiance to its chief. In 1959 many people continued to base their loyalty on the abolition of forced labor, an event that had taken place fourteen years earlier. As one member of the Legislative Assembly put it, "I shall continue to follow him blindly as long as he remains faithful to this principle." Today this principle is implemented by Houphouet-Boigny's continued efforts to secure for the Ivory Coast the greatest possible economic and social development at the least possible cost to its people.

3. SIERRA LEONE

By Martin Kilson

PARTY COMPETITION

Sierra Leone People's Party

The British colonial administration divided Sierra Leone into two distinct political areas, the colony (268 square miles) and the protectorate (27,540 square miles), which followed somewhat different patterns of colonial development. One important feature of the colony's development, which affected the colonial development of Sierra Leone as a whole, was the existence among its population of a community known as Creoles, now numbering 25,000, who were settled there as repatriated slaves in the late eighteenth century and the first half of the nineteenth century. Their early contact with Western culture and their access to Western education enabled the Creoles to attain a measure of wealth and influence in commerce, the professions, and the colonial civil service. Consequently the Creole community gained an early predominance in Sierra Leone politics vastly disproportionate to its small size.

The colony-protectorate division and its sociological consequences have substantially influenced the postwar development of party politics in Sierra Leone. The long-standing predominance of the Creoles, combined with their condescending attitude toward protectorate Africans, stimulated a deep-seated antagonism among educated protectorate groups. In the postwar period the protectorate African encountered the Creole as his major political opponent, and, with the broadening of the franchise to include protectorate Africans in 1951, the protectorate elite effectively exploited anti-Creole feelings among the masses to the advantage of their political party, the Sierra Leone People's Party (SLPP).

Since its foundation in 1951, the SLPP has been the majority party in Sierra Leone. In this period it has withstood a number of political crises, none of which originated from the competition of opposition parties. The crises stemmed, rather, from elements that, although generally favorable to the SLPP, had become dissatisfied with certain of its policies.

The capacity of the SLPP to overcome internal crises and to render competition from opposition parties relatively ineffective stems largely from its ability to attract the support of traditional leaders, who are

90

strongly represented in the structure of the SLPP and in the government. In its accommodation of paramount and other chiefs, the party has synchronized its policy of leadership recruitment with the rather slow pace of social change in Sierra Leone. There has been comparatively little development of education (about 5 to 10 per cent literacy, as compared with 25 to 30 per cent in Ghana) or commercialization of agriculture. In the absence of a strong infusion of Western forms of social and economic organization and activity, there has been no significant erosion of traditional attitudes and norms in regard to political authority. Consequently the vast majority of Sierra Leone's rural population tends to accept direction and advice from traditional leaders. So long as the tempo of social change remains slow, chiefs are likely to be a major source of SLPP predominance.

Sources of Opposition

Despite the influences of traditional ties and institutions on their political behavior, the protectorate masses have, on occasion, rejected the admonitions of their pro-SLPP chiefs. They do this mainly in crisis situations, as at the time of the violent tax disturbances from November, 1955, to March, 1956. On that occasion, peasants and town-dwelling wage laborers in most of the Northern Province of Sierra Leone and in parts of the southern provinces (especially Moyamba District) became angry at the rate of taxation as well as at the corruption, the extortion, and the inefficiency of its administration by native authorities.[1] Some of the peasants shifted their political loyalties from the SLPP to the opposition United Progressive Party (UPP), which, in the first general election in 1957, gained two seats in Port Loko District, one in Kambia District, and one in Moyamba District, all of them centers of the tax riots. The political significance of this disaffection with the SLPP and its chiefly supporters is further seen in the fact that the opposition UPP was a party, not of protectorate Africans, but of colony origin.

Dissatisfaction with the SLPP's leadership was, however, limited in extent and duration. Although some peasants shifted their support to the Creole-dominated UPP in the 1957 election, the SLPP nevertheless gained 44 per cent of the protectorate seats, some of them located in the areas of the tax riots (e.g., Bombali East and West, Tonkolili East and West, and Moyamba South). Also, within two years of the 1957 election most of the disenchanted protectorate voters had returned to the SLPP. In the local elections in October, 1959, the UPP won only 2 of 324 district council seats (0.6 per cent), whereas the People's National Party (PNP), founded by Albert Margai in 1958, won 33 seats (10.2 per cent) and the SLPP

---

[1] Sir Herbert Cox, *Report of the Commission of Enquiry into Disturbances in the Provinces, November 1955–March 1956* (Freetown, 1956).

won 232 seats (71.6 per cent). Independent candidates, all of whom later declared themselves SLPP councilors, won the remaining 57 seats (17.6 per cent).

In the 1962 general election, however, the SLPP was weakest in protectorate areas where peasants and wage laborers questioned their political relationship to traditional leaders and institutions. In the Northern Province districts of Kambia, Port Loko, Tonkolili, and Bombali, where the 1955–56 tax riots had reached their highest pitch, the opposition All People's Congress (APC), led by Siaka Stevens, a protectorate African, who had formerly been a leader of the protectorate United Mine Workers' Union, gained twelve seats (or more than half of the twenty seats it won out of sixty-two contested seats). Five of these were won in quasi-urban or town constituencies, and four of the eight seats the APC won outside the north were in even more distinctly urban constituencies in the Western Province (the new designation given in 1961 to the Southwestern Province, formerly the colony area). The APC won its remaining four seats in Kono District, Southeastern Province, where it was allied with the Sierra Leone Progressive Independence Movement (SLPIM). As the center of the diamond-mining industry, and the protectorate district where the peasantry has experienced the greatest degree of socioeconomic change, Kono has long been a crisis area. The relatively rapid social change has necessarily created conflict between the peasantry and the chiefs, which was sharply reflected in the 1960 district council election in Kono. The SLPP, winning only six of the thirty council seats, was soundly beaten by the militant opposition party, the SLPIM, which won twenty-four seats.

Nevertheless, the SLPP is still in effective control of Sierra Leone politics. In the 1962 general election it gained forty-two seats in the House of Representatives, although thirteen of them were actually won by independents who later declared themselves SLPP legislators. In Sierra Leone, however, candidates who stand as independents are fundamentally SLPP-oriented, for they have the same characteristics as SLPP candidates, such as political conservatism and kinship ties with chiefs. When elected to local or national office, independents invariably join the SLPP.

Problems of Opposition Parties

Certain organizational features of opposition parties have tended to compound their weak competitive position vis-à-vis the SLPP. Since the establishment of an elected unofficial majority in the Legislative and Executive councils in 1951, no less than eleven political parties, excluding the SLPP, have emerged.[2] The National Council (NC) and the Positive

---

[2] The National Council was organized in 1950. The eleven parties organized in 1951 or later, with dates of organization, are Positive Action Party, 1951; British

Action Party (PAP) have been so closely associated with the conservative elements of the Creole community in the colony that they have never been able to win support among protectorate Africans. Three of the parties served mainly as political platforms for their individual founders, and when an election was over they were either disbanded or were absorbed by other parties. For example, the British Koya Political Party (BKPP) was disbanded after J. C. O. Crowther used it to get elected to the legislature in 1951, and the Sierra Leone Independence Movement (SLIM) was absorbed by the KPM after its leader, Dr. Edward Blyden III, failed of election to the legislature in 1957.

Only the UPP, the PNP, and the APC have attempted to compete with the SLPP at the national level. The growth of the UPP has been inhibited because of its Creole origin, and all three of these parties have lacked the capacity to build nationwide organizations, mainly because of inadequate financial support. The PNP and the APC have solicited external financial help, a fact that could have significant consequences for the whole political system in Sierra Leone. In the spring of 1960 all the opposition parties, except the APC and a rump of the UPP, surrendered political opposition and accepted the SLPP's proposal to join it in the formation of the United National Front (UNF) and a coalition government.

HISTORICAL DEVELOPMENT OF POLITICAL PARTIES

The term "political party" means an organized group of persons which seeks to control the decision-making machinery of government, normally through elections. The political party in this sense is a relatively recent institution in Sierra Leone, simply because until 1951 the decision-making machinery of government was not freely accessible to organized groups of persons. Rather, this machinery was part of an authoritarian governmental arrangement under effective control of British colonial officials. Nonetheless, it was a principle of British colonial policy that nonofficial groups should be permitted to influence decision making, and, under certain circumstances, even to be represented in the government. In the late nineteenth and early twentieth centuries, pressure groups, protopolitical parties, and protonationalist parties were formed and sought to influence the colonial government in the interest of their members.

Pressure Groups and Protopolitical Parties

One of the first political pressure groups in colonial Africa was the Sierra Leone Mercantile Association, founded in the mid-1850's and sur-

---

Koya Political Party, 1951; UPP, 1954; Labour Party, 1955; KPM, 1957; Sierra Leone Independence Movement, 1957; SLPIM, 1958; PNP, 1958; Radical Democratic Party, 1958; Independent Progressive Party, 1960; All People's Congress, 1960.

viving for about ten years. As an association of wealthy African (Creole) merchants, its main goal was the attainment of favorable trade policies. In pursuit of this goal it sought representation in the colonial legislature, and in 1863 one of its members, John Ezzidio, was appointed as the first African member of the Legislative Council.[3] When the Mercantile Association declined in the mid-1860's, its work was assumed by another pressure group known as the Sierra Leone Native Association (1872–1882), and later by the Sierra Leone Association (1884–1888). The latter was the more influential, and its members, like those of the Mercantile Association, were mainly well-to-do merchants, though several lawyers and clergymen also belonged to it.[4] Its main aims were the expansion of trade and the development of agriculture. The Sierra Leone Association, however, differed from the Mercantile Association in having some contact, even though limited, with the poorer and the non-Creole elements of the Freetown community through its public meetings.

By the second decade of the twentieth century, mercantile pressure groups were replaced by protopolitical or protonationalist parties. These associations are so designated because, although contesting elections, they fell short of gaining control of the decision-making machinery of colonial government; the protonationalist party had the added feature of conceiving its activity in explicitly anticolonial and nationalist terms. The protopolitical party emerged in 1909 in the form of ratepayers' associations. Three such associations were formed in that year to nominate candidates to contest the Freetown City Council elections;[5] their members, as payers of the city rate, were predominantly Creoles. Very few, if any, indigenous Africans resident in Freetown qualified as electors. As political organizations, there is little doubt that the ratepayers' associations approximated parties in a modern sense, for they sought to control the municipal government of Freetown in the interest of their members and supporters.[6] The control of the central colonial government, however, was not yet possible, though the ratepayers' associations did contest elections to the Legislative Council in 1924 and 1929.

Existing simultaneously with the ratepayers' associations were the protonationalist parties. There were two major parties of this type before World War II: the Sierra Leone Branch of the National Congress of

[3] *Sierra Leone Government Blue Book, 1863* (Freetown, 1864).

[4] *Sierra Leone Weekly News,* Jan. 24, 1885, pp. 2–3.

[5] The City Council was established by ordinance in 1893, with an elected unofficial African majority of twelve members and three official members. For electoral purposes, Freetown, the capital city, was divided into three wards having, in 1900, a population of about 34,000, of whom 848 were eligible to vote.

[6] Cf. *Fifteenth Annual Minute of the Mayor of the City* (Freetown, 1910), p. 22: "I must severely condemn the party-spirit and antagonism for party purposes . . . which have manifested themselves during the year in Council meetings. . . . It is like a desire to secure the personal ends rather than . . . the interests of the City."

British West Africa (referred to hereafter as the Sierra Leone National Congress, or SLNC) and the West African Youth League, Sierra Leone Branch (referred to hereafter as the Sierra Leone Youth League, or SLYL). The SLNC was formed in 1920 (though originally conceived in Ghana in 1918) to provide machinery through which the colonial government could be persuaded to grant Africans broader representation in the legislature, and ultimately self-government.[7] It also sought more positions in the civil service for members of the emergent African middle class, who constituted the main body of the SLNC's members and supporters. The SLNC was more attentive to matters of organization than its predecessors had been, and developed liaison with such groups as teachers' associations, women's clubs, church groups, and trade unions. It also employed a variety of political techniques for pursuing its goals, which included public meetings, protest marches, submission of memoranda to the colonial government, deputations to the Secretary of State for the Colonies, and participation in the election of three representatives to the Legislative Council (as provided in the 1924 Constitution). SLNC candidates won most of the legislative elections, and participation in the Legislative Council proved an important outlet for its demands.

By the late 1930's the SLNC was eclipsed by the SLYL, founded in 1938 by I. T. A. Wallace-Johnson, a journalist. Like the SLNC, the SLYL sought increased African representation in the organs of colonial government and ultimate control of these organs by Africans. Its approach, however, was more radical than the SLNC's; through its newspaper, the *African Standard,* the SLYL launched militant attacks against the colonial regime. Moreover, although its leaders were members of the emergent middle class, the SLYL conceived of itself as a party of the masses, and attempted to expand its organization in accordance with this conception. It was the first Sierra Leone political group to establish branches in the protectorate, and within less than a year of its founding the SLYL claimed 7,000 members.[8] Another difference between the two parties was the SLYL's Marxist orientation, which originated in the educational experiences of its organizing secretary, Wallace-Johnson, who pursued higher education in Soviet Russia during the early 1930's. This orientation was revealed in the language and the thought which characterized the SLYL's propaganda against colonialism, in the use of the word "comrade" as the mode of address among its members, and in the subtitle of one of the two party organs, the *African Worker,* which read: "Being the Articulative

[7] *Constitution of the National Congress of British West Africa* (1923), Sec. 19: "The aims of the Congress shall be to aid in the development of the political institutions of British West Africa under the Union Jack, so as eventually to take her place beside the sister nations of the Empire, and in time, to ensure within her borders the government of the people, by the people, for the people."
[8] *Sierra Leone Weekly News,* Aug. 13, 1938, pp. 8–9.

Voice of the Toiling Masses." It was largely the SLYL's Marxist and militantly anticolonial orientation that prompted the colonial government to imprison its organizing secretary during World War II, and in the postwar period the party, unable to recapture its earlier dynamic quality, was absorbed by the NC, and later by the UPP.

Postwar Political Parties

In Sierra Leone, as elsewhere in West Africa, the pace of political change quickened in the postwar period. The expansion of education and the increasing number of university-trained professionals signalized, in part, a pressing need to associate Africans more and more with the decision-making machinery of government. Toward this end, proposals for constitutional reform were put forth by the colonial government in 1947. They provided for an African unofficial majority of fourteen in the Legislative Council of twenty-three members. These proposals were subsequently discarded because they satisfied neither the colony nor the protectorate political groups; the former considered the ten seats offered the protectorate too many, and the latter regarded them as too few. The conflict over these proposals, however, stimulated the formation of post·war nationalist parties.

National Council of the Colony of Sierra Leone.—The first major party to emerge in the postwar period was the National Council of the Colony of Sierra Leone (NC). It was formed in August, 1950, to represent colony interests in the constitutional conflict with the protectorate. Organizationally, the NC was composed of about seven political and semi-political associations, all of which were predominantly Creole in membership (e.g., the ratepayers' associations, the Nova Scotian and Maroon Descendants' Association, the Settlers' Descendants' Union, etc.). It also had close ties with other associations led by Creoles but composed mainly of emigrant Africans from the protectorate who were resident in Freetown (e.g., the Artisan and General Workers' Union). The NC's leaders, like those of the prewar parties, were members of the emergent middle class: the president was H. C. Bankole-Bright, a medical doctor who was also general organizing secretary and founder of the prewar SLNC; the vice-president was a lawyer, C. D. Hotobah During; and the general secretary, C. M. A. Thompson, was a businessman. The party, through its determination to prevent any erosion of Creole political and social supremacy, reflected the interests and the backgrounds of its leaders. In an election manifesto issued in 1951, the NC referred to protectorate Africans as "foreigners," objected to protectorate predominance in the Legislative Council, and even supported independence for the colony as a means of preventing its own political eclipse by protectorate Africans.

In pursuit of its goals, which were obviously unattainable, the NC followed a strategy that was essentially obstructionist: it contested in court the legality of the 1951 Constitution, which gave the protectorate majority representation in the legislature; it dispatched memorials and deputations to the Secretary of State for the Colonies and to the British Crown; and, through its four representatives in the 1951–1957 Legislative Council, it opposed nearly all the acts of the SLPP government, regardless of their worth. The futility of the NC's political behavior was seen in its complete defeat in the 1957 general election; all its candidates, including Bankole-Bright, were beaten. Since then the NC has modified both its goals and its strategy, and in 1960 it joined the SLPP government in forming the UNF to facilitate Sierra Leone's assumption of independence in 1961.

Sierra Leone People's Party.—The SLPP was formed in April, 1951, some eight months after the NC was organized, through the merger of three political associations: the People's Party (PP), the Protectorate Educational Progressive Union (PEPU), and the Sierra Leone Organization Society (SOS). Of these, the PP, founded in 1949 by a liberal Creole, Laminah Sankoh, contributed least to the character of the SLPP. The PEPU and the SOS, however, both originated in the protectorate. Although both were mainly improvement associations, the SOS had explicit political inclinations insofar as its ultimate goal was to attain an independent Sierra Leone. The SOS also differed from the PEPU in that it was organized by a small group of educated protectorate Africans, whereas the PEPU was organized, led, and financed largely by paramount chiefs, except for Dr. (later Sir) Milton Margai, its deputy president.[9] Only one of the SOS's founding members was a paramount chief, Julius Gulama, who was one of the thirty educated paramount chiefs among some two hundred in the protectorate. The other founders were John Karefa-Smart, a medical doctor; Siaka Stevens, a trade-union leader; J. D. Manley, a clergyman; and Doyle Sumner, T. M. Williams, and F. S. Anthony, all teachers.[10] Although the SOS did utilize chiefly institutions in organizational activities, its orientation was mainly antichief and antitraditional. This is suggested, for instance, in a memorandum it submitted to the colonial government concerning the 1948 constitutional proposals:

During the twenty-five years of the existence of the present Legislative Council constitution, Government has never nominated the "Progressive and younger element" outside the Chiefs' class to sit in the Legislative Council. . . . Such discrimination has been responsible for the present monopoly over Protectorate representation which the chiefs hold in the District Councils, the Protectorate Assembly, the Legislative Council and the Executive Council. . . . It is . . .

---

[9] "Minutes of the Moyamba District Council" (MS), March 14, 1947, p. 1.

[10] Sumner was also founder and president of the Protectorate Teachers' Union and editor of its organ, *Vacco;* Williams and Anthony were officers of the union.

necessary that definite provisions should be made for the inclusion of the new progressive and literate element into the membership of the new Legislative Council.[11]

When the SOS and the PEPU merged to form the SLPP in 1951, it was inevitable that the pattern of organization and the political orientation of each association would influence the character of the SLPP. Although officially the SLPP claimed to be an all–Sierra Leonean party recognizing neither regional nor tribal boundaries (e.g., it adopted the motto: "One Country, One People"), in point of fact it functioned largely in the interest of protectorate Africans. Indeed, its protectorate orientation was ensured through their assumption of its major offices. Sir Milton Margai was the first national chairman and parliamentary leader; Paramount Chief Bai Farima Tass II was deputy leader; A. J. Momoh, a retired civil servant, was vice-president; and Kandeh Bureh, a teacher and a Temne tribal headman in Freetown, was national treasurer. Margai, the most influential political personality among protectorate Africans, did insist, however, that the SLPP at least attempt to function as a national party at the leadership level. Consequently, two Creole leaders of liberal persuasion were given senior leadership roles in the SLPP: Laminah Sankoh became a second vice-president of the party; and H. E. B. John, a teacher who, like Sankoh, had supported the protectorate cause in the postwar constitutional dispute, was appointed national general secretary.

Within the protectorate itself, the Mende tribe predominated in the formation and the leadership of the SLPP, as they had in the PEPU and the SOS.[12] Five of the SLPP's national officers in 1951 were Mende from the south, and two, both Temne, were northerners. A similar pattern prevailed in the party's Executive Council, formed after the 1951 elections. Three members of the council were southerners and Mende (Milton Margai; Albert Margai, a lawyer; and A. G. Randle, a businessman); two were northerners, one a Temne and one a Limba (Paramount Chief Bai Farima Tass II, and Siaka Stevens); and one was an Aku Muslim (M. S. Mustapha, a businessman in the colony). Despite an occasional criticism by northerners, especially the Temne, that they should be granted more posts in the party and the government executive, the south-

---

[11] "S.O.S. Memorandum to the Secretary of State for the Colonies on the New Constitution" (typescript; Nov., 1949), p. 1. Cf. F. S. Anthony, "Memorandum of the S.O.S.," *Sierra Leone Weekly News*, Oct. 18, 1947, p. 3: "The District Councils and the Protectorate Assembly . . . are merely composed of the natural rulers . . . and therefore are not democratic institutions from which an electoral body can be formed for the peoples of the Protectorate."

[12] Of the founders of the SOS, four were southerners and Mende, and three were northerners of the Loko, Limba, and Temne tribes, respectively. All officers of the PEPU were southerners and Mende, as were all officers of the SOS with the exception of Karefa-Smart, who was a Temne from the north, though raised in Mende country where he had maternal kin.

ern and Mende hegemony in the SLPP has thus far not been significantly altered.

PARTY LEADERS, MEMBERS, AND SUPPORTERS

Patterns of Leadership Recruitment

At the level of party representation in the legislature, the two outstanding factors influencing leadership recruitment are occupation and tribe. Table 1 shows the occupational distribution of Sierra Leone's fifty-

TABLE 1

OCCUPATIONAL DISTRIBUTION OF SIERRA LEONEAN LEGISLATORS, 1960

Occupation	SLPP (39)	PNP-Alliance[a] (6)	IPP (4)	UPP (1)	Nominated members (2)	Total (52)
Professional						
Lawyer	2	2	0	1	0	5
Doctor	2	0	0	0	0	2
Druggist	2	1	0	0	1	4
Teacher	5	0	1	0	0	6
Accountant	0	1	1	0	0	2
Politician	0	1	1	0	0	2
Total	11	5	3	1	1	21
Business						
Produce merchant	2	1	0	0	0	3
Importer	1	0	0	0	0	1
Transporter	1	0	0	0	0	1
Trader	4	0	0	0	0	4
Hotel owner	2	0	0	0	0	2
Manager	0	0	0	0	1[b]	1
Total	10	1	0	0	1	12
Other						
Clerk	3	0	1	0	0	4
Civil servant	2	0	0	0	0	2
Native administration official	1	0	0	0	0	1
Chief	12	0	0	0	0	12
Total	18	0	1	0	0	19

[a] Created by the legislative merger of the SLPIM with the PNP.
[b] European manager of an iron ore–mining company.

two legislators in 1960. Twenty-one, or 40 per cent, are professionals; twelve, or 23 per cent, are businessmen; and thirteen, or 25 per cent, are native administration officials. Some 54 per cent of the SLPP legislators, all the UPP and the PNP-Alliance legislators, and all but one of the Independent Progressive Party (IPP) legislators are professionals and businessmen. The preponderance of these two categories (together they account for 63 per cent of Sierra Leone's legislators) is not unique to Sierra Leone; it is also found in other areas such as Nigeria and Ghana.[13] This circumstance is owing to the greater capacity of professional and business leaders to finance political activity, to their possession of the leisure time necessary for such activity, and to their superior educational attainments.

The importance of tribal affiliation in the recruitment of party legislators is shown in table 2. With 58 per cent, the Mende and the Temne

TABLE 2

TRIBAL AFFILIATION OF SIERRA LEONEAN LEGISLATORS, 1960

Tribe and population	Per cent of population[a]	SLPP	PNP	IPP	UPP	Nominated members[b]	Total	Per cent of legislators
Mende (815,000)	36.2	15	3	0	0	0	18	35
Temne (620,000)	27.5	12	0	0	0	0	12	23
Creole (25,000)	1.1	5	1	3	1	1	11	22
Kono (164,000)	7.2	1	2	0	0	0	3	6
Kuranko (80,000)	3.5	2	0	0	0	0	2	4
Loko (80,000)	3.5	1	0	0	0	0	1	2
Sherbro (90,000)	4.0	1	0	1	0	0	2	4
Mandinga (10,000)	0.4	1	0	0	0	0	1	2
Aku (5,000)	0.2	1	0	0	0	0	1	2
Total	83.6	39	6	4	1	1	51	100

[a] Population percentages are based upon a total population estimate of 2,250,000. Present census officials believe Sierra Leone's population to be nearer 3,000,000.

[b] One of the two nominated members was a European, and hence had no tribal affiliation. For this reason the total number of legislators included here is fifty-one instead of fifty-two.

together have a clear majority in legislative representation. This, of course, reflects their large proportion of the population, but the strength of the Mende representation is based also on their historical role in postwar politics and their higher educational development, and perhaps on certain political features of their traditional system. Creole legislative

[13] James S. Coleman, *Nigeria: Background to Nationalism* (Berkeley and Los Angeles: University of California Press, 1958), pp. 280–283; J. H. Price, "The Gold Coast's Legislators," *West Africa*, May 26, 1956, pp. 324–325.

representation (22 per cent) is less attributable to their demographic position than to their educational attainments, which make them better able to participate in politics (at least in the colony area).[14] On a party basis, it is worth noting that the Mende make up 38 per cent of the SLPP legislators, as against 30 per cent for the Temne, and that this pattern of Mende hegemony prevails throughout all spheres of the recruitment of SLPP leaders.

United Progressive Party and People's National Party.—Both the UPP and the PNP (the major opposition parties until the recent emergence of the APC) expressed the desire to ignore tribalism and regionalism as political weapons, especially in the sphere of recruiting leaders. Between its foundation in July, 1954, and the tax riots of 1955–56, the UPP was essentially a party of Creoles of liberal persuasion. At the time of the tax riots, however, the UPP saw an opportunity to penetrate the protectorate, a necessary development if it was to compete with the SLPP. Thus, at its national convention in 1956, and again in 1958, the UPP named several protectorate Africans, including two leaders of the tax riots, to important offices. The PNP found its leadership primarily among protectorate Africans; Albert Margai, its leader, Siaka Stevens, its deputy leader, S. T. Navo, its treasurer, Y. Sillah, its general secretary, and Maigore Kallon, its organizing secretary, were all from that group. Creole representation among the party's leadership was limited to the Executive and Steering committees. In regard to the social and educational attributes of their leaders, the UPP and the PNP were rather similar. The top leaders of both were men with university training; the organizers of both possessed secondary education.

Sierra Leone People's Party.—Africans of protectorate origin are prominent among the SLPP's leadership. In 1960, nine of the thirteen national officers of the party, ten of its thirteen ministers, and nearly all its representatives in the legislature were protectorate Africans. There has, moreover, been a tendency toward Mende predominance. In 1961, five of the party's fourteen national officers, including the Life President and the Parliamentary Leader, five of its ministers, including the Prime Minister, and 35 per cent of its legislators were Mende. The preëminence in the SLPP and in postwar politics stems partly from the educational

---

[14] Whereas in 1938 the colony, with a population of 96,422, had 82 schools (70 primary, 9 secondary, 3 vocational), and 57.6 per cent of its children (mainly Creole) attended school, the protectorate, with a population of 1,667,790, had 185 schools (183 primary, no secondary, 2 vocational), and only 3.25 per cent of its children attended school (*Annual Report of the Education Department, 1938* [Freetown, 1940], pp. 6–8). The same pattern prevailed a decade later, with the colony claiming 54 per cent of educational expenditures and having 55 per cent of its children in school, whereas the protectorate claimed only 29 per cent of such expenditures and had 4 per cent of its children in school (*Report on the Development of Education in Sierra Leone* [Freetown, 1948], p. 3).

advantages enjoyed by the Mende; missionary education came to them
in the mid-nineteenth century, before it came to other protectorate peoples, and the first government secondary school in the protectorate was
opened in 1906 at Bo, the cultural center of the Mende country. It was
not until after World War II that a similar school was begun in the Northern Province. Another reason for Mende political predominance in Sierra
Leone may be that their traditional political culture, more secular, open,
competitive, and participant-oriented than that of the Temne (the second-
largest tribal group) in the north, may have accustomed them to behavior
characteristic of modern territorial political systems.

Like the PNP and other parties, the SLPP has recruited its leaders
from among the groups that rank high socially and educationally, although in the latter respect SLPP leaders, at least its ministers, rank
somewhat below PNP leaders (see table 3 for comparative data).

TABLE 3

HIGHEST EDUCATIONAL LEVEL ATTAINED BY SELECTED POLITICAL LEADERS
IN SIERRA LEONE, 1960

Educational level	SLPP ministers		PNP legislators		IPP legislators	
	Number	Per cent	Number	Per cent	Number	Per cent
Primary	1	8	0	0	0	0
Secondary	8	61	2	33	3	75
College and university	4	31	4	67	1	25
Total	13	100	6	100	4	100

A particularly significant sociological feature of the SLPP's recruitment has been the prominent role of traditional leaders. Paramount and
other chiefs are important at various levels of the party organization; in
1961 two paramount chiefs were ministers and twelve were members of
the forty-member SLPP parliamentary party. Among the factors contributing to the important role of chiefs in the SLPP is that educated
SLPP leaders have kinship ties with the traditional ruling strata. Another
is that the constitutional changes of 1951 provided a major impetus for
chiefs to enter national politics; the responsibility of electing the protectorate's fourteen representatives to the Legislative Council was given to
local assemblies controlled by chiefs. Twelve of the fourteen were to be
elected by the twelve district councils dominated by paramount chiefs
and tribal authorities; the other two were to be elected by the Protectorate
Assembly, whose twenty-nine African members included eighteen paramount chiefs. In effect, the constitutional changes of 1951 made it impos-

sible for any party that did not have the support of traditional leadership to win the protectorate seats in the Legislative Council. In the 1951 Legislative Council, eight of the fourteen members were paramount chiefs, and all but one of the nonchiefly representatives had kinship ties with traditional rulers. Paramount chiefs were again granted substantial representation when the legislature was reconstituted in 1956–57, with 24 per cent of the seats being reserved for them. Thus, throughout the postwar period, the constitutional changes effected by the colonial authority gave the SLPP no alternative to the inclusion of chiefs in its leadership structure.

Another feature of SLPP leadership recruitment is related to the chiefly social strata. The party has drawn many leaders from educated or middle-class groups who have close kinship ties with chiefs. In 1961, five of the SLPP's national officers and ten of its thirteen ministers were kin (i.e., mainly sons, nephews, or grandsons, but also sons-in-law) to traditional ruling families. This kinship factor applies also to the recruitment of party organizers, for all the provincial propaganda secretaries in 1961 were kin to traditional rulers. It applies further to the recruitment of candidates for both local and national office. Table 4 shows that in protec-

TABLE 4

CANDIDATES WITH CHIEFLY KINSHIP TIES IN PROTECTORATE CONSTITUENCIES IN THE 1957 GENERAL ELECTION IN SIERRA LEONE

| Party | Total number of candidates | Candidates with chiefly kinship ties | | | | Per cent of number of candidates |
		South-western Province (21)[a]	South-eastern Province (20)[a]	Northern Province (23)[a]	Total	
SLPP	25	7	4	7	18	72
UPP	6	2	0	0	2	33
Independents	33	5	10	3	18	55
Total	64	14	14	10	38	59

[a] Figures in parentheses denote number of candidates in each province.

torate constituencies, in 1957, 72 per cent of the SLPP candidates, 33 per cent of the UPP candidates, 55 per cent of the independents, and 59 per cent of all candidates had chiefly kinship ties. There is little doubt that such kinship, despite the influence of modern forces such as education, occupation, and constitutional change, has been a significant force in the recruitment of SLPP leadership and a crucial variable in the party's political predominance.

Party Members and Supporters

In the 1957 general election in Sierra Leone, contested under a qualified franchise, there were 494,917 registered voters; under the 1960 electoral ordinance, which provided for universal suffrage, male and female, there were nearly 900,000 qualified voters. The actual recruitment of these qualified voters into party membership, however, has not been actively pursued by Sierra Leonean parties. Available data show that in 1961, when the country's population was approximately 2.5 million, the total membership of the three main parties was about 150,000, representing only 20 per cent of the qualified voters and 4 per cent of the population. The relative insignificance of the membership in the activities of Sierra Leonean parties is suggested by comparison with the Convention People's Party of Ghana, whose 1,000,583 members in 1955 [15] constituted 25 per cent of the country's total population of 4,000,000, and a major proportion of the number of registered voters. In 1960 the ruling party in Guinea, the Parti Démocratique de Guinée, had some 1,600,000 members in a total population that was about the same as Sierra Leone's.

Party membership has been of little importance to the SLPP (it numbered about 80,000 in 1960) because the party has relied upon such traditional institutions as paramount chiefs, tribal authorities, and Poro societies to ensure it adequate political support. When political need arises, these groups are called upon to gather audiences of chiefdom subjects, to instruct peasants to vote for SLPP candidates, to distribute party membership cards to peasants, and to perform other similar functions. In general, peasants are the most widely represented social category among the SLPP's members, though some urban and periurban workers, especially in Freetown, also support the party; many of the latter are recruited through the quasi-traditional institution of urban tribal headmen. Clerks, teachers, and professionals are also represented among the SLPP's members. Tribally, the Mende tend to dominate, with the Temne forming the second-largest tribal group.

The now-defunct PNP was like the SLPP in being basically a protectorate party, but its membership base differed from the SLPP's in two respects. Its members were younger, and they were largely urban. Both features reflected the origin of the PNP as a splinter party that broke with the SLPP over leadership issues between Milton Margai and his younger brother, Albert Margai. The former represented the older generation of leaders, who believed in a gradualist, constitutional approach; the latter was the leader of the younger elements, who were more militant. When Albert Margai left the SLPP in 1958 to form the PNP, he took with him

---

[15] David E. Apter, *The Gold Coast in Transition* (Princeton: Princeton University Press, 1955), p. 217.

most of his followers among the protectorate youth, mainly Mende and Temne, who had left their tribal areas to seek urban employment as clerks, teachers, workers, and so forth. Many of the members and supporters of Siaka Stevens' APC, basically the successor to the PNP, are in the same categories.

Commitment of Leaders and Members to Party Life

In general, Sierra Leone parties are marked by a very low degree of commitment, on the part of both leaders and members, to involvement in party life. There are a number of reasons for this apathy. First, there is a dearth of party machinery through which such involvement can be effected. Second, the relatively unaltered traditional outlook of many members hinders active participation in political life. Third, many persons have become party members, not as an act of personal will, but because a tribal authority official requested or demanded that they do so.

Normally, a small number of party members are active at election time, but they are educated persons who are often paid by candidates to canvass on their behalf. At times, also, a paramount chief summons several hundred peasants and workers in protectorate areas to a native court to welcome SLPP ministers who are making a tour of the provinces. But these gatherings, where peasants drum, dance, and sing in traditional idioms not particularly related to modern politics, seldom reflect serious political involvement.

As might be expected, participation in party life, by both leaders and members, is particularly energetic during a political crisis. UPP leaders, for instance, were most active on behalf of the party during the tax riots in 1955–56,[16] and at the founding of the party in the constitutional crisis of July–August, 1954, relating to electoral reform. SLPP leaders were equally active during the tax crisis, making frequent visits to the affected areas to present the party's policies to its members and supporters. The 1957 election (which may be viewed as an institutionalized crisis) also prompted SLPP leaders to an exceptional measure of activity. Numerous party rallies characterized the election campaign, and the party's leaders convened the first annual convention held in three years, though the SLPP constitution requires one every year.

Besides the close relationship between the SLPP and traditional leaders and institutions, other factors have limited party activity. Many of Sierra Leone's party leaders have been only part-time politicians, for they have simultaneously followed their professions. Sir Milton Margai, for example, carried on an active medical and surgical practice in Bo until 1955–56, and the PNP leader, Albert Margai, was busy with his legal practice. Furthermore, most party leaders conceive of their respec-

---

[16] *Sierra Leone Daily Mail*, March 26, 1956, p. 1.

tive parties primarily as instruments to contest elections rather than to achieve well-defined goals. Finally, owing to the absence of an effective opposition, the SLPP has not been stimulated to mobilize its resources in depth.

INTERNAL PARTY ORGANIZATION

Formal Structure

In formal structure, Sierra Leonean parties are rather similar. Each one holds an annual conference or convention which, constitutionally, is the governing and policy-formulating organ. The annual conference elects national officers, though this function has been significantly modified in both the UPP and the SLPP, which have instituted the office of life president of the party (the life president is also the life leader of the parliamentary party). Representation at the annual conference varies slightly from party to party, but all include representation of the "constituency party"; in the PNP and the UPP affiliated organizations are represented as well. In all parties, party legislators, national officers, and members of the national executive committee are represented, and the SLPP annual conference has a special provision for representation of local government bodies. As no party has very much in the way of constituency party organization and affiliated membership, representation at the annual conference is effectively dominated by national officers and party legislators. The SLPP annual conference, however, is an exception, for the 159 representatives of local government bodies (143 of whom represent tribal authorities) outweigh all others. This mode of representation—which was included in the SLPP constitution after the protracted struggle for leadership between the Margai brothers—was devised to ensure that Sir Milton would henceforth control the decisions of the annual conference. The other national governing bodies of Sierra Leone parties are the national executive committee, which executes conference policies; the central or steering committee, which executes the policies of the national executive; and the parliamentary party.

At the provincial level, both the UPP and the SLPP have vice-presidents who represent provinces as administrative regions. All parties have provincial organizers known as propaganda secretaries. At the district and town level, the PNP has one party branch in Freetown, one in Bo District, Southwestern Province, and one in Bombali District, Northern Province; the SLPP has two branches in Freetown and a branch in each of the twelve districts of the provinces, though most of these exist mainly on paper. Each SLPP district branch is governed by a district executive committee and has its own organizers. Most SLPP activity, however, is carried out by the tribal authorities and the chiefs, which means that party branches as such are of little importance.

Distribution of Power

In the UPP and the PNP, the central committee is the most powerful decision-making organ. Its function is "to act as the main Directorate of the National Executive Council," [17] which is the general administrative organ of the annual conference. It is composed of the party leader and ten members appointed by him. These members are normally the party's legislators, thus integrating the parliamentary party with the central committee. As the central committee is required to meet weekly, it is the only major party organ of both the UPP and the PNP which convenes regularly in the interval between successive annual conferences.

The SLPP's Central Committee, which is composed of the party's national officers, is supposed to "execute the decisions of the Executive Committee in closest collaboration with the Parliamentary Council." [18] In reality, however, neither the Central nor the Executive Committee is of any real consequence in decision making, especially in comparison with the SLPP cabinet. Nor is it likely that the Central Committee was ever intended to have any real influence, for the SLPP constitution does not even state what constitutes a quorum of the committee or how frequently it should meet, as do the UPP and PNP constitutions. It is noteworthy, however, that more than a third of the ministers in the SLPP cabinet are national officers of the party; to this extent the cabinet's membership is the same as that of the Central Committee.

Several other factors have operated to make the SLPP cabinet the party's main decision-making organ. Cabinet members reside in Freetown where they are in close touch with one another; thus they constitute the only regularly meeting party organ. Furthermore, the parliamentary party does not really attempt to compete with the cabinet in the decision-making process, although it has formal powers in this sphere. Rather, it accepts cabinet predominance, partly because 38 per cent of its members (including two ministerial secretaries) make up the cabinet, and because all the major interest groups within the parliamentary party (e.g., chiefs, Creoles, Mende, Temne, etc.) are represented in the cabinet. Perhaps the most important factor underlying the hegemony of the cabinet in the decision-making process is that it is presided over by Sir Milton Margai. Sir Milton's status as life president and leader gives him the widest authority within the cabinet, and it is generally believed that, save for

---

[17] *Constitution of the U.P.P.* (Freetown, 1956), Clause 15; *Constitution of the P.N.P.* (1959), Clause 7.
[18] *Constitution of the S.L.P.P.* (1958), Clause IV.

the advice of one or two trusted ministers and (until 1961) of his European secretaries, he alone determines most cabinet decisions. His power to appoint and dismiss ministers,[19] and his strong influence among chiefs, combined with his statutory powers over their very existence,[20] give Sir Milton nearly autocratic authority within the SLPP's main decision-making organ, as well as throughout the party structure.

Intraparty Communication

Intraparty communication raises two main questions: (1) How does a party communicate its aims, policies, and decisions to its members and supporters? (2) How are the component parts of a party connected with one another to form a coherent entity, and what are the political consequences of such an articulation? In Sierra Leone, as compared with Ghana or Guinea, for example, the latter aspect of intraparty communication is of little importance because the party organization proper is relatively insignificant in the political process.

Political communication within the SLPP is effected mainly through paramount chiefs and tribal authorities. One of many instances of such communication is found in a report on the SLPP local election campaign of 1959 in Kenema District. The author of the report, a propaganda secretary, observed: "I arrived in this town [Wando chiefdom] and held a meeting in the Chief's *barri* with the tribal authority. I read out the names of the applicants for the election. They unanimously declared that they would not allow a man staying outside the chiefdom to represent them in the council. . . . Section Chief Alfred Pekawa was unanimously appointed." SLPP ministers, especially the prime minister, Sir Milton Margai, make similar use of traditional institutions in the course of political tours of the provinces. Furthermore, the Prime Minister occasionally summons paramount chiefs to Freetown to discuss SLPP policies, which they then communicate to party members and supporters. At one such meeting in December, 1960, attended by twenty-five paramount chiefs, Sir Milton informed the chiefs "that they had a duty to perform in the dissemination of information on the meaning of independence in every quarter of their various chiefdoms," and he told them how to do it: "He said that their duty was to tell all the section chiefs about independence;

---

[19] It is an open secret that most ministers refrain from opposing Sir Milton Margai on pain of dismissal, which frequently would mean loss of a degree of affluence derived from ministerial office (e.g., £3,000 per annum income, ministerial house valued at £13,000 upward, entertainment allowance, etc.). Hitherto such affluence had never been attained. For instance, a teacher—there are four teachers in the cabinet—advances six times in income upon the assumption of ministerial office.

[20] *Protectorate Ordinance No. 13* (1955) gives the prime minister, who is also the minister of internal affairs, the authority to advise the governor upon the deposition of any chief.

the section chiefs in turn should educate the town headmen who should explain to the people."

Of course, SLPP leaders also utilize nontraditional agencies of political communication, such as political rallies, though even these are often organized through tribal authorities and, except in Freetown, invariably take place at the headquarters of such authorities.[21] The press and the radio seem to be the only SLPP media of political communication not associated with traditional institutions.

Neither of the party's two newspapers, however, has been of great importance in political communication. The *Sierra Leone Observer,* which was founded in 1949 and died in 1958, had a weekly circulation of 1,500; the *African Vanguard,* also founded in 1949 and still being published, circulates 3,000 copies biweekly. The radio, used primarily at election time, reaches a larger audience of party members and supporters than the press; there are some 23,000 radio receivers in Sierra Leone and between 150,000 and 200,000 listeners, as against 28,000 to 42,000 newspaper readers.

Thus, although the SLPP employs a combination of traditional and nontraditional agencies of political communication, the basic pattern may be characterized as a primary communication network. That is to say, in its system of political communication, the party employs the face-to-face associations which characterize relations between paramount chiefs and tribal authorities on the one hand, and their peasant subjects on the other; or between tribal headmen in the towns and urban centers and the still quasi-rural urban dwellers. This system is, in large measure, congruent with the tradition-oriented aims and policies of the SLPP, policies that seek modernity within a purposely slowly changing traditional context. Furthermore, the communication is facilitated by the fact that SLPP political interpreters share many of the values and norms, and much of the language, of the people with whom they communicate.[22]

Party Finance

Party finance in Sierra Leone has been primarily the responsibility of the same social groups that predominate in party leadership. There are two main reasons for this. No party has its membership sufficiently organized to be a regular and adequate source of income.[23] Second, the leaders

---

[21] See, e.g., *Sierra Leone Daily Mail,* Aug. 16, 1960, p. 3.

[22] The national leaders of the SLPP use English and Krio—a form of pidgin English—when addressing political rallies in Freetown, but often use an indigenous language when addressing local meetings in chiefdoms organized by tribal authorities.

[23] In contrast, the CPP in Ghana expected to raise £150,000 in fiscal 1960 from membership dues, which it claimed would more than cover its operating costs, estimated at £75,000 (see the CPP's monthly journal, *The Party* [Sept., 1960], p. 4).

of Sierra Leonean parties, as shown in table 5, are either professionals or businessmen[24] who belong to high-income groups and are thus capable of

TABLE 5

OCCUPATIONS OF PARTY LEADERS IN SIERRA LEONE

Party	Leader's name	Leader's occupation
National Council	H. C. Bankole-Bright	Doctor
Sierra Leone People's Party	Milton Margai	Doctor
British Koya Political Party	J. C. O. Crowther	Businessman
Positive Action Party	Otto During	Lawyer
United Progressive Party	C. Rogers-Wright	Lawyer
Labor Party	R. Beoku-Betts	Lawyer
Sierra Leone Independence Movement	Edward W. Blyden III	College lecturer
Kono Progressive Movement	T. S. Mbriwa	Druggist
Radical Democratic Party	I. T. A. Wallace-Johnson	Businessman
People's National Party	Albert Margai	Lawyer
Independent Progressive Party	B. Wilson	Accountant
All People's Congress	Siaka Stevens	Businessman

meeting a major part of their parties' financial needs. For instance, the party leader is often largely responsible for financing the party newspaper; H. C. Bankole-Bright was founder and owner of the NC's organ, the *Evening Despatch;* Cyril Rogers-Wright was owner of the UPP's *Shekpendeh;* and Sir Milton Margai was founder and owner of the SLPP's organ, the *Sierra Leone Observer.* The leader has also met much of his party's election expenses, though the candidates themselves have assumed most of their own campaign costs.

As the governing party, the SLPP has more lucrative sources of income than opposition parties; one of them is the salaries of legislators (see table 6). Before 1957 the SLPP tapped this source only when and if the legislators offered donations, but since then, by formal arrangement, each SLPP legislator contributes at least £6 a month to the party fund, with ministers, junior ministers, the deputy speaker, and the chief whip contributing somewhat more.[25] Another source available to the SLPP has been expatriate firms, one of which contributed to the founding fund of the party's newspaper. At times such donations are solicited through the agency of paramount chiefs, who circularize the firms located in chiefdom

---

[24] In the first general election in May, 1957, 40 per cent of the candidates were professionals and 25 per cent were businessmen.

[25] The regular payment of this contribution is ensured through a checkoff system; the SLPP legislators have empowered the auditor-general to deduct their contributions to the party fund from their monthly salaries.

TABLE 6

INCOME OF SIERRA LEONE LEGISLATORS, 1961
(In pounds)

Position	Salary	Allowances[a]
Prime minister	4,000	480
Minister	3,000	420
Minister without portfolio	2,000	300
Junior minister	1,500	240
Speaker	2,500	380
Deputy speaker	1,250	180
Chief whip	1,200	180
Leader of opposition	1,500	380
Member	900	180

[a] Excluding automobile allowances.

towns. Expatriate firms also contribute to the SLPP by advertising in its newspapers,[26] by giving it advances or credit to purchase equipment and matériel for party purposes, and by granting loans on generous terms.

Opposition parties, on the other hand, have available a much narrower range of financial resources. The UPP and the PNP allegedly received limited donations from Lebanese firms, and both European and Lebanese firms inserted advertisements in the UPP's newspaper, *Shekpendeh*. Each opposition party, however, had to rely mainly upon its leader for financial help, which has proved inadequate to the establishment of an organization able to compete effectively with the SLPP.

POLITICAL RELATIONSHIPS

Relationships between Parties and Governmental Institutions

One obvious form of political relationship in Sierra Leone is that between parties and governmental institutions. As of early 1961, all but two of Sierra Leone's parties had some representation in at least one governmental institution; the SLPP was by far the predominant party in this respect. As shown in table 7, the SLPP at that time had 83 per cent of all elected seats contested along party lines, as against 17 per cent for opposition parties. The nearest opposition party, the PNP, claimed only 8 per cent of the seats.

A more important facet of party relationships to governmental institutions is that a large proportion of party candidates in elections have had

---

[26] The income from the SLPP's newspapers has barely met the cost of their publication, and the *Sierra Leone Observer* was forced to cease publication in 1958.

TABLE 7

ELECTIVE SEATS HELD BY SIERRA LEONE PARTIES IN GOVERNMENTAL
INSTITUTIONS[a] EARLY IN 1961

Party	House of Representatives		District councils[b]		Freetown City Council		Total	
	Number	Per cent	Number	Per cent	Number	Per cent	Number	Per cent
SLPP	39	78	315	84	12	67	367	83
UPP	1		2		3		6	
PNP	4		33		0		37	
SLPIM	2	22	24	16	0	33	26	17
IPP	4		0		1		5	
APC	0		0		2		2	
Total	50[c]		374		18		443	

[a] The Bo Town Council, the Sherbro Urban Council, and the rural area councils of the colony are excluded.

[b] These are the twelve district councils in the protectorate.

[c] Nominated members are not included in this figure.

previous government experience.[27] In the 1957 general election, in the country as a whole, 77 of the 121 candidates, or 64 per cent, had had government experience; the corresponding figure for the colony was 49 per cent (28 of 57 candidates), and, for the protectorate, 77 per cent (49 of 64 candidates). The Creole-dominated NC, which contested only colony seats, had the largest proportion of candidates with government experience, 90 per cent, whereas 77 per cent of the independents and 72 per cent of the SLPP candidates had had such experience. Furthermore, 72 per cent of the successful SLPP candidates, 83 per cent of the successful independents, and 64 per cent of all successful candidates had had government experience. It is also noteworthy that most successful candidates continued to hold their local government posts, showing a clear tendency toward multiple office holding among Sierra Leonean legislators; several of them, in fact, held three or four elected offices at the same time. It need hardly be emphasized that this tendency, also apparent elsewhere in Africa, implies that a relatively small political elite may monopolize most governmental institutions at both central and local levels.

Previous government experience, which a significant proportion of successful candidates in the 1957 general election had had, enabled them

---

[27] The data that follow are based upon interviews with candidates, biographical information supplied by the Sierra Leone Ministry of Information and Broadcasting, and material culled from nomination forms supplied by the Ministry of Internal Affairs.

to campaign more effectively for votes. An equally important reason for their success was their relationship with chiefly families, which constitute the basis of the native authority system of local government. Of the successful SLPP candidates who had had government experience, 69 per cent were kin to chiefly families (mainly sons, nephews, or grandsons of chiefs), as were 70 per cent of the independents and 70 per cent of all successful candidates with previous government experience. Chiefly kinship is apparently a significant political factor in itself, as suggested by the data in table 4. Furthermore, in protectorate constituencies in the same election, all the successful SLPP candidates, 90 per cent of the successful independents, and 84 per cent of all successful candidates (i.e., 21 of 25) were kin to chiefs. From all these data emerges the crucial fact that kin relationship to the native authority system is a major determinant in the struggle for political power in Sierra Leone.

Relationships among Parties

Political alliances, mergers, and amalgamations have been important in the formation and development of Sierra Leonean parties. In fact, the SLPP's political predominance is the direct result of a series of alliances and mergers over the past decade. In the 1951 election the SLPP as a party won only two of the seven directly elected seats and four of the indirectly elected seats in the Legislative Council; independents gained the remaining ten indirectly elected seats. Consequently, no party had a majority in the council, although it was the first one to have an unofficial African majority. The governor thereupon announced that party government could not yet be introduced.[28] There was, however, a majority of protectorate, as against colony, representatives; after consultations, the ten independent protectorate representatives (eight of whom were paramount chiefs) agreed to merge with the SLPP representatives. The colonial authority then recognized the SLPP as the majority party among the twenty-three unofficial members of the council, and called upon it to form the first Executive Council with an African majority.[29]

In the 1957 general election, the SLPP won only eighteen of the thirty-nine directly elected seats; the UPP won nine, and independents won twelve.[30] At the first sitting of the new House of Representatives,

---

[28] *Legislative Council Debates, 1951–1952,* I (Freetown, 1952), 8–9: "Where there is a well developed 'party system' it is the practice . . . to send for the leader of the party which commands a majority and invite him to form a Government. Here in Sierra Leone today I am not sure that the party system is yet quite sufficiently developed for me to introduce a procedure modelled, *mutatis mutandis,* on that which I have described."

[29] *Ibid.,* pp. 271 ff.

[30] "Report on the Sierra Leone General Election, 1957" (mimeographed; Freetown: Ministry of Internal Affairs, 1957), Appendix D, pp. 1–6.

however, the independents and eleven paramount chiefs merged with the SLPP, which then had forty-one seats to the UPP's nine. Thus the party that has been the majority party in Sierra Leone for the past decade has never actually gained a majority of seats in an election, nor has it gained a majority of votes over opposition parties and independents.[31] Rather, the SLPP has become the governing party through a process of mergers with independents (most of whom were always basically SLPP-oriented) and chiefs within the legislature.

Alliances and mergers have also contributed to the formation of opposition parties. The PNP, for instance, gained most of its legislative seats in this manner. Within less than a month of its founding by Albert Margai in September, 1958, after his unsuccessful attempt to capture the leadership of the SLPP, three leading SLPP legislators (Maigore Kallon, a ministerial secretary; S. T. Navo, chief whip; and A. J. Massally, deputy speaker) joined Margai on the opposition bench. A year later, I. T. A. Wallace-Johnson brought his Radical Democratic Party (which he had created in July, 1958, as a party cover for himself within the legislature) into legislative alliance with the PNP. At the same time, Tamba S. Mbriwa and A. A. Mani of the SLPIM formed a legislative alliance with the PNP, called the PNP-Alliance. Another party that emerged within the legislature was the Independent Progressive Party (IPP). It was formed in December, 1959 and January, 1960, when five UPP members, who were opposed to what they called the autocratic rule of their leader, Cyril Rogers-Wright, regrouped and provided themselves with a new party cover. For the UPP, this was the culmination of a two-year process of disintegration which began in February, 1958, when two of its members joined the SLPP; it nearly marked the UPP's demise, leaving its leader as the only party representative in the legislature.

Outside the legislature, two parties and one coalition have resulted from mergers and alliances. In September, 1958, Edward Blyden's SLIM, which suffered complete defeat in the 1957 general election, merged with the KPM to form the SLPIM. Similarly, the All People's Congress (APC)

---

[31] In the 1957 election, the SLPP gained 75,575 out of 165,479 votes, or 46 per cent, as against 89,904 votes for all other parties, or 54 per cent. Furthermore, the UPP and the independents together gained 84,666 votes, or 51 per cent. Similarly, in the 1962 general election the SLPP gained, as a party, only 35 per cent of the total of 671,995 votes (this total represents 52 per cent of the qualified voters), whereas the opposition APC (which had an electoral alliance with the SLPIM in Kono District) gained 23 per cent and the independents gained 42 per cent. As in the 1957 election, however, the total share of what might be called SLPP-oriented votes was much larger than the number of votes gained by SLPP candidates proper, because most independents, especially those in provincial constituencies, are essentially SLPP-type persons who invariably join the SLPP upon election to the House of Representatives. Thus, in the 1962 election, the SLPP's real share of the vote, including the independents' share, may be put at 77 per cent (*General Election, 1962, Score Sheet* [Freetown: Electoral Commission, 1962], pp. 3–12).

was formed in August–September, 1960, when Siaka Stevens' Elections-before-Independence Movement merged with Wallace-Johnson's RDP.

The most far-reaching political alliance to come into being outside the legislature was the United National Front, formed in March, 1960, as a result of a series of all-party round-table talks preparatory to the 1960 Constitutional Conference. The opposition parties accepted a bid from the SLPP to join it in a coalition whose initial purpose would be to bring the resources of all political groups to bear on the problems to be considered at the conference.[32] Perhaps the most significant feature of the United Front was that all parties agreed to its formation "under the leadership of Sir Milton Margai . . . our Premier," which meant in effect that the opposition party leaders were submitting themselves to SLPP authority. In May, 1960, upon the successful conclusion of the Constitutional Conference (which chose April 27, 1961, as the date for Sierra Leone's independence), a coalition government was formed which brought the leaders of the main opposition parties into the SLPP cabinet. Albert Margai of the PNP became minister of natural resources; Rogers-Wright of the UPP became minister of housing and country planning; and G. Dickson Thomas of the IPP was appointed minister of social welfare. Since then the opposition parties have disbanded and have joined the SLPP, with the exception of the APC and a rump of the UPP.

Relationships between Parties and Nonparty Groups

All Sierra Leonean parties maintain formal connections with nonparty groups or voluntary associations through organizational membership. A more common pattern, however, is that established by interlocking leaderships. The leadership of political parties is often the same as that of nonparty associations, which means, of course, that certain individuals play multiple leadership roles. For instance, C. Rogers-Wright, leader of the UPP, was president and solicitor of the Railway Workers' Union from 1954 to 1956; John Karefa-Smart, SLPP minister of external affairs, is president of the 3,000-member Ex-Servicemen's Association; Paramount Chief R. B. S. Koker, formerly SLPP minister without portfolio, is secretary of the Sierra Leone National Association, an organization of chiefs, and president of the influential Old Bo School Boys' Association; M. S. Mustapha, SLPP minister of finance and party treasurer, is a leading member of the Muslim Congress; and Mrs. Constance Cummings-John, SLPP vice-president for the colony area, is founder and organizing secretary of the Sierra Leone Women's Movement. It should also be noted that tribal associations in Freetown, such as the Mende Tribal Committee and the Temne Tribal Union, are closely linked to the SLPP through tribal headmen who, though government servants, are

---

[32] *Sierra Leone Daily Mail,* March 26, 1960, p. 1.

utilized as party agents. Interlocking leadership prevails in this area as well: Madame Nancy Koroma, the Mende tribal headman and head of the Mende Tribal Committee, is a member of the SLPP's Executive Committee; and Kandeh Bureh, Temne tribal headman in Freetown until 1960 and the founder of numerous Temne tribal associations, is the SLPP's minister of works.[33]

The relationship between nonparty or voluntary associations and the SLPP is further strengthened through financial dependence, for the SLPP government pays for much of the operating cost of these associations. To mention only one of many examples, from 1957 through 1960 the Sierra Leone Ex-Servicemen's Association received annual grants from the government which totaled £4,433. There are also nonparty groups whose main or only link with the SLPP is one of financial dependence, such as the Boy Scouts' Association and the Girl Guides' Association, which received £3,000 and £900, respectively, in the period 1957–1960; in the same period the Sierra Leone Football Association shared in the £6,725 government grant to the Sierra Leone Sports Council, a quasi-governmental body. Incidentally, this pattern of binding voluntary groups to governing parties is quite widespread in West Africa, and is particularly well developed in the Ivory Coast. It is obvious, of course, that the most important consequence of the financial dependence of such groups is to reduce the threat of opposition by minimizing the possibility that opposition parties will be organized around them.

Relationships with External Parties and Alien Groups

In Sierra Leone, relations with external parties have been of significance only to opposition parties. They have appealed to the British Labour Party for assistance to redress grievances against the colonial government and the SLPP government, prior to independence. For instance, in 1960 the SLPIM asked the Labour Party to bring before the House of Commons the matter of the imprisonment of its leader, Tamba S. Mbriwa, for political activities. The most important external links of Sierra Leonean opposition parties, however, have connected them with parties in other African states. Both the APC and the PNP have been on friendly terms with the governing parties in Ghana and Guinea, and the PNP was represented at the first All-African People's Congress in Accra in December, 1958. Also, the PNP was the only Sierra Leonean party to be represented by an observer at the congress of Guinea's governing party in September, 1959; at the second All-African People's Congress in Tunis in January, 1960, it was represented by its

---

[33] Michael Banton, "Ambas Geda," *West Africa,* Oct. 24, 1953, p. 995.

leader, Albert Margai, whereas the SLPP was represented only by its propaganda secretary. It should also be noted that the PNP solicited and allegedly received financial support from Ghana and Guinea, and it is believed that the APC has had a similar relationship with the governing parties in these two states.

No Sierra Leonean party has a significant relationship with alien groups resident in the country, although a few Lebanese have been members of the SLPP, and in 1961 a Lebanese businessman of some note was among the SLPP representatives on the Bo Town Council. As previously noted, European and Lebanese firms have contributed financially to the SLPP and other parties, but, as exact amounts are not known, it is difficult to assess the political significance of such assistance. It was reliably reported to me that the SLPP borrowed £12,000 on easy terms from a well-known European bank in order to conduct its campaign for the 1962 general election, but the lack of information on the total cost of the campaign makes it difficult to determine the precise political value of the loan. It is likely, however, that political parties and their leaders have benefited from the overwhelming financial predominance of Europeans in Sierra Leone and other West African states, and in return have made political and other concessions to expatriate interests.

Another aspect of the political scene in Sierra Leone is the relationship of several alien groups with the Parti Démocratique de Guinée (PDG). These alien groups—the Foulah, Soussou, and Mandinga tribes —originated in Guinea and only temporarily reside in Sierra Leone. They play a major role in petty trade, and the skill with which they have ousted indigenous groups from much of this trade is an index of their fine intelligence and their capacity for hard work. They are concentrated largely in Freetown, where they constitute about 10 per cent of the population, and in 1957 a branch of the PDG was organized among them. These three tribes are also scattered throughout the Northern Province of Sierra Leone, especially in Kambia and Koinadugu districts, which border on Guinea; in October, 1959, another branch of the PDG was formed among those living in Kambia. Furthermore, these groups in general are sympathetic toward the PDG and its leadership; when President Sékou Touré visited Sierra Leone in December, 1960, the Foulah and the Soussou organized committees to welcome Touré as their president. It is yet too early to gauge precisely the influence that this political relationship may have in Sierra Leone, except to note that its very existence signifies a pro-PDG element in the country. But it is likely that the PDG leadership, with its militant nationalist and Pan-Africanist orientation, will not hesitate to turn to its own advantage whatever benefit may be derived from such a connection.

POLITICAL GOALS AND VALUES

General Party Goals

The over-all and officially stated goals and values of Sierra Leonean parties are rather similar. All have valued self-government as virtuous in itself, and as a necessary precondition to further modernization. Development or modernization is also highly esteemed, and its attainment is articulated as a primary goal of all parties. The SLPP proposes "to promote political, social and economic emancipation of the people";[34] the UPP plans "to improve the standard of living of every man, woman and child in relation to the economic resources of the country";[35] and the PNP claims as one of its primary goals the attainment of "the rapid advancement of the economic, educational, social and cultural development of the country."[36]

All parties also place a high value upon civil liberties. The PNP constitution, for example, expresses a desire "to protect the interests and freedom of all groups in the country," and the SLPP claims to believe in "the fundamental Human Rights . . . [and] that every man or woman must enjoy the benefits and equal rights of society, regardless of his or her colour, social background, tribe, race or creed."[37] At the Constitutional Conference in 1960, the SLPP government and the United National Front agreed that "certain vital provisions affecting fundamental rights and democratic liberties should be 'entrenched,' and that the procedure for their amendment should contain special safeguards for ensuring that the electorate were fully consulted."[38]

Sierra Leonean parties do not agree, however, on the methods necessary to secure these and other goals, and they have shown particularly wide differences over the role of traditional institutions in the pursuit of modern goals and values.

Modernization

As already noted, Sierra Leonean parties view modernization as both desirable and necessary. Agreement on this goal, however, does not necessarily imply accord on its ultimate content or on the manner of attaining it; on such questions as the role of priorities, the tempo of modernization, and its cost, there is wide disparity. The parties have taken conflicting positions, for instance, on the role of expatriate personnel in develop-

---

[34] *Constitution of the S.L.P.P.,* Clause III.
[35] *Constitution of the U.P.P.,* Clause 2.
[36] *Constitution of the P.N.P.,* Clause 2.
[37] *Election Manifesto of the Sierra Leone People's Party* (Freetown, 1957), p. 17.
[38] *Report of the Sierra Leone Constitutional Conference, 1960* (Freetown, 1960), p. 6.

ment; the SLPP places rather heavy reliance upon such personnel in administrative and technical posts and as advisers in policy making. The extent of this reliance may be gauged by comparison with Ghana where, in 1956, about 63 per cent of the senior service posts were held by Africans, whereas only 36 per cent of such posts were Africanized in Sierra Leone. By 1960, however, 56 per cent of the senior posts in Sierra Leone were in African hands. Set against the SLPP's approach to Africanization has been the PNP position, which opposes any significant reliance upon expatriate personnel in its modernizing policy; PNP leaders regard the use of expatriates as a limitation upon Sierra Leone's independence and as an undue burden upon her financial resources.[39] The PNP's approach to the role of expatriates, however, is not one of total rejection, but of suspicion. The party prefers to make limited use of their skills, accepting only those expatriates "who have a specific contribution to make to the advancement of Sierra Leone and who would be willing to work for us and with us on a basis of mutual respect." [40]

Similarly, the parties take divergent views on private enterprise and foreign capital in the modernization process. Although the PNP admits the need for foreign investment, and would "look outside and negotiate with anyone who is able to provide . . . the necessary capital," [41] it has been suspicious and quite critical of foreign businesses in Sierra Leone. The PNP has even suggested that when it obtained power it would extend government control over some of them. Private enterprise as such is also viewed critically by the PNP. The SLPP, on the other hand, has often declared that "it is Government's policy to encourage private enterprise." [42] For instance, the government established the Development of Industries Board which issues loans to African businessmen. The SLPP government has also purchased manufacturing machinery which was resold at less than the original cost to African entrepreneurs, and has given generous assistance to British mining concerns, whose activities produce more than 25 per cent of its revenue. Furthermore, in November, 1960, the SLPP government took the first major step toward attracting foreign enterprise by enacting the Development Ordinance. Among the benefits the ordinance extends to foreign entrepreneurs are a "tax holiday" and the right to import free of custom duty, or to purchase in Sierra Leone subject to refund of custom duty, the articles required for the development of any mine, plantation, plant, or factory.[43] As of 1961 the SLPP government had not yet instituted a systematic development plan

---

[39] *Liberty*, July 18, 1959, p. 8.

[40] Siaka Stevens, "The People's National Party and Expatriatism," *ibid.*, July 25, 1959, p. 5.

[41] *Ibid.*

[42] *House of Representatives Debates, 1957–1958*, p. 81.

[43] *Development Ordinance* (1960), Sec. 3.

embodying a hierarchy of priorities and prescribing the speed at which its objectives should be attained. Nevertheless, the expenditure of government funds over the past decade has given priority to education, medical services, and agriculture. As to the tempo of development, the SLPP has shown a rather moderate attitude. Heavily dependent upon chiefly institutions for political support, it seems unwilling to remove the many traditional fetters that prevent rapid socioeconomic development. Nor does the SLPP government seem inclined to utilize its official authority and machinery, or the institutions of the party, to organize human resources around specific development tasks, as has the Ghana government with its Workers' Brigades, or the Guinea government with its policy of *investissement humain.* In short, to the SLPP government modernization is largely a matter for private persons and organizations, with government simply rendering them assistance and accepting responsibility only for matters beyond the capacity of private groups, such as education, social services, communications, and so on.

Democracy and Authoritarianism

Elements of democracy have been part of the program of all Sierra Leonean parties, if for no other reason than that the anticolonial struggle required such an orientation. The claim of anticolonial groups for control of the state is put forward in the name of popular sovereignty and majority rule. Colonial nationalist parties tend to use the values of democracy—personal rights, universal suffrage, popular consent, and the like—as instruments in the struggle for power. Furthermore, the British colonial policy of establishing representative legislative and executive bodies preparatory to the transfer of power to indigenous groups requires that parties seeking such power conduct their political activity along more or less democratic lines. Sierra Leonean parties, like those elsewhere in British Africa, have had little alternative but to express democratic principles, at least during the period of transfer of power. There have, however, been significant variations. In general, the opposition parties, especially the PNP, seem more committed to democratic practices than the governing SLPP. This may stem simply from the fact that opposition parties would, by their very position, invoke democratic norms as a political technique. SLPP leaders also make democratic appeals, but they have put forward undemocratic proposals more frequently than have opposition leaders. Sir Milton Margai's defense of traditional chieftaincy in a government debate is a notable example:

I don't know what has brought this idea of "loss of confidence" [in chiefs]. I have only heard it in European countries where a Prime Minister brings up a motion and the backbenchers refuse to vote for it, and when the Government does not get the support it wants there is a "loss of confidence" and the party in power is thrown out. But to depose someone because of loss of confidence, I say it is a myth. . . . That idea of loss of confidence should be wiped out. . . . To come here and say that a chief has lost confidence is absolutely nonsense: the sooner we do away with that the better. . . . I know how this "loss of confidence" business goes about and it should not be allowed to ruin the Protectorate. If anybody is found causing trouble we ought to take the most vindictive steps in dealing with that one.[44]

This rather authoritarian view of the relationship of rulers to the ruled is partly a consequence of Sir Milton's traditionalist orientation and of his party's dependence upon chiefs for political support. Whatever its origin, an authoritarian element prevails throughout much of the thought and the practice of the SLPP. One need only mention here the relationship between paramount chiefs and the SLPP government, which is essentially authoritarian in character; they participate in the formulation of government policy as ministers, in its enactment as legislators, in its administration as native authorities, in its adjudication as members of native courts, and in its enforcement as members of native authorities that have police powers.[45]

Nationalism and Pan-Africanism

Nationalism of the militantly anticolonial variety has seldom characterized the political outlook and behavior of the SLPP. The words "colonialism" and "imperialism," or any derivatives thereof, are seldom, if ever, uttered by SLPP leaders at political rallies, in the legislature, or in other public places, save as an appellation for the administrative area known as the colony. The SLPP's lack of militant nationalism is further revealed by its conception of the political process by which colonial peoples ultimately gain control of the state apparatus. Whereas a militant nationalist party like the Convention People's Party in Ghana conceived of this process as a struggle by colonial people to wrest power from colonial authority,[46] the leaders of the SLPP viewed the process as one whereby power was granted by, not wrested from, the colonial authority, as the colonized peoples proved their ability to handle power properly. As Sir

[44] *Proceedings of the Eleventh Meeting of the Protectorate Assembly* (Freetown, 1955), pp. 13–14 *passim*. The same outlook is seen in the reaction of Paramount Chief Yumkella II, member of the house for Kambia District Council, to an opposition motion that incapacitated chiefs be retired on government pension; he maintained that "by bringing the motion to the House the mover was abusing the privilege of democracy" (*Summary of Proceedings of the House of Representatives*, Nov. 29, 1960, p. 2).

[45] Cf. *Report of the Sierra Leone Police Force, 1959* (Freetown: Government Printer, 1960), pp. 45–46; *Chiefdom Police Ordinance No. 195* (1961).

[46] "Give Kwame Nkrumah and the C.P.P. your mandate to complete the task of liberating Ghana from colonialism and foreign domination" (*Convention People's Party Manifesto for the General Election, 1954* [Accra, 1954], p. 20).

Milton Margai put it in the 1957 election campaign: "We were the first Ministers ever in Sierra Leone. We were pioneers. The evidence of how well we have done our jobs is seen in the readiness with which Her Majesty's Government has agreed for us to take another step toward self-government." [47]

Moderate nationalism tends toward moderate Pan-Africanism, or perhaps toward no Pan-Africanism at all. The militant nationalism of the dominant parties in Ghana, Guinea, and Mali has produced the radical Pan-Africanist objective of the immediate union of African states, but the moderate nationalism of the SLPP has been accompanied by a more qualified Pan-Africanist goal, "the possibility of unity and co-operation between African States, based on mutual respect for the sovereignty and territorial integrity of each State." [48] On the other hand, the more nationalistic PNP inclined toward the unity rather than the coöperation approach to Pan-African relations, thus resembling its counterpart in Ghana or Guinea. At the first All-African People's Congress in December, 1958, the PNP delegate made a strong plea for Pan-African unity, declaring that "we hope . . . this Conference will prove to be the first step towards the establishment of a United States of Africa." [49] A few young SLPP leaders, however, sympathize in private with the unity approach to Pan-African relations, and they were presumably influential in having reference to it included in a communiqué issued by Sir Milton Margai and President Touré in December, 1960.

Neutralism and Alignment

Just as moderate nationalism inclines toward moderate Pan-Africanism, so does the latter tend toward alignment rather than neutralism in the international politics of the cold war. A moderate Pan-Africanist government tends toward alignment partly as a reaction to radical Pan-Africanism, which is little concerned about such accepted precepts as "state sovereignty" and "territorial integrity." Other factors intensify the tendency toward alignment, such as dependence upon a metropolitan power for significant financial or military support. This would seem to be true of the moderately nationalist and Pan-Africanist Ivory Coast, Upper Volta, Niger, and Dahomey,[50] as well as of the SLPP government. In 1959–60 the British government paid for 71 per cent of Sierra Leone's military expenditures, and the Constitutional Conference in April, 1960,

---

[47] *Sierra Leone Daily Mail,* May 3, 1957, pp. 4–5. See also *ibid.,* May 30, 1957, p. 1.

[48] *Ibid.,* Dec. 19, 1960, pp. 6–7.

[49] *Ibid.,* Dec. 13, 1958, p. 1.

[50] Cf. Félix Houphouet-Boigny, "Discours de Politique générale," *Fraternité* (Abidjan), Jan. 13, 1961, pp. 2–10; Elliot J. Berg, "The Economic Basis of Political Choice in French West Africa," *American Political Science Review,* LIV (June, 1960), 391–405.

decided that, as Sierra Leone would confront problems during the first several years of independence "in such matters as defence and the compensation scheme, which it would be difficult to meet without outside assistance," the British government would "provide assistance in various ways, which would total about 7½ million pounds." [51]

The alignment factor implied in the foregoing was concretely expressed in another decision of the Constitutional Conference "providing for mutual co-operation in the field of defence" [52] between an independent Sierra Leone and Britain. Alignment rather than neutralism was also the main theme of Sir Milton Margai's statement at the conference. He observed that his government "would like to look first of all to our old friends. There are all too many offers from other sources which we would prefer not to encourage as long as our old and proven friends are prepared to stand by us and help us." [53] His statement, however, contained a conditional element which would presumably push the SLPP government toward neutralism should British assistance prove inadequate.[54] Perhaps a more explicit allusion to a neutralist orientation on the part of the SLPP government was the declaration by John Karefa-Smart, minister of external affairs (by far the most cosmopolitan and informed SLPP leader), that, although an independent Sierra Leone, like many other nations, would be far from self-sufficient, "this . . . does not mean that . . . Sierra Leone must toe the line of any particular Great Power or bloc of Powers. Whenever we are invited to take sides, we must objectively consider every such proposal and only decide to align our sympathies one way or the other or remain neutral after carefully weighing the pros and cons of the effect which any particular alliance will have on our country as a young State." [55] Despite all these suggestions of neutralism, the SLPP government has thus far pursued a policy approximating alignment with the West through Britain, and the two countries with which Sierra Leone has the closest ties in West Africa, Liberia and Nigeria, are similarly inclined.

POLITICAL STRATEGY AND TECHNIQUES

Acquisition of Power

The political strategy and techniques utilized by the SLPP in the acquisition of power have been largely shaped by ethnic differences, the relatively strong influence of traditional institutions among the masses,

---

[51] *Report of the Sierra Leone Constitutional Conference, 1960*, p. 8.
[52] *Ibid.*, p. 7.
[53] *Ibid.*, p. 14.
[54] Cf. Kwame Nkrumah, "African Prospect," *Foreign Affairs*, XXXVII (Oct., 1958), 53: "Africa has no choice. We have to modernize. Either we shall do so with the interest and support of the West or we shall be compelled to turn elsewhere."
[55] *Sierra Leone Daily Mail*, March 3, 1960, p. 2.

and the pattern of postwar constitutional change. The ethnic factor has centered on the colony-protectorate division which separates the Westernized Creole community from the largely traditional indigenous tribes. The latter developed a deeply rooted antagonism toward the former's predominance in the modern sector of Sierra Leonean society, and throughout the postwar period of decolonization the SLPP effectively exploited this antagonism for political purposes. The party's propaganda secretaries, for instance, conduct election campaigns with the claim that a vote for any party but the SLPP is a vote for "Creole domination." At the same time, however, the SLPP leadership has endeavored not to alienate Creoles completely, largely because it needs their educational skills; a few Creoles have accordingly been brought into the party leadership. This policy has required a modification of the anti-Creole campaign in colony elections, and the reservation of almost all the colony seats in the legislature to Creole SLPP candidates. In the 1957 general election, for instance, all but two of the twelve SLPP candidates in colony constituencies were Creoles, and in the 1962 general election, all but four were Creoles.

The continuing strength of traditional authority in the provinces has been largely responsible for the most significant aspect of the SLPP's political strategy, namely, its policy of courting traditional rulers, integrating them into the party's leadership structure, and employing them as the party's main medium of political communication. Although the chiefly kinship of SLPP leaders tended to predispose them toward this policy, it is also true that they recognized the ability of traditional authority to direct the political loyalties of most people toward the party. The pattern of postwar constitutional change also encouraged the strategy of integrating traditional rulers into the SLPP's leadership structure. When, in 1956, the 1951 Constitution was revised to grant greater African participation and wider suffrage, the SLPP government gained the colonial authority's agreement to reserve 24 per cent of the seats in the legislature for paramount chiefs, who later proved a key element in the party's success in the 1957 election. Interestingly enough, the more militantly nationalistic opposition parties have also attempted to orient their political strategy toward traditional rulers. As previously noted, the PNP leaders publicly supported the institution of chieftaincy and promised to give it an important role in the country's political development. Such overtures failed, however, because paramount chiefs distrusted the political consequences of the PNP's militant nationalism, and because they had already attained a satisfactory share of political power through their association with the SLPP.

Traditional forces have been particularly influential in shaping the election strategy of all parties that contest seats in protectorate constituencies. As noted above (see table 4), the factor of chiefly kinship was of enormous importance in the selection of candidates for the 1957 general election, and it also affected election results (see pp. 112–113, above). Just as a party would be unwise if it selected candidates without considering the factor of chiefly kinship, so it would run a risk of electoral defeat if its candidates were not "sons of the soil." Traditional and parochial considerations require that candidates be indigenous to the constituency they contest. In the 1957 election, for example, only 25 per cent of all the successful candidates in protectorate constituencies, and only 17 per cent of the successful SLPP candidates, were not sons of the soil. Another partly traditional factor in the election strategy of parties is the use of money or wealth to treat prospective voters to food, drink, and so on. In the traditional political system, such use of wealth by chiefly families to gain political power is rather common, and in the modern political system parties and candidates have found it to their advantage to continue the practice.

The Maintenance of Power

To maintain its power, the SLPP government, like every other government in West Africa, has inclined toward some restriction of opposition parties. Such restriction of the opposition is not an official policy, but it tends to be a consequence of the political strategy employed by the SLPP government. And this strategy, in certain respects, falls rather short of being democratic. The SLPP government utilizes paramount chiefs and tribal authorities as political agents even though they are, in effect, civil servants. On the other hand, other categories of civil servants are not permitted to participate in politics in behalf of opposition parties; in fact, in 1959 the Prime Minister strongly warned them not to do so. Moreover, the SLPP government has designated most of Sierra Leone's schoolteachers as civil servants, inasmuch as the central government pays 50 to 100 per cent of their salaries. It has thereby tremendously restricted the political activity of a group that is likely to support opposition parties in Sierra Leone.

The SLPP has also tried to weaken opposition parties by restricting their political meetings in the provinces. Under the Tribal Authorities Ordinance of 1946, which makes paramount chiefs and tribal authorities responsible for maintaining law and order at the chiefdom level, a political rally held by an opposition party may be construed as an attempt to undermine the lawful authority of the chief. If so construed, such a rally is a criminal act, punishable by six months' imprisonment. The full weight of this law was brought to bear against the opposition party in Kono District, the SLPIM, whose leader was imprisoned for six months by a native court on the ground that his political activity constituted a threat to the paramount chief's authority.[56] And in the local government elections in October, 1960, paramount chiefs hindered the election of the opposition PNP candidates.[57]

Another means used to reduce political opposition has been the rather liberal allocation of governmental posts, especially ministerial appointments, to opposition leaders. When it seemed that Sir Milton Margai might lose the leadership of the SLPP to his brother, Albert Margai, after the 1957 election, the former consolidated his position and undermined his opponents through a most astute allocation of ministerial portfolios. He gave three portfolios to Temne leaders who, although critical of their tribe's share of executive posts, had supported Sir Milton against his brother; a Creole was given the portfolio of education, which ranks high in the Creole value system; and the independents, some of whom were inclined toward Sir Milton's opponent, received one portfolio, one ministerial secretaryship, and the posts of chief whip and deputy speaker. Similarly, in 1958, the UPP's leading organizing secretary in the protectorate and its sometime deputy leader was, upon his resignation from the UPP, made a ministerial secretary in Sir Milton's Ministry of Internal Affairs. But the establishment of the United National Front in March, 1960, and the formation of a coalition government in May, constituted Sir Milton Margai's most striking effort to undermine opposition groups through a judicious allocation of ministerial portfolios and other government posts. After the coalition came into being, all existing opposition parties surrendered their right to engage in political activity against the SLPP.

CONCLUSION

As we have seen, forces stemming from the modern sector of Sierra Leone's developing colonial society have been important in determining the character and the behavior of political parties. Traditional forces, however, have also made their contribution. The leaders of the SLPP have high social rank not only in the modern sector of society, but also in traditional society as sons, nephews, or grandsons of chiefly families. Similarly, although SLPP leaders have relied on modern methods and institutions in their political activity, they have also drawn upon traditional means, as evidenced by their decision to articulate the party to institutions associated with paramount chiefs and other traditional leaders. This policy is based on the assumption that in Sierra Leone modern techniques would not, in themselves, bring political success. Despite the significant

---

[56] *Ibid.*, Nov. 11, 1960, p. 1.
[57] *Ibid.*, March 24, 1960, p. 1.

social and economic changes that have come about under colonial rule, the loyalties of most people are still shaped by traditional norms. Consequently, the SLPP linked itself to traditional institutions in order to control the expression of mass loyalties in elections.

There is little doubt that in the immediate future Sierra Leonean politics will continue to be influenced by traditional forces. In time, however, the strength of tradition in shaping peasant loyalties and behavior will decline. As further social and economic changes occur, one may expect these loyalties to become more autonomous. They will, in short, be detraditionalized. There is already evidence that this process is at work, as seen in the inability of traditional leaders to control the political expression of residents of areas where social change is occurring at a relatively rapid rate. In Kono District, for example, the employment of thousands of peasants and laborers in the mining industry has modified their traditional loyalties, helped them to develop new loyalties, and given them new outlets for expression. A similar situation prevails in the iron ore–mining towns in the Northern Province (Port Loko and Tonkolili districts), and it is precisely in such areas that the SLPP has met its strongest opposition from the APC. In general, the structure of the SLPP does not qualify it to compete with opposition parties in areas of relatively rapid social change. Hence the SLPP has tended to employ restrictive measures against opposition groups in these areas, and it is likely that such measures will increasingly characterize the SLPP's relationship to opposition parties like the APC and the SLPIM in Kono District.

Yet, even where restrictions have not applied, no opposition party has effectively challenged the combination of interests around which Sir Milton Margai so astutely organized the SLPP's hegemony. Sir Milton's untimely death in April, 1964, was a major loss, but it will not alter the party's basis of power. The succession of Albert Margai as premier slightly disturbed the balance between Temne and Mende tribal interests in the SLPP, and in the long run the imbalance may prove harmful. One influential Temne leader, Dr. John Karefa-Smart, opposed Albert Margai's succession; along with M. S. Mustapha, considered the second leading member in the SLPP cabinet at the time of Sir Milton's death, Karefa-Smart refused to enter the new government. Equally important Temne leaders, however, did join Albert Margai's government: Kandeh Bureh, perhaps the most influential Muslim political personality in the country and a powerful grass-roots Temne leader, and A. Wurie, a Temne educator who served for some years as a local government education leader in the north. A serious Temne-Mende split therefore seems unlikely, and there is little doubt that the SLPP's dominance in Sierra Leonean politics will prevail.

APPENDIX TABLE 1
Registered Voters, Total Vote, and Vote by Party in the 1957 General Election

Constituency	Registered voters	Valid votes Number	Valid votes Per cent[a]	SLPP	UPP[b]	NC	SLIM	LP[c]	IND[d]
COLONY	53,517	35,837	67	17,117	10,001	2,984	1,126	1,128	3,481
Freetown East	12,878	8,373	65	5,519	1,617	1,070	167	...	...
Freetown Central	11,458	10,596	92	5,465	3,598	618	536	236	143
Freetown West	10,283	8,756	85	3,799	3,401	541	423	440	152
Sherbro	3,642	2,671	73	...	...	...	...	...	2,671
Wilberforce	2,128	967	45	265	469	233	...	71	...
York	2,194	661	30	162	279	149	...	26	...
Kissy	3,262	996	31	430	244	296	...	...	...
Mountain	898	523	58	111	216	77	...	...	119
Waterloo	3,473	1,156	33	584	54	...	...	355	163
British Koya[a]	3,301	1,138	34	782	123	...	...	...	233
PROTECTORATE									
Northern Province	160,129	38,318	24	17,438	8,942	...	...	...	11,938
Bombali East	18,855	4,196	22	2,225	854	...	...	...	1,117
Bombali West	13,010	3,824	29	2,279	...	...	...	...	1,545
Koinadugu North	12,620	3,797	30	329	...	...	...	...	3,468
Koinadugu South	13,737	4,962	36	2,425	...	...	...	...	2,537
Port Loko East	29,181	5,919	20	2,381	1,357	...	...	...	2,181
Port Loko West	25,064	5,428	22	2,406	3,022	...	...	...	...
Kambia East	10,246	5,087	49	3,997	...	...	...	...	1,090
Kambia West	12,592	5,105	41	1,396	3,709	...	...	...	...
Tonkolili East[e]	10,492								
Tonkolili West[e]	14,332								

Southeastern Province	128,044	55,283	43	17,749	…	…	…	…	37,534
Kenema North	25,497	7,007	28	2,458	…	…	…	…	4,549
Kenema South[f]	25,819	14,289	55	6,322	…	…	…	…	7,967
Kono North	18,047	5,549	31	2,572	…	…	…	…	2,977
Kono South	16,754	6,166	37	3,105	…	…	…	…	3,061
Kailahun East	22,994	13,195	57	1,538	…	…	…	…	11,657
Kailahun West	18,933	9,077	48	1,754	…	…	…	…	7,323
Southwestern Province	153,227	36,041	24	23,271	1,992	…	…	…	10,778
Bonthe North	10,007	6,239	62	2,566	…	…	…	…	3,673
Bonthe South	10,792	3,859	36	3,262	…	…	…	…	597
Moyamba North	24,586	6,193	25	4,453	1,740	…	…	…	…
Moyamba South	28,008	7,444	27	7,192	252	…	…	…	…
Pujehun North	11,206	5,132	46	2,365	…	…	…	…	2,767
Pujehun South	10,319	5,457	53	2,773	…	…	…	…	2,684
Bo Town	4,681	1,717	37	660	…	…	…	…	1,057
Bo North[e]	27,206								
Bo South[e]	26,422								
Total	494,917	165,479	33	75,575	20,935	2,984	1,126	1,128	62,086

[a] The three Freetown constituencies and the Sherbro constituency were double-member constituencies in which each registered voter had two votes. All other constituencies, in both colony and protectorate, were single-member constituencies.
[b] The UPP was the only party of colony origin to contest seats in protectorate constituencies.
[c] Labor Party.
[d] Independents.
[e] The SLPP was unopposed in these constituencies.
[f] I have corrected the entry for Kenema South, on page 3 of the source cited below, as it incorrectly lists the successful candidate as a member of the SLPP, whereas in fact he was an independent.

SOURCE: "Report on the Sierra Leone General Election, 1957" (mimeographed; Freetown: Ministry of Internal Affairs, 1957).

Appendix Table 2

Percentage of Votes and Number of Legislative Council Seats Won, by Party, in 1957 General Election

Electoral area	Total number of seats	SLPP Per cent of votes	SLPP Number of seats[c]	UPP Per cent of votes	UPP Number of seats	NC Per cent of votes	NC Number of seats	SLIM Per cent of votes	SLIM Number of seats	LP[a] Per cent of votes	LP[a] Number of seats	IND[b] Per cent of votes	IND[b] Number of seats
COLONY	14	48	9	28	3	8	..	3	..	3	..	10	2
PROTECTORATE													
Northern Province	10	46	6	23	2							31	2
Bombali East	1	53	1	20	..							27	..
Bombali West	1	60	1	..	..							40	1
Koinadugu North	1	9	..	..	..							91[d]	1
Koinadugu South	1	49	1	..	..							51	1
Port Loko East	1	40	1	23	1							37	..
Port Loko West	1	44	1	56	1							..	..
Kambia East	1	79	1	..	..							21	..
Kambia West	1	27	..	73	1							..	..
Tonkolili East	1		1										
Tonkolili West	1		1										
Southeastern Province	6	32	2	..	..							68	4
Kenema North	1	35	1	..	..							65[e]	..
Kenema South	1	44	..	..	..							56	1
Kono North	1	46	..	..	..							54	1
Kono South	1	50	1	..	..							50	..
Kailahun East	1	12	..	..	..							88[f]	1
Kailahun West	1	19	..	..	..							81[g]	1

Southwestern Province	9	64	8	6	..		..	..	30	1
Bonthe North	1	41	1	..	..		..	..	59[h]	..
Bonthe South	1	85	1	..	..		..	..	15	..
Moyamba North	1	72	1	28	..		..	..	..	..
Moyamba South	1	97	1	3	..		..	..	54[i]	..
Pujehun North	1	46	1	..	..		..	..	49	..
Pujehun South	1	51	1	..	..		..	..	62	1
Bo Town	1	38	1	..	..		1	..		
Bo North									38	
Bo South	1		1							
Total	39[j]	46	25	12	5	2	1	1	38	9

[a] Labor Party.

[b] Independents.

[c] Figures for the number of seats won by the SLPP are those given in the source cited below. The SLPP, however, lost some of its seats to the UPP and to independents as a result of election petitions presented to the Supreme Court, and of by-elections ordered by the court. The UPP won two of the SLPP's nine colony seats in by-elections held in Freetown West and Freetown Central at the order of the court, one of its six seats in the Northern Province in a by-election held in Port Loko East, and one of its eight seats in the Southwestern Province in a by-election held in Moyamba North. The UPP, thus winning four additional seats, brought its total to nine instead of five. Independents took one seat from the SLPP in the Northern Province through an election petition in Bombali East, one in the Southeastern Province through a by-election in Kono South, and one in the Southwestern Province through an election petition in Bonthe North. By winning these three additional seats, the independents raised their total from nine to twelve. The SLPP, losing nine seats altogether, ended up with eighteen instead of the twenty-five given in the report on the election.

[d] Four independents contested Koinadugu North.

[e] Three independents contested Kenema North.

[f] Six independents contested Kailahun East.

[g] Two independents contested Kailahun West.

[h] Four independents contested Bonthe North.

[i] Three independents contested Pujehun North.

[j] In addition to the thirty-nine directly elected seats, there were twelve indirectly elected seats. These seats were reserved to paramount chiefs, who were elected by district councils. Only eleven chiefs were elected, however, as Tonkolili District failed to produce a literate chief, and literacy was a condition of election. The eleven indirectly elected chiefs, as well as the independents, joined with the SLPP in the legislature. There were also two nominated seats, filled by the governor with the advice of the premier.

SOURCE: "Report on the Sierra Leone General Election, 1957" (mimeographed; Freetown: Ministry of Internal Affairs, 1957).

4. CAMEROUN

By Victor T. Le Vine

INTRODUCTION

The Cameroun Federal Republic* comprises the East Cameroun (the former Cameroun Republic) and the West Cameroun (the former British Trust Territory of Southern Cameroons). Before federation, these two areas shared little except a common past as a German protectorate, a minor ethnic community, and a widely discussed feeling that the two Camerouns ought to be reunited. Forty years of separate administration under French and British tutelage had developed modern political systems that were almost mutually exclusive. Present constitutional arrangements uniting the two territories envisage a transitional period during which each unit has considerable political autonomy and can prevent passage by the Federal Assembly of laws it opposes. The original intention of the constitutional draftsmen seems to have been the maintenance of a period of loose association before the holding of federal elections, but events in 1962 pointed to political amalgamation on the federal level rather than to the preservation of distinctly regional party systems.

The East Cameroun

A key factor in the pattern of political groups in the East Cameroun is the fact that there has been no national party, like the Tanganyika National African Union or the Convention People's Party in Ghana, to carry the thrust of the country's movement to and beyond independence. Such country-wide organization was attempted in 1962, when the party in power, the Union Camerounaise, moved to create what President Ahmadou Ahidjo termed a "unified party" by attempting to suppress the major opposition parties. Before that time the several parties competing for power were regionally or ethnically based formations, loosely organ-

* In this essay "Cameroun," the Gallicized version of the name, will be used for general references. It is the official spelling presently employed to refer to the Federal Republic and its components. "Cameroon" or "Cameroons," the Anglicized spelling, refers to the British Cameroons and its two parts. It is still employed widely in the West Cameroun despite the official change. Other variants are: "Kamerun" (German), "Camaroñes" (Spanish), and "Camaroes" (Portuguese). "Cameroun" is also employed to denote the former French Trust Territory and its successor, the Cameroun Republic.

I gratefully acknowledge the support of the Ford Foundation, whose Foreign Area Fellowship Program underwrote field research in the Cameroons during 1960–61, and the support and assistance of the African Studies Center of the University of California, Los Angeles, which enabled me to visit the two Camerouns in 1959.

ized, more often than not coalescing around some local political personality rather than focusing on an ideology or a program.

The only genuinely national party with a dynamic organization, an ideological commitment, and a militant leadership—in short, the only party that might have grown into an all-Cameroun movement—dissipated its vitality by a premature attempt to seize power. This party, the Union des Populations du Cameroun (UPC), was outlawed in 1955 because of its recourse to violence. Its leadership either took to the bush, becoming self-styled *maquisards,* or fled abroad to the protection of more friendly African governments. After the republican constitution was approved in February, 1960, the ban against the UPC was removed, and a group of *rallié* UPC leaders were elected to the National Assembly of the Cameroun. However, the death of the party's president-in-exile, Dr. Félix Moumié, on October 28, 1960, left the UPC fragmented and unable to regain its former organizational vitality. The UPC deputies, whose number has been considerably reduced by imprisonment and arrest, constitute the principal opposition in the East Cameroun Assembly.

Also in opposition, although only since the loss of its three ministerial portfolios in October, 1960, is the smaller Parti des Démocrates Camerounais (PDC). This party is headed by André-Marie Mbida, a former prime minister whose varying political fortunes once took him out of the country and into an uneasy collaboration with Moumié's so-called "external" UPC. The Démocrates, of whom there are four left in the present Assembly, represent a large, predominantly Catholic, Bulu-Ewondo tribal clientele located in the south central part of the Cameroun, mainly around Yaoundé, the country's capital.

The official government party, now mustering a large block of nearly 90 deputies in the 100-man Eastern Assembly, is the Parti d'Union Camerounaise (UC).[1] The UC, led by the unprepossessing, but highly respected, president of the Republic, Ahmadou Ahidjo, is based on the massive support of the traditional Muslim hierarchies and chieftaincies of the north. Building upon the narrow legislative margin it had in 1960

---

[1] After the elections of April 14, 1960, the Cameroun National Assembly comprised 100 deputies. The number was reduced to 99 when Ahmadou Ahidjo resigned to accept the presidency. By December, 1960, the composition of the Assembly was as follows:

Government:		
Parti d'Union Camerounaise	50	seats
Groupe des Progressistes du Cameroun	10	"
Front Populaire pour l'Unité et la Paix	18	"
Opposition:		
Parti des Démocrates Camerounais	11	"
Union des Populations du Cameroun	8	"
Independents (Marcel Beybey-Eyidi and Douala Manga		
Bell; no affiliation)	2	"
	Total 99	seats

(50 of 100 seats), the UC has since established important organizational bases in the southern areas of the East Cameroun, hitherto considered the closed reserves of other parties or local groups. Its current preponderance of seats in the Assembly, however, is owing more to defections from opposition and independent parties (notably the Démocrates and the now-defunct Groupe des Progressistes du Cameroun and Front Populaire pour l'Unité et la Paix) than to gains in the by-elections of December, 1961, and January, 1962.

Before 1962 a small number of other parties participated in Cameroun political life, but they did not possess substantial electoral strength. The Groupe des Progressistes du Cameroun (GPC) was a legislative coalition of two such parties, the Mouvement d'Action Nationale du Cameroun (MANC), composed basically of intellectuals and political nonconformists, and the Parti Socialiste du Cameroun (PSC), which was formerly the local branch of the French Socialist Party (SFIO). The Groupe des Progressistes provided the present eastern government with its prime minister, Charles Assalé, and its former foreign minister, Charles Okala. Neither of the two parties, however, ever enjoyed much electoral good fortune; their successes lay in the personal appeal of and the effective tribal support mustered by their leaders.

Although the Cameroun had some ninety registered political "parties," most of them, with the exception of the foregoing, were but little more than *ad hoc* organizational adjuncts to local politicians. A number of parties are affiliates of the UPC, performing the function of incubating future UPC leaders and acting as centers for the dissemination of UPC propaganda. A sizable number of these groups are purely local or departmental organizations built solidly on ethnic bases and functioning as solidarity symbols and interest-articulating organs for the locality, the tribe, or the ethnic group involved. Still others are self-styled "traditional" organizations which have proven useful political springboards for not a few important Cameroun politicians. In the broad configuration of the Cameroun's parties, however, the basic pattern persists: (1) there are no national parties, although the UC now aspires to that status; (2) most of the parties are premised on personality, ethnic, or sectional considerations; and (3) parties with a genuine ideological commitment have been the exception, not the rule. That the present governing coalition has been a coalition of personalities as well as parties offers dramatic proof of the complex nature of the Cameroun's party system and of the manifold divisions within it.

The West Cameroun

Immediately before independence, the British Trust Territory of the Cameroons was divided into the Southern Cameroons and the Northern

Cameroons. The Southern Cameroons was a self-governing region within the Federation of Nigeria, complete with its own Legislative Assembly, House of Chiefs, and Council of Ministers. For the most part, politics in the trust territory meant politics in the Southern Cameroons; any historical analysis must give Southern (later West) Cameroonian politics primary emphasis. In the Northern Cameroons, now the Sardauna Province of the Northern Region of Nigeria, there was only nominal party activity, and that was limited to the period between the United Nations plebiscites in November, 1959, and February, 1961.

Three main and several minor parties constitute the dimensions of party life in the West Cameroun. Further, a number of tribal associations, coöperative societies, and labor unions, a cultural group (the Kamerun Society), and a student organization provide articulation within or without the parties for special social, economic, or political interests. The present governing party is the Kamerun National Democratic Party (KNDP), headed by western Prime Minister and federal Vice-President John Foncha. The first general elections to the West Cameroun Legislative Assembly held on December 30, 1961, produced a comfortable KNDP margin of twenty-five of the thirty-seven seats in the Assembly. The principal opposition party, the Cameroon People's National Convention (CPNC)[2] won ten seats; the One Kamerun Party (OK), also in opposition, one seat; and one seat went to an independent who, with the OK member, declared for the KNDP shortly after his election. The new KNDP majority contrasts with the slim, artificial majority (fourteen to the CPNC's thirteen) which bedeviled it before 1962.

Two factors help to explain the KNDP's domination over the West Camerounian political scene and, conversely, the relative weakness, even decline, of the opposition parties. One is that the KNDP is the party under whose leadership the Southern Cameroons "reunited" with the East Cameroun. The United Nations plebiscite, held on February 11, 1961, to determine whether the Southern Cameroons would join Nigeria or the Cameroun Republic, resulted in an overwhelming vote for unification with the Cameroun. As the party favoring the winning alternative, the KNDP could not help but reap the political benefits that accrued therefrom. The CPNC favored the Nigerian alternative, and the finality of its defeat on this issue (235,571 for the Cameroun; 97,741 for Nigeria) reduced even further its effectiveness as an opposition party. Even the OK, which was in agreement with the KNDP for the first time on the question of unification, suffered in the light of the KNDP's increased popu-

---

[2] The CPNC was formed by the merger of the Kamerun National Congress (KNC) and the Kamerun People's Party (KPP). The German spelling, "Kamerun," became a nationalist symbol for those advocating the unification of the two Cameroun territories.

larity. Although the OK won one seat in the January elections, it found itself losing its limited support within the West Cameroun to the victorious KNDP. The second factor is that the organizational and electoral base of the KNDP is in the three "grassfields" divisions of Bamenda, Wum, and Mamfe, which together contain slightly more than half of the West Cameroun's inhabitants. Using its solidly loyal grassfields constituencies as a fulcrum, the KNDP pried a number of coastal districts loose from the CPNC in the plebiscite. The CPNC, unable to make progress in the grassfields (except Nkambe division), and dispossessed of several crucial coastal electoral fiefdoms through the plebiscite, never regained its former strength.

HISTORICAL DEVELOPMENT OF PARTIES

The East (French) Cameroun

The early period, 1919–1946.—During most of the first two decades of its administration of the Cameroun, France felt little need to provide organized forms of political expression for the African elite it was nurturing in its schools and training in various official positions. Inasmuch as French colonial policy had always espoused assimilation of indigenous peoples as its goal—though in practice the policy has become "association by stages"—it was generally felt that when the African had become sufficiently *évolué* he would seek political expression within the French political system. This pattern was then emerging in Senegal and the Ivory Coast, and it was also expected to prevail in the French Cameroun, as well as elsewhere in *Afrique Noire*. Moreover, a centralized political administration, the *indigénat*, and the legal distinctions between Frenchmen and non-Frenchmen, effectively discouraged Camerounian Africans from organizing for political action against the system. Such local discontent or protest as came to the surface was both unprogrammatic and unorganized. As a consequence, the first formally organized Camerounian political groups developed in response to external rather than internal pressures and events.

Under the pressures of World War II and such events as the Brazzaville Conference of 1944, the French permitted the formation of a wide spectrum of political and quasi-political associations, ranging from Franco-Camerounian "patriotic" organizations to local branches of metropolitan parties. Wartime promises and political concessions by France were embodied in the French Constitution of 1946, which provided for the participation of Overseas France in metropolitan legislative organs and, later, for the creation of local legislatures. In the French Cameroun, as elsewhere, a plethora of parties and groups sprang up, ready to contest for seats in the newly created assemblies. The wartime patriotic formations and the new labor unions quickly became the nuclei of political groups which drew into them the most promising of the young Camerounian politicians.

After 1945 Cameroun branches of metropolitan parties were hastily organized, and by the beginning of 1947 some seven main political groups had seen electoral battle. Of the three locally inspired formations, the most important was the Union Camerounaise Française (Unicafra), successor to the prewar groups. The others were local branches of such French parties as the SFIO, the Mouvement Républicain Populaire (MRP), the Gaullist Rassemblement du Peuple Français (RPF), and the Front Intercolonial. These early political groups were extremely limited in both membership and electoral clientele. They represented attempts to transplant French models into the Camerounian context, and their organization, programs, and tactics were local replicas of the French originals. The leaders of these groups were invariably French-educated and French-trained Camerounians for whom political experience meant political experience on the French pattern. Further, the presence of a number of Frenchmen in these organizations reinforced their already heavy Gallic character.

With all their similarities to the metropolitan models, it is hardly surprising that the new parties failed to make much headway either in advancing their respective programs or in winning the stable loyalties of any sizable sections of the electorate. Fundamentally, of course, their weakness lay in the very "Frenchness" they had espoused. Their leadership had not yet come to understand that organizations, tactics, and programs which had found strong support in France would not necessarily command the same influence in a totally different social and political milieu. Moreover, very few Camerounians had any understanding of the new electoral activity, and many of those on whom the French were counting for leadership in the new era failed to grasp the significance of the new political developments. Finally, even though the parties had recruited and used most of the politically conscious elements in Camerounian society, these elements represented only a small proportion of the actual electorate and an even smaller segment of the potential electorate.[3] Only parties that could adapt tactically, organizationally, and programmatically to a rapidly expanding electorate could hope to survive. This was not fully understood until much later.

New directions, 1947–1949.—During the immediate postwar period, trade unions were the most politically active organizations in the French

---

[3] In 1946, of a total estimated population of 3,006,000, there were only 40,614 names on the electoral rolls. Of this number, 2,611 were of the first college (French citizens), and 38,003 were of the second college (qualified Africans). By 1956 the dual college system had been abolished and the new single roll contained 1,752,904 voters.

Cameroun. Soon after the legalization of trade-unionism in 1944, the Cameroun branch of the Confédération Générale du Travail (CGT) transformed itself into the Union des Syndicats Confédérés du Cameroun (USCC). In 1945 the USCC and other unions sought to excite popular feeling by staging strikes in Douala and by launching propaganda campaigns among the workers in the larger urban centers. The strikes did not profit the USCC, however; neither its membership nor its power had increased appreciably, and candidates whom it supported at the polls in 1946 were soundly beaten. In trying to use the doctrine of the class struggle as the main carrier of its message, the USCC had failed. The USCC, as well as other unions, realized that in a country whose population was overwhelmingly rural, with virtually no *bourgeoisie* and a very small urban technical proletariat, class consciousness was almost nonexistent and could not be exploited for political ends.

After 1946 the USCC began infiltrating two small local political organizations: the Unicafra and its successor, the Rassemblement Camerounais (Racam). By 1947 it had captured both groups. And in April, 1948, the trade-unionists, represented by former government clerk Ruben Um Nyobé, medical officer Dr. Félix Moumié, and several others, formed the Union des Populations du Cameroun. Within two months the UPC became the Cameroun branch of Félix Houphouet-Boigny's Rassemblement Démocratique Africain (RDA), and announced what was essentially a two-point program: unification of the two Camerouns, and rapid progress toward complete independence under the terms of the United Nations Charter. The emergence of the UPC signaled the beginning of a new era in the Cameroun's political development, an era of agitational, overt nationalism.

With its simple, direct program, as well as the backing of the RDA and the USCC, the UPC picked up momentum. Two influential traditional organizations, the Ngondo (Douala) and the Kumsze (Bamileké), threw their support to the new party.[4] The UPC began to build a tightly knit, hierarchically structured organization on the RDA pattern, and established liaisons with an organization of *émigré* Doualas living in the British Cameroons. Further, the UPC created a number of subsidiary formations with varying tactical roles, and began publishing a party newspaper, *La Voix du Peuple,* in which it attacked both the French administration and other political parties.

By November, 1949, when the first United Nations Visiting Mission

---

[4] By 1949 the Ngondo had become disenchanted with the UPC, and withdrew its support. The Kumsze followed suit in 1950. (*Ngondo* is the Douala term for the local councils that existed among the Douala long before the German occupation in 1884. *Kumsze* represents a similar tribal institution, found generally on the level of the chiefdom, with limited, though crucial, powers. The political formations bearing these names carry only the ethnic referent of the originals, not their characteristics.)

arrived in Douala, the UPC had become by all odds the best-organized political party in the Cameroun. It had taken on the coloration of a national Camerounian party and had developed the first effective body of doctrine based (at least the party so claimed) on exclusively Camerounian themes. Although the UPC had no representation in the local legislature, it could still claim to be the primary instrument of Camerounian nationalism. Certainly its tactical and organizational boldness lent much substance to the claim.

The multiplication of parties, 1949–1955.—The UPC had begun auspiciously by organizing itself on a broad geographic basis and by launching a program designed to attract the widest possible support. Its membership, however, was limited largely to the southwestern part of the country, and, despite its potentially irresistible program, the UPC was not yet in any sense a national party. Its inability to achieve national status gave heart to other Camerounian parties and politicians, and in the next five years a large number of political groups were organized. Not unexpectedly, their programs and strategies reflected attempts to pre-empt the theses and the tactics of the UPC. In a sense, the political battle lines drawn between 1949 and 1955 ranged the UPC and its affiliates against the other parties, which were using the local legislature as their sounding board, with both sides strongly emphasizing appeals to tribal and ethnic loyalties.

The first of the anti-UPC groups was organized early in 1948. In the Bamileké region, proadministration chiefs created the Union Bamileké to counter the pro-UPC Kumsze. In June, 1949, to offset widespread UPC activity among the Bassa people, the Evolution Sociale Camerounaise (Esocam) was organized in the Sanaga-Maritime region. Similarly, the Renaissance Camerounaise (Renaicam), whose aims parallel those of the Esocam, was formed in the East Cameroun. Like the Esocam, the Renaicam was ethnically based upon the Ewondo and Maka peoples.

In addition to these strictly anti-UPC groups, elected representatives had begun to form their own organizational adjuncts. Two of the most successful were Louis Aujoulat's Bloc Démocratique Camerounais (BDC) and Charles Assalé's Association Traditionelle Bantoue Efoula-Meyong, built upon a solid Bulu ethnic base. The success of Assalé's traditional organization, which he had used to sweep all opposition before him on his way to the Assembly in 1952, prompted other politicians to create similar structures in their constituencies, or to convert extant organizations into more useful political weapons. In this spirit, Prince Douala Manga Bell, Betota Akwa, and Paul Soppo-Priso seized upon the Ngondo in Douala for their own (successful) electoral ends. In the Bamileké region, Mathias Djoumessi reconstructed the Kumsze into a political party, and, by 1953, traditional organizations had been initiated among

the Bamoun, the Eton, the Ewondo and the Beti, the Fulani of N'Gaoundéré and Garoua (the two largest towns of the north), the Musgum, and
the Batanga. Two other groups of this period bear mentioning: Charles
Okala's Union Sociale Camerounaise (USC), formed in 1953 from the
remnants of an older Socialist group, and the Coordination des Indépendants Camerounais (Indecam), an anti-UPC organization operating
mainly in the Bassa tribal area. Neither party, however, had much electoral success; the former offered a program too diffuse to be attractive, and
the latter preferred leadership rivalries to electoral battles.

The elections of June, 1951, for the French National Assembly and
of March, 1952, for the Cameroun Territorial Assembly marked a victory
for the moderates, with the UPC again failing to win a single seat. Whatever the party felt privately about these successive defeats, publicly it
accused the Franco-Camerounian administration of foul play, claiming
that every device from ballot stuffing to the arrest of its agents had been
used against it. Failure at the polls, however, stimulated the UPC to
change its tactics, a move that came to have wide strategic and organizational repercussions among its opponents.

In 1952 the Togolese issue, brought into the United Nations by Ewe
petitioners, had begun to attract world-wide attention. The lesson was not
lost on the UPC. Not only did petitioners have unparalleled access to
world opinion through the publicity facilities of the UN, but the UN
itself almost automatically conferred status and the mantle of respectability upon those who appeared before it. It presented an opportunity to
acquire a legitimacy by association which not even success at the polls
could bring. In November, 1952, Um Nyobé made the first of several
appearances before the Fourth (Trusteeship) Committee of the General
Assembly, ostensibly to testify in connection with a number of UPC-
sponsored petitions.[5]

Um Nyobé returned home and immediately embarked on what UPC
chroniclers have called "a gloriously triumphant tour of the country,"
reporting on his alleged victories before the UN. One effect of his activities
was the formation of a number of UPC and non-UPC organizations, most

----

[5] The number of UPC petitions received by the United Nations has never been
totaled; conservative estimates put the number at 2,000 or 3,000, a figure that does
not include the almost 100,000 petitions received by the several visiting missions to
the Camerouns. Most of the latter petitions arrived in large bundles containing hundreds of handwritten notes or slogans, many of them illegible. Um Nyobé appeared
in New York in December, 1952, and December, 1953, and again in November, 1954.
At virtually every session of the General Assembly after 1952, UPC representatives
were present as petitioners, correspondents, or observers, and later, after the party's
leaders had been banished from the Camerouns, as members of the United Arab
Republic and Guinean delegations. Félix Moumié was probably better known, in the
beginning, outside the Camerouns than in them. Almost certainly, without the
free publicity and the quasi respectability afforded by his presence at the UN, he
would never have become so well known and so feared as he was.

of them designed solely to fulfill the organizational requirements for appearance before the UN. Between 1952 and 1959 increasingly larger numbers of Camerounian politicians made the trip to New York. The discussion of the Cameroun question at the United Nations in the spring of 1959 brought to New York no less than twenty-seven petitioners, representing some twenty-eight groups or organizations. Only about half of these organizations could actually have mustered a sizable membership or following.[6]

By the beginning of 1955, despite the impression it had created in New York and, by reflection, at home, the UPC had accomplished little of real substance. Its primary contribution to the Cameroun political scene had been catalytic. It had provided tactical and organizational models for its opponents to follow; by 1955 all the other parties, including the BDC, had accepted as their goals reunification of the Camerouns and the eventual independence of the country. The UPC had led all the rest in bringing Cameroun issues before the UN; before long other parties had established beachheads in New York. The war of preëmption had ended in a stalemate; moreover, by 1955 the extremism of the UPC had begun to attract the unfavorable attention of the administration. Having failed to achieve any measure of power by legal means, and checked on all levels by opponents, it is not surprising that the UPC leadership, in the early months of 1955, became increasingly receptive to the more revolutionary urgings of Moumié and his supporters.

Crisis and recovery, 1955–1960.—The events surrounding the abortive UPC-led revolt in May, 1955, are discussed at length elsewhere.[7] Insofar as these events reflected a UPC effort to ignite a nationwide insurrection, they clearly failed. The riots, demonstrations, and damage to property which occurred between May 22 and May 30 affected only Yaoundé, Douala, and the regions of the southwest. By June 5 calm had been restored to these areas. The failure of the UPC to overcome the antipathy of Muslim leaders resulted in a series of misfires in several northern towns where the UPC had tried to initiate demonstrations. In July the administration banned the UPC and its affiliate organizations, and soon thereafter the core of the UPC leadership crossed into the British Cameroons to set up emergency headquarters at Kumba. In September the UPC directorate split. One wing, led by Um Nyobé and Mayi Matip, decided

---

[6] The complete list of organizations in question may be found in the *United Nations Review* (April, 1959), p. 47.

[7] The most complete documentary record available on the events of 1955, though written from the administrating authority's viewpoint, is the French High Commission's white paper, *Les Emeutes de mai* (Yaoundé: Service de l'Information, 1955). See also *Report on the Cameroons under French Administration*, United Nations Visiting Mission to Trust Territories in West Africa, UN Doc. T/1240, Suppl. 4 (New York, 1956), and the unpublished manuscript by George Horner, "Response of Selected Camerounian Ethnic Groups to French Political Institutions" (1958).

to return to the French Cameroun and continue the revolt from within; the other wing, including party president Félix Moumié and most of the other leaders, opted to conduct the struggle from outside the Cameroun. Expelled from the British Cameroons in 1957, the Moumié group subsequently found asylum in Khartoum, then in Cairo, and finally, in 1958, in Conakry. The revolt ended party activity for the balance of 1955, leaving the air heavy with suspicion and recrimination. Many of the most vocal of the southern politicians seemed to be shocked into silence, and the UN Visiting Mission that toured the country in December observed that northern hostility to the south had been so aggravated as almost to endanger the unity of the country.[8]

In the spring of 1956, however, matters had calmed down sufficiently for political activity to be resumed. In March the Ngondo and the Association Traditionelle Bantoue merged to become the Mouvement d'Action Nationale du Cameroun under the leadership of Charles Assalé and David Mvondo. Other developments reflected a general impulse for "national rejuvenation" and "national reconciliation," and a willingness to forget the events of 1955 and to welcome the UPC and its affiliates back into Camerounian political life. In June, seventeen days before the Loi-Cadre was promulgated, Paul Soppo-Priso launched the Courant Mouvement d'Union Nationale (CMUN) as the organizational expression of the new spirit of reconciliation. The project was an ambitious one; it called for the rejection of the Loi-Cadre, unification of the Camerouns, reconstitution of the Assembly through universal suffrage, and the proclamation of a general amnesty throughout the territory. The movement, at first warmly received in the south, was joined by a large number of politically prominent people, including some of the leaders of the USC, the BDC, the Indecam, the Esocam, and the UPC. Mbida and Ahidjo, as well as most of the northern leaders, remained aloof and suspicious of the CMUN's authenticity.

The CMUN lasted only until November, 1956. Even though its participants agreed on general principles, they found themselves unable to decide on a common program of action. Moderates and radicals split on the question of participation in the forthcoming election of December, 1956; the UPC walked out and launched a campaign of boycott, leaving the others determined to contest the elections. Although its life span was only five months, the CMUN could claim two important achievements. First, it marked the general acceptance by most Cameroun parties of the full panoply of Camerounian nationalist symbols. Second, it gave the moderates revolutionary respectability through their alliance with the UPC, without having to embrace the more violent aspects of the UPC's program. The result of this experiment with national party solidarity was

[8] *Report on the Cameroons*, pp. 14–16.

a net gain for the moderates and, as it turned out, another setback for the UPC.

The elections of December, 1956, took place in an atmosphere of tension generated by the UPC. The outlawed party conducted its campaign for abstention by every means at its disposal: sabotage, arson, strikes, public demonstrations, and intimidation of voters. In the Sanaga-Maritime, which had become the heartland of the rebellion, and in the Wouri region, in which Douala is located, the UPC obtained high abstention percentages. But elsewhere participation was at a high level, except in the north where the abstentions were due not so much to the UPC's activities as to a lack of interest in the election itself. In all, about 55 per cent of the registered voters cast their ballots, and again the moderates swept the lists.

The new Assembly, organized according to the new Loi-Cadre rules which permitted the creation of political groups within legislatures, contained four main groups. Two reflected preëxisting alliances (Mbida's Groupe des Démocrates with twenty seats, and the MANC, with eight), and the other two represented regional voting blocs (the Paysans Indépendants from the Bamileké area, with nine seats, and the Union Camerounaise, from the north, with thirty seats). Soppo-Priso's MANC became the opposition, and the other groups formed a government under André-Marie Mbida. It is important to note that none of these groups except the MANC were political parties in the true sense; they were only parliamentary formations of deputies who had previously associated in earlier groups or parties or who had been elected from the same geographical areas, and therefore had a high degree of ethnic and political communality. It was only later, in 1958, that the four groups became full-fledged political parties with an extraparliamentary existence.

Mbida's government lasted less than a year. He started out well enough, but very soon managed to alienate his friends and infuriate his foes by a series of tactical blunders. His first difficulties stemmed from his uncompromising attitude toward the popular desire for reconciliation and for a *détente* between the UPC and the government. He cracked down on the UPC with what his detractors have called "unnecessary brutality." An even more impolitic move was his announcement that it would not be until after ten years of economic development that the question of the Cameroun's independence could be objectively broached. However reasonable this view might have been, it was not designed to make friends for Mbida among the politicians for whom early independence was an important electoral slogan. Finally, in September, 1957, fresh outbreaks of violence and terrorism occurred in the Sanaga-Maritime region. The new rebellion was put down by Cameroun and French troops, but Mbida's fate was already sealed. In January, 1958, the UC's five ministers resigned in the face of a government policy that seemed to put off both independence and reunification indefinitely, and in February Mbida himself resigned. Ahmadou Ahidjo, leader of the UC group, was appointed as the new prime minister.

The new government included, in addition to Ahidjo's UC, the Paysans Indépendants and several ministers drawn from the MANC, previously in opposition. The Union Camerounaise was now ascendant, and it acquired the enviable distinction of moving the Cameroun toward independence. As far as the parties were concerned, the political picture changed little during 1958 and 1959, except that both the Paysans and the Démocrates lost a number of their adherents in parliamentary shifts, and that several rallié UPC leaders were elected in 1959 by-elections on independent slates.

Two problems, however, continued to occupy the attention of the nation and its political leaders. One was the still unresolved problem of the UPC; the other was the future of the parties after independence was won. The difficult UPC problem presented the graver danger. Throughout 1958 sporadic violence broke out in the southwest, and continued despite the death of Um Nyobé in September. Directed from outside the country by the Cairo-Conakry–based Moumié group, and fed by social unrest in Douala, in Yaoundé, and, after 1958, in the Bamileké region, terrorist activities paralyzed much of the southwestern part of the territory. Crops went unharvested, movement between towns greatly diminished, and an atmosphere of fear pervaded daily life in urban centers such as Douala, Yaoundé, Dschang, and M'Balmayo. After Um Nyobé's death, terrorist activity virtually ceased in the Sanaga-Maritime, but grew in intensity in the Bamileké, Wouri, Mungo, and Nkam regions. Throughout 1959 the UPC kept up a constant drumfire at the United Nations, and almost managed to convince that body that general elections should be held before independence was attained on January 1, 1960. With Guinean, Ghanaian, and Egyptian support, the UPC sought to force itself into the power it had been denied at the polls.

Fortunately for the government, the UPC problem was intimately connected with the question of the future of the parties after independence. It became apparent that the real reason for the UPC's past failures had been its inability to retain control over key nationalist objectives, such as independence and reunification. As these had become part of the common political vocabulary of all parties, the UPC lost whatever it had gained by being the first to espouse them. The UPC's last chance clearly lay in seizing power before independence was attained; in this, too, it failed, even though the Independence Day celebrations were marred by terrorist gunfire in both Yaoundé and Douala. In simple terms, the survival of the non-UPC parties after independence depended on their moderation, for this quality permitted the sort of tactical suppleness which, once nationalist objectives had been realized, could form electoral appeals on the basis of less inspiring domestic goals. The extremist UPC, forged in the heat of nationalist fervor, simply lost its *raison-d'être* after independence, and no amount of warning that the new status was unreal and that the Cameroun was still a tool of French imperialism could blunt the edge of the *fact* of independence. As expected, the revolutionary UPC did not survive the Cameroun's independence; its erstwhile supporters deserted it, and its rallié members in the Cameroun reconstituted themselves into what was in fact only a pale image of the formerly vigorous party.

The move to the one-party state, 1960–1962.—Among the first acts of the government of the new republic was to confer legality once again upon the internal UPC, and to declare a general amnesty for all those in the opposition still at large and in prison for political offenses. The general elections of April, 1960, returned eight UPC and eighteen Bamileké deputies to the National Assembly, most of whom had previously been in the *maquis.* Mayi Matip and Dr. Marcel Beybey-Eyidi were both offered positions in Prime Minister Assalé's cabinet, but declined. The eighteen Bamileké deputies, united under the banner of the Front Populaire pour l'Unité et la Paix (FPUP), accepted collaboration with the government, and their leader, former maquis chief Pierre Kamdem-Ninyim, entered the Assalé government as a minister of state. In a similar spirit of reconciliation, the Démocrates entered the coalition and three of their members—but not Mbida, who turned down a portfolio—accepted minor ministries in the new government.

The incorporation of the FPUP and the PDC into the government marked the first stage in the progressive deterioration of oppositional strength. In October, 1960, the Démocrates lost their three portfolios and, in the next twenty-one months, all but four of the PDC's deputies either defected to the UC or lost their seats in by-elections. In April, 1961, Kamdem-Ninyim, soon to lose his ministry, signaled the disintegration of the FPUP by joining the Union Camerounaise. (In November, 1963, Kamdem-Ninyim was condemned to death for his complicity in the assassination of Deputy Mopen Noe.) During the next three months most of the FPUP's members were assimilated into the UC, and not long thereafter the Groupe des Progressistes, a loose amalgam of the MANC, the PSC, and independents, followed the FPUP by formally merging with the UC. Only Okala, titular leader of the Cameroun Socialists, declined to join the UC. As a result, in the ministerial reshuffle that followed the creation of the Cameroun Federal Republic in October, 1961, he lost his position as foreign minister, a post he had held since early 1960. In November, 1961, Ahidjo confirmed officially what had already become apparent during the preceding months, that he and his party had set their sights on the creation of a one-party system led by "a great unified national movement."

In January, 1962, the government dissolved the UPC congress in Yaoundé, the first indication that more forceful means would be employed to create national unity. The UPC, though favoring collaboration with the government, had rejected Ahidjo's *parti unifié*. In March, at the Socialist congress at Ntui, Okala bluntly condemned the parti unifié as a "play on words"—it was simply the *parti unique* in a different guise. By mid-May, 1962, Mayi Matip, Okala, Mbida, and Beybey-Eyidi agreed to the formation of a united national front, and, on June 23, the four opposition leaders issued a manifesto categorically condemning the proposed parti unifié and contending that unity could be achieved only by sabotaging their own parties for the benefit of the ruling UC. The parti unifié, they claimed, would ultimately culminate in a "fascist-type dictatorship." In July all four of the dissenting leaders were arrested, tried, and imprisoned under an antisubversion law promulgated only four months earlier. By mid-1962 the East Cameroun had become, to all intents and purposes, a one-party state. The remaining deputies of the opposition (UPC and PDC), now only a handful, had been reduced to leaderless and ineffective protest. Most observers of Cameroun politics agreed that their days were numbered.

The erosion of the political opposition must be viewed against a background of events which, taken together, served to strengthen the hand of Ahidjo and his ruling UC. Three interrelated events may be regarded as keys to this development: (1) the government's reconciliation policies during 1960; (2) the crystallization of the UC's organizational and ideological framework; and (3) the unification of the two Camerouns attendant upon the British Cameroons plebiscite of February, 1961, and the subsequent creation of the Federal Republic.

The "relegalization" of the UPC, together with the generally conciliatory attitude of the government during 1960, served further to weaken the UPC as an opposition party. The government policy had the effect not only of crystallizing the party's internal schisms, but also of forcing an open break between the external and internal factions. Moreover, the general amnesty provided former UPC maquis with an alternative access to public life; the FPUP members, once lost to the UPC, became easily convinced of the advantages of further integration into the dominant political party. Similar pressures eventually split the PDC, a split made easier by Mbida's obsessive dislike of Ahidjo and his colleagues.

Because of the weakening of the opposition and the scramble to get on the UC band wagon, the UC found its attempts to organize party units in formerly hostile opposition territory increasingly easier and, as a consequence, increasingly more successful. That the party held its fourth congress in Ebolowa in July, 1962, signified that Ahidjo and his colleagues considered much of the south to be theirs. Ebolowa, the home of eastern Prime Minister Assalé, was the center of MANC activity, and it remains the home base of the Association Traditionnelle Bantoue Efoula-Meyong, politicized by Assalé and speaking for most Bulu-Beti south of Yaoundé. For the first time the party began to outline an ideological position, a clear indication that it considered the political wars almost won.

The partial attainment of the nationalist goal of unification in 1961 further enhanced the prestige of the governing party and its political leadership. The February, 1961, plebiscite conducted under UN auspices in both the Northern and the Southern Cameroons, under British administration, resulted in the south in an overwhelming vote for unification with the Republic, and in the north in a substantial majority for integration with Nigeria. In May, Ahidjo and Premier John Foncha agreed on the formal constitution of a federal republic. On October 1, upon termination of the UN trusteeship, the Cameroun Federal Republic came into being. The political gains of the Ahidjo government in the plebiscite and the creation of the federation greatly enhanced the UC's prestige and emboldened it to move more decisively against its opponents.

In short, by the end of 1961 it seemed that Ahidjo held all the important political cards. His party could now play from a position of great strength, which enabled it to reject the compromises offered by the opposition. The opposition could either capitulate or coalesce in the hope of maximizing its dwindling strength. It chose the latter alternative, but even so it could do little to change the course set by the regime.

West (British) Cameroons

Organized political activity in the former Trust Territory of the Cameroons under British Administration did not commence until 1946, although there were a few quasi-political formations in existence before World War II. The postwar upsurge of political activity occurred partly because the Cameroons became a United Nations trust territory. The status of trusteeship, which differed markedly in its developmental emphasis from the prewar mandate system, stimulated an ever-increasing preoccupation with the political future of the territory among politically conscious Cameroonians. This autonomous growth of activity has accelerated and strengthened as a result of the Cameroons' administrative link with Nigeria, which was the scene of extensive nationalist ferment in the early postwar period. Indeed, some of the early Cameroon associations had close organizational and leadership ties with major political movements in Nigeria.

Second, after the war, organized political activity was heavily concentrated in the Southern Cameroons, largely because economic and social development was more advanced in the southern areas than in the relatively backward northern areas. This pattern was characteristic of the entire Guinea Coast. The Southern Cameroons was much better endowed with educational facilities, with an economic infrastructure, and, consequently, with "socially mobilized" elements of the population susceptible to political appeals and activity. By contrast, the Northern Cameroons was relatively untouched by modernizing forces until the mid-1950's, which reinforced the existing political quiescence characteristic of the rather rigidly conservative Muslim north.

The most important leader among the small group of politically conscious Southern Cameroonians active in the early postwar period was Dr. Emmanuel M. L. Endeley, a medical officer working in Nigeria. In 1946, after he was dropped from the rolls of the British Medical Association for malpractice, Endeley plunged into an active political career. He organized two tribal associations, the Bakweri Improvement Union and the Bakweri Land Committee, to articulate demands for the return of former German-owned lands ceded to the Cameroons Development Corporation. In 1947 he formed a political organization, the Cameroons Federal Union (CFU), to support demands for a separate Southern Cameroons region within Nigeria. Other Southern Cameroonians who had become politically active by this time included Peter M. Kale, with whom Endeley had formed the Cameroons Youth League (CYL) in Lagos, Nigeria, in 1941, and L. N. Namme and Namaso N. Mbile. These four leaders had participated in the founding of the National Council of Nigeria and the Cameroons (NCNC) in Lagos in 1944.[9]

Until 1948 the objective of the CFU, the CYL, and the various ethnic-centered associations was to assert the identity of the Cameroons within Nigeria, an objective strongly supported by the Nigerian pro-NCNC nationalist press. In 1948, however, the idea of the unification of the two Camerouns emerged and gathered support. The possibility of unification had been discussed before, but it was not until Jobea K. Dibonge and his French Camerouns Welfare Association formally raised the issue in 1948 that it became attractive to Endeley and the groups in which he was involved.

In May, 1949, a conference of political groups from both Camerouns met at Kumba to discuss common problems and to plan submissions to the first UN Visiting Mission, scheduled to arrive in the Cameroons in October. The conference attacked the British administration, pointing to

[9] "Because Cameroonian associations in Lagos desired to affiliate (that is, the Bamenda Improvement Association, the Bakweri Union, and the Cameroons Youth League), the name of the movement was changed to the National Council of Nigeria and the Cameroons (NCNC)" (James S. Coleman, *Nigeria: Background to Nationalism* [Berkeley and Los Angeles: University of California Press, 1958], p. 265).

what it claimed was the more rapid political and economic development in the French Camerouns, and demanded the transfer of the British Cameroons to French trusteeship. The presence of UPC representatives from the French Camerouns at the conference is significant, for it marked the first formal contact between French Cameroun nationalists and the nascent nationalist groups in the British trust territory. (The contact was strengthened at two important meetings held at Kumba in August and December, 1951, when the UPC and Southern Cameroons nationalist groups further elaborated joint political objectives.) An informal alliance between the French Camerouns Welfare Association and the UPC was concluded, and the unification theme became part of the political vocabulary of Southern Cameroons politicians. The 1949 conference had the additional important consequence of giving birth to the Cameroons National Federation (CNF) under the leadership of Endeley, Dibonge, Mbile, Solomon T. Muna, and S. A. George.

Despite Endeley's willingness to use unification as a slogan to mobilize support for the CNF, particularly among resident French Camerounians, his main preoccupation continued to be greater Southern Cameroons autonomy in Nigeria. By 1951, after several petitions to the UN Visiting Mission and the Trusteeship Council, it seemed to some Cameroonians, particularly Mbile, that Endeley was not pursuing unification with sufficient vigor. As a consequence, Mbile split with the CNF to form the Kamerun United National Congress (KUNC) to campaign for what had then become known as "reunification." But, toward the end of 1952, Mbile and Endeley had resolved their differences, and the CNF and the KUNC merged to become the Kamerun National Congress (KNC).

The formation and re-formation of Cameroonian political groups did not, however, sever the ties that Endeley, Mbile, and others maintained with the NCNC. That break did not occur until 1953, when the thirteen-man Cameroons bloc in the Eastern Regional House of Assembly split during the crisis over the issue of Nnamdi Azikiwe's leadership. Two separate parties emerged from the schism: the Kamerun National Congress, led by Endeley, Foncha, George, Muna, and C. Kangsen, stood for Southern Cameroonian administrative separation and eventual reunification with the French Cameroun; the Kamerun People's Party (KPP), led by Kale, Mbile, and Peter Motomby-Woleta, stood for the continued association of the Cameroons with the Eastern Region of Nigeria and the maintenance of close ties with the NCNC.

In December, 1953, the KNC won twelve of the thirteen seats in the Eastern House in an election in which the main issue was the demand for separate regional status. The 1954 Nigerian (Lyttleton) Constitution, taking the recent elections into consideration, made the Southern Cameroons a quasi-federal territory with its own house of assembly and its own executive. In October, 1954, the Southern Cameroons House of Assembly met for the first time with Endeley as leader of government business. With the passing of time, especially after the Southern Cameroons achieved its distinctive quasi-federal status, the KNC tended more and more to see the Southern Cameroons of the future as a self-governing region within an independent federation of Nigeria, and to relegate the goal of unification of the two Camerouns increasingly to the background. This swing toward an apparent permanent association with Nigeria cost the KNC the support of some of its strongest leaders. In 1955 John Foncha, who had served as secretary of both the CYL and the Bamenda Improvement Union and had organized the Bamenda section of the CNF, split with Endeley and organized the Kamerun National Democratic Party (KNDP) on a program of complete secession from Nigeria and reunification with the French Cameroun. In a sense, the KNDP had reverted to the old CNF program. The KNC suffered another blow in September, 1957, when Muna, who had held one of its seats in the House and in the Executive Council, resigned and joined the KNDP. He reportedly accused the KNC leadership of following a policy of "integration with Nigeria," even though the party was still committed to the policy of unification. Although the KNC had lost valuable support by its gradual shift away from unification, it had, by 1957, moved sufficiently close to the KPP's position to permit a KNC-KPP alliance and to present a united viewpoint to the 1958 UN Visiting Mission. On May 29, 1958, Endeley revealed that he had almost completely abandoned the unificationist goal by stating that he and his colleagues "still believed in the desirability of the ultimate unification of the two Cameroons, but that the intervening events and circumstances had removed the question of unification from the realm of urgency and priority." [10]

In contrast with the vacillations in objectives and leadership which plagued the KNC and the KPP, the KNDP, from its inception, displayed little outward change in its goals and grew both in strength and popular appeal. In January, 1959, it assumed power after a general election to the Southern Cameroons House of Assembly had returned fourteen KNDP members and only twelve KNC-KPP coalition members. Foncha was named premier and immediately launched discussions within the Southern Cameroons and at the United Nations headquarters in New York which led to the decision to hold a UN plebiscite in February, 1961, and to agreement on the questions to be submitted to the voters. During 1959 and 1960, as the plebiscite drew closer, Foncha's enthusiasm for reunification seemed to wane. Although he ultimately adhered to his declared

---

[10] "Report on the Trust Territory of the Cameroons under British Administration," United Nations Visiting Mission to Trust Territories in West Africa, UN Doc. T/1426 (mimeographed; New York, 1959), p. 43.

preference for the Cameroun Republic over association with Nigeria, he repeatedly demanded that the United Nations extend the trusteeship until a clearer perspective of political developments within the two neighboring states could be gained.[11]

Of the several minor Southern Cameroonian parties formed after 1950, only the One Kamerun assumed any importance; the others have been relatively short-lived, functioning as organizational handmaidens to various politicians and collapsing shortly after the elections for which they were created. The One Kamerun, headed by Ndeh Ntumazah, was formed in 1957 as the Southern Cameroons rump of the UPC after the latter party had been declared illegal and its leaders had been deported. It was unable to gain a seat in the Southern Cameroons legislature until January, 1962, when the House became the West Cameroun Assembly, and its limited appeal has largely dissipated in the wake of unification. Among the more ephemeral parties were the Kamerun United Commoners' Party, the Cameroons Muslim Congress, the Cameroons Commoners' Congress, the Cameroons Indigenes' Party, and the Kamerun United Party. The Kamerun United Party is of interest because it was created in 1960 by Peter M. Kale, one of the founders of the KNC and former president of the KPP, to agitate for separate independence for the Southern Cameroons. Kale dissolved his party after the UN plebiscite, joined the KNDP, and was named speaker of the West Cameroun Assembly in January, 1962.

PARTY LEADERS, MEMBERS, AND SUPPORTERS

Of the various political parties and groups in the two Camerouns, only the few noted in the introduction have had sufficient cohesion to affect elections or public policy making. The many local organizations, associations, clubs, and unions with political aims are mainly tributaries to the important parties, serving to arouse interest and exert pressure. Interesting as they may be, their influence is usually local, and they rarely appeal to larger audiences. Their limited goals, restricted membership, and parochial outlook prevent them from playing more significant roles.

It must, however, be noted that the larger parties have not yet lost their provincial air; their leadership, organization, and goals too often betray their local origins. It is in this halfway house between parochialism and national stature that most of the Cameroun's parties find themselves,

[11] For a fuller discussion of the Southern Cameroons' unsteady progress to unification, see Reuben Frodin, "Flies in the Trusteeship Ointment," *American Universities Field Staff Reports,* West Africa Series, Vol. IV, no. 1 (Feb., 1961). See also Edwin Ardener, "The Kamerun Idea," *West Africa,* June 7, 24, 1958; Victor T. Le Vine, "Unifying the Cameroons," *ibid.,* July 15, 1961, and "The Other Cameroons," *Africa Report,* VI (Feb., 1961), 5–6, 12. See also David Gardinier, *Cameroon: United Nations Challenge to French Policy* (London: Oxford University Press, 1963), pp. 103–136 *passim.*

and their singular, and often uncomfortable, plight is nowhere better seen than in the composition of leadership and membership, and in the character of party supporters.

The East Cameroun

None of the East Cameroun's parties are mass parties in the Western sense. Even though substantial numbers of voters may cast their ballots for one party rather than another, the choice is usually for an individual rather than for a party. The measure of electoral success in most instances is not party identification or even the program of the candidate, but the degree to which the candidate is known in the constituency and, very often, the extent to which he enjoys the support of traditional authorities. This generalization helps to explain, for example, the spectacular successes of the Parti d'Union Camerounaise in the northern part of the East Cameroun.

Parti d'Union Camerounaise.—In the elections to the first National Assembly of the Republic in April, 1960, the UC was unopposed in all seven of the northern departments (Adamawa, Benoué, Margui-Wandala, Diamaré, Mayo-Danai, Logone et Chari, and Bamoun). Originally formed from a number of local political groups in urban centers, the UC has since enjoyed a monopoly in the north for the simple reason that it has the full support of virtually all the northern traditional leaders. Because of the comparatively low level of education and the slow rate of social change, these leaders are in many instances still able to command the election of a deputy whom they favor.

As early as 1955 the northern *lamido*'s and sultans (traditional titles of rulers dating back to the beginning of the nineteenth century) realized that the modern political groups being formed in such northern towns as Garoua and N'Gaoundéré offered the best chance of ensuring their own political and social future. Recognizing that their traditional prerogatives and powers would eventually disappear with increasing modernization, the chiefs believed that the transition would be most gradual and painless if they backed the party that Ahmadou Ahidjo and Arouna Njoya created in 1958. In this belief they have not been disappointed. The party has given them a political voice as well as a share in controlling the rate of social change in the north. This is not to say, of course, that theirs is the decisive voice; the position of Ahidjo and his secular colleagues has become strong enough for him to depose one northern chief, and to administer occasional blunt warnings to the others to adapt to changing conditions or be swept aside.[12]

---

[12] "It is no secret to anyone that certain chiefs consider it almost profane, a violation of a forbidden reserve, that others than themselves organize and lead inhabitants in their chiefdoms. I solemnly call upon these chiefs to surpass themselves,

In short, then, the electoral base of the UC has been and continues to be the Cameroun north, whose seven departments contain slightly less than half the East Cameroun's population. Thus far the only voters who have managed to exercise their franchise have been the dominant Muslim Fulani peoples in and around the principal urban centers of Garoua, N'Gaoundéré, Maroua, and Yagoua, and their votes have been largely commandeered by the traditional authorities.[13] Under such circumstances, of course, opposition parties have found it almost impossible to operate in the north; a number of UPC organizers, for example, have found their stay in the north cut short by unceremonious deportations or imprisonments, or by physical hostility.

Like its electoral base, most of the UC's leaders are northern Muslims. The top echelon, headed by President Ahmadou Ahidjo (also president-general of the party), Minister of State Arouna Njoya (nephew of the powerful Sultan of Bamoun), and Moussa Yaya (first vice-president of the East Cameroun Assembly), includes at least ten lamidos, five sultans, and several dozen local chiefs. The decisive element within this stratum, however, includes men whose ties to the chiefs are only nominal, and who show little hesitation in taking effective leadership in national and party affairs.

Since 1958 the UC has been gathering support in the southern departments. At first the pace was slow. By 1960 only a handful of influential southern politicians had joined the party's ranks. After 1960, under the impetus of the circumstances noted above, increasing numbers of southern politicians joined the party, and by 1961 it could boast of strong local organizations in all southern departments. There is every indication that the extension of the UC into the southern and eastern departments has had a salutary effect on the party. Its northern-oriented outlook has been modified by the necessity of seeking support in non-Muslim, non-

---

to transcend themselves . . . so that they may fall in step with our imperatives, with our necessities. . . . If they will accept the necessary efforts, if they will consent, in a spirit of fair play, to certain sacrifices, they will avoid an evil whose symptoms are already becoming apparent. If they wait, if they resist certain measures, certain evolutionary measures, this evil, once unleashed, will be fatal to them" (Ahmadou Ahidjo to the Third Party Congress of the UC, Sept. 22, 1960, "Rapport du Politique générale" [mimeographed]). The Lamido of Maroua, one of the more powerful of the northern traditional chiefs, was the one who was deposed. He was removed (rumor has it by assassination) after a trial of strength with Ahidjo in September, 1959.

[13] This fact is disquieting. Of the approximately 1,500,000 inhabitants of the northern departments of the East Cameroun, only about 515,000 are Muslims. The rest are animist peoples (called *Kirdi,* or "pagan," by the Fulani), many of whom bear strong traditional animosities to the dominant Muslims. For the most part, this huge group of Kirdi is extremely backward and has had little or no political experience. What will happen when the Kirdi begin coming to the polls has given many a UC leader uncomfortable second thoughts. The extension of the party's activities to the south may well have been spurred by this potential threat.

northern areas, and its leadership has been enriched by the presence of personalities with different sets of values and experiences.

Contrasted with the other Camerounian parties, the UC has a relatively large membership; according to figures cited at the Fourth Party Congress, it was about 300,000. In the larger northern departments, party membership comprises a substantial percentage of the voting public. The department of Diamaré, for example, has a population of about 275,000 and a registered electorate of 174,004; in 1960 the UC had 25,015 members, all of them presumably carrying membership cards and paying dues. In the same year, in the department of Adamawa, also with about 275,000 inhabitants, 107,437 of whom are inscribed on the electoral rolls, the party claimed 20,242 members. Thus, about 14 per cent of Diamaré's and about 18 per cent of Adamawa's registered voters are party members.[14] Although these figures might suggest that the UC is in fact a true mass party, it must be remembered that in the northern departments the UC is not only the sole party, but often represents the only available channel to jobs, status, and even educational opportunities above the primary level. Thus, in the north, the UC's political monopoly allows it to recruit the area's most promising elements, to inculcate them with party values, and to train them according to the party's estimates of what it and the nation will need in the future. It can readily be seen that this one-track recruitment has inestimable benefits for the party, and certainly helps to explain its continuing domination in the north.

Parti des Démocrates Camerounais.—When the present Parti des Démocrates was first formed in 1958, suggestions were made to name it the Parti des Démocrates Chrétiens. Pressure on the party's leaders forced them to drop the religious link, but the suggested title went far to describe both the party's general orientation and its adherents. The base of the PDC, as noted previously, is the populous department of Nyong et Sanaga, of whose 460,000 inhabitants some 317,000 are members of the Archdiocese of Yaoundé, one of the largest Catholic aggregates in West Africa.[15] Most of the population belongs to the Ewondo, Bulu, and Eton ethnic groups, who are among the most vigorous of the southern ethnic stocks. Drawing upon this combined ethnic-sectarian base, the Démocrates regularly captured all or almost all the department's complement of deputies to the Cameroun legislature.

The party's electoral strength, even in a period of relative decline, may be seen in the results of the April 10, 1960, legislative elections in the Nyong et Sanaga. The department's twelve seats were contested by

---

[14] Electoral statistics were provided by M. Rambeau, Agence France-Presse, Yaoundé office. Party figures were taken from the departmental reports presented at the Third Party Congress.

[15] P. Mviena and J. Criaud, *Géographie du Cameroun* (Yaoundé: Imprimerie St. Paul, 1960), p. 100.

no less than 134 candidates running individually or on seventeen different lists. Of the 221,587 counted votes, the PDC's candidates received 139,780, or 63 per cent, and captured eleven of the twelve seats. This vote is all the more remarkable because, at the time of the elections, the party had not fully recovered from its defeats in the Assembly in 1958 and 1959; moreover, Mbida did not return from his self-imposed exile in Conakry until shortly before the election, and had had little time to regroup his forces. The Nyong et Sanaga is the only department where the PDC has commanded large-scale support.

Several factors help to explain the PDC's strength in the Nyong et Sanaga, and especially in the Yaoundé area. First, as early as 1951 the Catholic militants of the area had been politically mobilized by Louis Aujoulat's secular organization, Ad Lucem, and its political successor, the Mouvement Démocratique Camerounais (MDC). Even though Mbida broke with Aujoulat in 1953 to join forces with Soppo-Priso, he was able to build upon the support previously given Aujoulat by appealing to the same religious and ethnic sources that had given the MDC its strength. Second, Mbida also received support from traditional leaders in the area. Superior Chief Atangana and André Fouda, mayor of Yaoundé, were among his strongest supporters. Third, the PDC has maintained an excellent network of local structures, many of them at the village level, and several of these appeared from time to time as supporting political parties.

The direction of the PDC has been determined by Mbida himself; his single-mindedness and personal dynamism have thus far eclipsed his closest rivals for the PDC's leadership. A measure of his power in the party, and of the extent to which its vitality derives from him, was that the party remained moribund during his absence in Conakry, despite the efforts of Fouda and others to revive it. It is still impossible to predict how the reduction of the PDC's parliamentary forces and Mbida's recent trial and imprisonment will affect the party's electoral support. The by-elections in Djongolo-Yaoundé on December 24, 1961, are the only index of any change thus far, but they are of questionable value as a criterion. The UC candidate was declared the winner with 13,254 votes; the other two candidates, one running as PDC, the other (the Mayor of Yaoundé) closely associated with the PDC, together polled 14,061 votes. Some allegations have been made that the count was deliberately falsified, and that the PDC candidate had in fact won. True or not, it seems clear that the PDC has already lost much standing and will probably lose many votes in the future. One other circumstance reinforcing this impression is that Mbida supporters in the church hierarchy in the Yaoundé area have been removed or neutralized by Monseigneur Jean Zoa since his accession as archbishop of the Archdiocese of Yaoundé in December, 1961.

Union des Populations du Cameroun.—Beyond the fact that the

UPC's electoral support is concentrated in the heavily populated departments of the Cameroun southwest, it is not a party with a well-defined geographical referent, as are the UC and the PDC. Nor is its over-all strength based on any one population group, as it draws members and supporters from a wide variety of ethnic groups, social strata, and educational levels.

In the elections of April, 1960, the UPC polled approximately 91,000 votes in the eleven departments where it ran candidates, a figure representing about 6.7 per cent of the total votes cast throughout the country. In three departments its candidates obtained more than 60 per cent of the votes cast (Dja et Lobo, 60 per cent; Nyong et Kelle, 73 per cent; Sanaga-Maritime, 80 per cent), and in Kribi its candidate for the one seat won by a narrow margin. The party also obtained large blocs of votes in the Bamileké, Mungo, Wouri, and Nyong et Sanaga departments. As this was the second general election in which the UPC presented candidates under its own banner, and as the party was outlawed between July, 1955, and March, 1960, these results are particularly impressive. An unofficial estimate made in December, 1960, gave the UPC between 30,000 and 35,000 members.[16] It becomes crucial, therefore, to inquire into the basis of the party's remarkable staying power during a period when it was unable to organize or propagandize openly within the country. Four main focuses of influence may be distinguished with some clarity: the left-wing labor unions; the Bassa ethnic group, mostly in the Sanaga-Maritime; the Bamileké populations; and the so-called urban "strangers."

Initially, it will be recalled, the UPC established itself with the aid of several left-wing labor unions formed in Douala after the war. The union leaders and most of the union members remained loyal to the UPC during its proscription, and, in fact, constituted one of the UPC's main propaganda and agitational outlets. The most prominent of these unions is the Union des Syndicats Confédérés du Cameroun, led by Jacques N'Gom.

Once the party had gained a foothold, it directed its most intensive organizational efforts toward the Bassa peoples of the Sanaga-Maritime. Um Nyobé, himself a Bassa, was able to exploit both the Bassa's highly developed kinship feelings and their general discontent at their "poor-relative" position vis-à-vis the coastal Doualas, and thus to build up an effective party organization. After the party was banned in 1955 and the UPC directorate split, Um Nyobé took to the maquis among his Bassa brethren, and kept the region in open rebellion until his death in 1958.

---

[16] No reliable figures are available on the membership of the UPC; official party figures tend to exaggerate the number and to blur the distinction between *adhérent* (dues-paying member) and *sympathisant* (sympathizer), and are often deliberately falsified to prevent government interference.

It is hardly surprising, then, that one of his former lieutenants, Mayi Matip, at the head of the UPC ticket, managed to sweep a by-election in 1959 and the general elections in 1960. The key to Mayi's campaign was an effective dual appeal to Um's memory and Bassa pride.

Mayi, who acceded to the titular leadership of the party left vacant by Moumié's death, is paradoxically not a Bassa, but a Bamileké. Mayi's position becomes clear when one recognizes the preponderance of the Bamileké peoples in the southwestern and western Cameroun. From their traditional homes in the Bamileké region, the Bamileké, one of the most industrious and prolific of African ethnic groups, have been moving into adjoining areas in ever-larger numbers since the end of the 1920's. They have all but overwhelmed the populations in neighboring Mungo, and they now form the largest ethnic group in the city of Douala itself. The social and economic reasons that caused them to overflow their traditional boundaries made them ideal targets for the supercharged propaganda of the UPC, which promised radical changes and provided the Bamileké with a demonology to suit their discontent. The story of the UPC penetration into the Bamileké geographical and population sectors is extremely complex;[17] here it is sufficient to point out that after the UPC rebellion in the Sanaga-Maritime abated with Um's death, the party shifted its operations to the Bamileké region. Since then the Bamileké areas have been afflicted with almost continual terrorist activity, though it diminished somewhat in the latter part of 1960 and throughout 1961, and still more in 1962. Despite the vigorous and successful anti-UPC activities of a number of Bamileké leaders, the UPC was still able to attract widespread popular support among large segments of the Bamileké population.

The fourth important source of UPC influence has been the exogenous populations of the major urban centers in the Cameroun south. Mention has already been made of the large numbers of Bamileké in Douala; similar problems have been created in Yaoundé, N'Kongsamba, Ebolowa, and M'Balmayo, not only by the Bamileké, but also by immigrants of other ethnic stocks who come to the cities to find work. According to unofficial estimates, there are about 30,000 unemployed in Douala, or about one-fifth of the city's population. In other towns the percentage of unemployed is almost as high. Again, as in the Bamileké areas, the apocalyptic nature of UPC propaganda attracted many followers, large numbers of whom found release in the violence for which the UPC was responsible in 1955. Although the UPC's influence seems to be waning among the town "strangers," the party is still strong enough to command sizable

---

[17] Aside from official reports, most of which are confidential, collateral discussion of the Bamileké problem, from the viewpoint of a sociologist, is the perceptive book by Claude Tardits, *Les Bamileké de l'ouest Cameroun* (Paris: Editions Berger-Levrault, 1960).

electoral support. The election of Marcel Beybey-Eyidi, long associated with the UPC, represents the mobilization of just such a vote.

Currently the UPC leadership is divided among the so-called "external" UPC, which followed Moumié into exile, and two rallié UPC factions. Of the former group Abel Kingué and Ernest Ouandié are best known; they represent the vestiges of the old Comité Directeur of which Moumié was president. The rallié UPC are divided between the UPC deputies, headed by Mayi Matip, and a group of younger UPC leaders of whom Jean-Paul Sendé and Emah Otuh are the most important. The UPC's leadership dilemma, which the January, 1962, congress sought to resolve, may be regarded as a conflict between the old guard, who "fought the battles," and the young hopefuls, who are impatient with their elders. True to the classic pattern, the younger leaders are far more radical and revolutionary than the older ones, many of whom became quite content with the respectability conferred by legal reinstatement and membership in parliament. There are as yet no indications as to whether or not the forcible dissolution of the Yaoundé congress and the subsequent arrest of Mayi have healed these divisions. In any event, through internal splits, the ambiguity of its program, and the reduction of its leadership by arrest and imprisonment, the UPC has lost both its former militancy and considerable popular appeal. Several courses are now open to it: capitulation to the UC, dissolution, a return to underground opposition, or reactivation of terrorist activity. It seems unlikely that a party so long able to operate extralegally will select either or both of the first two choices. The latter two are likely if the UPC should suffer still greater attrition at the hands of the regime.

Other political formations.—The trend toward the one-party state in the East Cameroun has had, predictably, a constrictive effect on the number, the activities, and the impact of all political formations still outside the Union Camerounaise. First to be overwhelmed in the expansion of the dominant party were two parliamentary groupings which represented, for their creators, a flexible political base from which to maneuver vis-à-vis the government as well as future national organizations. Both the Front Populaire pour l'Unité et la Paix and the Groupe des Progressistes du Cameroun were formed after the 1960 general elections. The former represented a new tendency among Bamiléké leaders to depart from the old UPC ties and to attempt to solve their problems without going to extremes. The FPUP, composed, for the most part, of young men in their twenties and early thirties, reflected the gradual loss of UPC prestige among the Bamiléké population. Some of the FPUP members had UPC backgrounds, but except for some agreement on national objectives, most of them had little in common with even the "new" UPC. The group included Pierre Kamdem-Ninyim, Victor Kanga (now federal minister of national economy), Wandji Nkuimy (currently East Cameroun secretary of state for finance), Philippe Achinguy (former minister of national economy for animal husbandry), and Marc-Max Batonga, the group's president. By mid-1961 the FPUP had formally dissolved itself, and most of its members joined the UC.

The Progressistes, a coalition of two older parties (the PSC and the MANC), represented an interesting attempt to provide a nonpartisan environment for such important personalities as Assalé and Okala. Ultimately, the pressures for conformity proved too strong for the group; after unification it was no longer possible to remain outside the UC and still retain some influence within the regime. The Progressiste hopes for the creation of an extraparliamentary organization, shared by the FPUP, died with the dissolution of the group. The disintegration of the Progressistes was foreshadowed by the official capitulation of Prime Minister Assalé, who formally dissolved the MANC in February, 1961.

Many of the fringe political "parties" are little more than *ad hoc* organizational appendages to local political figures. Some of these figures deserve mention, if only because they reappear from time to time on the political stage. One of the most important is Paul Soppo-Priso, onetime president of the Assembly, former head of the MANC, and once considered a likely choice for the prime-ministership. Soppo-Priso, though losing his Douala seat to Prince Douala Manga Bell in April, 1960, retains considerable political influence in the Douala area. He now seems to be waiting in the wings, and may reappear as a national figure within the next year or two. Others include former Vice-Premier Michel Njiné, who has deep political roots among the Bamileké peasants and farmers and who threw his support to the UC in 1960, and André Fouda, a former minister in Ahidjo's cabinet, presently mayor of Yaoundé, and still an important figure in the ranks of the PDC.

The West Cameroun

Although the patterns of political life in the two constituent states of the Cameroun vary considerably one from the other, they are similar in that the principal parties in the West Cameroun have not yet become mass parties, but remain variously rooted in local, personality, and ethnic identifications. As noted elsewhere, "the only public issue to give shape to Southern Cameroons political alignments . . . [was] the grading of the various degrees of differentiation from or opposition to Nigeria." [18] Yet even this issue was eventually resolved, not on the merits of the Nigeria-Cameroun alternatives, but in relation to the more parochial circumstances of ethnic loyalty, local economic interest, and the popularity

[18] Edwin Ardener, "The Political History of Cameroun," *World Today* (Aug., 1962), p. 346.

of political leaders. Superficially, the One Kamerun Party seems not to have followed this pattern, but its failure to receive more than 7 per cent of the votes cast in any election up to and including the December, 1961, general elections tends to support rather than to weaken the generalization.

Kamerun National Democratic Party.—Originally organized in the Bamenda Plateau, the KNDP continues to draw most of its electoral support from the highland divisions of Bamenda, Wum, and Mamfe. The results of the December, 1961, elections were another confirmation of this fact (*vide* the general elections of January, 1959, and the plebiscite of February, 1961), and not even the increase in the number of Bamenda seats from six to thirteen or the surprisingly large OK and independent vote could vitiate its significance. Of the 140,347 votes cast for the KNDP in December, 1961 (of a total state-wide vote of 255,933, representing 80.85 per cent of the registered voters), 84,897 were cast in these three divisions. The figure is even more significant because it does not include KNDP candidates returned unopposed in two Bamenda constituencies which together had 14,069 registered voters. Not unexpectedly, more than half of the KNDP votes in the three divisions were cast in Bamenda (see table 1).

The KNDP's electoral success is attributable to the quality and the skill of its leaders and their ability to transform local ethnic, economic, and social issues into votes. The result of the February, 1961, UN plebiscite in the Southern Cameroons, for example, demonstrated their acumen. Agitating for reunification with the Cameroun Republic, Foncha, Muna, Augustine N. Jua, John H. Nganje, and Simon A. Mofor—all ethnically from the "grassfields"—converted on imperfectly articulated feeling of community with certain Cameroun peoples (Bamileké and Bamoun) into a conviction that "brothers" ought to be reunited. This feat was accomplished despite the opposition of at least two local *fon*'s (traditional rulers in Bamenda). Coupled with an appeal to a strong antipathy toward certain Nigerian peoples (particularly the Ibo), the campaign paid off handsomely in Bamenda and substantially in Mamfe and Wum (see table 2). The fact that about 60 per cent of the registered voters lived in these three divisions undoubtedly spurred the KNDP to concentrate its activities there; again, the decision was amply rewarded, for 60 per cent of the total vote for reunification was amassed in the three divisions. There are also indications that the strong appeal to ethnic loyalty swayed the large numbers of grassfielders residing in Victoria division (once a KNC-KPP stronghold), and that the anti-Ibo exhortations mobilized pro-Cameroun sentiment not only among grassfielders but among local ethnic groups in that division as well. Victoria, which had elected KNC-KPP candidates to three of four seats in 1959, gave the Cameroun alterna-

TABLE 1

RESULTS OF GENERAL ELECTIONS OF JANUARY 24, 1959, IN THE SOUTHERN CAMEROONS, AND OF DECEMBER 30, 1961, IN THE WEST CAMEROUN

Division	KNDP		CPNC		OK		Independents		Others	
	1959	1961	1959a	1961	1959	1961	1959	1961	1959	1961
Victoria	5,625 (1)b	22,776 (3)	9,260 (3)	8,652 (1)	0	5,244	0	0	71c	66
Kumba	11,031 (1)	22,418 (2)	11,471 (3)	28,650 (5)	0	5,266	247	2,850	0	111
Mamfe	14,900 (3)	20,416 (3)	12,716 (1)	8,079 (1)	0	3,370 (1)	2,062	2,248	0	557
Bamenda	30,227 (5)	44,173 (11)	6,504 (1)	3,123	1,940	3,420	7,389	20,867 (2)	0	1,026
Wum	6,771 (3)	20,308 (4)	3,338 (1)	5,924	0	433	736	1,527	0	141
Nkambe	4,780	10,256 (1)	8,665 (4)	14,030 (3)	81	0	0	0	0	0
Total	73,304 (13)	140,347 (24)	51,354 (13)	68,458 (10)	2,025	17,733 (1)	10,434	27,494 (2)	71	1,401
Number of candidates	25	35	27	22	2	16	11	26	1	5

a KNC–KPP coalition.
b Figures in parentheses indicate number of seats won.
c NCNC.

SOURCES: United Nations Visiting Mission to Trust Territories in West Africa, "Report on the Trust Territory of the Cameroons under British Administration," UN Doc. T/1246 (mimeographed; New York, 1959), Addendum 1, Feb. 6, 1959, p. 5; West Cameroun Information Service, Buea, Press Releases 1663 (Jan. 4, 1962) and 1669 (Jan. 10, 1962).

T ABLE 2

R ESULTS OF THE U NITED N ATIONS P LEBISCITE IN THE S OUTHERN C AMEROONS,
F EBRUARY 11, 1961

Division	Integration with Nigeria	Unification with the Cameroun Republic
Victoria	11,916	22,082
Kumba	32,733	27,600
Mamfe	10,050	33,267
Bamenda	12,341	108,485
Wum	8,784	27,115
Nkambe	21,917	15,022
Total	97,741	233,571

S OURCE: Southern Cameroons Information Service, Press Release 1217 (Feb. 17, 1961).

tive 22,082 votes to 11,916 in February, 1961; in December, 1961, it returned three KNDP candidates by a vote of 22,776 to 13,962 for all opposition candidates.

Leadership within the KNDP remains virtually uncontested in the hands of the group that has headed the party since 1957: Foncha, Muna, Jua, Peter M. Kemcha, Johannes M. Bokwe, Willie Effion, and two or three others. Foncha, certainly less articulate than Muna or Jua, is nonetheless the acknowledged leader of the group. His physical slightness and his quietness of manner give little indication of his remarkable ability to remain unruffled under provocation, of his will power, or of his sure grasp of grass-roots politics in the West Cameroun. Should there be any question of succession within the party, Jua or Muna would probably replace Foncha as the KNDP's leader. Both Jua and Muna, like Foncha, are moderate in outlook, and have displayed considerable effectiveness in various legislative and ministerial roles.

Cameroun People's National Convention.—In the December, 1961, elections, the CPNC seems to have retained its electoral support in the divisions of Kumba and Nkambe, where it won five (of seven) and three (of four) seats, respectively. It won only one seat in Victoria, but the constituency in question is that of Emmanuel Endeley, who has usually been able to mobilize his Bakweri followers to ensure his seat. The decline of the CPNC's fortunes in Victoria, interestingly enough, is in the loss of seats rather than of voting support, owing to an increase in the total number of voters caused by the influx of workers from the north. The CPNC's strength in Kumba rests solidly upon a number of forest peoples who recognize little communality with their grassfields neighbors to the north; their tribal ties are mostly with Nigerian ethnic groups. The CPNC's espousal of the Nigerian alternative therefore held strong attraction for many Kumba groups, particularly those in the western part of the division where Namaso N. Mbile, deputy leader of the CPNC, has his electoral fief. It is significant that Mbile, reflecting his constituency's ethnic orientations, agitated before and immediately after the plebiscite for a partition of the Southern Cameroons along ethnic lines, to permit those tribes wishing to join Nigeria to do so. Thus, insofar as the CPNC poses as the champion of the various separatisms of its ethnic constituents, it enjoys their support at the polls. In Nkambe, the CPNC's strength is based on several tribal groups that have long been mobilized electorally for the CPNC by the Reverend Andoh Seh.

Endeley and Mbile are the party's principal leaders. Until his death in the spring of 1962, Peter Motomby-Woleta, publisher of the CPNC's biweekly *Cameroons Champion*, shared in the party's leadership. Motomby, incidentally, suffered a surprising defeat in his Victoria constituency in the December, 1961, elections. Endeley's key role in the political development of the West Cameroun has already been noted; he is articulate and highly intelligent, but, according to some observers, lacks Mbile's grasp of political realities. Mbile himself is an effective campaigner, and has been credited with maintaining the party's electoral strength in the crucial Kumba constituencies.

One Kamerun Party.—Formed in the wake of the UPC's expulsion from the Southern Cameroons in 1957, the OK, by maintaining unwavering support for reunification and by assuming, at least rhetorically, a nationalist stance similar to the UPC's, has been able to capture the support of the disparate elements that make up the West Cameroun radical left. Among them are most university students pursuing their studies abroad (for which the National Union of Kamerun Students purports to speak); a significant number of urban migrants and workers, particularly in the Victoria and Kumba areas; and a scattering of local intellectuals, whose ties are principally with educational groups, labor unions, and coöperatives. In the December, 1961, elections—the first which the OK, with sixteen candidates, contested in strength—the party gained one seat and 17,733 votes, distributed mainly in Victoria, Kumba, Mamfe, and Bamenda divisions. The OK made surprisingly good showings in at least five other constituencies besides the one (Mamfe North) where it won a seat by a narrow margin. Significantly, it captured 10 per cent of the votes in Foncha's own constituency, and 24.6 per cent in another Bamenda constituency which returned an independent by a majority of 1,409 votes over the KNDP candidate.

Ndeh Ntumazah, a native of Mankon in Bamenda, is the OK's leader and principal spokesman. He spent four years (1944–1948) in the French

Cameroun with his brother, and while there became interested both in the prospects for unifying the two Camerouns and in the policies of the UPC. He returned to the British Cameroons in 1948 and at once became involved in politics. He joined the UPC in 1955, and in 1957 formed the One Kamerun Party. Ntumazah appeared frequently before the UN in New York to argue for reunification and for his party's views, developing noteworthy forensic skill, an urbane manner, and a polish that distinguishes him from the bulk of his following. In February, 1961, he claimed approximately 3,000 dues-paying members for the OK in the Southern Cameroons, but the figure may be somewhat inflated.

INTERNAL PARTY ORGANIZATION

Formation and Organization

Even a cursory examination of the development of political parties in the two Camerouns reveals a remarkable variety in scale, structure, and number. Thomas Hodgkin's schema of classification, by which parties are grouped according to scale, structure, and legal status (and combinations thereof) [19] breaks down in the face of a number of peculiarly Camerounian political circumstances. The extraordinary complexity of the ethnic picture (there are nearly 200 separate ethnic groups in the federation), for example, has had profound effects on the whole pattern of party building and party politics. There has been a pronounced tendency toward the creation of many rather short-lived ethnic-based parties, most of which are elite in character. Only those that successfully cross tribal lines in organization, recruitment, and programs manage to survive. Louis Aujoulat's MDC, for example, managed to break out of its primarily Yaoundé-Catholic-Ewondo bounds only when Mbida formed the PDC from it and appealed to northern as well as southern politicians on the basis of a broader, secularized program.

Large-scale, tribally oriented parties have been absent. The largest ethnic groups (such as the Bamileké and the Fulani) have never achieved sufficient cultural cohesiveness and self-consciousness to permit the emergence of leaders who could command broadly based Bamileké and Fulani identifications. In the north of the East Cameroun, the UC is an elite party, with a largely commandeered electorate. Bamileké politicians have preferred to build political groups on modern formations in which the organizational cement is economic interest rather than ethnic solidarity. Further, the fragmented nature of the Bamileké chiefdoms has precluded the rise of an all-Bamileké movement. Only the KNDP in the west has effectively mobilized a large ethnic group, the grass-fielders (ethnically

---

[19] Thomas Hodgkin, *African Political Parties* (Penguin Books, 1961), pp. 63–80 *passim*.

related, interestingly enough, to the Bamileké in the East Cameroun). Successful political parties in the Camerouns, even though, like the KNDP and the UC, they may rely on a single ethnic base for most of their strength, must nonetheless attempt to bridge wide ethnic gaps in their appeals. The dilemma produced by this imperative has meant that the party leadership tends to speak with one voice at home, and with another among other ethnic groups or in national contexts.

The organizational tasks of parties aspiring to mass status have been extremely difficult. The organizational development of the UC in the east, for example, owes as much to the band-wagon effect of being the party in power (bringing into the party numbers of influential southern politicians) as to any other single factor. The UPC, the only other eastern mass party, successfully crossed many ethnic boundaries, at least in the south, by actively recruiting and using cadres from a wide variety of ethnic groups. A conspicuous UPC failure, illustrating these difficulties, was Félix Moumié's almost total inability to mobilize his own group, the Bamoun.

Two other circumstances, uniquely Camerounian, have tended further to complicate the political picture. One has been the trusteeship status of the two territories. This status stimulated, particularly in the East Cameroun, the emergence of an unusually diverse array of fringe parties, groups, associations, clubs, leagues, movements, and the like. By 1962 most of these formations had disappeared in fact, but many remain on the registry books and occasionally reappear in new guises. The other circumstance has been the influence of the UPC, reflected not only in the programs, but also in the structure and the organization, of many of its competitors.

As a consequence of these factors, most Camerounian parties have experienced frequent internal reorganization, many of them have inaugurated subsidiary and affiliate organizations designed to reach sectors of the electorate with special needs or identifications, and almost all of them have engaged in virtually continual mutual absorption and incorporation. A few illustrations suffice to make these points. All the more important Cameroun parties have women's auxiliary organizations. Similarly, the parties have created youth organizations (e.g., the Jeunesse de l'Union Camerounaise is auxiliary to the UC; the Jeunesse Démocratique Camerounaise is allied with the UPC) which occasionally develop semiautonomous electoral support. Mention has already been made of the so-called "traditional organizations," such as the Anagsama Essomolo, the Union Bamoun, the Kumsze, the Ngondo, the Efoula-Meyong, and the like, whose principal function is to provide political parties with the legitimacy of an ethnic referent. Finally, the demise of such groups as the Paysans Indépendants, the Union Bamileké, the MANC, the FPUP, the GPC, and the Kamerun United Party points to the recurrent incorporation of one party by another.

Formal Structure

The broad reach of the Union Camerounaise enabled it to take advantage of existing administrative divisions in the Cameroun. It originally set itself up in 1958 on the basis of regions, within which were grouped *sous-sections* which corresponded in turn to the older officially defined *lamidat's*, cantons, and *groupements*. All the sous-sections in a region made up a *section*. After the administrative reorganization of the country in 1959, the party redesignated its organs to correspond to the new divisions. At present its organization follows a strictly hierarchical plan; the base is a large number of *cellules* grouped into *comités de base* and operating at the village or *quartier* level, and the apex is the annual party congress. The congress elects the Comité Directeur (Executive Committee), which is responsible for the execution of its proposals and resolutions. The sous-sections, next above the comités de base, are organized on the district or *arrondissement* level. All sous-sections in a *département* (the basic large administrative division in the Cameroun) make up a section. Once a year, all the sections send delegates to the party congress. As of 1962 the UC had sections in all the East Cameroun's twenty-five departments. In July, 1962, it claimed 300,000 dues-paying card-carrying members.

Also using existing administrative divisions, the MANC and the PSC created structures resembling that of the UC. Comités de base, functioning at the local level, unite into department-level *fédérations*, all of which send representatives to the annual congress or *conseil national*. The national congress in turn elects its Comité Directeur, which functions, as it does in the UC (and in almost all the other parties) as the executive and continuing organ of the party. Both the PSC and the MANC have used simpler organizational structures than the UC because of their smaller support and because of their need to subordinate organization to their leaders' personalities.

The structure of the UPC, in accordance with the party's special patterns of support, is not based on existing administrative divisions. In 1948 the party was organized along the recognized pattern of the Rassemblement Démocratique Africain (RDA), based on *comités de quartier* in the towns. In 1949 it was reorganized into a tightly knit, hierarchical party, along lines still followed today.[20] At the base of the pyramid are the comités de base with at least ten members each, located in the various quartiers of the urban centers and in some bush villages. Initially, almost half of the comités de base were in the Sanaga-Maritime region; next in

---

[20] *Statuts de l'UPC*, reprinted in *La Voix du Peuple*, June 16, 1960, pp. 2–3.

strength were the local organizations in and around the urban centers where trade-union activity flourished among laborers and plantation workers. At the second level are the *comités centraux* (each including at least five comités de base) whose essential function is to transmit orders from the higher echelons to the comités de base. The comités centraux are set up according to the number of UPC members in a given area, usually one to at least 600 members, and do not follow official administrative lines. Third are the sections or *secteurs*, designed to coördinate the activities of several central committees with the total membership (at least 3,500) in a section. Finally, according to the party constitution, at the top of the pyramid is the Comité Directeur, elected by the annual party congress and comprising a political bureau, a secretariat, and a treasury.

The problems posed for the UPC by the absence from the country of its president (Moumié), its two vice-presidents (Ouandié and Kingué), and a large part of the Comité Directeur were never satisfactorily resolved. At the beginning of December, 1960, three separate factions claimed to represent the sole directive apparatus for the party: one was the old Comité Directeur (minus Moumié) which on November 7, 1960, announced from Geneva that it would "continue the revolutionary struggle"; the second was the so-called Directoire Nationale Intersections (DNI), created on October 9, 1960, from a temporary secretariat (the Secrétariat Provisoire) which had been set up in February, 1960, after the party was relegalized; and the third was the rump Comité Directeur in the Cameroun, including by implication the bulk of the UPC deputies. On December 23, 1960, the DNI and the Cameroun-based Comité Directeur temporarily submerged their differences by forming the Bureau National Provisoire of twelve members, which sat until the party congress met early in 1962. The party congress held in Yaoundé in January, 1962, was forcibly dissolved by the government before it could decide on any new organizational reforms. Even though a number of its leaders have been jailed (Mayi Matip, "Prince" Dika Akwa, Owono Mimbo Simon), others have joined the UC (Pierre Kamdem-Ninyim), and the external UPC (Ouandié, Kingué, and others) has largely lost its influence, the party has not been dissolved; but continues to exist under increasingly uncomfortable circumstances. Its organizational inventiveness does not, however, seem to have faded. In January, 1961, it launched a journalists' association (Union Nationale des Journalistes), and undoubtedly contributed to the formation of Beybey-Eyidi's Parti Travailliste du Cameroun in April, 1962.

In the West Cameroun, both the KNDP and the KNC employ essentially similar organizational structures. Each party has created local branches at the village and town level, under the direction of a local secretary. The local secretary enjoys considerable latitude in organizing his branch and in recruiting party cadres. In some of the larger towns the parties have established more than one branch, usually corresponding to the distribution of various quarters or towns as defined on an ethnic basis. The local branches of both parties send representatives to the party national conventions, which usually meet once a year. The national conventions select the national executive, which consists of the president, the secretary-general, a number of functional secretaries, and, ex officio, all parliamentary members of the party. The continuing business of the party is handled by the national executive, whose decisions are, at least in theory, subject to review by the national convention. The OK follows the organizational pattern of the UPC, except that its Executive Committee is neither split nor temporary.

Power Distribution

Within the UC, the old hands are still at the helm; the generational difficulties that plague the UPC (now fifteen years old) have not yet come to disturb the UC (four years old). Yet even within the UC there are signs that the hegemony of the Ahidjo-Njoya-Yaya circle is not completely unchallenged. Some of the younger UC members, lately recruited to the party from the ranks of government administrators, have let it be known that they consider their metropolis-acquired *expertise* undervalued and underutilized in the making of party decisions. Whether or not their position will be reinforced remains in doubt; in any event, the party leadership, concentrated in the hands of President Ahidjo and his closest colleagues, brooks little diffusion or decentralization of power. A possible recognition by the UC of this potential threat is the presence in the Ahidjo government of Ministers Charles Onana Awana and Victor Kanga, two relatively young (in their thirties) technicians with limited political experience.

In the MANC, the PSC, and the PDC power has been concentrated simply and unequivocally in the hands of a dominant personality. It is difficult to envisage a PDC without Mbida, or a PSC without Okala; and the MANC disappeared when Soppo-Priso and Assalé left for other political pastures.

Because of its factional divisions, the patterns of power and influence within the UPC are rather more complex. Irrespective of the various groups competing for power, however, the UPC owes its continued existence in the Cameroun to the personal talents of Mayi Matip. Both competing directorates in the Cameroun claim his support obliquely or appeal to him for legitimacy. It was his unique position as Um Nyobé's lieutenant in the maquis which makes it necessary for the other UPC power aspirants to turn to him, however much they may dislike him. In the final analysis, it is probable that whatever organism he favors will assume the UPC reins; the fact is unassailable that he carries with him not only the other UPC deputies, but the support of a wide cross section of UPC members and electors. One other factor explains Matip's continued prestige: his popularity among the Bassa and his widespread support among the Bamileké. Other UPC leaders may disregard that sort of strength only at their peril.

Communication within Parties

Almost invariably the organizational pattern and the power distribution within each of the Cameroun's parties determine the extent to which there is effective communication among all echelons of the party. In the East Cameroun, the UPC, allegedly adhering to the principles of democratic centralism, has always permitted lively and open internal dialogue on important matters. A constant flow of literature ensures that the membership and all those interested are well informed on the party's doctrinal positions. Besides its own publications, which include a long series of pamphlets, the interior Cameroun UPC has its official newspapers (which change their names as they are banned by the government; currently the main organ is the weekly paper, *L'Etoile*), mimeographed "newspapers" issued by affiliated militants,[21] and the "Tribune Libre" section of the Cameroun's only daily paper (the *Presse du Cameroun*) to publicize both official and factional viewpoints.

The UC publishes an official weekly, *L'Unité,* on the government presses, and issues, also via the government presses, reports of its congresses, declarations by its leaders, and policy statements. In addition, a monthly bulletin is circulated within the party. The UC is less prone to air internal dialogues than the UPC; but it does, within the framework of the organization, make it relatively easy for the base comités to publicize their views. The other parties, including the Démocrates, are less able to disseminate printed materials because of their relative penury. They do, however, make use of the *Presse du Cameroun*'s columns, and occasionally issue bulletins and party newssheets. On the whole, however, the minor parties rely mainly on personal contact, and the available information indicates that internal communication is fairly open, both vertically and horizontally.

In the West Cameroun, only the KNDP enjoys the advantage of a printed party newspaper. The *Kamerun Times,* published in Victoria

---

[21]Among the other pro-UPC mimeographed, cyclographed, and roneotyped newspapers that appear are *Abolegé,* noted for the virulence of its attacks on the Catholic clergy and the PDC; *Le Crabe Noir* (the crab is one of the UPC symbols); and *La Nation.* For further details, see George R. Horner and Victor T. Le Vine, "Cameroun Newspapers, before and after Independence," *Africana Newsletter,* I (Spring, 1963), 8–12.

since 1960, is the only newspaper currently available on a regular basis in the western state. The *Times* is overtly KNDP-oriented and uses its columns to attack the opposition and reward political friends of the government. The CPNC operated a biweekly newspaper, the *Cameroons Champion*, from 1960 until the death of its founder, Peter Motomby-Woleta, in April, 1962. The CPNC and the OK publish occasional information sheets and propaganda material, and, like the KNDP, maintain intraparty communication by the use of party newsletters, memoranda, policy statements, and "inspirational" circulars.

Finances

The UC, like the governing party in most new African states, is financially secure. Not only does the party have access to government funds and agencies to disseminate its printed matter, but, possessing the largest membership and the largest number of deputies in the Assembly, it has resources that no other party can match. Like almost all the other eastern parties, the UC has six main sources of funds: (1) the *cotisation*, or assessment, which all parliamentary parties levy on their deputies (about 10 to 15 per cent of the annual salary) and on the sections for extraordinary expenses; (2) the normal *droit d'adhesion* or membership dues, which vary from 100 to 250 CFA francs; (3) the *contribution*, which is fixed according to the individual means of the members; (4) the *souscription*, or subscription, which is pledged by individual members; (5) gifts and legacies; and (6) the sale of party materials. The UPC realizes more through the last category than through all the others combined, but, according to one of its leaders, the receipts from such sales normally are only barely sufficient to cover the costs of printing and distribution. A seventh method of raising funds, though officially banned by all eastern parties, is the *prestation*, or forced contribution, which the parties at times accuse one another of levying. Unconfirmed reports indicate that during its period of proscription the UPC occasionally resorted to prestation in areas of heavy maquis activity.

PARTY RELATIONSHIPS

Other Parties

An examination of the relationships among the several major parties in the two Camerouns underscores the difficulties of analyzing African political phenomena. The Cameroun's political system is almost constantly in flux, as parties, associations, and groups continually form, re-form, and disintegrate. Understandably, then, the relationships of the main parties to the associational infrastructure, to the institutions of government, and to the society are likely at best to be unstable and transitory. The most that can be hazarded under these circumstances is to indicate the most stable of these relationships and to describe their essential lines. Such an analysis was undertaken in earlier sections for the main parties. Table 3 summarizes the most important of these relationships on the associational level in the East Cameroun. The West Cameroun's parties and their somewhat simpler associational relationships were examined earlier.

Three other relationship patterns not previously discussed remain to be briefly explored: relationships of parties to formal governmental institutions, to extra-Camerounian parties and groups, and to the special but significant categories of intellectuals and students. As before, the caveat must be made that the relationships noted are either the most conspicuous or the longest lasting, and that no conclusions as to their durability are to be drawn.

Governmental Institutions

The UC, as the government party in the East Cameroun, enjoys certain undoubted communication and financial advantages. The proprieties of a situation in which the government party uses civil servants to prepare its propaganda and the government presses to print it might be questioned in other contexts. Yet there has been no private or public criticism of the use of governmental institutions for party purposes; such practices are considered the normal procedure by most politicians. To some extent the parties that were members of the governmental coalition (FPUP, MANC, PSC) before 1961 enjoyed these same advantages, and, like the UC, saw little or no reason for drawing fine distinctions between governmental and political party activity.

The lack of such a distinction does, however, have marked disadvantages for opposition parties. In 1961 leaders of both the UPC and the PDC charged that the government, by imposing strict controls over public meetings, by banning publications that were too critical, and by limiting the opportunity to reply and to debate in the National Assembly, did not in fact permit the opposition to be constructive. Whether or not these charges were correct in substance, both parties felt, in view of the political events of 1960 and 1961, that they were constantly on the defensive, a posture that certainly increased their frustration and made recourse to desperate action more likely. It is somewhat ironic to recall the personal vendetta between Mayi Matip and Okala, who in 1960 and 1961 seized every opportunity to belabor the UPC, as an example of the dangers inherent in failing to exercise restraint in the use of the official rostrum for political purposes.[22]

---

[22] See *Journal Officiel des débats de l'Assemblée Nationale du Cameroun* (Première Législature, Année Législative 1960–1961, Première Session ordinaire), 14° Séance (Dec. 9, 1960), and 16° Séance (Dec. 16, 1960), *passim*.

Table 3

Representative Organizational and Associational Relationships of East Cameroun Parties

Party and branches	Other parties	Other modern formations	
		Economic and social interest groups (ga)[1]	Labor unions[2]
Union Camerounaise Jeunesse de l'UC	Union Bamoun (dc) MANC (pc until 1961) PSC (pc until 1961) FPUP (pc until 1961)[3] GPC (pc until 1961)[3] KNDP (ga, pc in Federal Assembly)	Action Paysanne Paysans Camerounais Association Amicale de la Benoué Ligue des Intérêts Economiques (Northern Cameroons) Association pour Progrès, etc. (PRONORD)	CASL-FO (n) USAC (ga) UCTC (n)
UPC JDC Union Démocratique des Femmes Camerounaises	Comité pour Regroupement des Forces Nationalistes (pa) One Kamerun[4] Mouvement Camerounais pour Défense de la Paix (ea) Parti Travailliste (la)	Association pour Défense des Chômeurs Bureau National Kamerunais de Conférences des Peuples Africains Union des Etudiants Kamerunais National Union of Kamerun Students Union Nationale des Journalistes	UGTK (ga) USCC (ga)
PDC	Rassemblement du Peuple Camerounais (ec) Comité du Coordination Camerounais (la) Forces Vifs d'Opposition (la) Mouvement Populaire Démocratique (la)		
MANC (dissolved Feb. 2, 1961, and merged into the UC)	UC (pc) PSC (ps) Cococam (la) Parti de la Jeunesse Nationale (la)		
PSC	MANC (pc until 1961) UC (pc until 1961) MSA (interterritorial)		

[1] Abbreviations: dc = departmental coalition; ea = electoral alliance; ec = electoral coalition; ga = general alliance; la = local alliance; n = nominal support; pa = parliamentary alliance; pc = parliamentary coalition.

[2] Labor-union abbreviations: CASL-FO = Confédération Africaine des Syndicats Libres–Force Ouvrière; USAC = Union des Syndicats Autonomes du Cameroun; UCTC = Union Camerounaise des Travailleurs Croyants; UGTK = Union Générale des Travailleurs Kamerunais; USCC = Union des Syndicats Confédérés du Cameroun (also known as CGKT = Confédération Générale Kamerunaise du Travail).

[3] Parliamentary grouping; not a true party.

[4] West Cameroun affiliation.

T A B L E 3 — *Continued*

	Traditional and semitraditional formations	
Other functional groups	*Tribal associations*	*Pseudo-traditional and semi-traditional associations*
Evolution des Femmes Camerounaises (ga) Conseil National des Femmes Camerounaises (ga) Businessmen's organizations in Douala and Yaoundé	Association Musulmane du Bamoun Assemblée Traditionelle du Peuple Bamoun After Feb., 1961, the tribal organizations affiliated with MANC (below)	Kumsze Mouvement du Salut Kribien
	Kolo-Beti	Union Traditionelle Boulou Union des Associations Traditionelles du Cameroun Association des Notables Bamileké Association Bamileké
	Anagsama-Essomolo Association Eton Manguissa-Batsenga	
	Ngondo Association Traditionelle Bantoue Efoula-Meyong Union Tribale Bantoue	

In the West Cameroun the parliamentary traditions, which allot both opposition and government well-defined areas of political responsibility, seem to have averted the problem the East Cameroun faces in trying to maintain the governmental-political dichotomy. In only a few instances does the dichotomy seem to have been blurred by the main parties.

Extra-Camerounian Parties

Among the West Cameroun's main parties, only the One Kamerun Party has maintained an outside liaison, and that was with the external Moumié faction of the UPC. Whether or not the OK has as close ties with the rallié UPC is not as yet clear. Nor is it clear whether or not the rallié UPC in the East Cameroun maintains or intends to maintain the wide range of outside liaisons which the former external UPC established before and during the period of its proscription, including ties with the Parti Communiste Français through the UPC's French-based representatives, with the CGT and the World Federation of Trade Unions through the Confédération Générale Kamerunaise du Travail (CGKT) and the USCC, and with a number of left-wing student organizations (such as the International Students' Union) through the Union Nationale des Etudiants Kamerunais (UNEK). These and other relationships with organizations and groups in the Communist world enabled UPC leaders like Moumié, Ouandié, Kingué, and Mayoa Beck to attend peace congresses, youth festivals, trade-union congresses, and other meetings in Moscow, Peking, Budapest, Prague, Warsaw, East Berlin, Vienna, and elsewhere.[23] Although the party invariably denied that it was a Communist party as such, or that its ties with Communist organizations represented anything more than a common front in pursuit of anticolonial and anti-imperialist aims, the French administration and later the Cameroun government remained largely unconvinced.

The only other party in the Cameroun with external contacts is the UC. The presence of "delegates" and "observers" from the Northern (British) Cameroons, Chad, and the Central African Republic at the Third Party Congress in 1960 indicates that the UC endeavored to extend its influence across its northern frontiers in both easterly and westerly directions. There is, for example, a sizable pro-UC Cameroun community in Bangui, Central African Republic. Moreover, since unification on October 1, 1961, the KNDP and the UC have been in increasingly close collaboration. The two parties are the only ones represented in the Federal Assembly, where they have formed a single parliamentary group. In August, 1962, the KNDP suggested to the CPNC that both parties be

---

[23] See "Moskau's Taktik im Schwarzen Erdteil," *Ost Probleme*, 12th year, no. 4 (Feb., 1960), 112–115; Zbigniew Brzezinski, ed., *Africa and the Communist World* (Stanford: Stanford University Press, 1963).

dissolved and subsequently merge with the east's UC. Although the CPNC rejected the proposal, there are indications that Foncha is still interested in some kind of formal alliance with the UC on the national level.

Students and Intellectuals

Some of the most vociferous antigovernment, pro-UPC propaganda to appear before 1960 was issued by the Union Nationale des Etudiants Kamerunais, which organized the more than 1,000 Cameroun students in French universities and technical colleges. The UNEK, in conjunction with the Cercle Culturel Camerounais, operated from a government-subsidized Foyer des Etudiants Camerounais and published the *Revue Camerounaise*, a monthly journal often sharply critical of the government. In April, 1960, the government closed the Foyer, withdrew financial support from a number of the more militant UNEK members, and insisted on dissolution of the organization.

Some of the UPC's strongest supporters are Cameroun students in France, most of whom are under government scholarships. The nationalist fervor of most French-speaking Africans in France was easily exploited by the UPC for its own ends, and the party's anticolonial, pro-independence, Pan-Africanist formulas found a ready echo in the students' impatience and latent discontent. The result was an extremely effective UPC-student alliance which permitted the party to bring into the Cameroun numbers of dedicated party militants. As elsewhere, however, most of these students were quickly absorbed into the civil service upon their return, and, in most instances, lost much of their radicalism when confronted with official responsibilities. Yet the fact remains that one of the reasons for the high degree of political awareness among civil servants in the Cameroun (about 60 of the 400 candidates in the April, 1960, elections were young civil servants) is the political initiation they received in France and within pro-UPC student groups.

PARTY GOALS AND PROGRAMS

Party goals, like structural relationships, are unstable and uncertain because of the dynamism of the two growing Camerounian political systems. When political groups appear and disappear with surprising rapidity, when political goals are constantly being reformulated to keep pace with current events, and when programs are created and presented according to heuristic needs, there has seemed to be little reason to formulate ideologies. Political mythmaking is subordinated to the pragmatic needs of the parties, that is, attainment of the positions of influence which, in the final analysis, count most in a changing situation. These generalizations require several reservations. (1) The postindependence period has permitted a more leisurely formulation of political goals and programs, simply because the more pressing demands of the preindependence period have been realized; those demands that have not been realized may be expressed in calmer, less emotional terms. (2) Despite the pressure of events, the main parties have crystallized recognizable positions on some of the major issues facing the country, positions that owe some of their explicitness to the actions, or the lack of action, of the Camerounian governments.

Three further observations are in point. First, a distinction should be made between goals and positions taken before independence in the East Cameroun, and those taken after. Preindependence goals, usually framed in apocalyptic terms, almost invariably submerged explicitness in emotion-laden rhetoric. This approach, of course, had a certain logic for political parties whose primary concern was not so much the shape of the future as the nature of their particular share of or role in it. Preindependence goals centered on the themes of independence, termination of trusteeship, reunification of the Camerouns, and on the position of the UPC in the political picture. Second, the impact of independence on the programs and the positions of the parties should not be minimized. Independence substantially reduced the content of common nationalist demonology (though not so markedly for the UC and the UPC as for other parties), and the old anti-French, anticolonialist slogans lost much of their meaning for both electorate and parties. There was a general softening of attitudes, and goals were reformulated in less heated and emotional terms. An excellent example is the UPC's acceptance, in effect, of the December, 1960, Franco-Camerounian coöperation agreements. Instead of rejecting the agreements, the party abstained from voting; it would not have gone even that far before independence. Third, a distinction must be made between party goals and programs before and after unification. Pre- and postindependence goals seem to have been retained virtually intact in both Camerouns, except for the emergence of the one-party system in the East Cameroun. The Union Camerounaise, once committed to the development of a multiparty, egalitarian parliamentary democracy, in 1961 began to move toward redefinition of its concept of political democracy.

Table 4 is a schematic presentation of the positions of the major Camerounian parties, as reflected in their program demands, on goals and issues in 1960 and 1962. It describes party positions on (1) five major goals more or less accepted by all parties, and (2) selected issues grouped according to these goals. That is, it elaborates the five major goals in terms of the major issues that have arisen in connection with them. The positions, as revealed in the program demands, are expressed in varying degrees of acceptance or rejection, or in terms of whether or not a position has been taken. The distinction between "silence" and "no position" is meaningful; the former indicates that a party deliberately says nothing on an issue, and the latter, that it actually has adopted no position. Table 5 gives party positions on particular issues identifiable in 1962 but not in 1960.

The five major goals were selected because the parties showed the greatest degree of consensus on them, and mentioned them the most often. They represent generalized statements of desirable national aims. Since 1955, at least, the principal parties have stressed such objectives as internal political peace, the pursuit of an "African" foreign policy (i.e., African coöperation in political and economic matters), and modernization (both social and economic). These goals still command wide popular sympathy, and have become part of the Cameroun's political culture. Unification, of course, has been achieved, but, as the touchstone of collaboration between the two states, it remains an identifiable goal in that it connotes a desire for continued unification. Only the CPNC in the West Cameroun continues to have reservations about unification, insisting that the wishes of those who favored integration with Nigeria were callously disregarded when the new federation was organized.

The deepest cleavage in the Camerounian political system became manifest in 1961–1962 over the substantive content of the goal of democratic institutions. In baldest terms, it is a dichotomy between those who favor the creation of a one-party state and those—the opposition parties —who see in this development portents of their political doom. Undoubtedly the events of June–July, 1962, in the East Cameroun served to mute their protests, but hardly eliminated their opposition.

The political systems of the two Camerouns reveal no "left-right" spectrum, either in the traditional European sense or in any commonly accepted sense. The general consensus on goals, the organizational fluidity of the parties, and the vagueness of party programs have permitted no stable alignments in terms of left and right. Not even the presence of the UPC permits a meaningful distinction to be drawn between radical and conservative parties. Only the external UPC exiles in Conakry and Accra pursue openly revolutionary aims; all other parties, including the rallié UPC, have accepted the new system, though with varying degrees of enthusiasm. The UPC's unconcealed Marxist vocabulary is no criterion for labeling it "leftist"; the UC, through President Ahidjo, now defines its ideology as a "socializing humanism, or, in other terms, African socialism." [24]

---

[24] *Effort Camerounaise,* July 15, 1962, p. 3, excerpted from Ahidjo's report to the Fourth Party Congress.

Table 4

Position of Principal Camerounian Parties on Major Goals and Related Issues, 1960 and 1962

Goal and issue	1960										1962						
	Cameroun						*Trust Territory*				*East Cameroun*				*West Cameroun*		
	Government				Opposition		Government		Opposition		Govt.	Opposition			Govt.	Opposition	
	UC	MANC	PSC	FPUP	UPC	PDC	KNDP	CPNC	KUNC	OK	UC	UPC	PDC	PSC	KNDP	CPNC	OK
UNIFICATION																	
Unification of Camerouns	A	A	A	A	A	E	A	R	R	A	A	A	A	A	A	CA	A
Integration with Nigeria	R	R	R	R	R	S	R	A	R	R	++	++	++	++	++	—	++
INTERNAL POLITICAL PEACE																	
End of terrorism	A	A	A	A	CA	A	A	A	A	CA	A	A	A	A	A	A	A
Unconditional *ralliément*	CR	CR	CR	A	A	R	—	—	—	—	CA	A	R	CA	CA	CA	CA
Conditional *ralliément*	A	CA	CA	CR	R	A	—	—	—	—	A	R	A	CR	CR	CR	R
Political amnesty	CA	CA	CA	CA	A	CA	—	A	A	A	CA	CA	CA	CA	CA	CA	A
National unity of parties	CA	CA	A	NP	A	CR	—	—	—	—	CA	CA	CA	CA	CR	R	A
Round table	CA	CA	CA	NP	A	CA	—	—	—	—	R	CA	CA	CA	R	CA	A
National government	A	A	A	A	A	A	A	A	A	A	CA	A	A	A	A	A	A
DEMOCRATIC INSTITUTIONS																	
Constitution of April, 1960																	
Referendum on	A	CA	CA	CA	R	R	—	—	—	—	++	++	++	++	++	++	++
Legality of drafting	A	CA	A	CA	R	R	—	—	—	—	A	R	R	R	A	CR	R
Sufficiency of political liberty	A	A	CA	A	CR	CA	—	—	—	—	A	R	R	R	A	CR	R
Administrative institutions																	
Too big and costly	CA	CA	CA	CA	A	A	R	R	R	A	CA	CA	CA	CA	R	R	R
Acceptable	CA	CA	CA	CA	R	R	A	A	A	R	CA	CR	CR	CR	CA	CA	CR
Expatriate staff																	
Immediate withdrawal	R	R	R	R	CR	A	R	CR	CR	A	R	CA	CA	R	R	R	R
Gradual replacement	A	A	A	A	CA	A	A	A	A	R	A	CA	CA	A	A	A	CA
Retention	R	R	R	R	R	R	R	R	R	R	CR	R	R	R	CR	R	CR
Camerounization too slow	R	CR	CR	CR	A	A	R	A	A	A	A	A	A	A	CA	CA	A

	1	2	3	4	5	6	7	8	9	10	11	12	13	14	15
'AFRICAN" FOREIGN POLICY															
Alignment															
With West	CA	CA	CA	CA	CA	CA	CR	CA	A	CA	CA	CA	CR	CA	CR
With East	CR	CR	CR	CR	CR	CA	CA	CR	R	CR	CA	CR	CA	CR	CA
Nonalignment	A	A	A	A	A	A	A	A	A	A	A	A	E	A	E
"Positive" neutrality	A	A	A	A	A	A	A	A	A	A	A	A	CA	A	A
European affiliations															
Community	R	R	R	R	R	R	R	R	—	—	R	R	R	R	R
OEEC¹	CA	CA	CA	CA	CA	CR	CR	CA	—	NP	CA	CA	CA	E	CR
Common market	CA	CA	CA	CA	CA	CR	CR	CA	—	NP	CA	CR	CR	E	CR
Zone franc or sterling															
area	CA	CA	CA	CA	CA	CR	CR	E	R	CR	A	A	CA	E	NP
African affiliations															
Pan-Africanism	A	A	A	A	A	A	A	A	A	A	A	A	A	A	A
Regional blocs	CA	CA	CA	CA	CA	A	A	A	NP	NP	CA	CA	CA	CA	CA
French-speaking															
countries	A	A	A	A	A	A	E	A	A	—	A	A	A	A	A
Foreign troops															
Immediate withdrawal	R	R	R	CR	CR	A	A	A	A	NP	A	R	R	A	A
Retain as needed	A	A	A	A	A	R	R	R	R	NP	R	A	A	CA	R
MODERNIZATION²															
Modalities															
Change land tenure	A	A	A	A	CA	A	A	CA	A	A	CA	A	A		
Reform chiefs'															
positions	CA	CA	CA	CA	CA	CA	CA	CA	A	NP	CA	CA	A		
Modify only	CA	CA	CA	A	A	A	CA	R	A	CA	CR	A	A		
Revise radically	R	R	R	R	R	R	R	CA	R	CA	CA	R	R		
Replace chiefs	CA	CA	A	CA	A	CA	CA	CA	A	CR	R	A	A		
External investments	CR	CR	CA	CA	CA	CA	CA	CA	CA	CA	CR	A	A		
Labor mobilization	CA	A	CA	CA	CA	CA	A	CA	A	CA	CA	A	CA		
Forced savings	CA	CA	A	A	NP	A	A	CA	A	CA	A	A	A		
Financial austerity	CR	CA	A	A	A	A	A	CR	A	NP	A	A	A		
Crop diversification	A	A	A	A	A	A	A	A	A	A	A	A	A		
Secondary industries	A	A	A	A	A	A	A	A	A	A	A	A	A		
Absorb unemployed	A	A	A	A	A	A	A	A	A	A	A	A	A		
Increased education	A	A	A	A	A	A	A	A	A	A	A	A	A		
National planning	CA	CA	CA	CA	CA	CA	CA	CA	CA	NP	CA	A	CA		
Tempo															
Gradual	CA	CA	CR	CR	R	R	A	CA	CA	NP	CA	R	CA	A	CR
Fast	CR	CR	A	A	A	A	A	CR	CR	NP	CR	A	CR	CA	CA
Priorities															
Infrastructure	H	H	H	H	M	H	H	H	H	R	H				
Heavy industry	L	L	L	L	L	L	L	L	L	A	L				
Secondary industry	M	M	M	M	M	M	M	M	M	H	M				
Social change	H	H	H	H	H	H	H	H	M	L	M				
Agricultural reform	H	H	H	H	H	H	H	H	H	M	H				

T A B L E   4 — *Concluded*

Key to abbreviations:

A = unequivocal acceptance	NP = no position
CA = conditional acceptance	− = not applicable
CR = conditional rejection	+ = no longer applicable
E = equivocation	H = high priority
R = rejection	M = medium priority
S = silence	L = low priority

[1] Organization for European Economic Cooperation, replaced in 1961 by the Organization for Economic Cooperation and Development (OECD).

[2] For the goal of modernization and its related issues, there was no change between 1960 and 1962.

SOURCES: *Presse du Cameroun*, 1959–1961; *Effort Camerounais*, 1960–1962; *Kamerun Times*, 1961–1962; *Cameroons Champion*, 1961–1962; *Bulletin Quotidien d'Agence Camerounaise du Presse*, 1961; *Le Monde*, 1960–1962; *Afrique Nouvelle*, 1961–1962; Southern Cameroons Information Service, newsletters and releases, 1959–1961; *Procès-verbaux de l'Assemblée Nationale du Cameroun*, 1960–1961. UC: reports and resolutions of Second Party Congress (N'Gaoundéré, July, 1939) and Third Party Congress (Maroua, Sept., 1961); *Premier Stage de Formation des Responsables de l'Union Camerounaise, Yaoundé, du 1er au 6 août 1961*; interviews with Ahmadou Ahidjo, Arouna Njoya, Victor Kanga, Charles Onana Awana, Moussa Yaya, and others, 1959, 1960–61. UPC: party journals, 1960–1962; party pamphlets, leaflets, and memoranda, 1959–1962; interviews with Mayi Matip, Jean-Paul Sendé, Zibi Abraham, and others, 1960–61. PCC: *Le Démocrate*, 1961; party brochures and leaflets, 1959–1961; interviews with André-Marie Mbida, 1959, 1960, 1961. FPUP, MANC, PSC: interviews with Victor Kanga, Pierre Kamdem-Ninyim, Charles Assalé, Paul Soppo-Priso, and Charles Okala, 1960–61. West Cameroun parties: *West Africa*, 1961–1962; *Daily Times* (Lagos), 1961–1962; *Citizen* (Zaria), 1961–1962; party brochures, leaflets, and memoranda; interviews with John Foncha, E. M. L. Endeley, Peter M. Kale, Jobea K. Dibonge, Solomon T. Muna, Augustine N. Jua, and Ndeh Ntumazah.

TABLE 5

POSITION OF PRINCIPAL CAMEROUNIAN PARTIES ON ISSUES RELATED TO THE GOAL
OF DEMOCRATIC INSTITUTIONS, 1962

Issue	East Cameroun				West Cameroun		
	Govern-ment	Opposition			Govern-ment	Opposition	
	UC	UPC	PDC	PSC	KNDP	CPNC	OK
Federal constitution, 1961	A	CA	CA	CA	A	CA	CA
Organization of powers	A	CA	CA	CA	A	CA	CA
Institutions	A	CA	CA	CA	A	CA	CA
Parties and political system							
One-party state	A	R	R	R	S	R	R
Parti unifié	A	R	R	R	A	CR	R
Multiparty system	R	CA	CA	CA	E	A	CA
National front	R	A	A	A	S	A	CA
Civil liberties							
Free speech	CA	A	A	A	A	A	A
Freedom of association	CA	A	A	A	A	A	A
Free press							
State supervision	A	R	R	R	CA	R	R
No supervision	R	A	A	A	CR	A	A

Key to abbreviations:
A = unequivocal acceptance   E = equivocation
CA = conditional acceptance   R = rejection
CR = conditional rejection   S = silence
SOURCES: See table 4.

POLITICAL STRATEGY AND TECHNIQUES

An observer of the Cameroun Republic's political scene commented rather trenchantly in 1960 on the singular appropriateness of the relative positions of the main parties, that is, that the UC, the PSC, the MANC, and the FPUP should be governing parties, and that the UPC and the PDC should be in opposition. Why? Because the UPC and the PDC always seemed to behave as if they were in opposition, even when the Démocrates were the governing party, and the others as if they were in power. The entire outlook of the UPC has been shaped by its view of itself as a revolutionary party whose ultimate aims have been complete elimination of the actual governmental institutions, whether French or Camerounian, and their replacement by a regime in which all things the UPC opposes will have been removed.

When the UPC first came into being, the negativism of its opposition had a basis in the current political situation, and the party was able to generate a dynamism and an *élan* which found a ready political echo in the country. It was inevitable, however, that the UPC's initial momentum could not survive some fifteen years of opposition, five of which were spent under the fetters of proscription. The long years of dwindling enthusiasm have produced a series of internal dichotomies from which the party has not yet shown signs of recovering. One such dichotomy is the conflict between the internal party's revolutionary, even Leninist, vocabulary, and the necessity of working within the constitutional framework of the postindependence period. In a word, the dilemma is how to be revolutionary and rallié at the same time. The result has been a virtually incessant internal dialogue over party policy and action, a dialogue perhaps interesting to the participants, but nonetheless sterile in outcome and content.

Under the circumstances the UPC has not been able to provide effective opposition on the major issues confronting the country. When a position is taken, the party invariably uses the old, preindependence slogans and phrases. Its electoral effectiveness has also suffered, and not simply because of government attacks. Although the UPC issues more literature than all other parties combined, its propaganda is uniformly dull and bears little relevance to actual events or conditions. In short, fifteen years is too long a time to wage a revolution, especially after the major revolutionary goals have already been achieved by others.

A similar inflexibility has rendered the PDC ineffective, both as a governing party and as a party in opposition. This inflexibility stems in a large part from the party's doctrinal origins. Mbida has declared, "I am a Catholic political leader. Our program finds its inspiration from the recommendations of the Holy Catholic Church and above all from the teaching of Pope Pius XII." [25] Mbida has always sought concordance between the Christian doctrinal position, as he saw it, and the actions of himself and of his party. However well-intentioned this policy may have been, it fostered a rigidity that made the party unable to adapt to changing political conditions. Doctrinal rigidity helped to make Mbida's tenure as premier unhappy, and vitiated the party's participation in the Ahidjo government before October, 1960. As a result of the conflict, the PDC lost its three portfolios and returned to the opposition. For the rest of 1960 and throughout 1961 the party and Mbida spent much of their time blaming the government, France, the United States, and the other parties (above all, the UPC, against which Mbida declared he would "fight to the end") for the PDC's uncomfortable predicament. Currently, with

---

[25] From a handbill entitled "Profession de Foi, Parti des Démocrates Camerounais," April, 1960.

Mbida in jail and the party suffering massive defections, the PDC seems to have entered a period of decline which may lead to its eventual demise.

In contrast, the UC has not only retained its ability to maneuver effectively on the political stage, but, thanks to its political successes and the effectiveness of its leaders, has virtually disposed of all challenges to its preëminence. The 1960–1961 Republic's French-style institutions (the 1960 Cameroun Constitution was almost a carbon copy of that of the Fifth French Republic) and a moderate view on political liberties enabled the party to rule with considerable flexibility. During this period it encouraged the growth of electoral participation and of public education, yet managed to keep the UPC and the rest of the opposition completely off balance. With unification and the creation of the Federal Republic, the UC further strengthened its hold on the polity.

The UC, viewing itself as the guardian of the national patrimony, has introduced liberal social and economic legislation. It did not hesitate, however, to pass an omnibus subversion law in March, 1962, to condone a certain amount of nepotism at the highest levels, to permit quiet exchanges of bribes, or highhandedly to arrest and try its political opponents. The party leadership has never recoiled from vigorous (some say "coercive") methods to insure its perpetuation in power. The opposition's bill of indictment has become quite lengthy, including the entire sequence of events that culminated in the arrest and imprisonment of all the major opposition leaders; questions about the propriety of the Ahidjo government's arrogating to itself *pleins pouvoirs* two months before independence; sending the Assembly on a holiday; creating a committee to draft the new constitution without the participation of the opposition; and, after independence, drafting and promulgating the electoral laws governing the April, 1960, elections. On the whole, the UC is characterized by a suppleness that readily harmonizes doctrinal considerations and the practical needs of the moment.

Of the three principal West Camerounian parties, only the KNDP has displayed a tactical agility on a par with that of the UC. Unencumbered by any extensive doctrinal commitments, Foncha and his colleagues have been able to seize upon heuristic situations and find positions that would win the widest support from the electorate. The February, 1961, plebiscite in the Southern Cameroons is an example. On that occasion the party exaggerated the threat posed by southern Nigerians in the Victoria and Kumba areas, and by Fulani herders in the grass fields, in order to mobilize large prounification blocs of votes. In the southern division, the party claimed that a vote for integration with Nigeria would invite perpetual domination by the Ibo, as well as loss of land, jobs, and liberties. In the grass fields, the party's propagandists promised that unification would permanently resolve the problem of the southward intrusion of Fulani herders and their cattle into the grass-lands. Unification has not, of course, removed the economic threat of the southern Nigerians, nor has it stopped the push of the Fulani pastoral-ists. The point is that, under the circumstances, such positions were in-telligible to and could garner the votes of thousands of people who under-stood neither the implications of the Cameroun-Cameroons merger nor the nature of the new union.[26]

In contrast, during the plebiscite the CPNC was unable to convince the voters that their future lay with Nigeria. The danger of merging with a country torn by violence—which Endeley stressed—was not very mean-ingful to most voters; a more immediate threat was allegedly posed by the Nigerian immigrants. In the West Cameroun context, the CPNC's insistence on parliamentary formalities and on respect for the opposition has had little popular response in the face of a governing party that could promise the impossible with impunity.

---

[26] Cf. Frodin, *op. cit.*

The Revolutionary-Centralizing Trend

5. GUINEA

By Victor D. Du Bois

Political activity in Guinea before World War II was the monopoly of a small group of French settlers and even fewer African *évolués* whose background, position, or education qualified them to be members of the small indigenous elite. Such political life as existed was closely bound up with politics in France. The dramatic postwar reforms embodied in the Constitution of the Fourth French Republic, however, ushered in an entirely new era. The relaxation of restrictions on political activity, the expansion of the electorate, and the very substantial increase in African representation in the First and Second Constituent Assemblies and, subsequently, in the National Assembly of the Fourth Republic, precipitated the birth of a variety of political parties throughout French *Afrique Noire.*

During the immediate postwar period political parties in Guinea were either overseas affiliates of the major parties in France, or parochial parties of an ethnic or a regional nature. The chief party of the resident Europeans was the Action Démocratique et Sociale, the Guinea branch of the Rassemblement du Peuple Français (RPF), the Gaullist party of metropolitan France. The other Guinea party linked to the French party system was the Démocratic Socialiste de Guinée (DSG), the local branch of the French Socialist Party (SFIO). Organized and led by Yacine Diallo, a Guinean, the DSG was mainly the party of the African évolué. The overwhelming majority of the eligible African electorate was affiliated with one or another of the purely indigenous parties.

Among the many African political groups which rapidly mushroomed into being as a consequence of the radically altered postwar political situation, at least four stand out. These coincided more or less with the four main geographical regions of Guinea: the Comité de la Basse-Guinée (Lower Guinea), the Amicale Gilbert Vieillard (middle Guinea or Fouta Djallon), the Union du Manding (Upper Guinea), and the Union Forestière (forest region in the south). Less important were the Foyer Sénégalais, the Foyer des Métis, the Union des Toucouleurs, and the Union des Insulaires. As all these names suggest, each political group had a linguistic, ethnic, regional, or similar type of parochial base. Moreover, little effort was made during this period by African party

186

leaders to organize support beyond the immediate group from which they derived their strength.

In the elections of 1946 and 1947 the DSG won about as many votes as the ethnic and regional parties combined. This near equilibrium in electoral strength between the two elements gave the French colonial administration a decisive role in determining the outcome of electoral contests, an advantage it rarely failed to grasp. Administrative intervention assumed many forms, including last-minute switches of polling booths, stuffing of ballot boxes, and compilation of fraudulent electoral rolls. When an electoral contest resulted in a close tally of votes between two candidates, the colonial administration would itself conduct the investigation and announce the victorious candidate, invariably an African who was amenable to French direction. These and other stratagems characterized the official determination to keep a tight control over Guinean political group life, a pattern that persisted until Guinea achieved independence in 1958.

The founding of the Rassemblement Démocratique Africain (RDA) at the Bamako Congress in 1946 was a critical turning point in the development of political groups in Guinea as well as in the rest of French *Afrique Noire*. Founded as a Pan-African interterritorial party to agitate more vigorously for the full realization of African rights, the RDA presented a potential challenge to the already established Démocratie Socialiste de Guinée as well as to the ethnic parties. It was several months, however, before the Guinean section of the RDA, the Parti Démocratique de Guinée (PDG), could be formed. From the outset its leaders faced formidable obstacles.

During its early existence the PDG was torn by factions reflecting old regional loyalties and the assertion of particularistic interests. Beneath the façade of unity exemplified at the highest level by the establishment of the Comité de Coordination, the organic base of the new party was no more than a conglomeration of fragmented local parties representing groups separated from one another by differences in language, ethnic origin, or region, and by mutual distrust. The many divisive elements that preëxisted Bamako were thus perpetuated within the framework of the new party. Increasingly disabled by these internal divisions, the PDG was in due course reduced to little more than a small group in the party that continued to strive for the goal of unity proclaimed at Bamako. Their efforts were strongly opposed by the colonial administration and the cantonal chiefs, as well as by the Guinea representatives in the French National Assembly. Fear of victimization by the administration as a consequence of being identified with the PDG led many African leaders and militants openly to disavow their affiliation; some even tacitly supported repressive measures by the government against the PDG. Top-heavy with intellectuals, most of them government functionaries, the party at the time lacked a base at the mass level on which it could depend for support. Little persistent effort was made to exploit latent but widespread anticolonial sentiment. Ambitious to be elected to office, yet fearful of antagonizing the colonial regime on which their jobs depended, candidates were often reluctant to pursue with vigor the principles they had enthusiastically endorsed at Bamako. Defeat in an election was often pessimistically interpreted by a candidate as dramatic proof that he should desist from further support of RDA policies.

Between 1950 and 1954 important political changes took place in Guinea. While the DSG's influence declined, the growth of the Action Démocratique et Sociale reflected the increase of the *petit blanc* population in Guinea's main towns: Conakry, Kindia, Labé, Mamou, Kankan, Boké, and Macenta. Although elsewhere in French West Africa the RDA steadily assumed a less radical air after its break with the Communists in 1950, the PDG in Guinea preserved its extremist character. Sékou Touré, leader of the PDG, continued his association with the French Communist-dominated Confédération Générale du Travail (CGT); in 1948 he was secretary-general of its Guinean chapter, and from 1950 on he was secretary-general of the Coördinating Committee of CGT unions for all French West Africa and Togo. He thereby remained very suspect in the eyes of the French colonial administration. His retention of these links with the Communists, even after Félix Houphouet-Boigny and other RDA chieftains had broken with them, led to his increasing alienation from the other leaders of his own party.

The elections in Guinea in June, 1954, pitted Touré against Barry Diawadou, head of the Bloc Africain de Guinée (BAG) for the late Yacine Diallo's seat in the National Assembly. Tensions that had been building up in Guinea over the preceding four years exploded in fierce street brawls. The election was the first contest between Guinean conservatives, backed by the colonial administration and the resident whites, and a resuscitated RDA, now strengthened by labor-union growth in the territory. Barry was declared the winner, and this was interpreted by many as evidence that the administration clearly regarded Touré as a dangerous opponent.

The growing influence of the RDA in Guinea alarmed conservative elements. Reactions to the new menace were varied. Local chiefs, fearful of the extent of RDA support among women and youth, organized an association that called for social reform, including the redistribution of land. European residents, foreseeing that their privileged position might very well be endangered by the RDA's growing power, organized a local chapter of the Présence Française and came out strongly against any further political reforms.[1] But Black Africa's impatience at last moved France, fearful of another Algeria, to undertake a vast new program of political reform.

THE LOI-CADRE AND SUBSEQUENT PARTY DEVELOPMENT IN GUINEA

The Loi-Cadre of June, 1956, laid the groundwork for fundamental changes in the West African political scene. By its proclamation of universal suffrage and extension of the single electoral college, the Loi-Cadre forced African parties to reappraise their capacity to contend for what became a new high stake in African politics, namely, control of the territorial assemblies, now clearly seen as precursors of sovereign governments. Realists in Africa and in France regarded it as inevitable that Africans would shortly be called upon to assume complete control of their own countries. Anticipating the power contest that would be precipitated, Guinean political parties began in earnest to streamline their internal structures and to expand their membership lists.

In Guinea, development of the RDA had long been hampered by three obstacles: the hostility of prominent political leaders of the territory, especially the Socialist Yacine Diallo;[2] an unsympathetic colonial administration; and the party's basic internal weaknesses. The first obstacle was removed in 1954 with the death of Diallo and the inability of the Socialists to find anyone of equal stature to replace him; the second was seriously weakened by the friendly relations that Sékou Touré succeeded in cultivating with Bernard Cornut-Gentille, a man of liberal disposition who was later to be Minister of Overseas France for the de Gaulle government. In overcoming the third obstacle, internal weaknesses, the RDA moved well ahead of its rivals in Guinea. By 1956 the party already controlled most of the political and quasi-political organizations in Guinea which clamored for an end to colonialism. It became the most vocal advocate of a federal association, freely entered into by Frenchmen and Africans for the advancement of their mutual interests. At the time, this was a revolutionary concept.

---

[1] The Présence Française in Conakry distributed hundreds of leaflets bearing the following message: "We [French] are witnessing the destruction of the magnificent empire which our fathers conquered at the cost of their lives. . . . Every day the pro-Negro policy of our rulers strikes another blow at the system. Soon, if we take no action, our country will have lost its colonies and be reduced to the status of Italy, Spain and Portugal. Frenchmen, are you prepared to accept that?" (quoted in *West Africa*, Nov. 5, 1955; cited in Virginia Thompson and Richard Adloff, *French West Africa* [Stanford: Stanford University Press, [1958?]], pp. 137–138).

[2] During this period (1951–1954) there was considerable opposition in other quarters to RDA expansion. The one other Socialist deputy, Mamba Sano, also opposed the RDA, as did the Cherif of Kankan, Fanta Mahdi, then the most prominent orthodox Muslim leader in French West Africa.

Aware of the shortcomings of political parties rooted in local and ethnic interests, RDA leaders revised the party's platform and widened its membership base. Proclaiming it the "authentic" African movement dedicated to the union of all Africans against colonialist reaction, they launched a campaign for social justice. The party's new program of political action rested on four principles:[3] (1) the peasant class, for whom the party had secured freedom of labor and of circulation and sale of its goods and services, was to be the social base of the RDA; (2) women were to be recruited as active participants in the political process, in keeping with the position merited by their dignity and political maturity; (3) youth would participate as equals in deliberations on national policy; and (4) labor would fight unceasingly, in close collaboration with other elements of Guinean society, for African unity and working-class interests. Labor unions, youth clubs, women's organizations, and veterans' groups were all assiduously courted to bring them into line behind the party militants, who would direct a movement representative not merely of one region or one ethnic group, but of the territory as a whole.

The PDG-RDA which emerged from these efforts was a very different party from the one organized at Bamako. By rapidly expanding its membership so as to decrease the proportion of intellectuals and government functionaries, it became more representative of the mass of the people. Purged of its links with the Communists, the party assumed a more genuinely African character. In this respect it enjoyed a marked advantage over its two principal rivals, the DSG and the BAG, the latter headed by Barry Diawadou. In the minds of many of the new voters, these two parties, in leadership and program, were closely identified with metropolitan parties, of which they seemed to be merely African appendages.[4] Unlike the PDG-RDA, which no longer hesitated to exploit popular anticolonialist sentiments, the BAG and the Socialists continued to endorse comparatively moderate policies which had little attraction for a people whose nationalist convictions were steadily mounting.

It was not that the Loi-Cadre meant less to these parties than it did to the PDG-RDA, but merely that their response to it was different. The PDG seized upon it as an opportunity to attract more members by campaigning vigorously for African unity and for the dismantling of the colonial structure. The other parties, less certain of the course of future developments, were not nearly so outspoken. Ibrahima Barry ("Barry III"), it is true, deplored the territorialization of the federations of French West Africa and of French Equatorial Africa which he feared would re-

---

[3] Sékou Touré, *L'Action politique du Parti Démocratique de Guinée pour l'émancipation africaine* (Conakry, 1958), I, 18–19.

[4] The Bloc Africain de Guinée was associated at first with the RPF, General de Gaulle's party. The DSG was still tied to the French Socialist Party.

sult from the Loi-Cadre. He advocated strengthening the powers of the Grand Conseil of the Federation of French West Africa in order to preserve interterritorial ties. At the same time, however, he resisted as premature Léopold Senghor's overtures to merge the DSG with other autonomous African parties to form a solid African front.[5]

Meanwhile, Barry Diawadou, perceiving that his party's *apparentement* to the RPF was no longer to its advantage, left the RPF and aligned the BAG with the Radical Socialists in the French National Assembly. At home he set about transforming the BAG into a party advocating a "confederation of autonomous republics tightly linked to France and oriented to the Western bloc." [6] Concomitantly with the rise of a socialist movement to power in France through the elections of January, 1956, the socialist party in French West Africa suffered a further decline. In Guinea the PDG-RDA candidate Sékou Touré was elected deputy to the French National Assembly over his Socialist rival.

Much of the success of the PDG-RDA over its opponents was due to its independence and assertiveness on the subject of colonial reforms. African Socialists finally realized that they could capture the initiative from the all-powerful RDA only by adopting a similarly independent stand on colonial issues. They called on Premier Guy Mollet (a fellow Socialist) to institute far-reaching reforms overseas without further delay. But Mollet, uneasy over the situation in Algeria, would grant no further concessions to the territories, fearing that such action might be construed in France as "giving away the empire" to implacable nationalist agitators. Disgruntled over Mollet's timidity, the African Socialists became convinced that only by taking the initiative, breaking with the SFIO, and forming an all-African socialist party could they once again capture support in West Africa. To this end a conference was held at Conakry in January, 1957; it was attended by delegates of the territories and by Pierre Comin, secretary-general of the metropolitan SFIO. Comin supported the Africans' desire to form their own interterritorial socialist movement. At the same time he urged his colleagues to maintain close ties in the National Assembly, a proposal they accepted. From this conference emerged the Mouvement Socialiste Africain (MSA), with which the

---

[5] Barry III similarly refused to consider merging with other parties in Guinea itself until such time as certain basic requirements were met. Among them were an agreement on certain legal and political guarantees in order to prevent any such merger from being exclusively to the advantage of any one party; the establishment of a provisional executive; the formulation of a political platform; and a promise that conservative parties would be excluded from such a union (see "Quelques Déclarations officielles de notre Camarade Barry III," *Le Populaire de Guinée* [Conakry], Sept. 15, 1956, pp. 1, 4).

[6] *Marchés Tropicaux du Monde,* Nov. 5, 1956, cited in Thompson and Adloff, *op. cit.,* p. 138.

DSG immediately affiliated.[7] In a resolution put forward at Conakry, the MSA proposed for French Black Africa "a political, cultural, economic, and social democracy assuring each individual of the full development of his personality, and leading to a true independence of peoples." [8]

Although the merger of most of the socialist parties in French West Africa lifted the sagging spirits of many African socialists, it failed to check the growing influence of the RDA and the downward slide of their own parties. In Guinea the elections of March, 1957, brought an overwhelming victory to the PDG, which won fifty-six of sixty seats in the Territorial Assembly.[9] Although Barry III bravely continued to speak of "resurgent strength," the reduction of Socialist representation in the Assembly to merely three members signaled the end of the DSG as a serious contender in Guinean politics.

Despite the organizational break with the SFIO, Guinean Socialists continued to vote with French Socialists in the National Assembly. But the metropolitan party leadership, absorbed in domestic problems, did not put its full weight behind programs of colonial reform. Its failure to do so was, of course, a tremendous disappointment to Africans, whose feelings were appreciated at least by a minority of the French party. Elements from both sides were at last able to convoke a series of round-table meetings in Paris (October–November, 1957), where every effort was made to close the breach and avoid a serious loss of party strength. When these conferences produced no tangible results, African socialists became convinced that they could successfully press claims for their people only in union with other African parties. They were deeply aware of the growing restiveness in Africa. They were concerned over the worsening situation in Algeria and the *immobilisme* that was paralyzing France. They even sensed the danger of a rightist coup. The African socialists took the initiative in calling a conference of all African parties, which met in Dakar on March 28, 1958, to consider how best to cope with the problems confronting Africa.

---

[7] The MSA also included local branches of the socialist party from other parts of Africa: French Soudan: Parti Progressiste Soudanais (PPS); Niger: Section Nigérienne du MSA (result of fusion between the Bloc Nigérien d'Action and the Union Démocratique Nigérienne); Ivory Coast: Section Ivoirienne du MSA; Mauritania: Section Mauritanienne du MSA; Cameroun: Union Sociale Camerounaise and Section MSA du Cameroun; Chad: Parti Socialiste Indépendant du Tchad; Middle Congo: Section MSA du Moyen Congo; Senegal: Parti Sénégalais d'Action Socialiste.

[8] Barry III, "Qu'est le M.S.A.?" *Le Populaire de Guinée* (published bimonthly by the DSG section of the MSA), April 15, 1957, p. 3.

[9] Of the 650,000 votes cast, the RDA received 500,000; the Socialists, 100,000; and the BAG (Barry Diawadou's party), less than 50,000. Despite their respectable showing of 100,000 votes, the Socialists lost out heavily in this election because a number of their men from certain areas of the territory (Kissidougou, Mali, Dinguiraye, Younkounkoun, and Faranah) ran as independent socialist candidates rather than under the banner of the DSG (see Barry III, "Remercîments," *ibid.*, p. 1).

While the socialists were pressing the issue of African unity, the RDA itself was similarly engaged. Already the most powerful party in all French Black Africa, the RDA in 1958 called on all African parties to join it in a consolidated effort to bring about a new federal relationship with France in which the territories might deal with the *métropole* as partners rather than as weak, disunited colonies. The socialists, balking at the idea of submerging their identity in a larger party in which they could hope to play only a subordinate role, turned down the RDA's appeal. Instead, joining other dissident parties, they formed the Parti du Regroupement Africain (PRA), the Guinean branch taking the name Union Progressiste Guinéenne (UPG), which embraced both the DSG of the Mouvement Socialiste Africain and Barry Diawadou's Bloc Africain de Guinée.

Despite the enthusiasm the parties displayed in formulating anticolonial programs and the vigor with which they pursued them, these were not at first anti-French manifestations, even in Guinea. They were aimed, not at destroying the relationship between France and Africa, but at reforming it. African parties did not seek through federalism to break the links that bound Africa to France, but rather to recast them so that the African personality could assert itself as legitimate, as something separate and distinct from the European personality, but not hostile to it. Indeed, Sékou Touré, the *enfant terrible* of French-African relations under the de Gaulle–Debré government, was for a time one of the most articulate champions of federalism.[10]

To most leaders of French Black Africa, the preservation of their respective federal structures loomed as an absolute imperative in any reorganization plan envisaged for the French Union. Seeing in any other scheme the Balkanization of Africa, the leaders of African parties, most notably those of the RDA, the PRA, and the Convention Africaine (successor to the Indépendants d'Outre-Mer), repeatedly appealed to the

---

[10] "Nous sommes pour la Communauté Franco-Africaine, au profit de laquelle les Etats Africains abandonneront une partie de leur souveraineté, parce que nous sommes conscients qu'à l'heure des grands ensembles l'Afrique n'a rien à gagner de son isolement, parce que nous sommes aussi conscients que la France sera notre partenaire le plus valable. ... Notre exigence pour l'institution d'un Exécutif fédéral doit signifier une volonté d'adhérer à la Communauté avec la France, comme bloc ayant les mêmes réalités, les mêmes espoirs, les mêmes problèmes. C'est en ce sens que la Révision Constitutionnelle est conçue par nous, notre idée n'est nullement celle d'une séparation avec la France, mais la signification de la confiance, de l'amour que nous portons à la France, confiance et amour qui passent à travers l'Afrique, que nous voulons autant que la France rendre bénéficiaire de leur association" ("La Loi-Cadre et l'Afrique Noire," in Touré, *op. cit.*, I, 24–25; see also "Rapport moral et politique," IVème Congrès du Parti Démocratique de Guinée, Conakry, 5–8 juin 1958, *ibid.*, p. 42; "Discours prononcé par Monsieur Sékou Touré, Président du Conseil de gouvernement à l'ouverture de la session extraordinaire de l'Assemblée Territoriale, 13–28 juillet 1958," *ibid.*, pp. 70–71).

French government to preserve the federal structures in any reorganization of territories under French rule.

Federalism was raised as a central issue at the RDA congress held in Conakry in June, 1955, which passed, and transmitted to the French government, a resolution calling for the establishment of a federal constitution. Early in 1956 representatives of all major African labor organizations, including the Confédération Générale du Travail (CGT), the Confédération Française des Travailleurs Chrétiens (CFTC), the Force-Ouvrière (FO), the Indépendants, and the Autonomes, meeting at Cotonou (Dahomey), passed a resolution calling for a new federal organization of France and the territories then composing the federations of French West Africa and of French Equatorial Africa, in which the principles of self-determination and independence would be recognized. In January, 1957, an MSA congress meeting at Conakry demanded that France acknowledge the right of independence for those territories that wanted it. At its congress at Dakar in the same month, the Convention Africaine issued a resolution calling for the constitution of two African states corresponding to the two federations.

In the ensuing year prominent leaders of all parties repeatedly appealed for a more satisfactory definition of Franco-African relationships, in which the right of self-determination, as an optional choice, would be recognized. These were either largely ignored by the French government or decried as "secessionist" by elements of the French Parliament and press. Yet all resolutions explicitly acknowledged the close ties between France and Africa and urged their preservation, although in a new form. Indeed, as late as August 25, 1958, scarcely one month before the fateful referendum, Touré himself supported the idea of a Franco-African community, provided that its constitution proclaim (1) the right to independence and the juridical equality of the associated peoples; (2) the right to "divorce" from "the Franco-African marriage"; and (3) the active solidarity of the peoples and of the associated states in order to accelerate and harmonize their evolution.[11]

The face-to-face encounter between General de Gaulle and Sékou Touré in Conakry on the day Touré made the foregoing demand marked the turning point in Franco-Guinean relations. Touré's speech, which strongly denounced colonialism, left no room for doubt that unless the new constitution contained the above provisions, Guinea would most assuredly vote "No" in the referendum and thereby sever her ties with France and with the other states of the French Community. De Gaulle, angered by Touré's attack on French colonial administration,[12] replied

[11] "Discours de Monsieur Sékou Touré, prononcés à l'occasion de l'arrivée du Général de Gaulle à Conakry, le 25 août 1958," in *ibid.,* p. 85.
[12] One of the things that most annoyed de Gaulle was Touré's remark that

in his speech before the Assembly that Guinea could opt for independence by voting "No" on September 28, but he made it clear that she would have to "assume the consequences" of such an act.[13]

Some weeks later, on September 14, 1958, the leaders of the RDA met at Conakry to formulate a common policy for voting in the impending referendum. Rallying behind Houphouet-Boigny, one after another, party leaders in the various territories declared their confidence in General de Gaulle and pledged their determination to vote "Yes." The PDG was the only exception; Sékou Touré asked for independence for his territory. That same day, at the PRA conference convened in Niamey (Niger) for the same purpose, the leaders of the Guinean section of the party, Barry III and Barry Diawadou, independently indicated their own decision to vote "No" in the coming referendum. Subsequent events moved swiftly in Guinea. On September 17, at the now-famous *réunion commune* at Conakry, Sékou Touré met with Barry Diawadou and Barry III, leaders, respectively, of the BAG and the DSG-MSA, the major opposition parties in Guinea. Together they planned a campaign for all-out mobilization of the masses to vote against the Constitution of the Fifth French Republic.

While a vigorous campaign was being waged throughout Guinea by the cadres of all three parties, Touré tried in vain to persuade Barry Diawadou and Barry III that their parties should merge with the PDG. Although for the moment unwilling to go so far, the two leaders did agree to issue a joint communiqué with Touré urging members of all three parties to vote "No." The communiqué was generally accepted for what in fact it was: a tacit recognition of the preëminent position of the PDG in Guinea (virtually undisputed after the elections of 1957) and of Touré's undisputed control over it. On September 28, 1958, the massive PDG organization, which over the preceding few years had meticulously built up a comprehensive system of communication in the bush, proved its worth; of a total of 1,405,986 registered voters (of whom 1,200,171 voted), 1,130,292 voted "No." These landslide figures were not only a *de facto* declaration of Guinean independence, but an overwhelming endorsement of Touré and his party.

It took the Guinean cadre of the PRA only two months to adjust itself to the new situation. On November 29, with Barry III as secretary-

<hr>

Guineans preferred "poverty in liberty to riches in slavery" ("Nous préférons la pauvreté dans la liberté à la richesse dans l'esclavage"; see *ibid.*, p. 80).

[13] "On a parlé d'indépendance, je dis ici plus haut encore qu'ailleurs que l'indépendance est à la disposition de la Guinée. Elle peut la prendre, elle peut la prendre le 28 septembre en disant 'Non' à la proposition qui lui est faite et dans ce cas je garantis que la métropole n'y fera pas obstacle. Elle en tirera, bien sûr, des conséquences, mais d'obstacles elle n'en fera pas et votre Territoire pourra comme il le voudra et dans les conditions qu'il voudra, suivre la route qu'il voudra" ("Discours du Général de Gaulle," in *ibid.*, p. 88).

general and Barry Diawadou as coördinating secretary, the party instructed its members to affiliate unconditionally with the PDG. On the same day the second national conference of the PDG passed a resolution acknowledging the absorption of the PRA into its ranks. Organized opposition to Sékou Touré and to the PDG had come to an end. Guinea was independent of France and had one political chief, absolute master of one monolithic political party.

The PDG and the RDA

Sékou Touré's rejection of the Constitution of the Fifth French Republic not only brought independence to his country, but isolated Guinea from the African countries that had voted to join the new French Community in the September, 1958, plebiscite. It completed Guinea's progressive estrangement from the RDA in the other territories, which had been developing for two years. Touré was convinced that to follow the lead of Félix Houphouet-Boigny, prime minister of the Ivory Coast and president of the RDA, in advocating a closer union with France would be to betray the ideals of Bamako. He became a natural champion, therefore, around whom rallied the more extreme anticolonialist elements in the RDA in all other territories. These two men, Houphouet-Boigny and Touré, symbolized, to many thousands of West Africans, two opposing policies. The Ivory Coast leader, mature, distinguished, and very much the African *grand seigneur,* personified the French-African assimilationist ideal. Touré, scion of an old African dynasty, was the young revolutionary, the champion of his people whom he sought to deliver from the chains of French imperialism. In reality, neither quite matched the portrait painted of him by the metropolitan press or by his opponents.[14] On many issues they were in far closer agreement than was generally recognized. Yet genuine differences did exist between the leadership of the PDG and that of the parent RDA. These centered chiefly on the form that the community should take and the degree of autonomy that its member states should enjoy.

The conflict between the PDG and the RDA came to a head on the day of the referendum, when, as a result of the vote in Guinea, the divergence of the two parties became definitive. On October 19, 1958, the PDG formally ended its affiliation with the RDA. In a special communiqué issued in Conakry on that date, its National Political Bureau declared that the PDG, in view of the RDA's affirmative position on the referendum, could no longer consider the RDA as embodying the real

---

[14] One of the harshest portraits of Sékou Touré was the one that appeared in the French newspaper *L'Aurore,* in a series of articles called "La Guinée sans les français." Touré was pictured as a Judas who had betrayed the nation that had reared him. See also Léonard Sainville, "The French Press and Guinea," *Présence Africaine* (English ed.), vol. 1 (n.d.).

interests of the African liberation movement, and that it was, therefore, severing its ties with the RDA:

> The Political Bureau of the Parti Démocratique de Guinée, after a profound examination of the political situation in Africa after the referendum, and after analyzing the conclusions of the meeting of the Bureau of the Coördinating Committee of the RDA held at Paris, October 7–9, 1958:
>
> Holds that the decision of the Bureau of the Coördinating Committee to compel adherence, territory by territory, to the community, denotes the definitive Balkanization of the federation and gravely compromises African unity, which all the sections of the RDA made the essential reason of their approval of the draft of the constitution.
>
> The PDG is stupefied by the unmistakable declarations of the President of the RDA defining the community, not as a means of emancipating the African masses in the sense of sovereignty and independence, but as a structure definitively integrating the fragmented African states into the French Community.
>
> The PDG affirms the manifest incompatibility between its conception of the personality and the dignity of the real aspirations of Africa and its adherence to the RDA, whose president now openly extols the maintenance of Africa in subordination, thereby sacrificing the African personality and renouncing the anticolonialist vocation of the movement.
>
> It is clear that this attitude on the part of the President of the RDA is clearly a retreat from the possibilities of option offered by the French Constitution.
>
> The Political Bureau of the PDG renders homage to the farsightedness of its secretary-general, Sékou Touré, whose political acumen has permitted Guinea to make a decisive choice giving to African unity its real meaning, and making a reality of the aspirations of the African masses to independence.
>
> On the platform of national independence and of full sovereignty for Guinea, the PDG solemnly proclaims that it no longer considers itself a part of the RDA, and that henceforth it is the natural ally of any section of the RDA or the PRA, or of any other democratic organization, which clearly aligns itself in the struggle for independence, in view of the final objective which historically remains the formation of the United States of Black Africa.[15]

Even after its secession from the RDA, the PDG continued to use "PDG-RDA" as its official title, apparently as a symbol of its retention of ideals whose sole trustee it felt it had become. The break with the RDA and the bitterness it engendered did much to polarize African sentiments around the two African leaders, Houphouet-Boigny and Touré.

Relations between the two adversaries improved, however, after the other French territories acquired independence in 1960. Since that time the remaining contentious issues that divided Guinea from its fellow states of French-speaking Black Africa have gradually disappeared, or

---

[15] "Communiqué du Bureau Politique National du PDG, 19 octobre 1958," in Touré, *op. cit.*, II, 140–141 (my translation).

have been resolved. The granting of independence to Algeria and the gradual settlement of the Congo conflict have removed two major obstacles to a *rapprochement*. Houphouet-Boigny's state visit to Guinea in November, 1962, at the invitation of President Sékou Touré, signaled the reconciliation of the two RDA leaders.

THE SOCIAL BASE OF THE PDG: LEADERS, MEMBERS, AND SUPPORTERS

Membership in the PDG is open to all who accept the statutes of the party, work actively for it, and pay their dues regularly. Admittance to the party is determined by its basic units (*comités de quartier* and *comités de village*). Groups may not join the party en bloc as admittance is allowed only on an individual basis. Upon payment of party dues at a rate fixed by the party congress, the individual receives a membership card bearing the signature of the party's secretary-general and of the treasurer of his local section.

Youth occupies an important position in the PDG. The national youth organization, the Jeunesse Rassemblement Démocratique Africain (JRDA), is considered an arm of the party and is a major source of its strength. Representatives of the JRDA take part in the formulation of national policy, attend party conferences, and in other ways participate actively in the political process. Through such schemes as *investissement humain* (volunteer labor programs for the construction of public works), Guinean youth is early imbued with a sense of responsibility toward the community, the nation, and the party.

Women also play a significant role in Guinean politics. Although women's associations had existed for some years before independence, these were largely *ad hoc*, and, like most Guinean organizations, were based mainly on region, ethnic or linguistic affiliation, or religion. Their activities were restricted to their members' home districts, and their influence in national politics was negligible. Concerned principally with organizing celebrations and social activities of various kinds, they seldom worked on projects of benefit or interest to the community in general. With the founding of the RDA in 1946, women began to assume a much more active role in politics.

As the PDG-RDA expanded into all parts of the territory, the organizing of women became one of its major aims; the results of its efforts were strikingly evident in the legislative elections of 1951, when women voted for the first time, and in large numbers. In 1954 the organizing of women throughout the territory was pursued even more earnestly by the PDG. In the 1956 legislative elections, women campaigned vigorously for the party's candidates. Largely as a result of their efforts, Sékou Touré was elected to the French National Assembly. Since that time women, promoted in large numbers to the rank of party militant, play a role of primary importance in the life of the country. Today women serve as mayors and as presidents of village councils in Guinea, and two are members of the National Political Bureau, the highest decision-making body in the national party.

From its earliest days the PDG has had to create and maintain a mass party organization which would be a true reflection of the ethnic, regional, religious, and political diversities of the nation. Before independence the problem was mainly one of creating from this social potpourri a well-organized, highly disciplined, mass political movement to check the divisive propensities of Guinean society. Since independence the problem has been to develop a national consciousness, a feeling among the citizens of the young republic that their destiny is somehow linked to that of other peoples with whom in the past they have never shared a sense of kinship or identity.

To give substance to its aim of becoming a genuinely popular political movement, the PDG made every effort to avoid the pitfalls shown by experience to be causes of failure. Leadership of political parties had rested almost exclusively in the hands of a small elite of intellectuals or functionaries having little in common with the mass of the electorate. The party therefore sought to democratize both the leadership and the rank and file, and to appeal to a mass electorate. Consequently, the ability to organize and to lead received much stronger emphasis in party doctrine and propaganda, and is today a far more important criterion for advancement in party ranks than formal education. Throughout Guinea, persons with little if any schooling hold positions of responsibility and authority.

No less important than the downgrading of the intellectuals has been the need to maintain an impartial balance of tribal and ethnic representation in the national government. Leaders of all three principal ethnic groups—Soussou, Malinke, and Foulah—are found in the highest councils of government both at home and in Guinea's diplomatic missions abroad.[16] A similarly liberal spirit has been shown with regard to occupation as a criterion of political recruitment. The modesty of an individual's position in no way impedes his advancement in party ranks, if he has proved himself by personal leadership and by demonstrations of loyalty to the party.

The vigorous pursuit of this policy and the pervasiveness of party life in Guinea have induced a degree of political involvement which is matched in few nations, except, perhaps, in those of the Communist

---

[16] In the National Political Bureau (the party's real power center) members of the Malinke nation, Touré's own ethnic affiliation, are by far in a majority. At the time of writing, the Political Bureau contained eleven Malinke, three Soussou, and one Toma. Only two members are from the Foulah, Guinea's largest single ethnic group (more than 1 million strong).

world. The national government and, more importantly, the party control the country's economy, its educational system, and its health facilities, and instigate any change that comes to Guinea. Thus they dictate the fortunes of the people. For the vast majority, government-cum-party offers virtually the sole hope for advancement. In such circumstances the government and the party tend to elicit an almost total commitment on the part of the individual citizen.

Despite the absolute authority that the state, or, more accurately, the party, exercises over the individual, certain mechanisms written into the party's doctrinal precepts permit dissent to be voiced and protest to be registered. Criticism and autocriticism, as basic concepts in the theory of democratic centralism, fulfill an important function. The PDG maintains that the traditionally communal nature of African society has aided enormously in the transition from a comparatively underdeveloped and mutually antagonistic society to a united, highly disciplined, and articulate body politic. Collective action is relied upon as the principal instrument for the achievement of the goals of this new society. The transition has been further eased by the fact that the party itself has acted as the main agent of change in the social system. This circumstance has given to its actions, and to the attempts at modernization carried out by the national government in its name, a sanction they would not possess if they were evoked solely by external pressures. Transcending old loyalties rooted deeply in tribe, region, or ethnic group, the party has tried, and to an impressive extent has succeeded, not in replacing these loyalties, but in superimposing upon them a more inclusive loyalty to the nation and to the party, a loyalty that has come to signify to the average Guinean citizen something new and hopeful in his political experience.

INTERNAL PARTY ORGANIZATION[17]

The PDG may be compared in general form to the Communist Party of the Soviet Union, with which it shares many organizational characteristics. A highly centralized, vertically structured party (see accompanying chart), it has six distinct levels of organization, each engaged in the performance of clearly defined functions. As in the Soviet Union, each level is accountable mainly to the level of authority immediately above it, although in the performance of its functions each level enjoys considerable autonomy. Each party unit has a dual responsibility:

---

[17] Statutes of the PDG-RDA, adopted in congress on June 14, 1947, and subsequently modified by the party's Third Congress at Conakry, Jan. 23–26, 1958; the Fourth Congress, June 2–4, 1958; Extraordinary National Congress of the PDG, Sept. 14, 1958; and the Fifth National Congress of the PDG-RDA, Sept. 14–17, 1959. See also "Statuts du PDG-RDA," in Sékou Touré, *La Lutte du Parti Démocratique de Guinée pour l'émancipation africaine,* IV (2d ed.; Conakry, [1960?]), 201–210.

to the organization that elected it, and to its immediate superior. All members of the party and all subordinate organizations are required to subscribe to party discipline and to implement the decisions taken by the party's directing organs. All elected officers, whatever their functions, are responsible to the directing organs of the party, and are pledged to

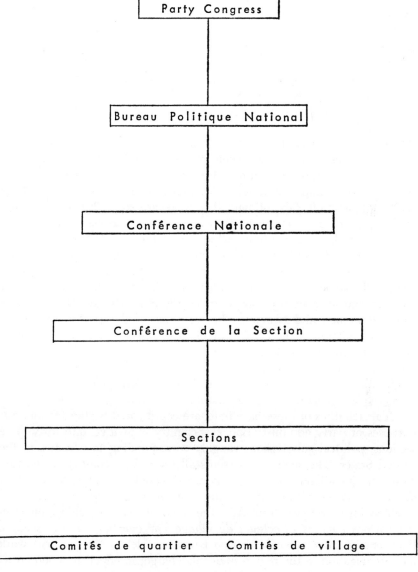

Organization of the Parti Démocratique de Guinée

conform to the policies adopted by its congress and to the general principles of discipline imposed upon all members. Elected officials must render to their electors periodic accounts of their mandates.

In theory, the party is democratically controlled. Each level of authority is elected by popular will, freely expressed by means of indirect universal suffrage exercised through elected delegates at sectional and regional conferences and at national congresses of the party. The decisions of each party organism, which are made by a majority of the members present, are not valid unless at least half of its organizations are represented. Communication within the party is a two-way process, from the summit to the base and from the base to the summit. Policy initiation tends to occur only by the former process. Policy modification, however, may result from pressures exerted from below.

The basic unit of party organization is the urban comité de quartier (neighborhood cell) or the rural comité de village (village cell). These are the most immediate symbols of party control with which the individual comes into contact. Their primary function is to organize the population, guarantee its support for party policies, and coördinate its efforts for their implementation. Although reliable statistics are not yet available, party officials estimate that there are some 25,000 such units in Guinea, each one comprising anywhere from a mere handful to several hundred members, depending on the size of the community.

Directing the actions of the comité de village is a group known as the *comité directeur*. It consists of ten persons: the chief or mayor of the village who is automatically a member, and nine other persons elected by popular vote for a term of one year. Of the nine who are elected, three must be women and two must be members of the JRDA. Except by special permission of the comité directeur of the *section*, the next higher unit in the Guinean party structure, only those persons with three years' experience as party militants are eligible for election to the village comité directeur. The local comité (whether of quartier or village) elects its own president.

The activities of these base units are coördinated by the section. For purposes of party administration, the country is divided into forty-three sections, political subdivisions roughly corresponding to counties in the United States. The section represents all the village committees located within its jurisdiction. Its activities are directed by a *comité directeur de la section*, consisting of seventeen members elected by a sectional congress for a two-year term from the ranks of persons holding office in the various *comités directeurs de village* (or *quartier*) in the section. Each comité directeur of a section is responsible for the political work and organization in the region under its charge; in effect, it functions as a local political bureau at the sectional level. This responsibility is determined by the unit immediately superior to it.

The party organism immediately above the section is the *conférence de la section*. It meets, in theory, twice a year, and includes the members of the comité directeur of the section and three delegates from each comité de quartier or comité de village. These three are the comité's president, the local women's head, and a representative of the youth of the community.

In addition to the conférence de la section, there is a *conférence régionale* which meets twice a year to discuss the implementation of party policy at the sectional level. The conférence régionale brings together the comités directeurs of the sections that make up the *région administrative*, members of the *conférence nationale* who reside in the region, three representatives from each comité de village in the region, regional commandants and heads of administrative posts, general councilors, presidents and directors of national coöperatives, heads of regional labor organizations, chiefs of the local services, and the commander of the local military camp.

The next level in the party hierarchy is the conférence nationale. Meeting twice a year, it comprises the members of the National Political Bureau; four delegates from each section, including the secretary-general and the political secretary; one woman representative; and one member from the section's youth group. Other persons who may attend the conférence nationale but whose presence is not mandatory are members of the national government; deputies to the National Assembly; commandants of régions administratives; presidents of general councils; village mayors; ambassadors of the Republic of Guinea; the commandant of the Guinean army; the head of the national labor organization, the Union Syndicale des Travailleurs de Guinée (USTG); the secretary-general of the National Council of the JRDA; the head of the Economic Chamber; and any other person or persons whose presence may be deemed desirable by the National Political Bureau. The principal function of the conférence nationale is to discuss methods for executing on a national scale the programs of the party in accordance with objectives adopted at party congresses. The conférence nationale also performs the very important duty of selecting the members of the National Political Bureau.

The National Political Bureau (Bureau Politique National) reposes at the top of the party hierarchy. Although nominally below the party congress and subordinate to it, it in fact functions as the policy-formulating, decision-making center of Guinean politics. As originally organized, the Political Bureau consisted of seventeen members elected by the conférence nationale for a term of three years. At the party's Sixth Congress (held in Conakry December 27–30, 1962) the seventeen original incumbents were reëlected to office. Their mandate was extended from three to five years. Although leaving the Political Bureau's outward composition intact, however, the congress altered its inner structure by agreeing to name Sékou Touré, his half-brother Ismael Touré, and a handful of others as permanent members of the group. These permanent members of the National Political Bureau now constitute the uppermost level of political authority in the country, and as such function as the country's chief holders of power.

As a group, the Political Bureau acts as the nerve center of Guinean politics. It formulates policy in keeping with the broad objectives of the party, and initiates proposals for specific programs of action which are transmitted down through the sections to the village level, where they are discussed by the mass membership before being sent back to the Political Bureau for final decision. The bureau directs the political activity of the party, organizes the work to be undertaken in the party's name, and orients and controls the activities of the elected officials and the press of its various agencies. Usually meeting once a month, the Political Bureau may be convened in extraordinary session upon the order of the secretary-general, or at the request of the permanent secretary.

According to Guinean ideology, the ultimate source of authority is the party congress. Originally, the party congress was required by statute to meet every three years. After the Sixth Party Congress, however, this formula was altered. Henceforward the congress is to be convened in regular session only once every five years. Other procedural statutes remain essentially the same. The party congress may also be convoked in extraordinary session on the initiative of the National Political Bureau or at the request of more than half of the sections. The notice of convocation, listing the agenda, is made public at least a month in advance of the meeting of the congress. Each section is represented by a maximum of ten delegates, among whom must be representatives of women's and youth groups. Each section has one vote.

According to Article 20 of the statutes of the PDG-RDA, the party congress "determines the political line of the party and the objectives to be attained in the period following its meeting." It also pronounces upon all political and organizational questions, and upon modifications of party statutes. It enjoys unlimited jurisdiction. In the interim between congresses, party decisions are made by the conférence nationale.

These two reforms in the party statutes—the creation of a core of permanent members in the Political Bureau and the lengthening of intervals between party congresses—reflect a shift in the power base within the PDG. At the expense of the other members of the National Political Bureau and the rank and file, they greatly strengthen President Touré's authority over the party and assure him a virtually dictatorial role in national affairs.

FINANCIAL SOURCES AND CONTROLS

Party finances derive from four principal sources: annual dues collected at a rate determined by the party congress; donations; gifts and legacies; and proceeds of party-sponsored events and activities. Funds are collected and managed by the directing body or official of each echelon. An accounting commission of the party may have access to the funds and the records of any echelon or unit at any time. Local treasurers and other directing officers are personally responsible for funds committed to their trust, and the party reserves the right to institute judicial proceedings against anyone suspected of mishandling funds entrusted to his care.

THE PDG AND THE NATIONAL GOVERNMENT

The relationship between the PDG and the national government in Guinea is more implicit than explicit. According to the nation's constitution, national sovereignty resides in the electorate, which exercises it through deputies elected by universal suffrage to the unicameral legislature, the National Assembly. Nowhere does the constitution refer to the party. Yet the party rather than the government is supreme in the political system. The constitutional organs of government, parliament and the council of ministers, occupy a subordinate position in the process of policy formulation. As previously noted, the real center of Guinean politics is the seventeen-member National Political Bureau of the PDG.

The preëminence accorded the party over the government is predicated on the view that the party is the crux of national unity. In its ranks the diverse ethnic elements of Guinean society come together to discuss, forge, and implement policy for the common good. Because the party organization is so pervasive, and impinges to so extraordinary an extent upon the daily activities of Guinean life, the party is a much more immediate reality to most people than the relatively remote national government in Conakry. As the champion of Guinean independence, the PDG enjoys a virtually unassailable position. At a time when other political parties talked of remaining within the framework of the newly reorganized French Community, the PDG campaigned for outright independence. Further, it has had exclusive control of the conduct of national affairs since its absorption of the opposition parties.

In contrast to the situation in many single-party states, where there is a power struggle (actual or potential) between party and government, in Guinea these two entities are reciprocally reinforcing rather than antagonistic. Each is conceived of, not as a check or balance to the other, but as a complement without which the nation could not be governed. This close relationship between party and government is deliberate. Through the initiative of its National Political Bureau and the discussion and the consent of the rank and file, the party determines national policy. The government is then entrusted with its execution. As the sole avenue of political advancement, the party exercises complete and absolute control over the fortunes of its members, thereby ensuring undeviating adherence to party policy.

The duality of political control is manifest at every level of political organization. The overlapping and interrelated systems of authority between party and government reinforce rather than threaten each other, as individuals holding positions of prominence in one invariably enjoy eminence in the other. The president of the Republic, Sékou Touré, is also secretary-general of the party. The vice-president of the Republic, and *ipso facto* president of the National Assembly, El Hadj Saifoulaye Diallo, is political secretary of the party. At different levels of political organization, party leaders are frequently tied to the government in an official capacity, as deputies to the National Assembly, as members of governmental commissions, or as members of other public bodies. Regional commanders, although they do not vote, attend meetings of the comités directeurs of the sections; presidents of village councils, leaders of municipal districts, and other civil employees keep in constant touch and work in close collaboration with party officials in their areas; members of the JRDA serve as active members of village councils.

DEMOCRATIC CENTRALISM IN GUINEA

The philosophical basis of politics in Guinea, as explained by Guinean leaders themselves,[18] is the theory of democratic centralism. The democratic aspect of this is the two-way communication, from narrow party summit to broad popular base and back again. Ideas are submitted by the National Political Bureau to the nation, descending the political hierarchy, echelon by echelon, until they reach the comité de quartier or the comité de village. The comité proposes the ideas to the inhabitants of the locality, whose opinion it then transmits back up the line to the National Political Bureau at the top of the whole structure. Apologists of the regime make much of the fact that no policy decision is made until this process of consultation has been allowed to function.[19]

---

[18] "Les Principes du centralisme démocratique," in Touré, *L'Action politique du Parti Démocratique de Guinée pour l'émancipation africaine,* III (Conakry, [1960]), 454.

[19] The broad consensus among Guineans in identifying the problems that confront their nation is, no doubt, a basic reason for the effectiveness of the system. It is not unnatural that, in so small a country, where so much remains to be accomplished, there should be a high degree of unanimity on such matters. This unanimity on

As formulated by Sékou Touré, the Guinean concept of democratic centralism is embodied in three main principles:

(1) Party leaders are directly and democratically chosen by the supporters, who all enjoy full liberty of conscience and of expression within the Party;

(2) The affairs of the State of Guinea are the affairs of all the citizens of Guinea. The programme of the Party is democratically discussed. As long as no decision has been made, each is free to say what he thinks or what he wishes. But when, after extensive discussions in congress or in assembly, a decision has been arrived at by a unanimous vote or by a majority, the supporters and leaders are bound to apply it correctly;

(3) The responsibility for leadership is not shared. Only the responsibility for a decision is shared. Thus, no breach of discipline can be permitted.[20]

The nation shares in the determination of broad policy objectives when party militants, exercising their democratic liberty, meet to define national problems and to recommend solutions. The party leadership, however, reserves the right to decide how these solutions may be effected in the practical circumstances of time, place, and the best available means.

Democratic centralism has enjoyed marked success in Guinea, owing to the flexibility it has shown in adapting itself to an African social system already communal in nature and possessing a long tradition of obedience to autocratic structures of authority. The dual character and the interrelationship of political control in Guinea—control by party and government and the absence of organized opposition—lend to the system a stability whose results in social progress and international prestige have become the envy of other recently independent states. The view once held in many parts of Africa that only a pluralistic society—one in which all political attitudes are given free expression and an individual may follow his own convictions—could achieve real social and political justice is fast declining. Political leaders are perceiving the short-term advantages likely to accrue to them from concerted action by a single-party system firmly directed from the top.

---

fundamentals makes for a minimum of friction within the political system itself. In like manner, a very large majority of the people evidently acquiesce in leaving it to the National Political Bureau to determine the solution to the problems and the specific means to be used therein. Having assumed this responsibility at the outset, the bureau exercises it indefatigably and guards it closely, always asserting that it rests upon the free consent of the Guinean people: "Au niveau d'un Comité de quartier, d'une Section du PDG et à celui de la Nation, cette dictature est acceptée. La discipline dans l'union des enfants du pays est un fait librement consenti" ("La Dictature populaire et la Pratique démocratique," *ibid.*, p. 323).

[20] "Les Principes du Centralisme démocratique," in *ibid.*, pp. 454–455. For the English version here quoted, see Sékou Touré, *Toward Full Re-Africanisation: Policy and Principles of the Guinea Democratic Party* (Paris: Présence Africaine, 1959), p. 91.

THE PDG AND ORGANIZED LABOR

The relationship between labor and politics in independent Guinea is an intimate one. This derives in part from the labor-union background of Sékou Touré, and from the active role played by the Union Générale des Travailleurs d'Afrique Noire (UGTAN), an amalgamation of the principal labor organizations in the country, in the achievement of Guinea's independence. From its inception at the Cotonou Conference in January, 1957, the UGTAN openly opposed colonialism and the exploitation of the African masses by European capitalist interests. Proclaiming itself the only organization truly representing the interests of African workers, it sought to organize them into a single union, independent of, although not opposed to, metropolitan labor organizations. The UGTAN early became a rallying point for other anticolonial elements in Guinea.[21] In the weeks immediately preceding the referendum, the organized efforts of the USTG, the Guinean section of the UGTAN, contributed importantly to the outcome of the vote.

As the PDG consolidated its control in independent Guinea, so too did the UGTAN, now the sole labor organization in the country. The ties binding Guinean labor to politics have grown steadily stronger, especially since Mamady Kaba, secretary-general of the USTG, was appointed to the National Political Bureau of the party. Through its intimate connection with the PDG, labor has moved into the decision-making area of politics. It now exercises a far more influential role in the direction of national policy than it ever did under the earlier system of fragmented, mutually antagonistic labor organizations.

Working intimately with the party, labor has come to be regarded as "an arm of the revolution"; it is an indispensable participant in planning social and economic reforms. So completely have its objectives become identified with those of party and state that they no longer seem to be uniquely labor's. It is questionable whether or not the labor movement in Guinea will again be able to act on its own volition and in the sole interest of its members, independent of party control.

THE PARTY AND THE INTELLECTUAL

The PDG's straightforward and uniformly sympathetic view of labor is in sharp contrast with its ambivalent attitude toward Guinean intellectuals. Acknowledged as an element essential to the direction of government, the intellectual has been the target of the party's displeasure

[21] Résolution sur le programme revendicatif," Conférence Syndicale Africaine, Cotonou (Dahomey), 16–19 janvier 1957. See also Alioune Cissé, "L'U.G.T.A.N. face à la Loi-Cadre," in *Unité, Mouvement Syndical Africain, revue U.G.T.A.N.* (Casablanca: Imprimerie de l'Union Marocaine du Travail, [1958?]), pp. 12–13, and "Conférence du 29–30 juin à Dakar sur la Loi-Cadre," in *ibid.*, pp. 11–12.

whenever his independent thought has run counter to the party line.

Guinea's decision on the referendum of 1958 understandably stirred up sympathy among students and intellectuals in many parts of Africa. Her leaders won the grudging admiration even of those intellectuals of the community who themselves had voted to cast their lot with France. For some time, no doubt, it will be an academic question whether or not the Guinean option is to be explained by the differing attraction of Gallic political institutions for men like Houphouet-Boigny and Sékou Touré. Their different views may also have arisen from profoundly opposed concepts of the role of the colonies vis-à-vis the métropole. There seems to be little reason, however, to doubt the substantial support that Touré received for his decision from West Africa's intelligentsia.

As the symbol of the new unity, of the new revolutionary force whose declared goal is the emancipation of all Africa, the PDG has become for many intellectuals in Guinea the incarnation of ideals that were unattainable under colonialism.[22] Their commitment to the party, to its values and methods as well as to its policies, is explained in part by this attitude. Their commitment also derives from the fact that the party, as the supreme authority in the nation, is also, in effect, almost the sole repository, and therefore the sole dispenser, of favors and rewards. It is the one hope for advancement within the system over which it reigns. So pervasive has its authority become, so immediate its presence in all phases of Guinean life, that existence outside its influence is virtually unthinkable.

The dominance of the party over the intellectual is further reinforced by the doctrines to which the intellectual must subscribe as a party member. The principles of democratic centralism, the philosophy of the PDG, do provide for free discussion of potential policy alternatives. But the efficacy of the intellectual in his role as critic is severely compromised by the compliance required of him by the second phase of democratic centralism. Once a policy has been adopted by a majority of the party militants, the intellectual must support it, however much he may disagree with it.

The unique responsibility that has been thrust upon the intellectual in Guinea has made of him something quite different from his counterpart in other countries. In contrast with the intellectual in many areas of Africa (as well as in Europe), where the new university graduate feels himself underutilized and often assumes the unconstructive role of

---

[22] This situation is like that in other underdeveloped nations where the intellectual, as the vanguard of social and political revolution, has become totally committed, intellectually as well as politically, to the cause he has espoused and which he can no longer abandon. For a discussion of the problem see Edward Shils, "The Intellectuals in the Political Development of the New States," *World Politics,* **XII** (April, 1960), 329–368.

nihilist in relation to society, the educated Guinean is actively caught up in a project he regards as historically momentous—the creation of a modern African state.[23] By thus structuring the national task, Touré has sought to integrate the intellectual into the government and the nationalist movement. It is Touré's hope that the Guinean intellectual will think of himself as a pioneering researcher, eager to rediscover a history and a cultural tradition which were ignored by a contemptuous colonial world.

It is too soon to assess the social and political implications for the future of the Guinean government's crash program of sending large numbers of Guinean students abroad to receive their education. The sending of students to institutions of higher learning both in the West and in Communist countries may create problems. Students going abroad will encounter a wide range of social and political systems. Each student will be impressed either positively or negatively by his experience and his observations. To what extent these differences in training and association will affect the ability of Guinea's future policy makers to achieve consensus is a matter of conjecture. Eventually a political pluralism of a type at present condemned and discouraged by the national party could develop in Guinea.

At present there is evidence of a growing dissatisfaction with the tight controls the party has imposed on the nation's budding intelligentsia. The antigovernment student demonstrations that occurred in Conakry and Labé in November, 1961, after the arrest and trial of five prominent intellectuals on charges of subversion, revealed a restiveness, of which few people had been aware, among certain elements of the nation's youth. Although Touré still enjoys great prestige among his people, his image was somewhat tarnished by the repressive measures he took to quell the student disturbances. Unless he is able again to elicit strong loyalty from the members of the expanding intelligentsia, or, failing that, is able to cow them sufficiently, he may eventually find among them the greatest challenge to his authority.

THE PDG AND TRADITIONAL CHIEFS

As in other areas of French West Africa, conflict between the traditional chiefs and the rapidly developing educated urban classes increased after World War II. The institution of chieftaincy in Guinea, weakened by the onslaught of a century of ambiguous French colonial policy, collapsed quickly when attacked on the eve of independence by reform-minded colonial administrators under the leadership of Governor Jean Ramadier, and by modern political leaders like Sékou Touré.

---

[23] The fact that the vast majority of the newly educated will almost certainly be absorbed into the governmental apparatus as teachers, doctors, administrators, or technicians will, in all likelihood, reinforce even further the commitment of the Guinean intelligentsia to the political system under which they live.

Despite its long tradition, chieftaincy broke down once it had become purposeless in the eyes of the French and obstructive in the eyes of the Guineans. For the French, the inadequacies of the system arose principally from the difficulty of applying it. Formerly, chiefs had been important agents of the colonial administration, particularly in the collection of taxes, the dispensing of justice, and the administration of local affairs. Their usefulness diminished, however, as the system itself began to pose vexing problems for the colonial government. It was frequently difficult to decide whether those with a traditional claim or those elected by their tribes should be recognized as chiefs. The compensation to be offered the several grades of chiefs in view of the services they performed and their varying responsibilities posed delicate problems. Complicated legal questions were involved in determining what protection should be afforded chiefs in civil suits, an issue never fully resolved by the territorial assemblies or by the National Assembly in Paris.

In Guinea, the problem of the chiefs was brought to the fore with the enactment of the Loi-Cadre in June, 1956. Although the law tended to shift political power from urban centers to rural areas, where the authority of the chiefs remained fairly intact, its over-all effect was to undermine their position. Accompanying the Loi-Cadre was a provision for the reorganization of the civil service. Functions formerly exercised by the chiefs were taken over by appointees of the administration. Centrifugal pressures, too, emanated from such groups within the territory as veterans' and students' organizations, and from educated city dwellers. Persons in all these categories were less and less willing to show deference to an institution that had become discredited in their eyes. They blamed its tradition-bound conservatism for obstructing the achievement of the goals that extratribal experience had taught them were both desirable and attainable. Moreover, with the increase in political activity resulting from the reforms of the Loi-Cadre, the PDG and other parties mobilized their members against the chiefs. In the system personified by the chiefs, the parties saw a grave obstacle to their own efforts to form a united party base, irrespective of regional, ethnic, or tribal loyalties.

As the problem of the chiefs was debated in Guinea,[24] the point at issue was not the abolition of the institution of chieftaincy; on this there was agreement. The problem was rather how, and how quickly, chieftaincy could be done away with. Both Governor Ramadier and his subordinates, as well as the Conseil de Gouvernement (made up mostly of PDG members), recognized that many of the 247 cantons in Guinea were ruled by capable and highly respected chiefs. It was decided to use

---

[24] For an account of the discussion between French colonial officials and Touré and other African members of the Guinean Territorial Assembly regarding the problem of the chiefs, see "Conférence des Commandants de cercle de la Guinée," in Sékou Touré, *Prélude à l'Indépendance* (Paris: Présence Africaine, 1959).

the experience and the authority of these men in some new capacity, perhaps as government functionaries. Each chief was accordingly considered on an individual basis, and his qualities and capabilities were evaluated in terms of previous performance. Those who were too old, or were deemed lacking in the essential qualities of leadership, were pensioned off; others were not reappointed when their terms expired.

The chiefs no longer present a serious problem in Guinea.[25] For the most part they have been replaced by village councils, each council presided over by a democratically elected president with the title of mayor. The village council is directly accountable to the administrative region which has replaced the former *cercle*. In an effort to break down the regional, ethnic, and language barriers that formerly divided the people, and to create, instead, a genuinely national unity among the diverse Guinean peoples, the government has followed a calculated policy of appointing as regional administrators (*commandants de régions*) persons alien to the particular areas over which they exercise jurisdiction.

This policy has proved advantageous in several ways. By deliberately putting in command of a region an official alien to the people under his charge, it has forced on the citizenry an acknowledgment of the authority of the national government. A large majority of the appointees have proved themselves sympathetic and understanding leaders as well as capable administrators. As a result, much of the suspicion and fear that ethnic groups formerly exhibited toward persons outside the group has been dissipated. A further advantage of this policy has been that the dispersion of leaders to areas alien to their own affinities and tribal loyalties has discouraged favoritism. It has prevented the possible crystallization of power around a person whose position of authority, reinforced by the loyalties of the tribe or the region under his command, might conceivably pose a threat to the party or to the government.

GOALS AND VALUES OF THE PDG

The PDG's broad objectives, proclaimed by Sékou Touré at the Fourth Party Congress in Conakry, June 5–8, 1958, are (1) the creation of a government by the people and for the people; (2) equal rights for women; (3) decolonization of the country; (4) democratization of all public organisms; (5) independence and unity for Guinea and Africa; and (6) assertion of the African personality.[26] Through the party, the

---

[25] So successful was the party's campaign against the chiefs that Sékou Touré was justified in exclaiming, early in January, 1958: "Oui! Le bastion de la féodalité indigène est tombé. La chefferie est supprimée à compter du 1er janvier 1958 et avec elle, ont disparu tous les abus dont elle se rendait coupable vis-à-vis des populations rurales" ("Les Assises du Parti Démocratique de Guinée. Bilan et conclusions," in Touré, *L'Action politique du Parti Démocratique*, I, 34).

[26] "IVe Congrès du Parti Démocratique de Guinée, Conakry, 5–8 juin, 1958,"

government has undertaken an ambitious program of social and economic development in Guinea, while abroad it has pursued an aggressive foreign policy based on two main objectives: the promotion of African unity and the maintenance of neutral status and noninvolvement in the power struggle between East and West.

Long-range domestic goals were announced at a national conference of the party held in Kankan on April 2–5, 1960.[27] At that time Guinea embarked on an ambitious three-year plan, designed to hasten its industrialization, expand its exports, and increase its educational and social facilities. The plan originally called for the expenditure of approximately $40 million, 50 per cent of which was to be devoted to increasing production in mining, light industry, and agriculture; 30 per cent was to be used for public welfare, such as the expansion of educational, health, and medical facilities; and the remaining 20 per cent was earmarked for administrative purposes.

The party took a firm position on the need for modernization and accordingly drafted extensive plans toward this end. Looming high among these was investissement humain, the use of volunteer labor for the construction of roads, schools, dispensaries, and other public works. More than 25 per cent of the national budget was to be allotted to construction and staffing of schools in order to cope with the country's gigantic illiteracy problem.

But Guinea's ambitious economic plans never got off the ground. From the very outset they were handicapped by the fact that the national money established when Guinea withdrew from the franc zone on March 1, 1960, was worthless outside the country. As the government tightened its control over the few private enterprises remaining in the country, most of which were French-owned, conditions grew worse. Foreign investment slowed to a trickle; unemployment became more widespread.

Nor did Guinea's investissement humain program fulfill the high hopes that were held for it. The zealousness and the idealism with which the program began could not be maintained. Frequently the difficulty lay in the fact that initial plans for civic improvements were overly ambitious or poorly conceived; in either event their realization was impossible. Sometimes promised aid from government agencies in Conakry did not appear, thus convincing the hinterland people that the government was not honoring its end of the bargain; often the trouble was

---

in Sékou Touré, *L'Expérience guinéenne et l'Unité africaine* (Paris: Présence Africaine, 1959), p. 43.

[27] *Rapport d'Orientation du Bureau Politique National*, Parti Démocratique de Guinée, Conférence Nationale (de planification économique), Kankan, les 2, 3, 4, et 5 avril 1960 (Conakry, 1960).

nothing more or less than Guinea's hot sun, which scorches the earth and makes protracted labor out of doors almost impossible.

Adding to the country's woes was the fact that the government frequently misused the resources it did have. Rather than putting available funds and matériel into productive enterprises which would have created permanent employment for people, thereby contributing to the national income, the government channeled such resources into the building of showcase projects such as a stadium, a printing plant, and private houses for top party functionaries and members of the ruling elite. The inevitable accompaniment to this mismanagement has been a certain amount of corruption openly practiced at the highest levels of government. Although President Touré has on many occasions spoken out against such corruption, he has done relatively little to put a stop to it. How long Guinea will be able to continue in its present state is open to conjecture. Although new accords were signed with France in May, 1963, settling certain outstanding financial problems, Guinea to date has shown no intention of reëntering the franc zone or of radically modifying her present monetary program.

The prestige enjoyed by President Touré both at home and abroad has won respectful consideration for his neutrality in the East-West struggle, and has made it seem a more viable policy than many of his critics had thought it. His decision to vote "No" in the 1958 referendum established his party as unequivocally opposed to the retention of colonial ties in any form. He himself was endowed with indisputable authority as an exponent of African nationalism and a champion of independence movements.

The nature of one-party rule in Guinea, the absence of any organized opposition, the extent and the type of aid received from countries of the Eastern bloc, and the truculence Sékou Touré has often displayed toward the West, particularly toward France, have given rise to many reports of his alleged Communist orientation and even of Communist domination of his country. Such appraisals have frequently rested on fragmentary or even hearsay evidence. They have often failed to take into account the peculiarities of the African cultural, political, and social milieu. They have not recognized to what extent patterns of traditional authority have determined the development of systems of control in Guinea and in other new African states. It has been difficult for the West, with its profoundly different traditions, to appreciate the communal patterns and the control structures which have emerged in Africa, and to comprehend their meaning and relevance to the African scene. Moreover, in Guinea, where certain factors such as the nature of the party structure, the common adherence to the principles of democratic centralism, the devotion to a state-controlled economy, and the absence of an organized opposition are ostensibly shared with nations of the Eastern bloc, a careful effort must be made to discover the nuances that, however subtle, distinguish Sékou Touré's African nationalism from Soviet Communism.

6. MALI

*By Thomas Hodgkin
and Ruth Schachter Morgenthau*

The party system in Mali* has several particularly interesting characteristics. First, the evidence for the influence of precolonial political
structures and ideas on modern forms of organization is reasonably clear.
Second, Mali is a state where a relatively well-developed two-party system, operating during the later stages of the colonial period, from 1946
to 1959, gave way, at about the time of independence, to a one-party
system. Hence an account of the evolution of the system should throw
some light both on the factors contributing to interparty conflict, and on
those tending to promote the rise of one-party states.[1] Third, the Union
Soudanaise deserves close study through the whole period of its history,
from 1946 to the present. Aspects to be considered include its internal
organization; its relations with the interterritorial parties of which it successively formed a part—the Rassemblement Démocratique Africain
(RDA), from 1946 to 1958, and the Parti de la Fédération Africaine

---

* Certain problems of nomenclature arise here. The term "Mali," or "modern
Mali," is used in this essay to refer to the independent Republic of Mali, established
on September 22, 1960. For periods before that date the antecedent state, or territory, is normally referred to as "Soudan." But we have not attempted to be entirely
consistent in regard to the use of these two terms. When we are referring, not to
the existing Mali Republic, but to the short-lived Federation of Mali (including
Soudan and Senegal) which functioned from January 17, 1959, until August 20,
1960, or to the medieval state of Mali, the distinction is, we hope, made clear in the
context. The term "Soudan," referring to the territory officially known as "Soudan
Français" during the colonial period, must, of course, be distinguished both from
"the Sudan" (the term traditionally used to refer to "the country of the Negroes,"
"the whole savanna belt of sub-Saharan Africa, stretching from the Atlantic to the
Red Sea") and from "the Republic of the Sudan" (the state formerly known as the
Anglo-Egyptian Sudan, which acquired its independence in 1955).

For the material contained in this essay we owe most to the many *maliens* and
maliennes who have over the past years given us all possible help toward the understanding of their party system in its historical and social context. We have also
learned much from discussions with Joseph Ki Zerbo, professor of history at the
Cours Normale, Wagadugu, Upper Volta, and visiting professor at the Institute of
African Studies, University of Ghana.

[1] From a comparative standpoint, L. Gray Cowan, "Guinea," in Gwendolen
Carter, ed., *African One-Party States* (Ithaca: Cornell University Press, 1962), is of
particular interest.

216

(PFA), from 1959 to 1960;[2] its connections with the machinery of government and administration; and, perhaps above all, its ideas. The Union Soudanaise has been particularly concerned with questions of theory and its application to the practical problems of, first, the anticolonial struggle and, later, government, economic planning, and external relations.

BACKGROUND

The Mali Republic extends over an area of about 470,000 square miles, and has a population estimated at about 4.2 million. Its northern frontier stretches deep into the Sahara. At its southern limits the desert gradually gives place to the Sahel. Farther south still is savanna country, the region of the Upper Niger, where the bulk of Mali's population is concentrated. About half the population consists of Malinke, Bambara, Dioula, and Khassonke, closely related peoples speaking variants of the Malinke language (which is used and understood by a much larger section). In addition, Mali includes about 280,000 Sarakolle, 230,000 Songhai (in the region of the Niger bend), 370,000 Senufo (toward the frontier with the Ivory Coast), 200,000 Dogon, 120,000 Sorko (or Bozo) and Somono (fishing peoples living beside the Niger and Bani rivers), 750,000 Fulani (widely distributed through the Sahel and the savanna), as well as about 350,000 Tuareg, Moors, and Arabs (nomadic peoples living in desert and near-desert areas). About two-thirds of the population are Muslims. Most of the remainder practice some form of animism, but here, as elsewhere, the border line between Islam and animism is not clearcut. Apart from the northern nomads and a relatively small urban population (Bamako, with 120,000, is the only large town by modern standards), most of the people are peasants, living in villages, occupied in farming and stock raising, in traditional crafts and small-scale commerce. The only major economic development carried through during the colonial period was irrigation for the production of rice and cotton, based on the Sansanding Dam on the Niger. Mali's exports are entirely agricultural (in the wide sense), consisting mainly of groundnuts, cattle and sheep, dried fish, millet, rice, and some cotton. The average per capita

---

[2] In attempting to examine the history, organization, and ideas of the Union Soudanaise in partial abstraction from the history of its parent party, the RDA, one is open to the criticism of omitting a great deal of relevant material. Similarly, aspects of the political history of Soudan are discussed or referred to here in isolation from the wider history of the former French West African Federation (AOF), and from the processes of constitutional change affecting the whole of *Afrique Noire,* a knowledge of which is to some extent assumed in the text. This kind of abstraction inevitably involves a certain distortion. The larger theme of the history and the structure of the RDA in its French West African context is dealt with in Ruth Schachter Morgenthau, *Political Parties in French-speaking West Africa* (Oxford: Clarendon Press, 1964); various accounts of the constitutional-historical background are presently available (see nn. 1, 25, 28, 29).

income, estimated at about $52 a year,[3] is extremely low, even by African standards.

For present purposes it may be convenient to consider the history of Soudan-Mali as falling into four main phases:

1) *Before 1898.*—The precolonial period, characterized by the existence of independent African states, with their own specific forms of political organization.

2) *From 1898 to 1945.*—The period of authoritarian colonial rule, during which political power was concentrated, locally, in the hands of the French administrators (governor, *commandants de cercle,* and *commandants de subdivision*), responsible ultimately to the government of France, and African political initiative, insofar as it existed, was expressed through protonationalist forms of organization.

3) *From 1945 to 1960.*—The period of limited colonial rule, during which Africans enjoyed certain civil and political liberties, including the rights of association and of representation at various levels (metropolitan, federal, territorial), even though political power remained ultimately in the hands of the French authorities. This made possible the emergence of political parties and of other forms of popular organization. The last two years of this period, from September 28, 1958, the date of President de Gaulle's referendum, to September 22, 1960, when the Republic of Mali came into existence, constitute a transitional phase during which the Federation of Mali was formed and later disintegrated.

4) *From September 22, 1960, to the present.*—The period of Mali's existence as an independent republic, with political power concentrated in the hands of a single dominant party, the Union Soudanaise–RDA.

This essay is naturally concerned primarily with the last two phases, during which parties have played a significant part in the political life of Soudan-Mali. But because any institutions, if they are to be understood, must be studied in their historical context, attention will be paid also to those aspects of the precolonial and early colonial systems which helped to determine the characteristics of modern parties.

Like most modern African states, and indeed to a greater extent than many, the Republic of Mali is in many respects a most unsatisfactory political unit. Its present frontiers have no particular significance beyond the fact that they were eventually so defined by the French colonial government. As a constituent territory of Afrique Occidentale Française (AOF), Soudan Français was established by decree on December 4, 1920. It comprised, in effect, the residue of the much more extensive French colony that had existed since 1904 under the name "Haut-Sénégal-

[3] *Rapport sur le plan quinquennal de développement économique et sociale de la République du Mali, 1961–65,* République du Mali, Ministère du Plan et de l'Economie Rurale, p. 7.

Niger," whose eastern sector (known as "the military territory of Zinder")
was detached in 1911 to form the Territory of Niger, and whose southern
sector was detached in 1919 to form part of the Territory of Upper Volta.[4]
Further amputations and frontier modifications followed. In 1932 Upper
Volta was eliminated as a separate territory and partitioned between the
Ivory Coast and Soudan, partly for reasons of economy, and partly in
response to pressure from French colonists in the Ivory Coast. In 1947
the pre-1932 situation was restored, and the Territory of Upper Volta
was re-created, mainly with a view to weakening the RDA (dominant at
that time in the Ivory Coast) and strengthening the position of the
Mogho Naba and Moshi traditionalists. Political motives have had a
bearing on the revisions of the frontier between Soudan and Mauritania,
including the transfer in July, 1944, of the northern parts of the Nioro
and Nara *cercles*, and the whole of the Nema-Timbedra *subdivisions*,
from Soudan to Mauritania (revised by the Treaty of Kayes of February,
1963).

Hence the history and the institutions of modern Mali cannot be
understood except in relation to the history of adjacent territories—
Mauritania, Algeria, Niger, Senegal, Guinea, Upper Volta, the Ivory
Coast—inhabited by peoples closely associated, in past history and
present culture, with the peoples of Mali. It is only these surviving colonial frontiers that distinguish the Tukulor of Senegal and southern Mauritania, the Tuareg of the Algerian Sahara, the Malinke of Guinea, the
Songhai of Niger, the Senufo of the Ivory Coast, and the Bobo of Upper
Volta from the same peoples in modern Mali. Moreover, the Malinke, the
dominant people of modern Mali who gave their name to the medieval
state, have penetrated as traders into neighboring West African countries
from Senegal to modern Ghana, whereas the Fulani, who have played a
major part in Mali history, are widely dispersed throughout the whole
West African region.

Nonetheless, modern Mali possesses a kind of national identity, as
the heartland of a succession of states and empires based upon the Upper
Niger, occupying varying sectors of the western Sudan, and extending
northward into the western Sahara. From the eighth century, at least, and
probably from a much earlier date, until about 1200, the empire of Ghana
was the dominant power in this western Sudanic region. Ancient Mali,
from which the modern state derives it name, was in existence probably
from the eleventh century, under a dynasty that was converted to Islam
about 1040. But it was not until the middle of the thirteenth century,
under the famous Mansa Sundiata—the semilegendary ruler who con-

---

[4] Georges Spitz, *Soudan Français* (Paris: Editions Maritimes et Coloniales, 1955),
p. 13. The term "Soudan Français" was used as early as 1890 to refer to the region
of the interior under French occupation administered from Kayes.

stantly recurs in the literature and the propaganda of modern Mali—
that ancient Mali established itself as a major power and an effective
successor state to Ghana. During the fourteenth century, under Mansa
Musa and his successors, the Mali empire extended its international connections, particularly with Morocco and Egypt, from which it drew expatriate civil servants and technical assistants. By the beginning of the
fifteenth century Mali's power was much reduced. From the mid-fifteenth
to the end of the sixteenth century the Songhai state, with its capital at
Gao on the Niger bend, under Sonni Ali (1466–1492) and the Askia
dynasty (1493–1591), became dominant throughout the western Sudan,
its authority stretching northward into the Sahara and eastward as far
as the Hausa states.

After the disintegration of the Songhai empire, following the defeat
of its army at the battle of Tondibi by a Moroccan expeditionary force
in 1591, the government of the region became fragmented. During the
seventeenth and eighteenth centuries Timbuktu and the surrounding
area were at first controlled by a succession of pashas of Moroccan, or
partly Moroccan, origin, whose authority later gave way to the political
and spiritual ascendancy of the Kunta Arabs. In the west of the region
the dominant states were the pagan Bambara kingdoms of Segu and
Kaarta. In the late eighteenth and early nineteenth centuries a new wave
of reform movements, under Fulani or Tukulor leadership, sought to
establish model Islamic states in territories controlled (from an orthodox
Muslim point of view) by pagan governments. This impulse led to the
organization of the state of Macina under Ahmadu Bari, known as Shehu
Ahmadu (who ruled from 1810 to 1844), and, a generation later, to the
establishment of the much more extensive empire of al-Hajj 'Umar
(whose period of rule lasted roughly from 1852 until his death in 1864).
Both these systems were of considerable significance, from the standpoint
of their ideas and institutions, for the founders of modern Mali.[5]

Although these successive states did not, of course, include precisely
the same segments of the population, or cover the same area, as modern
Mali—indeed, the authority of fourteenth-century Mali, sixteenth-cen-
tury Gao, and al-Hajj 'Umar's empire at the height of its power extended
in some directions over a much wider area—they were similarly based
upon the Upper Niger. Thus they may be, and by Malians normally
are, regarded as parent states of the modern system. This historically
grounded sense of identity, which Professor Ki Zerbo has called Mali's

[5] For a more detailed account of this period of history, and the main sources
from which it is derived, see J. S. Trimingham, *The History of Islam in the Western
Sudan* (London: Oxford University Press, 1962), chaps. 2, 3, 5. For a criticism of
certain aspects of Trimingham's approach, see Thomas Hodgkin, "Islam: History
and Politics," *Modern African Studies*, I (March, 1963), 91–97.

"tradition étatique," is reinforced by the continuity of certain types of social institutions. Specifically Islamic institutions, such as the hadj, the koranic school, the fast of Ramadan and the basic Islamic festivals, and the Sufi brotherhoods and their leaders, the Marabouts, have come to form a recognized part of the national life, even for those who are not, in any formal sense, Muslims. Other institutions, deeply rooted in Mali society, are Sudanic rather than Islamic in character, particularly such occupationally specialized social groups as blacksmiths, fishermen, butchers, and praise singers (*griots*), which are sometimes referred to as "castes." There is evidence that specialized groups of this kind, subject to special rules and prohibitions (in regard to marriage, for example), and owing definite obligations to the sovereign, existed in fourteenth-century Mali.[6] And although the present Mali government, with its egalitarian attitude, is attempting to eliminate traditional social distinctions, they have survived, in a somewhat modified form, into the modern period.

Thus political parties with a restricted ethnic or local appeal, though they did occasionally emerge in the period 1945–1960, never acquired much significance and tended to be drawn into the orbit of one or another of the major national parties. Given the particular character of Mali history and institutions, the concept of "tribalism" has relatively little use in explaining political oppositions and conflicts. At the same time, Mali's historic function as the cradle of the western Sudanic empires, the close connections of its people with the peoples of neighboring African territories, its tradition of involvement in long-distance trade and cultural relations with North Africa and the Middle East, were all factors tending to prevent the development of a limited territorial nationalism. They help to explain why the Union Soudanaise, of all the sections of the RDA, has been most consistently committed to the ideas of West African federation and "African unity."

PRECOLONIAL INFLUENCES

In what ways were the parties that emerged in Soudan after World War II affected by the ideas and the institutions of the precolonial period? One factor that deserves consideration is the "urban tradition." This tradition was associated particularly with the urban centers that developed, from the eleventh century on, from the international trade linking the western Sudan with the Maghrib and the Mediterranean world by way of the trans-Saharan trade routes, and with the centers of the extractive industries (in particular, gold) in the forest regions, such as

---

[6] See Mahmud al-Kati, *Tarikh al-Fattash*, translated into French by O. Houdas and M. Delafosse, Publications de l'Ecole des Langues Orientales Vivantes (Paris, 1913), pp. 107–113.

Ashanti and Bambuk-Bure, to the south.[7] Cities like Timbuktu, Jenne, Walata, and Gao acquired further significance as centers of Islamic culture and learning because, from the fourteenth century on, and increasingly in the fifteenth and sixteenth centuries, cadis, imams, koranic teachers, and administrators were trained there in the basic Islamic sciences. The term "city" seems applicable to these centers not only because of their size, but also because a substantial bourgeois class, composed of merchants and 'ulama', enjoyed some measure of internal autonomy and expressed sentiments of civic patriotism.[8]

The leadership of the political parties of modern Mali, and particularly of the Union Soudanaise, includes men who were associated with, or at least deeply interested in, this urban tradition. They derived from it a background of Islamic scholarship, training in the use of legal concepts and procedures, habits of keeping records and accounts, administrative skills, an interest in theological and philosophical disputation, and a cosmopolitan outlook. This background remained important during the colonial period despite the partial displacement of Islamic by French forms of education, the decline of the older urban centers, such as Timbuktu, Jenne, and Walata, and the rise of new commercial towns like Bamako and Mopti. The sense of pride in this older form of urban tradition was admirably expressed by Mahamane Alassane Haïdara, a Timbuktuan of Moroccan origin who was formerly a Union Soudanaise senator in the French Parliament and is now president of the Mali National Assembly, at the opening of the new Timbuktu airport on April 15, 1961:

"For her inhabitants, she [Timbuktu] was also the city of cities; to her they devoted a positive cult; and all the rest of the world, in the eyes of her sons, was the land of barbarians.

"Even in our days, we must admit, this feeling of attachment reveals itself spontaneously. When a Timbuctuan makes ready to tear himself away from her holy circle, to go far from her venerable walls with which he has never ceased to commune, he announces in a tone filled with disillusion and regret: 'I betake myself . . . to the bush,' even if he goes to Bamako." [9]

Another related factor contributing to the process of party building has been the existence of the Dioula commercial network which developed along the interior West African trade routes, probably starting in the fourteenth century. This network arose from the Malinke diaspora

---

[7] For a full description of these relationships see Ivor Wilks, *The Northern Factor in Ashanti History*, University of Ghana, Institute of African Studies (1961).

[8] Mahmud al-Kati, *op. cit.*, states that a survey of Gao in 1585 revealed the existence of 7,626 family compounds, which might imply a total population of 50,000 to 60,000. For evidence of civic patriotism see *ibid.*, and other works of the Timbuktu school.

[9] Quoted in Morgenthau, *op. cit.*, pp. 262–263.

(indeed, the terms "Dyula" and "Wangara" are normally used to refer to the Malinke of the diaspora). Malinke commercial colonies, which were at the same time secondary centers of Islamic culture and influence, were established deep in the Sudanic hinterland (now included in Guinea, northern Ivory Coast, Upper Volta, and northern Ghana). Towns such as Kankan, Odienné, Beyla, Bobo-Dioulasso, Kong, Bouna, Bego, and Wa were outposts where the Dioula built mosques in the Sudanic style, developed centers of Islamic studies, and at times acquired political ascendancy.[10] During the anticolonial struggle from 1946 to 1958, the Dioula undoubtedly made an important contribution to the building up of the RDA, not merely in Mali, but throughout Afrique Occidentale Française. As a community they possessed certain obvious advantages: economic and religious status; contact over a wide area with such artisan classes as butchers, woodcutters, blacksmiths, tailors, cobblers, jewelers, and the like; a certain radicalism of political outlook, frequently involving opposition to European commercial policies and interests; and the cosmopolitan attitude associated with their interterritorial form of organization. These were assets on which the RDA was able to draw so long as it functioned as an interterritorial organization. With the breakup of the French West African Federation—and of the interterritorial RDA—after 1958, and the realization of formal independence by its constituent territories, as well as the growth of ethnocentric attitudes in some of them, the political influence of the Dioula has tended to decline.[11]

We have already suggested that the political structure of the Union Soudanaise, and of Mali under Union Soudanaise rule, owes something to the Islamic reform movements of the nineteenth century. Essentially these seem to have been movements led by alienated intellectuals who seized political power as a means of reëstablishing the authority of an Islamic state in a region of the Muslim world which had been temporarily lost to pagan control. Shehu Ahmadu took the title of *amir al-mu'minin* and conceived himself as the twelfth imam, successor to Muhammad Askia, ruler of Gao in the late fifteenth century; the institutions of the state that he established were deliberately based on the Islamic model. In a modified form these institutions survived al-Hajj 'Umar's conquest and the subsequent period of civil and international war, ending with the defeat of Ahmadu Shehu, al-Hajj 'Umar's son and successor, by the French in 1893, and the destruction of the state.

The principle of collective leadership, to which the Union Soudanaise has attached particular importance, seems to have been well developed in Macina, at least in its earlier period. According to Amadou

---

[10] On the Malinke diaspora see Trimingham, *op. cit.*, pp. 186–189.

[11] The part played by the Dioula in the political history of West Africa is presently being studied in detail by Ruth Schachter Morgenthau.

Hampaté Bâ, ultimate authority in the state lay not with Shehu Ahmadu personally, but with the Great Council, or Council of Forty, and the Inner Council of Three, consisting of Shehu Ahmadu himself and two especially trusted members of the Council of Forty who were constantly with him. The Great Council was composed of *'ulama'* more than forty years old, selected for their moral and intellectual qualities. They were paid salaries from the *bayt al-mal* (state treasury), and were not allowed to go more than one day's journey from the capital without permission. During necessary absences they were replaced by alternates, from whom their successors were normally chosen. If allowance is made for the very different political conditions of 1810 and 1960, and the very different objectives of the governments of Shehu Ahmadu and Modibo Keita, one may see certain resemblances between the Council of Forty and the Comité Directeur of the Union Soudanaise, and between the Inner Council and the party's Bureau Politique.[12]

Another analogy may perhaps be traced in regard to the inspectorate. In Shehu Ahmadu's Macina there existed the institution of the *mutasibi* (derived from the Islamic *muhtasib*), or "censor of public morals." There was also a body known as the *sa'i*, described by Hampaté Bâ as "agents who had taken an oath, and who were dispatched discreetly to check on the exactions of public servants. They were recruited from among those companions of Shehu Ahmadu who had proved their contempt for influence and the goods of this world and who had never been convicted of corruption. They were generally known as *misikimbe nundube*, that is to say, 'the poor just ones.'" [13] There are certain resemblances between these institutions and the system of *commissaires politiques* introduced by the Union Soudanaise in 1961, one commissaire for each of the six regions of Mali, with responsibility for inquiring into everything relating to the party and the administration in their respective regions—as Modibo Keita put it, "No door was closed to them"—and reporting back to the Bureau Politique. Another institution in modern Mali with inspectoral functions of a more localized kind is the Brigades de Vigilance, recruited from the Union Soudanaise youth in the towns, whose functions begin at midnight, and who are responsible for maintaining public order and morality.

In drawing these comparisons one is not, of course, suggesting that there has been any direct carry-over of the institutions of an earlier period

---

[12] For the structure of the Macina state under Shehu Ahmadu, see A. Hampaté Bâ and J. Daget, *L'Empire Peul du Macina*, Vol. I (1818–1853) (2d ed.; Paris: Mouton, 1962), and Trimingham, *op. cit.*, pp. 177–181. The concept of "collective leadership," and the organization and the functions of the Comité Directeur and the Bureau Politique of the Union Soudanaise, are discussed on pages 246-252, below.

[13] Hampaté Bâ and Daget, *op. cit.*, p. 66.

into the modern system, but rather that, in developing its own form of collective leadership and its own inspectorate, the Union Soudanaise has been in some degree influenced by the institutions and the attitudes of the earlier period. Moreover, the Muslim reform movements of the nineteenth century have left a residue of moral values which have to some extent been built into the social philosophy of the Union Soudanaise: for example, its puritan outlook; its emphasis on austerity, discipline, individual responsibility, criticism, and self-criticism; the importance of "doing things in the right way." The Bureau Politique of the Union Soudanaise has been described as "democratic" because Modibo Keita is a "militant très discipliné." The party's theory of socialism itself is related to this Muslim reformist tradition: "Il n'y a pas de religion plus socialiste que la religion musulmane, parce qu'elle enseigne dans ses principes: aux riches, à donner, à partager, à soulager la souffrance des autres." [14] It is, however, important to note here that what is constantly emphasized is not Islamic values as such, but rather the values of the party, which are conceived as having their historical roots in the Sudanic Muslim tradition. This point was clearly put by Modibo Keita when addressing a conference of the Union Soudanaise in September, 1954: "Le R.D.A., l'Union Soudanaise, est une seconde religion qui trouve sa source dans la religion Musulmane qui veut qu'on aide les pauvres et qu'on défende les faibles. Aider les pauvres, défender les faibles, c'est que veut l'Union Soudanaise, c'est pourquoi nous acceptons tous ces souffrances." [15]

INFLUENCE OF THE EARLIER COLONIAL PERIOD

What were the consequences of the second phase of Mali history, the period of authoritarian colonial rule, for party organization, ideas, and relationships?

First, one must take into account the process by which French rule was imposed upon Soudan, and the scale and the character of Soudanese resistance to French penetration. Western writers have too often (in this as in other instances) been misled by the colonial myth, that "the military conquest of Soudan proved comparatively easy." [16] In fact, the process of conquest occupied most of two decades, lasting from 1881 (the beginning of the French wars with Samory Ture) to 1898 (the final capture of Samory and the sack of Sikasso). It cost the Soudanese heavy

---

[14] *Le Mali en marche* (édition du Secrétariat d'Etat à l'Information, 1962), p. 12, reporting an address made by Modibo Keita to the first Stage National de Formation Accélérée de Journalistes, held in Bamako from December 20, 1961, to March 23, 1962.

[15] *L'Essor*, Sept. 15, 1954.

[16] Virginia Thompson and Richard Adloff, *French West Africa* (Stanford: Stanford University Press, [1958?]).

losses in both manpower and property.[17] The main leaders of the resistance—Ahmadu Shehu, Samory Ture, Mamadu Lamïn (among the
Sarakolle), Tieba (ruler of Sikasso), and his brother and successor, Ba
Bemba—were Muslims whose power depended on a combination of
religious influence, appeal to national sentiment, and a capacity for
efficient military organization. True, the failure of these leaders to achieve
any kind of durable alliance, and the periodic conflicts within and between ruling families, worked to the advantage of French diplomacy
and French military power.[18] But the memory of this resistance, maintained over a long period, was used to good effect by the Union Soudanaise, which was able to present itself as renewing, under different
conditions and by different methods, the anticolonial struggle of the last
quarter of the nineteenth century.

Second, unlike the British in northern Nigeria, the French administration, once installed, rapidly set out to break the power of the dynasties
that had opposed it. The French administrative system, as it developed
after the transition from military to civil rule, involved the creation of the
Commandement Indigène, totally subordinate to the French commandants, and responsible for carrying out relatively menial duties.[19] It functioned mainly at two levels, that of the canton and the village. Those
who were appointed to the Commandement Indigène, particularly as
chefs de canton, were drawn for the most part from sections of the
Soudanese population—pagan Bambara; supporters of the former Segu
dynasty; Fulani adherents of the Macina regime, overthrown by al-Hajj
ʿUmar; the Agibu wing of the Tal family, which had come to terms with
the French invaders—which had been hostile to the ruling groups taking
part in the resistance. Thus the establishment of the French administration meant a reversal of political fortunes for those who, as members of
ruling families, traders, *talaba* (Muslim activists), or *sofa* (regular
cavalrymen), had supported the former dominant regimes and had
shared in their fate.

Third, the protonationalist organizations that emerged in the period

---

[17] Jean Suret-Canale, who discusses this topic at length in his *Afrique noire*
(Paris: Editions Sociales, 1958), asserts: "Si l'insuffisante précision des sources ne
permet pas d'affirmer, il est en tout cas extrêmement probable que les dix années de
guerre de 1890 à 1900 infligèrent au Soudan des pertes démographiques largement
supérieures à celles qu'avaient pu entraîner toutes les guerres locales antérieures au
cours du XIXᵉ siècle" (chap. iii, "La Conquête coloniale," p. 222).
[18] At one stage Ahmadu Shehu seems to have attempted unsuccessfully to organize a triple alliance with Samory and Tieba (*ibid.,* p. 211).
[19] For an account of the system of native administration in French West Africa
in the early colonial period, see Raymond L. Buell, *The Native Problem in Africa*
(2 vols.; New York: Macmillan, 1928), I, chaps. 60, 61. Cf. also Robert Delavignette,
Freedom and Authority in French West Africa (London: Oxford University Press,
1950), esp. chap. 5.

before 1945 were of two main types: movements of religious protest, which appealed in some degree to the mass of the population; and ostensibly cultural associations, which provided the Western-educated elite with limited opportunities to develop their own system of communications, and to discuss their own problems arising out of the colonial situation.

As resistance to French penetration in Soudan had been mainly organized under Muslim leadership and had made use of an Islamic ideology, it was natural that the first efforts to regroup the forces that had been broken up by the French occupation, and to restate fundamental principles, should have been made within an Islamic context. One of the most important of these was the development of a reformed Tijaniyya—the order that had been widely diffused through the western Sudan during al-Hajj 'Umar's ascendancy—under the leadership of Shaykh (or Sharif) Hamahu'llah (Hamallah) ibn Muhammad ibn Sayyidna 'Umar, after whom the reformed Tijaniyya came to be known, incorrectly in the view of its adherents, as "Hamalliyya." The center of the order was at Nioro in northwestern Soudan, near the Mauritanian frontier, where the Shaykh Sidi Muhammad ibn Ahmad ibn Abdallah (known as al-Sharif al-Akhdar) established himself in 1900, having come from Tuat in Algeria, propagating reformist ideas and highly critical of the existing Tijani establishment in Soudan. Shaykh Hamallah, the son of a Dioula trader from Tichit in Mauritania and married to a Fulani wife, studied with al-Sharif al-Akhdar, absorbed his ideas, and, on the death of his master in 1909, succeeded to the leadership of the order at the age of about twenty-five.

The reformed Tijaniyya represented an interesting amalgam of ideas. It contained a strong Sufi mystical element, with special emphasis on the value of esoteric knowledge and the symbolic importance of particular numbers. It attached great importance to austerity in personal life, and the main burden of its opposition to the established Tijani leaders was that, in becoming preoccupied with political power, they had lost sight of the essential ethical-religious message of Shaykh Ahmad al-Tijani (the Algerian founder of the order) and of al-Hajj 'Umar himself. The outward sign of acceptance of the reformist position was the recitation of the crucial Tijani prayer, *jawharat al-kamal* (Pearl of Perfection), eleven times—which, according to al-Sharif al-Akhdar, had been the practice of Ahmad al-Tijani in his later years—and not twelve times, the accepted practice of the unreformed Tijanis in Soudan.

The chain of causes which led to increasing conflict between the reformed Tijaniyya under Shaykh Hamallah's leadership and the French administration is somewhat obscure. In part, it seems to have been associated with the opposition of entrenched Muslim interests, which turned to the administration for support, to these reformist ideas, and the occasionally violent incidents to which this opposition gave rise. In part, it was connected with the growing popular influence of the movement in the period between the two world wars which, through the radical individualist interpretation it gave to Islam, seems to have had a special appeal for the more oppressed sections of the community, such as subject tribes, captives, women, and the young: "He [Shaykh Hamallah] prescribed the absolute independence of the child in the family and of the individual in society." [20]

Moreover, the movement benefited from the official persecution of its leader. Shaykh Hamallah was exiled to Mauritania from 1925 to 1930 and to the Ivory Coast from 1930 to 1935; he was arrested again in 1940 and exiled, first to Algeria and later to Montluçon in France, where he died in 1943. This victimization helped to transform him from the austere shaykh of a reforming order into a messianic figure. Hence the practices said to have developed within the order in its later period, which were criticized as deviant, do not seem always to have been sanctioned by the Shaykh himself. Among them were the substitution of two protestations for the normal three or four (with the implication that the relations between the Muslims of Soudan and the French infidels were characteristic of a jihad); the practice of facing west, toward Nioro (or France), rather than east, toward Mecca, during the performance of prayers; and the use of the formula, "There is no God but God, and our Shaykh is Hamallah," instead of the approved profession of faith, "There is no God but God, and Muhammad is his Prophet." In this later period the spread of the influence of the reformed Tijaniyya—not only within Soudan, but into the adjacent territories of Mauritania, Senegal, Guinea, Upper Volta, Niger, and northern Nigeria—was considerably assisted by the administration's policy of deporting its most active supporters.

After 1945 the reformed Tijaniyya survived mainly in its quietist form, that of emphasizing particularly the importance of the mystical "way" and of personal morality, of which Tierno Bokar, and his biographer, Amadou Hampaté Bâ, have been two of the principal exponents. Its radical attitude to the problems of West African society, and its militancy in its relations with the authorities, whether French or Muslim, were inherited in a secularized form by the Union Soudanaise–RDA.

---

[20] Quoted from J. L. Montézer, *L'Afrique et l'Islam* (Dakar: Grande Imprimerie Africaine, 1939), p. 42, by Alphonse Gouilly, *L'Islam dans l'Afrique Occidentale Française* (Paris: Larose, 1952), p. 145. We are here following Gouilly's interpretation, as he gives the best short account of Shaykh Hamallah and the reformed Tijani order under his leadership. See also the interesting personal account in A. Hampaté Bâ, *Tierno Bokar, le sage de Bandiagara* (Paris: Présence Africaine, 1957). An adequate assessment of the movement must, however, await the publication of the work on which Jamil Abun-Nasr of the American University of Beirut is engaged, based upon a study of Shaykh Hamallah's papers.

During the interwar period a Western-educated Soudanese elite began to emerge, though on an extremely small scale because "the total number of Soudanese to attend any AOF secondary, upper primary or vocational school between 1905 and 1947 was only 836." [21] Among these the most able and fortunate, such as Mamby Sidibé, Fily Dabo Sissoko, Mamadou Konaté, and, in a later generation, Ousmane Bâ and Modibo Keita, were admitted to the federal Ecole Normale–William Ponty at Dakar, and after graduation became for the most part *institu-teurs*.[22] Their interest in Soudanese history, and its documentary and oral sources, was stimulated by French administrator-scholars, such as Maurice Delafosse (author of the classic *Haut-Sénégal-Niger*). At the same time they became aware of the distortions in the approach of most French scholars to the problems of African history, particularly in the period of European penetration and conquest, and their hagiographic treatment of the French empire builders and military commanders of the late nineteenth century. For this reason Mamby Sidibé and other Soudanese intellectuals began to develop their own African-centered interpretation of their past.

Under the pre-1945 French colonial system this Soudanese elite, who were, almost without exception, *sujets* and not *citoyens*, were not permitted to form political associations of any kind.[23] But groupings of old boys, such as the Association des Anciens Elèves de Terrasson de Fougères, and social clubs like Espérance, founded in 1931 as "an association for fetes and receptions," existed under strict administrative surveillance. The return to power of the Popular Front government in France in 1936, its introduction of a cautious program of colonial reform (including limited recognition of African trade unions), and its appointment of a few men of the Left to posts in the French West African civil service, provided the stimulus for a new initiative on the part of the African intelligentsia.

In 1937 Mamadou Konaté, in coöperation with Ouezzin Coulibaly of Upper Volta, organized the first African Syndicat des Instituteurs. Even more important, on May 2, 1937, more than a hundred African teachers, civil servants, and employees in commercial firms held a meeting at the Maison de l'Espérance in Bamako, under the chairmanship of Mamby Sidibé, and decided to form an organization to be called the Association des Lettrés du Soudan. A week later a second general meet-

---

[21] Morgenthau, *op. cit.*, p. 269.

[22] For the importance of Ponty as the main educational center for the formation of a French-speaking African elite, in the period before 1945, see *ibid.*, pp. 10–16.

[23] For the distinction between "sujets" and "citoyens" in the pre-1945 AOF, see Kenneth Robinson, "Political Development in French West Africa," in Calvin W. Stillman, ed., *Africa in the Modern World* (Chicago: University of Chicago Press, 1955).

ing changed the name of the association to the Foyer du Soudan, and elected a committee, with Sidibé as president, to draft its constitution. On June 10 the committee submitted a constitution to the Governor, who instituted a confidential police inquiry to make sure that the association would not be "subversive" in character. On August 9 the French mayor of Bamako informed Sidibé that the government thought the association would be too large; its membership should be restricted to Bamako, and it should be made clear that it was *apolitique*. The government had no objection to Sidibé as president, as he would be able to exercise a restraining influence on the young; if he failed to do this, he would be imprisoned. On September 23, 1937, the revised constitution of the Foyer du Soudan was approved. The foundation of this officially apolitical association marked the entry of the younger generation of Western-educated Soudanese into politics. It was the "point de départ de libération des esprits," and the germ from which later developed the political parties of postwar Soudan.[24]

THE PARTY SYSTEM IN SOUDAN, 1945–1958

The collapse of France in 1940 and the establishment of the Vichy regime meant in Soudan, as throughout Vichy-controlled AOF, the withdrawal of the limited political concessions of the Popular Front period and intensification of administrative repression and racial discrimination. Forced labor, the requisition of local products (including animals), import shortages and the development of European-controlled black markets, and the efforts of the administration to cut trade connections with British West Africa stimulated popular discontent. Thus, after de Gaulle's provisional government took over control of French West Africa in 1943, and the Brazzaville Conference of January, 1944, outlined a new program of reforms for the overseas territories, there developed a climate of radicalism, encouraged by a few progressive French administrators and teachers and aided by the return of Soudanese ex-servicemen with new political ideas from Europe and North Africa. The Foyer du Soudan, with Mamadou Konaté as president, became again the main focus of radical opinion. And for a short period (as in several other territories) the Groupe d'Etudes Communistes (GEC) in Bamako provided opportunities for the study of Marxist theory and its application to the problems of colonial peoples.

The elections to the First Constituent Assembly in Paris, held in October and November, 1945, stimulated the creation of political parties and competition for election as deputies among members of the new elite who had already demonstrated, through the Foyer du Soudan, the

---

[24] The information contained in this paragraph was communicated personally by Mamby Sidibé.

trade unions, or the GEC, their capacity for leadership. In these elections Soudan and Niger combined as a single constituency to elect one second-college deputy on a restricted franchise.[25] The two principal contestants in these elections, and in subsequent elections for the next ten years, were Fily Dabo Sissoko and Mamadou Konaté. On this occasion Sissoko was elected by 11,277 votes to Konaté's 5,242. In the elections to the Second Constituent Assembly in June, 1946, Sissoko won by an even larger majority (17,032 votes to 4,307). In the First Constituent Assembly Sissoko associated himself with the French Radical Socialist Party, but in the second, after the defeat of the first (April, 1946) constitution in the referendum, he transferred his allegiance to the Union Républicaine des Résistants (URR). This group, to which Félix Houphouet-Boigny and the future founders of the Rassemblement Démocratique Africain belonged, was itself allied with the French Communist Party in the Assembly.

Meanwhile, in Soudan, the first political parties were in the process of formation. The Parti Soudanais Progressiste (PSP), set up in December, 1945, was led by Sissoko. With the encouragement of French Socialists, most of the candidates defeated in the fall elections of 1945 formed the Bloc Soudanais, led by Jean Silvandre, a Martiniquan, and including Mamadou Konaté. A third group, associated particularly with the GEC, formed the Parti Démocratique Soudanais (PDS). The founding congress of the interterritorial RDA was held at Bamako in October, 1946, partly in recognition of Soudan's historical significance for a *rassemblement* that sought to organize in a united anticolonial front "tous les peuples, toutes les races, tous les partis politiques, toutes les organisations ouvrières, tous les mouvements culturels et religieux de l'Afrique noire." [26] Influenced by the idea of unity in the struggle against colonialism in general and against reactionary forces in France, particularly in French West Africa, the delegates of the three Soudanese parties—PSP, Bloc Soudanais, and PDS—decided to establish a single unified party at the territorial level. This party, the Union Soudanaise, was recognized as the Soudanese section of the RDA.

From October, 1946, to January, 1947, the controlling committee of the Union Soudanaise included, in principle, representatives of the three parties that had combined to form it. But already, at the time of the

[25] For the constitutional background to the developments described above, and the meanings of the terms used, see Thomas Hodgkin and Ruth Schachter, *French-speaking West Africa in Transition*, Carnegie Endowment for International Peace, International Conciliation, no. 528 (May, 1960); K. E. Robinson, "Constitutional Reform in French Tropical Africa," *Political Studies* (London), VI (Feb., 1958); and K. E. Robinson, *The Public Law of Overseas France since the War* (Oxford: Institute of Commonwealth Studies, 1954).

[26] "Manifeste du Rassemblement Démocratique Africain," in *Le RDA dans la lutte anti-imperialiste* (Paris, 1948), p. 23.

Bamako Congress, Fily Dabo Sissoko made clear his unwillingness to identify himself with the RDA. Like the Senegalese Socialists, Lamine Guèye and Léopold Senghor (both of whom signed the manifesto calling the congress but failed to attend it), he was disturbed by what he regarded, or was persuaded by his friends among the French Socialists to regard, as Communist influences within the RDA. But, under pressure from his supporters, he participated in the congress and reluctantly presided over its first session. However, when the Union Soudanaise was faced, at the time of the November, 1946, elections, with the need to make nominations for the three seats in the National Assembly now allocated to Soudan, the split within the unified party was reopened. The PDS representatives proposed to nominate Sissoko, Konaté, and Gabriel d'Arboussier, the recently elected general secretary of the RDA. But Sissoko, rejecting d'Arboussier on the ground that he was a Communist, re-formed the PSP and stood for election with Jean Silvandre (who had dissolved his Bloc Soudanais and moved over to the PSP). The PSP won 60,759 votes in this election. Both Sissoko and Silvandre were elected deputies, and both became affiliated with the Socialist group, Section Française de l'International Ouvrière (SFIO), in the National Assembly. The Union Soudanaise obtained 27,653 votes, and its candidate, Konaté, was elected to the third seat. In the subsequent elections to the territorial General Council (conducted on the basis of a dual college) in November, 1946, the PSP maintained its clear lead; the Union Soudanaise won only two seats and 38 per cent of the votes cast. The pattern of Union Soudanaise–PSP rivalry which emerged from these elections continued to dominate Soudanese politics for the next twelve years.

The elections between 1946 and 1959 reveal a gradual decline of the PSP and a gradual strengthening of the Union Soudanaise. In the 1946 elections to the National Assembly, the Union Soudanaise won about 30 per cent of the total vote, and in June, 1951, it increased its share to about 34 per cent on a considerably enlarged franchise, winning 115,490 votes to the PSP's 201,866. But, of the four seats allocated to Soudan at this date, three were won by the PSP—Hamadoun Dicko joining Sissoko and Silvandre as PSP-Socialist deputies—while the Union Soudanaise continued to be represented by its single deputy, Mamadou Konaté. In the March, 1952, elections to the Territorial Assembly (the new name given the former General Council in 1947), the Union Soudanaise further improved its position, winning thirteen seats (with 101,-902 votes, about 40 per cent of the total), as contrasted with the PSP's twenty-seven seats (with 122,957 votes). In this situation the Union Soudanaise made a tactical and temporary alliance with the Rassemblement du Peuple Français (RPF) first-college (i.e., French) territorial assemblymen. As this coalition could outvote the PSP, the Union Soudanaise was able to nominate its representatives to a proportion of Territorial Assembly offices, and to secure the election of Mahamane Alassane Haïdara, the representative of Timbuktu, as senator to the Council of the Republic, and of Modibo Keita as councilor to the Assembly of the French Union.

By January, 1956, when the next general elections for the National Assembly were held, the balance had clearly swung in favor of the Union Soudanaise. It won approximately 50 per cent of the total poll and elected two deputies, Konaté (succeeded after his death in May, 1956, by Bocoum Barema) and Keita. The PSP, which obtained only 161,911 votes in contrast with the 215,419 won by the Union Soudanaise, was likewise represented by two deputies, Sissoko and Hamadoun Dicko. The Union Soudanaise also won all the municipal council seats in the newly created *communes* of Bamako, Kayes, Mopti, Sikasso, and Ségou. As a result of the March, 1957, elections to the Territorial Assembly (following the constitutional reforms introduced under the Loi-Cadre), the Union Soudanaise attained a position of overwhelming dominance, winning (with the support of seven representatives of the Union des Populations de Bandiagara, who came over to it) sixty-four seats to the PSP's six, and 472,208 votes to the PSP's 218,668. On this occasion Sissoko, Dicko, and other PSP leaders were defeated in their home constituencies. Finally, in March, 1959, the Union Soudanaise won all eighty seats in the elections to the Legislative Assembly (which had replaced the Territorial Assembly), although its 534,946 votes amounted to only 76 per cent of the total poll. The Parti du Regroupement Soudanais (PRS), successor to the PSP, won 170,428 votes.

At this point two related questions should be considered: (1) What were the main factors making for conflict between the Union Soudanaise and the PSP during the period 1946–1959? (2) What is the explanation for the gradual transformation of the Union Soudanaise from a minority into a dominant party, and of the PSP from a majority into a minority party, and ultimately of its elimination as a political force?

A study of the changing situation in the constituencies throws some light on the first question. Initially, in 1946, the only cercles in which the Union Soudanaise won seats were Kita, San, and Sikasso. By 1952 it had added Bamako, Gao, and Timbuktu, but had lost San. By 1956 the only cercles retained by the PSP were Bafoulabé, Nioro, Macina, Koutiala, Bougouni, and Goundam; in 1957 it retained only Bafoulabé, Macina, and Koutiala. This pattern suggests that at first the principal centers of Union Soudanaise strength were in the towns and along the main communication axes, the Dakar-Koulikoro railway and the Niger River. When the party began to extend its influence into the rural areas, its earliest support came primarily from the Malinke and the Songhai, and from constituencies where Islam had been well entrenched in the precolonial period, such as Timbuktu and Sikasso. The PSP, on the other hand, tended to be strongest in rural areas, away from the main commercial centers and trade routes, and among animist populations such as the Bambara. It was also able to rely on fairly solid and steady support from areas such as Koutiala and Bougouni, which had suffered at the hands of al-Hajj ʿUmar or Samory, and where there was a tendency to identify the RDA with a renascent militant Islam. Among Muslim communities the PSP was most closely associated with the Fulani, as in Macina, where the Fulani dynasty established by Shehu Ahmadu had been defeated by al-Hajj ʿUmar. Thus interparty conflict seems in part to have followed well-marked lines of historical, cultural, and religious division.

Furthermore, the PSP, though not strictly an administration party because it was established and maintained through Soudanese initiative, had connections with the French administrative hierarchy such as the Union Soudanaise never enjoyed. Fily Dabo Sissoko received active support from the administration in the elections of 1946. Moreover, the PSP early developed a close association with the Commandement Indigène; and the network of official chiefs, who had regular duties to perform in connection with the organization of elections, was used as a mechanism for securing the return of PSP candidates. Sissoko, who described himself as a "Malinke Islamized animist," was himself a chef de canton from Bafoulabé. Hamadoun Dicko was the son of a Fulani chef de canton from Douentza. Almamy Koreissy, one of Sissoko's lieutenants, was a Fulani chef de canton from Macina who played a major role in organizing the Syndicat des Chefs Coutumiers in 1956, and became its president. The large majority of the chefs de canton were PSP supporters, and were prepared to use their official position to promote the party's interests. Hence the party was naturally concerned with the protection of chiefly interests, and, by implication, because chiefs depended for their continuing tenure of office on the support of the French administration, was unwilling to take up positions that might bring it into serious conflict with the administration.

The Union Soudanaise lacked these connections with the official hierarchy, and the consequent advantages and disadvantages. It was therefore not inhibited by its composition or outlook from attacking either the administration or the Commandement Indigène on issues that in its opinion involved the popular interest. Indeed, in one of its aspects, the Union Soudanaise may be regarded as the party that sought to unite, and eventually succeeded in uniting, the various sections of the Soudanese population which were in opposition to the Commandement Indigène: wage and salary earners, teachers and junior civil servants, traders, artisans, the Muslim intelligentsia (particularly those with reformist tend-

encies), members of former ruling families displaced by the Commandement Indigène, and members of depressed social groups such as the
servile Bella in the region of the Niger bend and the Bozo fishermen.
This aspect of party conflict was reflected in the conduct of the Union
Soudanaise after it was firmly established in power. In 1958 it suppressed
the judicial functions of the chefs de canton by abolishing the *tribunaux
coutumiers,* and finally, in 1960, it eliminated them altogether from local
government.

Although its main roots thus lay in the local African situation, interparty conflict was intensified by external factors associated with the functioning of the French political system in the period of the Fourth Republic, and by the tendency of African political parties, or their leaders,
to ally themselves for parliamentary purposes with metropolitan parties.
For example, Fily Dabo Sissoko and other parliamentary representatives
of the PSP, as noted above, attached themselves to the Socialist group in
the French Parliament, which, during the period 1946–1958, usually
either participated in or supported successive French governments. Thus
the PSP became identified with the repressive policies that these governments followed in Madagascar, Viet-Nam, and North Africa, as well as
in *Afrique Noire.* The Union Soudanaise, on the other hand, was a section of the interterritorial RDA, which until 1950 was allied with the
URR and, at the metropolitan level, worked in close association with the
Parti Communiste Français (PCF). Although the RDA preserved considerable freedom of action in regard to specifically African questions,
on wider international issues it adhered fairly closely to the Communist
Party line during this period. Thus, from the standpoint of the Union
Soudanaise, Sissoko seemed to be a "colonialist lackey," whereas, from
the standpoint of the PSP, Mamadou Konaté could be represented as a
fellow traveler. This particular aspect of the conflict naturally became
more acute after May, 1947, when the PCF withdrew its representatives
from the French government and turned to a policy of thoroughgoing
opposition. It was further intensified in 1949 when the French administration in AOF attempted to break the power of the RDA. Though the repression of the period 1949–1950 was most severe in the Ivory Coast, it
had its repercussions also in Soudan, where leading members of the
Union Soudanaise were imprisoned, dismissed, transferred, or victimized
in other ways.

After 1950, when the RDA broke its association with the PCF—
shortly thereafter allying itself, at the French parliamentary level, with
a minor governmental party, the Union Démocratique et Sociale de la
Résistance (UDSR), led by René Pléven—and began to apply its new
policy of "constructive coöperation" with the administration, it might have
seemed that a major cause of interparty conflict in Soudan had been re-

moved. But, although the political distance separating the SFIO from the UDSR in France was not itself of major significance, the Union Soudanaise remained extremely conscious of its sacrifices, its martyrs, and its revolutionary objectives. Its leadership accepted the new policy, more perhaps from considerations of party loyalty than from conviction, but the attitude of the party militants to the struggle against the administration and the Commandement Indigène over local issues did not change. Moreover, the leadership itself insisted, as Secretary-General Keita put it in his report to the 1952 congress, that there is "no change in our aims, no fundamental aboutface in the methods of our struggle but rather an adaptation in the form our methods take, which is to say that we recognize through the emancipation of Africa the anti-colonial fight must take into account the international and above all, local realities." [27] And the administration on its side continued, until at least the mid-1950's, to regard the Union Soudanaise with the suspicion and the hostility which any colonial regime normally feels toward any radical nationalist party.

This point may be put in another way. There were basic differences in ideology and political objectives between the PSP and the Union Soudanaise which were not substantially affected by the various alliances they contracted with metropolitan parties, and which survived into the period after the Loi-Cadre reforms of 1956–1957, when these alliances lapsed. These differences might be crudely summarized by describing the PSP as a "traditionalist" or "conservative" party, and the Union Soudanaise as a "radical" or "progressive" party. Yet both appealed in their different ways to Soudanese tradition. But "tradition," as the PSP conceived it, meant the traditional status, rights, and privileges of those chiefs and Marabouts who had come to terms with the French administration and enjoyed its protection and support, whereas the "tradition" in which the Union Soudanaise was interested was the precolonial tradition of state and empire building, of Islamic universalism and brotherhood, of militancy and reform, associated in the popular mind with Sundiata, Muhammad Askia, and al-Hajj ʿUmar.

Perhaps the essential difference was that the Union Soudanaise believed that its function was to mobilize the masses and educate them for political action, whereas the PSP regarded the masses primarily as passive voters who should accept the directives of their leaders. The Union Soudanaise attacked social and economic privilege and "feudal" forms of authority, whereas the PSP defended them. The Union Soudanaise was concerned with promoting the unity of Africans and of colonial (or former colonial) peoples in general in the anticolonial struggle, whereas the PSP tended to limit its field of action to Soudan Français, and took for granted the necessity for a continuing close relationship between

---

[27] Quoted in Morgenthau, *op. cit.*, p. 293.

Soudan and France. The Union Soudanaise paid close attention to ideological questions, whereas the PSP, like conservative parties in other parts of the world, tended to regard ideologies as an unnecessary luxury. But, if in these respects the Union Soudanaise may reasonably be regarded as a "revolutionary-democratic" [28] party, at the same time it showed a kind of Fabian caution in the application of its ideology to specific situations.

Against this background it should be possible to explain how the PSP moved from a dominant to a minority position, and eventually lost its independent existence, while the Union Soudanaise succeeded in transforming itself from a minority into a dominant party, and eventually into the governing party of a one-party state. The following would seem to have been the main contributory factors.

First, the main initial asset of the PSP—the support of the chiefly interests and the availability of the Commandement Indigène as a ready-made electoral machine—became increasingly a liability, as popular opposition to the Commandement Indigène developed and could be expressed with greater freedom. Second, the steady widening of the franchise and the consequent expansion of the number of registered electors from 36,714 in June, 1946, to 916,944 in June, 1951, and to 2,090,048 in 1957, directly benefited the Union Soudanaise, though in some territories (e.g., Mauritania, and to some extent Upper Volta and Niger) it could be turned to the advantage of chiefs' parties. This expansion was associated with a third factor, the efficiency and the democratic character of the organization built up after 1946 by the Union Soudanaise, which showed itself to be far more capable of managing and mobilizing a mass electorate than the PSP, with its rudimentary patron-client type of structure. But perhaps the most significant change in the total political situation by 1957 was the fact that the administration, answerable to a French government which, from January, 1956, included Houphouet-Boigny, the president of the interterritorial RDA, abandoned its earlier policy of active intervention on the side of the PSP in favor of a genuine neutrality as between the two competing African parties. The effect of this radical change in French policy was not simply to remove the various official pressures that had formerly helped the PSP to maintain its majority, but, in a climate of growing anticolonial sentiment, to cause the PSP, as the party of "the collaborators," to be discredited, and the Union Soudanaise, as the party of "the resisters," to be vindicated.

The political developments of the period 1956–1959 may thus be regarded as a second reversal of fortunes. Just as, in the period after

---

[28] For the meaning of "revolutionary-democratic" in this context, see Thomas Hodgkin, *African Political Parties* (Penguin Books, 1961), chap. 7, and "A Note on the Language of African Nationalism," in *African Affairs*, no. 1, St. Antony's Papers, no. 10 (London: Chatto and Windus, 1961), pp. 39–40.

1898, the Soudanese governments that had resisted French penetration were dismantled and replaced by the French-controlled apparatus of the Commandement Indigène, so several generations later the Commandement Indigène, deprived of the underpinning that the French administration had provided, was dismantled, and the party that had been constructed around it was gradually eroded, to be replaced by the Union Soudanaise. The Union Soudanaise may not, of course, be regarded simply as the successor to the regimes and the movements that had formerly resisted French penetration. Essentially, as has been argued, the party was a new political force, though it included, among the elements it had fused into a single party, some that could trace a direct line of descent from the earlier resistance. By referring back to the memory of that resistance, the Union Soudanaise strengthened its appeal for popular support.

FROM THE REFERENDUM TO THE MALI REPUBLIC, 1958–1960

In order to understand the part played by the Union Soudanaise in the modern, postcolonial Republic of Mali, including the relations between party and state and the policies for which the party stands, it is necessary to pay some attention to the particular form of the transition to independence in Soudan-Mali, the problems that this transition raised, and the nature of the solutions found.

The RDA, at its frequently deferred Bamako Congress, held September 25–30, 1957, was confronted with the second major crisis in its history. The first crisis, in 1950, associated with the question of RDA-PCF relations, involved the choice between a revolutionary and a gradualist strategy. This second crisis, turning principally on the issues of independence and unity, raised equally fundamental questions of policy. First, should the interterritorial party press for the total independence of French-speaking Africa, or should it accept the limitations on independence which continued participation in some form of French community would be likely to involve? Second, should the RDA attempt to maintain the unity of the existing French West African Federation and therefore press for the establishment of a democratized federal executive, responsible to a federal parliament? Or should it be prepared to support, or acquiesce in, the breakup of the federation into its constituent territories (a process that had already come to be known as "Balkanization")?

In this controversy, Houphouet-Boigny and the Parti Démocratique de la Côte d'Ivoire (PDCI) were the main protagonists of territorial autonomy within a reconstructed French African community, while Sékou Touré and the Parti Démocratique de Guinée (PDG), supported by the great majority of delegates to the Bamako Congress, asserted the principle of independence for a West African federation, which would preserve its unity though ceasing to be French. The Union Soudanaise was naturally committed by its history and outlook to a basic sympathy with the PDG position, and the slogans with which the party's militants had decorated the congress hall clearly expressed this attitude. At the same time their desire to maintain the unity of the interterritorial party, as well as their role as hosts to the congress, led Modibo Keita and the party leadership to attempt insofar as possible to mediate between these conflicting standpoints.[29]

The actual resolutions of the Bamako Congress did little more than register the basic disagreement that in fact existed within the RDA. This disagreement had not been overcome by September 28, 1958, the date of the referendum on the Constitution of the Fifth French Republic, when the overseas territories were faced with the necessity of choosing, individually, between local autonomy within a new French-dominated community and independence outside it. With the decision of the PDG to vote "Non," and opt for independence, while all other territorial sections of the RDA decided to vote "Oui," the actual process of disintegration of the RDA, as an interterritorial organization, began.

Why did the Union Soudanaise, whose attitude to the related questions of unity and independence was not essentially different from that of the PDG, decide in favor of a "Oui" vote in the referendum, and, by giving the *mot d'ordre* to this effect to its members and supporters, ensure Soudanese support for the new constitution and adherence to the French community by an overwhelming majority? The decision was clearly a difficult one, and was reached only after a great deal of debate within the party. But, once it had been approved by the Bureau Politique, and confirmed by a special party congress in August, 1958, the whole weight of the party's organization and propaganda was thrown into the effort to explain the policy to its membership and to secure its implementation in the constituencies. Among the party leadership only Abdoulaye Diallo, leader in the Union Générale des Travailleurs d'Afrique Noire (UGTAN) and minister of labor in the 1957–1959 government of Soudan, broke party discipline by calling for a "Non" vote, and left for Guinea.

The main reason for the decision of the Union Soudanaise to vote "Oui" would appear to have been the strong commitment of its leadership to the idea of unity. Although unity and independence were objectives of equal importance, it was politically much to be preferred that the French-speaking West African territories should attain independence in unity rather than as separate states. Hence, as it was clear that most of

---

[29] For a useful account of the RDA's second Bamako Congress, and the subsequent political developments in AOF during the years 1957–1959, see Gil Dugué, *Vers les Etats-Unis d'Afrique* ([Dakar]: Lettres Africaines, 1960). Franz Ansprenger, *Politik im Schwarzen Afrika* (Cologne and Opladen: Westdeutscher Verlag, 1961), is well documented for this period.

the RDA territorial sections were either, like the PDCI, opposed in principle to the idea of independence, or not yet prepared to face the responsibilities and problems raised by *indépendance totale* (on the harsh terms laid down by President de Gaulle), the Union Soudanaise conceived it as its first duty to attempt to preserve unity, at the level both of the federation and of the interterritorial party, by voting with the main body of the RDA. This point of view was expressed in such statements as the following:

"L'unanimité de l'AEF autour du 'OUI,' et la forte majorité qui se dégage de la masse en AOF nous ont définitivement déterminé dans nos convictions."

"L'Unité doit se faire. Il importe qu'elle soit realisée autour du 'OUI' ou du 'NON.'"

"Nous aurions fait contre mauvaise fortune bon coeur si, contre notre pensée profonde, une majorité de 'NON's' s'étaient dégagée."

"Nous n'approuverons jamais ceux qui, par ambition personelle, ou par calcul (pour prendre dans l'avenir la tête d'une Fédération) risquent d'être les briseurs de cette unité dont par ironie ils se réclament les champions."

"Nous disons 'OUI' parce que notre 'OUI' entraînera un grand pas en avant de l'Histoire Africaine."

"Nous disons 'OUI' parce qu'autour de ce 'OUI' nous pourrons ensemble constituer de façon définitive l'Unité Africaine par la voie des Fédérations AOF et AEF, à condition, une fois de plus, que chaque responsable fasse taire ses ambitions personelles, et chaque Territoire ses particularismes locaux." [30]

At the same time the Union Soudanaise was influenced by practical considerations. Its main concern was not so much the serious economic and administrative problems which, as the experience of Guinea showed, would have faced Soudan in the event of total and immediate withdrawal of French aid (though this factor certainly counted), as the strength of its position in the country. If it gave the order to vote "Non," could it be sure that an overwhelming "Non" vote would be recorded? The opposition party, the PRS (formerly the PSP), was still functioning, and could continue to rally the support of a substantial number of chiefs. If the French administration in the cercles (which had not as yet been entirely Africanized) and the French army decided to intervene on the side of the conservative opposition and the chiefs in the referendum (as actually occurred in Niger), the Union Soudanaise leadership was not confident that the party was strong enough to withstand these combined pressures. At that time the Union Soudanaise frankly regarded its own position as less secure and less favorable than that of the PDG, which had already

---

[30] *L'Essor*, Sept. 27, 1958.

abolished the chefs de canton in Guinea, established effective control over the administration, and carried through a merger with the opposition parties. As one of the party leaders explained to a meeting of Union Soudanaise youth: "Notre but est resté le même que celui de la Guinée, mais notre organisation n'est pas suffisamment assise dans les masses pour pouvoir parer dans l'immédiat, à toutes éventualités." [31]

After the referendum the Union Soudanaise had quickly to rethink the strategy by which it could best work toward its objectives of unity and independence within the framework of a French community from which Guinea was now excluded, and which clearly implied the liquidation of AOF as a federal system. The constitution of the Fifth French Republic provided for the setting up of "primary federations," but it was clear that no such federation would emerge at a West African level without a new initiative from federal-minded governments and parties within the various territories. Otherwise the Balkanization which the Union Soudanaise had constantly struggled to prevent would become an accomplished fact. In the course of postreferendum discussions within the leadership of the interterritorial RDA (minus Sékou Touré and the PDG), it became clear that Houphouet-Boigny and the PDCI were still opposed to any move to re-create any form of West African federation. A similar position was taken by the Niger section of the RDA, the Parti Progressiste Nigérien (PPN), which had combined with the Niger chiefs to form the Union pour la Communauté Franco-Africaine (UCFA) and had succeeded in replacing the former governmental party, the federalist Sawaba, after the referendum. In Mauritania the government party, the Parti du Regroupement Mauritanien, had adopted a cautious, noncommittal attitude.

Thus only Senegal, Soudan, Upper Volta, and Dahomey participated in the Conférence des Fédéralistes at Bamako on December 28–29, 1958, which endorsed the principle of federation, and in the subsequent Constituent Assembly at Dakar on January 14–17, 1959, which approved a constitution for the new Fédération de Mali. But between January 17 and April 4, 1959, when the federal government of Mali held its first session in Dakar, the new federal capital, a combination of internal political maneuvers and external pressures (principally from the Ivory Coast and from France) led to the withdrawal of the Upper Volta and Dahomey governments. In this way the Mali Federation, which had been conceived as a new union of French-speaking West African states on the broadest possible basis, was transformed into a dialogue between Senegal and Soudan.

The Union Soudanaise was thus brought into close partnership with the only other governmental party that was strongly committed to the

---

[31] *Ibid.,* March 27, 1959.

federal idea, the Union Progressiste Sénégalaise (UPS) under the leadership of Léopold Senghor. This partnership, bringing to a temporary end twelve years of estrangement between the Soudan section of the RDA and the dominant party of Senegal, had a basis both in historical ties, as the new Mali covered an area roughly comparable to that of fourteenth-century Mali, and in contemporary economic facts, as Soudan, a landlocked territory, relied heavily on its communications with Senegal, by way of the Dakar-Niger railway, for its exports and imports.[32]

Its overwhelming victory in the Assembly elections of March 8, 1959, followed by its absorption of the opposition party, the PRS, put the Union Soudanaise in a position of effective control of the Soudan, and enabled it to devote itself to working out the logic of participation in the Mali Federation.[33] This meant, in the first place, detaching the party leader, Modibo Keita, to serve as president of the council in the federal government, with Mamadou Dia, Senghor's deputy, as vice-president. Of the total of six federal ministers, three others were Soudanese: Ousmane Bâ (*fonction publique*), Tidiani Traoré (information and security), and Aw Mamadou (public works). The Federal Assembly was composed of forty deputies, twenty from Soudan and twenty from Senegal.[34]

Second, the Union Soudanaise finally broke with what now became the rump of the RDA, though continuing to preserve "RDA" in the party title, and joined with the UPS, as well as with opposition parties in Dahomey, Upper Volta, Niger, and Mauritania, to set up a new interterritorial party committed to the principles of federation and independence, the Parti de la Fédération Africaine (PFA). The PFA, born at the Dakar Conférence des Fédéralistes Africains in March, 1959, held its constituent congress on April 1–3, electing Senghor as its president, Modibo Keita as its secretary-general, and Doudou Guèye, a Senegalese radical, as its organizing secretary.

Third, in September, 1959, after the decision of the PFA and its Comité Directeur, the government of the Mali Federation opened nego-

[32] See Elliot J. Berg, "The Economic Basis of Political Choice in French West Africa," *American Political Science Review*, LIV (June, 1960), 391–405. Berg adds, however, that Soudan, during the period of the French West African Federation, carried on "noticeable trade" with the Ivory Coast and Upper Volta, as well as with Senegal and Mauritania; it turned both ways in the labor market also, for Soudanese migrants went to work in both Senegal and the Ivory Coast.

[33] See page 233. Fily Dabo Sissoko, on behalf of the Bureau Politique of the PRS, announced the party's adherence to the Union Soudanaise and the RPF on March 31, 1959, after a three-day conference (*L'Essor*, April 3, 1959). A small group of irreconcilables continued to operate for a few months as the Parti du Rassemblement du Soudan under the leadership of Hamadoun Dicko, but this group also faded out when Dicko later rallied to the Union Soudanaise.

[34] *Fédération du Mali, Constitution Fédérale*, votée par l'Assemblée Constituante Fédérale le 17 janvier 1959, modifiée par la loi No. 59/1 du 4 avril 1959, et la loi No. 59/5 du 22 avril, de l'Assemblée Fédérale du Mali.

tiations with France for the recognition of its independence, within the framework of the community, by the method of transferring to Mali all the powers hitherto exercised by the community.[35] As a consequence of these negotiations the Mali Federation achieved its formal independence (limited in practice by a number of Franco-Malian agreements, in regard to such matters as defense, diplomatic relations, finance and currency, higher education, etc.) on June 20, 1960.[36] In this relatively rapid transition to independence, there is no doubt that the initiative of the Union Soudanaise within the PFA and the Mali federal government played an important part.[37]

The Federation of Mali, as an independent state, survived for exactly two months, from June 20 to August 20, 1960. Although the complex history of the events leading up to the *éclatement* of the federation does not directly concern us, it is important to consider what light the éclatement, and the tensions from which it arose, throw on the objectives and the policies of the Union Soudanaise at this period, and how these were affected by the failure of this first federal experiment.

Modibo Keita, in a reference to the breakup of the federation, said plainly: "Il y avait contradiction entre les systèmes économiques, politiques, sociaux auxquels appartenaient les dirigeants du Mali et du Sénégal." [38] What was the nature of these contradictions? The basic opposition lay in the fact that, in the terminology of the Union Soudanaise, the UPS was essentially a "bourgeois" party, whereas the Union Soudanaise was a "socialist" party. This distinction was connected with the fact that the early implantation of French colonial rule in Senegal had made possible the emergence there of a national *bourgeoisie,* from which the leadership of the UPS was mainly drawn, whereas in Soudan the French administration, "faithful to the colonial policy of immediate and maximum profit, and indifferent to the interests of our country, had not permitted the creation of a national *bourgeoisie,* of a national capitalism." [39]

---

[35] The powers reserved to the community, under Article 78 of the Constitution of the Fifth Republic, included foreign policy, defense, currency, common economic and financial policy, policy on strategic raw materials, and, unless specified by agreements, supervisory powers over tribunals, higher education, the general organization of external and intracommunity transportation, and telecommunications.

[36] "Accords franco-maliens," *Recueil Penant* (Paris), no. 679 (June, 1960), 330–354.

[37] This point was strongly put by Modibo Keita at the Union Soudanaise congress held on September 22, 1960, after the breakup of the federation (*Le Mali continue* . . . , République du Mali, Congrès Extraordinaire de l'USRDA, Sept. 22, 1960, p. 15): "Tout d'abord la Fédération du Mali a permis au Sénégal d'aller à l'indépendance parce que tout le monde sait que les dirigeants sénégalais, empêtrés dans leurs difficultés intérieures, isolés du reste de l'Afrique, et pour cause, ne pourraient pas, seuls, y conduire leur pays."

[38] *Le Mali en marche,* p. 17.

[39] *Ibid.,* p. 11.

Moreover, the Union Soudanaise conceived of itself as a "monolithic" party, whereas the UPS, particularly since the breaking away of its radical wing at the time of the referendum, was more like a federation of clans under various powerful clan leaders.[40] The Union Soudanaise, during its fourteen years of existence, had developed a strong tradition of anticolonial struggle, whereas the UPS had on the whole been favorably regarded by the colonial administration. Hence the UPS, in the view of the Union Soudanaise, was likely to be "noyauté" and "téléguidé" by neo-colonialist pressures of a kind that the Union Soudanaise was equipped, by its organization and experience, to resist.[41] Given so wide a divergence in the character and the standpoints of its two main components, the interterritorial PFA was hardly capable of developing the tightly knit structure, based on the principle of democratic centralism, which it set out to achieve. Instead of reconciling the tensions between its constituent territorial parties, it rather reflected them.

This basic opposition between the standpoints of the two parties jointly responsible for the government of the Mali Federation was expressed in a conflict over immediate objectives: "Notre position sur le problème algérien, notre détermination à construire un véritable socialisme, notre volonté de réaliser, avant toute autre association, une véritable communauté africaine, ont déterminé certains responsables français à conduire les dirigeants sénégalais à la sécession." [42] In addition to the issues referred to by Modibo Keita, the question as to whether Mali should develop as a unitary or as a federal state seems to have been a further source of disagreement. From the point of view of the UPS, a relatively loose constitutional structure would make it easier for the federation to gain the adherence of other French-speaking African states, and would at the same time enable Senegal to continue to preserve a fair degree of freedom of maneuver. For the Union Soudanaise, on the other hand, the existence of three governments in a state of some 7 million people was an unjustifiable extravagance. But the more centralized the Mali political system became, the more risk (from the UPS's point of view) that it might tend to pass under the effective control of the Union Soudanaise (and of those dissident radical elements in Senegal which shared its basic presuppositions). This outcome would have been a natural consequence of Modibo Keita's law, "Lorsque deux idées vont dans le même sens ou s'affrontent, l'avantage est toujours à l'idée la plus dynamique." [43]

---

[40] For the conception of "clans" in this context see Kenneth Robinson, "Senegal: The Elections to the Territorial Assembly, March 1957," in W. J. M. Mackenzie and Kenneth Robinson, eds., *Five Elections in Africa* (Oxford: Clarendon Press, 1960), pp. 340–345.

[41] *Le Mali en marche*, p. 19.

[42] Modibo Keita in *Le Mali continue.* . . .

[43] *Le Mali en marche*, p. 16.

However much the Union Soudanaise may have tended, after the éclatement, to emphasize the underlying divergencies of ideology and policy between the UPS and itself, there is no doubt of the strength of its commitment to the idea of the Mali Federation during its lifetime. It was Modibo Keita who, at the Dakar Constituent Assembly in January, 1959, called on the delegates to swear the famous threefold oath: "Si pour la Fédération du Mali, pour l'Unité politique, pour l'Unité africaine, je dois accepter l'ultime sacrifice, je ne hésiterai pas, je ne reculerai pas, je le jure." The official visits of Senghor and Mamadou Dia to Soudan were made the occasion for mass demonstrations in support of the principle of the federal state: "Un peuple, un but, une foi." Hence the disillusion-ment, the "grosse déception," consequent upon the breakup of the federa-tion were all the more intense. The implications of this new situation for the policy of the Union Soudanaise were various. There was inevitably a renewed emphasis on national identity: "Nous sommes devenus nous-mêmes." At the same time the economic difficulties arising out of the disruption of communications with Senegal, particularly the closing of the Dakar-Niger railway, strengthened the drive to construct a socialist economy within Soudan, no longer restrained by the "dead hand" of Senegal and its bourgeois leadership: "J'estime également que la sécession du Sénégal a été le ferment de la mobilisation générale des populations soudanaises. Elle permettra à la République Soudanaise de réaliser pleine-ment ses objectifs politiques, économiques, sociaux et culturels sur la base d'un véritable socialisme, et uniquement en fonction des intérêts des couches les plus défavorisées." [44]

The reasonable belief that France, or certain French interests, were at the root of the éclatement led not only to the repudiation of the whole body of Franco-Malian agreements, but to an intensification of Soudanese hostility to neocolonialism in all its forms. At the same time the govern-ment of the new Republic of Mali (Soudan having insisted on taking over this symbolic title from the extinct federation—"le Mali continue"), though forced into a position of temporary isolation, by no means aban-doned its commitment to the idea of African unity. It sought, rather, to achieve this objective by other means, first through the development of close relations with all those African states "qui seront désireux de promouvoir une politique d'union et de progrès, de s'engager résolu-ment dans la lutte pour la libération totale du Continent africain et l'établissement d'une paix durable entre tous les peuples." [45] For this reason Mali participated in the Ghana-Guinea-Mali Union and the Casa-blanca grouping of African states.

Finally, the difficulties inherent in the situation which the new Re-public of Mali and the Union Soudanaise faced led to a tightening of

[44] Modibo Keita in *Le Mali continue* . . . , p. 16.
[45] *Ibid.*, p. 18.

party discipline, a certain toughening of the party's attitude, and the restatement in sharper form of the principle of democratic centralism: "Les circonstances actuelles ne toléreront aucune défaillance, aucune erreur, aucune hésitation. Toute prise de position officieuse mettant en cause les décisions du Parti ou du Gouvernement sera considerée comme une trahison, et elle sera sévèrement reprimée." [46]

THE UNION SOUDANAISE: ORGANIZATION AND IDEOLOGY

In this section we shall describe the Union Soudanaise from the standpoint of its organization and its ideas, taking into account the whole period of its history, from 1946 to 1963, but paying particular attention to the most recent period, since the creation of the independent Republic of Mali on September 22, 1960.

The formal structure of the Union Soudanaise follows the normal pyramidal pattern of RDA territorial sections. It underwent little substantial change from its foundation until the meeting of the Sixth Party Congress in September, 1962. During this period the basic party units were the *comités de village* in the country and the *comités de quartier* in the towns. Both functioned through an *assemblée générale*, consisting in principle of all the adult inhabitants of a given village or quarter, and a *bureau exécutif* of three or more members elected by the assembly. Above the comités stood the *sous-sections,* covering an administrative district (a cercle or subdivision) and based on (*a*) a conference of sous-sections, whose members were elected from the various comités within the area; (*b*) a *comité directeur,* elected by the conference; and (*c*) an inner bureau exécutif. A similar pattern of authority existed at the national level: (*a*) the Conférence Nationale (or Conférence des Cadres), elected from sous-sections throughout the country; (*b*) the Comité Directeur and (*c*) the Bureau Exécutif (or Bureau Politique), both elected by (*d*) the party congress, the ultimate source of power within the party, which in principle met biennially. Extraordinary conferences could also be held to deal with particular crises; for example, one was held on September 22, 1960, to discuss the situation arising from the breakup of the Mali Federation. [47]

The division of functions among these various organs of the Union Soudanaise was, in theory at least, straightforward. At each level the most representative body—congress, conference, or assembly—was ultimately responsible for defining party policy or interpreting and applying

---

[46] Idrissa Diarra, address to the Congrès Extraordinaire de l'USRDA, in *Le Mali continue* . . . , p. 11.

[47] The information in regard to party structure contained in this and following paragraphs is based partly on Bakary Kamian, *Connaissance de la République du Mali,* Secrétariat de l'Etat d'Information et Tourisme du Mali (1962), pp. 101–106.

it within the local context. The day-to-day management of party affairs was entrusted to elected authorities which, at the district and national levels, took the form of two distinct organs: the bureau exécutif, which took the initiative and issued the directives, and the comité directeur, which received information and exercised control. Directives and mots d'ordre within the general framework of party policy, as laid down by the party congress, came down from the national Bureau Politique through the sous-sections to the comités de village and the comités de quartier. Proposals and resolutions came up from the comités through the sous-sections to the national organs. Thus every party member—indeed, every citizen—had the right and the opportunity to contribute to the making of party decisions. On the other hand, no party member, or citizen, might publicly oppose party decisions once they had been made. This, broadly, is what is understood by democratic centralism within the Union Soudanaise.

In addition to these vertical links connecting the basic units of the party with its central policy-making organs, there were horizontal links between the party proper and its various allied organizations: the youth (Jeunesse de l'Union Soudanaise–RDA), the women (Union des Femmes de Mali), and the trade unions (Union Nationale des Travailleurs Maliens), as well as the Anciens Combattants et Victimes de la Guerre, the Mouvement Soudanais de la Paix, and so forth. The unified youth movement (JUS-RDA) was brought into being in 1959 through the fusion of various existing youth associations into a single secular organization, working in close association with the party and organized on the same general pattern, but enjoying some real measure of autonomy and initiative. At the same time the JUS-RDA was able to exercise an influence on party policy because its supreme authority, the Bureau Exécutif National, was represented on the national Comité Directeur of the Union Soudanaise, and there was similar representation at the level of the sous-sections. The JUS-RDA embraced organizations with specialized functions—Pionniers, Milice Populaire, Brigades de Vigilance, Service Civique Rurale—concerned with drawing young people into socially useful activities such as illiteracy campaigns and the building of roads, schools, clinics, and the like. The Union des Femmes was linked with the Union Soudanaise in a roughly similar way; it was organized as an autonomous section of the party with representation on the comités directeurs at both national and district levels. It has been concerned particularly with women's education, the improvement of home conditions, the defense of women's interests (e.g., through the Code de Mariage, which limits polygamy, forbids divorce by repudiation, etc.). The trade-union organization (UNTM, formerly the Union des Travailleurs du Soudan) has also, throughout its history, been strongly represented in the policy-making

Mali

organs of the party, and tended, under the leadership of Abdoulaye Diallo and Lazare Coulibaly, to function as its radical wing.

This is far from being a complete account even of the formal structure of the party. Moreover, the structure, as described here, was modified in several quite important ways by the Sixth Party Congress, held at Bamako from September 10 to 13, 1962. First, the party organ functioning at the level of the cercle (the town of Bamako being regarded for this purpose as a cercle) became a section instead of a sous-section, and the term "sous-section" was transferred to party organs at the level of the *arrondissement* (or, in Bamako, the quartier). Second, comités directeurs were eliminated at the national and cercle levels; their functions were partly taken over by the existing conférences (national and sectional), meeting not less than once a year. Third, a new type of basic party unit was created, industrial rather than local, at the level of workshops and enterprises; these new units, known as *groupes politiques,* were to function as "brigades de travail dans la construction socialiste." Fourth, the Bureau Exécutif, hitherto the supreme authority of the JUS-RDA, was suppressed, and it was decided to integrate this organization and the Union des Femmes du Mali more closely with the party. The Bureau Politique of nineteen members elected by the party congress included in fact two representatives of youth (*commissaires à la jeunesse*), one representative of women (*commissaire à l'organisation des femmes*), and one representative of trade unions (*commissaire aux questions syndicales*).[48] So far as can be judged, the purpose of this reorganization was partly to simplify the structure and eliminate any party organs that seemed redundant; partly to tighten party discipline; and partly to develop a party organization that would be as well equipped as possible to solve the problems of socialist construction at the grass-roots level.

As to the relationship between party and state, there is no doubt about the ultimate supremacy of the organs of the party over the organs of government, in accordance with the principle described by Madeira Keita as the "dominance of the political machine over the administrative machine."[49] It has been said that "the Bureau Politique decides; the Assemblée Nationale ratifies; the Conseil de Gouvernement executes." This generalization is no doubt oversimplified. Indeed, in a state where the party is not only unique, but as all-pervasive as the Union Soudanaise, any attempt to draw a distinction between party and government is somewhat artificial. Major policy decisions in Mali are usually announced as

---

[48] For the data contained in this paragraph see the reports of the Sixth Party Congress published in *L'Essor,* Sept. 17, 1962.

[49] "La Prééminence de l'appareil politique sur l'appareil administratif," in Madeira Keita, "Le Parti unique en Afrique," *Présence Africaine,* n.s., no. 30 (Feb.-March, 1960), 12.

having been taken by "le parti et le Gouvernement," and the fact that about half of the members of the cabinet are normally also members of the Bureau Politique is a sufficient guarantee that cabinet decisions are in harmony with party policy, as defined by the Bureau Politique. Similarly, the eighty members of the National Assembly are all party militants having status within the party at either the national or the district level. Hence they are inevitably committed to support the party line. But, as representatives of their respective constituencies, they are also bound, on certain types of issues, to reflect the local or regional point of view. Moreover, through the various commissions that the Assembly sets up, or in plenary sessions of the Assembly, they are able to review and, if they wish, to criticize the decisions of individual ministers. If there is disagreement between a commission, or the Assembly, and a particular minister, the normal procedure is for both to present their respective points of view to the Bureau Politique, which in these, as in other matters of internal controversy, has the final say.

The structure of local administration has likewise to be understood in relation to this symbiosis of party and government. Formal administrative authority rests with the *gouverneurs* of the 6 regions into which Mali is now divided (Kayes, Bamako, Ségou, Sikasso, Mopti, Gao); with commandants de cercle in the 42 cercles; and with *chefs d'arrondissement* (or *chefs de poste*) in the 224 arrondissements into which the cercles are subdivided. All these officials are appointed by the central government. Villages are administered by *conseils de village,* whose members are all elected by universal suffrage, with the exception of the president, who is appointed by the government. Responsibility for the administration of nomadic tribes and *fractions* remains in the hands of chiefs, assisted by elected councils. There are also thirteen urban communes, with their own elected mayors and councils. Superficially the administrative structure seems to have changed little since the later period of French colonial rule, except for the interposition of regional governors between the government in Bamako and the commandants de cercle, and the introduction of elected councils at the village level. In practice, of course, the system has been radically transformed. The hierarchy of officials, from the regional governors to the chefs de poste, and indeed to the presidents of village councils, consists of party members, and in most instances of party militants of many years' experience, selected for their qualities of political understanding, integrity, reliability, and so on, as much as for their administrative ability. "Aussi avons-nous mis a la tête des circonscriptions des commis, des fonctionnaires africains qui ont fait leurs preuves à la tête des sections politiques ou à la tête des syndicats et qui se sont révélés les administrateurs efficaces." [50] At the same time

---

[50] *Ibid.*

these officials are accountable for all their decisions, immediately to the local organs of the party at the level of region, cercle, arrondissement, commune, village, or tribe, with which they are bound to work in close and constant association, and ultimately to the Bureau Politique and the national party.

This symbiotic relationship between administrative and party structures at every level naturally does not imply that no conflict arises between them. Indeed, one of the main preoccupations of the Union Soudanaise in the period since independence has been its effort to overcome such conflicts or to remove their basic causes. This purpose is partly served by the periodic conférence des cadres held at the regional level, in which not merely the administration, but also the technical officials (concerned with education, health services, *eaux et forêts,* agriculture, etc.), whose ties with the party may sometimes be relatively weak, meet and discuss common problems with representatives of the regional party and of its peripheral organizations of youth, women, trade unions, and the like.

It may be useful to supplement this rather bald account of the party structure with one or two comments of a more general kind. First, as has already been stressed, the Union Soudanaise has throughout its history laid particular emphasis on the principle of collective leadership. This principle was restated at the Sixth Party Congress in September, 1962: "Le Congrès, considérant que le Parti est la seule force dirigeante de la nation et que le principe de la collégialité régit tous ses organismes, ... précise que la Direction collective n'exclue pas la responsabilité individuelle dans l'accomplissement des devoirs." [51] Few African parties have succeeded in applying this principle so consistently as the Union Soudanaise. Each of the two successive party leaders—Mamadou Konaté (1946–1956) and Modibo Keita (1956 to the present)—has been regarded essentially as *primus inter pares,* partly because of the character and the attitude of the party leaders concerned, and partly because the Bureau Politique has included a number of exceptionally able politicians (e.g., Madeira Keita, Idrissa Diarra, Seydou Badian Kouyaté, Jean-Marie Koné, Mahamane Alassane Haïdara, at the present time). But it can equally well be argued that only a party that has developed so clear a conception of the importance of *collégialité* can provide a setting in which leaders of this type emerge. Certainly the Union Soudanaise has built into itself a variety of institutional checks to ensure the collective ascendancy of the Bureau Politique and counteract the natural tendency for a personality cult to emerge.

Another characteristic of the Union Soudanaise, and a source of its effectiveness as a party, is the efficiency of its system of communications.

---

[51] "Résolution de politique générale et d'orientation," *L'Essor,* Sept. 17, 1962.

No doubt this efficiency is partly a reflection of the "tradition étatique" referred to above, the tradition of belonging to and functioning within the framework of relatively large-scale political systems: "Nous sommes, ici au Mali, dans un pays qui a un long passé d'administration, un long passé de culture, un long passé d'organisation sociale et culturelle, un pays qui avait une organisation avancée à une époque où certains grands pays, qui sont actuellement à la pointe du progrès dans de nombreux domaines, n'avaient pas atteint ce même niveau." [52] National sentiment, identified with the idea of being a *Soudanais* or *Malien,* has been rein-forced by the succession of crises through which the party has passed: the repression of 1949–1950; the struggle for independence and unity, culminating in the formation of the Mali Federation, in 1957–1959; the disintegration of the federation, and the birth of the independent Re-public of Mali, in isolation, in 1960. On this foundation of national senti-ment the Union Soudanaise has built a superstructure of institutions and procedures, designed to ensure that the rank-and-file party militants in their villages and towns understand the decisions of the Bureau Politique and that the Bureau Politique is responsive to the views of the militants.

The party journal, *L'Essor,* published regularly since 1949 (in a duplicated form for the first ten years, and since then as a printed daily and weekly), has been one important instrument of this policy. *L'Essor* has sought to combine reports of party conferences and activities, state-ments by the party leadership, local and personal news, discussion of the major issues of the day—domestic, African, and international—with lead-ing articles in which the party line is simply and clearly expounded. The fact that the political direction of *L'Essor* was in the hands of Idrissa Diarra, the political secretary of the Union Soudanaise, ensured that it was the authoritative voice of the party and the Bureau Politique. Even when, in its duplicated form, it had a circulation of only some 800 copies, it reached a much wider section of the party membership than that figure would indicate, for it was constantly read aloud by the literate to the illiterate. In addition, the Bureau Politique from time to time issues direc-tives to the subordinate organs of the party, explaining policies and dis-cussing current problems with more frankness than is possible in a public journal.

Other methods have been used to ensure efficiency of party com-munications. One safeguard has been the fact that the management of the party machine, and the handling of internal party problems, have been the special responsibility of the political secretary, who is a promi-nent member of the Bureau Politique and who does not at the same time hold ministerial office. Another important institution has been the Com-mission des Conflits, whose members are periodically dispatched by the

---

[52] Modibo Keita in *Le Mali en marche,* p. 9.

Bureau Politique to inquire into difficulties arising in local party organs and to make judgments on the spot or report back. More recently, by the appointment of six commissaires politiques (see p. 224), the Bureau Politique has sought to ensure a direct and continuous flow of information, in regard to the state of the party and its relations with the administration, from the localities to the center. The purpose of this system would seem to be to supplement, but not to replace, the periodic conferences at the national or regional level, and the frequent tours of particular areas by the secretary-general and other members of the Bureau Politique, by which the party leadership tried in the past to keep in touch with local opinion, and to overcome tendencies toward deviation at the local level, or toward isolation at the national level.

The political theory of the Union Soudanaise belongs clearly to what we have elsewhere referred to as the "revolutionary-democratic" family.[53] It has the distinctive characteristics of all such theories: preoccupation with ethical principles such as dignity, justice, the liberation of man from oppression and exploitation, and the possibility of unlimited progress through the development of reason;[54] insistence on human equality, and the need to remove the social causes of actual inequalities; the conception of the party, and therefore the state, as the expression of the popular will (the Union Soudanaise has been described as the "conscience politique de la nation"); and belief in the brotherhood of man, implying a special kind of brotherhood among African peoples, and thus the concept of "African unity."

It will therefore be best to consider those particular aspects of Union Soudanaise theory which distinguish it from other African ideologies of the same general type. They may be grouped as (a) theories relating to the internal organization of the state, and (b) theories relating to its external relations with other states.

First, the Mali Republic is a one-party state, without apology, and without any supposal that it might develop any other form of political system in the foreseeable future. The reasons for regarding this type of system as better suited to the needs of Mali at this stage of history than any possible alternative have been clearly stated by Madeira Keita[55] and others. The fusion of the PRS with the Union Soudanaise in March, 1959, and the consequent disappearance of any opposition party, reflected the positive desire of the masses in both political camps for national unity.

---

[53] See n. 28, p. 237.

[54] "En tout cas, nous avons la conviction que la victoire appartient à la majorité, que la victoire appartient à l'homme exploité, que la victoire appartient à l'homme insuffisamment payé; et que les guerres n'arriveront jamais à étouffer cette volonté de libération de l'homme exploité par l'homme" (Modibo Keita in *Le Mali en marche*, p. 16).

[55] Madeira Keita, *op. cit.*

It was only at the level of the leadership—where interest in status and office and the play of personal rivalries were operating—that fusion seemed to raise difficulties. Moreover, without committing himself to Sékou Touré's thesis regarding the essentially classless character of African society, Madeira Keita argues that there is no objective social basis for interparty conflict in a system such as that of modern Mali:

> Nous ne pouvons évidemment affirmer que la société d'Afrique noire soit une société sans classe. Mais nous disons que la différenciation des classes en Afrique n'implique pas une diversification des intérêts et surtout une opposition des intérêts.[56]

> Nous n'avons pas de problèmes religieux, de problèmes philosophiques ou de problèmes de théorie économique qui nous divisent pour la construction et la direction de l'Etat.[57]

From a practical standpoint, a plurality of parties gives a handle to neo-colonial influences, as it did in the past to colonial influences, playing on party divisions: "Si nous analysons bien la situation—et même retenant que le colonialisme par son régime électoral, surtout par ses fraudes, par son truquage électoral divisait les Africains—nous constatons que rien de fondamental ne nous opposait les uns aux autres." [58] Multiparty systems are also likely to give rise to the kind of political instability which is incompatible with the mobilization of the people to construct a socialist economy. Finally, although "it must . . . be recognized that the system of a single party is not without its dangers," democracy, in the sense of "the management of public interests in accordance with the will of the masses" and with their active participation, can be realized in a one-party state like Mali, where the single party remains essentially democratic in its internal organization and its mode of functioning. The one-party state is, however, conceived of essentially as a means to an end, and the primary end is the realization of socialism. What is meant by "socialism" in the Mali context?

The socialist theory of the Union Soudanaise has multiple roots. In its origins it was naturally associated with the Marxist-Leninist view of the necessary connection between imperialism and monopoly capitalism ("les Trusts"), which the RDA in its initial militant phase took over from the Groupes d'Etudes Communistes. This view conceived of socialism as an ultimate, not an immediate, objective. (RDA leaders had learned in the GEC's to concentrate their main energies on agitation against those concrete manifestations of colonial capitalism which caused particular suffering and resentment among the various sectors of the population

[56] *Ibid.*, p. 9.
[57] *Ibid.*, p. 14.
[58] *Ibid.*, p. 9.

which they sought to mobilize, such as peasants, nomads, artisans, traders, wage and salary earners, women, and youth.) Commitment to socialist ideas was implicit also in the basic egalitarianism of the Union Soudanaise, revealed in its concern for the interests of the most oppressed and exploited social groupings, such as Somono fishermen, Bella captives, and women. The party tended to represent this concern as an expression of the social values of Islam rather than in the context of Marxist doctrine.[59]

The transition from a general acceptance of socialist principles to preoccupation with the construction of a socialist system was a direct consequence of the breakup of the Mali Federation. The mobilization of the people of Mali behind a program of socialist construction was seen as the only way of resolving the serious economic problems arising from the dislocation of its commercial ties with the West, of ensuring the "ravitaillement de la nation," and of providing a firm guarantee of Mali's future economic independence. Indeed, the strong emphasis placed by the Union Soudanaise on its socialist objectives after September, 1960, may be regarded in part as compensation for its failure to realize any form of West African union, and in part as insurance against the kind of capitalist pressures which, in its view, had been mainly responsible for reducing the original four states of Mali to one.

The practical outcome of this new direction in the strategy of the Union Soudanaise was the 1961–1965 Five-Year Plan, which sought to achieve, as rapidly as possible, "economic decolonization" by means of "socialist planning based upon the facts of African social life [une planification socialiste fondée sur les réalités africaines]." [60] The distinctive characteristics of the Mali plan are not so much its economic objectives —the development of agricultural and animal production, the laying of foundations for industrialization and a "diversified planned economy," investment in infrastructure, the training of cadres, and so forth—as the network of new institutions designed to ensure its socialist content. At the level of every village the plan provides for the creation of a rural cooperative called the Groupement Rural de Production et de Sécours Mutuel (GRPSM), which is responsible for the collective marketing of local products, the purchase of consumption goods, the provision of credit, the organization of communal labor, and so on, and a *champs collectif*, which is intended to function as the nucleus for the eventual collectivization of agriculture. Each group of village coöperatives is to be served by the district Zone d'Expansion Rurale (ZER), closely associated

[59] See p. 225, above.

[60] *Rapport sur le plan quinquennal*, p. 5. The Union Soudanaise was particularly concerned to dissociate itself from Senghor's brand of "African socialism," as expounded in *La Nation et la voie africaine du socialisme* (Paris: Présence Africaine, 1961). See Ruth Schachter Morgenthau, "African Socialism," paper presented at the annual meeting of the African Studies Association, Washington, D.C., October, 1962.

with the Centre Coopératif d'Education et de Modernisation Agricole (CCEMA), of which 150 are projected for the whole of Mali. The purpose of each ZER is to serve as an "active center for the popularization of agricultural techniques and rural education," and to train cadres who will be primarily responsible for the transformation of the pattern of farming and social life at the village level. Each CCEMA is to be equipped with a coöperative shop, agricultural stores and machinery, a center for literacy work, and an emergency medical center.[61]

This policy of giving priority to the development of coöperative institutions among the rural masses stems from the Union Soudanaise's view that the realization of socialism in a society such as that of Mali is impossible without the active, conscious participation of the peasantry, the main productive class. But, as a "coöperative consciousness" is one of the basic "human values of African civilization," these new institutions are "not to be regarded as set up in opposition to an older, traditional way of life, but rather as a means of adapting an existing coöperative outlook to the requirements of the present day." [62]

The system of rural coöperatives is tied in with, and subject to the general direction of, the organs of administration and party described above. (If a village GRPSM wants to build a school or a clinic, or to construct a road or a well, it must first consult the local *chef de poste administratif* to find out whether it can obtain the services of a teacher or an *infirmier*, or other specialist help.) It is also supplemented, at the national level, by the various state agencies set up since September, 1960, to ensure that the government and the party are able to exercise maximum control over economic development and policy. These include the Société Malienne d'Importation et d'Exportation (Somiex), which enjoys a monopoly of the export of groundnuts and of the import of certain key commodities, such as sugar, tea, soap, flour, salt, oil, petrol, cement, matches, sacks, and milk; the Pharmacie Populaire de Mali, which imports medicines and medical supplies and sells them at fixed prices throughout the country; the Librairie Populaire de Mali, which imports and distributes books and journals; the Régie des Transports de Mali; and the Banque Populaire de Mali pour le Développement. The central objective of all these agencies is to reduce Mali's dependence on foreign, and especially French, commercial and financial interests—the *grosses maisons de commerce*—and to provide the institutional techniques for achieving "economic decolonization" and national planning.[63]

The setting up of this new complex of institutions is, however, itself

[61] For the data contained in this paragraph, see *Rapport sur le plan quinquennal,* and *Action Rurale, Edition spéciale, Organisation du monde rurale en République du Mali,* Ministère du Plan et de l'Economic Rurale.

[62] *Action Rurale, Edition spéciale,* p. 4.

[63] For Somiex and the other state agencies referred to here, see *Rapport sur le plan quinquennal* and *Le Mali en marche.*

regarded as simply a means to the realization of a moral end: the creation of a new type of African man, who has consciously rejected bourgeois, individualist values, and has chosen socialist, coöperative values. It is significant that Modibo Keita has defined "bourgeois" in the contemporary African context in ethical (or theological) rather than in economic terms:

La bourgeoisie ... n'est pas un mode de vie, mais il y a un mode de pensée bourgeois. ...

La verité, c'est qu'on devient bourgeois, c'est qu'on est bourgeois le jour où on ne se définit plus en fonction du peuple, et qu'on s'assigne comme objectif la satisfaction de toutes les joies de ce monde, même si on doit écraser le peuple qui est l'instrument de cette satisfaction.[64]

To prevent these tendencies toward "bourgeoisification" in the individual (and particularly among the party *responsables*), institutions of a socialist type are not sufficient. They must be supplemented by constant self-criticism (*autocritique*) and education in the principles of "scientific socialism." [65]

With the breakup of the Mali Federation and the birth of the republic, the Union Soudanaise found itself for the first time in a position to follow an external, as well as a domestic, policy that expressed the ideas and objectives of the party leadership. But because, as Modibo Keita put it in his Chatham House address, the new republic initially "had to face a certain number of difficulties, both internal and external, in affirming its sovereignty and at the same time in maintaining its territorial boundaries," [66] its first preoccupation was to overcome these difficulties; and it was only gradually, in relation to specific situations and problems, that the party was able to define its foreign policy, which in fact is still in the process of evolution. The basic principles that seem so far to underlie it might, however, be summarized as follows:

1) Commitment to the struggle against colonialism and neocolonialism, implying, since September, 1960, active support for the Front de Libération Nationale in Algeria, for the Lumumba-Gizenga governments in the Congo, and for liberation movements in Angola and southern Africa generally.

2) An emphasis on the development of close relations with African states committed to similar anticolonial objectives (in particular, Guinea,

---

[64] *Le Mali en marche,* p. 11.

[65] The Sixth Party Congress of the Union Soudanaise–RDA, held in 1962, instructed the party to organize the education of all militants in "les données historiques, économiques et sociales du Mali, de l'Afrique et du monde, l'histoire et les principes du Parti, les principes du socialisme, sans la connaissance desquels un responsable ne peut affronter efficacement la construction socialiste de notre pays" ("Résolution de politique générale et d'orientation," *L'Essor,* Sept. 17, 1962).

[66] Modibo Keita, "The Foreign Policy of Mali," *International Affairs,* XXXVII (Oct., 1961), 432.

Ghana, and the other states with a radical orientation), combined with an effort to improve relations with other African states pursuing different international objectives, particularly with neighboring French-speaking states having close economic and cultural ties with Mali (e.g., the Ivory Coast, Upper Volta, and Niger).

3) A continuing commitment to the idea of African unity, with the proviso, based on the experience of the disintegration of the Mali Federation, that a durable political union can be realized in practice only by African states with similar social systems, ideologies, and objectives.[67]

4) Acceptance of the principle of nonalignment or positive neutralism as between the two major power blocs, implying (*a*) the elimination of French military bases, and of all forms of special diplomatic, strategic, economic, or cultural relations with France which are incompatible with genuine nonalignment, and (*b*) the development of new forms of relationship with states other than France, including, in particular, the states of the socialist (or Eastern) bloc.[68]

5) An effort to ensure that the *Tiers Monde*—the states in Africa, Asia, Europe, and America which are committed to positive neutralism—play the maximum part in helping to promote the peaceful coexistence of the two blocs.

Any such account of the social and international objectives and policies of a party is likely to be out-of-date by the time it is published. By contrast, what has remained relatively constant throughout the history of the Union Soudanaise is its basic attitude, its capacity to reconcile apparently conflicting standpoints. Although it has preserved, perhaps more faithfully than any other section, its loyalty to the RDA's original revolutionary principles, in practice it has tempered them with a certain cautious empiricism. Its commitment to the idea of African unity (embracing

[67] "We are convinced that the States of Africa will never be independent, in the full sense of the word, if they remain small States, more or less opposed to one another, each having its own policy, its own economy, each taking no account of the policy of the others.

"Our Constitution therefore provides for a total or partial abandonment of sovereignty in favour of a grouping of African States, but such an abandonment of sovereignty demands an identity of views with our fellow states. One cannot build a complete whole with contradictions. Certain common viewpoints on international policy and on economic policy are absolutely necessary" (*ibid.*, pp. 435–436).

[68] Modibo Keita has explained (*ibid.*, pp. 434–435) Mali's special interest in the development of its relations with the states of the Eastern bloc in the following terms: "We have come to the conclusion that when certain European countries afford help to the developing countries they often make such aid conditional, even if only by implication, on political option in their favour. . . . On the other hand, we have noted . . . that the countries of the Eastern bloc, whatever may be their reasons, unreservedly support the peoples struggling for liberation from the colonial yoke. . . . Moreover we have found that help from the Eastern bloc is always immediate help and does not offend the susceptibility or the dignity of the receiving country."

Arabic-speaking and English-speaking, as well as French-speaking, peoples) has not distracted it from the problems of nation building within Soudan-Mali, involving, since September, 1960, a positive effort to realize "socialism in one country." Its emphasis on "collective leadership" in the party and the state, and on the individual responsibility of party militants, has been combined with the determination to maintain an effective form of central government. Drawing the majority of its leaders from an intellectual, and to some extent a social, elite, it has consistently asserted the claims of the illiterate, the poor, the underprivileged. Very conscious of the millennium of cultural tradition which lies behind it, it has not hesitated to attack traditional ideas and archaic institutions which stand in the way of social progress, as the party understands it.

7. GHANA

By David E. Apter

Ghana* has proceeded far more slowly and haltingly than Mali toward the single-party monolithic state. A substantial body of opinion in Ghana, by no means restricted to intellectuals, remains basically unsympathetic to the mobilization objectives of the regime. Ghana's political development illustrates the creation of a one-party mobilization system which is, in many ways, a compromise between the views of militants and moderates. A far cry from totalitarianism, it is nevertheless a genuinely new form of society which is being created under the auspices of the party. To study the Convention People's Party (CPP) is to study the design for the country. Moreover, as Ghana was the first country in colonial Tropical Africa to obtain independence, and the CPP was among the first parties to effect mass politics in Africa, we now have a history that enables some perspective on the role of political parties in new polities.

On the twelfth anniversary of the Convention People's Party in Ghana, Kwame Nkrumah made the following statement:

> This anniversary meets the Party and the nation with me as General Secretary of the Party and President of the Republic.
>
> This fact constitutes a remarkable historical landmark for our people, for it shows that, as I have often said, the party and the nation are one and the same, namely: the Convention People's Party is Ghana and Ghana is the Convention People's Party.
>
> Comrades, it is needless for me to ask you, therefore, to recognize this outstanding fact: that a very grave responsibility lies on the shoulders of us all,

* Material for this paper was obtained on a number of field trips to Ghana under various auspices. Previously unpublished data on the political opposition and the 1956 general election were gathered on a field trip undertaken in 1957 under the auspices of the West African Comparative Analysis Project under a grant from the Carnegie Corporation. More recent material was obtained during a visit in 1962 through the assistance of the University of California and the Institute of International Studies. In addition, funds made available by the Institute of Industrial Relations provided time for the writing of this article. I am grateful to each of these scholarly bodies for their assistance and hasten to add that they share no responsibility for the remarks made herein. I would like to acknowledge the assistance of Dr. David Brokensha of the Institute of International Studies, who read the manuscript and gave me many helpful comments.

This discussion is confined largely to the development of party politics in Ghana. A more detailed analysis of the constitutional structure and the wider political picture is to be found in the new edition of my book, *Ghana in Transition* (New York: Atheneum Press, 1963).

259

not only as Ghanaians, but also as members of the Convention People's Party which, no matter what may be said by our detractors, remains right in front of the struggle for the total liberation of Africa and the union of the independent African states.[1]

In addition to stating the key role of the party in the state, Nkrumah emphasized that the dangers of neocolonialism require vigilance, sacrifice, determination, and courage on the part of Ghanaians. He pointed to Ghana as an example of African self-government, neutralism, and non-alignment, and attacked Balkanization. Finally, Nkrumah said, "the Convention People's Party must mobilize our total manpower for the industrial, economic, technological and scientific reconstruction of Ghana, so that we can produce the necessary conditions which shall mean an abundance of every good thing for our people and the greatest welfare of the masses." [2]

This statement illustrates important characteristics which the CPP holds in common with several governing African parties today. One characteristic is, of course, reliance on the single-party pattern.[3] A second is emphasis on an internal organization that is capable of withstanding neoimperialism. African leaders maintain that colonialism does not end when independence is achieved, but merely takes new and subtle forms. A policy of neutralism (as in the early days of the American Republic) represents as much a moral rejection of the "older" world as it does a practical device for maintaining freedom of action. Other themes include sacrifice and self-improvement, hard work, and a commitment to society rather than to self, which are expressed in the requirements of party loyalty, collective responsibility, and mass solidarity. The party, vigilant against neoimperialism and dedicated to the safeguarding of neutralism and autonomy in international affairs, directs the energies of the public toward economic development.

Ghana did not always follow this pattern. By what steps did she move in this direction, and why? To some extent Ghana shows the effects of a movement with a charismatic leader which transformed itself into a monopolistic party whose symbolic ritualization of leadership offset declining charisma and established legitimacy by subsuming the state under the party. But why was charisma possible in the first place? What has led to the present situation where opposition groups, voluntary associations, or ethnic groups can barely function in the political sphere without being branded as subversive? Can pluralism in the society be manifested within the party? Is there such a thing as one-party democracy?

---

[1] *The CPP Twelfth Anniversary: A Message by Osagyefo* (Accra: Government Printer, 1961).

[2] *Ibid.*

[3] Ghana is now a one-party state, and the CPP is the only constitutional party.

FROM FACTION TO PARTY

Political party history in Ghana began with the early emergence of factions and "clubs." Indeed, the early stages recapitulated the development of political parties in the West. A morphology of political party development in Ghana might look something like this:

A. Ethnic factions and pressure groups, 1870–1940
  1. Ethnic associations, such as the Fanti Confederacy
  2. Protective associations, such as the Aborigines' Rights Protection Society (ARPS)
  3. Improvement associations and old boys' clubs, such as the Young Men's Free and Mutual Improvement Society
  4. Literary and discussion groups, such as the Achimota Conferences
B. Factional coalitions for political objectives, 1920–1950
  1. Local coalitions, such as the Ratepayers' Association
  2. National coalitions, such as the West African National Congress
C. Representational political parties, 1945–1956
  1. Conservative nationalist parties, such as the United Gold Coast Convention (UGCC)
  2. Radical nationalist parties, such as the Convention People's Party (CPP)
D. The party of solidarity (the CPP), 1957–1960
E. Factions within the monolith
  1. Conservative wing, including constituency and branch organs
  2. Radical wing, including auxiliary organs
  3. Intellectuals
    a) Socialist militants
    b) Socialist opportunists

These general categories overlap, both in chronology and in organizational relationships. The various factions correspond to a prepolitical phase in Ghana's history in which groups could pressure local administrative authorities, district commissioners, and the provincial and central governments. In some instances local pressure was contagious and larger coalitions took form around specific issues such as opposition to the Crown Lands Bill of 1894 and the Forest Lands Bill of 1911, when deputations were sent to the British Parliament. From the first such deputation there developed the Aborigines' Rights Protection Society. Still other coalitions came into being, particularly after 1925, when direct elections on a limited franchise were held in the major coastal municipalities for seats in the Legislative Council. Factions at times fought with one another, and at times coöperated, as did political coalitions. The more stable and all-embracing coalitions after 1945 became representational political parties, and groups like the UGCC based their organization and practices on Western and parliamentary models. Indeed, in that instance, the party came in advance of the necessary parliamentary reforms that would have made it more fully like its British counterparts. Much of the nationalist agitation by the UGCC was directed not so much at self-government as toward establishing in the Gold Coast a parliamentary framework with all its ramifications.

Left to itself, the UGCC or its successor organizations might have been successful, if the CPP had not captured the imagination of the nascent Ghana society. Even the CPP was first a party of representation. It developed a form of leadership, however, which required the party to become more or less monopolistic, disciplining itself, abolishing its enemies, and generalizing itself into society, with the result that the representative parties disappeared as the CPP emerged victorious. The victory was not merely against other parties. It meant the triumph of a different party type: instead of the party of representation, the party of solidarity, which in turn altered the fundamental political outlines of the state.

The present stage of party development is interesting because there is a renewal of factionalism, but now it takes place within the context of the party of solidarity and the single-party system. When factionalism is excessive in the party of solidarity, however, what happens to solidarity itself? One answer is that the party becomes riddled with opportunists and sycophants. Another is that the leaders most relied on are the most loyal rather than the best suited for the job, with a resulting growth of political cynicism. This is one of the reasons that the party puts so much stress on the new generations. These are the ones the party must "socialize" and indoctrinate. It is in part a generational revolution that the party now seeks.

The Sources of Factions

The Gold Coast was, as its former name implies, a country whose seacoast was the scene of extensive trade. People lived mainly in hamlets and villages. Their social life was gregarious, centering on family and clan, with extensive internal pluralism and political diversity.[4] Wealth originally derived from the slave trade and later from cash crops such as cocoa permitted greater social and physical mobility. Towns grew and prospered. People moved easily between town and countryside. Yet the various groups composing the population preserved an atmosphere of

---

[4] In the Gold Coast the Ashantis, the most powerful ethnic group, fought the British and resisted education and other British efforts to modernize them. The southern part of the country, having long enjoyed trading and political relations with the West, became the center for a nontribal and urban elite. These southern elites often contended with the chiefs as well as with the British.

intimacy and communication. Even today everyone knows the tribe, the family background, and the education of prominent men.

A limited but superior educational system was established relatively early in Ghana. In addition to primary schools, the Gold Coast had, by 1925, Achimota, Mfantsipim, Adisadel, and St. Augustine colleges, all of them excellent secondary schools whose instruction showed a strong classical bias. These institutions produced an elite from whom came the first impetus to a nationalism that focused upon legislative and social reform.[5]

Two types of nationalists emerged: the chiefs, and the newly educated elites. The nationalism of the chiefs was linked to their councils, which were given formal powers. Its electoral significance was expressed in provincial councils, composed largely of chiefs. Chiefs were often arrayed against the more urbanized middle-class nationalists, lawyers and journalists from coastal towns who organized the Aborigines' Rights Protection Society and the West African National Congress. Some members of these associations were descended from old families of Creole origin, or were products of the extensive intermarriage that occurred in Cape Coast and Accra between Africans and Dutch, Danes, Germans, or English. These nationalities, besides introducing Western occupations, harbored traditions of education and values which helped set them apart from the chiefs.[6] Not only did they conflict with chiefs over purely political matters; they also differed on economic issues.

The Gold Coast economy, based on the single cash crop of cocoa, was hard hit by the depression. Despite this, the intellectuals, encased in their literary societies in Cape Coast, Accra, and Saltpond, and associated with the Aborigines' Rights Protection Society, gave surprisingly scant attention to economic matters. Although at an early date they had been interested in forestry and land policy, and were certainly anxious to expand the number of trading and clerical posts open to Africans both in government and elsewhere, their main concern was political. Preoccupied with widening the franchise and with constitutional reforms, they collided with the chiefs who also sought wider representation in the enlarged legislative council system and wider participation in the affairs of the country, and with the administration which regarded educated "natives" doubtfully, to say the least. By the 1930's the middle-class nationalists had lost interest in nonpolitical issues, but the chiefs remained directly involved in economic matters, and, through these, in politics. After having suffered an initial decline in prestige and support because of their somewhat

---

[5] See D. Kingsley Williams, *Achimota: The Early Years* (Accra: Longmans, 1962), esp. chap. 7 and Appendixes 1, 2, 4.

[6] J. W. de Graft-Johnson, *Towards Nationhood in West Africa* (London: Headley Brothers, 1928), chap. ix.

slippery dealings with the British authorities, they now sought to regain their prominence by putting forward economic and social grievances through their state councils and the regional councils. The great "cocoa holdup," a voluntary trade boycott which in 1937 halted the sale of cocoa to the great European marketing firms, was in part facilitated by the chiefs.[7] Moreover, as chiefs, they had to be concerned with the indebtedness of farmers, maladjustments in tenure and occupancy of land, the control of immigrants and other newcomers in rural towns, and the administration of local justice, coöperating with local administrative officers in their districts. Their nationalism was that of the successful negotiator who enhances the well-being of his community by the shrewdness of his dealings with others.

It would be wrong to regard the chiefs and the middle-class lawyers as always opposed to each other. Not only were they brought together in court cases against the government or private firms, but the middle-class nationalists tried to explain matters of land and custom to British authorities, and, by so doing, safeguarded stool land and ameliorated the conditions of administration. Indeed, to this day some of the most able discussion of customary law and traditions is to be found in books and articles written by lawyers like John Mensah Sarbah, Joseph Casely Hayford, and J. W. de Graft-Johnson.[8] But it was the chiefs who remained closer to economic realities, as lawyers became more concerned with constitutional reform.[9]

These brief comments provide some background to an understanding of party growth and development in Ghana. The two forms of nationalism in the Gold Coast reflected a very different set of social and traditional patterns. Urbanization, education, long contact with the West, the nature of tradition, the lack of religious conflict, and the absence of settlers were some of the characteristics of the Gold Coast. In an atmosphere of intimacy, alternative forms of life were rural or urban, tribal or modern. There were also choices regarding values and society resulting in differing concerns about what constituted political advance and elite status, and

---

[7] W. K. Hancock, *Survey of British Commonwealth Affairs* (London: Oxford University Press, 1942), Vol. II, Part II, pp. 207–231.

[8] John Mensah Sarbah, *Fanti Customary Laws* (London: William Clowes & Sons, 1904); J. Casely Hayford, *Gold Coast Land Tenure and the Forest Lands Bill, 1911* (London: Phillips, 1912), *Gold Coast Native Institutions* (London: Sweet & Maxwell, 1903), *The Truth about the West African Land Question* (London: Phillips, 1913), and *United West Africa* (London: Phillips, 1919); de Graft-Johnson, *op. cit.*

[9] One significant factor in the growth of Ghana politics was the absence of permanent European settlement. As the coastal elites were successful in enlarging their political roles and their participation in government, the devolution of authority could therefore not include European settlers, but, rather, was fought out between two African groups, the middle class and the chiefs.

indeed what it meant to be African. Increasingly, the middle class, and chiefly the nationalists, fought with one another to achieve political prominence in more or less "national" political institutions.

The cleavages produced by these conflicts were deep, and in the twenties, the thirties, and the forties led to ever-widening rifts between different groups in the population. In the Gold Coast what was needed to bring the people together was an all-embracing political movement containing within itself the vision of a new society. This was the circumstance that produced the CPP.[10]

The Nature of Factions

In the emerging pattern of politics, a range of organizations—some made up of chiefs and their representatives from various ethnic groups, others composed of tribal associations working for some particular aim or for the amelioration of local conditions and calling themselves committees or associations—wrote petitions, applied pressure, organized opinion, and made representations to authorities. Thus in 1871 the Fanti Confederacy, a grouping of the major Fanti states, put forward constitutional proposals to establish the confederation as a state with a president-king and a representative assembly. This led to the formation of the Aborigines' Rights Protection Society which, successfully opposing land bills at the end of the nineteenth century, turned its attention to political participation in municipalities. Chiefs were active members of the society, one of the first clearly political organizations in Tropical Africa. By 1912 the society had 100 members, mainly chiefs, lawyers, businessmen, and journalists.

After World War I, in 1920, the National Congress of British West Africa was established under the impetus of one of the leading members of the society, Joseph Casely Hayford, a lawyer. Its objectives included association with the Pan-Africanist movement founded in 1919 under the leadership of W. E. B. Du Bois. The congress was a West African body established in Accra, and at its inception included representatives from Sierra Leone, Gambia, and Nigeria, as well as the Gold Coast. These three associations—the Fanti Confederacy, the Aborigines' Rights Protection Society, and the National Congress of British West Africa—were organized expressions of nationalism. The chiefs and the middle-class elite sometimes joined together, while at other times they were at odds.[11] We may call them the *progressive chiefs* and the *constitutional progres-*

---

[10] Since this paper was completed, a detailed political history has appeared. David Kimble, *A Political History of Ghana, 1850–1928* (Oxford: Clarendon Press, 1963), an extremely useful and exhaustive study, is essential for an understanding of this early period.
[11] *Ibid.*, pp. 330–404.

sives, respectively. They represented the two durable groups in Gold Coast politics which were prepared to put pressure upon colonial authorities and administrators in order to achieve reform, wider political participation, and more political responsibility for Africans.[12]

The progressive chiefs were the main beneficiaries of the early activities of both the society and the congress. British authorities, hostile to the intellectuals, were prepared to work with the chiefs.[13] Provincial councils, composed of paramount chiefs, were established in the Eastern, Western, and Central provinces. These councils became electoral colleges for six of the nine African elected seats on the Legislative Council, as provided in the 1925 Constitution. The other three seats were to be filled by a municipal electorate in the three coastal townships that possessed town councils. These reforms not only enhanced the significance of the chiefs in the political life of the colony (the coastal part of the Gold Coast), but they also turned the attention of the intelligentsia to municipal matters. Interest in nationalist politics was found only in literary societies, study groups, and cultural organizations, and among journalists. Because of this, new semipolitical groups manifested a rising sense of political consciousness (more or less antagonistic toward chiefs), but within the bounds of a colonial system. Such a "nationalism" was essentially reformist and intellectual.[14] In contrast, the progressive chiefs sought to widen their powers in the new political institutions established for the colony area, and subsequently for the country as a whole. The Joint Provincial Council,

---

[12] Not without interest are some of the achievements of these associations. The confederacy, influenced by a parliamentary select committee report of 1865 which argued for eventual self-government for British West Africa, organized itself in order to prepare for the event. But instead of granting self-government, the British consolidated their authority in the Gold Coast. Many of the chiefs then joined the society, and together with the able lawyers agitated successfully against the Forest Lands Bill, which would have converted unoccupied land into crown land. The result was the Concessions Ordinance whereby land could not be alienated without an elaborate legal procedure. Finally, the demands of the congress for widening the African membership of the Legislative Council resulted in the 1925 Constitution, which gave representation to the chiefs, the congress, and the society. This constitution, however, because it was weighted heavily in favor of the chiefs, led to a conflict between them and the intelligentsia.

[13] J. B. Danquah, *Liberty: A Page from the Life of J. B.* (Accra: H. K. Akyeampong [1960]), p. 29.

[14] Virtually all this activity was confined to the coastal area. Ashanti, having actively opposed British intervention, was not represented in the Legislative Council until the Burns Constitution of 1946. Between 1901 and 1934 the old Ashanti Confederacy had been abolished. Much of the nationalist activity among the Ashantis was directed toward the reconstitution of the confederacy. Some divisions, such as Techiman Wam Atabubu, Jaman, Abease, and Berekum (i.e., Brong areas), which in the past had been troublesome, were by no means anxious to be included in the restored confederacy. Today Brong has been set up as a separate region. See Eva Meyerowitz, *At the Court of an African King* (London: Faber and Faber, 1962), *passim.*

created in 1936 out of sixty-five paramount chieftaincies grouped into five confederacies, was an example of successful coöperation among chieftaincies for political ends in the colony area.

One reason for the political strength of the progressive chiefs was that they were less vulnerable to the impact of the depression in the 1930's than were the constitutional progressives. The depression was felt especially in the urban areas where the intelligentsia lived. Not only did the latter depend upon salaries, but they had developed a style of living which did not allow an easy return to the more rustic life of the villages. The depression sharpened their grievances, but robbed them of their resources. The West African National Congress declined in strength, and the Aborigines' Rights Protection Society suffered from lack of funds. The progressive chiefs were in a more secure position, and, after the provincial councils had been established, they reached the height of their political influence. Their counsel and guidance were not only accepted by the British authorities, but were actively solicited. The chiefs were extremely influential in the Legislative Council; for example, the Native Administration Bill of 1927 was largely drafted by Nana Sir Ofori Atta I. The Native Administration Treasury Ordinance of 1934, sponsored by the chiefs, gave them the power to impose taxes. Moreover, their skillful participation in the activities of the Executive Council helped to make them the dominant group in political life.[15]

The constitutional progressives, who played a limited role in the Legislative Council, tried to displace chiefs in the legislature, and to enlarge the opportunities for Africans in administrative cadres. They also became involved in African international affairs.[16] Their support came largely from the Christian towns along the coast, where small political study groups were established which eventually formed two associations. One of these, organized by Dr. J. B. Danquah, was the Gold Coast Youth Conference. The other, launched by staff members of Achimota College, rapidly attracted a wide variety of participants concerned about the future of the Gold Coast. A political association, the Friends of African Freedom Society, and two political parties, the "radical" Mambii Party and the "conservative" Ratepayers' Association, were also organized.[17]

---

[15] The recent struggle against chieftaincy conducted by the Convention People's Party in Ghana is difficult to understand without knowledge of the central political role of the chiefs under British rule.

[16] In 1934, on political missions protesting certain laws in the Gold Coast, the chiefs represented the unofficial members of the Legislative Council and the intelligentsia represented the Aborigines' Rights Protection Society. The ARPS representatives helped to organize the International African Friends of Abyssinia after the attack by Italy.

[17] These parties and a few others, the Oman or National Party, for example, were primarily concerned with municipal matters. The conflict between the chiefs and the intelligentsia, however, centered in the municipalities. The Ratepayers'

Important newspapers of the period were, first, the *Times of West Africa,* edited by J. B. Danquah, and, later, the *African Sentinel,* edited by I. T. A. Wallace-Johnson, a Sierra Leonian who founded the Youth League, and the *Africa Morning Post,* under the aggressive editorship of Nnamdi Azikiwe. Azikiwe, after returning from his studies in America, was so dramatically outspoken in his editorials that he was imprisoned for sedition and libel in 1937.

Perhaps the most significant development was the series of conferences held by the Youth Conference. The first met at Achimota in 1930 to discuss progress and make plans. The second was held at Mfantsipim in 1938, and the third in Kumasi in 1939. There were two further conferences at Akropong and Sekondi. By careful organization, and with a continuation committee in office between conferences, the Youth Conference made strong efforts to bring together old boys from the major secondary schools, particularly Achimota and Mfantsipim, the Aborigines' Rights Protection Society, the intelligentsia, the chiefs, the Ashantis, and important groups in various cultural centers along the coast. The Youth Conference also published a number of pamphlets, one of the most noteworthy being *First Steps towards a National Fund,* edited by Danquah.[18]

Emergence of Political Parties

The efforts of the Gold Coast Youth Conference brought into being a loose network of political organizations which, emerging in the municipalities, soon spread to towns and villages, embracing chiefs, youth, and intelligentsia up and down the coast. Even Kumasi, the capital of Ashanti, hitherto more or less excluded from the political and social life of the country, now became more politically prominent. Achimota and Kumasi discussion groups continued the tradition of the Youth Conference during World War II, and helped to make a new generation politically sensitive. A markedly different political climate began to prevail, particularly among the youth. Efforts to bring political parties together made for greater effectiveness. The Ratepayers' Association and the Mambii Party combined under Dr. F. V. Nanka-Bruce to form the National Democratic Party, which stood for the slow but solid achievement of self-government. Ultrarespectable, serious, and dull as some of these groups were, they nevertheless made political parties part of the Gold Coast scene. Out of these experiences were to come the United Gold Coast Convention and the Convention People's Party.

The interwar period was thus marked by a proliferation of voluntary associations which were the most significant single source of political

Association supported the intelligentsia, who in fact made up the membership. The Oman Party supported the elites.

[18] For further discussion of this period see Apter, *op. cit.*

socialization. Inevitably, as grievances remained unsatisfied, various groups cast about for ways and means to further their objectives. They sought analogies to their condition in the political history of England, and to some extent in other countries as well. At the outbreak of the war, their loyalty to the Empire evoked the promise of radical reform in the colonial sphere, but, when peace had returned, a new postwar constitution proved a disappointment. Africans then turned to amateur constitution writing, and confronted colonial authorities with draft constitutions, petitions, and memoranda demanding political reforms. Their political expectations, evolving slowly in the interwar period, now emerged sharply as they concentrated on specific grievances, asking for political power, postwar benefits, action to curb the postwar inflationary spiral, cognizance of the political ambitions of ex-servicemen, and, finally, definition of the role of the intelligentsia. As politics gathered momentum, the chiefs were left behind. Over the years many chiefs had once again fallen into disrepute. Malpractice was common. They seemed to lag behind the times, despite efforts to modernize their role and to adopt new practices. With their position worsening, ethnic nationalism declined in the Gold Coast, as conditions permitting a more truly national consciousness evolved.

Two aspects of the interwar period were extremely important in Ghana. The first was the growth of voluntary associations with an increasingly political focus. The second was the development of political elites whose concern was constitutional advance and self-government. In the postwar period two other factors entered into the picture. One was the development of a professional corps of political organizers, who might be called "political entrepreneurs," and the other was the effort to build movements rather than parties.

These two latter factors are related in meaningful ways. A politician whose job it is to engage in public life on a full-time basis requires a governmental framework within which to operate. The system within which he works, must, however, specify his role, or at least demarcate the limits within which he may legitimately function. In any stable political system these two conditions are in harmony. In the postwar Gold Coast they were not. Hence the professional politician had to create an acceptable role for himself by changing the structure of government. In order to do that he had to destroy the legitimacy of colonial rule and establish both a new government and a new basis of authority. This process is one important feature of the ideologies of nationalism and revolution. Its moral dimension depends on its ability to provide a new basis of authority, from which derives a more harmonious relationship between political roles and governmental structure. Indeed, in many ways nationalist and revolutionary ideologies depend on their moral dimension rather than on programmatic or specific goals.[19] The colonial systems had, of course, been changing in response to the pressures of new elites as well as to the growing demands by chiefs for more formal powers. Professional politicians therefore found it necessary to widen their attack against colonialism so as to include both chiefs and elites, and thus they acquired a radical and populist orientation.

The Professional Politicians

In the postwar period the first two political groups, the nationalist-progressive chiefs and the constitutional progressives, were confronted with the emergence of a third group, composed of radical and populist nationalists. All three contended for greater authority. The first two believed that the devolution of authority to them by means of increasingly responsible government would allow a smooth and orderly transition to independence. Years of experience on legislative and provincial councils, not to speak of their positions of responsibility in the political and social structure of the country, gave sobriety and continuity to their demands. They could visualize their political roles as already fitted to the evolutionary structure of government.

In contrast, the group of radicals and populists had to destroy the position of prestige and dignity which the chiefs and the conservative elites commanded. Although each of the contending factions had a relatively stable following, the populists appealed especially to three classes in Ghana society: the growing intermediary group of partially educated, dissatisfied younger elements recently arrived in the urban areas; the small but articulate and status-conscious group of journalists, ex-servicemen, and teachers; and the rapidly growing number of semi-industrial workers who were excluded from the competition for urban status but were aware of their significance in the postwar climate of economic development.

These three groups were disliked both by the chiefs, who regarded them as upstarts, and by the conservative elites, who found them embarrassing. Anti-intellectuals living in slum or near-slum conditions, yet skilled in the ways of both town and bush and close to the economic realities of colonial society, became the backbone of the Convention People's Party. Among them were the professional CPP politicians—a hardcore group represented in all the main towns and villages—who were aggressive, militant, and quick to take offense, but remarkably hardworking and diligent.

---

[19] See the discussion of ideology and legitimacy in my introduction to *Ideology and Discontent* (New York: Free Press of Glencoe, 1964).

UNITED GOLD COAST CONVENTION AND CONVENTION PEOPLE'S PARTY

By 1949 there were four main political groups in the Gold Coast: the chiefs, who played an extremely influential role in their state councils, in provincial councils, and in the Legislative Council; the urban business groups in the National Democratic Party which carried on the conservative traditions of the old Ratepayers' Association; the United Gold Coast Convention, founded in 1947 by J. B. Danquah, a lawyer, George A. Grant, a businessman from Sekondi, Francis Awoonor Williams, and R. S. Blay; and the Convention People's Party, founded in June, 1949, and led by Kwame Nkrumah, the former general secretary of the UGCC.

The objective of the UGCC was "to ensure that the direction and control of government in the Gold Coast shall pass into the hands of the people and their Chiefs in the shortest possible time." The UGCC was organized around an executive committee, with major regions having headquarters at Sekondi, Cape Coast, and Accra. It made little headway in Ashanti, and no attempt was made to organize the north. The Asante Youth Association, before going over to the CPP, was its strongest ally in Ashanti. Although the UGCC had no press, strictly speaking, it received intermittent support from the *Africa Morning Post,* the *Spectator Daily,* and the *Daily Echo.*

In both the UGCC and the CPP, actual organization varied substantially from the ideal. During the period (1948–1949) that gave rise to the split between Danquah and the UGCC executive on the one hand, and Nkrumah, who had become its secretary, on the other, the organization took advantage of the opportunities presented by the Burns Constitution of 1946 to press for a greater degree of self-government. Popular unrest, resulting in the riots of 1948, was largely ignored, and even after the riots an atmosphere of conciliation prevailed. A new governor set up the "Coussey" Commission on Constitutional Reform, a measure viewed by the UGCC executive as a token of success for the policy of moderation. It was perhaps this success that made the split with Nkrumah inevitable. Although Nkrumah's primary responsibility was to build up the party's organization, he was neither fully admitted into the elite nor given control over UGCC funds. Consequently he formed the Committee on Youth Organization within the UGCC, which then broke away from the parent body to establish the CPP. Organized primarily in the towns, the CPP, with the assistance of lorry and taxi drivers, railway workers, market women, teachers and "Standard VII" boys, shopkeepers, and others, spread into the villages. Party members, representing groups of townsmen in coastal towns and villages, moving easily between rural and urban life and familiar with chieftaincy and tradition, were the brokers who stood between the elites, who were demanding recognition of their own status, and the wider range of associations—some traditional, some modern, some cultural, some economic—which had been formed in response to diverse pressures of social and political change. A newspaper was essential to publicize the activities of Nkrumah, K. A. Gbedemah, Kojo Botsio, James Markham, Kwame Afriyea, and Gamesu Amegbe; indeed, their organizational work centered on publication of the *Accra Evening News,* which had become the party's organizing instrument as well as an ordinary newspaper.

The UGCC, collaborating with the Coussey Commission, found itself working at cross-purposes with the Committee on Youth Organization (CYO). The UGCC called for a national constituent assembly to implement the Coussey report with certain amendments. It expanded its views, not to the public, but to the chiefs, telling them that "we desire to cooperate with you in your study of the proposals and recommendations of the Report, but as the time is short and we cannot visit every State or Divisional Council for this purpose, we submit the following views for your consideration." [20] Meanwhile the CYO, with Botsio as secretary, attacked the Coussey Commission root and branch: "As usual the appointment of the Coussey Commission to draw up a New Constitution smacks of the taint of out-moded imperialist Crown Colony system. . . . We unreservedly repudiate the idea of being 'trained' for Self Government. Self Government is acquired by practice, not otherwise." [21] From that time on, party politics in the Gold Coast assumed a mass populist form. The clumsy efforts of urban conservatives, chiefs, and intellectuals to denigrate Nkrumah only helped to enhance his popularity. After January 8, 1950, the day when positive action was declared, the Convention People's Party became a social movement as well as a political force.

The history of the organization and the rise of the CPP is well known and need not be recounted here. In effect, Nkrumah achieved what the UGCC had been unable to accomplish. And the youth organizations antedating the UGCC, particularly the General Council of the Youth Conference, whose general secretary had been J. B. Danquah, were restricted to the "quality" elite among the youth who were to become the next generation of middle-class urban professionals. Nkrumah built upon a wider base. Moreover, by focusing on the middle group that was taking form between urban elites and rural traditionalists, Nkrumah made the values of each of the latter more proximate and less antagonistic. He reduced the importance of the urban professional and thus eliminated him from membership in a new *Stand* composed of relatively inaccessible roles.

[20] *The Country's Demand,* United Gold Coast Convention (Accra: West African Graphic Ltd., 1950), p. 5.

[21] *The Ghana Youth Manifesto,* Committee on Youth Organization (Kumasi: Abura Printing Works, 1949), p. 5.

The Convention People's Party consisted of a number of different elements: journalists working on Nkrumah's newspaper, the *Accra Evening News,* of whom the most prominent was Gbedemah; youth groups, including representatives of the Youth Study Group in Accra, whose president was Gbedemah; the Asante Youth Association, whose secretary in Kumasi was Krobo Edusei (this association later combined to form the Committee on Youth Organization with Nkrumah as "promoter" and Kojo Botsio as secretary); ex-servicemen under the leadership of Dzenkle Dzewu, a former sergeant major in the army and general president of the Ex-Servicemen's Union; the market women, represented by Mrs. Hannah Cudjoe; and the young urban radicals of the League of Ghana Patriots under the leadership of Kofi Baako, editor of the *Cape Coast Daily Mail.* In addition, many voluntary and youth associations, such as the Sekondi Ghana Youth Association, the Tamale Youth Movement, the New Era Club, the Manya Krobo State Improvement Association, the Mandated Togo Farmers' Association, and the Ada Youth Association, either by supporting the CPP or by taking a direct interest in its affairs, helped to expand its network of organization.

The CPP was organized in two stages. First, an effective executive, composed of Nkrumah's associates both within the UGCC and outside it, was established. This meant building upon the CYO and the group of journalists associated with the *Accra Evening News.* Kofi Baako became the director of information. The second phase was to fashion Nkrumah into the symbol of liberation. The First National Delegates' Conference, held at Saltpond, appointed a committee of eight to draft a party constitution. At a second conference, held at Ho in 1951, the constitution was presented and the political spirit of the party was defined. "We shall not tolerate factionalism in our Party," said Nkrumah, pursuing a line that has continued to this day. "We shall expel from our ranks those individuals and those little caucuses who meet in their little holes and conspire against the backs of the Party. If they have any grievances against the Party let them come out in the open and defend their position. This, Comrades, is democratic centralism." [22]

The constitution established a national executive committee, and a central committee to serve as its "directorate." The annual delegates' conferences were concerned with major policy objectives. Regional committees with a regional conference, constituency organizations, and party branches completed the organizational structure. In addition, there was a national secretariat with a general secretary, a propaganda secretary, and other officers in charge of the administration of the CPP. Committees

---

[22] Kwame Nkrumah, *The New Stage* (Accra: Nyaniba Press and Publishing Co., 1952), p. 4.

of the national executive were responsible for ideology, education, international affairs, and other phases of party work.[23]

The three core organizational units were the national Executive Committee, the regional committees (for a time), and the party branches. By 1952 there were six regional committees, and at the end of a year 4,000 CPP branches had been established. A women's section was organized, and the Youth League, launched in 1951, had eighty-three branches by the end of 1952. Moreover, the National Association of Socialist Students' Organizations (NASSO) had begun the work of teaching socialism to study groups and classes, and had set up its own branches. By 1952 the combined registered membership of the CPP was 800,000.[24]

The fact that the CPP was able to contest elections from the very first contributed greatly to its organizational success. It won its first victories in municipal elections shortly after it came into existence as a political party, and these were soon followed by others. The Gold Coast Constitution of 1950 made provision for general elections on a wide franchise throughout the colony and Ashanti areas. Nkrumah's emphasis on effective party organization bore results in the first general election in the Gold Coast,[25] held while Nkrumah himself was in jail. The CPP won thirty-four of the thirty-eight municipal and rural seats, and its popular vote was roughly 59,000 against a combined opposition vote of 6,000. The UGCC obtained only two seats in the Legislative Assembly. Indeed, because of the mixed composition of the Assembly and the combination of direct and indirect methods of elections to it, it was the chiefs and their representatives who constituted the parliamentary opposition party. The CPP suddenly realized that its real rival was not the intelligentsia, but rather the traditional leaders, secure in their native administrations and entrenched in their state councils. Thus the new CPP government directed its first attack against the progressive chiefs, with whom the defeated constitutional progressives now made common cause.

The CPP made three efforts in this direction. First, it launched an organizational campaign which, following hard on the heels of the 1951 general election, was designed to set up a CPP branch in every village and town. Second, it enacted legislation which reformed the native authorities system so as to give power to elected local councils instead of to chiefs and their representatives. CPP organizational campaigns thus

---

[23] *Constitution of the Convention People's Party* (1st ed.; Accra: United Press, 1952).

[24] See "Freedom," *C.P.P. Monthly Magazine,* no. 1 (Dec., 1952). Kofi Baako was the editor of this journal.

[25] Indeed, the general election became identified with the CPP, even though it came about as a consequence of the constitutional recommendations of the Coussey Commission. The UGCC and the Coussey Commission were thus robbed of the fruits of their labors.

capitalized on local grievances against chiefs within each chieftaincy, and recruited many local party leaders on purely local grounds. Third, the CPP set out to change the country's constitution so that in the next general election all the seats in the legislature would be based on single-member constituencies and direct elections under universal suffrage; this would eliminate the indirect systems which favored chiefs and their representatives.

All three of these objectives were realized. The Local Government Ordinance, passed in 1951 over the strenuous opposition of the chiefs, made district and local councils two-thirds elective. The "Nkrumah" Constitution of 1954 provided that all members of the Legislative Assembly be elected by direct vote from single-member constituencies. This eliminated the political power of chiefs. Finally, the irresistible power of the CPP made possible the organization of new party branches in all parts of the country.

Opposition to the CPP

Nevertheless, there was opposition to the CPP. Although the National Democratic Party disappeared in all but name, and the UGCC had suffered a disaster from which it never recovered, it was not long before disaffected individuals such as Joe Appiah, Kwesi Lamptey, Dzenkle Dzewu, and others began to leave the ranks of the CPP. Some felt that they had been ignored by Nkrumah. Others disliked certain aspects of the party. Furthermore, older intellectuals of the Aborigines' Rights Protection Society, the National Democratic Party, and the UGCC now put an end to the years of strife with the chiefs; the latter, recognizing the seriousness of their conflict with Nkrumah, looked to the intellectual elites for leadership in a new kind of politics which left them with no direct political outlets.

Despite these efforts to organize against Nkrumah, however, the combined opposition refused to recognize the strength of populism and the effectiveness of the CPP organization. When attacked by local CPP politicians, the chiefs retired to sulk in their state councils, and one by one were eliminated by CPP adherents who helped destool them or otherwise render them impotent. The intellectuals issued manifestoes and argued with one another. They formed one group after another, but remained politically unsuccessful.

Opposition to the CPP took three forms. First, J. B. Danquah and others sought to show that the intellectuals and the chiefs had been the most active participants in the constitutional negotiations leading to the first African government in a colonial territory. It was they, not Nkrumah, who were the really effective nationalists of the country. Indeed, to underscore the point and to embarrass the new government, Danquah made a motion in the 1951 Assembly favoring the establishment of a constitutional committee. This proposal, which would have led to immediate self-government, the Nkrumah government had to turn down. In 1952 the UGCC issued a program for self-government and called for a national emergency council to declare the readiness of the Gold Coast for independence.[26]

Second, efforts were made to build a combined opposition to the CPP. A meeting of a committee for the formation of a united front, held on April 6, 1952, "with a view to preventing the rise of dictatorship and also to establishing a stable and democratic government," [27] was called by G. Ashie-Nikoi and Dzenkle Dzewu, both of whom had defected from the CPP. The committee included Ashie-Nikoi; Ako Adjei; Kwesi Lamptey; N. A. Ollennu, a prominent lawyer of the National Democratic Party; and two journalists, Henry B. Cole, a Liberian, and M. Therson-Cofie. Dr. Kofi A. Busia was later made a member. The committee proposed a loose association of all political parties and organizations to fight the CPP. Upon the committee's recommendation, the National Democratic Party and the UGCC did not merge, but were replaced by a new organization, the Ghana Congress Party (GCP). The word "Congress" was considered to be acceptable to the chiefs, and the name "Ghana" was taken to show that the party would have a nationalist outlook. Its program included general welfare measures of a reformist nature.

The GCP attempted to brand the CPP with corruption. It claimed that the government's plan for education was lowering standards. It wanted more fiscal austerity. In 1954 its slogan was: "Vote for the GCP— the party which will give the country real prosperity, peace and progress." [28] None of its proposals were likely to capture popular support. As the GCP was dedicated to fostering widespread disillusion with Nkrumah, it was never very successful. Busia, who became its leading figure, had trouble with older politicians like Lamptey and Danquah who resented one another. Danquah did not dissolve the UGCC for fear of being without a party of his own making. Instead of appearing as a reasonable alternative to the CPP, the GCP began to look more and more absurd. Despite the dignity of some of its leaders, it created the impression of being a carping, negativistic, and opportunistic set of dissidents. This in turn enhanced the prestige of the CPP.

Another attempt to form a combined opposition failed in 1954, when the Volta Charter was suggested. The language of the charter itself re-

---

[26] *The "P" Plan: UGCC's Seven-Point Scheme for Gold Coast Liberation* (Accra: Iona Press, 1952).

[27] "Deliberations of the Committee on the Formation of a United Front for Political Action in This Country" (mimeographed; Accra, 1952).

[28] *Manifesto of the Ghana Congress Party* (Accra: West African Graphic Co., 1954).

veals the predicament of the opposition more effectively than any description:

(1) We shall organize effectively on a common platform during the election campaign so as to sweep the polls at the forthcoming General Election. (2) The manifestoes already prepared by the various Parties shall be examined and embodied in one manifesto acceptable in principle by all the Allied Parties. (3) A Central Election and Finance Committee shall be set up. (4) A Central Co-ordinating Secretariat shall be set up in Accra with full-time staff to see to the successful running of the campaign. (5) In the event of our winning the election, which we pledge ourselves to help achieve, we shall form a National Coalition Government.[29]

The participating parties were the Togoland Congress, the Ghana Nationalist Party (founded by Obetsebi Lamptey after he was expelled from the GCP), the Ghana Action Party, the Gold Coast Muslim Association Party, the All-Ewe Conference, and the Ghana Congress Party. Because the representatives could not agree among themselves, the Volta Charter was never signed.

The third effort of the opposition was to collaborate with the chiefs. Here they came close to achieving their objective, particularly after the 1954 general election, when popular disaffection with Nkrumah was beginning to appear in parts of the north and in Ashanti. Indeed, the coalition between chiefs and certain of the GCP leaders was successful (particularly for Busia and Danquah, whose brother and cousin, respectively, were chiefs and members of royal families). A number of regional parties emerged, utilizing the only organizational device open to them—the traditional organization of the states. Robbed of their previous power, these traditional groups were ready for use as units of ethnic parties. In 1954 the National Liberation Movement (NLM) was formed in Ashanti under the patronage of the Asantehene (paramount chief of the Ashantis), and with the support of the Asanteman Council and the Ghana Congress Party, particularly K. A. Busia. Bafour Osei Akoto, a prominent cocoa farmer in Ashanti and the Asantehene's chief linguist, was chairman. He proclaimed the NLM as a national movement of Ashantis rather than a political party, and it was frankly an organ of Ashanti nationalism rallying around the Asanteman Council. Except in the coastal areas, where tribal feeling was weakest and urban population largest, ethnic and local forms of opposition became characteristic.

The new efforts of the opposition after 1954 were successful enough to attract much of the youth to its standard. Several factors helped to bring the Asante Youth Association over to the NLM, as well as to foster new anti-Nkrumah youth groups in the south. One was resentment over

---

[29] *The Volta Charter* (n.p., 1954).

the stiffening of the policy of recruitment of young men eligible to promotion within the CPP, for by 1954 the party had filled most of its available administrative and governmental posts and would be unable to
create additional positions until self-government was safely in its hands.
In the resulting competition for CPP positions, the Accra and Kumasi
youth who were unsuccessful became embittered. Another reason for the
defection of young people from the CPP was the harsher party discipline
imposed by Nkrumah. Youth groups were not disposed to take orders
from the Nkrumah government or from the party. Thus the bitterly anti-
Nkrumah Ghana Youth Federation, which collaborated closely with the
NLM, was formed in the coastal area in 1954.

Though the opposition was poorly organized, it continued to grow
in strength and reached the height of its effectiveness just before independence. It also gained the support of the chiefs, who, deprived of seats
in the Legislative Assembly after 1954, allied themselves with political
opposition groups. Some of them coöperated with the Muslim Association
Party, organized primarily among Muslim groups in Accra.[30] But once
again, as in the earlier days of the Coussey Commission, the prospect of
success divided them. Splintering along tribal lines and plagued by personality conflicts, the opposition could find no broad base for unity even
in coalition. More often than not, the older leaders looked back to the
organizations they had sired as the proper progenitors of nationalism and
independence, and bemoaned the fact that these had been usurped by
Nkrumah and his upstarts. Others, having split off from the CPP, sought
local strength in a combination of urban-ethnic minorities such as the
Ga Shifimo Kpee movement which arose in Accra in 1957 to oppose
Nkrumah in his own and adjacent constituencies. Such parties sprang
into being, flared briefly, and extinguished themselves, but a spark always
remained to smolder.

These ephemeral opposition parties contained three elements which
are illustrated by the Ga Shifimo Kpee (only one of many of its type).
The first was Ga and Andangme traditionalists who sought to reassert
the control of their people over land alienated to "foreigners" or to other
ethnic groups. (The objective was to gain control over tribal lands now
in the city of Accra.) The second element was young men who had
hitherto formed the backbone of the CPP "strong-arm" groups: tough,
poorly educated, truculent, and rootless Ga men who had received few
benefits from the CPP. Their complaint that "everyone else was able to

---

[30] The Muslim Association Party originally wanted to coöperate with the CPP.
In 1951 it offered to support CPP candidates and asked to participate in joint
nominations of candidates for both general elections and by-elections. The offer was
refused by the CPP. See *Manifesto of the Muslim Association Party* (Accra: Iona
Press, 1954).

get off the veranda but them" referred to the term "veranda boys," [31] which had once been contemptuously leveled at Nkrumah and his followers by the elites. The third group comprised earlier associates of Nkrumah, such as Dzenkle Dzewu and a former women's organizing secretary of the CPP who belonged to the Ga group; journalists, such as the West African editor of *Drum*, Henry Thompson, and his brother; older leaders of earlier parties, such as Obetsebi Lamptey; and, of course, most of the traditional leaders of the Ga peoples. Economic grievances, traditional issues, and disgruntlement over the lack of opportunities for advancement within the CPP formed the basis for the organization of an opposition party around a tribal group. Chiefs poured a libation in honor of young toughs whom they had only recently regarded with contempt. Young toughs identified themselves as members of Asafo companies (traditional warrior groups), and found a new organizational core from which to work. Old chiefs found their spokesmen in the intellectuals and journalists.

The Ga Shifimo Kpee movement, though highly localized, was one manifestation of dissatisfaction with the CPP, but the opposition groups could not combine successfully. Agreement upon issues could bring about unity among people only within the tribe, and could not phrase these issues in the universally ideological terms required if an opposition party was to succeed. Because the opposition was fragmented, local parties could be annihilated by the CPP one by one: by exploiting an existing conflict, as among Ga traditionalists; by eliminating a powerful chief, as with Nana Ofori Atta II, the former Omanhene of Akim Abuakwa, ruler of the single most powerful anti-CPP state in Ghana; or through promises and benefits, as with the paramount chiefs of Mamprusi and Dagomba who, before long, were soliciting subscriptions for the CPP treasuries.[32]

Despite its difficulties, the opposition continued to strive for a more effective organization. With the NLM as its core, the United Party was formed in October, 1957, under the leadership of Busia. Not long after the party was founded, however, Busia became Ghana's first political exile. Leading Nigerian merchants who had contributed funds to the United Party were deported to their home country. The political activities of the Asantehene were investigated, and many of the leading members of the party executive, particularly R. R. Amponsah, were accused of participating in a plot to assassinate President Nkrumah and were put

---

[31] The term is invidious, meaning people who slept on the veranda and had no home or room of their own.

[32] It is noteworthy that Ga opposition is still very strong. A large proportion of the CPP top officials presently in jail under preventive detention, such as Tawia Adamafio, Kofi Crabbe, Ako Adjei, and Boi Doku, are Ga.

in prison under preventive detention, one of a series of measures which the government took to ensure political control. The opposition was destroyed. In the process the CPP itself underwent fundamental changes. No longer a party of representation, it now became a party of solidarity, changing the basic quality of political life in Ghana.

Too late, the opposition was propelled toward a semblance of unity by the government in the summer of 1957, when the Avoidance of Discrimination Act made tribal and religious parties illegal. This forced the opposition groups—the National Liberation Movement, the Ga Shifimo Kpee, the Northern People's Party, the Togoland Congress, the Anlo Youth, and the Muslim Association Party—to come together in a better-organized body. But just as a loose unity seemed to obtain, the CPP eliminated by a variety of means the effective leadership of the United Party.

Opposition Ideologies

In his valuable discussion of the early relationship between the Working Committee of the United Gold Coast Convention and Kwame Nkrumah, Dennis Austin remarks:

> The broad nationalist front started under UGCC leadership fractured quickly along moderate versus radical lines—it is probably fair to add "along lines of economic and social interest" too. But the great advantage and the great strength of the political struggle in the Gold Coast at this time was the general agreement which existed between all sections of local society—the lawyers, the "young men," the farmers, even many of the chiefs (at least south of the Volta)—on the desirability of self-government. There were differences over methods and between leaders, but not on ends, not even—in 1949–50—on the form of self-government that the end should bring.[33]

To recapitulate, the expansion and the proliferation of political groups had begun in the twenties, and were accelerated in the thirties by the growth of cultural, youth, and old boys' associations. This led to a group division between constitutional progressives and progressive chiefs. The first group could be distinguished from the uneducated, and the second from the more old-fashioned traditionalists. Lawyers, journalists, and teachers, whose past associations were with the Aborigines' Rights Protection Society and the West African National Congress, composed the first group. Chiefs who had participated in the Legislative Council and had helped to frame reform legislation for local government formed the second group. Their past associations went back to the relationship between Nana Sir Ofori Atta I and Governor Sir Gordon Guggisberg, a

---

[33] Dennis Austin, "The Working Committee of the United Gold Coast Convention," *Journal of African History*, II, no. 2 (1961), 296–297.

relationship steadily reinforced by the political ideas that inspired indirect rule.[34] Indeed, the Gold Coast never had indirect rule in undiluted form, partly because the chiefs themselves were influential participants in central government affairs from 1925 onward.

We have already noted the rivalry that developed between the constitutional progressives and the progressive chiefs. Often their members came from the same families. Mainly drawn from the coast, the two groups were not a purely urban phenomenon. The constitutional progressives, for example, did not even have their headquarters in Accra. The ARPS had its office in Cape Coast. The office of the United Gold Coast Convention was at Saltpond, a small town on the coast. The chiefs had their headquarters at Dodowa, the site of the Joint Provincial Council. Leaders were scattered up and down the coast and inland by virtue of their professions or their state councils. There was little effective organization in the UGCC, despite wide sympathy from diverse associations and individuals. In contrast, local organization was strong among the chiefs through the modified structure of the state and provincial council system. Although never properly adapted for national political purposes, it participated increasingly in central government while carrying on local government.

The CPP was able to organize all those groups that, although peripheral to the constitutional progressives and the progressive chiefs, made up the bulk of the population. Younger groups were kept at arm's length by the chiefs as well as by the elderly leaders of the UGCC, such as George "Pa" Grant. As Thomas Hodgkin put it after the CPP electoral victory in 1951, "The measure of social revolution involved in the CPP's victory at the recent elections can be realized from a study of the election results. In the constituency of Assin–Upper Denkyira (Rural Area), for example, Alfred Pobee Biney, former locomotive engineer (CPP) obtained 51 votes from the electoral college, as compared with 13 votes for Nana Sir Tsibu Darku, Kt., O.B.E., Omanhene of Assin Attandansu. This defeat was typical of many." [35]

Local conflicts within state councils, however, created points of entry for CPP politics. Those in opposition to the chiefs, often because of local and family matters, were anxious for an alliance with outside forces. The most famous example occurred in the Brong areas of Ashanti. The Brongs had fought long and quite unsuccessfully against the Ashanti Confederacy (after its restoration in 1935). The CPP allied itself with the Brongs

---

[34] Even anthropology played an important role in this relationship; if the general policy of indirect rule was often reinforced by the observations of anthropologists, a more direct sympathy between the British administration and the chiefs for the modification of traditional situations was provided by the writings of R. S. Rattray.

[35] Thomas Hodgkin, *Freedom for the Gold Coast?* (London: Union of Democratic Control, 1951), p. 9.

against Ashanti.[36] Today the Brong-Ahafo region is separate from and larger than the Ashanti region, and is as well one of the strongest CPP areas in the country. The CPP also intervened in disputes over stool lands and in problems involving the destooling of chiefs, protests against taxes, unpopular European commercial activities in rural areas, and other key issues concerning chiefs and their followers. What occurred then was a conflict between the African "establishment" and those who wanted to enter it.

Indeed it was rather a long time before issues polarized themselves into basic conflicts over ideologies and aims. From 1949 to 1954 both the CPP and the opposition groups remained essentially parties of representation. Their aims were to widen the franchise, organize for elections, enlarge the sphere of representative government, and thereby gain control of the society. Political coalitions seeking unity among diverse groups remained the basis of both government and opposition politics for a long time.[37]

Typical political demands of the constitutional progressives may be found in the pamphlet, *The Country's Demand*, which is written in the form of a "Letter to Nananom [Chiefs] in Council." It called for a two-chambered legislature with the upper house of chiefs composed predominantly of elders who would represent them. The traditional state councils were to retain their powers. In effect, chieftaincy and its particularly Ghanaian form of traditional "democracy" were to continue to provide the major link between the state councils and the central government, while popularly elected representatives in the lower house would provide representation for the population as a whole.[38]

---

[36] Meyerowitz, *op. cit.*, *passim*.

[37] J. B. Danquah is an excellent symbol of the "coalitional nature" of the opposition, if only because he so clearly illustrates the qualities of its leadership and its pattern of activities.

His elder brother was Nana Sir Ofori Atta I. Danquah was well educated both in Ghana and London (second-class Honours B.A. in philosophy and a Ph.D. in ethics from London University). He became a lawyer, and helped found the Gold Coast Students' Association and the West African Students' Union in Great Britain. He belonged to various religious bodies; he worked both with chiefly bodies and with more urbanized political groups; he established the youth conferences in the thirties; he published the *Times of West Africa*, and wrote on Akan religion and Gold Coast politics; and he participated in the Joint Provincial Council, the Legislative Council, the legislature, and assemblies. Throughout his remarkable career his activities remained consistent with his belief in pluralism. His own party, the United Gold Coast Convention, was never more than a coalition, and his later participation in the Ghana Congress Party was based on the same principle. His later support of feudalism was a natural product of his belief in political pluralism.

There were many such figures in the opposition. Kofi A. Busia was another younger man who moved easily between the educated elite, of which he was a key member, and the progressive chiefs, of whom his brother was one. See Danquah, *op. cit.*

[38] George A. Grant, *The Country's Demand* (Saltpond: United Gold Coast Convention, 1950).

Two years later the opposition stated its program in a pamphlet, *The "P" Plan*. The program called for a national emergency council to declare dominion status and establish an interim constituent assembly in which seats were to be distributed as follows: Convention People's Party, 5; Joint Provincial Council, 3; Asanteman Council, 3; Northern Territorial Council, 3; British Togoland Council, 1; United Gold Coast Convention, 4; People's Democratic Party, 1; and Aborigines' Rights Protection Society, 3. Delegations from political parties were to speak at territorial councils, the trade-union council, University College, the teachers' union, churches, chambers of mines and commerce, and farmers' associations. Hence the "convention" aspect of the opposition, which was also present in the early stages of the CPP, stressed a kind of loose coalitional unity.[39] Notably absent was a concern that the people of the country be granted broad political participation. The appeal was always to a coalition of organized groups and interests.

It was only when the Ghana Congress Party was formed in 1952 that emphasis was placed on the electorate and the public. Then, however, the main objective was to capture support being given to the CPP. "The new Party should make no distinction between classes of people in our national community." But even this statement was diluted by a reference to chieftaincy: "Unlike the United Kingdom, the people and their Traditional Rulers *are one and the same people.*" In fact, the emphasis on chieftaincy soon became much stronger, partly because the structure of the Ghana Congress Party depended more and more on traditional organization and chieftaincy.[40] By 1956 it was chieftaincy that was keeping alive the most stubborn opposition. Rural groups, disenchanted with the government's cocoa policy and disturbed by the slow pace of development in the villages, rallied to the chiefs. This was particularly true in Ashanti.

The constitutional progressives, in keeping with their tradition of coalition, called for a federal union with an upper house composed of forty-eight members: ten from each of four regions to be elected by the territorial council of the region, one from each region to be appointed by the "federal government," and one from each region to be appointed by the governor-general on the advice of a council of state. In addition to an elective lower house and a federal prime minister and cabinet, there would be a council of state, consisting of the governor-general, the heads of the regions, the federal prime minister, prime ministers from each region, and the federal ministers of defense and external affairs, the interior, and justice. Each region would also have upper and lower houses. The upper houses, to consist of chiefs and their representatives,

[39] *The "P" Plan.*
[40] "Deliberations of the Committee on the Formation of a United Front for Political Action in This Country" (italics added).

would be built around the existing territorial councils; the lower houses would be elected by universal adult suffrage every four years. Enumerated powers for the federal government were to be relatively restricted, with residual powers remaining with the regional governments. The regional assemblies would play a key role in constitutional amendment.[41]

In summary, the constitutional progressives and the progressive chiefs had formed an alliance in defense of their interests. In this alliance the chiefs were in the ascendancy, drawing a large part of their strength from their ability to modify age-old institutions so as to reinforce their claims on the traditional loyalties of the rural population. Conflicts with the CPP over local issues were transformed into matters of deep national interest. "Ethnic" parties thus used "traditional" organization as the basis for electoral combat. Political party struggles became conflicts over basic beliefs as to the nature of Ghana society and its future political organization. Violence, always a good index of such conflicts, increased sharply just before independence. A new and younger political leadership, made up of such men as Victor Owusu, R. R. Amponsah, Joe Appiah, and others who were untainted by the earlier failures of the constitutional progressives, came forward to work with the chiefs. As they breathed new life into the opposition, events began to move more rapidly. Indeed, two events brought the conflict to a head and almost precipitated a revolution. One, before independence, was the 1956 general election, which many thought at the time would be the last free election in the country. The other, after independence, was the establishment of the republic with Nkrumah as president in 1960. The period between these two events was marked by a struggle between government and opposition over the nature of the state.

In general, the loose coalitional approach favored by constitutional progressives and progressive chiefs began to consolidate after 1954 into a tighter organizational structure. By 1957 the opposition parties, with their new leadership and their more popular appeal, had become one party of representation with real strength centered upon the institutions and the practices of traditional society. The proposals for federal forms of government represented the political stand of the progressive chiefs, the royalists who accepted innovation and were prepared to fight for it on the basis of pluralist democracy.

The CPP, originally a collection of diverse ethnic groups and associations balanced within a decentralized framework, also underwent changes. After coming into power in 1951, the party employed the full strength of government as well as the prestige of the civil service to

---

[41] *Proposals for a Federal Constitution for an Independent Gold Coast and Togoland* (Kumasi: Ahma Printing Works, 1956); see also *Statement by the National Liberation Movement and Its Allies* (Kumasi: Ahma Printing Works, 1956).

enhance its power and consolidate its position. Conscious manipulation of Nkrumah's charisma was blended into the pursuit of economic development, the expansion of education, and the achievement of self-government and independence. The sheer proliferation of membership in the party, an increase in the range of its political activities, and the all-inclusive quality of its political ambition brought significant changes. From a loose alliance of youth, economic, and social associations, as well as ethnic groups, with a strong political nucleus at the center, the CPP had become both a political movement and a political party. As a political movement it appealed to the whole of society in the name of the leader for independence. Radical in the speed with which it sought to achieve its political objectives and in the militancy it required of its members, it remained mainly middle class or rural in its following. Shortly after the CPP came to power, its leaders were "small middle-class people—petty traders, chemists, school teachers, farmers, journalists, etc. A few of them [came] from the Trade Union movement. There [were] also one or two lawyers among them. But the standard of living of most of them [was] not very far removed from that of the mass of the people." [42]

The CPP was a political party which more and more became a movement. As a movement, it claimed more than parties normally do. As a party, it remained a party of representation until independence. Better-organized than the opposition, it deliberately adopted policies designed to attract the support of diverse groups in the population on the basis of interests that were popularly generated or stimulated by its leaders. Inevitably, however, in the effort to please some, the party offended others. Indeed, just as the opposition forces were beginning to coalesce into a political party, the CPP was alienating increasingly large numbers of people. Ordinarily the two parties of representation would simply have competed for political power, but each drew its strength from completely contradictory sources of legitimacy. Behind the constitutional progressives were the chiefs and the manipulators of tradition, local, sectarian, and increasingly embittered. Behind the CPP as a party stood the CPP as a movement, monopolistic, demanding total loyalty, and defining its friends and its enemies in terms of that loyalty. In the end the political movement won. The parties of representation disappeared. A new militancy replaced the old popular appeal—a militancy with a strong quality of coercion about it. The CPP had become a party of solidarity. It is in the light of these changes that the elections in Ghana will be examined.

ELECTIONS

There are several reasons for the transformation of the CPP from a party of representation into a party of solidarity. As a party of repre-

---

[42] Hodgkin, *op. cit.*, p. 9.

sentation, it had to abide by certain principles of constitutional government. Moreover, its effectiveness in implementing programs depended upon substantial, if not overwhelming, electoral support. With major weaknesses in electoral strength, the CPP as a political movement remained unstable and vulnerable.

Before analyzing the general elections that have taken place since 1951, when the CPP came into power, it is vital to record some of the vast changes that occurred between 1951 and 1956 regarding the purposes and the composition of the legislature as well as the system of elections itself. Although the 1950 Constitution provided for a wider and more representative legislature than any previous colonial constitution, nonetheless it continued the representation of a number of significant political groups in the Gold Coast, particularly the chiefs and their representatives, and rural and urban groups. Rural members were indirectly elected, and the territorial councils elected representatives as well. The only direct elections were those in urban areas, based on a broad but by no means universal franchise. Moreover, a system of electoral colleges prevailed in the north. Not until 1954 did the legislature become a fully representative body with an assembly drawn from 104 single-member constituencies.[43] The change that occurred in 1954 was, therefore, almost as fundamental as that of 1950, when the nominated unofficials (mostly constitutional progressives), by providing for the direct election of urban members, occasioned their own removal from the Assembly. Some of them were then elected by territorial councils as representatives of the chiefs. But in 1954 the chiefs were unable to send representatives to the Assembly unless they were directly elected. This means that mass organization throughout the country was the only effective means of ensuring parliamentary victory.

Despite the organizational weakness of the opposition, however, its record in various elections shows how widespread was its support, a fact that the parliamentary successes of the CPP tend to disguise. In practice, the pluralities by which the CPP won most of its elections were not overwhelmingly larger than those usually found in stable two-party systems. In fact, before the CPP onslaught against all opposition groups, when it became abundantly clear to all that to vote for the opposition was idle or even dangerous, the opposition was more than holding its own. As the accompanying figure shows, in the period from 1954 to 1956 the presence of the British limited the use of political force by the CPP against the opposition. In the 1956 election, the "independence" election and presumably the particular inheritance of the CPP, the percentage of voting was highest where the opposition was strongest. In Ashanti, the

---

[43] In 1960, ten additional regional seats for women were added, bringing the total membership of the National Assembly to 114.

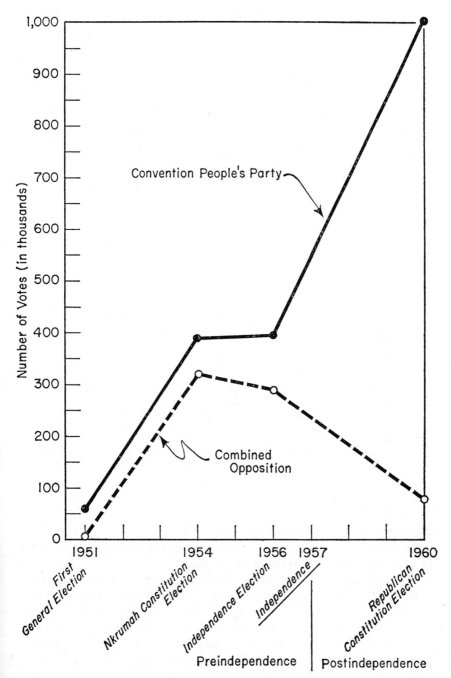

Ghanaian Elections, 1951–1960

NLM stronghold, 57 per cent voted; in Transvolta-Togo, 51 per cent voted; and in the Gold Coast colony or coastal area, where Nkrumah was especially strong, 47.5 per cent voted.[44]

The 1954 general election was the first popular election in the country. The opposition popular vote was relatively strong, totaling 324,822; the popular vote for the CPP was 391,720, or 20 per cent more than that for the opposition, with 59 per cent of the eligible voters actually voting. Parliamentary representation, however, presented a very different picture:

Party	*Number of seats*
Convention People's Party	71
Independents	16
Northern People's Party	12
Togoland Congress	2
Ghana Congress Party	1
Muslim Association Party	1
Anlo Youth Organization	1

After the 1954 election the Ghana Congress Party began to disintegrate, as personal conflicts among its leaders became sharp. Relations among opposition leaders had never been too harmonious: Obetsebi Lamptey had broken away to form the Ghana Nationalist Party; Danquah had refused to acknowledge the leadership of Busia; and Dzenkle Dzewu had withdrawn in disgust after the failure of the combined opposition to sign the Volta Charter the February preceding the 1954 general election.

The poor parliamentary showing of the opposition in the 1954 election (many of the independents were in fact CPP "rebels" who rejoined the CPP once in the Assembly) stimulated organization along ethnic lines. The National Liberation Movement, formed shortly after this election, illustrated the trend (see p. 277, above). Despite the growth of ethnic nationalism, however, the CPP was able to increase its over-all voting strength in the general election of 1956. It received 398,141 votes, and the combined opposition received 299,116. Thus the CPP won 38 per cent more of the popular vote than the opposition, an increase of 18 per cent over its record in the 1954 election.[45]

These figures, however, are somewhat misleading. A more detailed analysis of the 1956 election statistics shows that the opposition vote was heavily concentrated in the hinterland. Moreover, in some areas where the CPP won, the turnout was relatively low. For example, in Accra Municipal, the center of CPP support, only 31,840 of the 86,603 registered voters actually voted. In Accra Central, Nkrumah's own constituency,

---

[44] "Report on the General Election of 1956" (mimeographed).
[45] *Ibid.*

registered voters totaled 32,944, but Nkrumah received only 11,119 votes. His opponent, S. E. Odamtten, a constitutional progressive and a founding member of the Ghana Congress Party, received 1,865, and the turnout was only 39 per cent. This surprisingly low figure is subject to two interpretations, both of which are reasonable. One is that everyone knew that Nkrumah would win and therefore many did not bother to vote. The other is that in Accra Central, a strong Ga constituency, a quiet and unorganized opposition to Nkrumah was beginning to emerge, though it did not come into the open until several years later.[46]

In some areas where it had exploited traditional conflicts, the CPP gained its heaviest vote. For example, in the Brong area, where it had supported the Brongs against the Ashantis, not only was the vote large, but the CPP did exceptionally well, receiving 38,373 votes against 25,633 for the opposition. In Kumasi, where before 1954 the CPP had won overwhelmingly both in municipal elections and in the 1951 general election, the issues were bitterly disputed and loyalties and rivalries had been deeply inflamed, particularly in non-Brong areas in Ashanti and in the north. Southern Ghana, for instance, gave only 42,602 votes to the opposition, or 16 per cent of the votes cast, whereas the rest of the country gave it 256,514 votes, or 35 per cent of the total vote. This opposition vote, without benefit of well-organized parties, was indeed remarkable, particularly after effective rule by the CPP, which was asking for a vote of confidence to bring the country to independence. In fact, the CPP did not increase its number of seats until after independence, when opposition members began to cross the floor and the opposition as such was finally abolished. A more detailed breakdown of the 1956 general election, in which 50 per cent of the eligible voters went to the polls, is shown in table 1.[47]

The elections held after the 1956 general election, including by-elections, are particularly significant because they illustrate some of the major conflicts that arose between the CPP and the opposition. They also illuminate the rise of the United Party, the attack upon it by the CPP, and the circumstances under which the CPP developed from a political movement and a party of representation into a party of solidarity in a single-party state.

Kumasi South, a critical Ashanti area, illustrates the fluctuations in popular support of the CPP and the fickleness of the public in four elections: the 1954 and 1956 general elections, a 1958 municipal election, and a 1959 by-election (see table 2). This interesting constituency contained a relatively cosmopolitan but predominantly Ashanti population

---

[46] *Ibid.*

[47] Dennis Austin and William Tordoff, "Voting in an African Town," *Political Studies*, VIII (June, 1960), 130.

TABLE 1

GENERAL ELECTION OF 1956 IN GHANA

Region	Number of registered voters	Number of votes cast	CPP^a	Opposition parties							Total opposition vote
				NLM^b	NPP^c	MAP^d	FYO^e	TC^f	WYA^g	IND^h	
Accra Municipal	86,603	31,840	27,076	2,950	..	1,814	..	..	..	..	4,764
Western region	226,911	111,896	97,064	7,109	..	..	..	..	3,898	3,825	14,832
Eastern region	167,605	77,890	54,884	16,065	..	..	1,230	..	..	5,711	23,006
Transvolta-Togo	197,195	101,584	55,508	..	..	..	5,617	20,352	..	20,107	46,076
Ashanti	389,153	224,069	96,968	119,033	..	7,565	..	..	..	503	127,101
Northern territories	325,407	149,478	66,641	..	72,440	1,732	..	..	..	8,665	82,837
Total	1,392,874	696,757	398,141	141,157	72,440	11,111	6,847	20,352	3,898	38,811	298,616

REPRESENTATION IN LEGISLATURE

Number of seats won	1,392,874	99^i	66	12	15	1	1	2	..	2	33^j
Uncontested seats	66,869	5^k	5	..	..	..	..	..	..	..	..
Total	1,459,743	104^l	71	12	15	1	1	2	..	2	33^j

ᵃ Convention People's Party.
ᵇ National Liberation Movement.
ᶜ Northern People's Party.
ᵈ Muslim Association Party.
ᵉ Federation of Youth Organizations.
ᶠ Togoland Congress.
ᵍ Wassaw Youth Association.
ʰ Independents.
ⁱ Total number of seats won.
ʲ Number of seats won by opposition parties.
ᵏ Total number of uncontested seats.
ˡ Total number of seats in legislature.

SOURCE: "Report on the General Election of 1956" (mimeographed).

TABLE 2

FOUR ELECTIONS IN KUMASI SOUTH, 1954–1959

Election	Number of registered voters	Total votes cast	Per cent voting	Convention People's Party		Opposition		Independents	
				Number of votes	Per cent of votes cast	Number of votes	Per cent of votes cast	Number of votes	Per cent of votes cast
General, 1954	23,926	13,499	56.4	11,232	82.3	2,104	15.6	163	1.2
General, 1956	32,860	19,622	59.7	7,740	39.4	11,882	60.6	a	..
Municipal, 1958	38,890	26,741	68.2	14,849	55.5	11,687	43.7	205	0.8
By-election, 1959b	38,838	19,015	49.0	9,023	47.5	8,653	45.5	1,339	7.0

a No candidate.

b The 1959 by-election marks a change in the pattern. Owing to a split in the CPP branch, the extremely popular CPP candidate, B. E. Dwira, was ousted and therefore ran as an independent. He received 1,339 votes. The CPP candidate who replaced Dwira, Owusu-Afriyie, had the support of Nkrumah and of the party's Central Committee and won 9,023 votes. The opposition candidate, J. Fordwo of the United Party, received 8,653 votes. This by-election is particularly noteworthy because it shows that latent opposition continued to exist, and that interference from Accra, even in local CPP affairs, could cause the opposition vote to rise sharply. The significance lies in the facts that the opposition is thus more real than apparent, and that the electoral system may check the actions of CPP politicians. Source for the 1959 data was *West Africa*, April 25, 1959, p. 387; May 9, 1959, p. 449.

whose ties to the Asantehene were weakened by urbanization and by the influx of relatively stable and commercially or professionally successful strangers (non-Ashanti), particularly from the south, who had inter-married and settled down in the constituency.

In other areas the decline of the opposition after 1956 was over-whelming. In Sekyere West, for example, in the 1959 by-election, the United Party lost the seat formerly held by its secretary-general, R. R. Amponsah (who had been put in jail for alleged participation in a plot against Nkrumah). The CPP candidate, Kwaku Bonsu, received 10,840 votes to 5,153 for the opposition candidate, Kwasi Agyarko. In another striking illustration, K. A. Busia, leader of the opposition and Ghana's first political exile, lost his seat to his long-time political enemy, C. E. Donkoh.[48] In the violent campaign preceding the election, fifty-eight people were arrested and two CPP supporters were killed. The result was never in doubt. The vote was 13,676 for the CPP and only 1,589 for the United Party.

Everywhere, from 1957 on, the constituency organizations of the op-position were attacked root and branch. The leaders of the United Party were subjected to abuse, and many of them were jailed and expelled from the National Assembly. Finally, in the spring of 1960, in the last major election held, the effects of this policy were amply displayed. J. B. Danquah, who stood for maintenance of the *status quo* with the prime minister continuing to be responsible to Parliament and the Queen, was soundly beaten by Kwame Nkrumah, who campaigned for a change to republican status with himself as president under a new constitution. The vote for the republic was 1,000,740 to 131,425 against. Nkrumah received 1,016,076 votes for president; Danquah, 124,623. The rout was complete. A year and a half later, Danquah, the leading symbol of opposition and the person most responsible for bringing Nkrumah back to the Gold Coast from the West African secretariat, joined his colleagues in prison under preventive detention.[49]

The CPP as a Party of Solidarity

The CPP electoral successes have virtually eliminated the opposition as an electoral threat to the government. However, the effect on the CPP itself requires comment. Three tendencies have become apparent since 1960. First, the CPP constituency and branch organizations have declined, not in number, but certainly in significance within the party. Second, the auxiliary and functional organizations of the party have become more important. These two tendencies have led to a third, the increase in in-

---

[48] Busia's brother, the former chief of Wenchi who had been destooled, has also gone into exile.

[49] Danquah has since been released, and is currently president of the Ghana Bar Association.

ternal factionalism, in competition for influence, and in inner party intrigue. This in turn has caused Nkrumah to tighten his authority over
the entire party apparatus. These three changes have produced modifications in the organization of the party and its auxiliary agencies, which
serve as quasi-public bodies.

The Decline in Significance of Constituency and Branch Organizations

The disintegration of the United Party as an electoral force created
a new and unanticipated problem for the CPP. Branch leaders, no longer
attacking opposition forces in the constituencies, began instead to patch
up their differences with those they had vanquished. Efforts were made
to recruit former rank-and-file United Party adherents into the CPP in
order to swell the latter's membership, augment national and local treasuries, and build more effective solidarity for the local tasks confronting
both the party and the local government authorities. Opposition assemblymen crossed the floor in large numbers. Local party officials tried to mend
those ruptures in family and social life which had appeared at the height
of constitutional conflict. A new *rapprochement* took place between
chiefs, now overtly pro-CPP, and elders in the community.

As a result, many of the issues originally raised by the United Party
were taken up by the branch and constituency organizations of the CPP.
A new localism appeared. Branches were pitted against regions. At times
both would unite against the national secretariat. Conflicts arose between
them. Sometimes the Central Committee would oppose a constituency
organization's choice of candidate to the National Assembly, as happened
in Kumasi South. Other issues centered on demands for special funds for
development, or stemmed from resentment against district commissioners,
who were now political appointees. More frequently, resistance arose
against manipulation of local constituencies by central bodies through the
district commissioners, or by the local representatives of the United
Ghana Farmers' Council, the Trades Union Congress (TUC), and later
the Young Pioneers. The constituency organizations, no longer required
to fight hard to win by-elections, took on the political complexion of their
erstwhile opponents, and, as loyal CPP members, argued vigorously for
the issues formerly espoused by the United Party. Moreover, because they
were inside the CPP, they could argue such causes much more convincingly than the United Party ever could. This posed severe discipline problems for both regional and central authorities in the CPP.

The Growth of Auxiliary and Functional Organizations

Partly as an answer to the growth of localism in the constituency
parties, and partly as a basis for reorganizing society along lines of
Nkrumaism and socialism, functional and auxiliary organizations were

given much greater prominence than ever before. Under the general program of consolidating the revolution along the lines laid down by George Padmore in his *Pan-African Manifesto,* the two most important functional organizations so honored were the Trades Union Congress under its leader, John Tettegah, and the coöperatives. By the action of the government, which consolidated the trade-union movement and instituted an automatic checkoff system, and by the action of the party, which made Tettegah an ambassador extraordinary and minister plenipotentiary, with an office in the new CPP building in Accra, the TUC was transformed into a vanguard movement for the building of Nkrumaism.[50]

There was also a consolidation of the entire coöperative movement into a single organization. Among the reasons for this step was that more than a breath of scandal surrounded the operations of the Cocoa Marketing Board and the Cocoa Purchasing Commission, and local farmers' organizations were attacking the CPP for mismanagement and corruption. Indeed, one of the main grievances on which the opposition had been able to capitalize was the confused state of the various coöperative and marketing boards under CPP control.[51]

---

[50] The Trades Union Congress had been plagued by a series of internal conflicts between pro- and anti-CPP elements, and by a split within its own ranks. Moreover, a large number of strikes, not unrelated to political events, took place between 1956 and 1957. Pro-NLM labor leaders were gradually eliminated from the TUC, and the TUC was restructured by its General Council. As Tettegah said at the time, "We do not want to be bothered with Cambridge Essays on imaginary ILO standards, with undue emphasis on voluntary associations" (cited in L. Snowiss, "Democracy and Control in a Changing Society: The Case of Ghana" [unpublished M.A. thesis, University of Chicago, 1960]). Not only was the TUC made into an arm of the state and the party, but civil servants, who had been regarded as uncommitted to the CPP and often hostile to it, were now required to join the TUC as a form of "protection."

[51] A sample of the complaints is to be found in a petition of the National Liberation Movement: "The members of the Cocoa Marketing Board who are also Directors of the Cocoa Purchasing Company Limited are also the Leaders of the Convention Peoples Party and since its establishment in 1952 [*sic*] it has been taken for granted by the members of the Convention Peoples Party of which Dr. Kwame Nkrumah, [then] Prime Minister, is the Life Chairman, that the Cocoa Purchasing Company Limited, a Public Company run with public funds, is an organization affiliated with the Convention Peoples Party and a reservoir from which funds might be drawn to run the Convention Peoples Party. Indeed in a debate in the Assembly in 1954, Mr. Krobo Edusei, a member of the inner circle of the Convention Peoples Party, much to the embarrassment of the Ministers, unabashedly and shamelessly stated that the Cocoa Purchasing Company is the CPP and the CPP is the CPC, a statement not altogether unsupported by facts. For example, the week one Twumasi Ankrah, Regional Propaganda Secretary of the CPP Kumasi, went from Accra to Kumasi with Fifty pounds of CPC money, he openly boasted he had come with orders to kill the Leaders of the NLM. Four days later he murdered E. Y. Baffoe, Secretary of the National Liberation Movement, for which he was duly convicted by the Kumasi Assizes" (see *Why CMB-CPC Probe,* Petitions Submitted by the Asanteman Council, Farmers, NLM and Allies, and the Opposition in the Legislative Assembly [Kumasi: Abura Printing Works, n.d.], pp. 1–2).

The CPP farmers' organization—the United Ghana Farmers' Council —virtually eliminated the opposition National Farmers' Union and, in the aftermath of the investigation of irregularities in the Cocoa Purchasing Commission and other marketing organizations, became the nucleus of the new Ghana Cooperative Movement (GCM). Like the TUC, the GCM publishes its own newspaper (the *Co-operator*); the editor is Dorothy Padmore, widow of the late George Padmore. The leader of the movement is an ambassador extraordinary and minister plenipotentiary. Through its control of the entire coöperative movement, it implements the government's farm policies.[52]

In transforming the TUC and the coöperative movement into organs of party and state, the CPP had two objectives. First, it wanted to implement the new style of social and political life emerging in Ghana. The trade-union and coöperative movements both represent a type of organization or discipline through which each individual is linked to the state not only by the party, but by a voluntary association or an occupational grouping under party supervision. Participation in society extends beyond party membership to a relationship based on meaningful work in the significant areas of labor and agriculture. Second, these two organizations are functional, and cut across other forms of organization, such as ethnic and religious groups; thus they reduce the significance of the latter.

In order to make these movements effective, however, the CPP had to elevate the position of labor and agricultural organizations within the party. Nor were these the only groups to receive such attention. Postwar urban growth had been phenomenal.[53] A general movement from the villages to the towns had increased in tempo, because urban centers offered more skilled and semiskilled occupations and greater educational opportunities than rural areas. After independence, a sharp drop in cocoa prices helped encourage farm laborers to come to the towns, where they joined the ranks of the partially employed or the unemployed. Moreover, political conflict in the rural areas, often extremely bitter and intense, aggravated the flow of disgruntled villagers into the towns. Finally, the ex-servicemen were restive, many of them being unemployed. The Ghana Legion replaced the former Ex-Servicemen's League with a central council, whose chairman was appointed by the minister of defense. Builders' Brigades (now Workers' Brigades) were established to provide work for the unemployed on rural development schemes, housing projects, and

---

[52] The GCM emphasizes coöperative farming of various kinds, and has established the Kwame Nkrumah Cooperative College. See the *Co-operator*, I, no. 15 (Sept., 1961), for a review of GCM activities by the chairman of the National Cooperative Council, Martin Appiah Danquah.

[53] See *1960 Population Census of Ghana* (Accra: Government Printer, 1962), compiled by the Central Bureau of Statistics.

the like. These have had to be disciplined on several occasions, but they are given semimilitary training and indoctrination in Nkrumaism.

The same pattern held with respect to women's organizations and youth groups. All were abolished except the National Council of Ghana Women associated with the CPP. The Women's Organization Bureau was established at the highest echelons of the party, as was the Youth Bureau. The fluctuating loyalties of such organizations as the Asante Youth Association were no longer tolerated. The CPP made the National Association of Socialist Students' Organizations responsible for the ideological training of young people. It established a unit called the Vanguard Activists, whose members were to promote ideological devotion to the party, and the youth were organized in the Young Pioneers.

The effort by the CPP to penetrate every sector of organized life was by no means limited to the functional auxiliary bodies in Ghana. Various apostolic churches formed CPP branches within their congregations, as did the Anglican churches, with the full support of their bishops; some Presbyterian churches followed suit. Organizations such as the Kumasi Marketwomen's Association, which were affiliated with the National Council of Ghana Women (NCGW), also formed party units and CPP Study Groups. Instructions on forming party branches were published:

And this is what the harmonial national pattern will look like. For all upper and primary schools we have the young pioneers (teachers who are party enthusiasts here to form party branches). For all secondary schools we have the Party's Young Peoples League—PYPL (teachers who are party enthusiasts here to form party branches). For all offices, workshops and farms party branches may be formed by at least two party members. In very large concerns or well organized offices, the ideal is to form party branches in every department of the same establishment each with only an elected secretary. And all these branches teaming up to form the main party branch in the office with only an elected secretary convener to connect them with the general secretary of the party. There shall be no Serinkin Zongos. The party shall henceforth deal directly with tribal heads of the communities concerned. Moslem and Christian, non-Christian and non-Moslem should also form party branches wherever they congregate.[54]

The result of all these activities has been to proliferate party branches into more but smaller units. Some large and powerful branches have been broken up by the organization of more atomistic smaller ones.

The auxiliary and subordinate arms of the party may be categorized as follows:

1) *Ideological and youth organizations.*—These include the National Association of Socialist Students' Organizations, the Young Pioneers, the CPP Study Groups, the League of Ghana Patriots, and the

---

[54] *Evening News,* Oct. 26, 1961.

Kwame Nkrumah Ideological Institute at Winneba. Recently, as a consequence of the rise in autonomy within the party of the militant left, the NASSO and the CPP Study Groups have been abolished.[55] Since then, the main burden of political action has devolved upon the Young Pioneers and the Kwame Nkrumah Ideological Institute. Because of the extraordinary importance assigned to ideological training, seminars and discussion sessions are held at the school to train youth leaders and Young Pioneer activists who return periodically for refresher courses. Moreover, Young Pioneer branches are being set up in all the schools.[56] Interestingly enough, there is considerable opposition to the Young Pioneers not only from teachers and headmasters, but from the students as well; this is clear evidence that more intensive ideological work is necessary. As the party sees it, the requirement is not simply indoctrination, but rather the political socialization of a whole new generation. On that will stand or fall the program of the CPP.

2) *Trade unions and coöperatives.*—Originally the Trades Union Congress was independent of party politics. After a series of splits and maneuvers, it became an integral part of the CPP, and achieved an automatic checkoff system, a revised and more limited branch structure, and a senior position among party auxiliaries. Its president, John Tettegah, became an important party official. The right to strike is contingent on prior negotiation and government approval. The prevailing role of the TUC is perhaps best defined by Nkrumah himself:

In the United Kingdom, I organized colored workers to combat the exploitation of their labor power. What is more, my whole philosophy is Marxian, a fact which ranges me immediately on the side of any organization fighting to abolish the exploitation of man by man. I have actively encouraged since the beginning of our struggle, the building of a virile and responsible trade union movement because I believe that it is necessary to give correct leadership to the workers for the great exercise of the industrial and economic reconstruction of our country.

The Government which is formed by the Convention People's Party is a people's Government—indeed a government of the people—free, strong and independent, pursuing a socialist pattern of reconstruction. The interest of

[55] "Other things being equal, the Central Committee considers that the NASSO and the Party Study Groups have done their work and done it very well. They have stirred up great enthusiasm in the field of Party education and their activities have led to the general raising of the standard of enlightenment among the rank and file of the Party. Nevertheless, the time has come when Party education should be carried forward to its final stage—the stage of mass Party education. General Party education must reach the masses at the base" (Kwame Nkrumah, *Guide to Party Action* [Accra: Central Committee of the CPP, 1962], p. 3).

[56] The headmaster of Achimota College, Daniel Chapman, resisted the establishment of a Young Pioneer branch at Achimota and has now resigned his position in order to take a post with the United Nations. The CPP has announced that a powerful Young Pioneer branch will soon be established at Achimota.

workers is therefore well catered for by the State. The trade unions therefore have a different role from that of trade unions in a capitalist society.[57]

In May, 1961, the All-African Trade Union Federation (AATUF), with headquarters in Accra, was formed. It is the answer to international trade-union movements of both Western and Eastern countries: the International Confederation of Free Trade Unions and the World Federation of Trade Unions. The central roles of the TUC and the AATUF as militant instruments of party policy are clear enough.[58]

A key role has also been assigned to the United Ghana Farmers' Council. This organization was founded in 1953, when an earlier group, the Ghana Farmers' Congress (organized in 1950 by G. Ashie-Nikoi after his release from prison along with Nkrumah), bolted to the opposition. It also replaced older organizations of farmers, such as the Asante Farmers' Union, whose chief farmer and secretary had both joined the National Liberation Movement. Subsequently, the National Cooperative Council was established to supervise the coöperative movement. The United Ghana Farmers' Council was then given the main responsibility for running the coöperatives, as well as the new state farms that are being established under Israeli auspices. Martin Appiah Danquah was appointed general secretary of the United Ghana Farmers' Council, ambassador extraordinary and minister plenipotentiary, and chairman of the National Cooperative Council. Like the TUC, the United Ghana Farmers' Council is entrusted with the realization of important state objectives: "The United Ghana Farmers' Council has shown in many ways that it can be relied upon by the state to pursue vigorously the duties set before it." [59] And, like the AATUF, it has a Pan-African equivalent, the All-African Union of Farmers.

3) *Women's organizations.*—Ghana women have always played an extraordinary part in nationalist politics. This has been manifested by their financial support of the party and by their role in trade boycotts and marketing. Women's organizations have a long traditional history, and include singing and dancing societies, market women's associations, and the like. One of the original members of the Committee on Youth

[57] *Speech by Osagyefo Dr. Kwame Nkrumah, President of the Republic of Ghana at the Opening of the First Biennial Conference of the Ghana TUC at Kumasi, 26th March, 1962* (Accra: Government Printer, 1962). See also Kwame Nkrumah, *Towards Colonial Freedom* (London: Heinemann, 1962), a pamphlet written in 1947 but not published until 1962. Nkrumah claims in the preface that his views have not changed.

[58] Tettegah has been made secretary-general of the AATUF.

[59] *Inaugural Address by Osagyefo the President at the Ninth Annual National Delegates Conferences of the United Ghana Farmers' Council, Kumasi, 26th March, 1962* (Accra: Government Printer, 1962).

Organizations, Mrs. Hannah Cudjoe, had long been in charge of women's organizations in the CPP. The National Council of Ghana Women, established in 1960 as an integral part of the party, helps to select candidates for the ten regional parliamentary seats reserved for women, opens party branches within its own organization, and takes over other organizations of women. Just as the Young Pioneers have become the major youth organization (although the Boy Scouts continue to exist, with about 2,000 members), so the NCGW has superseded the YWCA and other women's organizations. Although many of these remain, they are slowly being weakened.

4) *Other organizations.*—Other groups have been brought either directly under the party or into a quasi-official relationship with it, such as the Workers' Brigades, the Central Organization of Sports, and the Ghana Legion. Among these organizations, the Bureau of African Affairs, under the leadership of Michael Dei-Anang, is particularly significant. It provides a liaison with other political parties in Africa, and helps to train party men from other countries at the Winneba Ideological School. The bureau has been instrumental in setting up various Pan-African conferences, including the Ban the Bomb Conference in 1962. It is increasingly an organ of militant Nkrumaism, and in 1962 it took a decisive step. After Nkrumah proposed a joint military command and an African army, navy, and air force, the bureau rejected nonviolent resistance as the only means of political action against colonialism.

5) *The party press.*—The party press is regarded as an instrument of ideology and training. The journalists who hold editorial positions are the most extreme party militants. They are on good terms with the militant left of the AATUF and the TUC, and were key figures in the party Study Groups before the latter were abolished.

Each major arm or auxiliary of the CPP has its own newspaper or journal. The most important papers remain the *Accra Evening News,* the *Ghanaian Times,* and *The Party,* which are controlled by persons at the ideological heart of the party. Recently a militant weekly, *The Spark* (taking its name from Lenin's newspaper, *Iskra*), has appeared. It is edited by Kofi Batsa, who also edits the *Voice of Africa,* organ of the Bureau of African Affairs. The bureau also publishes pamphlets, and speeches on Pan-Africanism; its director is A. K. Barden, a member of the militant left. The TUC publishes *Labour* under the editorship of another militant socialist, J. P. Addei. An international journal, the *African Worker,* is published in French and English by the AATUF. The *Co-operator* has already been mentioned.

There is at present no genuine opposition paper in Ghana, but the *Daily Graphic* has the distinction of not being a party newspaper. Formerly part of the *Daily Mirror* chain, it is now published by the Graphic Trust in Ghana. A former opposition paper, the *Ashanti Pioneer*, was made subject to censorship and eventually capitulated to the government.

Changes in Party Structure

A party reorganization that took place after 1959 was itself a product of the CPP's new role as a party of solidarity. In 1959 a new party structure was designed to consolidate changes in the party and articulate the goals of the new society. Not only was the party to protect the "revolution," but it was to create African socialism, establish the welfare state, and, through political means, bring about the economic and social reconstruction of the country. Under the new party structure, which came into effect simultaneously with the new constitution establishing the Republic of Ghana, Nkrumah became the first general secretary of the CPP. The Trades Union Congress, the United Ghana Farmers' Council, and the Cooperative Movement were given representation in the national executive with the right to send a specified number of delegates each to national delegates' conferences.

Under the new structure, the party modified its national secretariat. The secretariat presently consists of a general secretary, an administrative secretary, and a director of ideological studies; bureaus of information and publicity, organization, African and international affairs, local government, functions, education and anticorruption, national propaganda, finances, membership, youth, and women's organizations; a bureau for trade unions, coöperatives, and farmers; and a bureau of disciplinary control. The national secretariat, under the control of the Central Committee, is the key administrative organ of the party, linked closely with branches, constituencies, and regional executive committees and secretariats. Regional secretariat staff members are appointed by the Central Committee, and the broad mandate for the national Executive Committee of the Central Committee derives from the annual delegates' conference. Noticeable in the new national secretariat is the strong emphasis upon discipline, organization, and ideology.[60]

The branch executive committee remains the party's key organizational unit, and party branches are found in every village, ward, and rural area. Three key posts in the CPP are those of the secretary-general of the TUC, the general secretary of the United Ghana Farmers' Council, and the general secretary of the party. Hence a dual organization prevails: the party branch with its executive, the constituency, and the regional organization with its executive and secretariat reach out into each area; the functional organizations, particularly union locals and coöperative

---

[60] For a full discussion of the new structure, see Tawia Adamafio, "The New Party Structure," *The Party*, I (Sept., 1960), 9–10.

associations, cut across the geographically based party units. In addition, youth organizations, women's organizations, and others are associated with their own ideological units in schools and party branches, both functional and geographical.

What effects did the new structure have upon the party? There are several that are worth particular mention. By elevating the functional organizations, the party created a dualism that was to have almost disastrous results. Excessive pressure brought to bear on local branches and regional groups, which had become extremely localized and parochialized, and even oppositionist, resulted in a disenchantment with the party in local areas. The functional groups, which provided a new power base against the constituency and local organizations, stimulated competition between the leaders of the functional and ideological groups and those of the constituency organizations. At the same time it intensified conflict between ethnic and regional branches, on the one hand, and newer and centrally controlled functional groups on the other. This would be difficult enough under ordinary circumstances, where the desire of local and regional groups to enlarge their autonomy creates antagonism between them and the central party organization. In Ghana it resulted in tension between functional and other party groups, between ethnic and national loyalties, and between secretariat and field organizations, all within the party itself.

Intrigue, sycophancy, and mistrust at the center, and cynicism in the rural areas, became more common. In 1961 Nkrumah tried first to eliminate the corrosion within the party by attacking the right wing, which had been the most opportunistic and around which had swirled rumors of "deals," "negotiations," and corruption.[61] All party officials, ministers, and ministerial secretaries were required to submit their financial records to a committee, listing houses, cars, and land owned by them.[62] The resignation of K. A. Gbedemah, Kojo Botsio, E. Ayeh-Kumi, E. D. Dadson, W. A. Wiafe, and S. W. Yeboah were demanded. Botsio was read out of the party.[63] Gbedemah fled the country. Others have come back to positions of authority. Krobo Edusei was removed from office for a while and others were forced to relinquish property. In effect, this was a "purge" of the right wing. The militant left was jubilant. The party press singled out former old-guard party leaders for particular abuse.

---

[61] See the Dawn Speech, *Broadcast to the Nation* (Accra: Ghana Information Services, 1961).

[62] *Statement by the President Concerning Properties and Business Connections of Ministers and Ministerial Secretaries* (Accra: Government Printer, 1961). The statement directed that no minister or ministerial secretary should own more than two houses with a combined value of £20,000, more than two motor cars, and plots of land in addition to the first category with a total value above £500.

[63] He has now been reinstated and is at present Ghana's foreign minister.

After the purge, Nkrumah designated as the integral parts of the party the Trades Union Congress, the United Ghana Farmers' Council, the National Council of Ghana Women, the Ghana Young Pioneers, and the Cooperative Movement:

All these bodies have their various functions in the particular aspect of our national life in which they operate, but there is one strain running through all of them, which is basic and fundamental, namely, the membership of the Convention People's Party. Whatever they do the character of the Convention People's Party must be clearly manifested for all to see. They all have a single guiding light, the guiding light of our Party ideology. This light must constantly be kept bright and full of luster and must on no account be allowed to dim, for, as soon as this happens, we are bound to find ourselves in difficulties.

The emphasis was to be on discipline:

Why shouldn't the workers of the State, who are composed mainly of the laborer group, be put into uniform? It would give them an added incentive to serve the State, a reason to feel proud of their service and a sense of belonging. They can be employed on various national jobs by the State Construction Corporation. This will eliminate the present element of idleness which takes place when a particular job is completed and the workers await assignment of another job.

The Asafo Companies also, the members of which are almost all members of the Party individually, will come within this category. They should be properly uniformed and perform their traditional role in a modern manner.

Another group of workers whom we now call "Watchmen" will have a new orientation and come under this category. And why shouldn't they also be dressed in a smart uniform and be renamed "Civil Guards"?

All this will lead to one useful result—discipline. The whole nation from the President downwards will form one regiment of disciplined citizens.[64]

This, then, was to be the basis for building a new social order. The general secretary of the party was Tawia Adamafio, also a minister plenipotentiary and ambassador extraordinary. At the same time, the "cult of personality" was deliberately encouraged. No other leader had a public building or street named after him except Nkrumah. There were the Kwame Nkrumah leaders' schools, the Kwame Nkrumah state farms, Kwame Nkrumah Avenue in Accra, the Kwame Nkrumah University in Kumasi, and so forth. Hymns were sung in praise of Nkrumah, and Nkrumaism became the philosophy of the day.

This emphasis was a response to the various conflicts within the senior ranks of the party. Disciplining the complex party formations which had been built up, and which operated in local areas, both rural and urban, as well as at the center, required increasing obedience to

---

[64] Nkrumah, *Guide to Party Action,* pp. 7-8.

Nkrumah himself. Coördination and control became a major problem. Indeed, the more powerful the auxiliary, the greater the momentum it acquired within the party, and the more dangerous it was to the party as a whole. There were references to Nkrumah as "the Old Man," and sidelong looks for a successor. Adamafio was a possibility. So was Tettegah, the young and able trade-union leader. But there was no effective party opposition, for virtually all the dissidents were in jail or out of the country. Opposition could come only from within the party itself. Moreover, "foreigners" began to play a role; refugees from other parts of Africa, particularly South Africa, moved into party circles in growing numbers. The result was confusion.

The socialist militants, so clearly in the ascendancy, pressed for greater autonomy and strength within the party. The party press became more and more extreme. When lower echelons in the party objected, as in the Sekondi-Takoradi strikes of 1961, party discipline was immediately imposed.[65] Harsh government actions and an inadequately presented, extremely unpopular budget also spurred on the efforts of the socialist militants to reorganize the society. Non-Ghanaians, such as Abdoulaye Diallo, Guinea's minister to Ghana, represented a more austere and pure form of Marxism beside which the Ghanaian form seemed shabby and confused; this contrast helped to encourage the socialist militants.

With the right wing effectively downgraded, ideological as well as personal differences emerged between two groups of socialist militants. One group might be called the *socialist puritans;* the other, the *socialist opportunists.* The first was, on the whole, a studious and sincere group, not in the public eye, whose members were particularly interested in the study of Marxism and of Neo-Marxist thought. The second group consisted of slogan manipulators and emotional socialists in journalistic and party positions which brought their names before the public. Perhaps the largest group among the socialist militants fell between these two groups. But it was the socialist opportunists who contributed the most to building up Nkrumah, proclaiming their loyalty to him and arousing bitterness and cynicism in the party ranks. And it was they who established deification oaths for the Young Pioneers, according to which "Nkrumah will never die." Indeed, as cynicism within the party and among the public grew, as widespread rumblings from the constituency parties began to be heard, and as the ranks of the quietly disaffected expanded both inside and outside the party, a new emphasis on Nkrumaism was offered to the public.

---

[65] The strikes in the Sekondi-Takoradi area and elsewhere were a protest not only against government policy, but also against TUC leadership. Several of those put in jail under preventive detention were junior trade-union leaders, loyal party members who resented their own senior officials.

Party Ideology

A rather bitter, though socialist, ex-CPP adherent who had quarreled with Nkrumah has described the ideology of the party as "Nkrumaism, the highest stage of opportunism." This is an unfair description, except in one sense. Nkrumaism is not so much a consistent ideology or dogma as it is a search for perspective in the African revolution, and for a sense of destiny and purpose by means of which attention will be focused on the most important and significant events within Ghana and abroad. That it leaves much to be desired as an ideology is perhaps its greatest advantage, for pragmatism thus remains a feature of the new ideological look.

The easiest way to describe Nkrumaism is perhaps through examples. In a recent issue of the *Co-operator* there is a discussion of farm coöperatives and what they mean. After describing the main types—service coöperatives, coöperative tenant farming societies, joint farming societies, and collective farms—the article concludes:

Obviously each country must adopt the form or forms which are best suited to its environment, national or local customs and character. Farmers may find that a blend of types may be best suited; or they may choose a particular form and adapt it to the local conditions. This should not affect the general nature of Co-operative Farming, which is that those who participate are rewarded in proportion to the amount of work they put in.[66]

Again, the secretary of the CPP Bureau of Information and Publicity, O. B. Amankwah, argued that Nkrumaism looks on scientific socialism as the "basis for correcting the inequitable distribution of food, shelter and clothing—the basic necessities of life which are the legitimate right of every human being." Nkrumaism is anticapitalist; it postulates the "vigorous but systematic elimination of capitalism from society taking into account the prevailing situation in a given country." It is based on the "projection of the African personality which is one of the tenets of Pan-Africanism," and its philosophy is "embodied in the life and teachings of Kwame Nkrumah." [67]

Through the CPP Study Groups, the NASSO, the Winneba Ideological School (now the Nkrumah Institute), and, more recently, the organizations of branch chairmen and Young Pioneers, Nkrumaism has been strongly urged on the people. Preceding a series of articles on Nkrumaism, this message appeared in the *Evening News*:

Nkrumah is our Messiah. Whoever sees his brother's need and supplies it—not by casting off the discarded garment to him—but by giving him a

---

[66] *Co-operator*, I, no. 15 (Sept., 1961).
[67] O. B. Amankwah, "What Is Nkrumaism?" *The Party*, I (Sept., 1960), 12.

moral and spiritual standard by which he shall live; that is the Messiah, the Saviour, the Christ.

From time to time, individuals have caught glimpses of the Christ or the true idea of God, good. Long before Jesus, were men like Moses, Joshua, Elisha, etc. who demonstrated the true idea of sonship. This demonstration by no means ended with Jesus. Why! Karl Marx demonstrated the Christ, and so did Lenin of U.S.S.R., Ghandi of India, Moa [*sic*] of China and in our midst is Kwame Nkrumah.

When our history is recorded the man Kwame Nkrumah will be written of as the liberator, the Messiah, the Christ of our day, whose great love for mankind wrought changes in Ghana, in Africa, and in the world at large.[68]

Couched in spiritual language, this is clearly an effort to personalize morality, and to provide a sense of social mission in both moral and political terms. An example may be found in the series on Nkrumaism offered by the *Evening News*: "Nkrumaism is the quest for African unity and independence, a way of life that ensures security, abundance and prosperity for all through brotherly love one for another based on work and happiness not for a few but for all." That is the theme. Afterward come the variations.

Nkrumaism will introduce a society in which the exploitation of man by man has been abolished forever. A society in which the wealth and natural resources of the land belong to the people; a society in which there is no unemployment, a society in which there is no existence of economic crisis, a society where the standard of living of every individual citizen is appreciably high, a society that recognizes the creative ability of her citizens and pays them according to their production and standard of work, a society where neither tribalism nor race discrimination exist.[69]

In essence, this is a literature of morality. That there are doubters only increases the intensity and, at times, the shrillness of the CPP ideological drive. It ought not to be read in terms of its precision, its immediate content, or its prescriptive quality. Just as it venerates political good it castigates political evil, and particularly evildoers. The doubters and the antagonists are vilified and excoriated. For example, a once respected opposition leader who had fled to Togo, a former associate of K. A. Busia's, was named in the press as follows:

WANTED! OBETSEBI LAMPTEY [in banner headlines]! Description: Criminal, Scoundrel, Assassin, Coward, Nincompoop, Swindler and Desperate Political Lunatic!

Bloodthirsty, Obdurate Fiend, Heartless Looking, Addicted to the Opium of Tribalism, Vain Boasting and often suffering from fits of mad yelling and screaming and using his fists on innocent people.

---

[68] Oct. 14, 1961.
[69] Oct. 23, 1961.

REWARD: Any information leading to his immediate capture will be amply rewarded. Must be captured alive. Finder: hundred guineas.[70]

In another fall from grace, the once powerful minister of finance, K. A. Gbedemah, was dropped from his post; the bill of particulars included alleged irregularities in financial matters. The party press called him a "bloated vain frog." "We have a mission," the abusive article went on. "By your deeds you have given abundant evidence that you have no sympathy with the Party's missionary faith. And that is why you have been thrown out of the Party's high councils and indeed the Party itself if you continue to behave in the way you are doing at this moment." [71] Gbedemah found it expedient to leave the country to avoid possible imprisonment under preventive detention.

Exhortation, missionary work, equalitarianism, opportunism, Pan-Africanism—these are all key aspects of Nkrumaism. In short, it is a modern religious crusade, using political forms of religion.[72] Its critics complain about its fulsomeness, its inconsistency, and the poverty of its ideology. All these criticisms may be turned around. The fulsomeness of Nkrumaism must be taken as a language of morality and religion. Its inconsistency is a token of its lack of dogma and strictness. Its preaching, unlike the narrow dogmatism of modern Marxism-Leninism, does not drastically narrow the range of alternatives open to political leaders as they seek solutions to their problems. Its ideology is symbolic rather than precise, expressing commitment to honesty, to work, and to the community.

The language of Nkrumaism, although it grates on foreign ears, is perhaps less foreign than we may think. If one were to go back to the speeches from the pulpit, the exhortations by missionaries, the extravagant claims for Christian miracles, one would find a direct link between the religious language employed for a hundred years along the coast in Ghana, and the quasi-religious language of Nkrumaism today. Nor is the language purely emotional. In part it is directed at stamping out widespread corruption, both in the local organizations of the party and at the highest levels. Although there were obviously many reasons for his dismissal, Gbedemah was removed from his post because of alleged irregularities. The same reason was given for the dismissal of Kojo Botsio, the long-time confidant of Nkrumah's. It was also the charge against Krobo Edusei. In his famous "dawn" broadcast, Nkrumah pointed to the deeper issue, the cynicism that was emerging in the party:

[70] *Evening News,* Oct. 6, 1961. Lamptey returned secretly to Ghana and was arrested on preventive detention, and is presently in prison.
[71] *Ibid.,* Oct. 2, 1961.
[72] See my article, "Political Religion in the New Nations," in Clifford Geertz, ed., *Old Societies and New States* (New York: Free Press of Glencoe, 1963).

Let me turn to some other causes which I consider plague Ghanaian society generally and militate against undisturbed progress. A great deal of rumor-mongering goes on all over the country. "Berko said that the Odikro informed Asamani that the Ohene said he paid a sum of money to a party official to become a paramount chief."

"Kojo said that Mensah told him that Kweku took a bribe." "Abina stated that Edua said that Esi uses her relations with Kweku to get contracts through the District Commissioner with the support of the Regional Commissioner and the blessing of a minister in Accra."

So, day after day, night after night, all types and manner of wild allegations and rumors are circulated and they are always well sprinkled with: They say, They say . . .[73]

It is against the background of cynicism, private self-seeking, and local plunder that the lofty expressions of political morality must be viewed. Moreover, such an ideology is capable of adapting to the vast changes in the government now under way, which have transformed the role of the president; he has become a ritualized leader, a "president-monarch" in whom the trappings of monarchy and the executive authority of the supreme party leader were merged. Nkrumaism is the projection of the African personality:

The African personality to Nkrumah does not mean the policy of separatism or racial discrimination. Such ideas are a direct contradiction to the principles of communalism which is basic to African life. The projection of an African personality calls for a total integration of all that is best in Africa into all that is best from outside Africa. It demands a new way of thinking and a breakaway from former colonial dogmas under which we have existed so long. Having succeeded in decolonizing ourselves and gaining our sovereignty we have also to dementalize ourselves of the colonial mentality which shut our eyes against our self-respect and dignity and took away from us a sense of objectivity and national pride.[74]

Finally, the meaning of Nkrumaism in economic and political terms, and its value to the CPP, have been stated in the party's program: "This program has been formulated in the conviction that Socialism implies central planning in order to ensure that the entire resources of the State, both human and material, are employed in the best interests of all the people." Five sectors of the economy are recognized: (1) state enterprises; (2) enterprises owned by foreign and private interests; (3) enterprises jointly owned by the state and foreign private interests; (4) cooperatives; and (5) small-scale Ghanaian private enterprises.[75]

---

[73] Nkrumah, *Broadcast to the Nation.*

[74] Stephen Dzirasa, *The Political Thought of Dr. Kwame Nkrumah* (Accra: Guinea Press, 1962), p. 21.

[75] *For Work and Happiness,* Program of the Convention People's Party (Accra: Government Printer, 1962).

If the philosophy of Nkrumaism is by no means organized or pro-grammatic, it is clearly a language of socialism, progress, and develop-ment. Party and state are one. Despite internal conflicts the party of solidarity has shown the same buoyancy and optimism that characterized the socialist militants. By mid-1962 Ghana seemed well on the road to-ward building a popular one-party socialist state. In the context of na-tional struggle, Pan-Africanist successes, and anti-imperialism, closer links were sought with socialist countries. The National Council of Ghana Women became associated with the Union of Mali Women and the Union of Senegalese Women, and, at the Conakry Conference of 1961, established links with the Women's International Democratic Federation Affiliates. The All-African Trade Union Federation secretariat consists of eight members, seven of them supported by the World Federation of Trade Unions. The Ghana Cooperative Movement, through the National Cooperative Council, maintains affiliations with coöperative organizations in the Soviet Union, the German Democratic Republic, Poland, Yugo-slavia, Israel, Hungary, and Czechoslovakia. The council is a member of the International Federation of Agricultural Producers. All these are Communist-dominated international bodies.

Finally, on July 2, 1962, the *Evening News* reported: "This morning at the State House, Accra, the Nation's Founder and Fount of Honor, His High Dedication Osagyefo the President was presented with the 1961 Lenin Peace Prize." In the capitals of the West as well as in Ghana itself, observers wondered where it would end.

THE NEW FACTIONALISM

"The Convention People's Party is a powerful force, more powerful, indeed, than anything that has yet appeared in the history of Ghana. It is the uniting force that guides and pilots the nation, and is the nerve center of the positive operations in the struggle for African irredentism. Its supremacy cannot be challenged." [76]

On August 1, 1962, when Nkrumah was returning from talks with President Maurice Yameogo of Upper Volta, a bomb was thrown at him in the northern Ghanaian village of Kulungugu. Several people were killed and Nkrumah was injured. Shortly afterward, Tawia Adamafio, then minister of information and broadcasting, Ako Adjei, minister of foreign affairs, and several party leaders, Boi Doku, former propaganda secretary of the CPP, and Kofi Crabbe, were put in jail under preventive detention. Curfew was immediately established and road blocks were set up along roads leading into Accra.

Ghana was politically restless. Everyone wondered what would be the next step. Anti-CPP groups, consisting of exiles from the United

---

[76] Kwame Nkrumah, "What the Party Stands For," *The Party*, I, no. 1 (1960).

Party and other defeated organizations, had been forming in Togoland. The Ghana Democratic Party under the leadership of John Alex-Hamah, formerly a regional ideological secretary in the TUC, had been established in London with West African headquarters in Nigeria. Alex-Hamah, who had been sent to Peking, Leipzig, and Moscow to get special training, broke with the TUC upon his return from one of his visits, remaining in London to organize anti-CPP students before going on to Nigeria. Gbedemah, still abroad, was active in building an anti-Ghanaian coalition, and hoped to gain support for his policies from American and British authorities.

Inside the party, those appointed to high political positions by Adamafio were quiet. No one was quite sure who was a socialist puritan and who a socialist opportunist. N. A. Welbeck, long a loyal supporter of Nkrumah's (he had been under a cloud for failures in two important posts, first as Ghana's minister to Guinea and then as Ghana's ambassador to the Congo during the period of the Lumumba crisis), was made acting general secretary and then executive secretary. Krobo Edusei came back as minister of agriculture, and Kofi Baako, the originator of Nkrumaism, became minister of defense. Kojo Botsio returned as foreign minister.

More bombs were thrown, this time at a demonstration of public thanks that Nkrumah had not been killed in the August episode. An additional wall was put up around the President's residence, Flagstaff House. Rarely did the President venture forth from his home. In a speech to the Assembly, he declared:

"We must tighten our ranks ever closer. We must work as an organic whole, not only to hold our own against the onslaughts of those who desire our downfall, but to further that second revolution on which we embarked when we took the road of independent nationhood. . . . For this a revolutionary outlook is necessary in our thinking and actions which will engender absolute loyalty, absolute honesty and absolute sincerity. The country must be cleaned forever of corruption and nepotism. . . . The security of the State is not a matter for the police alone. It is the concern of every one of us. With vigilance on the part of us all, it should be impossible for anyone to set up within the Party, cells which are inimical to the safety and the welfare of our nation and our people." [77]

There exists today a new quiet in Ghana. The police are much in evidence. A guard stands behind the statue of the President in front of Parliament House. Police lines have been set up outside Flagstaff House. Yet it is the old group that is in power, however uneasily. Welbeck's links have always been with the constituency organizations of the party and the local branches, where he knew everyone. For the time being the

---

[77] *Ghanaian Times,* Oct. 3, 1962.

party is trying to repair the organizational damage that resulted from the strengthening of the functional auxiliaries. John Tettegah, picked up by the police for questioning and newly chastened, is head of the AATUF; in that post he is more remote from direct contact with the rank and file of the TUC. Not only are the moderates in power and the militants under a cloud, but the Soviet Cultural Center has been closed. A new emphasis is being placed on *African* socialism by several leaders: "Nkrumah is like a chief. His linguists are the key members of the Cabinet and the Party."

The Deputy Minister of Foreign Affairs put it another way. African politics remain in the context of clan and chief. Chieftaincy is the essence of the African personality. Duty is to the state because the state is the family and the clan, and any individual derives from a clan. African socialism implies that use rights may be allocated, but property belongs to the state as in traditional land tenure. There is personal property and there is property of the society. Anyone who uses the property of the society must pay for the privilege. One should not enrich one's personal property from excessive use of state property. Hence the high taxes on expatriate firms. If personal property becomes excessive it sets people apart from one another, destroys the basic unity of African life, and violates custom. Elections are simply a way of emphasizing that unity and of according recognition to a chief. Western elections are different.[78]

Hence there is a renewed effort to give meaning to the term "African socialism." There is greater caution in dealing with the Soviet Union. The socialist opportunists were the ones who were jailed, and the lesson is not lost on the socialist puritans. The CPP is undergoing a stocktaking and a realignment of factions. The socialist puritans play an important role in Pan-African affairs and the press. They scrutinize the civil servants, the African socialists, the expatriates, and the rest.

CONCLUSION

We have seen a series of radical transformations in the life of political parties in Ghana. Political factions in the early days of nationalist activity helped stimulate political awareness and participation. As these factions attempted to coalesce, major groupings appeared—the progressive chiefs and the progressive constitutionalists. Gradually the latter helped to form the first parties of representation. The Convention People's Party, itself a mixture of faction, party, and movement, developed steadily toward the latter, and attempted to blend party, state, and society in a single community, organically tied together through the various instruments of the party and sharing in a common loyalty to Nkrumah.

---

[78] Interviews with the Reverend Stephen Dzirasa in December, 1962.

The opposition parties of representation disappeared. Opposition appeared within the CPP: constituency organization against auxiliary, old guard against young militant, socialist puritan against right-wing opportunist and socialist opportunist. Around the President politics swirled as in the court of a king. Extravagant titles and praise disguised the intrigue. Disenchantment became more widespread.

Perhaps the wheel has come full circle. The party is not the monolithic organization it has often been portrayed as. The politics of faction, which predate political parties in Ghana, are now inside the CPP. Nor is tradition destroyed. Chiefs will never recover their position, but perhaps chieftaincy already has. Clearly Nkrumah is more than ever like a chief. The drums beat when he makes his appearance; libation is poured. These are not empty symbols. The traditionalization of authority has begun. Under the socialist slogans are the thousands of practical translations that ordinary people make in ordinary ways in terms familiar and comfortable. It is with these ordinary people and their ideas that the CPP and its leadership must make their peace.

POSTSCRIPT

On December 31, 1963, Nkrumah announced that a constitutional referendum would be held which would formally make Ghana a one-party state and give the President the right to dismiss judges of the Supreme Court and the High Court at any time. The news followed in the wake of the trial in which Ako Adjei and Tawiah Adamafio were acquitted of the charges of conspiring to commit treason. (Two other men were sentenced to death.) The acquitted were retained in custody. Sir Arku Korsah, the chief justice (once acting governor-general of Ghana), and the other judges were dismissed. In explaining the dismissal, Nkrumah said:

> The Judges of the special court by their failure to take me into their confidence meant to create discontent and terror throughout the country. You, the people of Ghana, have made me the conscience of the nation. My duty is not only to govern but to ease the conscience of the people by giving them peace of mind and tranquility. A nation cannot tolerate a dishonest and corrupt judiciary. I want to assure you all that there is the possibility of a retrial of the persons involved in this particular case, depending on the results of certain investigations now in progress.

Accordingly, the desired amendments to the constitution would "invest the President with 'power in his discretion to remove a Judge of the Supreme Court or a Judge of the High Court at any time for reasons which appear to him sufficient.'" As well to ensure a wider unity in the country, the amendments would also provide that "in conformity with the interests, welfare, and aspirations of the people and to 'develop the organizational initiative and political activity of the people, there shall be one national party in Ghana.' This party would be the 'vanguard of our people in their struggle to build a socialist society and the leading core of all organizations of the people.'" [79] For such changes Nkrumah wanted an unequivocal mandate for what is now called Marxist-Nkrumaism, to allow the party to "combat" all forms of "hostile ideology and propaganda emanating from Western imperialist countries, and at all times expose the total hollowness, corrupting influence, and decadent nature of capitalist-imperialist culture." In its broadest terms, then, the referendum was to be ideological: Marxist-Nkrumaism versus capitalist-imperialism.

The mass media were utilized to the fullest extent to mobilize a huge affirmative vote. Owners of motor vehicles were directed to report to the regional commissioner's office, or some other appropriate place, to obtain "Vote Yes on the Referendum" stickers to display on their automobiles. The result of the referendum was overwhelmingly in favor of the single-party state, with 2,773,920 affirmative and 2,454 negative votes;[80] there were charges that in several areas the number of "Yes" votes exceeded the number of voters. The poll itself included 95 per cent of the eligible voters.

Shortly thereafter, amid anti-American rioting (which ended with the expulsion of several American staff members of the university, as well as the temporary detention of others), it was announced that for "purposes of our revolution, the hallmark of good conduct in our universities should be close identification with the spirit and objects of the Party." The party suggested that the universities be "brought to heel." [81] At the same time a new seven-year plan was announced and five administrative committees were set up, the most important being a national planning

---

[79] *Times* (London), Jan. 1, 1964.

[80] The over-all results of the national referendum in each of the eight regions of the country and the Accra District were officially given as follows:

	Yes	No
Upper Region	325,859	186
Northern Region	201,781	30
Brong-Ahafo	368,369	—
Ashanti Region	425,022	—
Western Region	217,947	—
Central Region	441,041	—
Eastern Region	390,938	—
Volta Region	261,393	677
Accra District	141,570	1,559

[81] *Ghanaian Times*, Feb. 6, 1964.

committee, which is to be responsible for over-all planning. There will also be a state planning committee under the chairmanship of the President.

These events, representing a further stage in the development of monolithic political life in Ghana, are worthy of serious attention because they show the emergence of two major tendencies which until now have been latent in the political situation. The first of these involves the militant Left; the second, the administrative structure.

The militant Left, until now, derived its power largely from Nkrumah himself. Its adherents were concentrated mainly in the press, the Bureau of African Affairs, and, to some extent, the Young Pioneers. These groups have been given a much more central role in the party. In an effort to bypass the political generation that emerged just after independence—it might be called the Adamafio generation—the younger and more militant Left has acquired a mass following. What has emerged is a pattern of party control of the youth, the future cadres of Ghanaians. Despite the obvious reluctance of headmasters and teachers to attach much importance to the militant Left and the Young Pioneers, a strong effort will be made to build loyalty and conformity through the school system. The same reasoning guided the effort to take over the university (which has remained largely anti-CPP). Dubious about the brand of knowledge represented by the university, the socialist puritans hold as their ideal a working university with a much stronger emphasis on technical subjects and with humanistic subjects linked closely to the building of Ghanaian socialism. The socialist puritans will attempt to build a new party through the Young Pioneers, whose "inspiration" comes from a 1948 comment by Nkrumah: "Place the young at the head of the awakened masses. You do not know what strength, what magic influence the voice of the young have on the crowd. You will find in them apostles of the new social order. But youth lives on movement, grows great by example and emulation. Speak to them of country, of glory, of great Memories."

Equally important is the new administrative structure, which will downgrade the largely hostile and increasingly opportunistic civil service. What began as a career service in the British pattern has long been regarded by the socialist puritans as a stumbling block to the achievement of socialism. Well educated and, in living habits, residence, and traditions, very much in the British expatriate tradition, the civil servants have always taken a rather dim view of the CPP. Yet their standards of work and efficiency have been crucial to carrying out government policies. Now they are under direct attack. As the *Evening News* put it, the "appointment of anti-Party, anti-Socialist rascals on the basis of bourgeois qualifications alone leaves open the possibilities of creating so many agents of neo-colonialism in a State administration." [82] Calling civil servants "intellectual spivs" and the Civil Service Commission "semi-colonial," the party will establish planning bodies in the President's office which will become, along with the Ghana Bank, the critical administrative organs of the state.

Youth and administration, then, are the key concerns of the new Ghana. Party criticism will be allowed. Parliament will continue as a forum of debate. The Ghana flag will be the CPP flag with a black star added to it. The party is the guardian of the state. As Nkrumah's speech after the referendum made clear, the

Party is the rallying point of our political activity. Without the Party there would be no force through which to focus the needs and desires of the people. The Convention People's Party is this force. The Party, therefore, is the hard core of those who are so dedicated to its ideology and program, that they make their membership the most serious business of their lives. The Party is nothing but the vanguard of the people, the active organ of the people, working at all times in the service of the people.

All of us are now one in the acceptance of a One-Party State. Our task is to plan for progress in the interests of the whole people. To carry out this work of service to the people, the Party needs the assistance of everybody, even those who are not members. . . .

As long as we carry out these obligations, we can rest assured that we are doing the right thing and that no one can interfere with us. For we shall be interpreting the constitutional rights and duties vested in us as the source of power and the guardian of the State. [83]

This most recent stage in the evolution of the Convention People's Party is in some respects the most important of the long series of developments described in this essay. Whether or not the socialist puritans will succeed in transforming the political style of Ghanaian political life remains to be seen. One thing is clear. The alternatives in Ghana are rapidly shrinking. The billiard game of politics is being played on a table that constantly grows smaller. Ghana has been steadily using up her supply of political capital. Punishing her friends, she has chosen a lonely course. The job of building a new Ghana will now be more difficult. Even the party anticipates that it will operate in an atmosphere of suspicion and fear. "The Party must establish as a matter of urgency an anti-Rumor Squad to augment the Security Machinery of the Nation," says the referendum commentary in the *Evening News*. "Ghana lives. Osagyefo, the Generalissimo and Conqueror of Imperialism is determined with

[82] See the *Evening News*, Feb. 4, 1964, for a discussion of changes in the Civil Service Commission.
[83] *Ibid.*

the Party to lead our people to Socialism and the rumor-mongers will be ashamed of themselves. Listen to the Leader's word this morning as he met with high Party officials: 'We are not joking. We are moving forward.'" [84]

---

[84] *Ibid.*

The Control of Nonparty Groups

8. VOLUNTARY ASSOCIATIONS

By Immanuel Wallerstein

Traditional societies of Tropical Africa ranged in structure from small nomadic groupings which had a very simple political organization (like the Bambuti), and were almost synonymous with lineages, to societies with clearly defined boundaries and a complex political hierarchy (like the Ashanti).[1] The larger the unit in number of individuals and in territorial extension, the more likely the society was to have special groupings within the social structure which might be called "associations." As a general rule, "In simpler cultures individuals are not ranged solely according to kinship or localities; . . . they unite in associations according to sex, age, and religious and social interests."[2]

Entry into these associations was largely ascriptive (based on age and sex). Even if certain achievements were required for admittance, it was assumed that all, or almost all, persons would be able to meet the requirements. These associations were functional divisions of the tribe[3] for the attainment of certain traditional social objectives, such as the practice of warfare, the production of certain craft articles, and so forth. The associations were few in number and, in theory, were fixed entities. The individual did not in principle choose to enter; rather, he was assigned a certain social role which involved membership in a certain association. The associations operated on the same basis as the over-all political structure: the acceptance of traditional ways as the only legitimate activities of individuals within the society. The associations as such did not attempt to alter the social structure, nor was entry into them motivated by a desire to change it. They were, in effect, "extensions of the government."[4]

---

[1] See G. Murdock, *Africa: Its Peoples and Their Cultural History* (New York: McGraw-Hill, 1959), pp. 48–51, 256; P. Schebesta, *Among Congo Pigmies* (London: Hutchinson & Company, 1933); and R. S. Rattray, *Ashanti Law and Constitution* (London: Oxford University Press, 1929).

[2] Robert H. Lowie, "Social Organization," *Encyclopedia of the Social Sciences,* XIV, 146.

[3] On the difficulty of defining a "tribe," see A. S. Southall, "The Theory of Urban Sociology," a paper presented at the January, 1957, conference of the East African Institute of Social Research, Kampala.

[4] A. Rose, *Sociology* (Minneapolis: University of Minnesota Press, 1950), p. 307. For a detailed account of one society, see D. Forde, "The Governmental Role of Associations among the Yako," *Africa,* XXXI (Oct., 1961), 309–323.

The establishment of colonial administrative structures in Tropical Africa created an entirely new social situation based on a new territorial unit, the colony.[5] Colonial administration brought with it urbanization; participation in the world-market economy; modern technology, particularly in the fields of transportation and communications; and a modern educational system. These phenomena were entirely new to some areas, and were greatly expanded in others.

One of the basic implications of these changes was that large numbers of persons, formerly permanently resident in the tribal area, migrated to urban areas. Often the migration was temporary, but increasing numbers of migrants became permanent town dwellers. Urban areas were usually administrative or transportation centers, or were located near mines. Some of the migrants went to other rural areas where cash crops were grown; usually these areas had some urban facilities. The division of labor, in Tropical Africa as elsewhere, has meant urbanization. Technological change has not merely brought about greater population density and spatial redistribution of the population, but it has also established different values and norms from those of traditional societies. This process of modernization has led everywhere to the growth of a new form of social organization, the voluntary association, which is different in function and structure from the associations found in tribal societies.

One of the most striking aspects of the migration from the traditional rural to the modern urban area has been dislocation and disorientation for the individual. In the traditional rural society, the individual was certain that his minimum material needs would be met, insofar as the society's resources permitted. He knew that he would not be allowed to starve, and that the necessary expenses connected with the transitional ceremonies of the life cycle (birth, initiation, marriage, death) would be taken care of. The individual also had a fixed and clear role within the society. He knew his obligations and his rights. He was reasonably clear about the norms that governed social behavior, and he could plan his activities in the light of his expectations concerning the behavior of his fellows. Thus the tribe offered social security in the certainty of material existence, and psychological security in the certainty of normative patterns.

Migration out of the tribe upset these assurances and diminished the individual's sense of social and psychological security. In the city he could no longer be assured of the minimum goods needed for his maintenance. The entry of some of the urban migrants into the wage system evoked the specter of unemployment for a landless group. (The fact that

---

[5] For an over-all treatment of the changes and the reaction to them, see my *Africa: The Politics of Independence* (New York: Vintage Books, 1961), Part One.

they still retained land rights in a village that might be quite remote was irrelevant to their immediate economic needs.) In the city, the values and the norms of urban life were different and strange. The migrant did not understand them, and for a time was uncertain what behavior was expected of him and what he could expect of others.

In this new situation, to what agencies could the individual turn for the assurances he sought? His tribal ties had been weakened by sheer distance from the tribal setting, if for no other reason. In any event, the tribe in its traditional form was not fitted for solving urban problems. The family, too, was often, if not always, weakened by the migrant's separation from it. The colonial government had neither the resources nor the personnel to step into the breach. Even if it had been able to do so, it would still have lacked the kind of relationship with the new urban dweller which would have provided social and psychological security. The educational system touched only a tiny minority of individuals, and only those who were children. The occupational system was specific in its definition of the relations between employer and employee—or at least employers tried to make it so—and hence assumed limited functions. Furthermore, it affected only a minority of the population, and often demanded, as a prerequisite to entry, some readjustment of the individual.

New social institutions were obviously needed, by both the individual and the colonial social structure, to resolve the uncertainties of life for the new migrants. Everywhere in Tropical Africa new voluntary associations sprang up to perform the services that the tribe, the family, and the government could not perform. The voluntary association was, happily, a flexible instrument, capable of meeting almost every kind of demand that might be made upon it. It could, first of all, provide social security. In this area the most pressing need seems to have been for the payment of funeral expenses.[6] Marriages could be postponed for lack of funds, but burials could not. Moreover, funerals were too important as a mechanism of social reintegration to be easily dispensed with;[7] they prevented further isolation of the individual from meaningful participation in the social structure.

In a more positive sense, the voluntary associations helped the individual to adapt to urban mores.[8] In fact, they "developed partly in

---

[6] K. A. Busia, *Report on a Social Survey of Sekondi-Takoradi* (Accra: Government Printer, 1950), chap. vi, notes that all the different kinds of associations in Sekondi-Takoradi provided funeral benefits.

[7] "The moral support which [voluntary associations] . . . give to members when bereaved is at least as important as the financial assistance" (M. P. Banton, "Adaptation and Integration among the Temne Immigrants in Freetown," *Africa*, XXVI [Oct., 1956], 362).

[8] Cf. Kenneth Little, "The Role of Voluntary Associations in West African Urbanization," *American Anthropologist*, LIX (Aug., 1957), esp. 591–594.

response to the need for role differentiation—for developing in a confused situation a new structure of roles and statuses," [9] and in them "migrants learn the principles of conduct in an achievement-oriented society." [10] The associations taught new values even while they were
helping to create new solidarities to which the individual could belong.[11]
It was not only because of the need for learning how to enter the new
role structures that men formed associations. Often the new voluntary
associations derived directly from the declining function of the old tribal
associations. For example, the virtual destruction of the traditional
"youngmen" organizations (*asafo*'s) in Ashanti in the 1940's led many men
between thirty and fifty years of age to seek new outlets for their leadership by creating new religious cults.[12]

If the voluntary association helped the individual to define his role
vis-à-vis society, it also provided the colonial social structure with new
mechanisms to control the individual. For example, the Zion Youth Fellowship in Ghana was a "civilizing agency within church and community." [13] These organizations made men civil, that is, responsive to the
controls of the new social order. Some of them directly took over primary
mediating functions. "A notable feature of the constitutions of many
[voluntary associations] is the attempt to make members settle disputes
within the society." [14] That these associations were linked with the need
for social control finds some confirmation in the fact that observers in
towns as distant and as different as Freetown and Brazzaville noted a
correlation between the weakness of the tribal structure out of which
the individual came and the likelihood that he would form voluntary
associations.[15]

The movement began with the formation of a few associations in
the large towns. Later it spread to all parts of Tropical Africa, and the

---

[9] M. P. Banton, *West African City* (London: Oxford University Press, 1957), p.
182.

[10] *Ibid.*, p. 181.

[11] "[The various associations] . . . act as social agencies acquainting members
of the community with each other. This makes up for the social isolation which some
of them would otherwise feel" (Busia, *op. cit.*, p. 78).

[12] B. E. Ward, "Some Observations on Religious Cults in Ashanti," *Africa*, XXVI
(Jan., 1956), 47–61. By the late 1950's these same men would "find a measure of
satisfaction through the development of representative government, with the new
party organizations" (p. 58).

[13] D. K. Fiawoo, "Urbanisation and Religion in Eastern Ghana," *Sociological
Review*, VII (July, 1959), 92.

[14] Banton, *West African City*, p. 190.

[15] Banton notes of Freetown: "Other things being equal, the more devolution
of authority there is in tribal societies, the more rapidly contractual associations . . .
emerge" (*ibid.*, p. 195). G. Balandier notes of Brazzaville: "It is those elements most
cut off from their traditional base who were first forced to think up new modes of
organization" (*Sociologie des Brazzavilles noires* [Paris: Armand Colin, 1955], p.
122).

number of groups multiplied rapidly. Some groups were based on age, sex, or occupation: youth and student associations, women's organizations, craft guilds, professional societies, and trade unions. The objectives of some were political, economic, religious, or social: political parties, co-operatives, fellowships, social clubs, and sports groups. Some of the associations grouped people on the basis of a special life experience: old boys' associations and ex-servicemen's organizations. Tribal unions had an ethnic base, and friendly societies claimed to accept anyone. The forms were multiple, but all the organizations shared a common feature: they were formed within the colonial social structure for a limited objective by groups of individuals who were almost never recruited exclusively on a traditional base. The individual had to join these associations through a process of formal entry; he chose his leaders. Each organization had some form of responsible, autocephalous government. As it is difficult to find further criteria, an accurate definition of voluntary associations is not easily formulated. Many of their functions and characteristics were shared by religious groups, especially by the numerous syncretistic and revivalistic cults. But a precise definition is less important than an understanding of what the name means. The organizations are "voluntary" in that no one's membership was foreordained at birth, or automatic; they are "associations" in that they were formalized groupings from the point of view of both the member and the society as a whole, and they were smaller than the whole society.

Quite often, the earliest voluntary associations were inspired by European administrators acting in a personal capacity. For example, as early as 1787 an African minister in Cape Coast founded the Torridzonian Society, whose purposes were to promote conviviality and to open a school to educate twelve mulatto children. It had twenty-six members, including Europeans, and it met weekly.[16] Wherever colonial rule spread, small societies of this kind emerged in the major urban centers. The principal goal was usually defined in terms of promoting education or of advancing Christian practice. Sports clubs, at first usually for football (soccer), were also founded. Early in the twentieth century most African territories established small groups of Boy Scouts and Girl Guides for the few children in the formal school system. Indeed, in British Africa, the governor and his wife normally served as chief commissioners of the Scouts and the Guides, respectively.[17] Most of these early groups shared three main features. Europeans were prominent in the leadership, as

[16] F. L. Bartels, "Philip Quaque, 1741–1816," *Transactions of the Gold Coast and Togoland Historical Society*, Vol. I, Part V (1955), 161–162.

[17] Government officials could not so serve in French territories, where scouting was divided into three main sections (Catholic, Protestant, and laic), but official encouragement was offered.

advisers or even as officials. The African membership was recruited from among those who had received Western education or had otherwise entered into the higher social world of colonial society. The main function was to promote social change by direct and indirect instruction in the norms and the values of the modern world, provided that this instruction furthered the acceptance of the legitimacy of the colonial situation. Efforts for social change were encouraged, if no political changes were advocated.

By and large, the role of the colonial governments was an indirect one. They offered verbal and sometimes financial encouragement to the associations, but the associations remained voluntary. In the important rural sector, however, such limited intervention was insufficient. Colonial governments, anxious to promote modern agricultural and commercial techniques, could rely neither on interested Europeans nor on educated Africans to take any action, as they were too few. The burden of introducing coöperatives thus fell upon the administration.[18] Throughout French *Afrique Noire*, starting with Senegal in 1907, the administration formed *sociétés indigènes de prévoyance*.[19] They served as "useful intermediaries between the administration and the mass of farmers," and were "particularly efficacious in assisting the vulgarization of modern methods of agriculture." [20] But, as has been pointed out,

Had the African peasant any conception during these years of his role of member of a providential society? It is extremely doubtful whether he distinguished the subscription from the poll-tax, in spite of a different coloured receipt, or the administrator as president of the local section, collaborating with him as member of the administrative council, from the administrator as such, ordering him as village headman to organize the production of unheard-of crops for unimaginable markets.[21]

In fact, these societies were scarcely voluntary; their obligatory character was never questioned, and thus they ran counter to the basic spirit

---

[18] *African Labour Survey*, International Labour Organization (Geneva, 1958), chap. xii, "The Cooperative Movement," pp. 434–464.

[19] See Robert Delavignette, *Freedom and Authority in French West Africa* (London: Oxford University Press, 1950), pp. 126–136, and Kenneth Robinson, "The Sociétés de Prévoyance in French West Africa," *Journal of African Administration*, II, no. 4 (1950), 29–34. The idea of these societies was copied from the French administration in Algeria, where such groups were first formed in 1882, and was adopted in Tunisia in 1907 and in Morocco in 1917 (cf. P. Marthelot, "Histoire et réalité de la modernisation du monde rural au Maroc," *Tiers-Monde*, II [April-June, 1961], 141, and P. Vidaud, *Le Développement de la culture moderne et la naissance du crédit agricole mutuel en Guinée française* [Forcalquier: Imp. Ch. Testanière, 1928], pp. 67–85).

[20] Georges Spitz, *L'Ouest Africain Français: A.O.F. et Togo* (Paris: Société d'Editions Géographiques, Maritimes et Coloniales, 1947), p. 206.

[21] D. Trevor, "Native Providential Societies in French West Africa," *South African Journal of Economics*, V (1937), 247.

of coöperation.[22] Furthermore, this obligatory character would eventually discredit them. For later nationalists, these societies were, by their authoritarianism and paternalism, just another element of colonial repression.[23] Coöperative societies established by the government in British West Africa were equally paternalist.[24]

Thus the only important type of voluntary association in the rural areas was a semigovernment agency, and would remain so until a mass nationalist party, originating in the towns and spreading to the countryside, would radically change the line-up of forces. In the towns, however, the attempt by Africans to take over the direction of their own associations and hence to redefine their objectives was more gradual and more subtle. One of the first efforts along these lines was the establishment of alumni associations (of *anciens élèves,* or "old boys") by the educated elite.

An old boys' association comprised the graduates of a single school, usually the one offering the highest level of education in a given colonial territory. In this way the most strongly urbanized elements in the population were grouped together, and could find spiritual comfort in the company of their peers, a small minority who felt somewhat beleaguered.[25] These organizations had multiple purposes in the beginning. They served as incubators of political and syndical movements. They promoted educational advance by establishing literacy programs before the colonial authorities assumed this task.[26] The problem of disengaging from European control made its appearance early. The difficulties placed in the way of organizing the Association des Anciens Elèves de l'Ecole William Ponty were overcome only with the persistent support of the European principal, "and even then it [the association] had to be placed under the patronage of numerous important people. Its cradle was so covered with flowers that it almost seemed a coffin." [27] In time, however,

---

[22] See Mamadou Dia, *Contribution à l'étude du mouvement coopératif en Afrique noire* (Paris: Présence Africaine, 1952), pp. 22–23.

[23] See Abdoulaye Ly, *L'Etat et la production paysanne* (Paris: Présence Africaine, 1958), esp. p. 45.

[24] J. Stonehouse, "The Place of Cooperation in Africa," *United Asia,* VII (April, 1955), esp. 107.

[25] These associations sometimes opened their ranks to other "literates." The old boys' association of the Ecole des Pères de Scheut in Stanleyville allowed graduates of other schools to be admitted by its Executive Committee (P. Clément, "Social Patterns of Urban Life," in *Social Implications of Industrialization and Urbanization in Africa South of the Sahara,* International African Institute [Paris: UNESCO, 1956], p. 475).

[26] For example, in the Gold Coast, the Old Achimotans' Association founded a night school which taught literacy to adults before mass education began (P. W. DuSautoy, *Community Development in Ghana* [London: Oxford University Press, 1958], p. 83).

[27] B. Dadié, "Misère de l'enseignement en A.O.F.," *Présence Africaine,* n.s., no. 11 (Dec., 1956–Jan., 1957), 60.

the evolution that characterized Leopoldville—"Old boys' associations, although generally started by a European, [became] . . . more or less independent"[28]—took place everywhere.

Much later in the colonial era, just before and just after World War II, interested Europeans again played an important role in inspiring African voluntary associations, this time by encouraging and aiding the creation of political parties and trade unions. Sometimes, as in the earlier period, the interested European was an administrator, and occasionally the colonial authorities encouraged the formation of such organizations. But more often it was a new group of Europeans, the metropolitan radicals, who provided the stimulus. During and after the war the British Trades Union Congress and the French labor federations actively supported the organization of trade unions in their respective colonial empires.[29] They helped to secure the passage of favorable legislation in the metropolis, and exported personnel to serve directly with the fledgling trade unions and with the colonial government as labor commissioners or *inspecteurs de travail.*[30]

Direct European aid in the creation of political structures was not important in British territories. In French areas, however, Europeans resident in West Africa were prominent in initiating Groupes d'Etudes Communistes, which served as early training bases for Africans who later became active in the Rassemblement Démocratique Africain.[31] The links between French and African parties were not definitely broken until 1957.[32] Similarly, after 1954 Belgian parties encouraged the formation of linked groups in the Congo.[33] Soon, however, as a consequence of the rise of nationalism, European dominance and paternalism were rejected, even when metropolitan radicals were involved.

European-inspired voluntary associations were, however, only a small, if important, part of the picture. The new urban elements began to create other kinds of associations, more purely African in conception

---

[28] S. Comhaire-Sylvain, "Food and Leisure among the African Youth of Leopoldville," *Communications from the Cape Town University School of African Studies,* n.s., no. 25 (Dec., 1950), 101.

[29] Thomas Hodgkin, *Nationalism in Colonial Africa* (London: Frederick Muller, 1956), pp. 128 ff.; Georges Fischer, "Trade Unions and Decolonisation," *Présence Africaine* (English ed.), vol. 6/7 (1961), 121–169.

[30] The Belgian trade unions followed a similar pattern (see R. Poupart, *Première esquisse de l'évolution du syndicalisme au Congo* [Brussels: Ed. de l'Institut de Sociologie Solvay, 1960], esp. chaps. 4, 6, 8).

[31] Thomas Hodgkin and Ruth Schachter, *French-speaking West Africa in Transition,* Carnegie Endowment for International Peace, International Conciliation, no. 528 (May, 1960), p. 387.

[32] See *ibid., passim,* for links between French and African parties during the postwar period.

[33] See the brief discussion in Ruth Slade, *The Belgian Congo* (2d ed.; London: Oxford University Press, 1961), pp. 39–43.

and orientation. There were first of all the organizations of the educated elite, among which must be included, at least in their early stages, the ethnic associations (*associations d'originaires,* or improvement and tribal unions). These were groups formed to provide social and economic solidarity in the towns among persons coming from a given tribe, village, or district. But they were more than mutual-aid societies, for they offered educational assistance and political advice to their home-town units.[34] In this way the educated [35] helped to spread modern values and institutions among the traditional societies from which they had come. These groups gradually opened their ranks to uneducated urban dwellers, who thus gained access to the material benefits of social solidarity and enjoyed the prestige of association with the literate members of their community. For the educated person, the admission of his illiterate urban compatriot was a further extension of the educational and improvement goals of the association.

The influence of the educated on their urban environment was expressed in the formation of syndical organizations which later grew into trade unions. In the mid-nineteenth century an organization of palm-wine carriers existed in the Gold Coast.[36] In French West Africa, after World War I, workers organized in *amicales* engaged in work conflicts on the wharfs of Cotonou and Abidjan.[37] African occupational associations in Kenya, sometimes organized on a tribal basis, began "to take on the characteristics of trade union movements"; in most industries, trade unions were "said to be working 'underground.'"[38] In western Nigeria, traditional craft guilds were transformed into a more modern

[34] Ione Acquah, *Accra Survey* (London: University of London Press, 1958), p. 105; E. P. O. Offodile, "Growth and Influence of Tribal Unions," *West African Review,* XVIII, no. 239 (1947), 937–941.

[35] "Many of the members of these [improvement and tribal] unions [in eastern Nigeria] are among the best educated men in their communities, holding good posts in Government departments or the commercial houses" (Lord Hailey, *Native Administration in the British African Territories,* III [London: H.M.S.O., 1951], 19). "In nearly every Division in Ashanti, the educated young men have formed literary societies and 'Progress Unions' which are active political groups" (K. A. Busia, *The Position of the Chief in the Modern Political System of Ashanti* [London: Oxford University Press, 1951], p. 132).

[36] J. I. Roper, *Labour Problems in West Africa* (London: Penguin African Series, 1958), p. 48, citing Reindorf. Even if the palm-wine carriers were not formally educated, they represented a segment of the urban population which was familiar with modern norms and values. Formal organization was a direct outcome of this familiarity.

[37] *Code du Travail des Territoires d'Outre-Mer,* Secrétariat Social d'Outre-Mer (Paris: Société des Editions Africaines, 1953), p. 57.

[38] Mary Parker, "Political and Social Aspects of Municipal Government in Kenya, with Special Reference to Nairobi" (undated MS, *ca.* 1950–1955), reported in *Social Implications of Industrialization and Urbanization,* p. 130.

form and were "no longer composed of fathers and sons but of masters and journeymen or apprentices; and this is a difference of overwhelming importance both in craft industry and in society as a whole." [39] Even in Mozambique, "small craft brotherhoods" exist which are reported to be "quite distinct from modern trade-unionism, but analogous to medieval guilds, in that they are bound up with forms of the Catholic religion or that they look after their members in distress." [40]

In the early days, many of these syndical groups or artisans' guilds were in liaison with traditional structures.[41] Others grew out of alumni associations. For example, in the Anglo-Egyptian Sudan, "it was in the Technical School Old Boys' Club in Atbara that the Workers Affairs Association was born." [42] In the French Soudan (Mali), the Association des Anciens Elèves du Lycée Terrasson de Fougères at Bamako was "instrumental in bringing into being the first trade unions . . . in 1937." [43] Legalization of the right of trade unions to organize, which occurred in French, British, and Belgian territories just before, during, and after World War II,[44] gave a new character to syndical groups, enabling them to become mass organizations linked to the nationalist movement. Even during this later period, however, in Senegal in particular and in French West Africa in general, manual workers were the least organized and intellectual elements were the most organized.[45]

Traditional organizations were not always modified in a syndical direction. The traditional role of secret societies was to enforce the customs of the society and to assure social place to their members. Their degeneration under modern conditions sometimes turned them into antisocial groups "whose members seek to assume power by terror. These are then the famous societies of panther-men or crocodile-men." [46] But under other circumstances the antisocial tendencies of these secret societies were channeled in nationalist directions: "In the Ivory Coast, in the high

---

[39] P. C. Lloyd, "Craft Organization in Yoruba Towns," *Africa*, XXIII (Jan., 1953), 44.

[40] A. Moreira, "The 'Elites' of the Portuguese 'Tribal' Provinces (Guinea, Angola, Mozambique)," *International Social Science Bulletin*, VIII (1956), 477. R. J. H. Pogucki, *Gold Coast Land Tenure* (Accra: Government Printer, 1956), III, 9, speaks of "quasi-castes" of fishermen, market women, butchers, and motor drivers in Accra.

[41] Roper, *op. cit.*, pp. 23–27, 48–50; *Code du Travail des Territoires d'Outre-Mer*, p. 58.

[42] Saad Ed Din Fawzi, *The Labour Movement in the Sudan, 1946–1955* (London: Oxford University Press, 1957), p. 34.

[43] Hodgkin, *op. cit.*, pp. 88–89.

[44] *African Labour Survey*, pp. 220–231; Poupart, *op. cit.*, chap. 3.

[45] Paul Mercier, "La Vie politique dans les centres urbains du Sénégal," *Cahiers Internationaux de Sociologie*, n.s., XXVII (1959), 79.

[46] D. Paulme, *Les Civilisations africaines* (Paris: Presses Universitaires de France, 1953), p. 102.

country, the Rassemblement Démocratique Africain consolidates its dominance by utilizing an initiation society, that of Poro." [47]

Of the various associations that emerged from a traditional background, essentially new but often retaining a familiar format,[48] the most important and the most universal, because it best met the needs of the mass of noneducated urban dwellers, was the savings club (credit and thrift association, or contribution club). These clubs were known as *esusu* in Nigeria;[49] as *kitemo* in central Congo; as *osassa* among the Mboshi of the Congo; as *djana* among the Fang of the southern Camerouns,[50] or *jangi* or *njangi*;[51] as *ndjonu* in Dahomey;[52] as *bandoi* in Leopoldville;[53] as *adashi* among the Hausa of northern Nigeria;[54] and as "tontines" in Porto-Novo.[55] Similar groups are reported at Kampala[56] and Jinja[57] in Uganda. Although some of these groups limited themselves to mutual-benefit activities, such as payments on the occasion of marriage or burial,[58] others worked out a system of further contributions, which were pooled on a regular, usually a weekly, basis and distributed to each member in turn. This system enabled members to purchase capital goods (if they were petty merchants) or gifts of value. It was a form of small credit, a self-created banking facility. For this reason, despite a traditional veneer, these associations were basically urban phenomena. The adashi, for example, "are common among salaried workers of the Native Authori-

---

[47] Georges Balandier, "Afrique Ambiguë," *Les Temps Modernes*, XII (July, 1956), 71.

[48] Georges Balandier, "Les Modifications dans les structures sociales," *L'Eveil de l'Afrique noire*, supplement to *Preuves*, no. 88 (June, 1958), 25–26.

[49] For a detailed description of an esusu see S. G. Ardener, "The Social and Economic Significance of the Contribution Club among a Section of the Southern Ibo," *Proceedings of WAISER Annual Conference—Sociology Section* (Ibadan, March, 1953), pp. 128–142.

[50] J.-C. Pauvert, "Le Problème des classes sociales dans l'Afrique équatoriale," *Cahiers Internationaux de Sociologie*, XIX (1955), 89.

[51] J. Guilbot, "Petite étude sur la main d'oeuvre à Douala," *IFAN Mémoires*, no. 1 (1947), cited in *Social Implications of Industrialization and Urbanization*, p. 105; W. A. Warmington, "Savings and Indebtedness among Cameroons Plantation Workers," *Africa*, XXVII (Oct., 1958), 329–343.

[52] Guilbot, *op. cit.*

[53] Comhaire-Sylvain, *op. cit.*, p. 102.

[54] M. G. Smith, "Cooperation in Hausa Society," *Information*, X (Jan., 1957), 1–20.

[55] Claude Tardits, *Porto-Novo* (Paris: Mouton, 1958), p. 36.

[56] A. W. Southall and P. C. W. Gutkind, *Townsmen in the Making*, East African Studies no. 9 (Kampala, 1956), pp. 162–163.

[57] C. and R. Sofer, *Jinja Transformed*, East African Studies no. 4 (Kampala, 1955), p. 108.

[58] Burial ceremonies are said to be the chief stimulus for the formation of tribal associations in Mombasa and Freetown (Gordon Wilson, "Mombasa: A Modern Colonial Municipality," in A. S. Southall, ed., *Social Change in Modern Africa* [London: Oxford University Press, 1961], p. 111; M. P. Banton, "The Restructuring of Social Relationships," in *ibid.*, p. 120).

ties in the larger settlements [of Nigeria], and among other persons with regular but low weekly cash incomes. They are rarely found in the rural districts, for precisely this reason, that membership presupposes a regularity of cash income which peasants rarely enjoy."[59] Occasionally the credit facility was so overemphasized, to the detriment of the solidarity aspect, that the savings group did not meet at all, and its members were known only to the organizer.[60]

Like syndical and ethnic mutual-benefit groups, religious associations developed from organizations of the elite into mass organizations, first in the largest urban centers and later in the smaller towns. European rule meant, almost everywhere, the presence of missionaries and the spread of Christianity. The Christian church hierarchies were, until very recently, manned largely by Europeans, at least in the higher ranks. One way of reacting to the colonial situation was to create new religious organizations. African secessionist churches, though largely accepting the theology of the Western churches from which they seceded, desired an independent structure whose personnel would be African. Various Neo-Christian messianic movements and syncretistic cults also sprang into being.[61] Traditional practices were revived in the form of new cults, appealing primarily to those who had had some contact with modern life.[62]

These Neo-Christian and neotraditional (and even some Neo-Islamic) movements, often urban in derivation and taking the form of voluntary associations, were essentially one more expression of the need of the new urban elements to find new ways of re-creating the social and personal security that was jeopardized in the colonial situation.[63] Among the Bakongo, "the 'churches,' which are the product of 'separatist' Christians, serve the objectives of those social categories who wish to affirm themselves vis-à-vis the traditional authorities . . . and vis-à-vis those who have power 'delegated' by the colonizer."[64] Even the neotraditional groupings are modernist in many ways: "One reason for distinguishing

---

[59] Smith, *op. cit.*, p. 9.

[60] Banton, *West African City*, p. 188.

[61] A good summary discussion of these two types of Christian movements may be found in George Shepperson, "Ethiopianism and African Nationalism," *Phylon*, XIV (First Quarter, 1953), 9–18. Cf. also E. G. Parrinder, *Religion in an African City* (London: Oxford University Press, 1953), and A. J. F. Kobben, "Prophetic Movements as an Expression of Social Protest," *International Archives of Ethnography*, XLIX, no. 1 (1960), 117–164.

[62] See, for example, B. Holas, *Les Sénoufo* (Paris: Presses Universitaires de France, 1957), pp. 155–158; M. J. Field, *Akim-Kotoku* (London: Crown Agents for the Colonies, 1948), chap. xiii.

[63] Orthodox Christian groups sometimes functioned in the same way. For the description of a Presbyterian bible class as a benefit society, and Catholic secret lodges as mutual-aid organizations, see Fiawoo, *op. cit.*, pp. 92–93.

[64] Georges Balandier, *Sociologie actuelle de l'Afrique noire* (Paris: Presses Universitaires de France, 1955), pp. 478–479.

native churches from tribal societies . . . is that the former are strictly fundamentalist and puritanical, objecting to many popular practices." [65] These new religious organizations, as opposed to traditional religious, orthodox Western Christian groups, or the older Islamic sects,[66] seemed to be most flourishing where they served as outlets for protest, that is, where political suppression under colonial rule was the most severe.[67]

This growing network of voluntary associations performed many functions for the new social order. First of all, the associations provided social services, and in this area they were at least as important as the government.[68] They certainly did more than the government in instructing their members about the new urban norms that were part of a modern political and economic system. This objective was accomplished in various ways. For example, the organization, by creating a large number of offices,[69] simplified the performance of necessary tasks and at the same time gave its members experience in office holding. The emphasis was on standards of personal comportment within the organization: "The discipline which they impose upon their members makes them more ready to accept discipline in other spheres." [70] Sometimes, indeed, self-improvement was very conscious, as in this announcement by the tribunal clerks of Koforidua (Gold Coast) when they formed an association in 1915: "The Association aims at the amelioration of certain defects that have tinged with rusticity the prestige of Tribunal Clerks." [71] Dispensing social services, spreading the norms of the larger society, making the norms for the group itself, and arbitrating its conflicts[72]—these were the common functions of the new associations.[73] Moreover, the voluntary

[65] J. Comhaire, "Religious Trends in African and Afro-American Societies," *Anthropological Quarterly*, n.s., XXVI, no. 4 (1953), 98.

[66] For the impact of colonization on Islamic religious practice, see Alphonse Gouilly, *L'Islam dans l'Afrique Occidentale Française* (Paris: Larose, 1952), and the various works of J. Spencer Trimingham.

[67] Hodgkin, *op. cit.*, pp. 93–114; Georges Balandier, "Messianismes et nationalismes en Afrique noire," *Cahiers Internationaux de Sociologie*, XIV (1953), 41–65.

[68] In the Congo "social services frequently fell into two categories: 1. Services set up by the workers themselves; (*a*) recreational organizations. . . . ; (*b*) educational organizations. . . . 2. Services organized for the wives of workers" (A. Doucy and P. Feldheim, "Some Effects of Industrialization on the Districts of Equatoria Province," in *Social Implications of Industrialization and Urbanization*, p. 684).

[69] Fiawoo, *op. cit.*, p. 91; Banton, *West African City*, p. 171.

[70] Banton, *West African City*, p. 175. Elsewhere ("The Restructuring of Social Relationships," p. 119) Banton notes that some "associations make greater demands upon their members and they are respected accordingly."

[71] Cited in Roper, *op. cit.*, p. 55.

[72] On the importance of arbitration, see Kenneth Little, "The African Elite in British West Africa," in A. W. Lind, ed., *Race Relations in World Perspective* (Honolulu: University of Hawaii Press, 1955), p. 287.

[73] Even prostitutes organized groups that performed these functions (J. Rouch and E. Bernus, "Notes sur les prostitués 'toutou' de Treichville et d'Adjamé," *Etudes Eburnéennes*, VI [1957], 237).

associations represented for the new society an effective mechanism of crossing kin barriers and creating national groups. They combined the literate and the illiterate,[74] and the many ethnic and linguistic groups,[75] even at the village level.[76] A prime objective of ethnic groups was to raise their own prestige;[77] by doing so they tended to level differences and thus to eliminate the need for their continuance.

The number of these associations increased rapidly throughout the colonial era. No accurate statistics are available, although most observers would agree that it is not putting it too strongly, at least since World War II, to speak of "African societomania." [78] A high proportion of individuals in the cities belonged to voluntary associations, and the average individual belonged to several of them. The leadership, especially in the earlier days, was intertwining,[79] and the groups were often small[80] and short-lived.[81]

Over time, voluntary associations followed a discernible pattern. The movement was from European inspiration to African inspiration; from groups of the urban educated elite to mass organizations; from few groups to many; from small groups to large ones; from groups with vague and diffuse objectives to groups with specialized programs. In Tropical Africa this movement occurred in the colonial context. The emergence of the nationalist movement, in large part the outcome of the growth of voluntary associations, was to have a fundamental impact on the character and the activities of these associations.

---

[74] Busia, *Social Survey of Sekondi-Takoradi*, p. 79.

[75] On the effectiveness of the new religious groups in this regard, see the discussion on Harrism in B. Holas, "Bref aperçu sur les principaux cultes syncrétiques de la basse Côte d'Ivoire," *Africa*, XXIV (1954), 55.

[76] In the Gambia, "among the Wolof the *kompin* is the only village-wide association that bridges all of the local kinship groupings and social classes" (D. W. Ames, "Wolof Cooperative Work Groups," in W. R. Bascom and M. J. Herskovits, *Continuity and Change in African Cultures* [Chicago: University of Chicago Press, 1959], p. 237).

[77] Banton describes this process for the Temne in Freetown (*West African City*, pp. 162–183).

[78] J. Lombard, "Cotonou, Ville africaine," *Etudes Dahoméennes*, X (1953), 198. A poll taken in Dakar about 1953–1954 suggests that more than two-thirds of the population, a proportion as high among women as among men, belonged to a political party, not to speak of other organizations (Mercier, *op. cit.*, pp. 69, 72).

[79] According to T. Hodgkin ("Towards Self-Government in British West Africa," in B. Davidson and A. Ademola, *The New West Africa* [London: Allen & Unwin, 1953], p. 70), a house sign in Enugu explained that the house "was the headquarters of the Enugu branch of the N.C.N.C., of the Freedom Movement, of the African National Church and the Tenants' Union as well as the office of the Nigerian Miners' Union."

[80] Balandier (*Sociologie des Brazzavilles noires*, p. 123) estimates that the group of average size in Poto-Poto had fifty members.

[81] A. L. Epstein, *Politics in an Urban African Community* (Manchester: Manchester University Press, 1958), p. 66, argues that the groups fluctuated in a cycle of energy and apathy.

Even before the rise of the nationalist movement, the growth of voluntary associations may be fully appreciated only as a "double process: struggle against *dépaysement,* concealment from and opposition to the colonial society." [82] Occasionally, even in an early period, the colonial regime permitted the creation of an avowedly political organization, if not a party. A classic instance was the founding in 1897, in the Gold Coast, of the Aborigines' Rights Protection Society (ARPS) to oppose certain proposed land legislation. After its initial success the ARPS "continued . . . to lead the opposition to any government policies which it considered contrary to African rights." [83] In other instances political opposition was expressed by a syndical group. For example, in the Ivory Coast in 1944, the African farmers, seeking to revise government policies that favored European farmers, founded the Syndicat Agricole Africain.[84] In Uganda, in 1947, the fight against the European monopoly of the cotton industry led to the creation of the Uganda African Farmers' Union.[85] From the beginning the colonial authorities, well aware of the political implications of voluntary associations, were reluctant to allow freedom of association, especially for trade unions[86] and avowedly political organizations. In the Congo, "adult native societies other than mutual-aid associations were not allowed to exist without permission from the government." [87] In 1915 the Harris movement in the Ivory Coast, although religious, nonpolitical, and modernist, "soon became incompatible with the security measures necessitated by the state of war." [88] The colonial authorities in Northern Rhodesia debated the utility of using welfare societies as a means of sounding native opinion on political matters.[89] At a conference of district commissioners of Northern Rhodesia in 1936, "the feeling . . . was that the [African Welfare] Associations should be allowed to develop along the lines of debating societies, but that they should not discuss political matters." [90] The fear of the colonial authorities was quite apparent and easily understandable: "Any [social] re-

---

[82] Balandier, *Sociologie des Brazzavilles noires,* p. 270.
[83] F. M. Bourret, *The Gold Coast* (Stanford: Stanford University Press, 1952), p. 41.
[84] Cf. M. Fréchon, "Les Planteurs européens en Côte d'Ivoire," *Cahiers d'Outre-Mer,* III, no. 29 (Jan.-March, 1955), 76.
[85] A. B. Mukwaza, "The Rise of the Uganda African Farmers' Union in Buganda, 1947–1949," East African Institute of Social Research Conference, June, 1957 (mimeographed).
[86] *African Labour Survey,* chap. vii.
[87] Comhaire-Sylvain, *op. cit.,* p. 104.
[88] F. J. Amon d'Aby, *La Côte d'Ivoire dans la cité africaine* (Paris: Larose, 1951), p. 152.
[89] Epstein, *op. cit.,* chap. iii, esp. pp. 69–70.
[90] *Ibid.,* p. 47.

organization in modernist form . . . quickly reaches a threshold of alarm and calls down the opposition of the dominating society." [91]

Yet the colonial authorities could not dispense with voluntary associations. That they needed them as adjuncts of the administration was stated clearly and frankly at a British Colonial Office conference in 1948:

This association of Africans with voluntary work of all kinds might indeed provide the key to securing the active cooperation of the educated classes in government policy and in programs for social and economic betterment. In Siberia the Russians have obtained the support of the educated people by associating them closely with the work of the local Communist party. The lighting of the spark which may destroy inertia and secure wholehearted cooperation is a far more difficult task in Africa; but, if it can be lighted, many of the obstacles to political and social development would be removed.[92]

The colonial authorities needed voluntary associations to help them spread certain values essential to the direction of a modern economy, yet they feared that these groups would turn from promoting approved social change to advocating political change. Indeed, they were apprehensive that it was true that "voluntary associations act as unconscious nurseries of democratic life." [93]

These associations were training grounds for leaders, both in the technical skills of running an organization and in the substantive appreciation of political ideas. Cultural associations and youth movements in Senegal contributed to the formation of solid cadres: "The concern with political training in a very large sense, beyond the orientations of particular parties, is not absent. . . . By means of questions such as education and the languages of education, the organization of local communities, economic development, interracial marriage, and so on, the study of political problems deriving from the colonial situation comes strongly into play." [94] In Uganda, "the list of officers of the Old Budonians' Club for 1950 reads like a Who's Who of Buganda." [95] Even in Angola, in 1956, "signs are appearing of an associational movement which autonomously calls for leaders and whence there may in due course emerge an elite whose general attitude and tendencies cannot be foreseen." [96]

Voluntary associations also served as communications networks

---

[91] Balandier, *Sociologie actuelle de l'Afrique noire*, p. 496.

[92] *Colonial Office Summer Conference on African Administration*, African no. 1174 (London: H.M.S.O., 1948), p. 122.

[93] David Kimble, *The Machinery of Self-Government* (London: Penguin West African Series, 1953), p. 28.

[94] Mercier, *op. cit.*, p. 77.

[95] David E. Apter, *The Political Kingdom in Uganda* (Princeton: Princeton University Press, 1961), p. 243.

[96] Moreira, *op. cit.*, p. 477.

through which new ideas, even forbidden ideas, could circulate.[97] They often provided excuses for travel and contact; even football has "sociological importance" in that it provided "one of the few inter-territorial meeting-points for Africans." [98]

Furthermore, voluntary associations were a proving ground for political leaders, where they demonstrated the support they could garner among a significant segment in the population. In western Nigeria, "Office in the *egbe* gives no formal status in the town. Yet the qualities of leadership displayed by the officeholders do not pass unnoticed and may often mark out a likely candidate for a chieftaincy title or election to the local government council." [99] In Uganda, all African members of the Legislative Council of 1955–1958 "were affiliated with a large number of voluntary associations by which they increased their influence." [100]

That there was an important link between the development of a network of voluntary associations and the development of political consciousness may be seen most clearly in the growth of political organizations from nonpolitical associations. In Northern Rhodesia, the African National Congress "developed out of the African Welfare Society which in turn grew from an African reading circle formed in 1926." [101] In eastern Nigeria, "the growth of local political party organization was also assisted by the [tribal] unions." [102] In most Yoruba towns in western Nigeria, the progress unions "tended to assume party labels, and, in time, to become party branches." [103] The Gold Coast Youth Conference (1938), a predecessor of the nationalist movement, was made up of "Clubs Union and other literary and social clubs in the country," [104] and the Parti Démocratique de la Côte d'Ivoire grew out of the Syndicat Agricole Africain.[105] In Guinea the Amicale Gilbert Vieillard, itself the outgrowth of a newspaper published by Fulani students in Dakar, became the base of a political party, the Démocratie Socialiste de Guinée,[106] and the

---

[97] "For the illiterates, especially from the far north, the tribal association, as well as the tribal head, provides an avenue through which news circulates" (Acquah, *op. cit.*, p. 106).

[98] Hodgkin, *Nationalism in Colonial Africa,* p. 88.

[99] P. C. Lloyd, "The Yoruba Town Today," *Sociological Review,* VII (July, 1959), 52.

[100] Apter, *op. cit.*, p. 407.

[101] M. McCulloch, "A Social Survey of the African Population of Livingstone," *Rhodes-Livingstone Papers,* no. 26 (1956), 8; cf. also Epstein, *op. cit.*, chap. v, esp. pp. 159–160.

[102] L. Gray Cowan, *Local Government in West Africa* (New York: Columbia University Press, 1958), pp. 32–33.

[103] Lloyd, "The Yoruba Town Today," p. 56.

[104] J. B. Danquah, *Liberty: A Page from the Life of J.B.* (Accra: H. K. Akyeampong, [1960]), p. 24.

[105] Amon d'Aby, *op. cit.*, pp. 112–114; Hodgkin and Schachter, *op. cit.*, pp. 411–414.

[106] Hodgkin and Schachter, *op. cit.*, p. 386.

Uganda African Farmers' Union was the forerunner of the Uganda National Congress.[107] In the Congo, the Abako (Association pour le Maintien, l'Unité, et l'Expansion de la Kikongo) transformed itself from a cultural organization into a political party, and the Conakat, a political party, grew out of a confederation of tribal associations (Confédération des Associations Tribales du Katanga).[108]

Political organizations thus drew upon the wide base of associations already in existence. When, however, a radical nationalist movement did emerge as an overt political party, this wide base was itself profoundly affected. The problem for the nationalists was how to form a mass movement with support of sufficient intensity and sufficient geographical scope to force the colonial power to yield to their demands. The nationalist movements were revolutionary movements which rejected the basic political structure of the colony.

Revolutionary movements must always face up to the truth that the existing social order commands a certain legitimacy even among many who are discontented with the regime. Even if the loyalty is not strong, there remains what might be called the "inertia of loyalty," or the lack of active disloyalty, to a structure that exists *de facto*. This legitimacy, both internal and international, was a basic source of strength for the colonial regime in Africa, and it was buoyed up by the support that traditional political structures offered, by and large, to the colonial administrations. In order to overcome the inertia of loyalty, the nationalist movement took on the form of a deviant subculture systematically challenging the norms and the values of the colonial regime, including its adjuncts, the traditional chiefs. The nationalists sought to expand the audience for their message by turning the multiple grievances of ethnic and occupational groups into political demands.

But, to succeed, a national movement had to do more. It had to transform all those with actual or potential grievances, which was virtually the entire population, into consistent deviants. It had to undermine the internal legitimacy of the system by creating a situation in which the majority of the population responded more to its norms and sanctions than to those of the colonial regime. To gain these ends, the nationalist movement found it desirable to absorb the total time of the

---

[107] An intermediate group, the Federation of African Partnerships, replaced the Farmers' Union when the latter was banned in 1949, and became the base of the congress (Apter, *op. cit.*, p. 275).

[108] "The Abako, before becoming the first Congolese 'nationalist' party, was an ethnic association created, with the assistance of the Belgian authorities, for the unity, maintenance, and expansion of the Kikongo language" (J. Buchmann, "Le Problème des structures politiques en Afrique noire," *Etudes Congolaises*, no. 5 [Oct.-Nov., 1961], p. 11). On the Conakat, see *Congo 1959* (Brussels: Centre de Recherche et d'Information Socio-Politique, 1960), p. 279.

individual, to surround him with environments in which the new nationalist norms were the only valid ones. With this objective in mind, the nationalist movements in Tropical Africa sought to politicize a whole network of voluntary associations, to make them extensions of the nationalist movement, infused by its values, responding to its *mots d'ordre*. Not only did ostensibly nonpolitical organizations assume overtly political roles—for example, the Egba Women's Union successfully agitated for the abdication of the Alake of Abeokuta in 1948; the Mothers' Union and the YWCA in Uganda called for the return of the Kabaka of Buganda;[109] youth organizations, ethnic groups, and trade unions played political roles in the recent political life of Senegal;[110] and the Sudan Workers' Trade Union Federation was a focal point in the nationalist struggle in the Sudan[111]—but the political movements themselves took on nonpolitical forms. Examples are the creation of affiliated religious groupings along the littoral of the Ivory Coast[112] and the inclusion of purely social activities in the program of the Tanganyika African National Union.[113]

The colonial governments did not allow this tendency to develop without challenge. They argued the virtue of apoliticism for voluntary associations, which, in the colonial context, amounted to creating barriers to the spread of nationalist ideas. They used administrative machinery to fight increasing politicization. But throughout Tropical Africa, in the post–World War II period, the trend has been away from apoliticism. The growth of nationalist political organizations, and the affiliation with them of trade unions, youth and women's groups, ethnic organizations, mutual-benefit societies, and so on, have gone hand-in-hand. At a certain point in their development, most nationalist movements became mass movements, penetrating to the remotest villages, where "men who have never learned the advantages of shirt and pants come to blows sometimes because they do not vote for the same candidate." [114]

The struggle between nationalist movements and colonial governments in Tropical Africa over the orientation of voluntary associations took place also in the international arena. The national movements were not only interested in undermining the internal legitimacy of the various colonial administrations; they wished to undermine their international legitimacy as well. International legitimacy meant the acceptance by

---

[109] Hodgkin, *Nationalism in Colonial Africa*, pp. 90–91.

[110] Mercier, *op. cit.*, pp. 77–82.

[111] Fawzi, *op. cit.*, pp. 113–121.

[112] B. Holas, "La *Goumbé:* Une association de jeunesse musulmane en basse Côte d'Ivoire," *Kongo-Overzee*, XIX, no. 2/3 (1953), 116.

[113] R. G. Abrahams, "Kahama Township, Western Province, Tanganyika," in Southall, *Social Change in Modern Africa*, p. 250.

[114] E. Milcent, *L'A.O.F. entre en scène* (Paris: Ed. de l'Homme d'Action, 1958), p. 147.

governments and public opinion in countries outside a particular colonial empire of the justness or the inevitability of continuing the colonial administration in a given territory, at least for some time beyond the immediate present. These outside forces offered differing degrees of support, ranging according to national ideology and time. What was most important for a given nationalist movement, at the minimum, was to reduce the moral and, a fortiori, the political and economic support given to the colonial regime in its own particular country. There were various ways in which it could accomplish this objective. After Asian and Middle Eastern countries had become independent and were committed to an ideology of decolonization, they could place governmental pressure (for example, through such means as United Nations resolutions or the Bandung Conference) on the colonial powers of Africa, or on other countries (the United States or the Soviet Union, for instance) which could influence the European colonial powers. As one nation after another proceeded to independence after World War II, such pressure became increasingly more effective.

There was another important arena where the campaign against the legitimacy of colonial regimes took place, the arena of international nongovernmental organizations (trade unions, youth and student associations, coöperatives, women's groups, ex-servicemen's organizations, and religious groups). In 1945 most of these international associations were largely European or North American in membership and leadership. Yet even before decolonization, nongovernmental organizations began to seek affiliates in Asia and Africa. Often a colonial administration would encourage affiliation by a group that was "nonpolitical" and "moderate." As the nationalist movements came into being in Tropical Africa, and sought to establish a network of voluntary associations linked with them, they wanted to have their affiliate groups recognized internationally as the ones truly representative of the particular colony.

Access to membership in international groups by organizations sympathetic to African nationalism had the consequence of increasing the politicization of international organizations on questions relating to the process of decolonization. The nationalist cause in Tropical African countries received substantial support in the form of resolutions by international voluntary groups and of material aid to the nationalist network of organizations. It also received increasing support from homologous voluntary associations in the metropolitan countries, or in the countries of their allies, which in turn began to put pressure on their governments to speed the pace of decolonization. The politicization of the international associations was hastened by the polarization of international groups (into parallel Communist-dominated and non-Communist structures) because of tensions produced by the cold war. The resulting competition for nationalist affiliations led international associations more and more to accept nationalist-linked groups as representative. In turn, this acceptance sometimes reacted on the remaining apolitical voluntary associations in Tropical Africa, speeding their politicization.[115] Beginning in 1955, trade unions and youth groups in French West Africa which were affiliated with nationalist movements evolved another way of forcing international and metropolitan organizations to recognize their representativeness and to adopt positions that aided the process of decolonization. Their method was to disaffiliate from all international and French organizations and to insist on the right to be the sole legitimate observer without, however, becoming a member. These groups also attempted to build intra-African structures that would have increasing leverage in relation to international associations.[116]

The achievement of independence in Tropical African countries has not terminated the political role of voluntary associations. The problems of national integration facing a new government have led to an intensification of the process of politicization rather than to a loosening of the ties between the governing nationalist party and voluntary associations.[117] Increased pressure has been put on apolitical groups that were considered to have been effectively allied with the former colonial administration to change their character or dissolve. Such pressure is more telling now that the nationalist movement controls the machinery of the state. The trend toward a single-party system[118] has generated a parallel trend toward a single trade-union, youth, women's, students', and coöperative structure, in many instances forming an integral part of the party.[119]

The process of seeking internal and international legitimation of nationalist values did not end with independence: "With the transition to independence and the growing emphasis on wider administrative and power relations, there may arise a tendency to gear all new developments to the symbols of national identification. Autonomous development of various parties and social groups, therefore, may sometimes be viewed as interfering with the stabilization of the basic institutional frame-

---

[115] The ways in which international affiliations encouraged politicization in trade unions are discussed in Mercier, *op. cit.*, p. 81.

[116] Ruth Schachter, "Trade Unions Seek Autonomy," *West Africa,* Jan. 19, 26, 1957; Fischer, *op. cit.*

[117] For an over-all discussion of the process and the reasons that explain it, see Wallerstein, *op. cit.*, chap. v.

[118] For the theoretical justification of this system see Madeira Keita, "Le Parti unique en Afrique," *Présence Africaine,* no. 30 (Feb.-March, 1960), 3–24.

[119] In Ghana, in 1961, separate membership cards for the trade-union, farmers', coöperative, and women's movements were abolished, as membership in the Convention People's Party offered automatic membership in the linked groups (see the broadcast of President Kwame Nkrumah of April 8, 1961, reproduced in Ghana Press Release no. 107 [New York], April 10, 1961, p. 5).

work." [120] The close intermeshing of nationalist and Pan-African objectives has stimulated further tightening of the party's control over voluntary associations. Because African countries are divided as to the correct paths to ostensibly similar objectives, governments are unwilling to tolerate voluntary associations that adhere more closely to the point of view of an African government other than their own.[121] In the years immediately following independence, there has been an almost total politicization of voluntary associations. Yet their old frameworks are being maintained. National voluntary groups are in fact being strengthened in terms of finance and organization. Today they are closely linked to the single-party structure, but they remain separate organizations and may in fact serve as useful channels for the expression as well as the restraint of dissent. The trend toward specialization of voluntary associations, with its almost inevitable long-run consequence of depoliticization, has been checked or reversed by the growth of single-party structures to meet the problems of the postindependence era. With, however, the increased social differentiation that accompanies economic development, it is likely that voluntary associations will again turn in the direction of multiplicity, specificity, and autonomy.

---

[120] S. Eisenstadt, "Approaches to the Problem of Political Development in Non-Western Societies," *World Politics,* IX (April, 1957), 452–453.

[121] For an analysis of the reciprocal pressures on voluntary associations, see my "How Seven States Were Born in Former French West Africa," *Africa Report,* VI (March, 1961).

9. TRADE UNIONS

By Elliot J. Berg
and Jeffrey Butler

In the last few years there has been put into circulation a set of generalizations about the political role of labor movements in underdeveloped areas. These generalizations are so frequently repeated that they have become a kind of conventional wisdom, the main lines of which may easily be summarized. Trade unions in these countries are said to have developed and behaved more as political institutions than as economic or collective bargaining agencies. They arose in response not to capitalism or industrialism, as in the West, but to the colonial situation. They have always been intimately involved in politics, most commonly subordinated to political parties and nationalist movements; they are party instruments. Although their numbers are usually small and their organization is shoddy, they have great influence, for wage earners form one of the few readily identifiable and mobilizable interest groups in these societies. Because they do, the unions have been key elements in the struggle for independence, and are one of the most dynamic and significant institutions in postindependence political life.[1]

Although some of these generalizations are valid in some African countries, most of them require severe qualification when applied to Tropical Africa. In fact, what is most striking about the political role of labor movements in the countries of Tropical Africa is their failure to become politically involved during the colonial period, their limited political impact when they did become involved, and their restricted role after independence.

Part of the difficulty in analyzing the political aspects of trade-

---

[1] See, among the many expressions of all or some of these views, Everett Kassalow, "Unions in the New and Developing Countries," and S. Lowe, "The Role of Trade Unions in the Newly Independent Countries of Africa," in a forthcoming volume of National Institute of Labor Education seminar papers to be published by Northwestern University Press under Kassalow's editorship; Bruce H. Millen, *The Political Role of Labor in Developing Countries* (Washington: Brookings Institution, 1963); George C. Lodge, "Labor's Role in Newly Developing Countries," *Foreign Affairs*, XXXVII (July, 1959), 660–671; Georges Fischer, "Syndicats et Décolonisation," *Présence Africaine*, n.s., no. 34–35 (Oct., 1960–Jan., 1961), esp. pp. 23 ff.; M. Neufeld, "The Inevitability of Political Unionism in Underdeveloped Countries: Italy the Exemplar," *Industrial and Labor Relations Review*, XIII (April, 1960), 363–386.

unionism is semantic. Most discussions of trade unions and politics, in Africa as elsewhere, suffer from a failure to specify exactly what is meant by trade-union "politicalness." The literature is liberally sprinkled with statements that labor organizations are "highly political" or are "associated with a political party." But such statements have little meaning. What is important is the nature and the intensity of the commitment of unions to politics and parties. There are a number of different ways to proceed in evaluating this commitment. One is to look at the general political attitudes of the labor movement: its vision of the kind of world it wants and how it proposes to get it, in short, its ideology. We will not follow this path here, partly for reasons of space and partly because what a labor movement says about these matters is less significant than what it actually does.

We will, therefore, say little about ideology. Instead, three broad sets of questions will be examined: (1) What were the structural relations between trade unions and parties in preindependent Africa? How close was the relationship, and to what extent may it be said that parties dominated unions? (2) What concrete political acts did African trade-union movements engage in, and how effective were they? Did the labor movement call political strikes and demonstrations? Did it provide the party with manpower, or with material and organizational help? (3) What is the union position after independence?

With these questions to guide the analysis, we will try to show that the usual generalizations about labor's political role in developing or colonial countries are inappropriate in Tropical Africa. The generalizations should indeed be reversed. In the period before independence, African trade unions were rarely the instruments of political parties. To the extent that they entered the political arena their role was usually negligible. After independence they were quickly subdued by governing parties, and at least in the near future seem destined to play a subordinate role.

Because the basic elements in the situation change radically after independence is achieved, the colonial and postindependence periods are considered separately in the following analysis. The presentation must of necessity be schematic. Many of the facts remain unrecorded. But even such facts as are available can be dealt with only fleetingly in a discussion of so wide a scope in time and space. Summary treatment of complex relationships, coupled with sparsity of available information, exposes a venture of the sort tried here to large risks. But it is useful to attempt a preliminary interpretation of such strands of information and insight as are available. We can in this way contribute to the building of a base from which further exploration may be made into this uncharted field of African political life.

UNION-PARTY RELATIONS BEFORE INDEPENDENCE

Trade-union movements may adopt any number of postures with respect to political parties. They may oppose any coöperation with parties, as did the anarchosyndicalists of the late nineteenth and early twentieth centuries. They may engage in loose and sporadic coöperation with parties—a kind of positive neutralism in the Gompers sense. Or the labor movement may ally itself with a socialist or labor party, sometimes taking the initiative in forming the party, sometimes being formed or nurtured by it. Alliance is the most common situation in the modern world. Coöperation or alliance may take various forms. It may mean occasional joint ventures, or continuing collaboration. It may be reflected informally, as in France and Italy, in intermingling labor-union and political leadership. It may involve physical interpenetration of the two organizations, as in England and Scandinavia, with collective affiliation of union members, ex officio representation for labor spokesmen in party councils, and so on.

In Tropical Africa the formal affiliation of unions with parties, along British or Scandinavian lines, has been rare. Nigeria provides the major example of such collective affiliation. Between 1944 and 1950 the central labor organization in Nigeria was sporadically affiliated with the major political movement, the National Council of Nigeria and the Cameroons (NCNC). The first Trades Union Congress (TUC) in Nigeria, formed in 1943, seems to have been one of the initial affiliates of the NCNC, when the latter came into existence in 1944.[2] The relationship was irregularly maintained until 1950, when it was finally severed. Since 1950 only the Northern Peoples' Congress (NPC), the dominant party in northern Nigeria, has maintained trade-union affiliates, notably the Northern Mineworkers' Union.[3]

Other important instances of formal affiliation existed among white trade unions and white political parties in Central Africa. In Southern Rhodesia there was a strong labor party between the wars, and in 1941 Roy Welensky founded a labor party in Northern Rhodesia.[4] There have

---

[2] There is some disagreement as to whether or not the TUC was in fact affiliated with the NCNC in 1944. James S. Coleman, *Nigeria: Background to Nationalism* (Berkeley and Los Angeles: University of California Press, 1958), p. 265, says that unions were not affiliated, and explains in some detail why the labor movement did not join the NCNC. Richard Sklar, "Nigerian Political Parties" (unpublished Ph.D. dissertation, Princeton University, 1961), p. 829, points out, however, that although few unions were directly affiliated with the NCNC, the TUC, which claimed eighty-six unions, was affiliated.

[3] The NPC seems actually to have organized the Northern Mineworkers' Union in 1953. Two of the main leaders of the union, Audu Danladi and Alhaji Isa Haruna, are NPC activists. Haruna is an NPC member of the federal House of Representatives.

[4] The Rhodesian Labour Party (Southern Rhodesia) split during World War II on the issue of the admission of Africans. Welensky's Labour Party soon ceased to

also been some attempts by African labor unions to forge links with political parties. In Kenya, for example, the formal affiliation of the Kenya Federation of Labour (KFL) with the Kenya African National Union (KANU) was prevented in 1960 only because the government vetoed the KANU's request for registration so long as the KFL was affiliated with it.[5] Outside these examples, instances of formal affiliation of trade unions with parties are hard to find. The most common form of relationship has been one of informal alliance, usually cemented by an interlocking leadership.

The degree of intimacy in these informal ties varied widely among countries. At one extreme was Guinea, where relations between party and union were probably closer than in any other part of Tropical Africa. The Parti Démocratique de Guinée (PDG) and the Confédération Générale du Travail (CGT) and its successors—the CGTA and the UGTAN [6]—were throughout most of the preindependence period as tightly related as two divisions in the same army. The party structure and the trade-union structure were completely interwoven. Many of the same people sat as leaders of local PDG units and as regional or industrial representatives of the labor movement. Sékou Touré's dual role as leader of both party and labor movement was thus not only symbolic of the union-party ties; it had its counterpart on all levels. Even in its structural characteristics the labor movement in Guinea, more than in other areas, reflected a nonoccupational orientation. Wage earners were affiliated directly with the central labor organization, which was really "one big union." Organization was neglected at the shop, the company, or even the industry level.[7] In most African countries, however, the informal ties between unions and parties were much weaker. In some there were hardly any ties at all during much of the preindependence period, as in Nigeria after 1950. In others there has been actual hostility between trade-union

---

have any significance, as its leader took on a larger role as spokesman of the white community of Northern Rhodesia. See R. Gray, *The Two Nations* (London: Oxford University Press, 1960), pp. 98–99, 302–308; E. Clegg, *Race and Politics* (London: Oxford University Press, 1960), p. 112; C. Leys, *European Politics in Southern Rhodesia* (Oxford: Clarendon Press, 1959), pp. 183–188. Since World War II white labor parties have declined in the Rhodesias, as they have in South Africa. White unions have moved toward closer informal ties with white political parties. The relations of white unions to politics will not be further considered in this paper.

[5] *Keesing's Contemporary Archives*, XII (1959–1960), 17545. The KANU was finally registered in 1960 without the formal affiliation of the KFL.

[6] The Confédération Générale des Travailleurs Africains and the Union Générale des Travailleurs d'Afrique Noire.

[7] The labor inspector of the Territory of Guinea noted in his annual report in 1950: ". . . the CGT . . . feels it is sufficient to distribute cards of the regional federation [Union Régionale (CGT) de Conakry] which groups in an anarchic fashion a mass of individuals who belong to no particular group, except for some regularly constituted local unions mainly in the public service" ("Rapport Annuel," 1950, Inspection Territoriale de Travail de Guinée [mimeographed], p. 56).

leadership and leading nationalist spokesmen, as in Southern Rhodesia and, to some extent, in Northern Rhodesia and the former French Camerouns.

In the history of Nigerian labor there is a sharp division between the period 1945–1950, when one segment of the labor movement threw itself vigorously into political activity, and the period from 1950 to the present, during which the labor movement has been altogether outside the political mainstream. The 1944 affiliation of the Nigerian Trades Union Congress with the NCNC was the first major political act of the labor movement. Organized labor later was included in the National Emergency Committee (NEC), a coalition of nationalist forces formed after twenty-one miners had been killed in the Enugu disturbances in 1949. Not only were labor leaders active in the post-Enugu agitation, but they actually participated in the NEC's selection of candidates for the 1950 legislative council elections.[8] When the NEC broke up, the Nigerian Labour Congress (NLC), representing the more militant and radical wing of the labor movement, struck out in other political directions; it formed the Demo-Labour Alliance with the Nigerian National Democratic Party to contest the Lagos Town Council elections. The alliance won a smashing victory; eighteen of the twenty-four seats in the Town Council fell to its candidates, and four labor leaders won seats.[9]

Nigerian labor's political activity was most intense during the rise and fall of the Zikist Movement, from 1948 to 1950. The Zikists were a radical nationalist group that preached positive action and civil disobedience in order to win immediate independence.[10] One of the major Zikist leaders was Nduka Eze, the dominant personality in the labor movement in the late 1940's. Eze was the Zikists' first field secretary. In 1946 he founded the United Africa Company Workers' Union, and by 1950 had made it the second largest in Nigeria. In 1947 he led the fight to affiliate, or rather reaffiliate, the TUC with the NCNC. He was the driving force in the Nigerian National Federation of Labour and in the Nigerian Labour Congress. Both these organizations were affiliated with the NCNC, and NLC leaders played an important part in the agitational activities sponsored by the Zikist Movement.[11]

The Nigerian Labour Congress and trade-union involvement in the Zikist Movement represent the peak of labor radicalism in Nigeria; after

---

[8] The NEC appointed a committee of nine to select candidates for the Lagos Town Council elections in 1950. Three labor spokesmen were on this committee (Richard Sklar, unpublished manuscript on labor and politics in Nigeria).

[9] Address of J. M. Johnson, federal minister of labor, to the first annual conference of the Trades Union Congress, Nigeria, April 22, 1960, reprinted in *Ministry of Labour Quarterly Review* (Nigeria), I (March, 1960), 40; Sklar, unpublished manuscript. This alliance was really a "triple alliance," including the Lagos Market Women's Guild.

[10] Coleman, *op. cit.*, chap. 13.

[11] Nduka Eze, "Nigeria's Union Split." *West Africa*, Aug. 25, 1962, p. 935.

1950 the forces of the left wing in the labor movement became dispersed and lost their impact. They attempted sporadically to form labor parties —the Working Man's Party in 1954 and the Nigerian Labour Party in 1956—but neither seems to have done more than announce its existence and sink into obscurity. The NLC also marks the peak of labor participation in Nigerian political life. Its role as mainstay of the Zikist Movement, its affiliation with and influence within the NCNC, and its triumph in the 1950 Lagos election had no counterpart in the decade of the 1950's. Since 1950 the labor movement has been preoccupied with, and torn by, the question of international affiliation. Connections between unions and parties have been slight or nonexistent, and labor affiliation with the NCNC ended in 1950. Since 1951 labor representation in party executive organs has been limited to two or three members, who are there more as party militants than as representatives of trade unions.[12] These are mainly in the NCNC; no trade-unionists at all are represented on the Action Group federal executive, and there has been no appreciable Action Group activity in the labor area. Only in the north, where the NPC entered the trade-union arena on the Jos mine fields,[13] have the unions been given serious attention by the parties. Since 1951, then, unions and parties in Nigeria have largely gone their separate ways. Although at one point trade union–political party relations cooled to the point of mutual distaste, when the Zikist-led NCL and the NCNC broke in 1950, there has been little real hostility. The parties have tended simply to ignore the unions as inconsequential.[14]

In other countries there has been overt conflict and deep hostility between unions and parties. Perhaps the most striking example is in Southern Rhodesia, where, until 1959, trade unions had a curious legal position. As in South Africa, Africans were not considered "employees" in terms of the Southern Rhodesian Conciliation Act of 1934.[15] Unions

---

[12] Sklar ("Nigerian Political Parties," pp. 792 ff.) studied the biographies of seventy-one NCNC leaders, including members of the national Executive Committee and of the eastern and western working committees, and members of ministerial rank in the regional and federal governments. Two of this group had, or have, associations with the labor movement. Of the sixty-six comparable leaders of the Action Group, only one (Eze) had a trade-union background. None of the seventy-four people in NPC executive organs had a trade-union connection.

[13] The Action Group has made some attempts to break the NPC hold over the Jos mineworkers. The NPC claims that the Action Group has given money to leaders of the Amalgamated Tin Mines of Nigeria African Mineworkers' Union (*Kano Daily Mail*, Sept. 2, 1961).

[14] When the nationalist fervor of the Zikists rose to its height in 1950, and the British administration suppressed the movement, the NCNC leadership expelled its Zikist-oriented labor members from party executive organs, and the party ceased to have formal dealings with the central labor organization of the country.

[15] Lord Hailey, *An African Survey Revised 1956* (London: Oxford University Press, 1957), p. 1444.

were not illegal, but they were denied all recognition.[16] Some union activity developed, nevertheless, on the railways and elsewhere.[17] As there was no major African political organization, the problem of union-party relations did not arise. In 1959, however, the Industrial Conciliation Act, which aimed at the creation of multiracial unions, was passed. Although failing to achieve its objective,[18] the legislation has led to a rapid expansion in the number of Africans in trade unions. In 1959 there were an estimated 3,000 African union members; in 1962 the unions claimed 50,000.

An African nationalist movement had meanwhile emerged as a serious factor in Southern Rhodesian life. Its name changed—from the African National Congress (ANC) to the National Democratic Party (NDP) to the Zimbabwe African Peoples' Union (ZAPU)—as each group was successively banned by the government. The growing labor movement and the growing nationalist movement at first entertained friendly relations with each other. But a rift soon developed between Reuben Jamela, the secretary-general of the Southern Rhodesian Trades Union Congress (SRTUC), and the nationalist party under the leadership of Joshua Nkomo, himself a former trade-unionist.[19] Jamela was sympathetic to the ZAPU and its predecessors, but at the same time desired to maintain the autonomy of the labor movement. He and his followers were more moderate than the party leaders.[20] Perhaps some party leaders were also concerned about the possibility that Jamela's personal influence might threaten their positions.

Throughout 1961 and 1962 the relations between party and union deteriorated, and sporadic conflict broke out. The party steadily urged the unions to be more militant; Jamela and the SRTUC resisted. In 1961 the party pushed for a general strike aimed at increasing to £25 the monthly minimum wage, then less than £8. Jamela refused to go along.

---

[16] Gray, *op. cit.*, pp. 102, 320.

[17] The Railways Act of 1949 provided for a union of African workers. The Reformed Industrial and Commercial Workers' Union and the Federation of Bulawayo African Workers' Union, which were more movements of African protest than specifically union bodies, were not recognized (*ibid.*, pp. 311, 318–323).

[18] "Labour's Lost Love," *Central African Examiner*, VI (Oct., 1962), 15–22: "The S.R. Industrial Conciliation Act has failed to effect the Government's stated intention of achieving nonracial trade unions. In terms of the Act, all had nonracial constitutions. In fact, six of them are all African and the rest are European-led. A few . . . have African members, but most are all white."

[19] Robert Rotberg, "From Moderate to Militant," *Africa Report*, VII (March, 1962), 3.

[20] When the first Trades Union Congress was formed in Southern Rhodesia in 1954, Nkomo was president and Jamela was assistant secretary-general. In 1956 Jamela joined the Youth League, an important group in the African National Congress. He was never a leader of the ANC, but was an active member, and was arrested for political activities in February, 1959, with other union leaders ("Profile of Jamela," *Central African Examiner*, V [Oct., 1961], 14–15).

Late in the year there was talk in political circles of a "break industry" campaign, but Jamela had decided to work within the legal framework. He had, for example, urged registration of unions under the Industrial Conciliation Act, and he opposed a series of work stoppages in Bulawayo, whose main aim seems to have been political agitation. At the same time, ZAPU forces attempted to encourage breakaways by Jamela followers.

The issue came to a head early in 1962. In January a ZAPU-sponsored organization, the Southern Rhodesian African Trades Union Congress (SRATUC), was formed under the leadership of J. T. Maluleke, a ZAPU militant. Shortly thereafter a Salisbury rally of the Southern Rhodesian Trades Union Congress (Jamela group) was picketed by the ZAPU Youth League. In succeeding months there were intermittent violent clashes between the pro-Jamela elements in the labor movement and ZAPU supporters of the rival SRATUC or of the nationalist youth organization.[21]

Southern Rhodesia and Nigeria, on the one hand, and Guinea on the other, represent the extremes of a spectrum of union-party relationships. A union-party connection resembling that found in Guinea exists in Kenya, where the links between the Kenya African National Union and the Kenya Federation of Labour are particularly close. There is the same dominance of the federation over the unions, the same dual office holding (by Tom Mboya and lesser leaders), and the same confusion of union and party roles. Some men have been refused membership in unions because they were not KANU partisans, for example, and on at least one occasion grievances about the KFL role in a labor dispute have resulted in threats of withdrawal of political allegiance from the KANU.[22] Indeed, it might be claimed that in its early years the federation was a political movement in disguise. It came into existence in 1955 during the emergency, when political organizations were banned. When, later in the year, the restrictions were relaxed slightly to allow the formation of local (but not territorial) associations, the KFL remained the only organization of Africans operating on a territorial basis.[23] In 1960 Mboya was to claim proudly that it was the federation that had fought the battle for African freedom.[24] The mingling of political and union roles was recognized by

---

[21] See the white paper of the Southern Rhodesian government, *Report on the Zimbabwe African Peoples' Union* (published in Sept., 1962), for a detailed account of the violent incidents involving pro-Jamela forces and the ZAPU.

[22] *East African Standard*, Nov. 5, 1960; *Colonial Times*, Oct. 22, 27, 1960.

[23] G. Bennett and C. Rosberg, *The Kenyatta Election: Kenya 1960–1961* (London: Oxford University Press, 1961), pp. 32–33.

[24] "Report of the General Secretary, 1958–1960," Kenya Federation of Labour (mimeographed), p. 2: "Many may not now realize it, but perhaps one might ask what would have happened to Africans in those dark days of the emergency if there was not the Kenya Federation of Labour consistently, fearlessly and vigorously championing the interests of the workers and the African community at large."

the government, which took the KFL sharply to task in 1956 for the wide range of issues on which it was taking a public stand.[25] The links between union and party in Kenya, however close, were not so strong as in Guinea. Factionalism was more intense in Kenya; both the KFL and the KANU were deeply divided within themselves, and the colonial government played a much more active role in keeping the two organizations apart. In both party and union the authority of the leadership was much less secure than in Guinea.

The close union-party intimacy that exists in Guinea and Kenya is hard to find elsewhere. The extraordinary diversity of conditions and experience in sub-Saharan Africa rules out easy generalization, but some general statements may be made about the strength of union-party connections in these countries. In most of them the pattern of union-party ties resembled the Southern Rhodesian or Nigerian model more than the Guinean model. Union-party ties were closer in French Africa than elsewhere. And finally, even in countries where the labor movement was closely related to parties, the nature of the relationship was usually extremely complex. Frequently different parties (or factions within a single party) were involved, and more frequently a large segment of the labor movement did not share the political commitment made by officers of central labor organizations. As a too-general discussion of union-party ties would be meaningless, and as it is clearly impossible to treat in detail the many countries involved, we have chosen to deal with only a few important countries: Ghana, the French Camerouns, Northern Rhodesia, and some of the states in French West Africa.

The Ghana and the French Camerouns stories are of special interest. They are often taken as prime examples of political unionism and of the identification of unions with nationalist movements. Yet a close examination of the preindependence relationship between trade unions and the nationalist party reveals, in Ghana, limited participation of the labor movement in party and political affairs, and, in the Camerouns, a state of tension between party and unions erupting finally in an open break resembling the one in Southern Rhodesia.

Ghana's labor movement came into political prominence in January, 1950, when leaders of the Gold Coast Trades Union Congress called a general strike in support of the positive-action campaign of the Convention People's Party (CPP). The strike and its suppression led to the disintegration of the country's central labor organization. Under the guidance and the encouragement of the Labour Department, the TUC was

---

[25] See resolutions passed by the conference of the KFL in 1955 (*Africa Digest*, III [July-Aug., 1955], p. 6). For the action of the government, see Bennett and Rosberg, *op. cit.*, pp. 32–33.

reconstituted in 1951,[26] with leadership in the hands of nonpolitical moderates like S. Larbi-Odam, head of the UAC Workers' Union, and D. K. Foevie, the mineworkers' leader. In 1951, however, after the CPP's triumph at the general election, Kwame Nkrumah was released from jail. Several TUC leaders who worked within the CPP were released at the same time, and proceeded to form a rival federation called the Ghana Trades Union Congress. This organization was outspoken in its support of Nkrumah and the CPP. The Ghana TUC was, in fact, the creature of the CPP; many of its leading figures were CPP militants with little trade-union connection.[27] In 1953 the Ghana TUC merged with the Gold Coast TUC, under the name of the latter but with officers from both groups.

Between 1953 and 1959 three groups were involved in a peculiar struggle that took place within the labor movement. The first was the CPP, which sought to bring the labor movement more securely under its influence. The second was the relatively well-established unions of mineworkers, UAC workers, railway workers, and several others, who wanted to maintain trade-union independence from the government and the CPP. The third group consisted of leaders attached to the CPP, notably John Tettegah, who seems to have seen in control of the labor movement a road to high position in the CPP.

In this contest there were well-defined ground rules; circumstances enforced on each party a certain number of constraints. The CPP, for example, could not simply impose itself on the labor movement. Before independence it did not have the means to do so; and in any event such action would not have been in accord with Nkrumah's policy of reassuring the British and avoiding pretexts for the prolongation of British control.[28] The independent, politically neutral trade-unionists also had to proceed with caution. They could not afford, nor did they want, an all-out struggle which might alienate the party they knew would someday assume full power. Despite charges that some trade-union leaders supported opposition parties,[29] almost all union leaders were sympathetic to Nkrumah. The CPP activists in the TUC, particularly Tettegah, could not act without caution. They had no real base in the labor movement, for

---

[26] *Annual Report of the Labour Department, 1950–1951,* Gold Coast Ministry of Trade and Labour, pp. 4–5.

[27] The major figure in the Ghana TUC, E. C. Turkson-Ocran, was parliamentary secretary of the CPP, personal secretary to Nkrumah, and a member of the CPP Executive Committee.

[28] See David E. Apter, *The Gold Coast in Transition* (Princeton: Princeton University Press, 1955), p. 215. As part of this tactical-action policy, Nkrumah purged both the TUC and the CPP of extremist elements. In November, 1953, Turkson-Ocran, secretary-general of the TUC, was expelled from the TUC and the CPP, along with several other left-wing leaders.

[29] G. W. Wright, "Pan-Africanism and the Ghana Trades Union Congress" (unpublished M.A. thesis, Howard University, 1962), p. 40 n. 18.

they had no unions of their own.[30] Although they had friends in the cabinet, they also had enemies, CPP leaders who realized that Tettegah presented a serious potential threat. Tettegah and his CPP allies saw one avenue open to them: to push for centralization of authority in the TUC, which they would control. Many trade-unionists were dissatisfied with the division of the labor movement into numerous small, poorly financed unions;[31] by persuading smaller unions to reorganize into larger units, with authority centralized in the TUC, Tettegah and his allies could capitalize on this dissatisfaction.

The struggle began in 1954. In the guise of creating a new, centralized structure, Tettegah and the CPP attempted to assert control over the unions.[32] The major unions of the country fought against centralization, and consequent control by the CPP, through delaying tactics aimed at preventing transfer of power to the TUC. Before 1958 the TUC was merely a façade, although it claimed jurisdiction over most of the labor movement. Its constitution did, in fact, give it considerable power over the affairs of its affiliates; for example, it could intervene in all industrial disputes and could investigate the behavior of affiliates, with expulsion as a sanction.[33] Yet the TUC's effective control over the unions was negligible, as illustrated by its financial arrangements with them. According to the constitution, each union was to contribute 3d. per member per year, roughly 2 per cent of membership dues. But even this small contribution was rarely made. In 1953 the TUC received less than $300 from the unions, and in 1954, less than $900.[34]

Lack of finances and of genuine power did not prevent the CPP group in the TUC from attempting to dominate the unions, but they were not successful until after independence.[35] After 1953 the TUC leadership was periodically accused by the unions of discourteous and peremptory behavior. The internal turbulence continued until finally, in September,

---

[30] Tettegah was originally associated with a small company union, the G. B. Ollivant Employees' Union, which he reorganized after the positive-action strike. In 1952 he became general secretary of the Mercantile Workers' Federation, an organization that existed more on paper than in reality. In 1953 he became assistant secretary-general of the TUC, and assumed the secretary-generalship in November of that year, after the expulsion of Turkson-Ocran.

[31] In 1957 there were some 130 registered unions, with a total claimed membership of about 80,000. Of these, 21 had less than 50 members each, 31 had between 50 and 250, and 16 had between 250 and 1,000 (*Annual Report of the Ministry of Labour, 1957–1958*, Ghana).

[32] In "Report of the Organization Committee" (mimeographed), presented to the 11th annual conference of the Gold Coast Trades Union Congress in September, 1954, amalgamation into ten national unions was suggested.

[33] "The Gold Coast TUC, Constitution, Rules and Standing Orders, Revised and Operative from 16 October 1956" (mimeographed), Rules 9, 10.

[34] Presidential speech by F. E. Tachie-Menson to the 11th annual conference of the GCTUC in 1954 (mimeographed).

[35] See p. 369, below.

1955, the nonpolitical group split with the GCTUC and formed the Congress of Free Trade Unions, which stayed out for a year before reaffiliating with the parent body. Every year after 1954 the CPP group in the TUC introduced structural changes in the labor movement in order to facilitate party control, but the unions resisted any transfer of authority to the TUC.

It is hard to find in this story much evidence of serious trade-union involvement in preindependence politics. Certainly there was no trade union–party alliance in any meaningful sense. Regardless of what went on in the TUC, most of organized labor remained aloof from the party. The Ghana trade-union movement before 1958 not only had limited relations with the dominant political party, but was one of the least ideological labor movements in all Africa. It revealed little interest in broad political issues and goals.

In the French Camerouns, on the contrary, organized labor was highly ideological; important political issues were at the center of trade-union concerns. Nevertheless, relations between the labor organizations and the major political party were characterized by severe strain.

Of the four main labor centrals in the Camerouns, only two had real strength, and only one—the Confédération Générale Kamerunaise du Travail (CGKT)—had political significance.[36] The first central labor organization in the Camerouns was the Union des Syndicats Confédérés du Cameroun (USCC), formed in 1944 under the guidance of French Communist Party members and sympathizers in Douala, the main coastal city. The first African leader of the USCC was Reuben Um Nyobé, who in 1948 became secretary-general of the Union des Populations du Cameroun (UPC), a militant nationalist party. In 1948 Jacques N'Gom succeeded Nyobé as chief of the USCC, and remained its major figure throughout the ensuing years. In 1951, when the USCC affiliated with the Communist-dominated World Federation of Trade Unions (WFTU), an anti-Communist faction within the USCC withdrew and formed a rival union, the Union des Syndicats Autonomes du Cameroun. This was only the beginning of factional discord; from the early 1950's on, the USCC was torn by a bitter internal struggle between a N'Gom faction and one

---

[36] The total claimed membership of Camerounian unions in the middle and late 1950's was approximately 40,000. Of this number, the CGKT had about 45 per cent. The Union des Syndicats Autonomes du Cameroun (USAC) and the Force Ouvrière (FO) each claimed 25 per cent, and the Catholic union, Confédération Camerounaise des Syndicats Croyants (CCSC), had the remaining 5 per cent. The FO and the CCSC, as localized groups, had less influence than either the USAC or the CGKT; the latter was more influential than its share of claimed membership suggests.

led by Mayoa Beck.[37] In 1956 the USCC became the CGKT, which in 1957 split into a Beck-CGKT and a N'Gom-CGKT. In February, 1959, they came together to form a new organization, the Union Générale des Travailleurs Kamerunais (UGTK).

Until 1955 the USCC apparently coöperated with the nationalist party, the UPC; there were few outward signs of discord, and N'Gom was a leading member of the party's Executive Committee. In May, 1955, however, after the outbreaks of violence which accompanied its increasingly militant campaign for independence, the UPC was suppressed by the French. Early in 1956 N'Gom was jailed for a short period. After his release, a division became evident between N'Gom, leader of the CGKT, and the UPC leadership. On one issue after another N'Gom took a different, and usually a more moderate, position than the UPC. He established a newspaper which attacked the UPC for its violence, and which was in turn condemned by the UPC Executive Committee. In the fall of 1956 N'Gom was removed from the committee. At the inaugural convention of the CGKT in December, 1956, he tried in vain to get the Executive Committee of the labor organization to support participation in elections under the recently passed Loi-Cadre. In the December, 1956, elections for the Camerouns' legislative assembly, Beck and the UPC, accusing N'Gom of betraying the nationalist cause, opposed his candidacy. He was resoundingly defeated then, as he was later in the June, 1957, by-election for deputy to the French National Assembly, and in the 1960 elections for the legislature. In July, 1959, N'Gom expelled the pro-Beck elements from the UGTK and changed the "K" in its name (for Kamerun, a nationalist symbol) to "C" (for Cameroun, as the French called it), presumably to please the government of Ahmadou Ahidjo, which was coöperating with the French. The exiled leaders of the UPC bitterly attacked N'Gom,[38] and have continued to do so up to the present. N'Gom nonetheless retains an influential position within the labor movement.

---

[37] The sources of the conflict, though personal in part, were mainly ideological. Both Beck and N'Gom spoke the language of radical nationalism, at least until 1956. Both were in favor of WFTU affiliation, at least until 1959. But in 1953 Beck accused N'Gom of mishandling union funds, and, after 1955, of selling out to the French. Beck was also more clearly in favor of affiliation with the UGTAN after 1959, and was more disposed toward coöperation with the UPC. It should also be noted that internal conflict was rife in the other centrals. Both the USAC and the CCSC experienced splits in the late 1950's.

[38] In 1959 Félix Moumié, UPC head after Nyobé's death in 1958, charged that N'Gom (1) took 600,000 francs to sell out the workers, and hid "behind a vile mask of trade union nonpoliticalness"; (2) opposed a resolution at the UGTAN conference in Conakry urging the legalization of the UPC; (3) supported Ahidjo representatives at United Nations sessions; (4) discouraged strikes because he wanted to win the good will of the Ahidjo government, claiming to be a "reformist-type trade-unionist" (*La Rôle de la Classe ouvrière dans la révolution kamerounaise* [Cairo, 1959], a pamphlet signed by Moumié in the name of the Union des Populations du Cameroun's délégation à l'Etranger, Service de l'Information).

Northern Rhodesia has an economic and social structure conducive to stable unions and effective union-party coöperation. The population is concentrated, and there is stability of employment in two modern industries (railroads and mining). Serious racial conflict means that questions of wages and conditions of work, as well as general political and constitutional issues, have been marked by racial discrimination at almost every turn.[39] Yet no simple pattern of relations between unions and parties has emerged.

As in Southern Rhodesia and South Africa, the workers in Northern Rhodesia were early divided and organized along racial lines. In 1936 the white mineworkers' union in the Copperbelt came into existence, partly upon the initiative of the South African Mineworkers' Union.[40] In 1945 the white union made a halfhearted attempt to organize an African branch, but it was greeted with skepticism, and Africans proceeded to organize their own unions. In 1949 the Northern Rhodesian African Mineworkers' Union (AMU) came into existence; Lawrence Katilungu was its first president.[41]

At the same time other African organizations were emerging. The Federation of African Welfare Societies was formed in 1946; in 1951 it became the Northern Rhodesian African National Congress (ANC), the first African nationalist organization of major significance. It was led by the moderate Godwin Lewanika until 1951, when he was ousted by the more militant Harry Nkumbula, under whom the ANC rapidly became the spokesman of African national sentiment. In 1952 and 1953 it was presented with a major issue on which to mobilize its followers: the creation of the Federation of Rhodesia and Nyasaland.[42]

In the beginning the informal ties between the AMU and the ANC were close. Katilungu was an officeholder in the ANC,[43] and many of the branch officers of his union were active members. In 1950 the Trades Union Congress was formed with Katilungu as its first president,

[39] P. Mason, *Year of Decision* (London: Oxford University Press, 1960), pp. 93–98; A. L. Epstein, *Politics in an Urban African Community* (Manchester: Manchester University Press, 1958), pp. xi–xvii.

[40] The white union, despite its small size, has played a major role in Northern Rhodesian political and economic affairs. Taking advantage of the British government's wartime determination to have copper at almost any cost, it was able to win significant increases in wages, and, more important, at the end of the war it obtained a so-called closed-shop agreement which forbade alterations in the boundary between those occupations allotted to white labor and those allotted to African labor. Since the end of the war the white union has fought a prolonged rear-guard action on the issue of "advancement," i.e., the allocation of more occupations to Africans (see Clegg, *op. cit.*, pp. 99–102, 127; *Report of the Board of Enquiry Appointed to Enquire into the Advancement of Africans in the Copper Mining Industry in Northern Rhodesia* [1954]; *Africa Digest*, X [Aug., 1962]).

[41] Gray, *op. cit.*, pp. 350–351; Epstein, *op. cit.*, pp. 90–93.

[42] Epstein, *op. cit.*, pp. 71, 159–163.

[43] R. Segal, *Political Africa* (New York: Praeger, 1961), p. 129.

and in 1952 he became a member of the Supreme Action Council set up
by the ANC to coördinate African opposition to the proposed federation.
Of nine members on the council, five were appointed by the TUC, and
a central committee was set up in the Copperbelt to take action, including
a general strike if necessary.[44] At the beginning of 1953 Nkumbula committed chiefs and trade unions to definite action if federation was imposed; claiming that union leaders and chiefs were solidly behind the
ANC, he called for a "Two Day National Prayer." [45] The attempt at a
massive demonstration against federation was a complete failure; production continued at the mines. The result was a sharp setback for
African nationalist forces. Nkumbula turned on those who he felt had
failed to support him in the demonstrations, naming in particular Katilungu and the African members of the Legislative Council. Many ANC
branches withered, presumably because of the failure to prevent the
consummation of federation. For a time the congress leadership abandoned political and constitutional issues, and began to conduct a widespread campaign against discrimination in retail shops.[46]

The failure of the nationalist movement to launch and sustain a
major demonstration against federation marked a turning point in AMU-
ANC relations. The leaders of the AMU, notably Katilungu, seem to
have withdrawn from the political arena; industrial and union-oriented
issues absorbed their energies.[47] Partly as a result of this aloofness from
politics, relations between ANC and AMU leaders deteriorated, and
between 1953 and 1956 chilled to the point of open hostility. At the same
time events were placing Nkumbula and Katilungu in parallel positions.
Both were moving to the right (or standing still), while the members of
their respective organizations were being pushed leftward by growing
nationalist militancy. Both were thus cast as moderates or conservatives,
and serious dissatisfaction developed in the ranks of both organizations.
Many of the militant members of the AMU were members of the ANC,

---

[44] *Ibid.;* Clegg, *op. cit.,* pp. 173–174.
[45] Epstein, *op. cit.,* pp. 160–162.
[46] *Ibid.*
[47] A successful strike for higher wages in the mines had been conducted at the
end of 1952, but a year later AMU checkoff privileges (automatic deduction of union
dues by employers) were withdrawn by the mining companies. At the same time
a dispute arose over Africans in supervisory positions; with the active support of the
companies, these skilled men began to organize themselves into a separate union
which became the Mines African Staff Association (MASA). With this development,
advancement presented the leaders of the Mineworkers' Union with a real dilemma;
African accession to senior positions meant that the AMU might lose some of its
most educated members. It was only in 1955 that the AMU reluctantly recognized
the MASA (Clegg, *op. cit.,* pp. 200–203; Mason, *op. cit.,* p. 111; Segal, *op. cit.,*
p. 155). The dispute was complicated by tribal factors. Most of the clerks in the
Copperbelt are Nyasas; Katilungu was a leading Bemba (Epstein, *op. cit.,* pp. 92,
126).

and no doubt formed part of the anti-Nkumbula and anti-Katilungu faction within it. This led to a brief period of collaboration in 1956 between Nkumbula and Katilungu, as each tried to head off the gathering storm within his own organization.[48]

After 1956, however, the tempo of political change accelerated, and militant nationalist forces grew increasingly powerful. Neither Nkumbula nor Katilungu adapted to this development. Against the wishes of his most able lieutenants, Nkumbula adopted an accommodationist position which was out of tune with the times.[49] In 1958 he accepted the new territorial constitution for Northern Rhodesia, an act that led to a final break with Kenneth Kaunda and ultimately to the formation of the more aggressive United National Independence Party (UNIP).[50] By the end of 1960 the UNIP was clearly the strongest African political organization in the country.

It was at this time that Katilungu chose to take office in the ANC once again. His differences with Nkumbula had narrowed in the face of the UNIP's challenge. Katilungu, even more than Nkumbula, had long had propensities toward accommodation with the existing order,[51] and these became more marked with time. In the political sphere he took a position far more conservative than the UNIP's; he accepted a place on the Monckton Commission in 1959, and in a speech in 1960 he questioned the benefits of self-government. In the labor movement he used his dominant place in the Northern Rhodesian TUC to prevent the political involvement of unions. In fact, the TUC split on this issue in 1960; a rival pro-UNIP group was formed, the Reformed Trades Union Congress (RTUC), made up of unions that were largely paper organizations.[52] But Katilungu's position within the AMU had been undermined by his political posture;[53] at the end of 1960 the union suspended him, and in 1961 expelled him.

---

[48] Mason, *op. cit.*, pp. 116–117.

[49] In August, 1956, for example, Nkumbula made a cheerful speech expressing hope for the future of race relations and pledging coöperation with Europeans (*Africa Digest*, IV [Sept.-Oct., 1956], 59).

[50] Segal, *op. cit.*, p. 387.

[51] As early as 1955 he had appealed for faith in "partnership" (*Africa Digest*, II [Jan.-Feb., 1955], 24).

[52] Aside from the AMU, the only substantial labor organization in the late 1950's was the African Railway Workers' Union, whose leaders seem not to have taken an active part in this dispute.

[53] One reason Katilungu had been able to maintain his position for so long was that many of his rivals had been removed during the emergency of 1956. In June of that year, while Katilungu was out of the country, there occurred a series of "rolling strikes" aimed at the elimination of work rules that Africans felt were discriminatory. The government declared an emergency in the Copperbelt, and arrested and "rusticated"—i.e., exiled to remote regions—thirty-two central and branch union officers. When these officers returned, the mining companies refused to rehire them; by 1960 only one had been taken back. As most of the rusticated men were ANC members

The stage was set for effective union-party coöperation, and events seemed to point in that direction. The split in the TUC was mended and a new body, the United Trades Union Congress (UTUC), was formed with Jonathan Chivunga, a UNIP militant, as its president.[54] The new body committed itself to strike action in protest against the new territorial constitution, in line with the strong stand that the UNIP was taking on the same issue.[55] At the same time, the fact that Kaunda made use of the threat of strike action suggests the possibility of a union commitment to the party.[56]

Nonetheless, in mid-1962 a serious conflict developed between the party and the AMU. The union struck for three weeks in May in support of a wage demand. The party was opposed to the strike; Kaunda seems to have wanted to avoid rocking the political boat before the general elections under the new constitution.[57] The strikers returned while a commission of inquiry met, but when negotiations broke down again, the AMU threatened to renew the strike in July. Again the party exerted pressure on the union to accept the companies' offer. But the AMU leaders persisted, withdrew from the UTUC, and attacked Kaunda for interfering. The party ultimately prevailed and the strike was called off except at one mine.[58] After this incident the AMU and the party were reconciled once again. The president of the AMU, John Chisata, became a UNIP candidate in the election for the Legislative Council, and the union issued a call to its members to support the party.[59] Such events may presage closer relations in the future, although the AMU remains outside the orbit of total party control.[60]

---

and probably represented the leadership core of anti-Katilungu forces within the AMU, their removal temporarily strengthened Katilungu's hold over the union (Mason, *op. cit.*, pp. 116–118; Segal, *op. cit.*, pp. 129–130; *Africa Digest*, IV [Sept.-Oct., 1956], 58–59).

[54] *Africa Digest*, VIII (April, 1961), 135. The *Manchester Guardian*, Feb. 7, 1961, wrote: "The control of African trade unions . . . [has been taken over] by supporters of UNIP." This statement implies that the UTUC controlled its member unions, which was hardly true.

[55] *Africa Digest*, IX (Aug., 1961), 5.

[56] The *Christian Science Monitor*, June 28, 1961, reported a statement by Kaunda: "Remember we control the mines, the airways, and the shops."

[57] One explanation for Kaunda's caution is that he may have been anxious to avoid giving the federal government a pretext for intervention ("Tug of War on the Mines," *Central African Examiner*, VI [Aug., 1962], 7).

[58] The miners at Roan Antelope struck for five days. This was particularly interesting because the Roan mine is a strong UNIP center, and the branch chairman of the AMU is a UNIP officer, suggesting that political militancy is not inconsistent with resentment at party interference in union affairs (*ibid.*).

[59] *Central African Mail*, Aug. 28, Oct. 9, 1962.

[60] Chisata is reported to have made the following statement at the time of the disagreement over the July, 1962, Copperbelt dispute: "I reminded Kaunda he has no business interfering in an industrial dispute" (*Times*, July 10, 1962, cited in *Africa Digest*, X [Aug., 1962], 4). The *Central African Examiner*, VI (Aug., 1962),

In Nigeria, Ghana, the former French Camerouns, and the Rhodesias, the trade-union commitment to political parties was weak, intermittent, or nonexistent in the preindependence period. In the French states of West Africa, informal union-party alliances were more widespread and intensive. Ideological factors played a larger role in French-speaking areas than in English-speaking ones; concern with wider political ideas and goals was more persistent. Although the law placed some general restrictions on trade-union political activity, these were hardly excessive, and the French were more permissive than the British in regard to the participation of civil servants in trade-unionism and in politics. In this environment the intermingling of union and political leadership became commonplace. In particular, many leaders in the most important labor organization, the CGT, and its successors, the CGTA and the UGTAN, were active in the territorial sections of the leading political organization in French West Africa, the Rassemblement Démocratique Africain (RDA).[61]

Even here, however, the pattern of union-party relations failed to develop along clear-cut lines of alliance and collaboration. First, a number of trade-union leaders were not associated with any party, or were only mildly interested in party affairs. This was true of most of the Catholic union leaders (CATC), of some of the unaffiliated union heads (notably among the railway unions), and even of some leading CGT figures. Abdoulaye Diallo, head of the Soudan (now Mali) CGT and at the same time vice-president of the WFTU, was not a member of the Executive Committee of the Union Soudanaise, the RDA section in the Soudan, nor does it seem that he even enjoyed the support of the party.[62]

Second, not all of those who were politically engaged were committed to the RDA, or, indeed, to any single party. Even in Guinea, where the intimacy between the CGT (or its successors) and the RDA was

7–8, commented on the situation as follows: "Far from showing that UNIP now controls the AMU, the crisis arose because the party did not have this control and had to resort to desperate means to get its way. The events have highlighted, not settled, the continuing conflict between straight African nationalism and African trade-unionism which in almost every other case has developed only after African self-government." This statement should be qualified by pointing out that the conflict was more widespread before self-government than is implied here.

[61] Throughout the postwar period there were four main groups in the French West African labor movement: the CGT; the Catholic union, Confédération Africaine des Travailleurs Croyants (CATC); the CGT–Force Ouvrière; and the autonomous organizations (those unaffiliated with any metropolitan center). The CGT (and, after 1957, the UGTAN) and the autonomous groups were the most important. The latter included territorial federations in Upper Volta and Togo, and some railway unions. In the period just before independence, UGTAN influence was dominant in about 75 per cent of the labor movement.

[62] It is hard to explain his defeat at the 1956 municipal elections in Bamako, a Union Soudanaise stronghold, on any other grounds (Ruth Schachter, "French West African Trade Unions, 1956" [unpublished manuscript]).

closest, several key union figures remained outside the party. Keita Koumandian, for example, head of the influential teachers' union, was secretary-general of the Bloc Africain de Guinée, the major rival of the RDA. And from 1951 to 1957 the head of the well-organized railway union was not an RDA militant.[63] In Senegal, trade-unionists were to be found among the leadership of most of the major parties. Most CGT (later UGTAN) spokesmen, however, were associated with the Union Démocratique Sénégalaise (UDS) and its successors, not with the RDA section in Senegal nor with the dominant party in Senegal, the Bloc Populaire Sénégalais (BPS).[64] In Niger, the CGT leader, Bakary Djibo, broke with the RDA in 1950 on the issue of its disaffiliation from the Communist Party in France. In the Ivory Coast a number of leading trade-unionists were unsympathetic to Félix Houphouet-Boigny's brand of RDA politics.

One aspect of union-party relations remains to be considered: were the labor movements that were in informal alliance with parties or nationalist movements autonomous agents, or were they simply party instruments? Much of the above discussion has obvious bearing on this question; the prevalence of loose ties or actual hostility between unions and parties implies a large measure of trade-union independence. But the power relations between unions and parties have many nuances, even where hostility has been the rule.

Two generalizations may be made. First, party influence tended to be focused on trade-union congresses, or federations. But federations rarely had effective control over component unions, and, as might be expected, the strongest, best-organized unions tended to be the most chary of political adventures and hence the most reluctant to transfer authority to the federations.[65] We have already seen that in Ghana the TUC was the agency through which the CPP sought control over individual unions. Most of the stronger unions in the country (in the mines, on the railways, and in the United Africa Company) opposed CPP control and political activity in general. In Nigeria, similarly, even during the period when labor was politically active, a substantial part of the labor movement opposed trade-union participation in politics.[66] A stand by the Nigerian

---

[63] *Ibid.*

[64] The UDS consisted largely of radical elements expelled from the RDA in the early 1950's. In 1957 they effected an uneasy merger with the BPS, which became the Bloc Démocratique Sénégalais and, ultimately, the present governing party, the Union Progressiste Sénégalaise.

[65] There is a clear difference in this respect between French and British African labor movements. In French Africa, decision-making power was centralized in the territorial federation, a geographically based organization. In most of British Africa, power was much more decentralized, residing almost invariably in the individual union often organized along company lines.

[66] Coleman (*op. cit.,* pp. 257–258) has pointed out that of the seventeen unions

central labor organization on a political issue, or, indeed, any major TUC-led venture, almost invariably accentuated disintegrative tendencies within the labor movement.[67]

In East and Central Africa much the same pattern may be discerned. The situation in Tanganyika was somewhat different from that in Northern Rhodesia. Before 1960 there was little friction between the Tanganyika Federation of Labour, with its component unions, and the Tanganyika African National Union. Early in 1960, however, the party moved to tighten its hold on the unions. The method was like that used in Ghana: first, assure party control of the federation, and then arrange for the federation to assume decision-making power within the labor movement. More than half of the significant unions in the country resisted this procedure, most notably the Tanganyika Railway African Union, headed by C. S. K. Tumbo.

That this pattern reappears frequently is of relevance in considering the question of trade union–party power relations. A second observation suggested by the available evidence is that, even in countries where the union-party alliance was most firmly cemented and reached down to the unions themselves, the labor organizations usually maintained an autonomous position. In some instances, as in Guinea, where the top leadership made little distinction between union and party (or youth organization), this was less true; the party was clearly dominant, at least in the sense that party strategy and directives determined important issues of trade-union policy. In most other French West African states the distinction between union and party leadership was real enough, but was blurred by shared goals and strategies. There is little doubt that decisions made in party councils influenced union action. The 1955 decision of the autonomist wing of the CGT to sever connections with the French CGT, for example, was not unrelated to a call for an autonomous trade-unionism made by the Indépendants d'Outre-Mer in 1953, and, more significantly, by the RDA Coördinating Committee in 1954 and 1955.[68] In general,

---

in Nigeria with a claimed membership of more than 500 in 1944, only five were affiliated with the TUC. In the late 1950's as many as half of the registered unions were apparently unaffiliated with any central labor organization.

[67] The affiliation of the TUC with the NCNC, combined with the failure of the TUC to take control of the 1945 general strike, led to the first split in the TUC in 1946. When Nduka Eze induced the reconstituted TUC to affiliate with the NCNC in 1947, the decision was overturned by the TUC conference of 1948, which in turn led the left wing to withdraw and form the Nigerian National Federation of Labour in 1949. The Nigerian Labour Congress, formed in 1950, was supposedly a merger. But the left wing under Eze was in complete control, and the more moderate unions refused to participate. Thus the TUC and other important merging groups failed to transfer their assets to the NLC, and that organization never had the allegiance, even on paper, of many of the major unions in Nigeria.

[68] Ruth Schachter, "Trade Unions Seek Autonomy," *West Africa,* Jan. 19, 1957, p. 55.

however, the trade unions in most of these territories maintained, with respect to political parties, a large degree of autonomy and independence.

One indication of this autonomy is the fact that, as indicated above, some important trade-unionists were on the margin of party affairs, or were sympathetic to minority factions within the dominant party. This seems to have been true of Abdoulaye Diallo in the Soudan, of some trade-union leaders in the civil service in the Ivory Coast, and of most union leaders in Senegal. But probably the most suggestive evidence is to be found in the heated debate that took place after 1956 on the question as to whether or not trade-union leaders should retain their union posts when they accepted ministerial or other public office. Opposition within the labor movement to this dualism was strong and widespread, even among those most closely associated with political parties.[69]

In Kenya, finally, the pervasive personal influence of Tom Mboya in both the Kenya African National Union and the Kenya Federation of Labour makes it difficult to evaluate the extent of party influence over the labor movement. The personal relationship undoubtedly reflects a real interpenetration of the two institutions, and there is no question that the party has much to say about KFL policy. It is also likely that the KFL has had greater control over its member unions than central labor organizations in most of the other English-speaking colonial areas; the KFL has actually been the spearhead of union organizing efforts since 1957.[70]

Even in Kenya, however, there have been restraints on party control.

---

[69] At the Conakry convention of the UGTAN in January, 1959, Abdoulaye Thiaw, CGT leader in Senegal, presented arguments in support of an "incompatibility thesis" which held that simultaneous possession of union and political office was incompatible with the interests of the labor movement. His arguments were based partly on principle, but also pointed to experience in Senegal, where former trade-unionists in places of political authority had taken drastic action against strikers. Sékou Touré made a heated defense of the dual role of the union leader–politician. The interests of the working class, he said, are best defended when its representatives are in positions of political responsibility. If at times union leader–politicians have acted in a manner contrary to the interests of the workers, it is not because there is any basic conflict of roles, but because these are wicked men, traitors to the working class.

The convention accepted these arguments with little open protest; insistence on the incompatibility thesis was not too healthy in the environment of the Conakry convention. Touré had written in 1958 that anyone who believed union office incompatible with political responsibility was a tool of the colonialists and an "enemy." Nonetheless, it seems that many important delegates were silently unconvinced, and, although a final resolution presented Touré's arguments, it did so in a considerably less forceful form than the version originally presented to the convention by Touré (*Rapport d'Orientation et de doctrine, Congrès Général de l'UGTAN,* Republic of Guinea, Jan. 15–18, 1959).

[70] Between January, 1958, and August, 1960, fifteen African trade unions were registered, of which at least eleven either had their offices in Solidarity House (KFL headquarters) or had received assistance from the KFL.

The existence of sharp factional disputes within both the KFL and the KANU have prevented the emergence of monolithic structural ties between the two organizations. It was possible in 1960 for Arthur Ochwada, a leader of both the KFL and the KANU, to withdraw from the KFL and set up a rival federation, the Kenya Trades Union Congress, while at the same time retaining his position in the KANU.[71] The component unions, moreover, are by no means mere rubber stamps; they have more than once refused to accept party and KFL directives. In 1960, for example, several unions rejected a strike proposal made by the Nairobi People's Convention Party, and in February, 1961, there was little union response when the KFL ordered a general strike to obtain the release of Jomo Kenyatta from detention.[72] More recently, KFL leaders have been outspoken in asserting union independence from political control.[73]

THE TRADE-UNION POLITICAL IMPACT

The political impact of a labor movement, or its contribution to political affairs, may be judged by different criteria: the number and the quality of men it makes available to parties, and to political life generally; the money it supplies to parties; the extent to which parties rely on the trade-union apparatus as a political machine; the extent and the effectiveness of union participation in strikes, demonstrations, and other activities in support of political goals.

The presence of many former trade-unionists in high political office is frequently cited as evidence that the labor movements of Africa have been institutions of wide political influence. The list of African political leaders with previous trade-union experience is indeed impressive: Sékou Touré in Guinea; Reuben Um Nyobé in the French Camerouns; Ouezzin Coulibaly, a founder of the teachers' union in French Africa and later second-in-command to Houphouet-Boigny, in the Ivory Coast; Cyrille Adoula in the Congo; Tom Mboya in Kenya; Rashidi Kawawa in Tanganyika; Joshua Nkomo in Southern Rhodesia. And others could be named.

But caution is required in interpreting the presence of numerous trade-unionists in positions of political responsibility. One may not conclude—as is so commonly done—that the labor movement has been a prolific source of political leadership. In the first place, some of those

---

[71] The Kenya TUC, unable to win many unions away from the KFL, existed mainly on paper. A recent decision by Luo elements to form a Kenya labor party may herald more serious dualism within the labor movement (see the *Newsletter* of the Institute of Race Relations in London [Sept., 1962], p. 26).

[72] *East African Standard,* April 14, 1960; Bennett and Rosberg, *op. cit.,* pp. 131–132.

[73] Peter Kibisu, former secretary-general of the KFL, has made a number of speeches calling for coöperative but independent relationships between government and the labor movement. He has also attacked Kenyatta, accusing him of "personal ambitions that tend towards dictatorship" (*Newsletter* [Sept., 1962], p. 25).

usually included in the category of former union leaders do not really belong there; if those whose energies were not primarily devoted to the labor movement are eliminated, the list would dwindle appreciably.[74] Second, for many of these men the trade union was simply one of many organizational channels used by them in their rise to power. They were often youth leaders and party militants before or at the same time that they were trade-union activists. In this sense they are not trade-unionists become politicians so much as political men in the labor movement.[75] Finally, the preëminence of those with trade-union backgrounds in high political office should not obscure the meager representation of trade-unionists among lower-level political leaders. Except in the states of French West Africa, where in 1957 eight trade-unionists were named to cabinet positions as ministers of labor and/or civil service,[76] few labor leaders found their way to political office. In the executive organs and the legislative assemblies of the new African governments, men with labor backgrounds are extremely rare. Even in French Africa, of 473 representatives in parliamentary bodies in 1958, only four could be identified as former trade-unionists.[77] In the Ghana National Assembly no more than five representatives have trade-union backgrounds.[78] In Nigeria, of eighty-four Eastern and Western Regional members in the 1957 federal House of Representatives, only three had had trade-union experience.[79]

---

[74] In some enthusiastic accounts even Kwame Nkrumah and Nnamdi Azikiwe are included as sons of the labor movement, mainly because they held cards in American labor organizations while they were students in the United States (see speech by Clement K. Lubemba, deputy secretary-general of the Kenya Federation of Labour, "The Role of Trade Union Movements in Africa," in *Educational Institutions and International Labor,* report of conference held at Michigan State University in March, 1962).

[75] Nor, for what it is worth, are they proletarians in any meaningful sense. There are few manual workers among them, few sons of the working class risen from the workbench. Most of them are relatively well-educated men who started life as clerks, teachers, or civil servants.

[76] Jean-Louis Seurin, "Elites sociales et Partis politiques d'A.O.F.," *Annales Africaines* (1958), p. 147.

[77] *Ibid.,* p. 154.

[78] L. Trachtman, "The Labor Movement of Ghana: A Study in Political Unionism," *Economic Development and Cultural Change,* X (Jan., 1962), 190. See, however, J. H. Price, "The Gold Coast's Legislators," *West Africa,* May 26, 1956, where, for the parliaments of the early 1950's, the category "trade-union office" is not even listed.

[79] *Who's Who of the Federal House of Representatives* (Lagos, 1958). Coleman (*op. cit.,* p. 379) says that about 12 per cent of the members from the southern regions had had experience as trade-union officials. This statement is not borne out by the *Who's Who* cited above. Sklar ("Nigerian Political Parties," pp. 792 ff.) has studied the biographies of 480 members of local government councils in Lagos and eight urban areas in the Eastern and Western regions. Only five were "agents of occupational, cultural and political organizations," the category into which trade-union officials would fall.

In the Kenya election of 1961 only three of eighty-eight candidates were listed as labor leaders "by dominant occupation." [80]

The labor movements have supplied even less in the way of financial resources. It is worth recalling that in the union-party alliances of European countries, it is the financial nexus that gives strength to the relationship; European labor or social democratic parties tend to rely heavily on trade-union financial support. In Africa there were, and are, few comparable arrangements. The unions have always been too poor to support even their own meager bureaucracies. Most of them have been helped by international labor organizations, such as the International Confederation of Free Trade Unions (ICFTU) and the WFTU. Or, as in French Africa, they depended on the colonial administration for aid in two forms: subsidies to "representative" labor organizations for the construction of headquarters buildings; and the privilege of "detachment," which allowed civil servants who were union officials to serve full time at their union jobs, while continuing to receive their regular salaries.

Union assistance to parties in other forms was likewise limited by the poverty of the labor organizations. In French Africa the detachment privilege, though allowing some time for party work, freed only a small number of trade-unionists. The whole burden of union work—grievance handling and the negotiation of agreements—fell on the shoulders of full-time officers, leaving them relatively little time for other activity. In Kenya, Mboya has benefited in both political and labor activities from the aid made available by the ICFTU and other foreign trade-union organizations. Solidarity House, the KFL headquarters in Nairobi, was built with outside funds; it provides superb facilities for union as well as political activities.[81] It is probable, too, that the KANU has benefited from the use of KFL automobiles. Similarly, it has been argued that Bakary Djibo's control of the chauffeurs' union in the Republic of Niger contributed to his political success in the early and middle 1950's.[82] In Nigeria, during the Zikist period (1948–1950) and in the Lagos Town Council elections of 1950, the trade-union organization did serve as a

---

[80] Bennett and Rosberg, *op. cit.*, p. 143. These writers go on to say: ". . . but recruitment from the labour movement . . . has been an important aspect of Kenya politics; . . . many minor political leaders have come up through the trade unions." This may be so. But the labor movement is very young in Kenya, and "come up through" is a phrase that should mean more than simply membership in a union at one time. How many "minor" leaders owed their positions primarily to their union experience?

[81] See "Report of the General Secretary, 1958–1960," Kenya, Federation of Labour, p. 2. Mboya's overwhelming victory in Nairobi in the 1961 election was celebrated at Solidarity House; this was, it should be noted, a victory over enemies within his own party (see Bennett and Rosberg, *op. cit.*, p. 80).

[82] Schachter, "French West African Trade Unions, 1956."

useful political vehicle. But, on the whole, little concrete evidence exists that unions gave significant assistance to political parties, and there are few instances where a party relied heavily on a union as a political machine.

The paucity of trade-union experience in direct political action is perhaps the clearest indication of the limited political effectiveness of unions. Labor organizations engaged in relatively few "political" strikes and demonstrations, and those that did occur were not notably successful. Unions were rarely able to compete with political parties; in independent political ventures, or in conflicts with parties, the labor movement almost invariably came out badly. To distinguish between political and other strikes is obviously difficult, for the causation in all work stoppages is complex. There may be profound political elements in the most humdrum of wage disputes. In a colonial situation, moreover, most work stoppages represent challenges to the colonial presence, and as such have political implications. But this does not mean that every stoppage is politically motivated, nor that political strikes cannot be distinguished from others.

We define a political work stoppage as one whose main objectives are not directly related to the short-run occupational interests of the wage earners concerned. Such work stoppages have occasionally taken place in most of Africa. The general strike of January, 1950, in Ghana was politically inspired, as indicated by its tie-in with the positive-action campaign and by the demands of the strikers for self-government and for the right of civil servants to engage in politics.[83] The 1950 strike in Nigeria against major trading firms seems to have been part of the Zikist (radical nationalist) agitation. In the Ivory Coast in 1950, the CGT engaged in a series of work stoppages which were connected more with the current political struggle than with any occupational questions.[84] The attempted general strikes in Southern Rhodesia in 1948 and 1961 were largely political, as were the strikes in Kenya in 1960, directed at winning the release of Jomo Kenyatta from detention. In most of French Africa the demonstrations carried out by the UGTAN for a "No" vote at the September, 1958, referendum also clearly fall into the category of nonoccupational action.

There are other examples. What is significant, however, is not that such examples exist, but that there are so few of them. Relative to the total number of work stoppages and to the total activity of most labor organizations, the political strike has been a minor factor. This is not to deny that political elements or implications colored most work stoppages,

---

[83] *Annual Report of the Labour Department, 1949–1950,* Gold Coast Ministry of Trade and Labour, p. 8.

[84] Elliot Berg, "French West Africa," in Walter Galenson, ed., *Labor and Economic Development* (New York: John Wiley & Sons, 1959), p. 251 n. 73.

or that much of the activity of trade unions involved conflict with the state. It is simply that strikes for well-defined political goals unrelated to the short-term interests of wage earners are the exception in preindependence Africa, not the rule.[85]

The relatively few strikes and demonstrations of a closely political nature have not been particularly effective. The impact of strikes, especially those with well-defined political objectives, has usually been questionable. Most of them were only partly implemented, either because some union leaders would not go along or because workers did not obey the strike call. The general strikes in Southern Rhodesia in 1948 and 1961, the protests against federation in Northern Rhodesia in 1953, and the attempted general strike of 1960 in Kenya, over the issue of Kenyatta's detention, were hardly effective.[86] When political strikes and demonstrations were successful in the sense of being effective work stoppages, they often led to the destruction of central labor organizations, as in Ghana after the positive-action strike of 1950. Or they led to the destruction of participating unions, as after the Zikist-sponsored mercantile workers' strike in Nigeria in 1950, or to a purging of union leadership, as in the Ivory Coast after a strike of civil servants in 1959.

The ineffectiveness of labor's ventures in the nonindustrial sphere is further emphasized by the relative insignificance of union efforts other than work stoppages and demonstrations. When, under union inspiration, attempts were made to form labor parties (as in Nigeria in 1954 and 1956, and in Sierra Leone in 1955), the record is one of failure.[87] Furthermore, trade-unionists who were not supported by a party in an electoral contest almost invariably went down to defeat. Abdoulaye Diallo's defeat in 1956 in the Bamako municipal elections presumably resulted from lack

---

[85] The French African experience seems to be in direct conflict with this argument; labor unions in French Africa were continually embroiled in disputes with the government. But this does not mean that their actions were political in the proper sense of the word. The state is the largest single employer of wage labor in French Africa, and thus directly determines wages and working conditions of some 30 per cent of the recorded wage-earning force. The system of wage determination, furthermore, was such that the government, in fixing statutory minimum wage rates, determined the wages of all unskilled labor in the economy, and indirectly exercised decisive influence on the rates of skilled labor. Finally, disputes arose over the application of labor laws by the government on matters of immediate occupational interest. Although most of the labor movement's energies were for these reasons devoted to pressure against the state, its objectives were essentially economic.

[86] Gray, *op. cit.*, pp. 302–306, 326–328; Mason, *op. cit.*, pp. 93–98.

[87] The 1950 Lagos experience (see p. 344, above) has few counterparts elsewhere. In Sierra Leone the electoral performance of the Labour Party was extremely poor. In the 1957 elections it ran five candidates; three lost their deposits and the other two did badly (see Martin Kilson, "Sierra Leone Politics: The Approach to Independence," *West Africa*, July 2, 1960, p. 744; D. J. R. Scott, "The Sierra Leone Election, May 1957," in W. J. M. Mackenzie and Kenneth Robinson, eds., *Five Elections in Africa* [Oxford: Clarendon Press, 1960], pp. 186, 207).

of support by the dominant party, the Union Soudanaise; Jacques N'Gom, CGKT head in the French Camerouns, repeatedly lost at the polls because of the opposition of the militant nationalist party, the UPC.

The most striking example of the ineffectiveness of trade-union mass organization is to be found in French Africa on the occasion of the referendum of September, 1958. The UGTAN was directly concerned in the option of independence offered by the French in the referendum. Most of the political parties of French Africa decided against immediate independence; the Parti Démocratique de Guinée and Bakary Djibo's Sawaba Party in Niger were the main dissenters. The interterritorial committee of the UGTAN, deciding to follow the Guinean path, campaigned for immediate independence; only its Ivory Coast section refused to go along. The labor organization thus came into direct conflict with the ruling parties in most of the territories. In the key territory of Senegal, where UGTAN unions were strongest and their potential political influence seemed most challenging, the struggle was particularly bitter. But in Senegal the UGTAN, with the other groups pushing for independence, was soundly beaten. Only in Niger did the "No" forces win a substantial part of the vote.

THE TRADE-UNION POLITICAL POSITION
AFTER INDEPENDENCE

The unions in Tropical Africa were of even less significance after independence than they had been before, at least in domestic politics. Almost everywhere in the continent, labor organizations were taken over by the governing parties, once independence was achieved. The process is already under way in countries that are nearing independence. It differs in degree; the levers of control are manipulated more gently and discreetly in Senegal and the Ivory Coast than in Guinea or Ghana. But in most countries the result is the same. The labor movement, if not completely subordinate to the party, is at least pliable and responsive to party pressures.

The process by which the party gains control over the labor movement varies from country to country. Everywhere the party brings to bear a combination of rewards and punishments: rewards for unions and union leaders who are prepared to accept the role designated by the party, and punishments and harassments for those who are recalcitrant. Once in power, the party has at its command a wide variety of gifts and an abundance of penalties, and can quickly bend the most determined trade-unionists to its will.

As rewards, the governing party first of all can offer money. It may grant the unions direct subsidies, or may build bright and imposing new headquarters, as in Ghana. It may give indirect help by establishing the checkoff system, as in Ghana, Kenya, and Tanganyika.[88] Even more important, the party can offer the choicest political plums to union leaders: ambassadorships, places on executive and consultative agencies, seats in the parliament. It is probably no coincidence that Alioune Cissé, a former CGT militant who became a prime mover in the creation of a labor organization friendly to the Senegalese government, was later appointed ambassador to Guinea. In Northern Rhodesia, the recent reconciliation of the African Mineworkers' Union with the UNIP-dominated United Trades Union Congress was not unrelated to the selection of the mineworkers' leader, John Chisata, as a candidate in the 1962 elections. The nascent opposition to the TANU which existed in the Tanganyika Federation of Labour was dissipated, at least temporarily, by the appointment of C. S. K. Tumbo as high commissioner in London and of Michael Kamaliza as minister of health and labor.[89]

These rewards are powerful instruments, and frequently suffice to bring understanding between trade unions and governing parties. When they do not, the parties have not hesitated to bring into play all the power of the new state machinery under their control. They have, first, taken a strong stand against strikes. In January, 1959, in Senegal, and in October, 1959, in the Ivory Coast, walkouts by civil servants, who in both states formed the core of the antigovernment, pro-UGTAN elements, were severely repressed.[90] In French Equatorial Africa, the process was much the same. In Brazzaville, in the Congo, the government jailed leading trade-unionists in May, 1960, on the ground that they had taken part in a Communist plot. Shortly thereafter, new laws were passed to regulate public meetings, to authorize dissolution of organizations potentially threatening the public interest, and to allow the arrest and expulsion of people regarded as dangerous to the security of the state.[91] In Nyasaland, a strike that greeted the new African administration immediately after

---

[88] In Ghana, the checkoff has been made obligatory by legislation.

[89] Tumbo soon resigned his position, but his absence during the debate on Tanganyika's new industrial relations legislation allowed for easier passage of the law regulating unions.

[90] In Senegal the government warned all nonestablished government employees that they would be discharged if they participated in the strike. This was enough to keep all but 15 per cent of them at work; the 700 who disregarded the warning were fired. To deal with the established civil servants the government pushed through a requisition law calling all essential men back to work. It is noteworthy that this requisition law was the first act of the new legislature of the new state of Senegal. The strike soon lost momentum and most of the men returned to work before the unions issued a back-to-work call. This was the first time in the postwar period that measures so harsh had been adopted in a labor dispute in Senegal.

The strike of the Ivory Coast civil servants was triggered by the arrest of Yao Ngo Blaise, a pro-UGTAN civil servant and union leader. More than 500 established civil servants were discharged and another 300 were suspended for a month (*Afrique Nouvelle,* Nov. 6, 1959, p. 3). Many of those discharged were later rehired.

[91] See summary of events in *ibid.,* May 18, 1960, p. 8.

it took office in 1961 brought a sharp reaction from the Malawi Congress Party (MCP), which was in control of the government; the party, appealing directly to the workers to return to work, made dark threats against the union leadership.[92]

Second, when unions are regarded as irreconcilable, the party has encouraged a split in the labor movement and created a rival union more friendly to the government. Senegal is a classic example,[93] and the same process may be seen in the Rhodesias. In Northern Rhodesia, UNIP militants set up the Reformed Trades Union Congress to combat the NRTUC which was controlled by Lawrence Katilungu, the former leader of the mineworkers, who was at odds with the UNIP. The Southern Rhodesian African Trades Union Congress is a creature of the ZAPU, designed to fight Reuben Jamela's SRTUC.

There is, third, the weapon of imprisonment and exile, used most commonly in French Africa. In December, 1960, several leading UGTAN figures in Senegal were imprisoned on the charge of fomenting an illegal strike. In Niger, early in 1959, Saloum Traoré, a UGTAN-Conakry leader and former minister of labor, was exiled. In 1959 the Ivory Coast government arrested some trade-unionists and exiled others.[94] Disturbances in Guinea late in 1961 led to the trial and imprisonment of prominent leaders of the teachers' union.[95]

---

[92] In September, 1961, the Transport and Allied Workers' Union struck eight major trucking firms; their main objective was to win the checkoff. The strike did not shut down trucking operations, but did antagonize the first African minister of labor, who had been in office less than a week. The *Malawi News*, organ of the MCP, then published a number of articles attacking "selfish" and irresponsible union leadership. The headline of the first article was MALAWI URGES STRIKERS TO GO TO WORK NOW. A later article said that the party identified itself with no trade union, and recommended that the Malawi Congress of Labour change its "misleading title" (see *Malawi News*, Sept. 14, 21, 1961, and, for background, C. D. Mkandawire, "Nyasaland Unions in Turmoil," *Free Labour World* [April, 1961], pp. 164–166).

[93] At the time of the 1958 referendum campaign, the Union Progressiste Sénégalaise (UPS) encouraged the formation of a splinter organization, the UGTAN-Autonome, under the leadership of Abbas Guèye, the UPS deputy and a former labor leader. In mid-1959 another segment of Senegal's UGTAN, named the UGTAN-Unitaire, broke away under the guidance of Alioune Cissé, a prominent trade-union figure and formerly secretary-general of the interterritorial UGTAN. In October, 1959, a new national organization, the Union Générale des Travailleurs Sénégalais (UGTS), came into being. Most of the old-line UGTAN leaders remained outside this organization. By 1961 the government had effectively isolated the orthodox UGTAN, and had created a Senegalese labor movement decidedly more friendly to it.

The same pattern was followed in other states of French West Africa. In Niger, for example, seventeen unions broke away from the UGTAN-Conakry in March, 1959, to form the UGTAN-Autonome of Niger.

[94] A striking instance of mingling rewards and punishments occurred in the Ivory Coast. Shortly after his release from jail, a union leader was nominated by the party as a candidate for election to parliament.

[95] The teachers' disturbances apparently originated in deteriorating wage scales

Finally, the legislative weapon, which is really a combination of the others, has been used in Ghana and, more recently, in Tanganyika. In Ghana the union-party *Anschluss* was effected through legislation. Despite great pressure from the CPP group in the TUC leadership, the unions resisted political control until 1958. At the 1958 convention of the TUC, which was supposed to authorize a new and centralized structure for the labor movement, John Tettegah's opponents fought a temporarily successful rear-guard action, thus postponing the decision. The government, finally forced to act directly, passed the Industrial Relations Act of 1958 which centralized power in the TUC and assured government control of the recalcitrant unions. When this proved insufficient to bring all the unions into line, stronger measures were passed, successively limiting the possibility of autonomous existence for any union.[96]

It would be a mistake, however, to conclude that labor organizations in independent Africa are or will be completely subordinate to government parties, and will lack any independent influence. In some countries, especially in Nigeria and Dahomey, the unions remain free of government control. In others—Senegal, the Ivory Coast, Tanganyika—the reins are loosely held, and the unions retain some maneuverability. In some countries, notably Kenya, the decentralization of the political structure, reflecting deep ethnic and other divisions, may prevent the emergence of single-party national governments and thus diminish the likelihood of party- or government-controlled labor movements, as it has in Nigeria.

Even in those countries where the absorption of unions by party and state has been most complete, the unions have not been mere puppets. In Ghana and Guinea strikes have occurred despite government control, and it has proved difficult to define the respective spheres of activity of party and union; the party has found it necessary to purge and control top union leadership (after the 1961 teachers' strike in Guinea, and early in

---

and fringe benefits. At their own meetings, and at meetings of the Confédération Nationale du Travail Guinéen (CNTG), the teachers made known their dissatisfaction. A memorandum outlining their requests was circulated among party leaders, and sent abroad as well; President Touré claimed that the teachers gave it to certain embassies also. At the November, 1961, national convention of the CNTG, the teachers' grievances dominated the discussions. The party suspended the Executive Committee of the union and sentenced two leaders to ten years and three others to five years in jail on charges of subversion. (It is interesting that one of those sentenced was Keita Koumandian, old enemy of the RDA before independence.) A number of sympathy strikes by secondary school students were suppressed by the RDA youth organization and the army. The government closed all the secondary schools for two months.

[96] For an outline of the main provisions of the law, and its amendments, see L. Trachtman, "Ghanaian Labor Legislation since Independence," *Labor Law Journal*, XII (June, 1961), 547–556, and D. Rimmer, "The New Industrial Relations in Ghana," *Industrial and Labor Relations Review*, XIV (Jan., 1961), 206–226.

1962 in Ghana).[97] In all instances the unions are allowed some expression of opinion, and often proclaim a leftist ideology, favoring socialism, more rapid Africanization, a centralized government instead of federalism, and Pan-Africanism. But it is only on party sufferance that they are given a role to play, and they are constrained to be "reasonable" and "responsible" organizations which emphasize productivity and hard work.

EXPLANATORY FACTORS

Reasons for the postindependence developments described above are not hard to find. The relationship between parties and unions is best understood as an outcome of the centralization of power by the new African governments, and of their drive for economic development. The independent African governments do not relish the existence of potential sources of opposition, for they see them as threats to fragile national entities. In the single-party systems that characterize most of the newly independent states, all interest groups are viewed as integral parts of the governing-party mechanism. Furthermore, economic growth demands reform of wage structures and changes in work attitudes and habits; it will also demand restraint in the increasing of personal incomes. Most political leaders feel that these readjustments may best be made with the coöperation of friendly trade-union organizations.

The explanation of preindependence patterns of trade-union political relations is more complicated. We have tried to show that most of the conventional generalizations about the political tendencies and the political importance of African labor movements are not borne out by the facts. Trade unions in colonial Africa were by no means political organizations; more commonly than not, trade-union energies were largely devoted, however ineffectively, to economic or bargaining activities. On the other hand, politics preoccupied not only central labor organizations, which were more often than not without power, but also the leaders of small and weak unions, who were really union leaders without unions. In general, the most solidly implanted unions have been least disposed to political activity; mineworkers and railway men everywhere in Africa, for

---

[97] After the teachers' disturbances in late 1961, the Guinea government threatened to turn the union headquarters over to the youth movement, and tightened party control over union meetings and trade-union international contacts. The Executive Committee of the teachers' union was replaced by party loyalists; preliminary steps to introduce the checkoff were abandoned; and Mamady Kaba, secretary-general of the CNTG, has been subjected to greater control by the party and by the Ministry of Labor.

In Ghana, John Tettegah was quietly removed from effective leadership of the TUC in the spring of 1962. By party decision, his internal functions were given to a party regular, S. Magnus-George. Tettegah's activities are restricted to international labor affairs.

example, have usually had the best organization and the least political commitment.[98]

Whatever the extent of their commitment to politics and political action, the unions were rarely the instruments of political parties. In some countries they were allied with parties through intermingling leadership, but in others they had little to do with parties; in still others they had strained relations with political groups. In very few instances were unions completely dominated by parties; as a general rule they were autonomous, independent bases of power and influence. But whether the unions were autonomous or not, their political significance was relatively slight. Although they provided some of Africa's leading statesmen, they contributed little to political leadership at the lower levels. They did not provide money or an effective electoral machine. They undertook relatively few political activities, and when they did, they were seldom notably successful or effective.

On the basis of available information, it is impossible to give a fully satisfactory explanation of the preindependence relationship between trade unions and parties. All that can be done here is to suggest certain factors that seem to have been of major significance in shaping the pattern.

Timing.—In most countries in Africa, trade unions arose earlier than, or at the same time as, political parties and nationalist movements. In Nigeria more than eighty trade unions were in existence in 1944, when the NCNC was established; some of these, like the unions of teachers and railway workers, were well entrenched. In Ghana, it was not until 1949 that the CPP came into being; its antecedent, the United Gold Coast Convention, had ignored the trade unions, so that by the time the mass party arose some unions had already had a decade or more of independent development and experience. In Northern Rhodesia, the Mineworkers' Union emerged in 1949, shortly before the African National Congress and other parties became significant political elements. In Southern Rhodesia, the African Railway Workers' Union and several other labor organizations functioned during much of the postwar period, when there were no legal African parties. In Tanganyika, the TANU was created in 1955, whereas the major unions had been in existence since the early 1950's. The fact that labor organizations antedated political parties is obviously important. It means, among other things, that unions did not owe their formation to nonindustrial groups. The unions in these countries, unlike those in India and Indonesia, had an opportunity to develop their own leadership; the parties could not truthfully claim proprietary stewardship over them.

---

[98] There are some important exceptions. Unions of civil servants, particularly teachers, were the best organized as well as the most politically committed unions in French Africa.

The argument pointing to the independent development of trade unions and political parties must of course be qualified. In many, if not most, instances, union leaders did coöperate with parties when they arose, though as more or less independent agents. Moreover, the picture is not always clear. In French Africa, for example, unions and parties developed at roughly the same time—in 1944 and 1945 in French West Africa.[99] But, in this area, the existence of Communist training groups—the Groupes d'Etudes Communistes—stimulated closer trade union–party connections. Many of the trade-union and political leaders of French West Africa attended courses organized by these groups during World War II, and continued until 1949 or 1950. They absorbed there a common ideological disposition, and common notions of strategy and tactics, which served to cement their personal relations even though some stayed on the political path and others remained in the trade-union movement.[100] In Kenya, and also possibly in Tanganyika, the timing factor seems to have been different. In the early postwar years, when the East African Trades Union Congress made its appearance, its connection with Kenyatta's Kenya African National Union was close. In the late 1950's KANU militants occasionally organized labor unions; for example, Dennis Akumu, a KANU activist, was responsible for organizing the Mombasa Dockworkers' Union. Recently, Julius Nyerere has claimed that the same process occurred in Tanganyika, but the evidence seems less convincing than it is for Kenya.[101]

Political environment.—On the whole, the transition from colonial to independent status was achieved with remarkably little violence in West and East Africa. In English-speaking areas, except Kenya, the rules of the game were fairly clear, and its outcome was certain. Independence was the acknowledged goal; the only question was its timing. In French

[99] Trade-union growth was probably more rapid than party growth. By the end of 1946 there were 175 registered labor organizations in French West Africa. The local sections of the RDA and other parties probably did not put down roots so fast.

[100] Common experience in the Communist study groups had effects similar to common attendance at the Ecole William Ponty, from which many of French West Africa's political leaders emerged (see Ruth Schachter Morgenthau, *Political Parties in French-speaking West Africa* [Oxford: Clarendon Press, 1964]).

[101] Julius Nyerere, "The Task Ahead of Our African Trade Unions," *Labour* (organ of the Ghana Trades Union Congress) (June, 1961), p. 28: "[The TANU] had an officer in the organization whose special duty it was to stimulate and help the growth of Trade Unionism. Once firmly established, the Trade Union Movement was, and is, part and parcel of the whole Nationalist Movement. In the early days, when a trade union went on strike, for instance, and its members were in direct need of funds to help them keep going, we saw no doctrine which would be abrogated by our giving financial support from the political wing to the industrial wing of the same Nationalist Movement." Despite this statement, some unions did antedate the party in Tanganyika, and there is little evidence to indicate that the TANU played a role in early union organizing, though there was considerable interlocking of personnel.

Africa the goals were less clear, but the ground rules were also well understood by the groups concerned; independence was not a legitimate subject of political discourse before 1956, but African political groups devoted themselves to consolidating their local organizations and preparing the way for independence. French suppression did occur, and violence was not unknown, particularly in 1949–1950 in the Ivory Coast and in 1954–1956 in Guinea. But in French Africa, as in British East and West Africa, violence was minimal. In most countries political institutions provided a channel for the expression of protest, and these institutions were modified when pressures became intense (in 1945, 1956, and 1958 in French Africa; more regularly throughout the late 1940's and the 1950's in British West and East Africa). It is surely no coincidence that in the two countries where trade-union political commitments were most intense—Guinea and Kenya—channels of legitimate political expression were least available. In Kenya the Mau Mau emergency after 1952 hindered the development of legalized political activity by Africans on a national basis, and distorted such activity as was permitted. In Guinea the French administration took a hostile attitude toward Sékou Touré's RDA party, refusing until 1956 to allow it to play the role in Guinean political life which its popular support justified.

Several related features of the political environment are relevant. In French Africa, the fact that until 1956 there were no overt nationalist movements demanding independence meant that territorial labor movements had few opportunities to engage directly in nationalist struggles. In British Africa national political movements existed, but participation by the labor movement in their activities was strenuously discouraged by the law, by British colonial administrators, and by the private advisers sent out by the British Trades Union Congress or, on a smaller scale, by the International Confederation of Free Trade Unions. In most British territories these advisers and local labor department officials worked closely with evolving labor organizations. Almost invariably their cardinal principle was that the labor movement must "stay out of politics." By ceaselessly hammering on this theme, they convinced some trade-unionists, especially those in the best-organized unions, that trade-union independence from parties and trade-union political neutrality were necessary and desirable.

The attitudes and the policies of the colonial governments were important in another way. Although "responsible" (that is, nonpolitical) African trade-unionism was tolerated or even encouraged in most areas, government reaction to any wandering from the nonpolitical path was usually extremely sharp. Not uncommonly, even work stoppages that had no political tinge resulted in violent suppression, particularly in East and Central Africa; the history of African labor disputes is punctuated by the eruption of bloody incidents.[102] If political elements were evident, a particularly harsh reaction was likely to follow. Thus trade-union political ventures were exposed to grave risks.

Finally, the existence of competing political parties was a strong deterrent to too-close commitment by trade unions to any single party. As it was likely that some trade-union leaders and many members would prefer different political groups, attempts to ally the unions to any one group commonly stimulated factionalism and rival unionism. In fact, division often followed attempts to politicize the labor movement or a segment of it; the tendency was more pronounced when political parties had a regional or tribal basis. This situation is most clearly illustrated in Nigeria, where trade-union nonpoliticalness was the only practicable alternative to a regionally divided labor movement. The effect of multiparty political situations, which were general in the preindependence period, was to dilute tendencies toward trade-union political commitment.

Union vulnerability.—African trade-unionism is of very recent origin. Before World War II there were no continuing organizations to speak of, mainly because of the lack of legal recognition of the right to organize, the hostility of colonial governments, and the nature of African societies and economies. In East and Central Africa it was not until the 1950's that any significant African trade-unionism made its appearance; in the Congo unions were not freed of crippling restrictions until 1957, and in Southern Rhodesia they were not made legal for Africans until 1959. In West Africa, few labor organizations are more than fifteen years old.

In this brief span of time, many of these organizations made tremendous headway in sinking roots among wage-earning groups. In some industries unions of real substance developed, mainly among railway men, mineworkers, commercial employees in large trading firms, and some groups of civil servants, such as teachers. Nobody who has seen at first hand an African union in convention could fail to be impressed by the way its leaders have come to grips with the enormously complex job of organizing and maintaining a workers' organization. Many labor organizations have engaged in effective negotiations with employers, and have provided machinery for the redress of wage earners' grievances. They have mounted impressive work stoppages, even ones that required close coördination, such as the railway men's strike of 1947–48 and the Labor Code strikes in 1952 and 1953 in French Africa, the rolling strikes on the Northern Rhodesian Copperbelt in 1956, the Ghana mineworkers' strikes in 1947 and 1956, and others. In these achievements, African labor organizations telescoped a hundred years of development into two decades. Moreover, in this relatively brief life span, they have had to deal with

---

[102] For a highly colored account, see Jack Woddis, *Africa: The Lion Awakes* (London: Lawrence and Wishart, 1961), chap. 2.

problems much more difficult than those faced by the labor movements of industrial countries in comparable periods of development.

One of the problems is the character of the labor force. It is largely migrant, comprising peasants who are temporarily in wage employment.[103] It is an unskilled labor force; perhaps 60 or 70 per cent of the African wage earners are men with little or no skill. It is a heterogeneous labor force, composed of men from many different ethnic groups.

A second difficulty is in the area of leadership. The richest source of trade-union leadership in most industrial countries is the skilled-worker categories. But the ranks of African skilled workers are very thin, owing partly to the structure of production in most countries; except for a large services sector, the agricultural and mineral sectors, both of which employ mainly unskilled labor, predominate in African economies. Furthermore, many of the available skilled-labor jobs were filled by expatriates, especially in French-speaking Africa, or, in East Africa, by Asians.[104] Finally, the labor movement lost many of its able people to other occupations; those who received formal training or education under trade-union auspices were likely to find new and more economically rewarding opportunities, and did not return to the labor movement.[105]

A third facet of union weakness was financial. Most of the unions had few members who paid dues regularly, and therefore could not raise adequate revenues to support full-time union officials and administrative offices.[106] The unions were thus dependent on nonunion support. In French Africa they relied directly on the government to release civil servants for full-time union work (with government salaries continuing) and to provide subsidies for the construction of headquarters; everywhere

---

[103] In West Africa, probably between one-half and three-fourths of those in paid employment may be regarded as migrant workers. It has been claimed that in Southern Rhodesia, in 1957, "90 per cent of the indigenous labor force still has one foot in the Reserves." The Committee on African Wages in Kenya estimated that in 1953 about half the wage earners in the country were migrants (see Berg, *op. cit.*, pp. 199 ff.; J. B. Heigham, "Notes on Labour in the Gold Coast" [mimeographed; Accra, 1952], sec. 3; *Report of the Southern Rhodesian Department of Labour for the Calendar Year 1957* [Salisbury, 1959], p. 24; *Report of the Committee on African Wages*, Kenya Colony [Nairobi, 1954], p. 13).

[104] Cf. C. Sofer, "Working Groups in a Plural Society," *Industrial and Labor Relations Review*, VIII (Oct., 1954), 68–78.

[105] In Nigeria, for example, only two of the ten trade-unionists who were awarded scholarships for trade-union education in the United Kingdom in 1950–1952 remained with the labor movement; several stayed in England for further study, four became personnel officers in the government, and two joined private firms (Sklar, unpublished manuscript).

[106] In Nigeria, the annual income of all unions in the five years between 1952 and 1956 averaged about $90,000 (data from unpublished manuscript by T. M. Yesufu). In Ghana, in 1957, less than 20,000 union members of a claimed total of more than 80,000 could be considered as paid up. For Rhodesia, see the Branigan Report (*Report of the Commissioner to Enquire into the Unrest in the Mining Industry in Northern Rhodesia in Recent Months* [Lusaka, 1956], pp. 47 ff.).

in Africa unions depended on subsidies from metropolitan and international labor organizations. In a number of countries (Ghana, Nigeria, and Northern Rhodesia, among others) they imported the idea of the American checkoff system.

The inability to finance their operations through voluntary dues payments subjected the unions to numerous restraints. The possibility of government withdrawal of assistance in French Africa was instrumental in keeping the unions within accepted bounds of behavior; indeed, in many French African states these privileges were withdrawn shortly after the achievement of self-government, with consequent disarray among the trade unions. The need for, or the reliance on, external finance exposed the labor movement to continuous internal dissension over the question of international affiliation, and over the handling of funds transmitted to leaders from abroad; when more than one source of outside assistance was available, ideological differences were exaggerated. The reliance on checkoff, combined with explicit management threats to withdraw checkoff arrangements if the unions turned to politics, could dampen enthusiasm for political adventures among union leaders. In the Northern Rhodesian mines, for example, the checkoff was eliminated by the mining companies in 1953 and was not restored until 1958.

For all these reasons the unions were exceedingly vulnerable: their clientele was heterogeneous and largely disinterested; their treasuries were perpetually empty; their leaders were few in number and subject to the appeal of other jobs; their internal cohesiveness was strained by dissension originating from within and without. It is no surprise that their organizational foothold was shaky. Nor is it surprising that breakaways and the growth of rival unionism have marked the history of most African labor movements. Sometimes tribal elements were at work. Personal rivalries arose frequently. The question of international affiliation was, and in many countries remains, a source of discord. And, most important, underlying most of the other disputes were political or ideological differences which strengthened the tendency toward factionalism.

The dilution of worker protest.—In any modernizing society, economic change brings with it inevitable strains. These strains are particularly intense among wage-earning groups newly recruited to paid employment. Certain features of the African economic environment, however, served to reduce and dilute the potential sources of protest among African wage earners. The postwar years were characterized almost everywhere in the continent by unparalleled economic growth, at least during the 1950's. Postwar aid from metropolitan countries, good prices for Africa's raw materials, the reinvestment of corporate earnings, and, in some areas, the inflow of capital accompanying European immigrants all contributed to raising rates of investment far beyond those of the prewar years, and indeed far beyond those in most other underdeveloped areas of the world. Thus, in the middle years of the decade, almost one-third of the national product of the former Belgian Congo was put aside for capital formation; in the Rhodesias, in the early 1950's, gross investment was more than 40 per cent of national output. In French Tropical Africa the figure was probably near 20 per cent, and in few African countries was it less than 15 per cent. The result of capital formation on this scale was rapid expansion of the money economy.[107]

Expansion of the money economy rapidly increased employment opportunities for Africans. In many countries the recorded number of Africans in paid employment doubled between the late 1940's and the late 1950's. The labor market, even for unskilled labor, was buoyant over most of the decade; in the early 1950's there were acute shortages in some countries. The high level of demand for labor, combined with the introduction of social legislation and the desire of many colonial administrations to "avoid trouble," led to rising levels of real wages in many countries. These rises, following the sharp deterioration of real wages during World War II and the immediate postwar years, had a particularly strong impact.[108]

At the same time, political change combined with expansionary economic trends to create an enormous need for skilled African workers and high-level personnel. For anyone with training there was, and is, unlimited room at the top, or at least near the top.[109] Africa has never known the problem of unemployed intellectuals, as have India and other parts of the world,[110] and has therefore not suffered from the cumulative frustrations arising from blocked ambition. This is not to say that causes of frustration were absent. Among African civil servants, the feeling was widespread that Africanization was too slow, and that expatriates retained too many key jobs. In French Africa, the presence of a poor white

[107] *Economic Survey of Africa since 1950* (New York: United Nations, 1959), chap. 4.

[108] See Elliot J. Berg, "Real Income Trends in West Africa, 1939–1960," in M. J. Herskovits and M. Harwitz, eds., *Economic Transition in Africa* (Evanston: Northwestern University Press, 1963). See also Monckton Commission report, *Report of the Advisory Commission on the Review of the Constitution of Rhodesia and Nyasaland*, Appendix VI, Cmnd. 1149 (London, 1960).

[109] The Rhodesias, where the color bar persisted until the end of the 1950's and has not yet disappeared, are an exception.

[110] There is only one remotely analogous situation. In Ghana and Nigeria massive education programs produced, by the mid-1950's, thousands of primary- and middle-school graduates who could not find the clerical jobs to which people with comparable education had gravitated in earlier years. Few of them would accept unskilled manual labor. As there was no room for them in secondary schools, many remain unemployed or partially employed in Accra, Lagos, and other cities.

(*petit blanc*) class, composed of people with little skill, did obstruct the promotion of Africans to better positions.[111] The color bar in Central Africa and the Asian presence in East Africa created similar, even more acute, tensions. But in most countries the demand for skilled and educated Africans was so urgent, relative to the supply, that upward movement was rapid and easy, particularly as the march toward self-government picked up momentum. Expanding employment opportunities, rising real wages, and wide possibilities for the advancement of skilled and educated Africans served to diminish the tendencies toward dissatisfaction and protest common among newly created labor forces, which were strongly accentuated by the indignities and the inequities of the colonial situation.[112]

Two other factors, of even more basic significance, helped to reduce propensities to protest. The first was the persistence of the migrant labor system. In most of Tropical Africa, the majority of unskilled workers and wage earners are "uncommitted"; they retain a base in their home villages. They are rarely ejected willy-nilly from the rural sector to feed a growing industrial machine. They are peasants, most of them possessing rights over land, who are temporarily in paid employment. They are poor raw material for urban protest movements. Second, the urban wage earner in most of Africa, whether permanently committed to wage employment or not, enjoyed more of the benefits of economic growth than any other major segment of African society. His money income was, and is, much higher than that of his rural cousin. He enjoys more of the amenities of modern life, including better opportunities for his children in school and in finding jobs. During the 1950's, furthermore, his income seems to have increased more rapidly than that of cash-crop growers or other groups.[113]

Competing channels for meeting workers' needs.—All the above-mentioned factors tended to reduce wage earners' dissatisfaction in the postwar period. But the colonial situation and the dislocations of economic and social change nonetheless gave rise to numerous grievances. If the African trade unions had been alone in the field of "protest management,"[114] they would have had ample opportunity to gain the loyalties

---

[111] Berg, "French West Africa," p. 202.

[112] This picture is very broadly drawn. A finer analysis would require many modifications. Possibly the most important distinction is between the period before 1950 and the period after it. In most countries the rise in real wages occurred mainly after 1950; in some countries the period from the end of World War II to 1950 was characterized by declining real incomes for wage earners. It is probably no coincidence that most of the massive protest movements of the postwar period occurred in 1949 or 1950, at the end of a decade of stagnant or deteriorating real wages.

[113] Cf. Berg, "Real Income Trends in West Africa, 1939–1960."

[114] See Clark Kerr, F. H. Harbison, J. T. Dunlop, and C. A. Meyers, "Industrialization and Industrial Man," *International Labour Review,* XXXII (Sept., 1960), 1–15, and their book of the same title published by Harvard University Press in 1960.

of wage earners. But they were not alone. Other organizations and institutions existed for meeting the needs of workers.

Of these, probably the most important and pervasive was the tribal or ethnic association. In most African cities, mining compounds, and industrial centers, tribally based organizations flower. In them, the newcomer to employment finds men who speak his language in every way, men who understand his customs and traditions, men who provide a network of social relations of great vitality. These organizations perform the mutual-benefit functions that were so important in the early development of British and American trade unions. They provide wedding presents, burial services, contact with the villages, gifts for newborn children —the whole range of services performed by family and kin groups in the villages. In most towns, almost everyone belongs to one of these associations, and pays dues that are usually appreciably higher than those demanded by trade unions.

In addition to the tribal union, there is the mass party itself. Organized in every village and neighborhood, the party is an omnipresent claimant of allegiance. The trade-union presence was rarely felt, even in the plant. The party presence was everywhere. The party could provide services requiring political leverage when the wage earner required it.

There was, third, the colonial state. In the twilight period of colonial rule, a strong strain of benevolent paternalism appeared in many colonies. In French and Belgian Africa, it expressed itself most clearly in the form of advanced social legislation, minimum wage laws, and so on. The legal provision for family allowances and a three-week paid vacation in French Africa are illustrative. In British Africa, social legislation was much less developed. But here, as in French Africa, government labor officers, serving as mediating agencies, were active in the broad range of industrial relations problems.

Finally, in much of the continent, paternalism was the predominant management philosophy. The Belgian Congo was, of course, the classic example, with its employer-provided houses, schools, rations, blankets, recreation rooms, medical facilities, and the like. But many large employers elsewhere, particularly mining firms, followed policies not far removed from those of the Belgians.

Other organizations and institutions, then, preëmpted much of the potential union role in meeting workers' needs. The trade union was in fact less effective in this respect than its competitors. The tribal unions performed an acclimatizing function, and provided welfare benefits as well as continuity with the village culture. The mass party made all grievances its province, and was able to touch masses of people with an intensity matched by few other organizations. The party attracted able leaders who quickly produced results in the form of concessions from the colonial power. In the one area where the trade union has a unique and distinctive contribution to make—grievance handling at the shop level—it was rarely active.

We have tried in this paper to show that the image of the African trade union as a political instrument, and as an instrument of great significance, is not in accord with the facts in most of Africa. Some of the factors helpful in explaining the trade-union political role have been outlined above: the fact that unions came into existence before or at the same time as parties, the nature of the political environment, the vulnerability of the unions, the dilution of protest as a result of postwar economic changes, and the existence of other agencies ministering to workers' needs. For all these reasons, African trade unions enjoyed in most countries a large measure of autonomy from parties, and tended at the same time to speak with a small political voice during most of the preindependence period; after independence, they lacked the strength to resist being taken over by governing parties.

The gap between image and reality is so wide in this matter that it is worthwhile to ask how it came into existence. One reason is that Guinea and Kenya, where the image most closely approximates reality, are often taken as typical, whereas they are in fact atypical. But there is a more fundamental reason. All the players on the labor scene in Africa during the colonial period were prone to give the labor movement a political cloak, even when it did not bear one. The colonial administrations, quick to see all African organized effort in political terms, would cry "Politics!" at every turn.[115] The employers were no different: the habit of denouncing all trade-union action as political was prevalent in all African countries, even when political elements were remote. The political parties were hardly averse to claiming trade-union action as their own, and the unions, though denying politicalness at the time, have not objected to an ex post facto glorification of their political role during the colonial period.

This ascription of a political quality to labor unions by all groups

---

[115] After the 1949 incidents at Enugu in Nigeria, the investigating commission wrote: "We consider that the Chief Commissioner and the Committee of officers who advised him, erred in diagnosing and treating the miners' dispute as a political agitation rather than what in our opinion it was—an industrial dispute. We fully appreciate the difficulty of drawing a dividing line, particularly in view of the background; . . . but in the conditions now prevailing in West Africa one of the major problems is to draw that line and the true test of the efficiency of the administration is the ability to do so. . . . There was not a scintilla of evidence to show that, as far as the miners were concerned, there was anything originally political behind the dispute" (*Report of the Commission of Enquiry into the Disorders in the Eastern Provinces of Nigeria, November, 1949,* Colonial no. 256 [London, 1950], pp. 34, 36).

concerned has deceived many outside observers. But observers have often been willingly fooled. They tended to seek out the political quality, to take as typical instances in which it could be found, to exaggerate it when it was in reality insignificant, and to ignore instances in which it was hardly present at all. Most frequently the tendency to highlight and overrate the political aspect of labor organizations springs from an a priori conviction that the labor movement in an underdeveloped, colonial country must be politically involved and significant, that it must be the leading edge of the nationalist reaction. In this sense we have all become Marxists. But the role of the labor movement, and its impact, depend on the particular conditions in a given society, on the historical evolution of relations between unions and parties in that society, and on the special features of its political and economic environment. There is no inner logic that invariably gives wage-earning groups a special political inclination or makes them a particularly strategic element in political life.

10. TRADITIONAL RULERS

By Peter C. Lloyd

In a volume focusing upon the political parties of the modern African state and the groups that have contributed to their growth, it may seem a little odd to include a chapter on the traditional rulers of the indigenous kingdoms, who have been associated with traditionalism and with many of the forces that hinder the development of the modern state. And, of course, it is true that the chiefs have not been in the van of the nationalist movement, at least in recent decades; some writers would see the first nationalist struggles in nineteenth-century encounters between African chiefs and the colonial powers. Yet the picture so often presented of a straight fight between elderly illiterate chiefs, living in the past, and modern Western-educated politicians is not in accord with the facts.

Sociologists often discuss the incompatibility between the norms inherent in a modern parliamentary state and the traditional values of African societies, and such discussions most certainly do have their uses. But they have, I believe, tended to obscure the changes that have taken place in chieftaincy under a half century or more of colonial rule. Today many of Africa's traditional rulers are men who have acquired a substantial amount of Western education; the Western Region of Nigeria and Ghana each counts a barrister among its rulers, and others came to their thrones as wealthy traders. The personal backgrounds of traditional rulers are not unlike those of many of the political leaders, with whom they share an ardent desire to modernize their countries economically and to bring the benefits of the welfare state. Yet they do have a vested interest in retaining the chieftaincy. There are still, of course, many aged and illiterate rulers; but, inasmuch as the chiefs form a group to protect their own interests, it is to the educated ones that leadership falls.

In each African state the emergent political leaders have had the same problem to face: how to turn the allegiance of the masses from their tribe to the state, from their chiefs and elders to the parliamentary leaders. The problem is most serious when the party leaders are largely drawn from an elite which, in its education and ways of thought, and in its style of life, is divorced from the masses. Yet the politicians must recognize the loyalty of the people to their chiefs. In 1947 Obafemi Awolowo wrote:

Events of history and in Europe in recent times have shown conclusively that kings or Paramount Chiefs are not the divine creatures that uncivilised mankind thought them, and that, in the long run, the machinery of government works much more smoothly and swiftly without them than with them. . . . Whatever may be the shortcomings of individual Chiefs, the fact remains that the masses of the people think the world of the office. To them it is inconceivable how the members of a community could cohere together as a political unit without the binding influence of Chiefs as they know them. They revere the office, and regard it as divine. They look upon the Chiefs (who were styled "kings" before the days of British rule) as the representatives of God on earth —the symbols of authority and power and the fountains of law, order, justice. To abolish the office, therefore, would be to remove the keystone which sustains the arch of the local government in the Yoruba-speaking West and the Hausa-speaking North of Nigeria. . . .

But, in a more practical vein, Awolowo continued:

We are concerned primarily with the present and the immediate future. During this period the office of Chiefs will continue to have incalculable sentimental value for the masses in Western and Northern Nigeria. This being so, it is imperative, as a matter of practical politics, that we use the most effective means ready to hand for organising masses for rapid political advancement.[1]

This was Awolowo's blueprint for the future. Thirteen years later, in writing his autobiography, he outlined, in retrospect, the problems that had faced him and his small party in 1951:

A large section of the community whose affairs I was to administer had no faith in my party; and this meant a good deal in a society such as ours where people can be insensate and unreasoning in their likes and dislikes.

Besides, I had to reckon with the Obas and Chiefs who were very jealous of and extremely sensitive about their traditional rights and privileges. In spite of agitation here and there against this or that Oba or Chief, the institution of Obaship and Chieftaincy was still held in high esteem by the people. But the traditional rights and privileges which the Obas and Chiefs wished to preserve were antithetic to democratic concepts and to the yearnings and aspirations of the people. To make a frontal attack on these rights and privileges would be the surest way of bringing a host of hornets' nests about our ears. To compromise with them, on the other hand, would mean death to our new party. The problem which faced me, therefore, was that whilst I must strive to harness the influence of the Obas and Chiefs for our purposes, I must, at the same time, take the earliest possible steps to modify their rights and abrogate such of their privileges as were considered repugnant, to an extent that would both satisfy the commonalty and make the Obas and Chiefs feel secure in their traditional offices.[2]

---

[1] Obafemi Awolowo, *Path to Nigerian Freedom* (London: Faber, 1947), pp. 65–66.

[2] Obafemi Awolowo, *Awo: The Autobiography of Chief Obafemi Awolowo* (London: Cambridge University Press, 1960), pp. 261–262.

In these paragraphs Awolowo vividly outlines the politician's dilemma. How does one, when one's party organization is still underdeveloped, use the traditional rulers to ensure that taxes are collected and that votes are cast for the party while, at the same time, slowly pushing them into the background? Furthermore, how does one reduce the traditional rights of the chiefs as antithetical to democracy while stressing the traditional elements in one's own nationalism? In their attempts to build the new states, political leaders have freely emphasized the glory of Africa's past and the African personality. Furthermore, they have themselves adopted the traditional symbols of authority, such as chieftaincy titles, and Kwame Nkrumah has even assumed royal regalia.

In no two states has the same solution been found. For there are always three variables: the nature of the traditional political system, the effect on it of colonial administration, and the composition and organization of the political party in power. With such variables it is obviously rash to attempt any generalizations about the role of traditional rulers in modern Africa. I shall therefore present three case studies. That of the Yoruba of the Western Region of Nigeria I give at greater length, for it is here that I have carried out my own field work. The Akan kingdoms of Ghana and the Hausa-Fulani emirates of the Northern Region of Nigeria I know only from the literature and from brief visits. These three areas provide an interesting contrast. In Ibadan the Oni of Ife, paramount among the Yoruba *oba*'s, became the first governor of the Western Region, emphasizing both the dignity of the traditional rulers and their role as "constitutional monarchs." In the Northern Region of Nigeria the Northern Peoples' Congress is loosely termed, though not without all justification, the emirs' party. Ghana falls at the other extreme, with the traditional rulers reduced to impotence and with President Nkrumah assuming the title of Osagyefo and such regalia as to suggest that he is the traditional ruler of all Ghana.

THE YORUBA OBA

When we speak of the traditional role of the ruler we are apt to confuse three separate aspects of it. Sometimes we refer to the role actually performed at a point in the historical past, usually in the period preceding colonial rule. At other times we mean those aspects of the current role which are derived from the past and are not in contrast, new roles, or new interpretations of past roles. Third, we may mean the role that people today believe their rulers performed in the past, an idealized role that is given sanctity by its supposed antiquity. In analyzing the position of the oba today, it is this idealized traditional role that is constantly before us, for this is the role that the rulers are continually trying to reinterpret to satisfy the varying and often conflicting expectations of their people, their subordinate chiefs, and the political party leaders. Yet one cannot appreciate this current conflict between traditional rulers and political leaders outside its historical context. Such has been the speed of political change that the reigns of most rulers span several distinct periods. For instance, the late Deji of Akure was enthroned before the British arrived in his town in the early 1890's, and he lived until 1957. He is unique in having lived through the entire period of colonial administration in his town; yet many other rulers, among whom were several educated men, came to their thrones in the 1920's and 1930's in the heyday of indirect rule and native administration.

I shall first outline the traditional role of the Yoruba oba, in terms so general as to embrace the historical and idealized roles of the past and the role that is still performed today. I shall then sketch the pattern of colonial administration so that we may appreciate the actual role of the oba in the mid-twentieth century, when his encounter with modern political activity begins. Finally, I shall describe some of the moves made in the past decade in the very restrained struggle for the supremacy of the political party and its leaders over the traditional rulers.

The Sacred Oba

The Yoruba oba is a sacred king.[3] He is a direct descendant of the original founder of his town, a man whom the myths describe, usually, as one of the sons of Oduduwa, the progenitor of the Yoruba people. The royal title is confined to descendants of this founder-ancestor, that is, to members of the royal lineage. Frequently, only those men born to a reigning oba are eligible to contest the throne. Members of the other lineages that compose the town also trace their descent from immigrant ancestors, but not from Oduduwa. Yet, as all Yoruba are presumed to have descended from Oduduwa, there is no royal clan.

The pattern of the subordinate chieftaincies varies considerably from one town to another. A common pattern in northern Yoruba towns is described briefly. Most titles are hereditary within the lineages, each lineage having one of the major titles and perhaps one or two titles of a minor grade. On the death of a subordinate chief, the members of his lineage meet and select a successor, who is ultimately installed by the oba. The oba himself is selected ultimately by these subordinate chiefs, who, as we have seen, represent the mass of the people. Upon the death of the oba, the elders of the royal lineage present all the eligible candidates to the senior chiefs; these consult the *ifa* oracle to establish the length and the prosperity of the reign of each candidate, should he be chosen. With these predictions and their own personal knowledge of the

---

[3] P. C. Lloyd, "Sacred Kingship and Government among the Yoruba," *Africa*, XXX (1960), 221–237.

candidates, the chiefs make the final choice and set in train the installation ceremonies. In most Yoruba towns the members of the royal lineage
may take no chieftaincy titles that give political power, nor may they
exercise any control over the choice of a successor to the throne.

It is by his installation rites that the oba assumes the sacred powers
of his predecessors. He is often led into the town by the route that the
founder is said to have taken; he performs ceremonies symbolizing the
founder's rebirth; he eats (or used to eat) the excised heart of his predecessor; he is secluded for three months to learn the art of government,
before being finally crowned and led into the palace. Here, in the past,
he lived in seclusion, seen by the public only at major religious festivals.
Government rested with the chiefs, meeting daily on the palace veranda.
The oba was expected to ordain their decisions with his royal sanction. A
delicate balance existed; the oba might divide his chiefs by intrigue, or
they could ultimately depose him, ordering him to die and thus to make
way for a successor. Yet deposition was rare in most towns, for it was
the popular belief that the consecrated ruler would not rule other than
wisely.

The oba is the personification of his town. "Without the oba there
could be no town" say the Yoruba. He maintains peace, for without him
the lineages are presumed to fall to fighting. He is the ritual head of the
town, though not a priest. At annual ceremonies he receives the blessings
of the royal ancestors and of the hill spirits guarding the town, and in
turn he conveys these blessings to his chiefs and his people. He must
provide sacrifices to a host of lesser deities, and it is on the proper performance of such rituals that the prosperity of the town was, in the past,
thought to rest.

The Pattern of Indirect Rule

Hugh Clapperton and the Lander brothers, Richard and John, crossed
the Yoruba country in the 1820's, and mission stations were opened in
Abeokuta in the 1840's and at Ibadan in the following decade. But
European penetration was slow, for the mid-nineteenth century was a
period of incessant tribal wars, with Ibadan raiding eastward for slaves,
holding the Fulani back in the north and struggling with the Ijebu and
the Egba for control of the trade routes to the coast. Between 1886 and
1893 British consular officials visited most of the Yoruba kingdoms,
signing treaties of friendship, peace, and protection; it seems that their
terms were openly debated by the obas and the chiefs. The proclamation of a British protectorate in 1901 was almost certainly without the
explicit knowledge of the obas, and they and their people were probably
unaware of their sudden loss of sovereignty. In the ensuing years British
administrative officers intervened directly in the affairs of the towns where

they were resident. Some obas were protected against the rebellions of their chiefs; others were punished by exile; all learned to regard the administrative officer as their protector whose commands were to be obeyed.

Although British policy, as clearly enunciated, was to uphold the traditional rulers, no real attempt to build a native authority structure was made until Sir Frederick Lugard became governor-general in 1914. Lugard was appalled by the administrative confusion in the Yoruba provinces, and, although it is not clear whether or not he fully appreciated the difference in structure between the Yoruba kingdoms and the Fulani emirates, his subordinates copied the native administration of the latter and constituted the obas as sole native authorities.[4] Not until Sir Donald Cameron's term as governor (1930–1935) were the native authorities reformed so as to include the oba and his chiefs sitting in council. But although this recognition of subordinate chiefs produced councils more akin to those of the traditional system, administrative officers continued to interact closely with the obas, to train them as educated and intelligent chief executive officers of their kingdoms. In 1936 the first of a series of annual chiefs' conferences was held. To attend these meetings many obas left their towns for the first time since their installation. Government policy was discussed, yet the impression was never created that the government was using the obas to propagate its less popular actions, nor were the obas identified with colonial policy.

Lugard and Cameron both felt that they had constructed a system of native administration which would safeguard the status of the oba for many years to come. They intended that the educated African should direct all his political energies into his own local government, and as late as 1937 Margery Perham was echoing their hopes that Nigerians would not enter the colonial administrative service, for this was a superstructure that would ultimately be withdrawn.[5] Their dreams were of an independent Nigeria composed of a federation of native authorities. But the politically conscious Yoruba scorned native administration. The native authorities were made up almost entirely of aged illiterate chiefs; they were small in scale and poverty-ridden, and had few practical powers; they offered little attraction to the clerk, compared with the posts available in Lagos and Ibadan, and tended to attract to their staffs those who were not fit even to be primary school teachers. In the postwar years the idea that a central government could be built upon a federation of native authorities was tacitly dropped by the British. Furthermore, it became

---

[4] Margery Perham, *Lugard: The Years of Authority, 1898–1945* (London: Collins, 1960), chap. xxii.

[5] Margery Perham, *Native Administration in Nigeria* (London: Oxford University Press, 1937), p. 361.

obvious that the native authorities, as constituted, were incapable of organizing social services on the scale demanded. The Colonial Office, in 1947, issued a directive that the needed efficiency, together with a democratic system at the lowest level of government, should be provided by the establishment of English-type local government councils. These were introduced gradually under existing legislation; but it was not until 1953 that, in the Local Government Law, the Action Group's first major enactment, a detailed and uniform framework was set in operation.

The Oba in Mid-Century

At the present time more than three-fourths of the obas of the larger Yoruba kingdoms are men with at least a full primary school education. Most of these came to their thrones when comparatively young—in their thirties or forties—and had spent several years working as teachers or clerks. They live in modern houses which they themselves have built within their traditional palaces. They invariably wear voluminous Yoruba robes and preserve the traditional symbols of royalty, the beaded crown and the staff; but they have also assumed the modern status symbols of wealth—the large house, the big car, and the education of children in England. The modern oba is no longer secluded within the palace, but moves about his town with that restricted freedom enjoyed by English royalty. He rarely makes private visits to the homes of his subjects. He travels frequently to Ibadan; state visits to Lagos are becoming popular, and a trip to England is eagerly sought.

Until the decade of the 1950's the oba was not only the wealthiest man in the town—a position enjoyed by the traditional oba—but he was frequently the best-educated native of the town who lived at home, others having emigrated. This superiority merely enhanced the autocratic role created for him by the administrative officers. Thus the oba converted one or two rooms in the old palace into his office, and furnished them as his status required. Here he sat for a few hours each day with his files, interviewing petitioners, with the telephone at his elbow to consult the administrative officer. Educated men of royal lineage sought the throne not only because they were anxious to preserve it within their own lineage segments, but also because the office gave them the opportunity to bring the benefits of the modern world to their towns. In other words, the educated oba represented not the forces of conservatism, which he had to combat in his subordinate chiefs, but the forces of progress in his town.

The educated oba had to reinterpret the role ascribed to the oba by tradition in the light of the changed economy and the new administrative pattern of the twentieth-century colonial period. He was only partly successful, for though he usually found a role acceptable to his people, he came into conflict with his subordinate chiefs. Whereas the avowed British policy was to preserve the traditional political institutions, the effect of the system of native administration was radically to alter the relationship between the oba and his subordinate chiefs. Instead of the oba being dependent on the advice of his chiefs, he leaned on the initiative of the administrative officer and feared the latter's power of deposition far more than that of his chiefs; the prevalent practice was for the administrative officer to protect the oba from the criticisms of his chiefs and his people.

Most of the chiefs were, as before, elderly and illiterate, and the young and inexperienced oba tended to ignore them; wiser rulers made more display of consulting their chiefs. The chiefs felt, with some justification, that their oba was ultimately responsible (in that the British officials relied heavily on his advice) for their appointment and their salary grading. The newly enthroned oba often tried to purge of corruption the native courts, from which the chiefs drew part of their salaries and numerous perquisites. He encouraged his people to bring their problems directly to him, and no longer to plead through their chiefs; thus another source of income was denied to the chiefs. While the obas became relatively wealthier, the chiefs became poorer, and with their impotence recognized by their own people, they suffered a further loss of prestige. But in the 1930's and the 1940's they still retained sufficient influence to canalize any local discontent against the oba, and most educated rulers have been forced to abdicate their thrones for short periods of time. The obas in turn have endeavored to manipulate the selection of chiefs so as to favor educated men who would be more sympathetic to them. These chiefs, however, with salaries rarely more than a tenth as large as those of their obas, are even more prone to corruption and public disgrace, as they attempt to live in the style that their titles and their education demand.

But if the oba became an autocratic ruler, he was nevertheless a benevolent one, and was usually much loved by his people. Colonial rule was not oppressive; scarcely any measures, at the local level, were unpopular. The oba continued to be the "father of all his people," for his town was not divided into factions. Opposition to colonial rule was largely confined to Lagos, and the very few literates in the provincial towns who were politically active were regarded by most people as irresponsible youths. At best they founded "improvement unions," with which the educated oba actively coöperated. The oba was not often described as a "stooge of the British" by his own people. While ostensibly upholding their own principles of justice, the administrative officers protected the obas from overt criticism by their people.

The expected role of the oba is today reinterpreted by his people. The good oba is one who maintains peace in his town; the need to call a riot squad of police is a serious blot on his record. He brings prosperity by increasing the social services in his town; the most loved oba is one who so badgers the administrative officers that he obtains more schools, dispensaries, and roads than the rival neighboring town. His own wealth, displayed by the modern status symbols, reflects the wealth of his town. It is still expected that the oba should be a legitimate ruler, but the administrative officers have been fairly scrupulous in ensuring that only those candidates eligible under customary law are encouraged to contest for the throne and gain official approval.

The modern oba has little interest in the ritual sacrifices expected of him, and is content to leave them to old women and palace servants. His indifference is shared by most of his people. The mystic aura that surrounded the sacred oba of the past is, of course, fast disappearing. Yet the major annual ceremonies are still performed with much pomp. Today the oba is, in addition, the leader in Christian and Muslim worship; he attends the weekly services of his own faith and his installation ceremonies are usually concluded with services in either church or mosque, or in both. When, however, the people are disappointed in their oba, they are still ready to explain his shortcomings by his inattention to certain traditional rituals or by his lack of legitimacy.

One of the oba's major problems is the upbringing of his children. In the past the royal offspring went to the farm to work, and the entire income of the oba was spent within the palace; all investments in new buildings or regalia passed to his successor in office. The modern oba wishes to give a good education to his children—and he usually has a score or more by his several wives. To do so he must divert the income of the "throne" to the use of his private family; even the most virtuous ruler follows this policy, despite cries of protest from his chiefs and his people. Corrupt obas, who may make excessive demands of their people, are unpopular, but it was difficult, under colonial rule, to remove them permanently by exile. Lesser measures, such as pressing for a reduction in the oba's salary, were not liked because they would presumably punish equally the more popular successors to the throne. And it seems to have been difficult to organize any concerted opposition to the oba; at the crucial moment leaders changed sides.

Thus, in mid-century, when the Action Group came to power, the oba was an autocrat; yet he often was well educated and efficient, and popular with his people. And so it was the task of the new political leaders to combat the autocracy, while depending heavily on the influence and the popularity of the obas to achieve their own programs.

The New Role of the Oba

In 1951 the Action Group won the parliamentary elections in the Western Region, and its leader, Obafemi Awolowo, a brilliant lawyer of somewhat puritanical habits and little charismatic appeal, became the

391   *Traditional Rulers*

minister of local government.[6] As he inferred in the quotation given earlier, his party did not have widespread popular support. The main tasks he confronted were to weld the elected members into a party, to establish support for the party among the masses, and to bring local administration under the firm control of the regional government.[7]

Nationalist politicians in Lagos had seen the traditional rulers as their rivals for power, as colonial administrators had dreamed of powerful native authorities federating in a self-governing Nigeria. Yet by 1945 the fear of traditional rulers was dated. In competing with the obas for power and popular allegiance, the politicians seized instead upon the conflicts between individual obas and their people, describing these as the direct and inevitable result of British rule. "Today, however," wrote Awolowo in 1947, "the constitutional position of a Yoruba Chief is the opposite of the traditional one. . . . [Peace] can only be achieved by restoring as far as is compatible with present-day development the traditional relationship between Chief and people." [8] At this time he advocated that an oba should be deposed if two-thirds of the members of the native authority council voted in favor of such a step. In 1950 the Action Group's policy paper on local government stressed the same themes.

Though anxious to achieve power for themselves, most Action Group legislators had grown up as responsible citizens of their home towns and retained a deep reverence for kingship. The Action Group itself had adopted many of the political aims of the Egbe Omo Oduduwa, the cultural association of which Awolowo was secretary. (The Egbe soon became defunct as the cultural organization of the elite; but it has been revived in recent years as an annual conference of hundreds of obas and chiefs, who meet to hear ministers explain government policy.) Soon after Awolowo became a minister, chieftaincy titles were bestowed upon him by his home town and other towns; it has become the practice for each minister to obtain a title, either a traditionally recognized or a newly created one; to be addressed as "Chief, the Honourable"; and to wear the coral necklace symbolic of chieftaincy. Traditional office thus legitimizes the authority of the new political leaders.

---

[6] In 1962 a split occurred in the Action Group. The federal government declared a state of emergency to exist in the Western Region, and appointed an administrator and commissioners to exercise the functions of government within the region. Parliamentary government was restored at the beginning of 1963 with the creation of a coalition between one faction of the Action Group—the United People's Party (UPP), led by the earlier Action Group premier, Chief S. L. Akintola—and the National Convention of Nigerian Citizens (NCNC). Those members of the Action Group who remained loyal to Awolowo constituted the opposition. In this interparty contest the obas were not identified, as a group, with either faction. They are overtly loyal to the new UPP-NCNC coalition government of the Western Region.

[7] P. C. Lloyd, "The Development of Political Parties in Western Nigeria," *American Political Science Review*, XLIX (Sept., 1955), 693–707.

[8] Awolowo, *Path to Nigerian Freedom*, pp. 73, 75.

The Oni of Ife is regarded as the father of all the Yoruba obas. It is therefore significant, though it was a historical accident, that the Oni installed in 1930 was a well-educated man. Sir Adesoji Aderemi became a prominent member of the old Legislative Council and of several government boards, and ultimately a loyal supporter of the Action Group. He became a federal minister in 1953, later president of the Western House of Chiefs, and ultimately, in 1960, governor of the region, thus subtly combining the highest posts in both the traditional and the modern hierarchies, and emphasizing the continuing dignity and prestige of the former.

The statements of the politicians that they wanted to preserve Yoruba kingship must not be regarded as mere hypocrisy. The legislation of the decade does, however, illustrate the role that the party intends for the oba.

In the debates that preceded the introduction of the Macpherson Constitution of 1951, the future role of the traditional rulers was a central issue. Some argued that obas would lose their prestige if they had to mix on equal terms with politicians, many of whom were thought of as the rabble of their towns. Others feared that if the obas were reduced to an ineffectual status, their frustration would breed discontent and opposition. The chiefs' conferences had been abolished in 1947, though obas continued to sit in the House of Assembly from that date. In 1951 it was decided to set up the House of Chiefs, modeled constitutionally on the British House of Lords. Meeting together, the obas have developed a much stronger sense of their unity as a group. Although all have nominally been Action Group supporters, and although the House of Chiefs has been anxious not to oppose any measure of the lower house and thus cause an open rift between obas and politicians, the obas have exerted considerable pressure in committee meetings in support of their own interests.

The Local Government Law of 1952 established councils on an English model. Not more than one-fourth of the council members were selected by and from among the traditional chiefs of the area; the remaining members were elected by secret ballot. The House of Chiefs raised a weak and ineffectual protest that traditional members should constitute one-third of the total council membership. In the initial bill it was proposed that the oba should be president of the council, and should perform ceremonial functions. This was contested in the lower house, and the law stipulated that the oba might preside at all council meetings, taking precedence over the elected chairman. The amending law of 1957 provided that the oba might be a candidate for the office of chairman, but, if not elected, should preside over meetings only when invited to do so by the council.

Earlier pronouncements notwithstanding, the Action Group retained for the government full control over the appointment and the deposition of obas and chiefs, resisting any suggestion that local government councils might have these powers in order to express "the popular will." As in colonial days, decisions of the government in such matters may not be questioned in the courts. But the provisions of the relevant law have aroused controversy. Initially a declaration of the customary law relating to chieftaincy was to be made by the relevant local government council; that is, the elected councilors were given the controlling voice. As later amended, the law provides that the president and the traditional members alone shall make the declaration. The obas defeated a provision in the original bill that councilors should sit with the chiefs in selecting the oba. Another provision, stipulating that preference should be given to a candidate for a throne who was literate in English, was dropped in amending legislation. The original clause was justified by government speakers on the ground that the oba had important functions in the government of his town, but it perhaps reflected a feeling that literate obas were more loyal to the Action Group.

The Communal Land Rights (Vesting in Trustees) Law of 1958 enables the government to appoint boards of trustees to manage so-called "communal land." The intention of the government that local government councils might be appointed as trustees was frustrated by the obas, and it was enacted that where land was vested under customary law in an oba and chiefs, these persons should be appointed as the trustees. The government, however, has the right to dictate, within the terms of the instrument it grants, the use of any revenue. This law was passed to meet a few specific local problems and does not suggest widespread mismanagement of land by obas and chiefs.

Under the Customary Court Law of 1957, which places such courts under the control of the attorney general and the Ministry of Justice, only the statutory criminal code may be administered in the courts; no longer may the courts recognize offenses known only to customary law, such as disrespect to an oba or a chief. The courts retain considerable civil jurisdiction, and customary law is still followed in cases involving land and personal status. Thus an oba no longer has the legal means to enforce the orders he gives in the traditional manner. In fact, an oba usually expresses his reforms through local government bylaws, and he has not been slow, along with councilors and others in positions of power, to realize the potentialities of victimizing one's opponents through offenses against such bylaws or through the punishment of tax defaulters in the courts.

At the end of the decade the government set up a committee of obas and chiefs which advises it on all matters relating to chieftaincy; the prestige of the traditional rulers, the politicians claim, will thus be preserved. The failure of the politicians to gain direct control over obas and chiefs should not, however, be seen as a defeat. Initially they sought such control, but as the party gained power over local government councils and over the local judicial system, and as the obas accepted the new regime with fewer signs of reluctance, the need for it has disappeared. At present the government could probably oppose the obas with impunity, though there is no need for so rash a measure. The less intelligent obas in the House of Chiefs have repeatedly asked the government to define their role; such a definition would certainly not be in their interests, and none has been given. These legislative changes have, however, indirectly affected the status of the oba in his home town, reducing in most instances his popularity and thus rendering him a less useful agent of the government and the party.

The introduction of local government councils, first by the colonial administration and then by the Action Group government, was a matter of policy and did not reflect, in most areas, any local demand for change. But once the councils were inaugurated, their personnel have tended to exploit their potentialities to the full.

In the past decade local government councils have become much wealthier bodies than the native authorities which they displaced. Tax rates have been increased fivefold, and more government grants-in-aid are available. The caliber of the council staff has been greatly improved. And, most significantly, the level of wealth and of education of the councilors is higher; in most towns there are few illiterates on the councils, and frequently university graduates have been elected. With the expansion of education and social services, many more of the well-educated Yoruba now live and work in their home towns. The oba no longer occupies the preëminent position that he held in the 1930's and 1940's.

The elected councilors have often had exaggerated ideas of the powers of their council. Instead of seeing it as a body with powers limited by statute, they regard it as a local parliament with sovereign authority, and adopt English parliamentary procedure in their debates. Again they presume that they have inherited all the powers wielded by the former native authority, including the traditional rights of the oba and the chief. The Ministry of Local Government has been active in preserving these rights for their customary holders. Local councilors have been even more interested than national politicians in curbing the autocracy of the oba. Initially the obas presided over council meetings, but more recently they have given way to the elected chairmen. In some towns the councilors have exacted from their oba a promise that he would not communicate with the administrative officer without their consent; in one town they appropriated the oba's typewriter in order to immobilize him. The councilors have argued, with justification, that it was incongruous for the oba to continue to sign all manner of permits—for building, drumming, cutting down trees—as they should be signed by the competent council officials; these officials and the councilors now pocket the perquisites hitherto received by the oba! The educated oba, naturally reluctant to see effective power slipping from his grasp, has often attempted to resist the changes. Frequently the council's response is to attempt to cut the oba's salary, which they now control. Here again ministry officials step in to protect the oba. But the new councils have been reluctant to make salary increases for obas proportionate to general salary increases within the country.

When the colonial administrative officers became advisers to the local government councils, their active support of the oba was suddenly withdrawn. Most of them, as expatriates uncertain of their future in an independent Nigeria, were quite anxious not to become involved in local political struggles. The oba has therefore turned for support to the government and to the party in power. Although the educated oba has probably felt considerable personal sympathy for the Action Group policies, he has also felt that he must display his support of the party so that he would be protected against attacks by the councilors. For its own part, the Action Group tended to win political support by gaining the allegiance of men locally influential, rather than by campaigning at mass meetings. Party leaders have usually behaved respectfully to obas whose towns they visit. The NCNC was of course always ready to accuse its rival of lowering the prestige of the traditional rulers; this could have been a powerful election weapon early in the decade. The government was embarrassed when Action Group councils openly opposed an Action Group oba, for it had to resolve the quarrel without losing the support of either faction.

All has not been gentle. Just as the first decade of this century saw a rather turbulent adjustment by the obas to British rule, so in the 1950's obas had to adjust to Action Group rewards or punishments. In 1954 the government deported the Alafin of Oyo, ruler of the largest Yoruba kingdom, "in the interests of peace, order and good government"—the hallowed colonial formula. His fault was that he allowed the NCNC to hold a meeting in his palace—the majority of his people at the time being NCNC supporters—which resulted in a riot. The commission of inquiry that was appointed to investigate revealed the existence of a petty autocracy, yet proved none of the graver charges against the Alafin. Educated obas had frequently pleaded with the aged and illiterate Alafin to mend his ways; his deposition was a warning to other obas.[9] On the other hand, the Action Group government recently dissolved the NCNC-dominated

---

[9] "A Crown Falls," *West Africa,* June 25, 1955, p. 583.

Ilesha District Council on the ground that it exceeded its powers in trying to depose the Action Group Oba of Ilesha. Not all dissolutions of councils have been for political reasons; the Action Group government has also dissolved them for inefficiency in carrying out their statutory duties.

Several obas supported by the Action Group have been rulers of towns in which the NCNC has the support of the majority, or of a large minority, of the people. Such men have been in an invidious position. Party politics has divided the town into factions as British rule never did; the oba can no longer be father to all his people. In his conflicts with his people he has leaned more heavily on government support, thereby losing even more prestige. It is perhaps significant that most of the obas who have been made ministers without portfolio in the regional government suffer conflicts of this nature. Their new offices give them an excuse to spend much of their time in Ibadan; yet they are on a downward spiral, and party patronage is, in fact, the kiss of death for them.

The oba is sometimes asked to choose between the interests of his town and those of the party he supports. During the discussion of the future status of Lagos in 1953, the Awujale of Ijebu was pressed by the NCNC faction in his town to campaign for the restoration of the lagoon-side town of Epe to his kingdom, and thus indirectly to further the cause of making Lagos the federal capital. He remained silent on the issue, preferring to risk the displeasure of one segment of his people rather than that of the Action Group.

No longer the wealthiest men in their towns, no longer the ostensible creators of peace, prosperity, and progress, the modern obas are not able to perform the traditional roles expected of them. In spite of the recent legislation, party politics intrude into the selection of obas and chiefs more overtly than British intervention ever did in the past. But as their old roles became impossible to perform, no new ones seem to be evolving, in the manner, for instance, that the British royal family has become the paradigm of family life. Even as ceremonial figureheads, they are often eclipsed by ministers and local politicians who want to be in the limelight themselves.

The Action Group government has stressed the notion that, by removing the oba from active participation in local government, it is restoring him to his traditional status and thus eliminating the bases of conflict with his people; the obas should therefore gain in prestige and popularity. Yet the government seems not to have worked out the full implications of its policy. Nor in fact need it have done so, for, whereas the British colonial administration aimed to rule through obas and chiefs, the Action Group built up an administrative structure separate from them. The party, in its early period of development, used the traditional rulers to win mass support. When it had gained this end it could treat the obas as archaic survivals, to be used, honored, and even respected so long as they were so respected by their people. The educated oba himself feels that kingship will probably survive his own reign, but not much longer.

THE FULANI EMIRS

In the years following 1804 the jihad swept across northern Nigeria. Power in the ancient Hausa or Habe kingdoms was seized by coalitions of Fulani *mallam*'s and pastoral Fulani headsmen. In each kingdom a similar pattern emerged: a learned mallam assumed the leadership, receiving his authority from Othman dan Fodio, the instigator of the jihad, at Sokoto; his sons in turn assumed the royal title of *seriki* (now rendered as emir). Thus northern Nigeria—the Hausa-speaking states, together with those of the Nupe at Bida, of the Yoruba at Ilorin, and of the Fulani and others in Adamawa—was united under a set of rulers with a common faith, Islam, vigorous and proselyting, owing allegiance to the *shehu* or sultan of Sokoto, and receiving from him military support. Later in the century the spiritual leadership of Sokoto was emphasized, its ruler having taken the title of *seriki musulmani,* or ruler of all the Muslims. In ensuing decades Fulani rule was consolidated with the conquest of non-Muslim groups living on the periphery of the Hausa states. And the Fulani assumed within the emirates almost all positions of political power, becoming in fact a feudal aristocracy.

The country was divided into fiefs held by members of the lineages of the emir himself and of the descendants of other Fulani prominent in the original conquest. The fief holders, bearers of chiefly titles, were appointed by the emirs; they in turn chose their own subordinates from their junior kin and their slaves, selecting as village heads local men of whom they approved. Some of the non-Muslim vassal states, however, continued to be governed by their indigenous rulers, subject to the authority of the emirs.

The emir ruled as an autocrat; unlike the Yoruba oba and his chiefs, he had no formal council of advisers which held regular meetings. In his government he was, of course, influenced by the opinions of his chiefs; he felt obliged to rule within the principles of Islam, and ultimately he could be deposed. But Sokoto was ever anxious to prevent any crisis that might weaken the fabric of the Fulani empire. In Zaria, for example, where the emir's title rotated among four royal lineages, each new ruler deposed the chiefs from lineages other than his own, consolidating his power by appointing in their places his own near kin and clients.[10]

---

[10] M. G. Smith, *Government in Zazzau, 1800–1950* (London: Oxford University Press, 1960), gives the only detailed account of the government of a Hausa-Fulani emirate.

The common peasantry, the *talakawa,* did not participate directly in the government of their emirate. They had no part in the selection of the emirs or of his chiefs. Against administrative malpractices, their only safeguard lay in a system of patronage. A man became the client of a minor official (who was in turn the client of a more important one, and so on to the emir himself) who would use his influence to protect his follower. Justice was administered, according to Islamic law, by the *alkali,* though the highest court was that of the emir himself. M. G. Smith believes that in the nineteenth century the alkali's courts were relatively free from political control.

At the turn of the century these emirates were conquered by British troops. On assuming the governorship of Northern Nigeria in 1900, Lugard was anxious to extend his rule to the limits of the protectorate, as defined by the British; his justification was the responsibility of Britain to eradicate slavery. The Fulani autocracy fled from their towns, and the talakawa offered no resistance. The restoration of the original Hausa rulers was postulated, but discarded as creating ethnographic problems far too large for Lugard's handful of political officers. Reigning emirs were therefore deposed, to be replaced, in most instances, by their dynastic rivals, as yet untainted by rule. Lugard saw the possibilities of the indigenous system of administration in formulating his own theories of native administration by indirect rule. In his autocratic and pragmatic manner he would have probably held the emirs under a firm rein and introduced Western education as quickly as possible. His successors, however, were more impressed by the indigenous culture and sought to preserve rather than reform it. Change was held to threaten the status of the emir and thus of the whole structure of native administration, a possibility not to be contemplated when, by the 1920's and 1930's, the emirates were the showpieces of British imperial policy.[11]

The emir, designated as sole native authority, remained an autocrat, subject to British overrule. The emirate was divided into territorial districts over which senior chiefs were appointed as district heads; they in turn selected new village heads whom the emirs then appointed. There were few jobs for minor chiefs. But the number of offices in the emir's patronage was maintained by his right of appointment of the head of each native administration department. These departmental heads in turn selected their own subordinates. The British insisted that officeholders could be deposed only for maladministration, and not for belonging to the wrong dynastic faction; the emirs soon learned how to manipulate the new situation. Once validly dismissed, however, men were rarely reappointed to office; thus a reigning emir could sharply reduce the

---

[11] Perham, *Lugard: The Years of Authority,* chaps. v–viii; Perham, *Native Administration in Nigeria,* chaps. v, vii–viii.

chance that a rival lineage would ever again achieve power. To control dismissals, the emir had to control the judicial system; the emir of Zaria achieved this by making the office of chief alkali subject to political maneuvering. Thus in 1945 the staff of the Zaria Native Authority comprised 529 northerners, of whom 120 belonged to the emir's own lineage, 124 to the three other royal lineages and that of the chief alkali, 99 to other Fulani lineages, and only 186 to non-Fulani (i.e., talakawa) families.[12]

In 1950 the government of the Zaria Emirate was "an autocracy ineffectively supervised by the British."[13] The native authorities, controlled by the emirs, were large and powerful bodies. Their scale is suggested by the fact that the largest one, in Kano, today spends £2 million annually. Services that are provided by the regional governments in the Eastern and Western regions, with their small fragmentary units, are, in the north, controlled by the native authorities; they run hospitals, secondary schools, and waterworks. Almost all prisons in the Northern Region are controlled by native authorities, and it is usual for the emirates to be policed by their own forces (ultimately under the emirs' control), whereas the federal Nigeria police are posted to the non-Muslim areas. When the British administrators dreamed of a self-governing Nigeria as a federation of native authorities, they were thinking of such units as the emirates; the impossibility of creating them in the Ibo country frustrated their hopes. The Northern Region has, in addition, remained economically backward. Far poorer than either the Eastern or the Western Region, its export crops—cotton and groundnuts—come mainly from the Katsina, Kano, and Zaria areas; two-thirds of the farmers of the region grow no export cash crop. Only 2 per cent of the children of school age in Sokoto Province attend school, though the Kano Emirate is planning universal primary education. Most technical posts and offices in the federal government departments have, in the past, been filled by southerners, or at best by northerners from the Middle Belt (and particularly by Yoruba from Kabba and Ilorin provinces), where education is far more widespread. Within the emirates the educated Fulani youth tends to seek employment in the native administration, where his birth offers him better opportunities of promotion to chiefly office. But Lugard's plan, that the future rulers of the country be given the kind of education available in the best English public schools, was possible of realization, given the political condition of the emirates; it was not, of course, practicable in the Yoruba kingdoms, where it is impossible to predict upon whom the mantle of kingship or chieftaincy might fall. In recent years a number of well-educated emirs have been installed, and many native authority depart-

[12] Smith, *op. cit.*, p. 273.
[13] *Ibid.*, p. 291.

ment heads are men of considerable ability. Most are products of Katsina College. These rulers, like their Yoruba counterparts, are progressive inasmuch as they seek such improved social services for their emirates as can be afforded. But, again like the obas, they are prepared to promote reforms only within the framework of the existing political system.

The Emirs and the Government Today

The Northern Peoples' Congress (NPC) began as a group of moderate radicals, most of whom were either Fulani by birth or were sons of slave officeholders and thus in positions of clientage to the emirs.[14] Yet these men were intensely critical of the native administration system as it existed in 1950. At that time Abubakar Tafawa Balewa, now federal prime minister but then an unofficial member of the Northern House of Assembly, introduced a motion for an independent inquiry into native administration. In a scathing but concisely argued speech, he attacked the inefficiency, the illiteracy, and the corruption of the native authority staff, the autocracy of the emirs, and the British administration which protected such abuses:

> One of the biggest defects of the [native authority] system is the complete ignorance of everyone from top to bottom about his rights, his obligations, and his powers. . . . The people must be made to realize they too have a share in their own government. . . . In the past their views have never been sought, their welfare seldom regarded and their helplessness shockingly abused. . . . There is hardly a single district head in the North who sits in his district with the full knowledge of his work and who can send comprehensive regular reports about his district. . . . Native Administrative servants have monetary obligations to their immediate superiors and to their sole Native Authorities [i.e., the emirs]. . . . Much of the attraction of a post lies in the opportunities it offers for extortion of one form or another.[15]

Balewa cited the progress made in local government in the Eastern and Western regions, and protested that his plea was for reform, not for destruction of the native authority system. As president of the House of Assembly, the lieutenant governor of the region replied, stating his government's aim of continued reform but vehemently objecting to such an inquiry as Balewa had proposed. The remaining unofficial members, including men who are still prominent, such as Muhammadu Ribadu (federal minister of defense) and Shettima Kashim (governor of the Northern Region), voted unanimously for the motion. It was carried by one vote against the equally unanimous vote of the official members, the

---

[14] See James S. Coleman, *Nigeria: Background to Nationalism* (Berkeley and Los Angeles: University of California Press, 1958), chap. 17.

[15] *Northern Region House of Assembly Debates,* Aug. 19, 1950, pp. 91–98 *passim.*

most senior civil servants and residents. But the proposed inquiry was never carried out.

With the establishment of parliamentary government in the Northern Region, the control of the Northern Peoples' Congress passed from the moderate radicals to the emirs and their supporters. The majority of the elected representatives were Fulani; many were close kin of the emirs, and most of them held native administration offices. No NPC candidate is likely to be successful without the support of his emir. In effect, membership in a legislature has become one of the offices within the emirs' patronage. To many ministers their offices are steppingstones on the way to senior offices in their home towns; their loyalty is given first to their emirates, and second to the region. (Shettima Kashim, for example, passed from being a federal minister to become, first, the Waziri of Bornu and, later, the first Nigerian governor of the Northern Region; the present Emir of Bida, the Etsu Nupe, was earlier a federal minister.) Throughout the decade of the 1950's the party's local organization was weak. In default of an alternative source of literate men, elections are supervised by the native authority staff; order is maintained by native authority police. The air of the north is thick with tales of vicious intimidation; their truth is immaterial, inasmuch as they are believed by most would-be supporters of any opposition party.

Since 1952, when leadership of the party passed to Ahmadu Bello, Sardauna of Sokoto and widely expected to be successor to the Sultan, radical critics have tended to be banished, whether as legislators or bureaucrats, to Lagos. In 1950 the program of the NPC contained a proposal that there should be a wider representation on the committee electing an emir; the deletion of this proposal in 1952 was a significant token of the change of emphasis in party policy. The clause proposing the reform of native administration within the emirate system was reinforced by the phrase, "according to tradition and custom."

The past decade has seen little general change in the status of the Fulani emirs. They are no longer sole native authorities; the emir with his council is now the gazetted authority. Yet the emir's selection of his chiefs remains unaltered. Various suggested local government reforms have not been implemented. A written criminal code, based on both Muslim and English law, is now in operation, and higher courts of appeal in Muslim law have been set up. But the lower courts of the emirs and the alkalis function much as before. Yet the government has demonstrated its ultimate power over the emirs. Some minor rulers have been deposed for corruption or old age, although no major ruler so suffered until 1963. In that year an inquiry into the affairs of the Kano Native Authority by a senior expatriate administrative officer revealed so much corruption that the Emir of Kano was obliged, under strong pressure from the Northern Region government, to resign and live in exile outside his kingdom. It is believed that the government allowed him, nevertheless, a handsome gratuity and pension. The immediate successor to the throne died after a reign of a few months. He has now been succeeded by Alhaji Ado Bayero, younger brother of the deposed Emir. At thirty-three years of age he has already served as head of Kano Native Authority police and as Nigerian ambassador to Senegal. Of radical political views, he will certainly redefine the role of emir. Other rulers owe their thrones to government influence indirectly wielded; the new Emir of Ilorin, whose right to rule was locally questioned, had been a senior native authority official and the town's leading NPC organizer.

Scholars who have studied Fulani rule have been so impressed by its stability that they have considered it impregnable; as late as 1959 one of them wrote: "It is unlikely that this quality of the regime will change significantly in the near future without considerable pressure." [16] Others, perhaps more in hope than in anticipation, think that an explosive revolution against autocracy is inevitable in the near future. Certainly it is difficult to see at the present time any definite cracks in the structure; yet it does seem most likely that the party will seek for and achieve power through methods very like those adopted by the Action Group in the Western Region. The party still contains its original moderate radicals, even though their radicalism seems to have been tempered. Many party officials belong to the talakawa, and not only do these men not owe their posts to their emirs, but they tend to be very critical of their autocracy.

In its attempt to control the whole of the Northern Region, and thus virtually prevent an Action Group–NCNC coalition from ever assuming power in the federal government, the NPC must seek the allegiance of the tribal unions that control the votes of the Middle Belt; it must give party and ministerial offices to their leaders, men who have no sympathy with the emirate system. The vigorous campaigning of the Action Group forced the NPC into the field to make a popular appeal to the masses; the northern party tends to emphasize loyalty to Islam and prevention of infiltration of southern faiths, persons, habits, and parties. The usual identification of the NPC with the emirs lead some to overlook the party's success in organizing the mineworkers into a trade union, which supports the party. The NPC is becoming much more broadly based.

As the regional civil service increases in size, there is a tendency for its members to be drawn from better-educated groups in the Middle Belt and from the talakawa. It is commonly believed now, however, that preference is being given to men from the emirates, who will be more sympathetic toward the existing regimes. Yet these men also are not

[16] Smith, *op. cit.*, p. 293.

within the patronage system of the emirs, and they are anxious to wield power. Ministers who do not aspire to offices in their emirates are loath to remain without effective power, watching the social services for which they are responsible being managed exclusively by the native authorities. Clashes have occurred when the regional government has sought to take control of waterworks and hospitals. The emirs are, of course, reluctant to lose control over any office formerly within their patronage.

Although the native authorities of the emirates remain almost unchanged, local government councils have been widely introduced in the Middle Belt. They were even started in the Ilorin Emirate, though here the Yoruba population elected a council with a majority supporting a local opposition party (allied with the Action Group). The council, which soon came into conflict with the emir and his chiefs and with the native authority staff, was dissolved by the regional government. This experience may serve as a deterrent to other emirates. Yet it is hard to see how they can resist such reforms for many more years. The experience of the Western Region has shown how quickly local government councils can erode the autocracy of the traditional rulers, for the two institutions are completely incompatible. The spread of education and of other services, though having little immediate apparent effect, will surely begin to stir the mass of the peasantry into believing that they too have a right to participate in their local government. Their interpretations of Islam may no longer stress obedience to their traditional rulers.

Neither the regional government nor the Northern Peoples' Congress seems to have any plans for the future of local government in the emirates, nor for the status of the emirs themselves. Open conflict between the government and the party, on the one hand, and the emirs on the other is at present checked by the Sardauna, the leader of both groups. The pattern of change may well parallel that in the Western Region, with the political leaders continually assuring the traditional rulers of their loyalty and support, preserving to them many traditional prerogatives, yet effectively withdrawing their autocracy from them.

THE RULERS OF SOUTHERN GHANA

The two preceding sections have dealt with rulers of kingdoms having ethnic homogeneity with one another; in Ghana the field is limited by the modern political boundaries of the erstwhile colony, comprising the Eastern and Western provinces and the province of Ashanti. Here we have the Akan rulers, termed *ohene*, together with the rulers of the Ga and Adangme kingdoms. Yet writers have not differentiated between these rulers in discussing their response to British rule or to the politically independent state; I, in turn, feel that the generalizations possible within this short section may apply throughout the area.

The type of chieftaincy and the economy in southern Ghana are very similar to those of Yoruba country. The main task here, therefore, is to show why the traditional rulers of Ghana have become more impotent, apparently, than the Yoruba obas.

The Akan ohene (and I here include all the rulers covered in this section) is a sacred king.[17] He must be chosen from the lineage of the founder of the town; his advisers, termed elders in his area, are the heads of the other lineages comprised by the town. He must be guided by their decisions, and he may be destooled by them. Like the Yoruba oba, he is the father of his people, the embodiment of the town's life, its peace and prosperity; the rituals he performs ensure the well-being of the town. The kingdoms were in many instances grouped into military confederacies, in which each one maintained its traditional internal government. The largest confederacy, with a high degree of cohesion, was that of Ashanti, and the Asantehene was its paramount ruler. The present population of the Ashanti confederacy is more than a million.

In the present century southern Ghana has become a country of moderately prosperous, by African standards, peasant cocoa farmers. Mission education is widespread. There are, however, important differences from the Yoruba kingdoms. Southern Ghana is small in area and many of its kingdoms lie close to the coast. Their rulers and people have long had contact with Europeans. Whereas in Nigeria the influence of the old Lagos families—mainly Yoruba of Sierra Leonean and Brazilian origin—has been completely eclipsed, the families of Cape Coast and the neighboring towns continue to be relatively important in Ghanaian political life. The coastal kingdoms were intermittently at war with the European powers in the nineteenth century. Ashanti was subdued in a series of battles and occupied by the British, and the Asantehene was exiled to the Seychelles for many years. One result of this closer contact with Britain is, of course, the much longer history of education in the coastal kingdoms than in most Yoruba towns.

The cocoa belt of Ghana lies away from the coast; it is an area much less densely populated than that of the Yoruba. To the forests have migrated thousands of farmers, seeking land suitable for cocoa. The market towns that have grown up in the present century are largely peopled by strangers, many of the younger ones being the "veranda boys" from whom the Convention People's Party (CPP) derived much of its early support. In 1948 more than half of the 78,000 inhabitants of Kumasi, capital of Ashanti, were non-Ashanti, and less than half of the remainder were

---

[17] R. S. Rattray, *Ashanti* (London: Milford, 1923); M. J. Field, *Akim-Kotoku* (London: Crown Agents for the Colonies, 1948); K. A. Busia, *The Position of the Chief in the Modern Political System of Ashanti* (London: Oxford University Press, 1951).

natives of the Kumasi town and kingdom.[18] These strangers feel no allegiance to the rulers in whose kingdoms they reside. This situation is in marked contrast with the Yoruba towns where, Ibadan excepted, more than 90 per cent of the population is native. Land is rented to the immigrant strangers by those rulers and elders in whom is vested the vacant land of town (or stool) and lineage, and they receive enormous incomes from this source. These are further augmented by fees and royalties paid by expatriate firms for rights to exploit timber and minerals. Such wealth, held to belong to the whole community, has in fact been largely used to maintain the rulers and their elders in comparative luxury; it has also been one of the prime reasons for the slow development of native administration in Ghana.

The Gold Coast Colony was created in 1874. Four years later the Native Jurisdiction Ordinance was passed, but it was not put into force until it was amended and reënacted in 1883.[19] Thus the history of British administration in Ghana antedates that in Northern Nigeria by twenty-five years. In Ghana, government through local rulers was interpreted in a laissez-faire manner, allowing the rulers and their councils to function in the traditional fashion and granting them only such extra functions as seemed expedient. The 1883 law did little more than give British recognition to the indigenous rulers and elders, allowing them to make bylaws and to exercise limited civil and criminal jurisdiction. No tax was imposed. This law remained in force until 1927, though it was quite inadequate to meet the social and economic changes of the twentieth century. Rulers, fearing destoolment, were reluctant to make bylaws or to enforce them; yet the colonial administrative officer had no authority to intervene, for only by a government ordinance could the colonial power institute local regulations. The income from stool lands was administered by the rulers without any supervision; they and their chiefs similarly shared the court fees. No provision existed for the creation of native treasuries, the keystones of native administration. A law of 1904 empowered the government to confirm the installation of a ruler and so render his position unassailable in law; but it did not prohibit a traditional ruler from exercising legal powers until formally recognized as a native authority.

---

[18] David E. Apter, *The Gold Coast in Transition* (Princeton: Princeton University Press, 1955), p. 163.
[19] The development of local government in southern Ghana is discussed in Lord Hailey, *Native Administration in the British African Territories* (London: H.M.S.O., 1951), Part III, chap. viii, secs. i, ii; Raymond L. Buell, *The Native Problem in Africa* (2 vols.; New York: Macmillan, 1928); F. M. Bourret, *Ghana: The Road to Independence, 1919–1957* (rev. ed.; London: Oxford University Press, 1960); Busia, *op. cit.;* George Padmore, *The Gold Coast Revolution* (London: Dobson, 1953), chap. ix; and David Kimble, *A Political History of Ghana* (Oxford: Clarendon Press, 1963).

By 1927 the Gold Coast government felt constrained to reform native administration, following the principles adopted in Northern Nigeria and elsewhere, but the intelligentsia opposed any move that would transform the traditional rulers into autocrats and delay the introduction of elected parliaments and courts subordinate to the Supreme Court. The Native Administration (Colony) Ordinance of 1927 was, therefore, a compromise. It again did little more than regularize the traditional councils of rulers and elders, termed state councils; again there was no provision for native treasuries to control stool funds, nor were the powers of state councils delimited by the government. Not until 1939 was a law passed providing for the establishment of treasuries that would be subject to administrative control.

This move paved the way for the more comprehensive reforms of 1944. The state councils were recognized, and their rights in ceremonial, social, and ritual functions were preserved to them. But the traditional ruler and his state council were also gazetted as the native authority controlled by the colonial administration; treasuries were set up and local taxation was introduced. Having at last gained control over local expenditures, the government was prepared to make grants-in-aid to enable the new native authorities to maintain their social services.

Parallel with this laissez-faire attitude toward the traditional rulers in the government of their own towns was the attempt to draw them more into the government of the Gold Coast as a whole. Provincial councils of rulers and elders were set up (in Ashanti, the Confederacy Council) to discuss not only matters affecting their own status and common problems, but also the policies of the government; their role, however, was purely advisory. From 1926 on, the provincial councils elected from among their own members representatives to the Legislative Assembly; these rulers represented the mass of the population in the rural areas, and the municipalities sent as their own elected representatives the more politically conscious members of the Assembly. In 1942 Governor Sir Alan Burns appointed Nana Ofori Atta, ruler of Akim Abuakwa, to the Executive Council; the Asantehene declined the invitation on the ground that tradition demanded that he should report all proceedings to his elders—an impossible condition. The traditional rulers and especially the educated ones began to see themselves as the heirs of British rule; election to a stool was thus a first step toward a position of national leadership.

The relationship between the traditional rulers and the intellectual elite of the early political groups has fluctuated between coöperation and antagonism. At times, as in the early years of the twentieth century, when the colonial government sought to gain more control over land and over indigenous institutions of government, the two groups united in opposition to the British. Nana Ofori Atta was one of the leaders of the popular movement against the fixing of cocoa prices in 1936; the ensuing cocoa boycott by the farmers lasted several months. The politicians, however, were hotly opposed to the introduction of native administration, viewing it as a step backward. But the divergence between the two groups was never wide; both looked forward to a gradual assumption of power. Both were equally opposed to the programs and the tactics of the CPP in the early 1950's, and it is significant that most of the opposition members of the House of Assembly at this period were elected not by popular vote but by the provincial councils.

In mid-century the traditional rulers of southern Ghana were probably better educated than their Yoruba counterparts. With their income from land they were also much wealthier. To judge from the writings of ethnographers, they still devoted much time to traditional rituals; but many of them wore European dress on occasion, and those who were members of provincial councils and similar bodies spent much time away from their home towns, often in Accra or Kumasi. As Lord Hailey says, they have not seen themselves as agencies of local government; they have seemed to be much more interested in land and chieftaincy affairs than in dispensaries, roads, and schools.

The high value of land has led to rampant litigation between stools, sometimes financed by the rents received but often, when these prove insufficient, by local levies. The wealth of the rulers has also led to bitter competition for titles. As the government has little direct interest in the security of the rulers, destoolments have been frequent. Of five rulers of Goaso between 1920 and 1937, only one died in office,[20] and in the Ashanti confederacy one in seven chiefs, on the average, was deposed each year.[21] The most frequent charge was misappropriation of stool funds. Office in a native authority or as a member of a provincial council or the Legislative Assembly did, however, render the rulers more secure and therefore added to the attractions of the office. Today the fact that a ruler is known to favor the opposition encourages the CPP majority in his town to find fault with his rule. Many rulers, however, support the CPP.

As anti-British feeling developed in the postwar years, the traditional rulers, along with the older middle-class politicians, were dubbed stooges of the British and implements of colonial policy. The low prestige of the rulers and the lack of an efficient system of local government were cited as being among the causes of popular discontent.

---

[20] R. Lystad, *The Ashanti: A Proud People* (New Brunswick: Rutgers University Press, 1958), p. 114.

[21] Busia, *op. cit.*, p. 216.

Traditional Rulers in the 1950's

The postwar agitation culminated in the appointment of a commission, headed by Justice J. H. Coussey, to inquire into constitutional reform. The members, all Gold Coastians, were drawn overwhelmingly from the ranks of traditional rulers and middle-class moderate political leaders. They recommended, *inter alia*, the introduction of a local government system. Further committees filled in the details, and the bill that was later presented to the new House of Assembly substantially conformed to these earlier recommendations. It had obviously not occurred to the members of the earlier committees that the new law would strike a grievous blow at the traditional rulers; only after the CPP victory was it appreciated how powerful a weapon was being placed in the hands of the party in power. The opposition was thus somewhat subdued during the parliamentary debates.

The provisions had seemed to be moderate enough. Local government councils would carry out all functions proper to them, while the state councils, officially recognized, would be continued. One-third of the local government council representatives would be traditional members, and the president would be a traditional ruler, though with ceremonial functions only. Later legislation protected the salaries of rulers by making them a first charge on annual revenues; the minister of local government would decide what was a fair salary, should a dispute arise. The most contentious issue was control of the stool lands. The law preserved to the rulers their traditional rights of ownership in trust for the community, but stipulated that all alienation of land receive the consent of the local government council, and that the council staff collect the revenue, paying an agreed proportion to the stool council. The latter provision has been difficult to implement, owing to the complex nature of land rights.

Thus, in the name of democracy and of reforming obvious abuses in the management of stool land, the new government removed the traditional rulers not only from active participation in the local government of their towns but also, to a considerable extent, from the control of stool lands. In claiming that it had merely restored to the rulers their traditional status, it had effectively weakened them. Nevertheless, a substantial income remained to the state councils, the use of which is neither supervised by the government nor subject to popular control.

As the CPP grew in strength, it had less need either to attack or to placate the traditional rulers. The rising demand for a federal constitution, however, revived tribal sentiments and brought the rulers, especially those of Ashanti, again to the fore. CPP strength lay in the colony areas; in the rest of the country, people felt that they did not receive enough of the benefits brought by the new government. The possibility of a federal constitution under which the CPP would control only one of the five probable regions was so serious a threat to the party that the idea had to be completely smashed. In Ashanti, the Asantehene was identified with the demand for federalism; he and other senior rulers petitioned the Queen for a commission of inquiry into the constitution in October, 1954. The new party of opposition, the National Liberation Movement (NLM), was led by one of the Asantehene's linguists.

Eventually the government promised the formation of regional houses of assembly and of chiefs. Houses of assembly were set up in August, 1958, but were abolished in February, 1959. Houses of chiefs were set up later in 1958, and the provincial councils, which had continued to this date, were at the same time abolished. The houses of chiefs are purely advisory bodies whose function is to discuss matters affecting the chieftaincy and other customary affairs within their own areas. In this period the government made further attacks on traditional rulers. In 1955 the Asantehene had destooled a number of lesser rulers who were CPP sympathizers; hitherto there had been no appeal from a decision of the Confederacy Council, but a new law enabled a deposed ohene to appeal to the government. In similar vein, another law, passed in 1959, made the governor-general the final arbiter in disputes over enstoolment, and enabled him to prohibit any traditional ruler from exercising his functions.

The strong measures adopted by the government in 1958 to quell opposition included an onslaught against traditional rulers. A number of commissions were set up to inquire into malpractices, the most publicized being the one that investigated affairs at Akim Abuakwa and looked into the activities of its ruler, Nana Ofori Atta II (successor to the ruler who had once been a member of the Executive Council). In the 1954 elections all seats for Akim Abuakwa in the House of Assembly had been won by the CPP. Yet the ruler was an active opposition member, supported by the veteran J. B. Danquah, whose home is in Akim Abuakwa. The commissioner, Justice Jackson, found (1) that in 1955 Nana Ofori Atta II had diverted stool funds, properly allocated to pay the salaries of lesser rulers and officeholders, to the coffers of the NLM for use in equipping the "Action Groupers," an armed band of thugs, and (2) that he had sworn oaths with his subordinates to ensure their allegiance to the NLM. The commissioner, though most appreciative of the difficulties facing the modern ruler, deemed the activities of Nana Ofori Atta II an abuse of power,[22] and the government withdrew its recognition of him. He was arrested in September, 1958, for refusing to deliver his state stool to the queen mother. In 1958 the government also took control of the Kumasi stool lands. A grave insult to the whole Ashanti people was the reprieve and the public welcome given to the only survivor of the four men who had

---

[22] *Report of a Commission Approved To Enquire into the Affairs of the Akim Abuakwa State, by Commissioner J. Jackson* (Accra, 1958).

despoiled the golden stool in 1920, and whose death penalty had been commuted by the governor to exile. In 1959 traditional members were removed from local government councils.

Yet throughout the decade the political leaders continued to voice their respect for natural rulers. In 1950 Kwame Nkrumah said at a public rally: "I am not in the Gold Coast to abolish chieftaincy. All that the people expect our natural rulers to do is to respect the wishes of their people. I plead for mutual respect between chiefs and people. Let me make it plain that when the CPP has been able to achieve self-government for Ghana, there will still be chieftaincy in the Gold Coast." [23] Later, in 1954, though averring that the disappearance of chieftaincy would spell disaster, he pointed out that "at the same time, the government believes that chieftaincy, in common with other human institutions, cannot remain static, but that it must in large measure adapt itself to the changing requirement of the changing time." [24] Article 14 of the presidential declaration on the assumption of office is, "That chieftaincy in Ghana should be guaranteed and preserved."

Yet in Ghana, too, the political leaders, while preserving to the traditional rulers many of their customary rights, have made no attempt to define a positive role for them in the new society. There is now so little to occupy an active ruler in his home town that some of them have virtually quit their kingdoms to seek other forms of public office. Nana Nketsia IV of Sekondi spent several years studying social anthropology at Oxford University, and is now cultural adviser to President Nkrumah; the late Nana Kwabena Kenna was Ghana's ambassador in Delhi.

Kwame Nkrumah is now termed the Osagyefo—the victorious leader. On July 1, 1960, he became president of the Republic of Ghana. For the occasion the House of Assembly had been furnished with a throne modeled on the traditional Akan stool; the President was greeted at the door by the linguists of each region; he took his oath upon a sword of traditional design; outside, music was played, not by the army and police bands, but by a team of drummers and praise singers. The new symbolism was predominantly Akan, though elements from other Ghanaian cultures had been incorporated. All the symbols are those of a traditional ruler.

If we were to present a reasonably complete picture of the role of the traditional ruler in the modern African state, we should add sections on the territories of the former French colonial empire, on the Bantu kingdoms of East Africa, and on peoples, such as the Ibo of eastern Nigeria, among whom only village chieftaincy exists. But the three studies given

---

[23] Kwame Nkrumah, *I Speak of Freedom* (London: Heinemann, 1960), p. 24.
[24] *Ibid.*, p. 35.

here do illustrate the problem faced by political leaders in attracting the allegiance of the masses.

Nobody pretends that the traditional rulers have been in the van of constitutional progress; at best, they have allied themselves with the more moderate political leaders. Yet one proposition that seems to emerge from these three studies is that the state of chieftaincy in the three areas, in the vital year 1950, had a determining influence on the type of political party which was later to emerge victorious. Would the CPP have grown so strong, one asks, had not traditional rulers been so weak? How else does one account for the success of the more radical CPP in Ghana, when the Action Group of the Western Region of Nigeria won power as a party representing the very elements—the intelligentsia—which lost support in Ghana?

In all these areas the traditional rulers in mid-century have been men better educated, on the average, than the masses. Their aims, to modernize their towns, have been little different from those of the politicians. Yet they have sought to effect these changes while preserving the chieftaincy. With the status of native authority bestowed on them by colonial administrators, and with their superior education and experience, they soon became autocrats, albeit very benevolent ones.

The political leaders of Ghana and the Western Region of Nigeria have, throughout the past decade, stressed the importance of chieftaincy as one of the traditional institutions that must be preserved. They probably mean what they say, but it is also true that their promises serve to maintain the support of the traditional rulers. Yet they attack the autocracy of the rulers, claiming that the traditional relationship—that of a ruler advised by his subordinate chiefs and people and responsible to them—should be restored. Such a restoration would remove the conflicts in which so many rulers find themselves.

In both Ghana and the Western Region, the local government legislation of the new government was based upon foundations laid earlier, and its importance in affecting the status of the traditional ruler and enabling the party to win mass support was not immediately realized. Yet this legislation has removed the rulers from active participation in the government of their towns. The politicians, in stressing the restoration of the ruler to his traditional status, quietly overlook the fact that his role was to govern his town. This is now denied him. Should the emirs, in the near future, be unable to assure the Northern Peoples' Congress of electoral victory, the party there will also be obliged to seek more direct popular support; it may well gain such support by setting up local government councils in the emirates. The autocracy of the emirs would then suffer the same onslaught as has that of the rulers of western Nigeria and of southern Ghana.

The new governments have maintained as much control over the traditional rulers as did the colonial administration, or perhaps more. They urge the rulers to be nonpolitical, yet they punish those who lean toward the opposition parties and reward those who openly favor their own. Participation in party politics is today destroying the prestige of the rulers just as did too close an association with the colonial administrators in past decades.

"Preserve chieftaincy!" cry the political leaders, yet they define no new roles for the traditional rulers. They leave to them merely the ritual and ceremonial aspects of chieftaincy, thus preserving a cultural heritage to which, as nationalists, they can appeal. Yet it is the insistence on this archaic aspect of the role which renders it even more difficult for the ruler to create a new and more modern role, symbolizing the norms, not of bygone ages, but of the second half of the twentieth century.

11. STUDENTS

By William John Hanna

University students* in Anglo-American countries (with the recent exception of American Negroes) usually do not seek political power, and their influence upon public policy is slight. Many are indifferent to the political process. In contrast, students in many Asian, Latin-American, and Middle Eastern countries are highly politicized and often intervene in the political process. Korea, Colombia, Cuba, Venezuela, and Turkey are among the countries in which students have participated in recent political revolutions. And Negro students are actively participating in the politics of revolutionary race relations. The role of students in the politics of most African countries seems to lie somewhere between these two contrasting patterns.

The characteristics, behavior, and opinions of university students in African countries are of central concern to the political analyst for at least four reasons. One is that Western education tends to be the determinant base value of the new (i.e., nontraditional) African elite. As university students are recipients of the most advanced Western education available, they understandably consider themselves, and are regarded as, actual or prospective members of this elite. They are conscious of their exclusiveness and their preëminence, and are often deferred to and imitated by the masses.[1] Second, as intellectuals, students have been in contact with a modern intellectual culture which "carries with it a partial transformation of the self and a changed relationship to the authority of the dead and the living."[2] They are aware of the divergence between intellectual currents and public policies. And they are highly politicized, an outlook that has been attributed to concern with relationships to

* This study was supported by grants from the African Studies Center, University of California, Los Angeles, and the Office of International Programs, Michigan State University. I am grateful for assistance from the students and the faculty of the University of Ibadan, Nigeria, and the staff of the Nigerian Institute of Social and Economic Research.

[1] Cf. S. F. Nadel, "The Concept of Social Elites," *International Social Science Bulletin*, VIII (1956), 413–424.

[2] Edward Shils, "The Intellectuals in the Political Development of the New States," *World Politics*, XII (April, 1960), 333. According to Shils's definition of the term, the students are intellectuals. As many of the students' comments on Nigerian politics are explicitly "anti-intellectual," a behavioral definition of "intellectual" will probably be used in future research.

authority, to the opportunity for achievement and effectiveness which politics provides for the intellectual, and to an incivility that breeds excessive partisanship.[3] Third, students, who constitute a large proportion of the intellectuals outside the government, are thus relatively free to offer independent criticism and public-opinion leadership. Fourth, as youths, they are in generational revolt, and they constitute the reservoir from which future national political leaders will be drawn. Their political relevance as a categoric group has been very aptly described:

For some time now, Africa has occupied a place in the forefront of current events, and quite rightly, most of the attention has been focused on the movements, declarations and positions of her leaders. For today, and this even is true in the territories not yet autonomous, the thoughts and actions of these leaders are decisive for the destiny of the Continent and for peace in the world.

But there is another category of African leaders, about whom there seems to be hardly any concern: African students. They have not yet come to grips with the concrete situation in Africa, they are devoid of immediate responsibility. And what is more, still untested, they often lack moderation.

Nonetheless, they are the natural cadres and the leaders of tomorrow's Africa, an Africa which by then will have acquired even greater weight, deepened its political reflection, assured a legitimate awareness of its forces and more fully assumed its place among nations. The decisions of this Africa of the future will have a much greater effect and more far-reaching international repercussions than those of today. . . .

Thus, our duty is to listen to their voice and to discern in the midst of the adolescent extravagances and the sometimes clumsy movements of their thought, the first echoes of the voice of Africa 1970.[4]

In this essay I discuss students and politics at the University of Ibadan, Nigeria (called UCI, and previously known as the University College, Ibadan).[5] The study was conducted in the spring of 1960, when

---

[3] *Ibid.*, pp. 338–342.

[4] "Their Voice," *Présence Africaine* (English ed.), vol. 6/7 (1961), p. 5 (quoted with permission of the editors).

[5] Data for this study were collected from the following sources: (1) files of the registrar, which give age, tribe, home division, and sponsor; (2) partially structured interviews with a nonprobability sample of 73 students, some of whom were met socially, whereas others were included in a roughly drawn quota sample; (3) interviews with UCI faculty members; (4) interviews with party officials in Ibadan; (5) newspaper reports, student periodicals, and other published materials relating to UCI and its students; and (6) a questionnaire administered to 351 of the 985 male students recorded in the registrar's files as of May 1, 1960.

Of the 351 students who completed the questionnaire, 80 were selected randomly and 271 volunteered. This compromise between probability sampling methods and sample size was necessary because I did not have time before the UCI end-of-term examinations to interview a large enough random sample of students to make cell N's satisfactory. Compromise permitted the identification of biases in the total sample, and it produced the necessary N's.

independence was assured but not yet achieved. As few data are available for a comparison between Nigerian university students and those in other African countries,[6] no claim is made that this student population is politically representative of most student populations in Africa. Nigerian students, however, seem to be similar to their counterparts in other African countries where political competition is legitimate, and where the transition to or toward independence has been nonviolent.

All students in the random sample of 80 were contacted and they all coöperated by completing the questionnaire. (Occasionally more than ten call-backs were necessary!) An attempt was made to contact (personally or by note) the other 905 students, and each was urged to fill out the same questionnaire; few call-backs were made for this group. Completed questionnaires were returned by 271 of these students, or 30 per cent. This voluntary sample percentage is low, but not unsatisfactory because (1) the questionnaire was distributed at the end of the term when students were studying for examinations, and (2) Nigerian students had had little experience in completing questionnaires on a voluntary basis.

An important consideration in evaluating the data from this study is the bias introduced by including a voluntary sample. What qualities of the volunteers differentiated them from a representative sample? There are no statistically significant differences between the random group and the voluntary group on characterological attributes. Some important contrasts do develop relative to political activity. These are suggested by the following table.

ACTIVITY BIAS
(In percentages)

Sample	Non-Affiliates (N = 22)	Affiliates (N = 267)	Action Group				National Convention of Nigerian Citizens			
			Nominals (N = 46)	Occasionals (N = 53)	Actives (N = 29)	Total (N = 128)	Nominals (N = 58)	Occasionals (N = 52)	Actives (N = 29)	Total (N = 139)
Random	27	22	28	26	14	24	25	17	17	19
Voluntary	73	78	72	74	86	76	75	83	83	81

Students who volunteered to complete the questionnaire were more active, regardless of party affiliation (though the contrast is sharper among Action Groupers), and were more likely to be affiliated with the NCNC. A bias was also introduced by excluding the 62 students who fell outside the Action Group/Non-Affiliate/NCNC trichotomy. Exclusion facilitated the analysis of contrasts, but the study thereby becomes less descriptive and more explanatory. These and corollary biases should be kept in mind when considering the quantitative data.

[6] Useful studies of African university students include Gustav Jahoda, "The Social Background of a West African Student Population," *British Journal of Sociology*, V (Dec., 1954), 355–365; VI (March, 1955), 71–79; and Dwaine Marvick, "Higher Education in the Development of Future West African Leaders," in James S. Coleman, ed., *Education and Political Development* (Princeton: Princeton University Press, in press).

The analysis of UCI students is divided into three parts: (1) the characteristics of the partisans, (2) their political activities, and (3) their political opinions. The cells of analysis are based upon the students' political party affiliations and their level of activity for these political parties. By dividing the student population according to party affiliation, a control against variations stemming from the characteristics of one political party is introduced. Insights into the nature of the political parties are also obtained. By stratifying according to activity level, associations between variables and attributes may more easily be assessed.

There are three major political parties in Nigeria: the Action Group (AG), the National Convention of Nigerian Citizens (NCNC), and the Northern Peoples' Congress (NPC). Only the students affiliated with the NCNC and the Action Group are considered in this report because only a small percentage of students from the north, where the NPC flourishes, attend UCI. The small northern representation reflects the fact that the north is, educationally, far less developed. Classification of the UCI students as "Action Groupers," "NCNCers," or "Non-Affiliates" was based upon the answers to two questionnaire items: (1) "Did you have a preference among political parties in the [1959] federal elections?" (2) "In general, do you have a preference among political parties?" Students who consistently answered "AG," "NCNC," or "No preference," were so classified. The following totals were obtained:

Action Groupers	128
NCNCers	139
Non-Affiliates	22
	289

As the total sample was 351, 62 students fell outside this trichotomy. The residual group is not further considered in this report.

The second step in student classification was to rate the level of partisan activity. Activity was chosen instead of power because of the methodological difficulties involved in determining the latter. There is probably a high correlation between activity, on the one hand, and power or involvement on the other, but the only objective data obtained which support this belief are (1) the activity level of officers in the student wings of political parties (15 of the 17 officers were classified as Actives in the scheme described below), and (2) the correlation of .81 between activity level and self-evaluation of political interest. The classification is based upon an index developed from the following items:

1) Membership in the party
2) Membership in the student wing of the party

3) Attendance at party meetings off campus
4) Attendance at party or student wing meetings on campus
5) Campaigning during the 1959 federal election off campus
6) Campaigning during the 1959 federal election on campus

The items were rated equally (they do not Guttman scale) and a trichotomy was developed:

Nominal	0 points
Occasional	1–3 points
Active	4–6 points

This produced the following groups:

	AG	NCNC
Nominals	46	58
Occasionals	53	52
Actives	29	29
	128	139

CHARACTERISTICS OF THE PARTISANS

The 289 students observed were divided into Action Groupers, NCNCers, and Non-Affiliates; the Affiliates were further divided into Nominals, Occasionals, and Actives. In this section differences among these groups are explored. The following factors are considered: ethnic group, region, home-town population, father's or guardian's occupation, university sponsor, expected occupation after UCI, and years at UCI. In many instances association suggests causation; however, interpretations in terms of the latter must be viewed tentatively because of insufficient data pertaining to intervening factors.

Ethnic Group and Region

The three largest ethnic groups in Nigeria are the Hausa (18 per cent), the Ibo (18 per cent), and the Yoruba (17 per cent). Each is concentrated in one of the three regions of the country; before the Western Region emergency, each group dominated one of the three major political parties, each of which controlled a regional government. Thus, the three largest Nigerian ethnic groups have strong governmental and party associations. All three parties, it should be emphasized, have tried to universalize their appeals and their bases of support.

Despite these attempts, ethnicity, or "tribalism," to use the popular term, is an important factor in Nigerian politics. Many party campaign appeals seek to capitalize on ethnic identifications. Illustrative are the following: "Who desires enslavement by the Hausas?" "The salvation of the Binis, Ijaws, Itsekiris, the Urhobos, etc., is in the hands of the Action Group." [7] One student commented, "The results of the last Federal election showed clearly that . . . voting is essentially on tribal bases. A party is voted for . . . because the leader comes from a particular tribe." [8]

Tribalism is also operative within the student body. In 1960 an editorial in a student newspaper said: "The events surrounding the last student presidential elections are, to say the least, most distressing. We were treated to a most shameless display of tribalism and sectionalism; . . . if as the 'undergrads' of Nigeria's only University, we cannot grow out of tribal loyalties and petty tribal prejudices, then there is very little reason for optimism in the New Nigeria of our dreams." [9] Although the tribal character of the election was somewhat exceptional, it indicates underlying divisions.

The two major southern Nigerian ethnic groups are overrepresented in the UCI student body: 42 per cent of the students are Yoruba, 36 per cent are Ibo, and only 1 per cent are Hausa-Fulani. The southern groups are, of course, also overrepresented among the Affiliates of the major southern political parties (see table 1): 50 per cent of the Non-Affiliates are from these two groups, but 83 per cent of the Affiliates are Yoruba or Ibo. This finding is accentuated when the activity level is examined. Ten per cent of the Action Groupers are from other ethnic groups, but none are in the active stratum. Similarly, the percentages for the NCNC are 22 and 15. A picture of Yoruba and Ibo dominance clearly emerges.

Because of the usual processes of recruitment to the active minority, and because of the importance of ethnic identifications, it was expected that the more active the stratum, the more predominant would be the students from the ethnic group that dominates the party nationally. This expectation is supported by an examination of the Action Group strata: 78 per cent of the AG Nominals, 87 per cent of the Occasionals, and 100 per cent of the Actives are Yoruba. Within the NCNC, however, the dominant group, the Ibo, has a relatively small representation in the Active stratum. Again, the Yoruba increase proportionately with activity. (The percentages are 7, 13, and 40.) There are two explanations for the increased role of the Yoruba. One is the character of the proximate electorate; more than 96 per cent of the population of Ibadan Division, where the UCI is located, are Yoruba. Yoruba are more effective campaigners among other Yoruba than Ibo are among Yoruba. And long-standing

---

[7] The second appeal is quoted in Philip Whitaker, "The Western Region of Nigeria, May 1956," in W. J. M. Mackenzie and Kenneth Robinson, eds., *Five Elections in Africa* (Oxford: Clarendon Press, 1960), p. 92.

[8] Editorial in *The Bug*, May 29, 1959, p. 2.

[9] "Looking Back in Anger," *The Beacon* (March, 1960), p. 2.

TABLE 1: CHARACTERISTICS OF THE PARTISAN STUDENTS (in percentages[a])

Factor	Non-Affiliates	Affiliates	Action Group				NCNC			
			Nominals	Occasionals	Actives	Total	Nominals	Occasionals	Actives	Total
	(18)	(198)	(36)	(38)	(20)	(94)	(46)	(38)	(20)	(104)
ETHNIC GROUP										
Western Region										
Yoruba	22	47	72	82	100	82	7	13	40	15
Ibo	6	6	3	3	0	2	7	10	10	9
Other	22	10	3	8	0	4	20	10	10	14
Eastern Region										
Yoruba	0	0	0	0	0	0	0	0	0	0
Ibo	17	29	3	0	0	1	58	59	35	54
Other	28	6	11	3	0	5	7	8	5	7
Northern Region										
Yoruba	6	2	6	5	0	4	0	0	0	0
Ibo	0	0	0	0	0	0	0	0	0	0
Other	0	1	3	0	0	1	2	0	0	1
HOME-TOWN POPULATION	(17)	(230)	(39)	(49)	(25)	(113)	(44)	(47)	(26)	(117)
Less than 5,000	18	27	31	24	24	27	23	32	31	28
Between 5,000 and 14,999	47	27	38	22	32	30	23	28	19	24
Between 15,000 and 49,999	29	21	10	20	16	16	36	15	27	26
50,000 or more	6	25	21	33	28	27	18	26	23	22
OCCUPATIONAL STATUS OF FATHER OR GUARDIAN	(18)	(192)	(35)	(35)	(19)	(89)	(45)	(38)	(20)	(103)
Higher	61	37	28	37	21	31	47	55	25	44
Lower	39	63	72	63	79	69	53	45	75	56
EXPECTED OCCUPATION AND SPONSOR	(18)	(187)	(34)	(37)	(19)	(90)	(42)	(35)	(20)	(97)
Professional										
Private	22	11	12	11	0	9	10	17	10	12
Federal government	17	4	3	5	0	3	10	0	0	4
Other government	0	2	6	3	0	3	2	0	0	1
Teaching										
Private	11	38	38	30	67	41	31	31	50	35
Federal government	0	4	3	5	5	4	5	3	5	4
Other government	11	7	12	14	5	11	5	0	10	4
Government										
Private	11	14	6	14	0	8	19	26	15	21
Federal government	17	16	15	17	11	14	17	20	10	17
Other government	11	4	6	3	11	6	2	3	0	2
YEARS AT UCI	(22)	(266)	(46)	(53)	(28)	(127)	(58)	(52)	(29)	(139)
One	27	24	20	25	21	22	22	21	38	25
Two	27	30	24	28	36	28	34	35	21	32
Three	23	25	26	30	29	28	16	27	28	22
Four or more	23	21	30	17	14	21	28	17	14	21

[a] Figures in parentheses indicate number of students in each category for each factor.

traditional conflicts among Yoruba have driven many Ibadan members into the non-Yoruba NCNC. A second explanation relates to the type of Yoruba recruited to the NCNC. They have been described as "the more radical elements. These include those who were, in the provincial towns, advocating self-government when the masses were still unaware of such aims, those who were 'misfits' in their society and rebelled against the tribal elders or British administrators, and, at a higher level, those who had been to England and returned with left-wing political ideologies." [10] Thus, one of the reasons the Yoruba students who affiliated with the NCNC are among the more active is that they are by the nature of their self-recruitment radical and activist.

Home region is also associated with partisan activity. Because UCI is located in the Western Region, it was physically and economically easier for students from the region to travel to their home areas to campaign than it was for those from the other two regions. Table 1 shows that the more active students are more likely to come from the Western Region, and less likely to come from either of the other regions. As further evidence, all 19 students from Ibadan Division whose ethnic group was ascertained were Yoruba, and their activity strata were: Nominal, 5; Occasional, 7; Active, 6 (one was a Non-Affiliate).

The relationship among ethnic group, home region, and partisan activity may be specified. The few Yoruba from outside the Western Region were among the Non-Affiliates and the less active. Both in the Action Group and the NCNC, however, the number of Yoruba from the Western Region rose proportionately with the activity stratum. Home region also had an influence upon Ibo participation; those from the west were relatively more active than those from the east. The western Ibo, however, were relatively less active in both parties than were the western Yoruba. Home region did not seem to be a factor in the participation of members of other ethnic groups.

Home-Town Population

African towns are the setting for acculturation and nation building. It is therefore not surprising that 24 per cent of the students at UCI came from urban areas with a population of 50,000 or more, and that 74 per cent came from areas with 5,000 or more, although the figures for all Nigeria are probably less than 10 and 15 per cent, respectively. Because "African politics are primarily urban politics," [11] it was expected

---

[10] P. C. Lloyd, "The Development of Political Parties in Western Nigeria," *American Political Science Review*, XLIX (Sept., 1955), 695.

[11] James S. Coleman, "The Politics of Sub-Saharan Africa," in Gabriel Almond and James S. Coleman, eds., *The Politics of the Developing Areas* (Princeton: Princeton University Press, 1960), p. 270.

that size of home town and partisan activity would be associated. Social-ization and recruitment to partisan politics would seem to be more in-tense in the larger towns. The results of the study, however, do not support this expectation. The figures in table 1 indicate that size of home town is not associated with partisan activity (nor is it associated with opinion leadership). Apparently, educational experience equalizes (is dominant over) disparities owing to urban-rural backgrounds.

Father's or Guardian's Occupational Status

It has been suggested that the power seeker "pursues power as a means of compensation against deprivation. Power is expected to over-come low estimates of the self." [12] Deprivation is operative among those from lower positions in the social stratification system, who turn to overt politics to obtain what those in upper positions already have and are able to maintain through influence. If those in lower positions are well educated, and therefore have broadened their world view, they tend to develop an awareness of the gap between position and potential, that is, a low estimate of self. In the context of the developing countries, the "intense politicization of the intellectual is accentuated by the provision, through politics, of opportunities for individual effectiveness and achieve-ment." [13]

For these reasons it was expected that the more active partisan students would be those whose fathers or guardians had occupations with relatively low prestige or material rewards. The following occupa-tional classification was used to determine status: the professions, in-cluding teaching, and technical governmental, religious, and political positions were classified as higher status; business, trading, farming, fish-ing, blue-collar work, and skilled labor were classified as lower status. Businessmen and traders were put in the second category because of the presumed antichrematistic attitude held by many Nigerians. Students were disproportionately drawn from higher-status backgrounds; approxi-mately 3 per cent of Nigeria's male population is engaged in administra-tive, professional, and technical work, whereas 39 per cent of the stu-dents' fathers or guardians were so engaged. Table 1 suggests that there is an association between occupational status and partisan activity. The Non-Affiliates tended to come from backgrounds of higher occupational status, and the Actives were most likely to have a father or guardian in a lower-status occupation. The relationship is not linear, however; the higher-status background of the Occasionals introduces an "error."

---

[12] Harold D. Lasswell, "Power and Personality," in Heinz Eulau, Samuel J. Eldersveld, and Morris Janowitz, eds., *Political Behavior* (Glencoe: Free Press, 1956), p. 98 (italics removed).

[13] Shils, *op. cit.*, p. 341.

Sponsor and Expected Occupation after Leaving UCI

Only about one in four students at UCI at the time of this study had their educational expenses paid by a private individual (a relative, a guardian, or a friend acting in a private capacity). The rest were sponsored by organizations: 13 per cent by schools (grammar schools, secondary schools, etc.), 13 per cent by religious institutions (churches, religious orders, etc.), 2 per cent by private businesses, 1 per cent by private organizations (tribal unions, progressive unions, etc.), and 42 per cent by various governments. In addition, 2 per cent were sponsored from outside Nigeria. Those students who were sponsored by a government divided as follows: federal government, 52 per cent; Western Regional government, 15 per cent; Eastern Regional government, 9 per cent; Northern Regional government, 15 per cent; other governmental units and corporations, 9 per cent. In return for support while attending UCI, a sponsored student often contracted to work for his sponsor for a number of years, usually five. Contracts, however, are not always fulfilled.

The belief developed among many UCI students and faculty members alike that political mistakes might lead to the withdrawal of sponsorship and might jeopardize future job opportunities. On the other hand, students seemed not to believe that correct political behavior would automatically further their careers, probably because they were uncertain as to who would employ them after they left UCI. No student or faculty member could, or would, cite a concrete example of support being withdrawn (many allusions were made), but so long as a belief is operative, behavior is affected. "The Nigerian student feels that he may be penalized if he should be too outspoken in the expression of his political and social convictions; . . . this is not unconnected with the source of his support and his hope for the future." [14] Two comments made by students during interviews illustrate this belief: "The present deterrent to political activity on the part of a government scholar is fear of victimization"; "Many students at UCI are under government scholarships. They feel restricted, afraid to criticize the government. One student's scholarship was withdrawn when he criticized the government."

Table 1 suggests that there is an association between participation and source of support. Among those who were not affiliated with a political party, 44 per cent were privately sponsored, 34 per cent had federal support, and 22 per cent were supported by other governments. This contrasts with the Affiliates, among whom 63 per cent were privately sponsored, 24 per cent were sponsored by the federal government, and

---

[14] H. A. Oluwasanmi, "Nigerian Students' Role in Their Society," *World University Service Bulletin*, XXI (Winter, 1960), 6.

13 per cent were sponsored by other governments. The association between sponsor and participation is clearer when Affiliates are divided into
activity strata. For both the Action Group and the NCNC, the Actives
had the highest percentage of privately sponsored students and the
lowest percentage of federally sponsored students. Those sponsored by
other governments tended relatively to be more active in the NCNC than
in the Action Group.

Partisan activity is also associated with expected occupation after
leaving UCI. Almost half the students (48 per cent) expected to become
secondary or primary school teachers after finishing their education, 31
per cent expected to go into other professions, 18 per cent, into government, and 4 per cent, into other occupations. The future teachers were
absolutely and relatively the most active in partisan Nigerian politics.
Furthermore, among those students who expected to be teaching ten
years after their education was completed, 54 per cent answered "Yes"
to the question, "Do you expect to be active in politics after leaving
University College?" No other career group registered more than 34 per
cent on this question. The explanation for the teachers' highly politicized
behavior and expectations probably lies in the nature of the teaching
profession in Nigeria; a high commitment is not necessary, restrictions
on political activity are minimal, and much free time is available. Furthermore, the "turnover of teachers is very high. The teaching profession has
been an avenue for movement into private industry, the government civil
service, and public office. . . . The teaching profession is a sort of
preparation for positions in other sectors." [15] Among UCI students
planning to become teachers after the completion of their education,
only 48 per cent expected to be teaching ten years later. The occupational continuity of the professionals was 82 per cent, and, for those
going into government work, 55 per cent.

It is possible to specify the relationships among sponsor, expected
occupation, and partisan activity. The only subgroup significantly associated with high partisan activity was the privately sponsored future
teachers. Apparently, only one restricting factor (government sponsorship, professional commitment, or future work in the government) needed
to be operative to discourage a student politically.

Years at UCI

Institutions of higher learning do more than provide their students
with vocational skills through classroom experiences. They also provide
the setting, in and out of the classroom, for political socialization (induc-

---

[15] Frederick Harbison, "High-Level Manpower for Nigeria's Future," in *Investment in Education,* Commission on Post-School Certificate and Higher Education
in Nigeria (Lagos: Federal Ministry of Education, 1960), p. 60.

tion into the political culture) and recruitment (induction into the specialized roles of the political system). Students "are exposed to a variety of political and ideological influences. They listen to political lectures in their classes, discuss politics and political philosophy, react to the communications of the mass media." [16] There is reason to believe, therefore, that the longer a student is at a university, the more active he will become. There are, however, countervailing factors. First, the longer a student participates in higher education, the less a "free-floating" intellectual he is and the more he tends to become a chemist, a teacher, or the like. Second, the average quality of students changes at each succeeding educational level as the poorer and less interested students drop out. Thus, after two or three years, the better and more professionally oriented students tend to remain. Third, the better and professionally committed students are unlikely to devote time both to education and politics.

Evidence for the third factor comes from a variety of sources. In the chaotic weeks immediately following the independence of the Republic of the Congo, the students of Lovanium University at Leopoldville studied and sat for their examinations, not visibly affected by the events surrounding them. At a high school near Nairobi, Kenya, whose students are predominantly Kikuyu, there was little effect upon school behavior or academic performance during the Mau Mau emergency. The reason for the devotion to education at UCI is that learning "becomes a fierce struggle for survival in a society in which a degree is an important index of social and intellectual success. . . . A student's failure to earn his degree will not only dash his hopes for a higher status in life, but will constitute an indelible stigma on his family." [17]

These factors suggest that political activity, when examined in terms of number of years at a university, should increase and then decrease. The UCI data support this expectation in part. Students who had been at UCI for four or more years were the least active; the more active the stratum, the further the proportion declines (see table 1). No trend is manifest among the other class groups, but a striking finding is the bunching of Actives within particular class groups. Of the Action Group Actives, 36 per cent were second-year men, and 38 per cent of the NCNC Actives were first-year men. Although the data are no more than suggestive, they do point to a low stage of class-clique development.

Another available measure of the differences among students who have been at UCI for differing periods of time is the frequency with which they talked about politics, and the people with whom they talked. Each student was asked how frequently he spoke with other students,

---

[16] Rose K. Goldsen, Morris Rosenberg, Robin M. Williams, Jr., and Edward A. Suchman, *What College Students Think* (New York: Van Nostrand, 1960), p. 116.

[17] Oluwasanmi, *op. cit.*, p. 6.

relatives, and nonstudent friends about Nigerian politics and international politics. The results indicate that "old-timers" talked about politics more frequently than did newcomers, but that the increase was registered almost exclusively by talks with other students. This suggests an estrangement between students and nonstudents, especially relatives. In future research, the previously assumed high degree of educational "filter-down" should be more carefully examined.

POLITICAL ACTIVITIES

In this section student partisan and nonpartisan political activities are analyzed. Included are voting, party membership, attendance at party meetings, campaigning, and participation in public demonstrations and protests. These activities do not, of course, exhaust the variety of student political behavior; they have been selected for analysis because of their measurability and assumed political importance.

Voting

In Nigeria the basic voting requirement is to be twenty-one years of age. As UCI students were comparatively old, only three students among those classified as Non-Affiliates, Action Groupers, or NCNCers were ineligible by the criterion of age.[18] Of those who were eligible, 73 per cent registered to vote and 52 per cent voted. These figures are very close to those for the adult Nigerian population. As it was possible for the students to register and vote at Ibadan, only those who had registered elsewhere were handicapped. They could either travel home to vote or change their place of registration (the latter choice was not always perceived). As table 2 indicates, Affiliates were more likely to register than Non-Affiliates (75 per cent to 31 per cent), and, having registered, they were more likely to vote (72 per cent to 16 per cent). Among the Action Groupers, the more active students were more likely to register and more likely to follow through by voting. Among the NCNCers, only the association between activity and registration holds; for those who registered, activity is not associated with voting. There was little difference between the party Affiliates in the over-all percentage of those who registered (AG, 74 per cent; NCNC, 75 per cent), and in the percentage of those registered who voted (AG, 75 per cent; NCNC, 71 per cent).

Party Organizational Activity

Touring party teams and rallies constitute the core of political campaigning in Nigeria. The teams, consisting of a party luminary, the local

---

[18] Some students were probably ineligible on other grounds, but their number was presumed so small that the additional data necessary to identify them were not collected.

TABLE 2
POLITICAL ACTIVITIES OF STUDENTS
(In percentages[a])

Factor	Action Group						NCNC			
	Non-Affiliates	Affiliates	Nomi-nals	Occa-sionals	Actives	Total	Nomi-nals	Occa-sionals	Actives	Total
VOTING	(19)	(267)	(46)	(53)	(29)	(128)	(58)	(52)	(29)	(139)
Voted	5	54	41	57	76	55	43	54	69	53
Registered but did not vote	26	21	20	17	21	19	21	21	28	22
Did not register	68	25	39	26	3	26	36	25	3	25
PARTISAN ORGANIZATIONAL ACTIVITY										
Membership	(22)	(267)	(46)	(53)	(29)	(128)	(58)	(52)	(29)	(139)
In party and student wing	0	20	0	9	72	20	0	15	69	20
In party only	0	3	0	4	3	2	0	6	10	4
In student wing only	0	16	0	40	24	22	0	25	10	12
In neither	100	60	100	47	0	55	100	54	10	64
Attendance at meetings	(22)	(263)	(45)	(52)	(29)	(126)	(57)	(51)	(29)	(137)
Off and on campus	0	19	0	8	59	17	0	16	69	20
Off campus only	0	5	0	8	3	4	0	16	3	7
On campus only	0	22	0	42	34	25	0	37	24	19
Did not attend	100	54	100	42	3	54	100	31	3	54
Campaigning	(22)	(265)	(45)	(53)	(29)	(127)	(58)	(51)	(29)	(138)
Off and on campus	0	14	0	4	52	13	0	4	62	14
Off campus only	0	6	0	17	0	7	0	8	7	4
On campus only	0	17	0	30	48	24	0	18	24	12
Did not campaign	100	63	100	49	0	56	100	71	7	70
DEMONSTRATIONS ON INTERNATIONAL ISSUES	(22)	(262)	(45)	(53)	(29)	(127)	(57)	(49)	(29)	(135)
Demonstrated	52	50	42	43	62	47	40	57	65	52
Did not demonstrate	48	50	58	57	38	53	60	43	35	48

[a] Figures in parentheses indicate number of students in each category for each factor.

candidate or candidates, and several functionaries, usually campaign at prearranged locations where from several dozen to several thousand local inhabitants gather. The tour routes are usually drawn in advance to maximize effectiveness within the party and minimize conflict among parties. This mode of campaigning, in contrast to the leaflet and door-to-door methods heavily relied upon in the United States, does not require a large corps of rank-and-file members, such as students help to supply in other countries.

Another characteristic of Nigerian election campaigns is that appeals are highly localized; few national issues are stressed. Therefore, except for party luminaries, those not brought up in an area are usually not effective campaigners in it. Because most campaigning for the 1959 federal elections took place during the school term (the election was held on December 12, 1959, the day the first term ended), many students were not able to campaign in their home areas.

Perhaps the most important reason for the students' minimum off-campus campaign participation was their relationship with the masses. Some students were "elitists" and did not like to associate with the masses, who often perceived and resented this attitude. Having a higher Western education makes students "feel that they have acquired some extremely valuable qualities which entitle them to the respect of others. . . . Those who do not have it tend to feel inferior to those who do, and to feel cut off from them." [19]

The gap between students and the masses, however, was far from unbridgeable. First, some students were willing and able to associate with the masses; one aspect of this is a "populism" that developed as a reaction to the education gap and the consequent distance from their people. Second, the students' ideas of social justice, a product of their Western and traditional educations, were viewed favorably by the masses. Third, traditional ties bound men from all levels of the modern stratification system. And fourth, higher education was very much respected.

The political value of students to political parties varied because of these conflicting elements. It was probably worthwhile to have a student return to his village to speak for the chosen political party, but unless a family or community tie existed, the effect might have been the opposite of that desired. Many Nigerians have reacted negatively to partisan propaganda delivered by young students. Such experiences kept some students from further participation in active campaigning off the campus.

Although on-campus involvement in the federal election campaign was not impressively high,[20] Affiliates of both the Action Group and the

---

[19] Edward Shils, "Political Development in the New States," *Comparative Studies in Society and History*, II (1960), 272.

[20] "The Federal elections did not disturb the College to any great extent, though the Halls displayed numerous posters exhorting us to vote this way or that, and

NCNC were more active on campus than off. More students attended meetings on campus than off, more campaigned on campus than off, and, perhaps as a result, more were members of the student wings than of the parties themselves (see table 2). The student wings of the Action Group and the NCNC met throughout the year, but except during election campaigns and on other special occasions, attendance was limited to a core group of from six to twelve students. There was little interest in having party sympathizers attend. At regular sessions, national party policy was discussed and representatives to the national party meetings were selected. Activities of and participation in the student wings increased considerably during the 1959 federal election campaign. Although the modal size of the meetings was still small (between twenty and thirty), attendance occasionally jumped to the hundreds (including some for whom curiosity was the only motive). The student wings were directly in charge of campaigning on campus, although there was some supervision from party headquarters. Campaigning off campus, however, was under the direction of regular party organizations.

There was little difference between the political organizational activity patterns of the Action Groupers and the NCNCers. The former were slightly more active on campus (more were members of the student wing, more attended meetings on campus, and more campaigned on campus), whereas the off-campus activities of the two groups were quantitatively the same, except that the NCNCers attended a few more meetings.

Yoruba were generally more active than were the members of other ethnic groups. This pattern was not particular as to setting or as to specific activity. Off campus and on, by membership, attendance at meetings, and campaigning, the Yoruba were the most active group.

The specific campaign activities listed by the students in an open-end question suggest the nature of their participation. Among the off-campus activities were traveling to neighboring villages to talk, organizing party dances, addressing party meetings, distributing placards, making campaign tours in the division, working in the party organization, and campaigning house to house. Among the on-campus activities were campaigning room to room, talking to small groups, enrolling supporters' names, writing posters and newspaper releases, helping with membership drives, taking students to attend election talks, and distributing placards among students and stewards. These activities may be classified as agitational (e.g., speaking) and administrative (e.g., mailing literature or planning). When a further division is made on the basis of on- and off-campus campaigning, clear differences appear be-

various polling stations were set up on the compound" ("The Term at Ibadan," editorial in *Ibadan*, VIII [March, 1960], 33).

tween Action Group and NCNC Affiliates. On campus, 31 per cent of the NCNCers who could be classified in terms of this dichotomy were administrators; off campus, the figure was 50 per cent. In the Action Group, 18 per cent of the students active on campus were administrators; off campus there were none. These percentages suggest differences in the character of the two national party organizations. The strength of the Action Group was organization; its weakness was its lack of appeal to the masses.[21] Students were therefore called upon to remedy this failing. On the contrary, the strength of the NCNC was mass appeal and its weakness was poor organization. Thus the student NCNCers were called upon for administrative roles.

Student activity patterns, in terms of the agitator-administrator dichotomy, contrast sharply with the roles the students wanted to fill after leaving UCI (or after completing their bond). Most NCNC Affiliates wanted to be agitators and most Action Group Affiliates wanted to be administrators. These hopes conform with the images the students had of the strengths (or the valued characteristics) of their parties, and indicate an identification process.

Student Demonstrations and Protests

The November 29, 1960, issue of the Lagos newspaper, *West African Pilot,* carried the front-page headline: STUDENTS STORM PARLIAMENT— POLICE USE TEAR GAS ON DEMONSTRATORS. Several hundred students from UCI (joined by other students) had demonstrated and forced their way into the reception hall leading to the chambers of the federal legislature to protest the defense pact between Nigeria and the United Kingdom.

The public demonstration or protest was probably the most effective means of political intervention available to students. Some students sat on political party councils and other policy-making groups; more participated at the lower organizational levels. But their influence in these organizations and through them on the country's power elite was quite limited. Demonstrations, on the other hand, were noted throughout the country and perhaps throughout the world. One politician commented: "The students' efforts have certainly been felt. When they protested against the Eastern pension bill, . . . the bill was immediately withdrawn and Zik stated that the students were right. The student protest against the Western Government did not affect a change of policy but at least the issue of right or wrong became a national one and well publicized." The student demonstration or protest had considerable influence for the same reasons that students in general played an important political role in Nigeria: the dearth of nongovernmental intellectuals and

---

[21] See pp. 434–435, below.

the resulting lack of "an effectively critical evaluation" [22] of government policies.

UCI students engaged in five major demonstrations or protests between January, 1959, and June, 1960: against Prime Minister Harold Macmillan for the United Kingdom's passive attitude toward *apartheid* and African nationalism, against the South Africans for the Sharpeville shootings, against the French for testing atomic weapons in the Sahara, against the Eastern Regional government for a pension bill, and against the Western Regional government for a housing bill.

In order to convey the impact of student action (as well as to illustrate other points made in this paper), the Western Regional protest will be described in some detail. On May 1, 1959, a group of UCI students met and approved a memorandum to Chief Obafemi Awolowo, then premier of the Western Region. (Although I found no concrete evidence that the action was organized by Affiliates of one political party, members of the NCNC were at least pleased by the developments.) The memorandum protested a new £800 housing allowance for Awolowo. The incident was reported on page 1 of the Lagos *Sunday Times* of May 3 under the headline, UCI STUDENTS CONDEMN MINISTERIAL ALLOWANCES. The story read: "More than 700 students of the University College, Ibadan, at a meeting on Friday night, approved a protest memorandum to Chief Obafemi Awolowo, Premier of Western Nigeria, on what they describe as the 'fantastic and anti-nationalistic catapulting of the housing allowance paid to him by the Government of the West.'" [23] The next day the NCNC *Southern Nigeria Defender* (Ibadan) printed most of the text of the memorandum under the headline, UCI STUDENTS PROTEST AGAINST HOUSE ALLOWANCE TO AWO. The flavor is apparent from these passages:

It would be realized that fantastic salaries as are being paid to Nigerian politicians have helped to produce a type of professional politician who is more interested in the pay than in the public service.

Let us appeal to Chief Awolowo not to continue to exploit the indifference with which the people of the West treat all governmental activities in his process of establishing a country where all the state money is spent to enrich the purses of politicians.[24]

Awolowo was quick to reply to the students:

---

[22] Cf. Edward Shils, "Intellectuals, Public Opinion, and Economic Development," *World Politics*, X (Jan., 1958), 232–255.

[23] The *Sunday Times* is owned by an English newspaper syndicate and is independent in Nigerian politics.

[24] Pp. 1–2.

AWO HITS CLAIMS OF UCI STUDENTS

Cites Figures To Show Charges of Luxury False

The Premier of the Western Region, Chief Obafemi Awolowo, said today that "it is anti-nationalistic to enjoin Ministers to live apart from their own people in reservations. . . . It is unpatriotic and utterly insincere to suggest that this evil heritage of the past should be perpetuated and enhanced by erecting palaces for Ministers in these exclusive areas." [25]

The students in turn answered Awolowo:

UCI STUDENTS REPLY TO AWOLOWO

. . . .

"The statement of Chief Obafemi Awolowo, Premier of the Western Region, on our humble suggestion to him to forego the fantastic housing allowance paid to him, has raised grave issues. . . .

"The students are interested in influencing the Nigerian public." [26]

After the exchange between the students and Awolowo, the Action Group newspaper questioned the size and the make-up of the original protesting group under the headline, UCI: NOT 700 BUT JUST 27,[27] and the NCNC press suggested that the Action Group was threatening those who held Western Regional scholarships:

DOES AG PLAN TO PUNISH STUDENTS?

. . . .

It was reliably learned yesterday that certain Action Group topnotchers had been frequenting the University College Campus only to issue threats to the students under the Western Government scholarship to coerce them to dissociate themselves from the memorandum submitted to Chief Obafemi Awolowo, . . . or their scholarships would be withdrawn.[28]

The final comment in this exchange appeared in the Action Group newspaper, whose editorialist, "John West," struck an anti-intellectual note:

THERE IS NOT ENOUGH THINKING AT THE UNIVERSITY COLLEGE

. . . Nigeria is not the first country to have the experience of undergraduates who seek to run Governments of their respective countries from their University Campus.

Therefore Nigerian students in the University College, Ibadan, and in other institutions who in their enthusiasm and ignorance endeavour to apply to our public affairs data copied from text books are only following a tradition.[29]

The Western Region protest was centered at UCI; participation by other

---

[25] Lagos *Daily Service* (AG newspaper), May 4, 1959, p. 1.
[26] *Southern Nigeria Defender,* May 8, 1959, pp. 2–3 (italics added).
[27] *Nigerian Tribune,* May 8, 1959, p. 1.
[28] *Southern Nigeria Defender,* May 9, 1959, pp. 1, 3.
[29] *Daily Service,* May 9, 1959, p. 6.

Nigerian groups was limited. In the end the protest had no effect upon the housing allowance bill.

The other incursion UCI students made into Nigerian domestic politics was a protest against clauses in the Eastern Region Legislative Houses Bill, which provided pensions for high political officeholders. Again there was a meeting, protest telegrams, and newspaper coverage. A significant difference in this second instance was broader participation by other Nigerian groups. As a result, the regional legislature withdrew the protested clauses.

There is little difference in the percentages of Non-Affiliates and Affiliates who participated in the international demonstrations (the students were not asked about their participation in the domestic protests because the necessary questions were judged to be too sensitive), but activity level is associated with participation (see table 2). Almost two-thirds of the Actives in each party participated in at least one demonstration in the period covered by the inquiry. Slightly more NCNCers than Action Groupers participated in a demonstration, but the small margin of difference suggests that neither party monopolized this mode of influence.

STUDENT OPINIONS

In this section selected student opinions about Nigerian politics are reported. The questionnaire included one item designed to establish which students took part in political conversations, and eight items calling for evaluations of the leadership, ideology, vote-getting ability, and governing ability of the Action Group and the NCNC. These items were quantitatively analyzed. In the partially structured interviews with a non-probability sample of 73 students, some opinions were emphatically and frequently voiced, suggesting that they were probably representative of the student body as a whole. Because of the sampling procedure employed, these opinions are not (with the exception of "more-or-less" statements) quantitatively analyzed.

The classification of a student as "political conversationalist," "non-conversationalist," or in the middle categories was based upon an index developed from answers to questions asking how often he talked with fellow students, other friends, and relatives about Nigerian political issues. Table 3 shows that those affiliated with a political party, and among the Affiliates the Actives, conversed the most. The NCNC group included slightly more conversationalists than did the Action Group. The characteristics of the conversationalists were similar to those of the partisans. There were more Yoruba (46 per cent) than Ibo (37 per cent), more from the west (58 per cent) than from the east (36 per cent), equal numbers from the four home-town population categories, more from

Table 3

POLITICAL OPINIONS OF STUDENTS
(In percentages[a])

Factor	Non-Affiliates	Affiliates	Action Group Nominals	Action Group Occasionals	Action Group Actives	Action Group Total	NCNC Nominals	NCNC Occasionals	NCNC Actives	NCNC Total
DEGREE OF PARTICIPATION IN POLITICAL DISCUSSIONS	(22)	(267)	(46)	(53)	(29)	(128)	(58)	(52)	(29)	(139)
Conversationalists	14	28	20	15	48	24	21	35	48	32
High middle	23	21	30	25	17	25	12	17	24	17
Low middle	23	30	28	36	21	30	33	33	17	28
Nonconversationalists	41	22	22	25	14	21	34	15	10	22
IMAGE OF OWN PARTY										
Leadership			(44)	(53)	(29)	(126)	(52)	(49)	(29)	(126)
Good			43	42	52	44	25	43	57	39
Fair			50	57	48	52	58	46	39	49
Poor			7	2	0	3	17	11	4	12
Ideology			(42)	(53)	(28)	(123)	(51)	(49)	(29)	(129)
Good			43	34	64	44	44	72	76	61
Fair			48	64	36	52	48	28	24	35
Poor			10	2	0	4	8	0	0	3
Vote-getting ability			(42)	(53)	(28)	(123)	(51)	(49)	(28)	(128)
Good			31	26	50	33	49	67	71	61
Fair			55	57	39	52	41	31	29	34
Poor			14	17	11	15	10	2	0	5
Governing ability			(42)	(53)	(29)	(124)	(51)	(49)	(28)	(129)
Good			57	60	83	64	25	43	61	40
Fair			40	40	17	35	62	47	36	50
Poor			2	0	0	2	13	10	4	10
IMAGE OF OPPOSITION PARTY										
Leadership			(42)	(45)	(28)	(115)	(52)	(41)	(26)	(119)
Good			0	7	0	3	8	22	15	14
Fair			64	31	64	51	63	63	62	63
Poor			36	62	36	46	29	15	23	23
Ideology			(39)	(44)	(28)	(111)	(52)	(39)	(26)	(117)
Good			3	5	0	3	2	3	4	3
Fair			33	43	54	42	29	36	42	34
Poor			64	52	46	55	69	62	54	63
Vote-getting ability			(41)	(45)	(29)	(115)	(52)	(41)	(26)	(119)
Good			24	13	25	20	13	20	12	15
Fair			46	60	59	55	46	49	65	51
Poor			29	27	17	25	40	32	23	34
Governing ability			(42)	(45)	(29)	(116)	(52)	(41)	(26)	(119)
Good			0	2	0	1	2	5	4	4
Fair			16	7	21	14	31	40	42	36
Poor			84	91	79	85	67	56	54	60

[a] Figures in parentheses indicate number of students in each category for each factor.

lower-status backgrounds (69 per cent) than from higher-status backgrounds, more privately sponsored (67 per cent) than government-sponsored, more going into teaching (54 per cent) than not, and more newcomers (59 per cent) than old-timers. The similarity suggests both overlap and substitutability of behavior.

Images of Parties

The Action Group and the NCNC have frequently been compared as to governing ability, leadership, ideology, and vote-getting ability. The Action Group, at least at the time of this study, usually ranked higher on the first two. To explore the students' attitudes toward political parties, eight items in the questionnaire called for an evaluation of the parties (good, fair, or poor) on each of the foregoing points. Table 3 shows that supporters rating their own parties view the Action Group as better at governing and the NCNC as possessing a better ideology and superior vote-getting ability. The leadership of the Action Group was rated slightly higher than that of the NCNC. Students' images of the opposition (see table 3) differed only slightly from those of supporters. Again, in comparing the ratings, the Action Group was regarded as the better governing party and as having better leadership. The NCNC was rated slightly higher on ideology and vote getting.

Comments recorded during the interviews support these quantitative patterns. Action Groupers stated that their party has "a definite plan" and "accomplishes its programs." Members of the NCNC spoke of their opposition as having "good stability, organization, and planning" and "discipline in its rank and file." NCNC Affiliates emphasized their party's ideology. One supporter commented, "I think that the NCNC has a policy which would . . . benefit the whole nation and strengthen national solidarity." Another referred to "the great ideology of the NCNC." Members of the Action Group also identified the NCNC with ideology, although it was often attacked as a sham (e.g., "The ideology says one thing and the activities quite another"). Perhaps the best summary statement of the governing and ideological contrasts between the parties was provided by an NCNC Nominal: "Frankly, I do not think there is much to choose between . . . [the parties], for while the ideology of the NCNC is unquestionably the best, the organization of the Action Group certainly is very admirable."

Action Groupers tended to talk more about the vote-getting abilities of the two parties. "The NCNC," said one, "is able to whip up the emotional forces of nationalism, which still accounts for its ascendancy in Nigerian politics." Comments on their own party included: "[It] is years ahead of the people," and "My party is very good at getting votes of the intelligentsia . . . but rather poor at catching votes of the uneducated masses." Comments recorded during the interviews also confirm the higher rating of Action Group leadership. Some students viewed Nnamdi Azikiwe and the NCNC leadership favorably (e.g., "The [NCNC] leadership is highly dynamic, brilliant, and the champion of Nigerian nationalism"). But a larger number of supporters and opponents viewed it otherwise. An NCNC Occasional spoke of the "weakening leadership of the party," and a Nominal said, "It would appear at present that the NCNC leadership, by which I mean not only Dr. Azikiwe but also the ministers, is puny beside the great ideology of that party." This similarity in partisan images parallels an observation about Republicans and Democrats in the United States: "The picture of the two candidates as seen through the eyes of the voters was fairly similar for Republicans and Democrats. . . . The majority of both groups looked upon Willkie as a businessman's and Roosevelt as the working man's champion." [30]

In both parties the Actives rated their own party higher on all four dimensions than did the Occasionals or the Nominals. Thus, belief in the worth of a party was associated with activity for the party. A recent study has found that leaders divide more sharply than their followers on political issues, for, with their "greater awareness and responsibility, and their greater need to defend their party's stands, they have more interest in developing a consistent set of attitudes" than the followers who are "often ignorant of the issues and their consequences." [31] The Actives of both parties also tended to be less critical of their opposition than did those in the less active strata. This suggests that the Actives may have realistically perceived "grays" rather than only "blacks and whites" in the game of politics. A similar conclusion is based on the study of a nationwide sample of American community leaders and followers: "All categories of community leaders . . . tend on the average to be *more respectful of the civil rights of those of whom they disapprove* than the average person in the general population, either of the same cities from which the leaders come or of the nation as a whole." [32]

Contemporary Politics

The opinions of most UCI students about contemporary politics were negative. Targets of the negativism included politics itself, politicians, and political parties. This approach was in part a manifestation of the intellectuals' oppositionalism often found in developing countries:

---

[30] Paul F. Lazarsfeld, Bernard Berelson, and Hazel Gaudet, *The People's Choice* (New York: Columbia University Press, 1944), pp. 28–29.

[31] Herbert McClosky, Paul J. Hoffman, and Rosemary O'Hara, "Issue Conflict and Consensus among Party Leaders and Followers," *American Political Science Review*, LIV (June, 1960), 420.

[32] See Samuel A. Stouffer, *Communism, Conformity and Civil Liberties* (New York: Doubleday, 1955), esp. chap. 2. The quotation appears on p. 27.

The intellectuals of the underdeveloped countries since they acquired independence, insofar as they are not in authority, do incline toward an anti-political, oppositional attitude. They are disgruntled. The form of the constitution does not please them and they are reluctant to play the constitutional game. Many of them desire to obstruct the government or give up the game of politics altogether, retiring into a negative state of mind about all institutional politics or at least about any political regime which does not promise a "clean sweep" of the inherited order.[33]

The students' political negativism was also an outlet for adolescent and young-adult revolt, which is intensified in a transitional society where conflict between tradition and modernity fuses with the ambivalence of youth toward authority. Finally, the negativism must be viewed in terms of the students' prospective career patterns. Many were going into the public services where their political activities would be restricted and, in the word of one student, where they themselves would be "governmentalized." The students were protesting the imminent "capture" of their intellect.

Politics.—The main theme running through the students' negative comments on politics was that it was "dirty" and therefore something to be avoided. One student said, "In order that my hands will ever remain clean I have decided not to be an active partisan in national politics." A member of the faculty observed that "students do not want to dirty themselves in the political arena." And an official of the NCNC suggested that the students "did not want to dirty their hands in politics." This attitude was probably due in part to the students' elitism, and consequently to an unwillingness to get into the rough-and-tumble of the game of politics. It may have been crystallized by a few jostlings that UCI students received in the town of Ibadan.

Politicians.—The students frequently and sharply criticized contemporary Nigerian politicians. The usual theme was that they were out to benefit themselves—that is, they were out for more money and the good life—rather than the nation. One student commented: "Many of us feel that most of those who want to be elected are not really moved by the true desire to serve but by selfish interests. We choose to give them a deaf ear." Charges of corruption were often made, ranging from the general—"Most politicians everywhere are corrupt!"—to the particular: "The Constitutional Convention was held in London so the Nigerian Ministers could get money by padding their expense accounts."

On several occasions the contrast between the contemporary political mammon and the students' ideal was pointed out: "People continue to regard politics as a money-making career rather than a sacrifice in the

---

[33] Shils, "The Intellectuals in the Political Development of the New States," p. 353.

interest of the nation," and "Even the few good politicians have all become money-conscious. . . . Let them clear out so that the people with
a mission can do their work in their life span." Sometimes Nigerian politicians who do and say the "right" thing are seen as "putting up a front."
One student used the phrase "gangs of pseudo nationalists" to indicate
what he thought about contemporary politicians.

One of the more important reasons for the students' attitudes toward
politicians is that the latter had the power that the students coveted.
The students, using their higher education as a base value, desired and
were moving toward power. The conflict was thus between a contemporary elite and a challenging group. In order to forestall the students' rise, many politicians attempted to keep student participation at
a minimum, although exploiting it when advantageous. According to one
party official, "The politicians are afraid of . . . [the students] and want
to keep them 'in their place.'" The youth of Africa are "ambitious to
attain the high offices now held by the older generation of nationalist
agitators. . . . They are confronted, however, with an entrenched elite
determined to hold on to high office and the affluence derived therefrom." [34]

Another reason that politicians hold student participation to a minimum is the limited number of jobs in party organizations. As most officeholders in both party and government were young, few openings developed: "At the very time that large numbers of a new and politically
ambitious generation are commencing to flow into the political arena,
there is likely to be increased restrictiveness in admission to the ranks of
the national political elite." [35]

Political parties.—Political parties were also the target of student
attacks. Although some of the negative comments were general, most of
them centered on tribalism. "When some individuals wanted to partake
of the glories of public office," said one student, "political parties which
appeal to tribal sentiments came into being. . . . An appeal to tribal
sentiments is the easiest way for getting votes." The desire was for a
party of unity: "The political party I prefer is not at present existing in
the country. It is one that will be open to all the tribes, work for the good
of all the tribes, . . . [and] make the various people feel and act as a
nation with malice to none, alien or natives, and fairness to all for
Nigeria." And from another student: "I strongly believe that Nigeria has
not had the right national political party yet. Certainly, all three major
parties today are not fulfilling the important task of instilling into the
minds of the people the spirit and essence of a Nigerian unity." These
quotations might suggest that the evidence has been weighted in favor

[34] Coleman, "The Politics of Sub-Saharan Africa," pp. 344–345.
[35] *Ibid.*, p. 345.

of the "anti's." But the fact is that when politics, politicians, or political parties were discussed during interviews, the comments were usually negative. If the student was an Affiliate, comments about his own political party were usually favorable, but the political arena in general was treated negatively.

Political Issues

The UCI students included in the sample were generally hostile toward ethnic institutions, the remnants of colonialism, and Western parliamentary democracy. They favored directed socialism. These opinions are described and illustrated below.

Ethnic institutions.—Most African leaders, it has been asserted, call for "the weakening of traditional loyalties . . . in favour of the new loyalties, to the emergent nation, the new State, the party, the party leader (or leaders), and the wider objectives of African emancipation."[36] This was also the students' position. The essence of their attacks on the tribalism of political parties was expressed in the previously quoted anonymous student editorial: "The events of the last few weeks have revealed certain ugly facts about our society. Who would have thought that tribalism is still a potent force in our community?" Only one student spoke favorably of the "historical institutions of obaships and emirates," whereas remarks such as the following were common: "All houses of chiefs should be disbanded," and "The Government should do away with the innumerable petty chiefs now parading the country."

Replies to questions about the institutions of family and community were less negative. Several students spoke or wrote about them favorably, as in this comment: "I believe that tribalism, like family loyalty, is a natural feeling. . . . In its good form it ought not to be antithetical to the greater loyalty to the state."[37] Distinguishing among "loyalty to the family: loyalty to the tribal community: and loyalty to the tribal government, or chief," Wallerstein says that urban Africans are most loyal to family and community, but that "they tend to lose some of their respect for the authority of the chief."[38] The UCI students seem to have conformed to this picture of the urban African.

Colonial remnants.—Nigerian students at UCI were learning about Western culture in a Western language; their status in society was and will be based primarily upon the knowledge, the skills, and the symbolic diploma attained. Yet their hostility toward many of the remnants of Western colonialism was intense. A dynamic relationship probably existed

[36] Thomas Hodgkin, *African Political Parties* (Penguin Books, 1961), p. 157.
[37] Ukpabi Asika, "The Nigerian Scene—As I See It," *The Beacon* (March, 1960), p. 7.
[38] Immanuel Wallerstein, "Ethnicity and National Integration in West Africa," *Cahiers d'Etudes Africaines*, no. 3 (Oct., 1960), 130.

between their attempt to overcome the feeling of dependence upon Western culture and the intense and hostile demands for independence in other areas.

Colonial administrators imposed many political institutions upon Nigeria, sometimes with African consent. The following comments illustrate how some of these institutions were viewed by the UCI students: "Nigeria, as soon as possible after independence, must be declared a republic with a president as the head of the country. . . . We do not wish to have the Queen as the head of our sovereign state after independence," and "The federal type of government is a relic of imperialist manoeuver to weaken an up-surging Nigeria."

Independence was also demanded for the personality. What was needed was a "Nigerian personality" or an "African personality." It has been said that Alioune Diop gave the clearest articulation of the later concept: "The African personality, which is the basis and foundation of our humanism, aspires . . . to being freed from the Western grip." [39] One student asserted, "The Nigerian personality and the African personality must be realized." And another, writing in a student newspaper, said, "What is needed today in the West African political scene is time; time to repair the damage done to the personality of the individual by the imperial master over several years of bondage and servitude, time to readjust the inhibitions of the people to their own sense of respect to constituted authority." [40]

Parliamentary democracy.—"Rejection of dictatorship and belief in the democratic ideal are attitudes common to virtually all African leaders." [41] Yet many UCI students were skeptical about the possibility or the advisability of democracy, at least in its parliamentary form, in Nigeria. "At least at the present stage of Nigerian development," said one student," "I personally do not support too much of democracy. Positive action is needed now to save the country from rising as a weak giant in the continent of Africa." Why was democracy not considered advisable? Illiteracy and diversity were the reasons most often given: "Nigeria is still an illiterate country and that is why democracy has virtually failed in the country," and "I feel that the peoples of Nigeria are so diverse, many different languages and dialects, varying culture, different historical backgrounds, different religions, that parliamentary democracy will never solve Nigeria's problems." Democracy as practiced in countries outside Africa was often discussed at the interviews with students. It was difficult to turn conversations from South Africa and the South in the United States. The usual view was represented in this comment: "The so-

---

[39] Colin Legum, *Pan-Africanism* (New York: Praeger, 1962), p. 118.

[40] Obiajunwa Wali, "Lesson from Ghana," *The Beacon* (Easter, 1958), p. 2.

[41] Legum, *op. cit.*, p. 121.

called Western democracy is a sham. In no part of the world is there anything like democracy. The word should be forgotten."

It is important to emphasize that the students' opposition to democracy was directed chiefly against its parliamentary form. The present prime minister of Nigeria, Sir Abubakar Tafawa Balewa, asserts that "democracy is essentially government by discussion." [42] In practice the UCI students did not always permit discussion, but they usually championed it. The following appeared in a student newspaper: "Go to any meeting and try to express an opinion not acceptable to the majority and you are at once shouted down. . . . It is a disgrace to us." [43] Democracy also meant the transfer of power from the colonial administrators to the African *demos*, "exercised on its behalf by the party and its leadership, as the most effective organized expression of the aspirations and demands of the *demos*." [44] This was clearly linked to the students' opinions about directed socialism.

Directed socialism.—Regarding Western parliamentary democracy as unsuitable, many students called for dynamic centralized leadership and a socialist state. The need for a dynamic, selfless leader was voiced more often, in comments like these: "I strongly advocate any form of government where one individual can work almost like an executive"; "I would like to see a Nigeria led by a very strong, powerful, dynamic, educated, and honest president"; and "If Nigeria were to have an unprejudiced patriot as a leader, for just a decade, it would advance the country a century ahead of its present conditions." These observations suggest the truth of the statement that the "socialism of the intellectuals of the under-developed countries grows, fundamentally, from their feeling for charismatic authority, from their common humanity, and from the anti-chrematistic traditions of their indigenous culture. More immediately, it is a product of the conditions and substance of their education, and of their nationalistic sensibility." [45]

Students argued that politicians were corrupt and that there was too wide a disparity between the rich and the poor, and that therefore the country needed socialism: "For survival, Nigeria needs a socialist government for some years after independence. There is already too much corruption in the country and only such a government will relieve us of some of these evils and the doers of the evils," and "My preference is for a party that advocates a socialist state. This should not be interpreted to mean a communist state. In Nigeria today, the disparity between the

---

[42] Quoted in *ibid.*, p. 122.
[43] Editorial in *The Bug*, Feb. 21, 1959, p. 2.
[44] Hodgkin, *op. cit.*, p. 156.
[45] Shils, "The Intellectuals in the Political Development of the New States," p. 345.

few capitalists and well-off people and the poor, poverty-ridden masses is so great that something should be done to establish an equitable condition for everybody. A socialist state, a state where the welfare and equity of every rightful citizen exists, must be created." It should be emphasized that the students unequivocally rejected communism and Soviet leadership. The kind of socialism that they wanted—African socialism—remains to be developed in detail.

SUMMARY AND CONCLUSION

The students of the University of Ibadan had backgrounds that were not representative of the Nigerian population. They were, to name three important differences, drawn disproportionately from the Yoruba and Ibo ethnic groups, from urban areas, and from families of higher occupational status. Characteristics of those in the student body who were most active in partisan affairs included (1) membership in the Yoruba or the Ibo ethnic groups, which dominate the two major political parties of southern Nigeria; (2) lower occupational status, suggesting that power was pursued to compensate for status deprivation; (3) private sponsorship at UCI and intention to become teachers, indicating that government employment or sponsorship, and professional (excluding teaching) aspirations, minimized activity; and (4) their recent arrival at UCI, suggesting that the old-timers were more professionalized.

The students were deeply involved in politics. On almost all indicators used in this study—political discussions; organizational membership, attendance at meetings, and active campaign work; and participation in demonstrations and protests—the students seemed to be more politically involved than their counterparts in Anglo-American countries (except for American Negroes). The campus, however, was the primary setting for most of the students' activities. Political discussions were usually restricted to all-student groups, registration and voting percentages were not relatively high, and most of the students' party organizational activities were on the UCI campus. Even the demonstrations and protests were essentially campus affairs, for they were organized on the campus and at all stages their personnel were exclusively students.

Politics, politicians, and political parties were viewed negatively, and relationships between students and both politicians and the masses were poor (the students' elitism was a factor). These were among the causes for the campus setting of political activities. The students' images of political parties, however, indicate that they were socialized to national political issues. The most active students displayed considerable realism in their images of the opposition party. The more intensely and frequently expressed opinions about political issues included hostility toward ethnic institutions, the remnants of colonialism, and Western parliamentary democracy, and support for a socialist system with strong leadership.

The two primary aspects of the role of students in Nigerian politics are independent criticism and public-opinion leadership. The UCI students were numerically insignificant and they had little organizational power. Their votes, membership, attendance of meetings, and campaigning all had relatively slight impact. But their demonstrations and protests rallied and focused public opinion on symbolically or substantively important issues. The international demonstrations had considerable impact in Nigeria and were noted in the world press. (There are unconfirmed reports that Prime Minister Macmillan rewrote his speech to the South African Parliament after witnessing the UCI demonstration.) The protests on domestic issues met with varying success, but in both instances government action was exposed to public scrutiny.

The results of this study have important implications for the Nigerian political system in the coming decades. With the passing of the generation of elites which attained independence, Nigerian university graduates will probably assume many of the important posts in the political system. Almost half of them expected to be politically active in the future. Although the students will then be older and more professionalized, several developments seem likely. (1) An urban educated class, separated psychically, socially, and geographically from the masses, seems to be developing. Not only were a disproportionate number of students drawn from educated (based on father's or guardian's occupation) urban families, but they were even then elitist in self-image and narrow in the domain of their political communications. (2) If the students' political opinions may be used as indicators of their future political actions, decision making will continue to be the exclusive province of the educated urban elite, and the masses will remain the objects of modernization. The formalities of parliamentary democracy will be superseded by a directed socialism. (3) Southern minorities and the northern Hausa-Fulani will feel increasingly threatened. The data indicate that (a) the disparity in power and education between the two major southern ethnic groups and other southern groups is increasing, and (b) the minority groups in the Northern Region are advancing educationally more rapidly than are the powerful Hausa-Fulani. Of the twenty-four northerners whose tribal identification was known, only five were Hausa-Fulani. This situation could easily lead to revolt or repression unless a closer approach to parity is achieved in the distribution of the values of power and education. Such parity might come about through the recent establishment of four new universities in Nigeria.

This projected picture of Nigeria's future probably does not contrast significantly with those that might be drawn for other African countries.

Most have comparable gaps in their social, class, educational, and ecologic structures, and their new generation of elites have many of the same perspectives. Although independence has been gained by constitutional reformation, revolutionary transformations should not be ruled out in the future.

PART II

PARTIES AND NATIONAL INTEGRATION

The Transformation of Historic Oligarchies

12. LIBERIA

By J. Gus Liebenow

Liberia,[*] which has existed as an independent republic since 1847, is the only area of Tropical Africa where the history of political party competition may be reckoned in terms of decades rather than years or merely months. Indeed, almost from the establishment of Liberia in 1822 as a refuge for freed American slaves, partisanship has been a dominant social characteristic of the Americo-Liberians, as the settler community came to be called.

Superficially, at least, the party system as it developed in Liberia may be regarded as the prototype of the one-party system which is becoming the norm in the newer states of Africa. After a brief period of interparty rivalry in the nineteenth century, the True Whig Party captured control of all branches of government in Liberia, and has successfully weathered all foreign and domestic threats to its supremacy during the past eighty-five years. The party's monopoly in the political realm has permitted it to maintain control as well over all other forms of organization within the Republic. This, too, has become a feature of the political systems of Ghana, Guinea, and other new states.

The superficial resemblance of the True Whig Party to other dominant parties in Africa is, however, far outshadowed by the dissimilarities in objectives and tactics. The leaders of the Convention People's Party in Ghana and of the Tanganyika African National Union are seeking to bring about the rapid mobilization of all segments of a highly heterogeneous and tradition-oriented population in terms of modern and well-integrated political, social, and economic structures. In contrast with these revolutionary parties, the True Whig Party of Liberia is attempting to forestall or at least to moderate an inevitable revolution within the ranks of the twenty or more tribal groupings that comprise the majority of the population. Although the façade of mass support for the party is currently maintained, the minority associated with the alien settlement of Liberia, through its control over the decision-making process within the True

[*] This manuscript is based on field research conducted in Liberia during 1960–61. I am indebted to the Social Science Research Council and to the Indiana University Research Foundation for their generous assistance. Some of the observations made here have appeared previously in modified form in my contribution to Gwendolen Carter, ed., *African One-Party States* (Ithaca: Cornell University Press, 1962), pp. 325–395.

448

Whig Party, remains dominant.[1] Moreover, the manipulation of electoral processes, the subordination of all other forms of social interaction to the dictates of the party, and the party monopoly over governmental patronage have made it impossible for any competing group to pose an effective challenge to Americo-Liberian domination of the political scene.

HISTORICAL DEVELOPMENT OF THE PARTY SYSTEM

The all-absorbing concern of the Americo-Liberian community with politics and the law was an attitude of mind detectable almost from the founding of Liberia. As early as 1823, a year after the first settlement had been made near Monrovia, the colonists presented a petition to the American Colonization Society expressing their dissatisfaction with the paternalistic form of government provided by the society's founders. In ensuing years political protest found additional outlets, as the settlers were permitted to elect the vice-agent and the members of the Advisory Council, who were to be consulted by the white American agent in the administration of the colony.

With the expansion of the channels for protest, the circles of partisanship moved steadily beyond concern with personalities and such minor issues as the allocation of house plots and the regulation of conduct to concern with more basic cleavages within the ranks of the settlers. The principal line of factionalism divided the commercial elements of Monrovia from the more conservative agricultural groups down the coast, who chafed at the trade policies adopted by the administration. As the Monrovia group usually supported the agent in his policies, he indulged in some manipulation of the electoral machinery to ensure that the Monrovia faction elected the vice-agent and the majority of council members during the colonial period (1822–1839).[2]

It was not until the commonwealth period of limited self-rule (1839–1847) that an inchoate two-party system became observable, with Vice-Agent Joseph Jenkins Roberts leading the proadministration adherents and the Reverend John Seys leading the opposition within the commonwealth legislature. Seys carried out a vigorous harassment of the administration. He used his pulpit, his newspaper, town meetings, and the floor of the legislature to take Governor Thomas Buchanan and his successor, Roberts, to task for their policies and actions in the fields of health, relations with the native chiefs, foreign commerce, and taxation. Despite the

---

[1] In the absence of a census, the population of Liberia has been variously estimated to be as high as 3 million or as low as 800,000. The official estimate supplied for the United Nations *Demographic Yearbook* (1958) places the population at 1,250,000. Unofficial estimates of the ratio between tribal Africans and the Americo-Liberian minority are in the neighborhood of 20 to 1.

[2] G. S. Stockwell, *The Republic of Liberia* (New York: Barnes and Co., 1868), pp. 89–90.

fanaticism of Seys's followers and their occasional resort to violence, his party found itself unable to dislodge the Monrovia group from control of the commonwealth government. Although the opposition party apparently concurred in the decision of 1847 to break the ties binding the settlers to the American Colonization Society, it vigorously opposed the ratification of the proposed constitution for the Republic of Liberia and threatened to have Grand Bassa secede from the new state.[3]

After ratification of the constitution, the partisans of Governor Roberts assumed the name of the True Liberian, or Republic, Party. Roberts' victory over Samuel Benedict, the new leader of the Anti-Administration Party, in the first presidential election was repeated in the two subsequent elections. In the face of Roberts' popularity it was not surprising that the Anti-Administration Party presented only an ineffective threat to the Republicans and gradually faded out of existence. It is perhaps significant, however, for the future style of Liberian politics to record that Roberts named his defeated opponent as the first chief justice of the Liberian Supreme Court.

The successful challenge to President Roberts came from within his own party as he attempted to capture a fifth two-year term in the election of 1855. In view of the circumstances of Liberia's founding, it is ironic that the issue that brought his downfall and was to become a continuing source of political conflict was the matter of racial extraction. Roberts was an octoroon and of considerably lighter complexion than Stephen A. Benson, who was also of mixed parentage. This difference was apparently significant in bringing Benson the support of the poorer Americo-Liberians and the Congoes (liberated Africans who had been taken from slaving ships intercepted on the high seas), for both groups had long resented the aristocratic ways of persons of "brighter" skin color.[4]

The cleavage within the Republican Party over the issue of ancestry and skin pigmentation ultimately led to the victory of the True Whig Party, which had been formed in 1869 as the champion of the still vigorous commercial middle class and of those who felt the need to be liberated from "Toryism, Royalism and Castle distinctions symbolic of the then ruling Republican Party."[5] The victorious candidate, Edward J. Roye, became the country's first full-blooded Negro president. The success of Roye and his party was short-lived, however. In 1871 the resurgent Republicans took advantage of Roye's loss of popularity after a notorious loan agreement with British bankers and Roye's attempt to extend his term of office by unconstitutional means. He was ousted by a Republican

---

[3] Charles Henry Huberich, *The Political and Legislative History of Liberia* (New York: Central Book Co., 1947), I, 670 ff., 728–729, 841–842.

[4] Frederick Starr, *Liberia* (Chicago, 1913), p. 90.

[5] *Liberia Today*, VIII (May, 1959), 10.

junta, was incarcerated, and apparently died while attempting to escape from prison. His martyrdom is to be ensured by the decision of the True Whig Party in 1962 to erect its new national headquarters building on the site where he was imprisoned.

The Republican junta of 1871 also ousted Vice-President James S. Smith and brought back ex-President Roberts, who served until 1875 and was succeeded by ex-President Spriggs Payne. In the election of 1877 the True Whigs repeated history by defeating Payne, and began what has now become eighty-five years of uninterrupted control of the government of Liberia. The supremacy of the Whigs over the Republicans and all other parties was not really assured, however, until the election of Hilary R. W. Johnson in 1883. Johnson, the son of one of the pioneer heroes and the first presidential candidate to have been born in Liberia, was endorsed by both the True Whig and the Republican parties in the election. It was only after his victory that he declared himself a Whig and began the consolidation of his party's control of the Liberian political system.[6]

Thus the only period of really effective two-party competition in Liberia was the decade and a half from 1869 to 1884. Thereafter, Americo-Liberians found themselves captives of the very situation they had created through expansion of the republic into the hostile tribal hinterland beyond the five coastal counties and the subsequent conflicts with the British and the French, who were coveting the same areas. It was the need for solidarity in meeting the twin threats to their supremacy, posed by tribal rebellion and foreign occupation, which convinced Americo-Liberian leaders of the value of the single-party system. Periodically, incidents such as the Kru uprising in World War I, or the League of Nations inquiry into the problems of slavery in Liberia in the early 1930's, have reinforced the Americo-Liberian faith in the wisdom of this decision. When pressed to the wall, the party leadership has made tactical retreats and jettisoned its standard-bearer, as it did with President William D. Coleman in 1900 and again with President Charles D. B. King and Vice-President Allen N. Yancy in 1930. But the strategy of using the True Whig Party as the vehicle of Americo-Liberian supremacy has remained intact.

The changes brought by World War II, however, in the political, social, and economic milieu of Liberia's West African neighbors, and of Liberia itself, necessitated strategic as well as tactical shifts on the part of the True Whig leadership. Otherwise the Americo-Liberians could hardly hope to stay the tide of nationalism which was sweeping alien minorities from their positions of privilege elsewhere on the continent. The Whigs could not ignore the latent political forces unleashed by the

---

[6] Abayomi Karnga, *History of Liberia* (Liverpool: D. H. Tyte, 1926), p. 50.

launching of the Firestone Plantations Company in the 1920's, the League of Nations inquiry, the presence of American troops during World War II, and by the rise of mass-based parties and the introduction of development schemes in the British and French colonies of West Africa.

The election of William V. S. Tubman in 1943 signaled the departure from the previous strategy of isolating the tribal majority from alien contacts and of largely excluding them from participation in the affairs of the Liberian polity. The open-door policy was to bring in a flood of foreign investors, technicians, and businessmen to develop the iron ore and other natural resources of the Liberian hinterland. The Whig leaders recognized the political dangers inherent in the exposure of the tribal people to Westernization, industrialization, and urbanization, but they hoped not only to avoid the dangers but also to put the open-door policy to work in perpetuating the supremacy of the Americo-Liberian ruling class.

The second major strategic change was the nominal extension of the principles of representation and suffrage to the tribal majority. At the turn of the century, Arthur Barclay, in a move to forestall British encroachments on the northwest frontier, had given the tribal people Liberian citizenship; this action had cost the Americo-Liberians nothing in terms of real power. Equally inexpensive, but highly significant in terms of propaganda value for the Tubman regime, were the granting of representation in the lower house of the legislature to the three hinterland provinces and the elimination of most barriers to universal adult suffrage. The continued control by the True Whig Party over the electoral process, patronage, and voluntary group activity made these "victories" for the tribal people hollow indeed. Without ignoring the need for force, or for elaborate legal technicalities in dealing with political dissent on the part of the tribal people or from within the ranks of the Americo-Liberian class itself, the party has been able to maintain the appearance of having overwhelming popular support.

The third, and perhaps the most important, pillar of the new strategy of the Whig Party has been the unification policy proclaimed by Tubman, which consists in the psychological identification of the tribal people with the objectives of the True Whig Party leadership. Prior to Tubman's regime, the Interior Department, in its "native" policy, placed major emphasis upon sanctions of a coercive nature. The Liberian Frontier Force was organized to instill fear and to deter tribal rebellion. The payment of hut taxes, the control over residence and population movements, the compulsory labor system, and extralegal exactions of money and services made by Liberian officials stressed the superiority of the Americo-Liberian elite over the tribal people. A modified system of indirect rule, moreover, not only kept the tribal people divided into twenty or more distinct ethnic groupings, but provided the Whigs with a rationale for excluding them from participation in the national life of the Liberian state. The personality of the tribal individual was to be developed within the context of traditional institutions. In respect to landholding, marriage and divorce, application of criminal and civil law, political rights, and the enjoyment of economic and welfare benefits provided by the central government, there have been, both in law and in fact, two distinct classes in Liberia—the Americo-Liberians and the tribal people.

Since the advent of Tubman, the lot of the tribal people has been significantly improved. To overcome the abuses that arose from lax administration of the interior, Tubman has held executive councils in the provinces at frequent intervals and has meted out swift justice even to those closely related to him. He has also announced new programs for the tribal people in the fields of health and education. In 1954, and again in 1959, he convened the National Unification Council and invited all elements within the country to attend it, in order to evaluate and criticize the implementation of the unification policy. Another facet of the policy is the naming of persons of tribal background to the executive, legislative, and judicial branches of the government. Many of the legal distinctions, at least, which have separated the two classes have been eliminated from the Liberian Code, and the paired usage of such terms as "civilized" and "uncivilized" or "Americo-Liberian" and "native" has been officially proscribed. The impact of the change in attitude is best underscored by the very real personal popularity that Tubman seems to enjoy wherever he journeys in the interior. Nevertheless, as a group of leading True Whigs themselves recently acknowledged, "the lines of cleavage are beginning to lessen somewhat, but the distinctions still remain. . . . It would be inaccurate to say that at this time members of the tribal groups are not at a disadvantage."[7]

PARTY LEADERS, MEMBERS, AND SUPPORTERS

Nominally, at least, the extension of the suffrage to women and the reduction of the property qualification for voting to the payment of a hut tax have opened the membership of the True Whig Party to every adult citizen of the Republic, regardless of his cultural origins. The only residents excluded from this largest circle of party involvement are minors, those disfranchised on moral or mental grounds, and aliens. For aliens the exclusion may be temporary or permanent, depending upon

---

[7] John P. Mitchell, ed., *Changing Liberia: A Challenge to the Christian*, report of the United Christian Fellowship Conference of Liberia, Switzerland, 1959, p. 12. The conference included, among others, the present secretaries of the treasury and education and the wife of the Speaker of the House.

whether or not the individual meets the constitutional requirement that limits citizenship to persons of Negro ancestry. The procedures of affiliation with the party are perhaps purposely vague. Although one may formally be read out of the party by a local or national convention of the True Whig Party for commission of certain acts, affiliation is not signaled by any formal action. One becomes a member of this largest circle of membership by voting for the party's candidates in the biennial elections for members of the legislature, and in the octennial or quadrennial elections for the presidency; by participating in precinct or other local True Whig meetings; by contributing funds to the organization or to individual candidates; by participating in party parades; or by giving, in other ways, outward signs of being a partisan in good standing.

Even within this widest circle, where each citizen has only a single vote, there is a qualitative distinction. Assuming the importance of the legislature in the national decision-making process, it is apparent that the tribal majority of the hinterland is grossly underrepresented. The ten members of the Senate are selected solely by the citizens of the five coastal counties (Grand Cape Mount, Montserrado, Grand Bassa, Sinoe, and Maryland). Moreover, only six of the thirty-nine members of the lower house in 1961 were selected by the people of the Western, Central, and Eastern provinces; the remainder represented the five counties and the four coastal territories (Marshall, River Cess, Kru Coast, and Sasstown). Even within the coastal strip, however, the preference given to Monrovia and the surrounding Montserrado County is evident, for almost one-fourth of the total membership came from Montserrado. In theory, seats are to be allocated on the basis of population as ascertained in a "true census," but to date no true census has been taken or published. Despite the absence of a national census, however, the legislature felt no qualms in 1959 in deciding that the increase in the population of Monrovia alone warranted the allocation of two additional seats to Montserrado County.[8] A similar bias in favor of Montserrado County (as well as of President Tubman's own Maryland County) is evident in the assignment of committee chairmanships in the legislature.

The second circle of political involvement is narrowed to those who participate in the nominating conventions for members of the legislature. Although in theory a county convention is open to all who can make the journey to the county headquarters, in fact the conventions are often limited to elected and appointed officials of the Liberian government, former officials, prominent private citizens, and "camp followers" of the leading committed candidates. Although the semblance of decisional autonomy is maintained, for the most part the nominations have been agreed upon by the True Whig leadership in advance of the convention.

---

[8] *Daily Listener,* Jan. 22, 1959, p. 1.

In the selection of representatives from the provinces, the convention frequently is an informal gathering of the leading chiefs and representatives of the Interior Department who decide upon a "safe" candidate.

The third circle of involvement comprises mainly those who hold or have held important posts in the government of Liberia. This circle is the bulwark of the True Whig Party and of the Americo-Liberian class, even though access is permitted to some who were not born into the class. Members of this group are held in high esteem, and entry into it is signified by one's being referred to as "Honourable" on public occasions or in the local press. Another outward and visible sign is the "knighting" of outstanding citizens by the president, a practice initiated by Anthony Gardiner in 1879 with the establishment of the Humane Order of African Redemption. The most recent addition to this odd trapping for a republic was Tubman's creation in 1955 of the Most Venerable Order of Knighthood of the Pioneers of Liberia.

Office holding is important not merely for prestige purposes, however. Public office provides access to the important sources of patronage. In addition to the traditional "dash," which is expected for the rendering of a public service, and the forgiveness of taxes or of payment for governmental services received by the official and his family, even more significant forms of patronage have appeared in the postwar period of economic development. Free housing and automobiles, frequent trips abroad on government business, preference in the awarding of foreign scholarships, access to presidential favor in the acquisition of land in the tribal hinterland, and the privilege of receiving exorbitant tax-free rentals on private buildings leased by the government are all part of the patronage system which enables the Americo-Liberian class to maintain a higher standard of living than the tribal majority.

Undoubtedly the unification policy of President Tubman and the sheer magnitude of the economic development of Liberia have enlarged the second and third circles of involvement, and recruitment is no longer strictly related to either culture or birth. Nevertheless, the latter factors are still of vital importance in restricting individual mobility within the Liberian political system. The movement from the first to the second circle of involvement is essentially a cultural transition. It is a passage from a tribal dialect or pidgin English to a modified form of American English; from ancestor worship or Islam to Protestant Christianity; from a subsistence economy based upon communal ownership to a cash-crop economy based upon private ownership of property; from acceptance of traditional political institutions based upon one of the twenty or more parochial tribal units to acceptance of political institutions bearing at least a superficial resemblance to those of the United States; and from acceptance of tribal to adoption of Westernized forms of food, dress, and architecture.

Passage from the second to the third circle is based upon much more narrowly ascriptive grounds—identification by birth or marriage with the pioneer founders of Liberia. It is for this reason that exact knowledge of the ancestral and connubial relationships of one's associates is essential for survival and advancement in the Liberian political fray. Regionally, certain families such as the Grigsbys in Sinoe, the Morgans in Grand Bassa, or the Gibsons in Maryland have greater prominence than others and tend to monopolize elective and appointive posts within their respective counties. Several families, on the other hand, enjoy national preëminence. These include not only the leading families of Monrovia or Montserrado County, such as the Barclays, the Colemans, the Grimeses, and the Kings, but also the Tubmans and the Yancys of Maryland and the Shermans of Cape Mount.

Marriage among the Americo-Liberians is as much a political act as it is a social or economic one and establishes more than a bond between two individuals. It interrelates a series of corporate groups to whom the parties to the marriage may turn for political allies, for information regarding changes in the political climate, and for access to the spoils available to the True Whig leadership. The corporate alliances may be established directly by the individual or through the marriages of his siblings or offspring to the members of other leading families. Conversely, divorce becomes a weapon of group conflict, and the sequence of marriages of some of the leading political personalities bears a rough approximation to the rise and fall in the political fortunes of the families of one's past, present, and prospective marriage partners.

The analysis of the genealogies of the leading officers in the Liberian government provides the objective observer, as well as the active participant, with the most significant map of the Liberian political terrain. In 1961 President Tubman, Vice-President William R. Tolbert, and Secretary of the Treasury Charles D. Sherman stood at the center of three sprawling yet overlapping dynasties. Earlier in the Tubman administration branches of the Dennis and Cooper extended families enjoyed a temporary preëminence over other dynastic groupings. Perhaps the family with the greatest resilience, however, is that including the descendants of Arthur Barclay, who emigrated to Liberia from the West Indies in 1865. Among his heirs there have been two presidents, several justices of the Supreme Court, and a host of legislators and cabinet members. Mrs. Tubman, the present secretary of state, the director of the National Public Health Service, and the recent ambassador to the United States are all members of the Barclay clan.

The recruitment of one's kinsmen to office gives the Whig patron increased status within the party as well as broader access to other forms of patronage. It is, however, a double-edged sword, for it increases the vulnerability of the key patron vis-à-vis other family leaders and the president himself. There is always a possibility that a minor member of the clan will commit an indiscretion and thus embarrass the key patron. The position of the president, too, is considerably enhanced by his role as the indispensable arbiter of interfamily conflicts. He may, moreover, indirectly put a major challenger to presidential authority on notice by removing some of his lesser kinsmen from office. In this way the equilibrium so essential to the maintenance of Whig supremacy is not seriously disturbed.

The recruitment of new political leadership from the lower-class Americo-Liberian families, from the Negro immigrant group, and from the tribal sector of the population takes place at a much slower rate. Good works, however, may have their reward, and one who occupies a minor post in government may by perseverance come to the attention of a leading politician who will serve as his patron. Many of the brighter tribal youths, for example, are adopted as wards by prominent Americo-Liberians and, upon maturity, such a ward may be given all the perquisites of the "Honourable" class and even the family name of his patron. One of the present members of the legislature is a tribal ward of former President Edwin Barclay. It may be, too, that a scarce talent, required quickly to fill a national need, can be found only outside the Honourable class. On this score the desirability of naming French-speaking ambassadors to Haiti and former French dependencies in Africa has permitted certain immigrants to achieve recognition on a par with sons of the First Families. Other talents, such as the gift of oratory, so characteristic of the Liberian political style, may be a factor in the political advancement of a teacher or a preacher from a lower-class Americo-Liberian family.

Those who advance on the basis of merit alone, or in spite of a tribal or alien background, are a potential threat to the regime. Advancement from outside the third circle not only constitutes an attack upon the rules of political preferment, but also presents the possibility that the new entrant will become attractive to the tribal majority. This accounts for the early and occasionally ruthless political demise of officials whose tribal antecedents have been unduly emphasized and who, as a consequence, have achieved a mass appeal. Three cabinet members in the years 1959–1963 suffered such a fate. The threat presented by the new entrant is diminished to the extent that he is legitimized by the establishment of marriage ties with a leading family. Such a connection is obviously valuable to him, as is also to the maintenance of the system, for it gives the newcomer a vested interest in the preservation of the privileged status of the ruling group and supplies him, too, with a set of relatives who will attempt to ensure that his adopted loyalties take precedence over his loyalties to his former tribe, kinsmen, or country.

In analyzing the characteristics of the Whig Party leadership which stands at the core of the third circle of political involvement—in effect, the fourth circle—one is struck not only by the emphasis upon family ties. As a group its members have had a greater per capita exposure to higher education than the leadership group in any of the newer African states. The establishment of Liberia College (now the University of Liberia) around 1858–1862 gave Liberia a substantial lead over its neighbors. Its position was enhanced in the postwar period by the establishment of Cuttington College in the interior and Our Lady of Fatima College in Maryland County, as well as by a veritable exodus of Liberian youths to study in the United States, Western Europe, Israel, and Asia under missionary, American government, and other types of scholarships. Although Tubman did not receive a university education, his use of the title "Doctor" suggests the high value placed upon even an honorary degree from the University of Liberia. More than two-thirds of the officials holding cabinet or subcabinet rank have at least one college degree, and roughly half of this group have received some higher education abroad.

One is impressed, too, with the youthful character of those holding key government posts. Admittedly, many of the old guard continue to exercise influence in the party behind the scenes. Inevitably, however, the occupants of government offices tend to monopolize patronage and hence power within the party. In 1962 the cabinet members in charge of the departments of State, National Defense, Education, National Public Health Service, Public Works and Utilities, and Justice ranged between thirty and forty-two years of age. The same image of youth and vitality is evidenced in the diplomatic personnel now being dispatched to the four corners of the globe to represent Liberia's growing economic and political interests.

Finally, the fourth circle is characterized by a high degree of full-time commitment to politics. The reasons for antipathy or disdain toward commerce and agriculture are discussed below. Suffice it to note here that a Liberian becomes involved in business and agriculture as a by-product of his involvement in politics; the reverse is seldom true. The preference for politics and the law is clearly reflected in the degrees received by Liberian students at home and abroad, and in the almost immediate pursuit of political office by one who, by the requirements of his scholarship, was compelled to take a technical course of education.

Recruitment for the Presidency

In many ways the editorial question posed to Tubman in the August 15, 1960, issue of the *Liberian Age*—"Who Are You Grooming for the Presidency?"—is one that cannot safely be answered. Indeed, even in a highly democratic society it is the exception to find a chief executive encouraging competition for his mantle. There is the real possibility of a shift of influence before the incumbent is prepared to sacrifice his power. An examination of the critical role the presidency plays in balancing the various forces within the Liberian political system makes it quite clear that presidential authority is not divisible. This is a lesson that ex-Presidents Arthur Barclay, Daniel Howard, and Charles D. B. King learned to their sorrow as they attempted to control the actions of their successors.

The style of Liberian politics seldom permits the question of succession to be raised. It is assumed that a president will attempt to succeed himself even when the constitution seems to deny him this privilege, as it did in Edwin Barclay's second term and William Tubman's first term. From the outset of a given term of office, the incumbent is besieged with resolutions from local chapters of the True Whig Party urging him to seek reëlection. Indeed, the first resolution urging Tubman to run for a fifth term came two weeks after his renomination by the party convention in 1959 for a fourth term![9]

Although Tubman's inauguration to a fifth term as president in 1964 seems to preclude immediate consideration of the choice of a successor, it is possible that death or retirement (Tubman was born in 1895) may compel the Whig Party leadership to make an earlier decision. Constitutionally, Vice-President William Tolbert is next in line. On three occasions in Liberian history (1871, 1900, and 1930), however, the constitutional successor in a time of crisis was bypassed in favor of one more acceptable to the dominant political forces of the day. Tolbert's problem is whether or not he fits the image of the presidency which has been constructed by Tubman under his unification policy. The Tubman image clearly differs radically from the one created by his predecessors. To maintain the present political system the president must be acceptable to both the Americo-Liberians and the tribal element without being too closely identified with the primary interests of either one. He must exhibit the appreciation of pomp and ceremony which the aristocratic-minded Whigs demand of their leader and yet possess the human foibles —indeed, the ability to act the clown—which have enhanced Tubman's reputation with the tribal masses. It is apparent that Tolbert does not

---

[9] *Ibid.*, Feb. 10, 1959, p. 1.

fit the Tubman image, for his appeal has been largely to the Americo-Liberian elite.

Private speculation about long-term successors frequently centers upon Secretary of the Treasury Charles Sherman, who undoubtedly has one of the keenest minds in Liberia. His credentials among Americo-Liberians are of the best sort, for his father, General Reginald A. Sherman, several times saved the settlers from defeat at the hands of tribal rebels. On the other hand, Sherman does not conceal the fact that his mother was a tribal woman. Other younger men, such as Secretary of State Rudolph Grimes and Secretary of Education John P. Mitchell, have attempted to stress their tribal antecedents or their concern about the lot of the tribal people, while maintaining the correct posture with their fellow Americo-Liberians.

Inevitably, discussion turns upon the future of "Shad Jr.," President Tubman's son by an earlier marriage. He has both youth and a good education, having only recently completed his B.A. in America. As president-general of the Labour Congress of Industrial Organization, moreover, he can control as well as become identified with the lot of those who pose the greatest threat to Whig supremacy—the lower middle classes and the tribalized elements of Monrovia. With success, he may build the same popular image that his father did years ago as an attorney in Maryland County who always took without fee the cases of the destitute. Shad Jr. has used his position to advantage in speaking before civic clubs or at school exercises. His recurrent theme is that the enemy of the working class is not the True Whig Party leadership, but rather the Lebanese and other foreign entrepreneurs in Liberia.[10] His marriage to the daughter of Vice-President Tolbert in 1961 was taken by several observers to indicate that Tolbert's possible succession would constitute a mere holding operation for Tubman's son.

INTERNAL PARTY ORGANIZATION

The True Whig Party is the only political organization in Liberia which functions on a continuing basis. Opposition parties are highly personalized groups which are organized to compete in specific elections and rally under the banner of a disaffected Whig. At least four times in this century the opposition leader has been a former president. The hastily contrived campaign staff is disbanded once the party has met its inevitable defeat, and a new band of dissidents takes up the opposition cudgel in a subsequent election. Although there was a measure of continuity in leadership between the People's Party of 1923 and that of 1927, the repeated use of popular opposition labels gives a false impression of continuity between, for example, the Republican Party of 1883 and

---

[10] *Ibid.*, July 2, 1962, p. 3.

that of 1911, the People's Party of 1927 and that of 1943, the Unit Whig Party of 1935 and that of 1943, or the Reformation Party of 1951 and that of 1955. The informality of opposition party procedures is illustrated by the convention of the Independent True Whig Party, which was formed in 1955. A hundred or more dissident Whigs met in the home of ex-President Edwin Barclay to nominate him for the presidency. So pressed was Barclay for fellow partisans that the convention nominated candidates for the legislature without first obtaining their approval. Normally an opposition party limits its campaign geographically to Montserrado and perhaps an additional county, and it concentrates upon the main prize, the presidency. For this reason the opposition parties seldom make an appearance in the biennial elections for the legislature.

In contrast with the ephemeral organization of the renegade Whigs, the apparatus of the True Whig Party has survived through more than forty elections since its founding in 1869. There are various principles of organization evident in the party effort. Since the beginning of Tubman's regime, for example, various specialized wings, based upon age or sex, have been formed to provide additional focuses for party activities. The primary principle of organization, however, is geographic. With the extension of legislative representation and almost universal suffrage to the people of the hinterland, every voting precinct within the Republic of Liberia is potentially capable of being organized into a local chapter of the True Whig Party. The local chapters are loosely affiliated with (what are in effect) two separate Whig parties. The first is the national Whig Party which meets every eight or four years to nominate presidential and vice-presidential candidates. The second is the county, territorial, or provincial Whig Party which meets at least every two years in convention to nominate candidates for the legislature. The theoretical autonomy of each of these sets of conventions was revealed in the 1959 county conventions, which met after the national convention had renominated President Tubman. Resolutions endorsing the nominations made by the national conclave were objected to by various delegates as an attempt by the county party to review the decisions of the national party.[11]

The national convention meets every eight or four years, depending upon whether the president is in his first or a subsequent term. Normally, the meeting is held in Monrovia in January, more than three months in advance of the May elections and more than eleven months before the beginning of a new administration. Only once in the past forty years, however, has lame-duckism been a problem in Liberia. The principal task of the convention is to nominate presidential and vice-presidential candidates; the dumping of a vice-president by the president gives the

[11] *Ibid.*, Feb. 27, 1959, *et seq.*

convention a wider choice in the selection of this candidate than it has in
the naming of a national standard-bearer. Only four times in the present
century has an incumbent president decided to retire and permit the convention to name a candidate. At least publicly, the conventions of 1919
and 1943 seemed to be lively affairs with several contenders competing
for the votes of the delegates. In 1943, for example, Clarence Simpson,
S. David Coleman, James F. Cooper, and Louis A. Grimes were actively
considered, and various individuals were placed in nomination. Actually,
the *African Nationalist,* a leading paper during the Barclay administration,
provided a clue as to Barclay's possible choice through its detailed reporting of every movement of Associate Justice William V. S. Tubman during
1940 and 1941. More than fifteen months before the convention of 1943, the
editor picked Tubman as the leading aspirant, noting that he "has the
whole of Maryland County, and not a minor part of Montserrado, and
everywhere his name is heard, it has a captivating charm, because he is
a natural mixer of men, good manners, and some persons say—liquors." [12]

Although the convention choice was apparently determined in advance, the intraparty struggle manifest at the convention left scars that
compelled Tubman to accept Simpson as his running mate and to name
members from the opposition parties to his first administration. Thus a
latent function of the national convention at the time of a succession is
to reveal the lines of factionalism within the party. Its ineffectiveness as
a constituent body that makes decisions independently of those arrived
at by the party leadership is seen in the lack of concern over rigid rules
regarding membership in it. There is no allocation of a fixed number of
seats to county, territorial, or provincial units of the party. There is an
informal understanding that those whose Whig credentials are in order
should be permitted to attend the convention. The number of delegates
may range from as low as three or four hundred, as in 1959, to several
thousand, as in 1955 when Tubman wanted to undercut the threat posed
by the candidacy of former President Edwin Barclay.

Other less-publicized tasks are performed by the national convention. The party platform, for example, is formulated by leaders of the
party and presented for approval. The relative unimportance of the
platform is revealed by the failure of the leading papers to report its
contents. Finally, the convention elects the officers of the True Whig
Party who will assist the president in the management of party affairs
between conventions. The national chairman, the national vice-chairman,
the general secretary, the general treasurer, and the other elected members of the Executive Committee not only are the trusted friends of the
president but tend also to represent the old guard within the party.[13] The

[12] Nov. 8, 1941, p. 1.
[13] The convention of 1959 elected Senator Edwin Morgan as national chairman,

Executive Committee of the party also includes the president, leading members of the cabinet and the legislature, and influential private citizens whom the president feels should be included from time to time. The institution is loosely structured and its proceedings and its significance vary according to the whim of the president, who during the present century at least has been the *de facto* head of the True Whig Party.

Following an occasional American pattern, the national chairman of the True Whig Party has frequently been given the office of postmaster general, although the predecessor of the present chairman was the president pro tempore of the Senate. The continued confidence of Tubman in Chairman McKinley DeShield is obvious in that he is the only cabinet officer who has survived the many shake-ups since Tubman took office in 1944. The national chairman of the party today, however, does not possess the same power in the field of patronage and other essential party matters as chairmen and general secretaries enjoyed before the presidency of Arthur Barclay (1904–1912). Indeed, the resignation of President Coleman in 1900, for example, was in great measure forced by the public stand taken against Coleman's hinterland policies by T. W. Howard, who was national chairman of the party and treasurer of the Republic, and by his son, Daniel E. Howard, who was at that time party secretary and governor of Montserrado County. Daniel Howard, in turn, was national chairman at the time of his election as president in 1911. Then his knowledge of patronage allocations and party decisions aided him in consolidating his position and preventing the strong-willed and very popular Arthur Barclay from exercising power behind the scenes after his retirement. It was Howard's experience, undoubtedly, which brought about the eclipse in the power of the national chairman and has left the office in the hands of those who have a strong allegiance to the president. Aside from the chairman's role in the investment and allocation of party funds, and in the mediation of contests over candidacies for seats in the legislature, his duties relate largely to the organization of the national convention, the management of the presidential campaign, and the appointment of registrars and other election officials.

The constituent body for the county, provincial, and territorial units of the True Whig Party is the biennial convention which meets to nominate candidates for the legislature. The selection of the one or two representatives to which each province or territory is entitled is accomplished quickly. The county conventions, on the other hand, are much more active gatherings, because the absence of clearly demarcated sena-

Wilkin Tyler as national vice-chairman, Postmaster General McKinley DeShield as general secretary, and former Secretary of the Treasury William Dennis as general treasurer. DeShield became national chairman upon the death of Morgan.

torial or representative districts compels the convention to adopt a single slate for the county at large, if it is to prevent the opposition from making inroads at the polls. Certain principles have evolved to limit the intraparty struggle. There is a fairly rigid rule that "each side of the river" within the county is to be represented by a senator. Second, an unwritten rule stipulates that a senator or a representative is entitled to a second term, so that the issue of succession is foreclosed for eight or four years, as the case may be. Although the tacit counterpart of this second rule has been that no legislator is entitled to more than two terms, Speaker of the House Richard Henries and Representative J. J. Mends-Cole—to cite two exceptions—ran in 1963 for their eleventh and seventh terms, respectively. Tubman, moreover, made it explicit to a group from Montserrado County in 1962 that "there is no limit to the number of times a legislator may be re-elected to the House of Representatives." [14]

Aside from these two rules, there is a broad basis for intraparty conflict over how geographic areas within the county should be represented in the House, and the "Letters to the Editor" section of the *Liberian Age* reflects the discontent in certain areas regarding this matter.[15] This regional struggle is a second crosscurrent; the interfamily struggle discussed earlier is the first. As a consequence, it is not always possible to predict the outcome of a county convention. In Sinoe in 1959, for example, the preconvention caucus found Representative William Witherspoon turning back the challenge of H. C. Williamson, the inspector of mines, by 223 votes to 84. Witherspoon's name was supposed to be the only one presented to the county convention to represent the precincts involved, yet in the end the convention nominated Williamson.[16]

Although the appearance of decisional autonomy is thus maintained, contradictory evidence suggests that the national party leadership maintains a firm hand over the county convention proceedings. For example, the March 4, 1955, issue of the *Daily Listener*, owned and edited by Charles C. Dennis, who was nominated as a candidate for the House of Representatives by the Montserrado County Convention, stated that the "result of the nomination was a bedrock conclusion that had been reached a day previous when shrewd politicians of the True Whig Party met at a caucus held at the Executive Mansion, the seat of the TWP standard bearer." [17] Furthermore, in 1959 the national party leadership vetoed the unanimous choice of the Grand Bassa County Convention for

[14] *Liberian Age,* Sept. 3, 1962, p. 7.
[15] *Ibid.,* March 2, 1959, p. 1.
[16] *Daily Listener,* Feb. 27, 1959, p. 1.
[17] P. 1.

a senatorial candidate. A second convention had to be held to renominate the incumbent senator, who irritated his constituents by his failure to visit Bassa between sessions. The reversal by Tubman was justified on the grounds that both the two-term rule and the stipulation that both sides of the St. John River were to be represented had been violated.[18]

There is no established pattern in the election of officers for the county organizations. The chairman may be the senior senator or the senior representative, or he may hold an executive position, such as that of county superintendent. The chairman, the secretary, and other key officers are usually those who are acceptable to the leading families within the county. In Montserrado County, which occupies so pivotal a role in Liberian politics, the confidence of the president is one of the key factors in selecting party officers for the county organization.

At the lowest level of party organization is the local branch, which may be limited to a single town or may embrace all the towns and precincts included within one of the vaguely defined representative districts. The most obvious function of the local branches is to pass resolutions of support for presidential and legislative candidates. A new aspirant to office usually argues his case to the national leadership on the basis of the number of resolutions he has received from local branches of the party within his area. Certain local chapters of the party constitute very powerful units of the national and the county parties, and control over the organization is essential for the future of key politicians. Speaker of the House Richard Henries, for example, has maintained his influence in national affairs through his chairmanship of the vital Monrovia local party, a position he assumed in 1944.

In the past few years the geographic units of the True Whig Party have been complemented by the establishment of specialized units to mobilize the energies of individuals who might not be adequately represented in the county or the national party. In 1958, for example, the Young People's Political Association of the Whig Party was formed in Maryland County and has since spread to the other counties. The youth association held its own convention shortly after the national convention met in 1959, and has been active in legislative elections, but it is not likely to become a focal point for opposition to the old guard. President Tubman's personal secretary, until his recent death in an auto accident, was the first national chairman of the group.

A second specialized organization is the inevitable outgrowth of the granting of female suffrage by the Tubman administration. The Liberian Women's Social and Political Movement was formed a few years ago by Sarah Simpson George, sister of Tubman's first vice-president and wife

---

[18] *Liberian Age*, Feb. 27, 1959, p. 1; March 2, 1959, p. 1; March 13, 1959, p. 10; *Daily Listener*, March 3, 1959, p. 1.

of one of the more influential representatives from Montserrado County. Its present chairman is the wife of Speaker Henries. Its primary goals are to interest the women of Liberia in politics and to agitate for greater representation of women in the government of Liberia.

The method of financing the True Whig Party has remained substantially the same for several decades, although the details may change. Raymond Buell in 1928 reported that the treasurer of Liberia automatically deducted 10 per cent of the monthly salary of every government employee until the expenses of the preceding presidential campaign had been met.[19] Doris Duncan Grimes, wife of the present secretary of state and daughter of a former cabinet officer, indicated even more recently that a yearly tax of one month's salary over a two-month period was levied upon every public employee.[20] There are other ways, too, in which the party coffers are kept replenished. After a candidate is nominated for office, he is expected to make generous contributions to the national and the county parties. The loser in a party struggle may also make a public offering to the party as evidence of his desire to heal the breach and remain a member in good standing. Finally, Lebanese businessmen and other foreign entrepreneurs are expected to make contributions to the party in the form of cash or by picking up the tab for party and official entertainment. According to Mrs. Grimes, there had never been a public accounting of party funds. Various sources have indicated that a European trading company in Monrovia serves as the bank for the party.

In contrast to the True Whig Party, the patronage-poor opposition party must be financed largely out of the personal fortunes of its leaders. Every effort is made by the Whig leadership to drain the opposition of its limited resources by constant litigation. In 1955, after Edwin Barclay's attempt to have the legislature investigate the conduct of the election, the legislature decided that Barclay should pay $19,000, the estimated cost of the farcical and futile special session.

TRUE WHIG PARTY IN RELATION TO OTHER STRUCTURES OF SOCIETY

There is a tendency for Whig Party leadership and governmental leadership to be equated in Liberia. It is apparent, however, that many prominent Whigs are permanently or temporarily outside the formal governmental establishment. In 1960 this was certainly true of former Vice-President Simpson, the late C. D. B. King, and several of the retired justices of the Supreme Court. Conversely, a number of governmental

---

[19] *The Native Problem in Africa* (2 vols.; New York: Macmillan, 1928), II, 712.
[20] "Economic Development on Liberia" (unpublished M.A. thesis, New York University, 1955), p. 6.

posts carrying prestige value did not bring correspondingly high standing in the party apparatus. This was true of tribal members of the legislature and of persons who had been given administrative or diplomatic posts to further an ideological goal or to satisfy a dissident element within the party.

In furthering Whig objectives, the presidency has become a vastly more significant governmental institution than the legislative and judicial branches, even though the speaker of the House, the president pro tempore of the Senate, and the chief justice may personally exercise considerably greater influence than many cabinet officials. The emergence of the president as a strong man in the party and the country, however, is a development of the present century. Of eighteen presidents before Tubman, five failed in their bids for reëlection or renomination by their parties, four were forced to resign, and one was actually deposed. The factors that have contributed to the rise of a strong president are various. It is obvious that control over patronage within the unitary political system has strengthened the president at the expense of regional challengers to his power. And the significance of patronage has been greatly heightened as economic development schemes have provided more and more new jobs, contracts, and other perquisites that may be employed to reward the party faithful and woo the following of the opposition leadership—if not the leadership itself! Postwar economic development and the consequent improvement in transportation and communications have likewise improved the national executive's control over his subordinates in the field.

Undoubtedly the crises, both foreign and domestic, which threatened Americo-Liberian supremacy within the state compelled the Whigs to rely upon the single-minded leadership that could be provided by the president, in contrast with the many-headed and regionally oriented legislature. Even before Tubman's attempt to cast himself in the role of a charismatic leader, the presidency was being insulated against public criticism. The gradual extension of presidential tenure from two years to an initial eight-year term, followed by an unlimited number of four-year terms, has relieved the president from the constant pressures of having publicly to defend his policies and programs. It has also freed the political system of the discord that a campaign invites. Criticism is further proscribed by provisions of the Penal Code which come close to equating criticism of the president with sedition, conspiracy against the state, and criminal libel.[21] The Whigs have permitted the development of what several leading officials acknowledge to be a "cult of the presi-

---

[21] *Liberian Code of Laws of 1956* (Ithaca: Cornell University Press, 1957), Title 27, chap. 3, secs. 52–57.

dency." "One must be," they recognized, "either for or against the regime, and often there is little room for honest differences of opinion." [22]

Government subsidization of the adulation of President Tubman is in evidence everywhere: the erection of statues of him at various points in the country; the naming of bridges, streets, and public buildings after him, or his wife, or his mother; the requirement that Tubman's picture be displayed in every commercial establishment; and the observance of public holidays to commemorate his birth as well as events in his life, such as the failure of the assassination attempt in 1955. At times the claque that precedes him on every public occasion borders on blasphemy in its attempt to emphasize the extraordinary character of the Tubman personality. The *Liberian Age*, too, frequently publishes such contributions from its readers as the "Ten Commandments of Tubmanism," and the paper dutifully reported that during one of Tubman's appearances "blue heaven sent a light shower of blessing upon the partisans." [23] The adulation extends occasionally to Mrs. Tubman, who was greeted upon her return from a trip to Europe in 1960 by a huge banner in downtown Monrovia proclaiming: "Welcome Back Our Blessed Lady Antoinette."

There are still significant pockets of political autonomy within the Liberian system which permit subordinate executive officials to pursue policies contrary to the dictates of the President and even contrary to the interests of the Whig Party. Legislators, too, may feel that their regional and family alliances give them independent bases for political support and may challenge the President. A recent example was the Senate's objections to various provisions in the proposed Mount Coffee Hydro Agreement.[24] In most instances, however, the legislature has little more than the power to delay passage or to alter details. The manifestations of independence are often deceptive and may actually be encouraged by the executive to strengthen its hand in dealing with foreign entrepreneurs or native elements.

The relations between the True Whig Party and other political parties are curiously ambivalent. The most consistent posture is one of hostility, and opposition to the party is equated with treason to the state. The intemperate language used in berating opposition parties during an election reaches an excessively high level.[25] Yet the Whig Party abhors continued controversy, and frequently extends forgiveness to dissident Whigs who provide opposition parties with leadership. It is a

[22] Mitchell, *op. cit.*, p. 79.

[23] Aug. 12, 1960, p. 3; May 6, 1960, p. 11.

[24] *Liberian Age*, Dec. 21, 1962, p. 2.

[25] Cf. Reginald E. Townsend, ed., *President Tubman of Liberia Speaks* (London: Consolidated Publications, 1959), pp. 95–100, 119–121, for examples of Tubman's 1951 and 1955 campaign speeches.

constant feature of Liberian politics that yesterday's opposition leader is today's ambassador or justice of the Supreme Court. In his first administration, Tubman went so far as to establish a coalition cabinet by naming leaders of the Unit Whig Party and the People's Party to executive posts, including the very important secretaryship of the Department of the Interior. The experiment was short-lived, however, for it had the undesired effect of giving second parties public status and access to patronage.

Relations with Voluntary Associations

The control exercised by the True Whig Party over the machinery of government and interparty competition tends also to affect the functioning of voluntary associations within the Liberian polity. The Whigs' greatest fear is that social and economic associations of tribal people may make an indirect assault upon the political bastion presently monopolized by the Americo-Liberian class. Whig antipathies to traditional organizations, so evident in the nineteenth century, have been somewhat modified, as the policy of indirect rule has brought about an alliance between the Whig leadership and the traditional tribal aristocracy. An absolute ban still prevails, of course, against such groups as the Human Leopard Society, which are organized to commit murder, cannibalism, and other crimes. Equally proscribed is the Mende tribe's Baboon Society, which in the immediate pre-Tubman era was implicated in an alleged plot to destroy the Americo-Liberian aristocracy.[26]

The most prominent and the most numerous tribal traditional organizations—the men's Poro and the women's Zande societies—have, however, been permitted to function now that they have been brought under government control. The historic fears of the Americo-Liberians regarding the power of the Poro were probably not exaggerated. It was the Poro societies that fomented the uprisings of 1898 in neighboring Sierra Leone against the extension of British and Creole influence into the tribal hinterland of that country. The alliance between the Whigs and the traditional chiefs, the administrative division of some of the larger tribal groupings, and other measures have been helpful in emasculating the political powers of the Poro leadership. The naming of President Tubman as the head of all Poros has not only broadened the base of his popularity, but has also given the executive a measure of supervisory control. As educational, health, and other facilities of the national government are extended to the interior, the functions of the Poro will be more and more reduced. Ultimately, it may come to have

---

[26] Accounts of the arrest and trial of currently prominent persons who were implicated in the plot against Barclay are contained in the 1940 issues of *African Nationalist* (Library of Congress microfilm).

the same curiosity and propaganda value for the unification policy as the Vai script, which the Liberian government is taking great pains today to preserve. Because the Poro constitutes no political threat, and because its bush schools, medicine, and community dancing keep the tribal people contented, the government feels it can view the institution with indulgence.

A similar indulgence is displayed toward the thrift, improvement, and burial associations which are so popular among the Bassa, the Kru, and other indigenous people who have gravitated to Monrovia and other urbanized centers. The limited economic and social objectives of these groupings have been rigidly maintained by government-appointed leaders, who regulate the conduct of their fellow tribesmen who have moved to the cities. Also kept in line by the urban tribal leaders are the nativistic religious societies, such as the Bassa Community Church, which could challenge the Christian leadership of Liberia.

The membership of tribal people in more modern forms of economic associations is, on the other hand, viewed with open hostility by the Whig leadership. Obviously mindful of the role played by the cocoa coöperatives of Ghana and the coffee coöperatives of Tanganyika in the rise of nationalist movements, President Tubman indicated to me, not surprisingly, that the people of Liberia were not yet ready for coöperative societies! In the absence of government support of coöperatives, the cash-crop economy seems destined to remain, for some time to come, under the control of foreign entrepreneurs and leaders of the Americo-Liberian class, with little competition from peasant cultivators.

Superficially at least, the tribal people have been more effective in organizing the industrial sector of the economy. Trade unions have been formed among tribal persons (especially the Kru) in shipping, mining, and other new industries. The unions are, however, carefully controlled by the True Whig leadership, as evidenced by the appointment of the President's son, William V. S. Tubman, Jr., as president-general of the Labour Congress of Industrial Organization. Although the members of a union may present petitions of grievances, and may engage in negotiations for improvement in wages and conditions of labor, the ultimate weapons of unionism—the strike and the boycott—are viewed with deep suspicion. Technically, a strike is illegal until a dispute has been submitted to a labor court. Inasmuch as no labor court has as yet been established, all strikes are illegal. The fears on the part of the Whigs that a walkout over wages could be converted into a general protest against the Americo-Liberian aristocracy came close to realization in the general strike of September, 1961, which occurred shortly after Tubman's son had gone abroad for his honeymoon. The work stoppage was accompanied by violence and demonstrations in Monrovia. Alarmed, the Whig leaders quickly arrested several union leaders on charges of sedition and conspiracy against the state. Before the dust had settled, moreover, a score or more persons had been arrested, officials of both the Ghanaian and United Arab Republic embassies had been expelled from the country, and charges of Russian incitement of the youth and tribal people against the government filled the air.[27]

The circumspect posture of the Whig leadership vis-à-vis voluntary associations extends even to those whose membership is limited largely to Americo-Liberians. The marked failure, for example, of the Liberian National Businessmen's Association to become an effective force in Liberian politics is all the more curious when viewed against the remarkable economic developments taking place in the country today. The fact is that few Liberians prefer, or are permitted, to become wealthy through the management of agricultural, industrial, or commercial enterprises. A man who does reap the benefits of the current economic development does so as a by-product of his participation in the affairs of the True Whig Party. The high value placed upon politics by the Americo-Liberian elite has been recorded by many previous observers of the Liberian scene. For example, in 1912 Professor Frederick Starr wrote: "In Liberia there is a general desire to feed at the public trough; it makes no difference what a man is or what he has accomplished, every one is ready to go into politics; neither trade, agriculture, nor professional life restrains a man who has political opportunities presented to him; everybody of ability wants office." [28] The preference for politics over business has been attributed variously to the missionary origins of many of Liberia's early settlements, to the early settlers' emulation of the genteel style of living of Southern planters in the United States, and to the series of world-wide depressions in the second half of the nineteenth century which destroyed Liberian planters, shippers, and other members of a burgeoning middle class.[29]

Whatever the basis for the preference for politics over business, the attitude serves a useful function in maintaining Whig political solidarity. Instead of using his economic position as a base from which to make particularistic demands upon the political system, an Americo-Liberian uses his political position to make demands for a larger share in the productivity of the economy. He becomes a politician first and a businessman second. Anyone who attempts to reverse the procedure, or who prefers to remain entirely aloof from the political system, is usually doomed to failure and is invariably regarded with suspicion. The obvious

---

[27] Cf. *Liberian Age*, Sept. 8, 1961, *et seq.*
[28] *Op. cit.*, pp. 210–211.
[29] George W. Ellis, "Political Institutions in Liberia," *American Political Science Review*, V (1911), 216.

antipathy of the Liberian government toward Liberian businessmen was acknowledged by several officials who agreed that as "a rule the government does not do business with Liberian businessmen." [30] Even the Secretary of Commerce, in his capacity as a private businessman, talks about subsidizing Japanese fishermen instead of encouraging Liberian fishermen to expand their operations.

How, then, does one account for the economic survival of Liberia and its current economic boom? Except for the tribal people, who have been employed in the past on various projects on a compulsory labor basis and who still work largely for marginal wages, the economy has been supported by external sources. American and other missionary societies have from the outset supplied funds, equipment, and personnel for education and health in Liberia. It was not until the Tubman administration began that any considerable portion of the government's budget had to be allocated to these ends. Similarly, the capital and the managerial skill required to exploit Liberia's agricultural and mineral resources have been secured from foreign sources; Firestone Plantations, the Liberian American-Swedish Minerals Company, the Deutsch-Liberian Mining Company, and other concessions are owned and operated by Americans, Germans, Scandinavians, Swiss, and other non-Liberians. The merchandising of commodities is largely in the hands of Lebanese and Syrians. Even many of the large rubber and fruit plantations owned by the Americo-Liberian elite are managed by West Indians, Sierra Leoneans, and other non-Liberian Negroes. Finally, it must be noted that the various foreign aid programs of the American and other friendly governments have been providing capital, technical skill, and education on an increasing scale since the end of World War II.

Obviously, the alien supporters of Liberia feel that there are worthwhile goals to be achieved by continuing to buttress the economy. For each venture, however, the Americo-Liberian group demands an exaction. Even the missionary whose goal is the winning of converts to Christianity is required by law to establish a school before he may pursue his calling. Each new concession agreement or renewal of an old agreement brings increased benefits for the Whig-controlled government, or new positions and enterprises that will accrue to the Whig leadership. The advantages for the Whig Party in dealing with alien entrepreneurs rather than with middle-class Liberians is that the former are in the country on sufferance. As aliens (and non-Negroes, who are ineligible for citizenship, are permanent aliens), the 20,000 Americans, Lebanese, Europeans, and Israeli cannot own real estate, engage in certain reserved occupations, or participate in the political process as members of a political party or pressure group. The depoliticization of the most sig-

---

[30] Mitchell, *op. cit.*, p. 51.

nificant groups in the Liberian economy thus serves as a safety valve for the Whigs against a nationalist revolution achieving its goal via the economic route.

As with economic groupings, the potentially independent role that religious associations might play in the Liberian political process is narrowly circumscribed. A loose form of interlocking directorate ensures that the clergy within most Protestant churches, the lay organization within the Episcopal and Roman churches, and the officers of the YMCA and other semireligious societies remain under Whig Party control. It is possible for a small community preacher to use his pulpit as a springboard for political advancement, but in most instances political prominence serves as a springboard for advancement within a religious organization. Almost by right, one who has achieved high political station has a claim upon religious office. Thus, Vice-President William Tolbert was elected president of the Liberian Baptist Missionary and Educational Convention, replacing another political leader who was merely a member of the House of Representatives. Another representative, J. J. Mends-Cole, is head moderator of the Presbyterian Church. Similarly, the last fourteen worshipful grand masters of the Masonic Order in Liberia include three presidents, one vice-president, a speaker of the House, a chief justice and an associate justice of the Supreme Court, an attorney general, and other leading officials.

Religious office undoubtedly reinforces the political standing of an individual, for the style of Liberian politics requires officials to attend church, to preach sermons or to read the lesson, and to give generously to church building programs. The speeches of President Tubman (who is himself a Methodist preacher) are laced through with Biblical references. When, for example, he was asked in May, 1962, about his intentions regarding a fifth term, he sent reporters to their Bibles to discover the message of Isaiah 49:8: "Thus saith the Lord, In an acceptable time have I heard thee, and in a day of salvation have I helped thee: and I will preserve thee, and give thee for a covenant of the people."

The military establishment is also firmly under Whig control. Patronage prevails over professionalism in the appointment of officers, and the enlisted men within the Liberian Frontier Force, who are drawn from the tribal sector of the country, are not considered a discontented group. The awe in which they are held by the people of the interior and the license permitted them in living off the tribal villages more than compensate for their low pay and their exclusion from officer ranks. In spite of itself, however, the Whig leadership may soon be compelled to construct a more efficient military organization. The poor showing of Liberian troops in the Congo, as well as the potential threat to the Americo-Liberians implicit in the military machines in the more militantly na-

tionalist states of West Africa, has underscored the advice of the United
States Military Mission that professionalism is now indispensable.

A further source of discord for the Whig regime is the student group,
especially those individuals who have gone abroad and have been exposed to liberal ideas as well as to the criticism of Liberia voiced by
other African students. The magnitude of foreign fellowship programs
makes it impossible any longer to limit the grants to Americo-Liberians,
to slant the curriculums in favor of politics and law, or to dissipate completely the liberal ideas of the returned graduate by enmeshing him in
the patronage system. The Liberian leadership showed its concern by
insisting, in September, 1962, that all foreign fellowships, from whatever
source, be channeled through and awarded by the Liberian government.

Students who are educated in Liberia, however, may be equally
disturbing, especially because the foreign fellowship program strengthens
the possibility that persons from the tribal area or from lower-class Americo-Liberian families will be admitted to the University of Liberia or to
mission-run schools. The restiveness of students at Cuttington (Episcopal)
College and the Seventh-Day Adventist Konala Academy has led to
strikes, which prompted President Tubman in 1960 to warn the students
that political activity on their part would be dealt with in a forthright
manner.

Goals and Values

In any political system there is inevitably a discrepancy between the
stated goals of the governing elite and their ability or their actual intent
to accomplish these goals. In a general way, then, the True Whig Party
of Liberia resembles any other governing party. What sets the Liberian
system apart from many others, however, is the continual widening of
the gap separating the public profession of goals and observable performance. From an examination of the political system, one very basic,
but unstated, goal of the Whig Party leadership remains constant: the
preservation of a state in which the descendants of the alien founders of
Liberia remain in control of the system. The success of nationalist movements in the rest of Africa as well as the impossibility of insulating the
tribal majority of Liberia against economic and social change, however,
has compelled the Whig leadership to take these altered circumstances
into account. It has responded to them by publicly espousing its adherence
to the standards embraced by the world community or by its African
neighbors.

Thus, the party priorities listed by President Tubman after his electoral victory in 1959 sound very modern and progressive. They were as
follows:[31]

[31] *Daily Listener,* May 20, 1959, p. 1.

1. Continuation of the unification and integration policy
2. Eradication of illiteracy and ignorance
3. Extension of Liberia's road and communication program, linking all sectors of the country
4. Improvement in the health of all citizens and an increase in Liberia's population
5. Development of all human and natural resources of the nation
6. Continuation of the open-door policy, encouraging and protecting the investment of foreign capital to the mutual benefit of Liberia and the investors
7. Pursuit of a sound foreign policy of peace and of respect for individual national sovereignty
8. Continued concern for human dignity and the inherent right of all to liberty, freedom, justice, and independence without discrimination

Although the leaders of the Casablanca bloc may differ with Tubman's emphasis on the sixth and seventh points, they would undoubtedly subscribe to the remaining goals. The leaders of the Brazzaville and Monrovia groups, on the other hand, might well support the entire list and give each item the same priority rating. It is in the implementation of these goals that the True Whig leadership might find itself at variance not only with Ghana and Guinea but also with Nigeria, Sierra Leone, and Senegal.

From what has been said earlier, it is apparent that despite twenty years of Tubman's unification policy the access of tribal people to the citadels of political and economic power in Liberia is still limited. True, public arrogance toward tribal people and the flagrant abuse of their rights have diminished considerably since Tubman assumed office. The tribal people themselves feel that they need no longer be ashamed of their antecedents, their distinct cultures, or even their traditional names. Moreover, as a popular political figure who has shown warmth, humor, and the ability to render substantive justice, Tubman has done much to bridge the gap separating the two communities in the country. But Tubman is not a dictator; he is, rather, the managing director of the Americo-Liberian class, and he cannot stray radically far from the interests of the group that provides him with his main political support. Where integration has been permitted, it is largely on Americo-Liberian terms and by the adherence of others to Americo-Liberian norms.

Examining the truly remarkable progress that Liberia has made with respect to Tubman's next four goals (education, transportation and communications, health, and development of human and natural resources), one is impressed not only by the dramatic physical changes in Liberia but equally by the absence of distributive justice. It is the coastal area rather than the tribal hinterland, where the majority of the population resides, which continues to receive a disproportionate share of new schools, clinics, roads, markets, and other benefits of economic development.

Modernization of the Economy

In regard to the strategies of development (the fifth and sixth goals), it should be noted that Tubman introduced the open-door policy over the concerted objection of the old guard within the party, who felt that this would only accelerate the processes of change among the tribal people. The skillful use of expatriate staff and foreign capital, however, has permitted the Whig elite to reap the benefits of industrialization without having to pay the penalties. Moreover, to offset the preponderant influence of the United States in the Liberian economy, arising from the pre-Tubman Firestone Plantations venture and the subsequent American development of the rich iron ore deposits in Liberia, the government has been steadily encouraging a diversification of the national sources of investment and personnel. Swedish, Swiss, Israeli, West German, and other groups are undertaking an increasingly larger share in the development of Liberia.

In terms of human involvement, agriculture is perhaps given the highest priority, inasmuch as an estimated 90 per cent of the population still engages in subsistence agriculture or the production of cash crops. In the latter category rubber has remained the most important single item of export, even though citrus fruits, piassava, cocoa, and other crops are being encouraged under a diversification program.

In terms of the rapid accumulation of wealth and the underwriting of education and other programs of government, however, mining is given a higher long-range priority than agriculture. Iron ore is not only abundant in Liberia, but is also of very high quality. By 1962 annual production had reached 5 million tons, and the amount of ore in reserve was estimated at 300 million tons. Liberia also has sizable deposits of manganese, bauxite, lead, corundum, diamonds, and gold.

The public statements of President Tubman, Secretary of the Treasury Charles D. Sherman, and Secretary of Commerce Stephen Tolbert on the organization of production in Liberia differ substantially from those of Kwame Nkrumah, Léopold Senghor, Julius Nyerere, and other advocates of African socialism. Although the Whig leaders describe the economy as capitalistic, it is certainly capitalism with a distinction. Americo-Liberians, it is true, place a high value on the private ownership of land, and, ancillary to their government employment, many officials operate small rubber farms on the coast or in the interior. Their capitalistic tendencies are also manifest in their surprising enthusiasm for subscribing to shares in the National Iron Ore Company, the Liberian American-Swedish Minerals Company, and certain other foreign concessions operating in Liberia. The retail and wholesale merchandising of commodities by Lebanese, moreover, is also along free-enterprise lines. There is a radical departure from capitalism, however, in several phases of production. The majority of the tribal people in the hinterland, for example, continue to hold their land on a usufructuary right-of-occupancy basis, and the Whig leadership apparently has no desire to disturb the tenancy pattern, as its disruption would only swell the ranks of the urbanized unemployed. Nor is there a desire radically to alter the subsistence character of the tribal economy or the bartering of commodities, which goes on in spite of the law. In the significant core areas in the money economy, further questions arise as to the capitalistic character of the Liberian economy. Production is largely in the hands of a few foreign concessionaires who operate large-scale plantations or mining operations under renewable agreements with the Liberian government. The agreements cover the geographic areas for exploitation, the type of production which may be engaged in, the conditions of labor, the extent of taxation, and other details. In recent agreements the Liberian government has insisted upon ownership of a considerable fraction of the shares in the company. Thus, without having to resort to nationalization of the basic sources of wealth, the government is in a strong position to regulate the economy toward whatever ends it may desire.

Liberian Foreign Policy

Although foreign policy was given seventh place among Tubman's objectives in 1959, it has high priority in the Whig system of values today. Even without defense expenditures, the 1961 Liberian budget allocated $1 million more to the operations of the Department of State, international conferences, and the maintenance of embassies and consulates abroad than it did to Liberian education on all levels. The lure of a foreign assignment draws off many of the best-trained Liberian men and women, and the opportunities are vast. Liberia has embassies in every African state as well as in the major countries of North America, Western Europe, the Middle East, and Asia. The junketing by executive, legislative, and judicial leaders to far-flung conferences on subjects ranging from accounting procedures to midwifery is nothing short of phenomenal. Liberia is a member of most of the United Nations specialized agencies, has sent troops to the Congo, and has attempted to assume the leadership of the African bloc in the General Assembly by virtue of its seniority of membership in the United Nations. Outside the United Nations, it has attempted to strengthen its political and economic ties with the United States while at the same time establishing new or stronger links with Britain, West Germany, the Scandinavian countries, Israel, and other states that could contribute to the economic development of Africa.

In the long run, however, it is Liberia's new-found interest in its African neighbors which will be most significant for the True Whig Party. As independence came to the new African states, the Whig leadership found itself at a disadvantage. In terms of economic development, Liberia was in danger of lagging behind. As Ambassador C. T. O. King phrased it in his historic statement to the United Nations in 1957, "Liberia did not have the advantages of colonial rule." The open-door policy had been introduced only after decades of mistrust (undoubtedly well founded) on the part of European investors and commercial interests in Liberia. Second, although the colonial systems of France and Britain did permit some contacts among the leaders of territories within the respective imperial systems, Liberia had been isolated as a result of its unique independent status within a colonial Africa. Third, the Whigs realized that many of the leaders of the new states had held Liberia in contempt because of its lack of development, its inefficient civil service, its strong dependence upon American governmental and missionary support, and especially because of the Whig treatment of the tribal majority.

Thus the intense desire of Liberian leaders to establish a vast complex of bilateral and multilateral relationships with the new African states stems from their need to neutralize a hostile environment, if not to recruit genuinely friendly allies. In this respect, strangely enough, Liberia's involvement in sub-Saharan Africa resembles that of Israel. It wants to present an image of a state whose leaders are wise in the ways of international diplomacy, stand for all things modern and progressive, will take up the cudgels against South African *apartheid* in the United Nations, and can secure the needed economic assistance from abroad while still maintaining their country's independence.

One of the Whigs' greatest fears is Pan-Africanism, whether on a continental or a regional scale. Although Liberia must maintain a vague public commitment to Pan-Africanism if it hopes to keep its position of leadership in the African camp, it has attempted to dilute the more militant version advocated by the leaders of the Casablanca bloc by insisting upon different means and ends. The Tubman plan would call for an ultimate confederation of African states in which the national sovereignty of each member would be recognized. The political union, moreover, would be attained only after a series of multilateral cultural, economic, social, and other agreements had prepared the way. Liberia's adroitness in pursuing its approach was demonstrated not only at the Monrovia Conference of May, 1961, but even earlier at the Sanniquellie Conference of 1959. There the proposed union between Ghana and Guinea lost its

vital momentum and was submerged in the looser Tubman proposal for
a community of independent African states.

POLITICAL STRATEGY, TECHNIQUES, AND STYLE

The unification policy and the increased welfare benefits allocated
to the tribal people under the Tubman administration constitute a basic
departure from the previous Whig strategy of controlling the tribal people through coercive sanctions and isolation. With respect to the Americo-
Liberian class itself, however, the Whig leadership has, for more than
eight years, relied upon patronage as its principal weapon in keeping
the party faithful in line and in undermining the opposition by wooing
away its qualified leadership. Indeed, with the postwar economic development and with United Nations and other foreign aid programs, the arsenal
of patronage is filled to overflowing. An opposition party leadership may
make promises; only the True Whig Party seems prepared to deliver.

Despite tight economic control, the True Whig Party feels obliged
to give more than perfunctory attention to the observance of the cardinal
democratic procedure of holding elections. The elaborate and extended
ritual of petitioning the President and other candidates to seek reëlection,
the lively nominating conventions, the campaigning that carries candidates into the smallest backwater communities, the colorful and often
humorous political posters, and the element of suspense regarding the
counting of votes on election day might convince the casual observer that
the results of the election were actually in doubt and that the opposition
party had an outside chance of unseating the Whig candidates. Little,
however, is left to chance, for the party fears that the period of license
permitted the opposition during an election might encourage the latter
to regard a substantial electoral showing as a precursor of better things
to come, or might encourage it to take advantage of cleavages within the
ranks of the Americo-Liberians and resort to violence in achieving its
objectives. The assassination attempt against Tubman in 1955 reveals that
violence is indeed a possibility, especially when the opposition feels that
the channels for orderly change of government personnel are closed.[32]

The control over the electoral system begins with the naming of the
Elections Commission. In theory the commission is nonpartisan, and the
façade is maintained by the requirement that members must, when appointed, renounce all party affiliations. True Whig dominance, however,
is assured by the proviso that the president not only names the chairman
and the Whig Party representative to the commission, but also selects
the third member from a list of candidates submitted by the opposition
parties. One of the key duties of the commission is to determine whether

---

[32] For an official version of the attempt see *The Plot That Failed,* Liberian Information Service (London: Consolidated Publications, 1959).

or not a candidate or a party is entitled to a place on the official ballot. In 1951 it decided that Didhwo Twe and the Reformation Party did not legally qualify in contesting Tubman's second-term bid. In 1955 the legislature made the decision easier for the commission by enacting a statute outlawing both the Independent True Whig and the Reformation parties "because of their dangerous, unpatriotic, unconstitutional, illegal, and conscienceless acts." [33]

Even if an opposition group is permitted a place on the ballot, the lack of patronage puts it at a decided disadvantage. Moreover, the principal channels of communication are Whig-controlled. The government-owned *Liberian Age* and the subsidized *Daily Listener* observe almost a studied silence with respect to opposition parties that threaten to be even moderately successful. Opposition newspapers are short-lived; they fail either because they lack financial support or because they quickly run afoul of the highly restrictive libel law regarding criticism of the President. The *Friend* in 1954 and the *Independent* in 1955, for example, were banned because they opposed Tubman's third term, and members of their staffs were imprisoned. The harassing of the opposition may extend even to the standard-bearer of the party. In 1951 Didhwo Twe was forced to flee the country during the campaign. The next opponent to Tubman, ex-President Edwin Barclay, found his campaigning impeded by an official investigation based on a vague charge of attempted murder. Finally, throughout every campaign, the activities of opposition partisans are reported to the President by his liaison and relations officers, who are stationed in every county, territory, and province. The appointment of these officers is authorized by the Liberian Code for the purpose of preventing "subversive activity and dissemination of dangerous propaganda." [34] The secretary of the treasury has a statutory mandate to pay their salaries.

If an opposition party does persevere until election day, it has no assurance that its partisans will be permitted to vote or that their votes will even be counted. In the 1955 election, the ballots cast for the Independent True Whig Party were counted in only two counties. If the ballots are counted and a majority is recorded, there is no assurance that the victory will be recognized. After the 1931 election in Maryland County the legislature refused to seat the candidates of the People's Party who had defeated the True Whigs by 1,676 votes to 367. [35]

Although elections do not give the electorate a clear-cut choice between two or more alternative governing groups, Liberian elections are not entirely meaningless. There is, first of all, the observance of constitu-

[33] *Liberian Code*, Title 12, chap. 8, sec. 216.
[34] Title 13, sec. 12.
[35] *African Nationalist*, Nov. 8, 1941, p. 3.

tional norms, which apparently has a high value to the legal-minded Americo-Liberians. Second, an election does permit at least a biennial discussion of the party's goals, and gives the party an opportunity to secure the enthusiastic adherence of new generations of voters. Not only are policies altered as a result of this active discussion, but the personnel of government is changed as well. After each election the President considers that he has a new mandate and may shuffle executive appointments without having to justify dismissals and additions, as he would be expected to do if he made major changes in mid-term.

The most significant function of elections in Liberia, however, is the maintenance of a good image abroad. Despite their trepidations about elections and their efforts to emasculate the opposition, Whig leaders publicly insist that opposition is healthy for the Republic. On the eve of both the 1955 and the 1959 elections, for example, President Tubman said that he was going to vote for his opponent, "even though it may not be in accordance with the law." His opponent, Circuit Court Judge William O. Davies-Bright, was a True Whig running as an independent on a platform of "sincerity, purity, and peace." He stated after the election of 1955 that had he known that Tubman would vote for him, he would have voted for Tubman. With only 16 votes to Tubman's 244,937, Davies-Bright had very few to spare! In the election of 1959 he received 55 votes to Tubman's 530,566. As the Judge stated, he ran only in response to Tubman's call for "fair and friendly competition." [36]

---

[36] *Liberian Age,* May 6, 1959, p. 1; *Daily Listener,* Feb. 21, 1959, p. 1; Feb. 24, 1959, p. 1.

13. ZANZIBAR

By Michael F. Lofchie

Immigrant minorities have frequently sought to preserve a privileged position in African societies. Their basic technique has been to avoid any liberalization of the institutions of government so as to deprive the African majorities of access to political power. In this respect Zanzibar is unique, for here minority domination has survived the introduction of full parliamentary democracy. Majoritarian politics have necessitated the illusion of multiracialism, but real political power remains in the hands of Zanzibar's Arab minority.

This community constitutes, in proportion to the total population, the second largest immigrant minority in Africa south of the Sahara. Comprising about 17 per cent of the slightly more than 300,000 inhabitants, it numbers more than 50,000. Only the white minority of South Africa (more than 20 per cent) is larger. A large part of the Arab community forms a sort of political aristocracy whose high economic and social position is based upon landownership, clove growing, commerce, and government employment.

The Arab aristocracy takes its origin in the first half of the nineteenth century when the ruler of Muscat established a sultanate in Zanzibar. During the remainder of the century Zanzibar became a sovereign and fully developed Arab state which possessed an army, a judiciary, a civil service, and a system of native administration for the indigenous African population. When Zanzibar became a protectorate in 1890, Great Britain gave special recognition to the political paramountcy of the resident Arab population. Later this recognition was reflected in the large representation Arabs enjoyed in the Legislative Council and other governing bodies, and in the priority given them for top government posts.

The descendants of the early Arab migrants now form a self-regenerating elite group. Their decisive advantages in wealth and style of life enable the younger generation to achieve superior education and thereby to qualify more easily for the highest positions in government and commerce. By allowing Asians to fill the intermediate and clerical levels of the civil service, the Arabs have prevented the emergence of an African elite. In this way, and through nepotism, favoritism, and other forms of preferential treatment, they monopolize the strategic sectors of

482

the administration and retain firm control over the entire state apparatus, the educational system, and the clove industry. Through this control they regulate the pace of African advancement so that it does not threaten their own position.

The determination of the Arab minority to remain at the political and social apex of Zanzibar society has been the most important factor affecting nationalism and the development of political parties in Zanzibar.[1] Indeed, the Arab community, not the African majority, was the creator of contemporary Zanzibar nationalism. And for several years, beginning in the spring of 1954, Arabs were the only nationalists.

That the Arabs should have become nationalistic at a time when there were no other nationalists in Zanzibar is puzzling. British colonialism had in no way impaired their privileged political and social status, and, under a system of racial representation in the Legislative Council, the Arab Association enjoyed greater representation than any other ethnic body. Further, Arab leaders were fully aware that, if Zanzibar should become a democratically self-governing state, the overwhelming African majority, approximately 80 per cent of the population, could politically swamp the Arab minority.

The essence of the dilemma facing Arab leaders was that by 1954 Great Britain was already clearly committed to a policy of introducing democratic political institutions and eventual independence in all colonies where there was no substantial resident white population. This meant that the elite status of the Arab community could not be preserved either through an indefinite postponement of independence or through the creation of a polity that was other than egalitarian. The forward-looking leaders of the Arab Association could not possibly have avoided the conclusion that, if an immigrant aristocracy was to survive as such within a framework of parliamentary democracy, it would have to win support and acceptance from a substantial part of the African majority. This realization would suggest the political strategy of wresting political power from the British before growing African nationalism on the continent should spread to Zanzibar.

No other hypothesis explains the suddenness or the militancy with which Arab nationalism emerged in the spring of 1954. As late as March the Arab Association had officially accepted constitutional proposals recommending a continuation of communal representation in the Legislative Council, and its leaders had indicated agreement with the administration's belief that a direct confrontation between Arab and African in the political arena could only create racial tension. Less than three months

---

[1] For a more extensive historical treatment of the emergence of nationalism and the development of party politics in Zanzibar, see my article, "Party Conflict in Zanzibar," *Journal of Modern African Studies,* I (June, 1963), 185–207.

later the Arab Association, completely reversing its position, put forward a series of demands for immediate constitutional reform. These included common-roll elections, universal suffrage, and the introduction of a ministerial system.

The Arab Association's rejection of the communal-roll system was the only course of action consistent with a view that the ultimate position of the Arab in Zanzibar depended upon his ability to command the political allegiance of large numbers of Africans. Racial representation would at best have afforded only a temporary means of stabilizing the political structure of Zanzibar society by offering Arabs a guaranteed place in the councils of government. In the long run, however, it would have been disastrous, for it would have fostered a pattern of political loyalties based exclusively on racial identity.

The ultimate objective of progressive Arab leaders was the creation of a multiracial nationalist movement with sufficient African support to prevent any appearance of excessive Arab influence. The immediate problem was how to gain the confidence of the Africans. The technique devised was a political martyrdom, the notion being that, if the Arab community suffered in the cause of nationalism, it could not easily be suspected of having self-interested motives. In the spring of 1954 the Arab Association deliberately courted arrest and imprisonment by publishing a series of virulently anti-British articles in its official newspaper, *Al Falaq* (*The Dawn*). In June the entire Executive Committee was found guilty of sedition and fined heavily.

Unexpectedly, the *Al Falaq* case also resolved a disagreement among the leaders of the association over the wisdom of Arab-inspired nationalism. An influential group of moderates within the Executive Committee had felt that the Zanzibar Arab ought to be prepared to abdicate his position of political preëminence as a way of averting political and racial antagonisms. The British decision to arrest the entire committee, however, led its moderate members to support their nationalist colleagues. So united had the association become during the trial that virtually complete unanimity marked its decision to boycott the Legislative Council and all other government bodies in order to dramatize the Arabs' demand for a common-roll election and to intensify their pressure for the withdrawal of British influence.

By the end of 1955 the British government had unofficially agreed to put aside its proposals for racial representation and to hold a common-roll election. This decision placed the Arab Association in an awkward and perplexing situation; with an election imminent it was more than ever essential to form a broadly based political party which had the support of Africans. Arab leaders realized, however, that if they openly launched a party themselves, the Arab Association would be accused of trying to dominate it. This would make it impossible to win nationwide support.

In late 1955 a political party called the Nationalist Party of the Subjects of the Sultan of Zanzibar (Hizbu l'Watan l'Riaia Sultan Zanzibar) was formed by a small group of peasant farmers. At its inception the party was purely a protest movement stimulated by local grievances and composed of semiliterate villagers. Soon, however, it began to echo the Arab Association's demand for an end to communal representation in the Legislative Council. The exact relationship between the Arab Association and the founders of the Nationalist Party of His Highness' Subjects is obscure. They knew of the association's boycott and of the political demands behind it, and by December they were in informal contact with Ali Muhsin, a member of the association's Executive Committee who had emerged as the foremost spokesman of Arab nationalism. Their unfamiliarity with the exact meaning of the terms "common roll" or "universal suffrage," their opposition to the elaborate proposals for communal representation put forward by the British resident, and their personal contact with the leading proponent of the common-roll policy all suggest that their constitutional demands were inspired by those of the Arab Association.

Shortly after the party had attracted some public attention Arabs began to join it, and soon became its real leaders. They changed its name to the Zanzibar Nationalist Party (ZNP), and transformed it from a rural peasant league into an Arab-dominated urban nationalist movement. It had in any event been completely vulnerable to such a take-over. Its founders and first members were farmers and cattle herders, remote from political life and altogether lacking in leadership that could give wide public expression to their views. More important, it completely suited the Arab need for a political party that could legitimately claim African origin.

The ZNP has ever since reserved the positions of party president and vice-president for its African founder members, and this practice is advertised as evidence of the party's multiracial character. It is a purely symbolic gesture, however, and has no relationship to the actual distribution of effective influence within the ZNP's national executive. Here interethnic power relations could more accurately be described in terms of the domination of the highly educated, politically sophisticated Arab intellectual over the simple peasant villager. This pattern has been a permanent feature of the ZNP throughout its development as a nationalist movement.

The ZNP next proceeded to create a nationwide organization of local branches which could recruit African supporters for the coming election campaign. As the sole nationalist organization in the country, it enjoyed the singular advantage of having no opposition when it appealed for members in rural African villages and settlements. From the very beginning it was able to preëmpt completely the symbols of nationalism, and at once became exclusively identified with the call for "Freedom, now." On the international level as well the ZNP was able to present itself as the only nationalistic party in Zanzibar, and thereby to gain the financial and moral support of various world bodies committed to the cause of African nationalism.

The ZNP also benefited substantially from ethnic differences within the African community. A long-standing division has existed between those Africans who consider themselves the indigenous inhabitants of Zanzibar and those of more recent mainland origin.[2] The former prefer the name "Shirazi" to the name "African" as a generic appellation because it distinguishes them in terms of descent and length of residence from relatively recent mainland arrivals.[3] Many Shirazis even believe that they are descended in part from Persian immigrants who came to Zanzibar between the tenth and twelfth centuries and prefer to think of it not as a part of Africa but as an independent geographical entity. By portraying the mainlander as an unwanted intruder in a land where Shirazi and Arab have always lived together in peace, the ZNP was able to employ the Shirazis' sense of separateness as a means of gaining their political support.

The ZNP was aided in its drive to recruit Shirazis by the conservative attitude of some mainland African leaders. In their own deputations to the British authorities mainlanders had argued that constitutional progress ought to be delayed until further educational advancement would enable all Africans to compete on equal terms with Arabs in a representative system of government. Arab leaders in the ZNP publicly interpreted this position as the worst sort of racism, an admission of racial inferiority, and appealed to Shirazis to repudiate it by joining their party. Inasmuch as Shirazis tend to look upon themselves as the heirs of a rich cultural legacy, a sense of shame at the constitutional conservatism of their mainland brethren became a powerful impetus to their joining with Arabs in the ZNP in order to demand immediate constitutional reform.

Perhaps the most important factor contributing to the ultimate suc-

---

[2] The mainland African community of Zanzibar includes descendants of numerous tribes of continental Africa, but especially the Nyamwezi, the Nyasa, and the Yao. Its presence in Zanzibar is the result of the slave trade and the practice of recruiting migratory laborers on the mainland for work in the clove plantations.

[3] Although the Shirazis of Zanzibar are not a tribe in the usually accepted sense of the term, the Shirazi community does comprise three quasi-tribal groups: the Hadimu, who inhabit southern and eastern Zanzibar; the Tumbatu, who dwell on Tumbatu Island just off the northwest coast of Zanzibar, and who also have communities in northern Zanzibar and southern Pemba; and the Pemba, the indigenous inhabitants of Pemba Island.

cess of the Arab drive toward a seizure of power was the absence of an educated African elite. Within the ZNP, therefore, Arabs would inevitably be the most effective and influential leaders, no matter how many Africans joined the party. Among the African majority there were no politically informed individuals with sufficient organizational experience to begin a nationalist movement, and the formation of an African party was delayed for more than a year after the organization of the ZNP. When an African party did appear, its impetus was far less an enlightened awareness of the revolutionary changes occurring elsewhere in Africa than a deeply rooted fear that if the British presence was removed the Arab community would be able permanently to consolidate its position as the ruling class.

In February, 1957, only five months before the scheduled general election to which the British had agreed in 1955, leaders of the African and Shirazi associations met together in response to the threat of Arab domination posed by the ZNP. They hoped to form a joint political party, but very little unity was achieved. Although they agreed to form the Afro-Shirazi Union and to coöperate during the election campaign, there was to be no merger of the two associations. And, further, even this modest agreement covered only the African and Shirazi associations of Zanzibar and not those of Pemba, the sister island of Zanzibar in the protectorate.

The inability of mainlanders and Shirazis to coöperate in a single political movement was possibly the result of factors that separated them long before the era of party politics. Differing occupational structures and residential patterns, for example, had probably created a sense of social distance between them. Mainland Africans tend predominantly to be engaged in urban employment, either in domestic service or as manual workers for the government. If they become engaged in agriculture it is usually as squatter farmers on land in which they have no permanent rights. Shirazis tend predominantly to be fishermen and agriculturists on privately owned or community-held land.

The major reason why Shirazis and Africans could not coöperate, however, was precisely that the sole motive for coöperation was resentment of the Arab community. Since the emergence of the ZNP, the place of the Arab in Zanzibar had become the sole issue around which the country's African politics revolved. For a variety of historical reasons, this was the one issue on which Shirazis and Africans had completely different attitudes and which could not possibly unite them.

Many Shirazis tend to look back upon a history of warm and friendly relations with the Arabs of Zanzibar. They recall with pride that they served as local administrators for the sultanate government, or as seamen in the Indian Ocean trade. Shirazis were very rarely bought and sold as slaves, and to a large extent their lives were unchanged by the establishment of an Arab sultanate in Zanzibar. And numerous Shirazis, especially in remote rural areas, have come to accept Arabs as the rightful and legitimate rulers of Zanzibar. For all these reasons, large numbers of Shirazis were profoundly reluctant to enter into any political party predicated upon the notion that the purpose of African unity was to defeat and overthrow the immigrant Arab minority.

The most vivid memory of the mainland African community is that Arabs were the instigators of the East African slave trade. Mainlanders are frequently aware that their own presence as a community in Zanzibar is largely attributable either to the Arab slave trade or to the need for migrant agricultural labor in the Arab clove fields. They are strangers in Zanzibar who are unable to regard it as their home, and yet are often removed by several generations from their countries of origin; furthermore, they occupy the lowest place in the social structure. For all this the immigrant Arab aristocracy seems to be to blame, and there is little other reason for entering politics than to defeat it, and create an African state. The Pemba Shirazis in particular refused as a group to join the newly formed Afro-Shirazi Union. Their leaders had been conspicuously absent from the meeting at which it was founded, and soon came to regard it as excessively influenced by mainland Africans. Equally repelled by the Arab-dominated ZNP, their objective was to launch a political party that would avoid both extremes and would be based on Zanzibar's Shirazi majority.

The two most influential Shirazi leaders of Pemba, Muhammad Shamte, a retired school principal, and Ali Sharif, a landowner, inaugurated a political group which they called the People's Party (Ittihad ul 'Umma). It never became a fully organized political party because it failed to attract the support of Zanzibar Shirazis, who preferred to exercise a moderating influence on the Afro-Shirazi Union. The People's Party was therefore disbanded just before the July election. Despite its failure, its two founders were successful as independent candidates, and its brief existence exercised a lasting influence on Zanzibar politics. In expressing a Shirazi determination to pursue an independent course midway between mainlander and Arab immigrant minorities, it provided the political inspiration for the later formation of Zanzibar's third political party, the Zanzibar and Pemba People's Party (ZPPP).

In the election the ZNP was completely defeated. It contested five out of six constituencies and did not gain a single seat. Although it had campaigned as a multiracial nationalist movement and had advocated immediate independence, it polled only about 22 per cent of the popular vote. The ZNP's total defeat is best explained by the fact that it had come to be widely identified as an Arab-dominated party.[4] In Zanzibar, where it won all three seats it contested and gained more than 60 per cent of the popular vote, the Afro-Shirazi Union emerged as the dominant political force. Campaigning strongly as the party of the oppressed African masses, it had advocated gradual constitutional progress. Its victory was the result of its ability to tap long-latent resentment of Arab social and political preëminence.

Not until several months after the election did the African and Shirazi associations of Pemba agree on political coöperation. The two elected representatives from Pemba would join the Afro-Shirazi Union, renamed the Afro-Shirazi Party (ASP), and sit in the Legislative Council as its members. Despite the tentative merger, however, the Shirazi Association insisted on the right to maintain separate organizational facilities, a demand symbolizing the deep disagreement between the two communities over the race question.

On a national scale, the election results did not represent a clear victory for the anti-Arab party. Rather, they revealed the presence of a communal pattern of voting behavior. The three victorious candidates who were not affiliated with the Afro-Shirazi Union had all been sponsored by communal bodies. In Stonetown, a constituency in Zanzibar Township, Cher Muhammad Chowdray, a lawyer, was the candidate of the Muslim Association. The two Pemba seats were won by Muhammad Shamte and Ali Sharif who, after the dissolution of the People's Party, and in the absence of a merger between the African and Shirazi associations, ran as independent candidates with the full support of the Shirazi Association.

Simple feelings of ethnic loyalty were, in balance, probably a far stronger determinant of voting behavior than anti-Arab prejudice. Communal identity had been virtually institutionalized as the sole basis of political and social organization since long before the era of nationalism. The strength of communal separatism was exemplified in the broad acceptance of the practice of racial representation in the Legislative Council, in the presence of innumerable racial and communal associations, and in the fact that even sports, social life, and the local press were organized on racial lines. In Zanzibar this tradition of communalism was of considerable assistance to the Afro-Shirazi Union, which was able to present itself as the legitimate heir of the African and Shirazi associations. In the last analysis, the election revealed the strength of communal

---

[4] For a fuller report on the 1957 election see *Report of the Supervisor of Elections on the Elections in Zanzibar, 1957* (Zanzibar: Government Printer, 1958). In this report Muhammad Shamte and Ali Sharif are incorrectly listed as Afro-Shirazi Union candidates. Sharif was opposed in his constituency by a candidate of the African Association.

feelings in general, and not of anti-Arab feelings in particular. This distinction has been of decisive significance in the subsequent history of the ZNP, for its leaders have recognized that as a matter of practical party strategy they need campaign only for broad acceptance of the idea of multiracialism, and need not excuse themselves for being Arabs.

During the year after the election race relations in Zanzibar seriously deteriorated. Politically inspired tension existed both in rural areas, where Arab landowners were evicting African squatters, and in the towns, where an African boycott of Arab shops forced many shopkeepers out of business. This racial crisis furnished the ZNP with an ideal occasion to work for wider public acceptance. If it could portray communalism as the real cause of racial antagonism and bring it into widespread disrepute as an impediment to independence, it would weaken the party loyalty of ASP supporters.

The ZNP had for some time pursued a policy of cultivating overseas contacts with African nationalist parties in order to win recognition as a genuine nationalist movement. It now convinced the Pan-African Freedom Movement of East and Central Africa (PAFMECA), of which it was a charter member, that the ASP was harming the cause of nationalism in Zanzibar by its unwillingness to demand immediate independence. ZNP leaders persuaded the PAFMECA to ask the ASP to abandon its conservatism and its anti-Arab views. Because the PAFMECA representatives in Zanzibar were inclined to accept the militant nationalism of the ZNP at face value, they were critical of the ASP. They concluded that it was allowing its racial feelings to delay Zanzibar's independence, and recommended that ASP leaders should form a united front with the ZNP to work for racial harmony and immediate independence.

These recommendations were a triumph for the ZNP. If the ASP refused, it would be cutting itself off from the mainstream of East African nationalism. If it accepted, it faced the ignominious task of changing its constitutional and racial policies to bring them into line with those of a party that it had far surpassed at the polls. ASP leaders chose the latter course, and early in 1959 joined with the ZNP in the Freedom Committee. They urged their followers to forget old racial differences, and changed their target date for independence from 1963 to 1960. Throughout the fifteen months that the Freedom Committee survived, the ASP presented the spectacle of a party publicly repenting of its past errors and conceding the superior virtue of the policies of its chief rival. As a result, the ZNP increased its stature immeasurably in the eyes of Africans.

Not all ASP leaders accepted the party's decision to abide by the PAFMECA recommendations. A small group of dissident leaders argued that the ASP was undermining the morale of its supporters by its espousal of ZNP policies, and that the ZNP was simply exploiting the Freedom Committee in order to win over formerly hostile ASP supporters. This group advocated withdrawal from the committee and a resumption of the party's old policies. The Freedom Committee dispute within the ASP eventually led to a catastrophic split in the party. Ameri Tajo, an Islamic theologian of the Shirazi community, was an influential ASP parliamentary leader. Suspected of being sympathetic with the dissidents, he was expelled from the party under deeply humiliating circumstances. In protest at this treatment of Tajo, the two Shirazi leaders from Pemba, Muhammad Shamte and Ali Sharif, resigned, and together the three men formed the Zanzibar and Pemba People's Party. Only two of the ASP's five parliamentarians remained in the party. More important, even the fragile unity between Africans and Shirazis which had been achieved in 1957 was lost. The ASP was to enter Zanzibar's second general election, scheduled for July, 1960, in desperate straits—bereft of leadership, divided over policy, and torn by internal ethnic conflicts.

The ASP withdrew from the Freedom Committee early in 1960 and attempted to rebuild its rapidly dwindling membership. But the results of the election, which was postponed until January, 1961, revealed that the ZNP had profited considerably from its participation in the Freedom Committee. The ASP gained only ten of a total of twenty-two constituencies. Its basic weakness lay in Pemba, where it received less than one-fourth of the popular vote and won only two of nine constituencies. The ZNP remained fairly weak in Zanzibar, where it gained only five of thirteen constituencies, but it also won four seats in Pemba, making a total of nine, or only one seat less than the ASP's total. The most important feature of the election was that the newly formed ZPPP, which won the three remaining Pemba seats, held the balance of power, and was in a position to decide which of the major parties would form a government.

The three ZPPP members split. The party president, Muhammad Shamte, still resentful over the ASP's expulsion of Ameri Tajo, was adamant against coöperating with a party that was led even in part by mainland Africans. He decided that the ZPPP would form a coalition government with the ZNP. Ali Sharif, however, refused to accept Shamte's decision, resigned from the ZPPP, and rejoined the ASP. As a result the Legislative Council was deadlocked eleven to eleven, and another election had to be called for June.

Table 1, indicating the distribution of Legislative Council seats in the January and June elections, shows that there were no significant changes in party strength between the two elections. There was an additional seat in Pemba in June because the British authorities decided to add an extra constituency so as to avoid a repetition of the deadlock.

TABLE 1

DISTRIBUTION OF SEATS IN THE ZANZIBAR LEGISLATIVE COUNCIL,
JANUARY AND JUNE, 1961

Party	January			June		
	Zanzibar	Pemba	Total	Zanzibar	Pemba	Total
ASP	8	2	10	8	2	10
ZNP	5	4	9	5	5	10
ZPPP	0	3	3	0	3	3
Total	13	9	22	13	10	23

SOURCES: *Reports of the Supervisors of Elections on the Registration of Voters and the Elections Held in January, 1961* (Zanzibar: Government Printer, 1961); *Report of the Supervisors of Elections, June, 1961* (Zanzibar: Government Printer, 1961).

Even the formation of an electoral alliance between the ZNP and the ZPPP changed the result in only one constituency. What in effect determined the outcome of the election was a preëlection agreement between the ZNP and the ZPPP that they would form a coalition government. Having gained thirteen of the twenty-three seats, they possessed a clear legislative majority. The June election precipitated several days of anti-ZNP rioting in Zanzibar. ASP supporters had been subjected to nearly two years of intensely anti-Arab propaganda. When word that the ZNP-ZPPP alliance had won reached rural villages in Zanzibar where there were ASP majorities, armed bands of Africans began a rampage of murder and looting. Nearly a hundred persons were killed, almost all of them Arab ZNP supporters.[5]

Since the June, 1961, election, the ZNP and the ZPPP in close coalition have formed the government of Zanzibar. The ASP is in opposition. For nearly two years after the election these parties disagreed profoundly over the priorities and the timing for the next stage of constitutional advance. The two coalition parties argued that self-government and independence should be introduced immediately, before the holding of an election which they felt would delay constitutional progress. The opposition argued that an election was necessary to determine which political party would lead the country into independence, and that further constitutional progress should be delayed until it could be held. The inability of the three parties to compromise their differences on this issue brought about a constitutional stalemate.

In the early spring of 1963 Secretary of State for the Colonies Dun-

---

[5] For a fuller discussion see *Report of a Commission of Enquiry into Disturbances in Zanzibar during June, 1961,* Colonial no. 353 (London: H.M.S.O., 1961).

can Sandys visited Zanzibar in an effort to end the deadlock. After consulting with the leaders of all parties, he announced a compromise procedure whereby constitutional progress might be resumed. Internal self-government would be introduced two weeks before a new general election, to be held in July; the granting of full independence, however, would await the outcome of the election.

For the independence election, Zanzibar was divided into thirty-one constituencies, seventeen in Zanzibar and fourteen in Pemba. In the election, conducted on the basis of universal adult suffrage, approximately 165,000 people, more than half of the total population of the protectorate, registered and voted. A poll of more than 99 per cent of the population reflected the widely held belief that this election would determine the future rulers of Zanzibar, for the victorious party would likely consolidate and entrench its position after independence. The coalition of the ZNP and the ZPPP gained a total of eighteen seats, the ZNP winning six in Zanzibar and six in Pemba, and the ZPPP winning six, all in Pemba. The ASP won thirteen seats, eleven in Zanzibar and two in Pemba. The significant feature of the election was that the ZNP-ZPPP alliance increased its majority by five in the National Assembly, even though the ASP won more than 54 per cent of the popular vote. Coalition leaders, feeling that the election nevertheless had strengthened their legislative position, refused to form a three-party national government.

Because choice of party in Zanzibar is basically a response to ethnic feelings, and because all parties have come to symbolize clearly differentiated racial attitudes, personalism has influenced the voting behavior of Zanzibaris far less than party loyalty. Pervasive commitment to party has been the foundation of the ZNP-ZPPP electoral coalition, as the supporters of each party could generally be depended upon not to bolt even when asked to vote for candidates of a different party. There has been only one major exception to this pattern. In Pandani constituency in Pemba, Ali Sharif, who was victorious as a ZPPP candidate in January, 1961, and again as an ASP candidate in June, had essentially the same body of supporters on both occasions. In practically every other instance party fortunes have scarcely been affected by changes of candidates, and each party has been able to count on its safe and weak constituencies almost irrespective of the candidates it places on the ballot.

Table 2 shows the comparative strength of political parties in the four general elections in Zanzibar, Pemba, and the protectorate as a whole. Voting behavior in Zanzibar Island has been stable throughout, with the electorate divided roughly 60 to 40 between the ASP and its opponents in every election, despite a more than fourfold increase of the electorate between 1957 and 1963. Here the ASP finds its strongest sup-

TABLE 2

POLITICAL PARTY STRENGTH IN FOUR GENERAL ELECTIONS
IN THE PROTECTORATE OF ZANZIBAR
(In percentages of total valid vote cast)

Election	Zanzibar				Pemba				Protectorate			
	ASP	ZNP	ZPPP	Others	ASP	ZNP	ZPPP	Others	ASP	ZNP	ZPPP	Others
1957	62.8	15.7	a	21.5[b]	c	29.9	a	70.2[b]	35.1	21.9	a	43.0[b]
January, 1961	61.1	34.6	4.3		23.3	43.0	34.0		43.2	38.5	18.3	
June, 1961	63.6	32.4	4.0		36.6	38.8	24.6		50.6	35.5	13.9	
1963	63.09	31.49	5.42		44.39	28.03	27.58		54.21	29.85	15.94	

a The ZPPP was not organized until 1959.
b These figures include the two victorious independents, as well as a number of other candidates.
c There were no official Afro-Shirazi Union candidates in Pemba in the 1957 election, as the African and Shirazi associations had not yet merged.
SOURCES: *Report of the Supervisor of Elections on the Elections in Zanzibar, 1957* (Zanzibar: Government Printer, 1958); *Reports of the Supervisors of Elections on the Registration of Voters and the Elections Held in January, 1961* (Zanzibar: Government Printer, 1961); *Report of the Supervisors of Elections, June, 1961* (Zanzibar: Government Printer, 1961); official government press release on the 1963 election.

port among ethnic groups responsive to an anti-Arab appeal, the mainland Africans, and the vast majority of Hadimu Shirazis. In the two 1961 elections and in 1963, the ASP swept the north central, central, eastern, and southern areas of the island, where the population is almost entirely Hadimu. In Zanzibar Township, the ASP scored victories only in constituencies where the population is overwhelmingly mainland African. The ZNP has consistently won the predominantly non-African seats in Zanzibar Township; two represent constituencies in the Stonetown area, where Zanzibar's Asian and Arab commercial and middle-class elements live, and the third is a constituency with a preponderance of Comorians and Ismaili Asians. All the rural constituencies won by the ZNP in Zanzibar are located in the north and northwestern areas of the island, where there is a majority of Tumbatu Shirazis. The ZNP has some strength in the fertile areas, where there are few Shirazis and where Arab plantation owners sympathetic to the party have strong local influence.

Voting behavior in Pemba is almost exactly the reverse of that in Zanzibar; in the two 1961 elections the ZNP and the ZPPP gained nearly two-thirds of the popular vote in Pemba, and in both 1961 and 1963 the coalition parties won all but two seats. Despite recent ASP gains among the Pemba and Tumbatu communities, these Shirazis have consistently preferred the coalition parties. The tendency to support them instead of the ASP is the political reflection of the Shirazis' low esteem for mainland Africans and their general good will toward the Arab minority.

The vast differences in the voting behavior of Pemba and Hadimu

Shirazis may stem from their respective relationships with mainland Africans (see table 3 for data on the Shirazi, African, and Arab popula-

TABLE 3

POPULATION OF THE PROTECTORATE OF ZANZIBAR
BY ETHNIC COMMUNITY, 1948

Community	Zanzibar		Pemba		Protectorate	
	Number	Per cent	Number	Per cent	Number	Per cent
Shirazi	81,150	61.2	67,330	60.2	148,480	60.8
African	37,502	28.3	13,878	12.4	51,380	21.0
Arab	13,977	10.5	30,583	27.4	44,560	18.2
Total	132,629	100.0	111,791	100.0	244,420	100.0

SOURCE: *Notes on the Census of the Zanzibar Protectorate, 1948* (Zanzibar: Government Printer, 1953).

tions of Zanzibar and Pemba). In Zanzibar there are more than twice as many mainland Africans as Arabs, and there has been extensive social contact between them and Hadimu Shirazis. The latter frequently migrate to Zanzibar Town, where they become socially and politically assimilated into the community of mainland Africans, and pick up its racial views.[6] Many migrants return to their villages and strengthen existing anti-Arab sentiments. This system of mutual reinforcement has created an almost impenetrable ASP stronghold in the Hadimu areas of Zanzibar Island. In Pemba there are far fewer mainland Africans, and they are widely dispersed over the island. There is no urban concentration of mainlanders to function as a center for the dissemination of ASP-style nationalism. Here the mainland African—not the Arab—is more commonly regarded as an alien and an unknown stranger, and his racial views and political attitudes have gained little currency with the indigenous population.

The antipathies of many Pemba Shirazis toward mainland Africans are rooted in a kind of social prejudice. Although almost all the mainland community is of the Muslim faith, Shirazis tend to view the mainland in terms of a strongly Christianized Tanganyika, and hence to disapprove of the mainland immigrant as a potential Christian influence. Shirazis frequently feel that the mainland Africans' national loyalties, especially among the more recent immigrants, may not ultimately be attached to

[6] The Hadimu account for more than four-fifths of the Shirazi migrants to Zanzibar Town, and more than one-tenth of the entire Hadimu population now resides there.

Zanzibar. Proud that they have lived in peace with the Arab minority, many Pemba Shirazis strongly disapprove of the mainland Africans' antipathy to the Arabs. In recent years Shirazis have perceived the mainlanders as playing a prominent role in incidents of political violence, and have added to their former biases an image of the mainland African as a troublemaker. Economic issues have aggravated these feelings; there is a growing sense that the mainland African is a cheapener of labor, and that Shirazis, as indigenes, ought to have special priority for government and other jobs.

The differences in racial attitude and hence in voting behavior among Pemba and Zanzibar Shirazis also reflect their widely varying patterns of historic, social, and economic relations with the immigrant Arab minority. When, in the first half of the nineteenth century, the Omani sultanate government was transferred from Arabia to Zanzibar, and Zanzibar Town was established as its administrative center, Arab control of Zanzibar Island at once became highly effective. Within a short time Arab immigrants had displaced the few indigenous Africans from the fertile land area surrounding the town, and practically monopolized the best arable land.[7] In this way the Shirazis of Zanzibar came to know the Omani Arab as administrator and colonial settler. With the Arab population concentrated on Zanzibar's fertile quadrangle in the close vicinity of Zanzibar Town, and the Shirazi population heavily concentrated in the distant coastal fishing villages or in small settlements peripheral to the arable area, geographic and social relations between Arab and Shirazi were remote from the start.

It is likely that Zanzibar's fertile area was, in fact, very sparsely settled before the arrival of the Omani settlers. The land, covered by dense forests heavily infected with malaria, had been little used; it was the Arab colonist who first introduced the clove tree to Zanzibar.[8] Whether the concentration of Zanzibar's Arab community on the best cultivable soil was by historical accident, by legitimate acquisition, or by force, the fact is that Zanzibar Shirazis have come to reside in a kind of native reserve, on land unsuitable for the intensive cultivation of cloves or coconuts. An additional element of strain has thereby been introduced into Shirazi-Arab relations in Zanzibar, and a political myth of major importance has been fostered. The Zanzibar Shirazi believes, rightly or wrongly, that he was forcibly and illegitimately deprived of his land by the Arab intruder. The present relative poverty of the rural coastal fishing villages in contrast with the moderate prosperity of the clove and coconut areas, and the hardship of country life in contrast with the com-

[7] Sir John Gray, *History of Zanzibar from the Middle Ages to 1856* (London: Oxford University Press, 1962), pp. 167–168.

[8] John Middleton, *Land Tenure in Zanzibar* (London: H.M.S.O., 1961), p. 11.

parative luxury of an urban existence (the Arab population of Zanzibar is 52 per cent urbanized), combined with the Shirazis' belief that they were forcibly evicted from the best land, have generated among many Shirazis of Zanzibar Island the conviction that, because of Arab colonialism, they enjoy at best the status of poor relations in their own land.

Relations between Shirazis and Arabs in Pemba have been entirely different. Because of Pemba's remoteness from Zanzibar and the limited number of early Arab settlers, the Arab administration of Pemba was, from the beginning, far less thorough and effective than that in Zanzibar. The Pemba Shirazi did not experience the immigrant Arab as an intruding colonial administrator, but rather as a fellow farmer and neighbor on the land. Two important factors have reinforced this view. First, the Arab population of Pemba is mainly rural; the proportion of the Arab community in Pemba's largest towns is smaller than the proportion of Arabs to the total population of the island. Pemba Shirazis and Arabs live side by side in the rural areas, and friendly personal relations are common. There has not developed that sense of social estrangement based on variant patterns of residence which figures so prominently in Zanzibar. Second, clove and coconut soils of good quality are almost universal throughout Pemba. Both Arabs and Shirazis occupy soils of similar arability, and the Pemba Shirazis do not feel that the immigrant Arab minority enjoys exclusive occupation of the best land. The first dramatic expression of this friendly relationship was the refusal of Pemba Shirazi leaders to join in the Afro-Shirazi Union. Its present importance lies in the inability of the ASP to gain more than isolated pockets of support among the Pemba electorate.

The prophetic feature of the two 1961 elections was the emergence of the ZNP as a major national political power. Since its utter defeat in 1957, the ZNP had nearly doubled its share of the popular vote, and was able to command electoral majorities in nearly half of the constituencies. For more than three years the party had engaged in intensive organizational activity, and had entered the 1961 elections as a highly disciplined, well-financed, and organizationally integrated body. Its swelling popularity was evidence as well of its growing ability to capture the mood of Zanzibaris with multiple political and religious appeals. Further, an almost unanimous confidence among ZNP supporters in the virtues and the policies of party leaders endowed the ZNP with a unique spirit of optimism and solidarity.

The ASP had emerged from the 1961 elections in undisputed possession of the largest single popular following, and the increase of nearly 7 per cent in the share of the vote between January and June gave it a slight majority of the electorate. In the election of July, 1963, it received more than 54 per cent of the votes cast, gaining 13,000 votes more than the coalition parties combined. Its failure to translate this vast electoral support into a proportionate number of seats in the National Assembly is owing to a variety of factors. The delimitation of constituencies has favored the ZNP, which in 1961 won three seats with votes of less than 2,000, as opposed to one such seat won by the ASP. In both the 1961 and 1963 elections, the ZNP was able to win easily in the two Stonetown constituencies which have a very small number of voters. The ASP has also been hurt by the success of the ZNP-ZPPP electoral alliance, for co-alition candidates of either party draw upon additional anti-ASP voters in close constituencies. Finally, the ASP has been consistently unable to command the financial and technological resources necessary to conduct a modern, nationwide campaign.

Structurally, there are no major differences between the ASP and the ZNP. Each has an ascending hierarchy of branches, branch commit-tees, and regional councils, at the apex of which stands the party execu-tive. Each party has organized a youth league and a women's section, which function under the loose supervision of the national executive, and both have established official relations with trade unions. Both parties also operate a double national executive committee—a pure party execu-tive and an expanded executive which includes representatives of the youth movement and of affiliated trade unions. Since the formation of an electoral alliance and a coalition government by the ZNP and the ZPPP, the ZNP's expanded executive has also included the parliamentary lead-ers and the general secretary of its political partner. Both parties have also instituted thoroughly democratic procedures for the selection of all party officers at local, regional, and national levels. All these similarities notwithstanding, vast differences in organizational strength and effective-ness separate the two parties.

The ZNP possesses an enormous political advantage in the power and the refinement of its party structure. Although it has never been more than a minority party, its better organization has enabled it to make maximum use of a limited popular following. This organizational su-periority does not stem simply from differences in its formal constitution, but from the fact that its membership and leadership alike are infused with a spirit of militancy and dedication. This spirit has been accom-panied by a zealous and relentless devotion to the day-to-day tasks of raising funds, issuing political propaganda, and recruiting members. Un-remitting attention to the smallest organizational details has transformed the ZNP from an electoral caucus of like-minded notables into a crusad-ing instrument of anticolonial nationalism. In the ZNP's progression from total defeat to national prominence, no other single factor was so de-cisively important as the excellence of its organization.

The 1957 election was a major catalyst to the organizational development of the ZNP. The totality of its defeat dispelled any lingering illusions about the ease of recruiting a multiracial party, and focused the attention of party leaders directly on the task of creating a more effective electoral apparatus. From that early moment in its history, the party was spurred to recruit new leaders and organizers among Zanzibar's educated elite. And, as a result, from 1957 on the ZNP benefited from a steady influx of younger men—journalists, teachers, and government servants—and soon became richly endowed with organizational skill, a resource unduplicated by any other party in Zanzibar.

Throughout its period of gestation, and subsequently, the ZNP has enjoyed the nearly unanimous support of Zanzibar's plantation-owning class. This group, mainly Arab, has been particularly helpful in rural areas. More financially independent than either squatter farmers or small farmers, and therefore free of the necessity of daily labor, this leisure class has been able to devote considerable time to political activities. As liaison between city and country, and in the execution of its party's organizational policies, it has furnished the ZNP with the equivalent of a full-time professional staff.

Organization was built from the center outward, the local branches and committees being set up in an organizing campaign that emanated from the party's urban nucleus. Even the ZNP's trade-union affiliate, the Federation of Progressive Trade Unions (FPTU), owes its origin to the party's program of building a nationwide network of branches and affiliated bodies. This pattern of development has enabled the top leadership to permit complete procedural democracy at the local levels, while at the same time reserving for itself the greatest possible degree of autonomy. The party's organizers were, from the start, in a position to specify the range of activities of local branches, restricting the discretion of local leaders to matters of organization building and recruitment. They thereby retained for the central executive unfettered flexibility in decision making on matters of policy and tactics.

Certain distinctive structural features of the ZNP help it to maintain the tightest unity within its now massive network of branches, and among its far-flung and disparate membership. The party's practice of convening all branch secretaries in a weekly meeting, attended by a representative of the national executive, facilitates rapid two-way communication between branches and top leaders, keeping the party executive continuously informed of the state of affairs in local areas, and providing for the dissemination of party policies throughout the organization. Still more important, the weekly meeting of branch secretaries engenders among local party leaders a strong sense of the party as a nationwide organization with national objectives. This all-pervasive sense of national purpose discourages wasteful jealousies and rivalries among regional interests within the party. The ZNP also convenes a weekly meeting of all the branch committees of Zanzibar Town. At first glance this gathering might seem superfluous, but its function is altogether different from that of the branch secretaries' meeting. Although the party's youth movement, the Youths' Own Union (YOU), and the FPTU have numerous members in rural areas, it is in the city that they are most active in party affairs. The frequent meetings of urban branch committees serve to integrate youth leaders and trade-unionists into the over-all party structure.

The most impressive structural feature of the ZNP, however, is its administration of numerous philanthropic and benevolent operations. Through an elaborate system of interlocking subcommittees and voluntary groups, the party engages in a ceaseless round of these parapolitical activities. Its programs of charity and welfare work, medical care, and adult education are so extensive as to place the ZNP in competition with the government itself as a dispenser of social services. These activities furnish the party with a superb medium for the recruitment of new members. They are even more significant to the internal functioning of the party organization, for the administration of philanthropic and benevolent services absorbs the energies and the attention of innumerable minor party leaders and officials. This has exactly the same consequences for the operation of the party structure as the restriction of local leadership to matters of organization; that is, it endows the top leadership of the Executive Committee with virtually unchallenged authority over matters of party policy and tactics.

The origin of the ZNP as a rural protest movement is dramatized by its custom of reserving the highest party offices, the presidency and the vice-presidency, for founding members of the Nationalist Party of the Subjects of the Sultan of Zanzibar. These official posts are thus solely honorariums, and those who occupy them have little actual influence on decision making. The ZNP president, Vuai Kiteweo (a Shirazi), continues to reside in his home village of Jambiani, travels to party meetings in the city only infrequently, and takes little interest in party affairs. The ZNP's acknowledged, and certainly its most influential, leader is Ali Muhsin, who holds no official party position beyond membership on the Executive Committee. This complete separation of formal office from effective influence lends decision making within the ZNP its distinctive quality as a collegial and consensual process. For there is no position within the executive which affords its occupant any special authority over party policy, and there is no struggle for power over the purely ceremonial posts. Effective influence depends on one's ability to persuade his colleagues. Collegial decision making has placed a high value on the collective responsibility of Executive Committee members for the party's policies. The most serious offense against the party is publicly to criticize its principles or leaders. Thus conflict has been contained within the Executive Committee, policies have had the unanimous public endorsement of party leaders, and party followers have been inspired with the solidarity of their cause.

The ZNP's appeal to Zanzibaris has been dictated by the present context of bitterly divided nationalisms, in which the Islamic religion provides the only potential bond among members of all racial communities. The ZNP has sought to present party affiliation as the sole allegiance consistent with the principles of the faith, and as the inevitable accompaniment to religious piety. Multiracialism, loyalty to the sultanate, and patriotism have all been expressed in the religious idiom, particularly in the rural areas where religious sentiments are strong. The most constant theme of the ZNP press and of its public speakers has been that Zanzibaris of every race must unite in a common struggle. Party spokesmen have stressed the spiritual meaning of this policy by quoting koranic precepts on the divine purpose of racial multiplicity.[9] The party has also given deep spiritual meaning to its role as guardian of the sultanate, which is portrayed as a religious obligation to established authority.[10] Commonly regarded as the preferred party of the royal family, the ZNP has benefited both from the high public esteem in which the Sultan is held, and from the belief that political loyalty is the sacred duty of devout believers. Party ideology frequently identifies the ZNP as the defender of Islam in a Muslim country threatened by powerful Christian enemies, and envisions the consequence of its electoral defeat as the destruction of the Islamic faith in Zanzibar. Wherever these appeals have been successful, the ZNP enjoys a commitment, deeply religious in character, which stems from the conviction that the political philosophy of the party embodies the social and moral teachings of Islam.

The appeal of the ZNP has a more political connotation in Zanzibar Township. In three key municipal constituencies, the party is dependent upon voting majorities of Asian and Comorian descent, whose advantageous positions in government and commerce and whose status as alien minorities have given rise to deep apprehensions about the future. Here the multiracial composition of the party, with membership based solely on Zanzibar citizenship, is stressed, as is also the fact that ZNP policies do not interpret Zanzibar's social structure in racial terms. The plain implication that social change must not be accompanied by discrimination against immigrant ethnic minorities is clearly suited to ease Asian, Arab, and Comorian fears of government policies that might give special economic priority to socially underprivileged racial groups.

The ZNP's assertion that Zanzibar citizenship is the chief political

---

[9] Koran 30:21.
[10] Koran 4:62.

virtue has attracted many Shirazis to its cause. Insistence on this point of ideology has given its nationalistic ethic a spirit of patriotic loyalty to country, which provides Shirazis with political outlets for expressing their cultural pride in being the first Zanzibaris. By dramatizing the alien and potentially disloyal character of its main rival, the ASP, it furnishes Shirazis who are in competition with mainland Africans for employment and social services a political rationale for their claim to first preference. The over-all effect of this appeal has been to integrate within the party a multiracial and socioeconomically diverse body of supporters. Shirazi farmers and fishermen, plantation owners and urban commercial and middle-class elements, have all been united in a league of patriots who serve the Sultan, his subjects, and the faith.

Probably the most important reason for the ASP's defeat in the 1961 and 1963 elections was its erratic and uncoördinated organization. In the period between the elections of 1957 and 1961, the party did very little to recruit supporters or to establish local branches in areas where the ZNP was strong. Perhaps of greatest importance was the party's failure to grasp the significance of the 1959 split and the emergence of the ZPPP, for that split stripped the party of its Pemba leadership and of most of its organizational strength in Pemba. The result has been a fatal structural imbalance: in Zanzibar, the ASP has a gratuitously powerful organization which produced needlessly overwhelming majorities; in Pemba its organization is so weak as to be almost wholly dependent on the personal magnetism of its candidates.

The ASP suffered organizational failure because of its chronic inability to transform the loose electoral coalition of 1957 into an integrated and disciplined political movement. The fact that the party was created through the fusion of two autonomous associations has affected every aspect of its development. The party organization is a purely electoral apparatus limited almost solely to the function of selecting candidates and assisting their campaigns. ASP local organization virtually disappears between elections, and all the assorted political tasks which demand a permanent rural staff—fund raising, propaganda, intelligence work, and recruitment—are left undone. Throughout the period after the first general election, ASP leadership remained largely uninformed of the extent of the ZNP's growth, and in both 1961 and 1963 the party was forced to plan election campaigns on the basis of unrealistic and often exaggerated appraisals of its own regional strength.

The view of the ASP as strictly an electoral machine, widely held among its leadership, has created conflict within the Executive Committee. Any attempt by the executive to expand its authority to include the right of making policy decisions binding on members has been strongly resisted. The debate over participation in the Freedom Committee, for example, was largely fought out within the party over the issue of whether or not all Executive Committee members should be compelled to abide by the party's decision to coöperate with the ZNP. And the secession of Pemba Shirazi leaders which preceded the formation of the ZPPP, was, in effect, provoked by what they regarded as an unwarranted exercise of party discipline. In the absence of a sense that all leaders must ultimately come to share collective responsibility for party policies, conflicts within the ASP resist final resolution, and factional squabbles are protracted over long periods of time. These have drained off energies and talents which could more profitably have been devoted to improving the party's organization, and have also demoralized its supporters.

The ASP is wracked by regional, ethnic, and ideological conflicts. Regional tensions over the distribution of party equipment and funds have crippled the Executive Committee's ability to plan the most efficient utilization of the party's slim resources. Pemba officials especially feel that they have been slighted in the allocation of finances, and argue bitterly that if sacrifices must be made, they should be made in Zanzibar where party support would remain constant. Conflicting regional interests, however, have often forced the party to plan the logistics of its campaigns on the basis of placating dissident local leaders rather than on the basis of winning the largest possible number of seats.

Superimposed over a complex pattern of regional jealousies is an endemic power struggle between mainland African and Shirazi leaders which splits the ASP into two large warring factions engaged in an interminable conflict over control of the party organization. This conflict has numerous dimensions, including that of private and personal animosities, but its fundamental components are a Shirazi belief that so long as the ASP is dominated by mainlanders it can never attract the vast majority of Shirazis, and a mainlander determination to prevent control of the party from falling into the hands of men whose loyalty to the cause of African nationalism is suspect. The tenuous and uncertain unity between these two groups has been preserved only by their maintaining an even balance of members on the party executive.

The ideological disunity of the ASP has expressed itself most clearly in a conflict of generations between its parliamentary group and the young members of the party's trade-union affiliate, the Zanzibar and Pemba Federation of Labor (ZPFL). The trade-union leaders, some of whom have received higher education in Eastern bloc countries, have wanted the party to abandon its gradualist approach to constitutional development and to take, instead, a more militant and socialist stand on both domestic and international political issues. Their demand for a larger representation on the party's branch and regional committees and on its Executive Committee, and their ability to coerce the party into adopting intransigent and extremist positions by threatening to withdraw their support, have antagonized the more conservative parliamentary leaders. These various patterns of conflict have fragmented the ASP into a series of isolated power blocs, each bent on altering the party to suit its own political aspirations. In the planning of campaigns, in the selection of top leaders, and in the formulation of its policy, the party is nearly paralyzed by its own internal opposition.

The ASP has consistently failed to recruit leadership that would enable it to compete on even terms with the more smoothly organized ZNP. The quality of its local leadership is particularly poor. In rural areas it is a party of fishermen, small farmers, and squatters; in the city, of houseboys and manual laborers. As a result the ASP has had to staff its local branches with leaders who lack administrative ability and who are unskilled in the strategies of agitational politics. At the level of the central executive, ASP elite leadership has been recruited late in the party's history. The party's most effective spokesmen and organizers did not join it until immediately before the January, 1961, election. Thus they have had very little opportunity, free from the pressure of campaigning, to accomplish the fundamental structural reforms necessary to improve communications between constituency organs and the center, and to recruit members in areas where the party is weak.

Frequently accused of being a purely racial party, the ASP has in fact combined the idea of African unity with the view that in Zanzibar the Africans constitute an economically deprived community. ASP leaders have sought to evoke an image of the ZNP as dominated by the well-to-do Arab minority, and as dedicated to the interests of non-African upper-class elements whose affluence depends upon the economic misery of the African majority. In effect more a protest movement of the impoverished urban and rural masses than a revolutionary party, the ASP denounces the religiosity and the patriotism of the ZNP as attempts to disguise the stratification of Zanzibar society along racial lines. Because of their memories of slavery and of the privileged political position historically enjoyed by the Arab minority, ASP leaders have singled out this group as the real enemies of African social progress. The ideology of the ASP asserts that Zanzibar suffers from two colonialisms, Arab and British, and that it would be meaningless to achieve freedom only from the latter because the political condition of Africans would remain unchanged.

This appeal lacks universality and has alienated from the party most of the ethnic minorities of Zanzibar. The party has virtually no Arab supporters, and receives only token allegiance from the Comorian community. Within the Asian community, it has attracted significant support only among Parsees and Hindus who, as religious minorities, approve the ASP's desire to separate religion and politics. Numerous Shirazis, particularly in Pemba, have also been alienated from the party, as their racial discontent with the Arab minority is slight. The party's effort to create a spirit of communality between Zanzibar African nationalism and continental African nationalism has had limited success among the many Shirazis who have little affinity with the African mainland. Their sense of a distinct Shirazi identity leads them to prefer the ZPPP.

The ZPPP is a party in trouble. The parliamentary negotiations of January, 1961, and the decision of the party president, Muhammad Shamte, to form a ZNP-ZPPP coalition government split the party and led to an exodus to the ASP of some of its most effective leaders. Among those who left the ZPPP and joined the ASP were four of its parliamentary candidates and its general secretary. Their departure weakened the party, which in any event had achieved only the bare beginnings of an organization and had destroyed its hopes of ever becoming an independent third force in Zanzibar politics. The ZPPP is an effective electoral force only in Pemba, where more than four-fifths of its voting support is concentrated, and where its ability to command the allegiance of between one-fourth and one-third of the electorate creates an almost evenly balanced three-party system. On Zanzibar Island, the party has virtually no popular support, and in most areas maintains only a token organization, or no organization at all. The only ZPPP stronghold in Zanzibar is the village of Makunduchi in the southern part of the island, the birthplace and home of the party's vice-president, Ameri Tajo. Here, however, its strength is largely a function of Tajo's personal popularity, and the party has been unable to extend its support sufficiently to pose an electoral threat in Makunduchi constituency.

The party has no major ancillary organizations, such as trade unions or youth movements, and consequently has had great difficulty in replenishing its faltering organization with a fresh flow of vigorous new leadership. The decision to expand its relationship with the ZNP from government coalition to full electoral partnership revealed that by June, 1961, the ZPPP had become almost wholly dependent upon the ZNP for organizational strength. Since that election its own organization has become so inextricably merged with that of the ZNP that, in terms of party structure, it has almost ceased to possess separate identity.

Further, the ZPPP has been unable to formulate a basis of appeal which would distinguish it from its partner. In the past it recruited members only among Shirazis dissatisfied with the ASP and the ZNP, who were attracted by the notion of a party of indigenous Zanzibar Africans opposed to both Arab and mainlander minorities. As the party is now completely identified with the ZNP, it can no longer appeal on that basis, and it has lost its chief source of popular support. Defectors from the

ZPPP probably account for a sizable part of the gain registered by the ASP in Pemba in the 1963 election.

The ZPPP now faces a perplexing, and possibly insoluble, political dilemma. Its candidates have become dependent on the support of ZNP voters. ZNP candidates, however, have represented the coalition in a larger number of constituencies than have ZPPP candidates, and in all these constituencies ZPPP supporters are being asked to vote for ZNP candidates on the ground that the objectives and the principles of the two parties are identical. The danger is that, in the absence of any clear policy differences between the two, ZPPP members will be drawn away by the more powerfully organized and more actively proselytizing ZNP. Similarly, many ZPPP supporters, when confronted with a clear choice between the ZNP and the ASP, seem to prefer the ASP. If the ZPPP should leave the coalition to travel a more autonomous road, it might invite disaster at the polls. If it remains, it faces a gradual, but no less fatal, attrition of its popular following.

With the virtual merger of the ZNP and the ZPPP, Zanzibar politics have hardened into an almost evenly balanced two-party system, but there is little prospect of political stability. In the ferocity of their competition, the parties have totally politicized Zanzibar society, and everyday social relations are more and more segregated along party lines. Sports, social life, and even marketing have become partisan activities. There is no network of politically neutral clubs or activities to bind individuals to one another outside politics, and thereby provide a kind of social unity which transcends political divisions. Nor is there any sizable social group subject to conflicting political cross-pressures which might induce the parties to bring their views into closer harmony. Individual Zanzibaris misunderstand and misinterpret one another's parties to a degree that makes mutual accommodation impossible.

The parties are not separated by disparate attitudes toward foreign or domestic affairs, but by elemental and irreducible racial fears. ZNP members see in the ASP disrespect for the Muslim faith, the unbridled use of political power to reverse the social structure of the country, and, ultimately, political domination of Zanzibar by the African mainland. To ASP supporters, the ZNP symbolizes perpetual economic servitude and political subjection to a racial minority. To them the ZNP victory of 1963 means the end of hope for a better life.

The apparent decision of the ZPPP to continue its dependent relationship to the ZNP has played into the hands of Arab ZNP leaders. For they are now able to exert the same sort of influence over their coalition partner as they enjoy within their own party, namely, the domination of the political sophisticate over those with limited political experience. This influence extends over the entire range of public policy, and even includes such questions as recruitment into the higher civil service and redistribution of land. In both these areas drastic reform is necessary if Shirazis or Africans are to advance. It has become the unspoken premise of all public policy that there must be no social or political change that threatens the position of Zanzibar's entrenched minority.

This premise explains the ZNP-ZPPP coalition's decision not to accept the ASP's offer to form a national government, for a national government would have meant that Africans independent of Arab influence could control important ministries. By this decision, however, the government has created a situation of ominous instability. Well above half of the population voted against the ZNP-ZPPP coalition, and in Zanzibar, the seat of government, the figure approaches two-thirds. The ASP is also supported by Zanzibar's most powerful trade unions, and, within both the party and its trade-union affiliates, the coalition's refusal has strengthened the position of militant and extremist leaders. These leaders believe that peaceful constitutional processes will never enable Zanzibar to be rid of its Arab rulers.

POSTSCRIPT

On January 13, 1964, approximately one month after independence, armed African insurgents seized control of Zanzibar, overthrew the ZNP-ZPPP government, and installed in power a revolutionary council headed by leaders of the ASP. Among the earliest acts of the revolutionary government was the mass arrest and internment of thousands of Arabs and the confiscation or destruction of large amounts of Arab property. With the permanent banishment of the Sultan and the proscription of all parties but the ASP, the new regime completed the political and economic destruction of the Arab oligarchy.

The revolution was not entirely unforeseen, for the strength and solidarity of antigovernment groups had become the most conspicuous feature of Zanzibar politics during the months immediately before independence. The most significant group was a new political party, Umma (The Masses), launched just before the July election. This party was created by Abdul Muhammed (Babu), former general secretary of the ZNP, and two other defecting members of the ZNP Executive Committee. Umma never gained a large popular following and did not stand candidates in the election. Its importance lay in the ability of Babu and his close personal associates to build a unified political movement out of a myriad of opposition elements.

Among the first supporters of Umma were the leaders of the Federation of Progressive Trade Unions (FPTU). Almost overnight the FPTU ceased to be a ZNP affiliate and identified itself with Umma. This action left the government without trade-union support. As a party largely inspired by a militantly Marxist ideology, Umma also attracted the sympathy of revolution-minded leaders within the ASP and its supporting trade unions, and soon became the organizational meeting ground of extremist antigovernment sentiments. Under Umma influence, the concept of violent political change was seriously considered by ASP leaders who had already been deeply embittered by election defeat and rejection of their appeal for a "national" government.

Under the pressure of dwindling popular support and increasingly effective opposition, the government attempted to rebuild its trade-union support by organizing government-sponsored unions among the split rank and file of the FPTU. When this effort met with only limited success, the government resorted to authoritarian methods to ensure its stability. The activities of the opposition were severely restricted, including travel to mainland and European countries. Concerned with the loyalty of the police force, the Ministry of Home and Legal Affairs, under Ali Muhsin, initiated a program of repatriating policemen of mainland origin, and began to replace them with Arab and Asian youths or with carefully selected indigenous Africans.

Despite all its precautions the ZNP-ZPPP regime remained extremely vulnerable to a coup. Nearly all its popular support was in Pemba or in the remotest areas of Zanzibar. The Stonetown area, which contains the Sultan's palace, the government office buildings, and ministerial residences, is located on a peninsula and is enclosed by massive areas of ASP followers. ZNP-ZPPP leaders were thus geographically cut off from their popular following. Lacking defense arrangements with Great Britain or nearby mainland countries, they could rally no one to their assistance once internal police resistance had been overcome.

The seizure of power was swiftly executed, and the new regime consolidated its political position within a day or two after the coup. Umma was dissolved and merged with the ASP, and the trade-union affiliates of the two parties also joined in a single national organization, the Federation of Revolutionary Trade Unions (FRTU). Abedi Karume, president of the ASP, assumed the position of president in the reconstituted People's Republic of Zanzibar and Pemba; Abdulla Hanga, deputy general secretary of the ASP, was named vice-president; and Babu, founder and leader of Umma, became minister for defense and external affairs. The remaining ministries were assumed by various parliamentary leaders of the ASP.

The new ASP regime was determined to complete the political revolution by bringing about a rapid restratification of the Zanzibar population. Its objective was to transform Zanzibar into a wholly egalitarian society so that the African community would achieve full social and economic parity with other ethnic groups. The Revolutionary Council, which included former Umma members and representatives of the FRTU as well as the ASP group, initiated a series of policies designed to ameliorate the social position of the African majority. It recruited African personnel into the administrative levels of the civil service and nationalized all land in preparation for a large-scale program of land redistribution. In order to elicit mass popular enthusiasm for its policies, the council sought to infuse Zanzibar society with a radical and militant political ethos.

The revolutionary government began to face critical problems, however, in consummating the African social revolution. These problems stemmed in part from the depressed condition of Zanzibar's economy, and in part from the difficulty of maintaining political viability in so small a state. President Karume looked to the mainland countries for support. The ASP had traditionally enjoyed cordial and close relations with the Tanganyika African National Union, and the social reforms it desired had the sympathy of Tanganyika's president, Julius Nyerere. Karume and Nyerere concluded a constitutional merger of their two countries in late April, 1964, about three months after the revolution.

The new nation is called the United Republic of Tanganyika and Zanzibar. Nyerere became its president, and there are two vice-presidents: Karume and Rashidi Kawawa, who had been vice-president of Tanganyika. The United Republic's constitution is strongly unitary in character. Zanzibar has been allowed to retain, for a time, its own parliament and executive, but these bodies are to have power only over limited local matters. Most major areas of policy are the responsibility of the National Assembly of the United Republic. These include defense and foreign affairs, tax and trade policies, and citizenship and immigration. Under this constitutional arrangement, Zanzibar became an integral part of a new African nation.

The Expansion in Political Scale

14. SOMALI REPUBLIC

By A. A. Castagno, Jr.

INTRODUCTION

In the Somali Republic,* a variety of factors have shaped political parties in forms different from those found in the rest of Tropical Africa. First, the Somali Republic is the only Tropical African territory that has a relatively homogeneous traditional culture. The majority of Somalis— nomads or seminomads who move in wide orbits with their herds—do not recognize the validity of international boundaries. The Pan-Somali movement, which seeks to unite all Somalis of the "horn" of Africa, is itself singular as a transterritorial movement among Tropical African states because it is identified with state policy and with all political parties. And yet in no other Tropical African territory is the social system so factious, so fissionable, and so highly segmented as it is in the Somali Republic. Only the Nuer in the Sudan bear some resemblance to the Somali in this respect, but they do not constitute a nation-state and do not have their own political parties.

The Somalis live in a Malthusian region where the struggle for survival against the elements of nature and the contrivances of man is severe. In order to survive, man joins with man in a complex and vast network of lineage groups which divide and unite and unite and divide as expedience requires. Stability, a rather relative term, is found almost exclusively in the *dia*-paying groups which bind men of common ancestry through formal treaty commitments to pay and receive blood compensation. New values, ideologies, and institutions have been introduced in the past seventy-five years, but even those Somalis who have taken the plunge into modernity have found themselves inextricably bound up with their

---

* In this text, Somalia means the former Trust Territory of Somalia, and Somaliland means the former British Somaliland. The Somali Republic includes both sections; the former is now called the Southern Region, and the latter, the Northern Region. Because of the unusual ethnic complexity of the Somali Republic, a map of the area has been included.

I conducted research in the Somali areas during 1957–1958 and the summer of 1962, spending most of my time in Somalia. I am particularly indebted to the Ford Foundation and to the Social Science Research Council, which sponsored my research, and to the many Somali, Italian, and British officials, educators, and party leaders who were generous with their time and research materials. I also wish to express gratitude to Dr. I. M. Lewis, Dr. Michael Pirone, Dr. S. Benardelli, and Dr. Lucy Mair for the assistance they gave me.

512

dia-paying groups. The hand of history is a heavy one, and it has pressed hard on the modern political parties.

Foreign influences in the Somali territories, especially on modern political parties, also differ from those found in other Tropical African territories. Britain, Italy, France, Ethiopia, the United Arab Republic, and, to a much lesser extent, the United States and the Soviet Union have had influence in the "horn." A unique factor in Somalia is the intervention of the United Nations, which in 1950 took the unprecedented step of establishing an independence timetable of ten years, imposing on the trusteeship authority a "Declaration of Constitutional Principles," and of stationing a watchdog committee, the United Nations Advisory Council, in Mogadiscio, the capital. No other trust territory has been watched over so jealously by its international guardian as has Somalia, which has long been viewed as the special ward of the United Nations. In this paper I do not seek to evaluate the multiple aspects of these external influences on Somali political development, but I do suggest their relationships.

It is because of these factors, and because little material on the Somalis as a whole is available, that I have departed from the conceptual analyses found in other contributions to this volume. My approach is basically historical, informational, and interpretative. Somali parties may be understood, I believe, only through knowledge of the socioeconomic background, the nature and extent of foreign rule and influence, and the history of their own emergence. One underlying theme is particularly significant: Somali political parties are intermeshed with a social system that is strikingly affected by the vacillating pattern of clan associations and cleavages. An understanding of the modern political system requires an appreciation of the agnatic lineage society that underpins it, for Somali political parties are essentially consortia of competitive kinship groups. The relationships between the parties and the traditional groups are major conditioning forces in the political process.

SOCIOECONOMIC ENVIRONMENT

As used in the traditional sense, the name "Somali" refers to two genealogical groups, the Samaale and the Sab (see table 1), both of whom claim descent from Aquil Abu Taalib of the Qurayshitic lineage. The Samaale group comprises four main clan families, the Daarood, the Dir, the Ishaaq, and the Hawiye. The Sab consists of two clan families, the Digil and the Rahanweyn; the Mirifle confederacy, the most numerous group, is often considered synonymous with the Rahanweyn. Among the Samaale clan families, the Daarood are regarded as having directly descended, in their own right, from Aquil Abu Taalib; they claim only an affinal relationship to the Samaale through the Daarood marriage with the Dir, the oldest Samaale group. Outside the two main genealogical

TABLE 1

SOME SOMALI ETHNIC GROUPS

SAMAALE			
Daarood	*Dir*	*Hawiye*	*Ishaaq*
Aulihan	Bimal	Abgal	Arap
Dulbahante	Gadabursi	Averghedir	Eidegalla
Harti	Iise	Aer	Habr Awal
Marehan		Saad	Iise Muuse
Muhammad Zubeir		Soleiman	Saad Muuse
Omar Mahmud		Hauadle	Habr Toljaala
Osman Mahmud		Galgial	Habr Yunis
Iise Mahmud		Murosada	
Warsangeli		Sheikhal	

SAB		OTHERS	
Rahanweyn (Mirifle)	Digil	Bagiuni	
Elai	Dabarre	Shidle	
Gassar Judda	Giddu	Rer Hamar	
Ghelidle	Irole	Rer Baraawa	
Hadama		Rer Merca	
Leisan			

groups there are a number of minority communities of non-Somali or part-Somali origin, the majority of which are found in Somalia: Asians, Negroids, Bantu, and mixed populations having unique cultural characteristics. Of these four main minority groups, the Asians have been the least influenced culturally by the Somalis.[1]

---

[1] The most significant works on Somali anthropology have been written by I. M. Lewis: "Clanship and Contract in Northern Somaliland," *Africa*, XXIX (July, 1959); "The Somali Lineage System and the Total Genealogy: A General Introduction to Basic Principles of Somali Political Institutions" (mimeographed; Hargeisa, 1957); "Modern Political Movements in Somaliland," *Africa*, XXVIII (July–Oct., 1958); "Sufism in Somaliland: A Study in Tribal Islam," *Bulletin of the School of Oriental and African Studies*, XVII–XVIII (1956). Some of Lewis' observations in *Peoples of the Horn of Africa* (London: International African Institute, 1955) have been revised in his later studies. Lewis concentrated his field work on British Somaliland. His latest work, *A Pastoral Democracy: A Study of Pastoralism and Politics among the Northern Somali of the Horn of Africa* (London: Oxford University Press, 1961), is a significant contribution to anthropology and political theory.

The *doyen* of Cushitic studies is Enrico Cerulli. Some of his writings are compiled in *Somalia: Scritti Vari Editi ed Inediti* (Rome: Istituto poligrafico dello Stato, 1957); others may be found in *Archivo per l'Antropologia: Rassegna di Studi Etiopici* and *Rivista degli Studi Orientali*. Massimo Colucci, *Principi di diritto consuetudinario della Somalia Italiana Meridionale* (Florence: La Voce, 1924), remains the most substantial source on southern Somalia. N. Puccioni, *Antropologia e Etnografia delle genti*

The physical base of the Somali social system follows the contours of migratory movements which began in the fourteenth century from the northern coastal area of Somaliland and proceeded in a general south-westerly direction, stopping ultimately at the foothills of the Ethiopian mountains in the west and at the Tana River in the south. European and Ethiopian authorities have set these outer migratory limits and have established boundaries that today juridically divide the Somalis. As these limits have contemporary significance, the estimates of Somali population distribution in table 2 include Somalis in Ethiopia, Kenya, and French Somaliland as well as those in the Somali Republic.

TABLE 2

ESTIMATED POPULATION DISTRIBUTION OF THE SOMALIS

| Ethnic group | Somali Republic | | French Somaliland | Ethiopia | Kenya (Northern Province) |
	Somalia	Somaliland			
SAMAALE					
Ishaaq		420,000	10,000	?	2,000
Daarood	270,000	120,000		400,000	31,000
Hawiye	480,000			?	29,000
Dir	40,000	100,000	20,000	?	
SAB					
Rahanweyn	340,000			?	8,000
Digil	50,000				
MINORITY COMMUNITIES					
Negroid and Bantu	70,000				
Arabs	30,000				
Indian and Pakistani	1,500				
Bagiuni (southern coast)	1,500				
Amarani (Rer Baraawa)	7,000				
Total	1,290,000	640,000	30,000	500,000	70,000

SOURCE: Estimates were compiled from official data, none of which, however, are based on accurate census-taking procedures. Population statistics cited are conservative.

In the Somali Republic, the Ishaaq are found mainly in central Somaliland; the Daarood, in the Migiurtinia, Mudugh, and Lower Giuba provinces of Somalia and east of the Ishaaq in Somaliland; the Hawiye, in central Somalia (Mudugh, Benadir, and Hiran provinces, and along

della Somalia, Vols. I, III (Bologna: N. Zanichelli, 1931, 1936), is an important ethnographic study.

See also *Bibliografia Somala*, Camera di Commercio, Industria ed Agricoltura della Somalia (Mogadiscio, 1958), and Helen F. Conover, *Official Publications of Somaliland, 1941–1959: A Guide* (Washington: Library of Congress, 1960), for bibliographical data.

the Uebi Scebelle River) between the Sab and the northern Daarood; the Sab, between the Hawiye and the southern Daarood in the relatively fertile area of the Upper Giuba between the Uebi Scebelle and Giuba rivers; and the Dir, mainly in the eastern part of Somaliland and in the southern coastal districts of Somalia. Several Hawiye groups and a few Daarood are found among the Sab, and some Hawiye reside among the southern Daarood. The Negroid and Bantu groups of cultivators inhabit

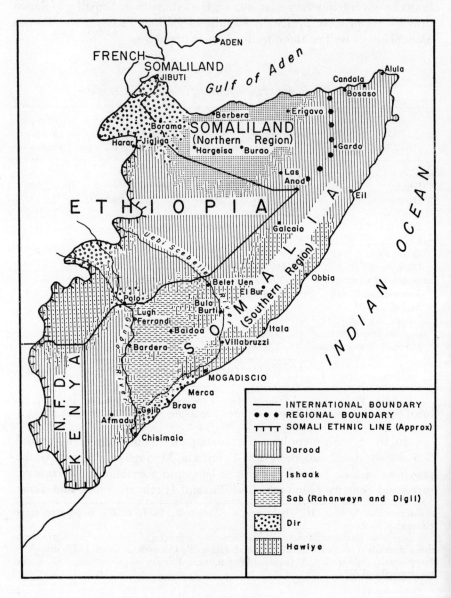

the region along the two rivers, and the European and Asian populations are found almost entirely in a few main cities (see map).

The genealogical cleavage between the Samaale and the Sab has been exacerbated by forceful intrusions of the Samaale into the fertile area of the Upper Giuba inhabited by the Sab. The schism also has its counterpart on social and political levels. The Samaale, with the main exception of some Hawiye along the Uebi Scebelle, are nomads or semi-nomads, whereas many of the Sab are engaged in sedentary agriculture and pursue some pastoral activities. The "noble" Samaale nomads have regarded the Sab as inferior, and many do not include them in the total Somali genealogy. Linguistically, the Sab and the Samaale are as far apart as are northern Italians and Sicilians. Differences are also found in traditional political organizations. Generally, the political units of the Sab tend to be larger than those of the Samaale, and, because of closer territorial attachment in the sedentary areas, the Sab political system, in contrast with the quasi-acephalous structure of nomadic society, lends itself to some degree of hierarchical organization.[2] Despite these differences, the character of the political leadership of the two groups does not vary significantly. Chieftainship, including the category of traditional chiefs, is based on the principle of *primus inter pares*, and is always subject to the will of the jural unit as expressed in *ad hoc* assemblies (*shir's*).

The traditional Samaale-Sab cleavage has set the broad framework of ideological antagonisms in the Somali nation, but animosities have also obtained among the Samaale, particularly between the Daarood and the Hawiye and between the Daarood and the Ishaaq. As lengthy migrations for pasturage and water result in a wide dispersion of agnatic lineages, the pattern of competition may follow the full spectrum of segmentation from the clan family to the smallest social unit, the *rer* (extended family). Clan-family association is insufficient to motivate the segments into concerted political action on a permanent basis. Yet the ideological link of a common eponymous ancestor in the clan family, or more particularly in the clan, may become a rallying point in the struggle for water, pasturage, prestige, or power. The dia-paying group, however, has the highest degree of social, jural, and political cohesion, because it is invariably the optimum unit for operating in a nomadic environment.[3]

---

[2] See Colucci, *op. cit.*, pp. 49–67; Lewis, "Modern Political Movements in Somaliland" and "Clanship and Contract in Northern Somaliland." The Sab are regarded as "tribal" and thus are less bound by genealogical fiction than the Samaale, but it does not necessarily follow that Sab traditional leaders have greater control over the dia-paying groups than do the Samaale. In my analysis of the elections of 650 chiefs, I found the percentage of those who were elected unanimously higher among the Samaale than among the Sab.

[3] There are 650 dia-paying groups in Somalia and 361 in Somaliland. The dia-paying group may be the rer, the subclan, or the clan. The average number of male voters in the dia-paying group is approximately 1,500, and ranges from 120 to 9,000. On

Britain, Italy, and now the Somali Republic have made strong efforts to mollify the extremes of the agnatic cleavages. Although interclan conflict is less endemic in Somalia than in Somaliland, the most crucial decisions in the traditional society still deal with matters of war, blood compensation, arbitration, alliances, and peace. Lineage associations are important in the alignment process, but they may not always be the determining factor; political expedience may require related lineages to assume positions of neutrality toward one another, or even to join the opposition. Disputes are usually on the subclan or clan level. It is extremely rare for whole clan families to be in conflict with one another, but when members of a clan family reside as a minority group in the area of another clan family, disputes between the two coexisting clan families may arise, as, for example, between the Hawiye and the Daarood in the Lower Giuba, or between the Hawiye and the Rahanweyn-Digil in the Upper Giuba. When such conflict arises, the disputants may be able to elicit sympathy from their respective coclansmen, wherever they reside.

Elements of modern Somali nationalism, an ideology antithetical to the parochialism of clanship, may be found in three main sources: a relatively common language, Islam, and Westernization. Although the language has not been reduced to a commonly accepted written form, there is considerable homogeneity in the Somali dialects, except for that of the Sab. As to religion, all Somalis, with the exception of a few converts to Christianity, subscribe to the Sunnite sect of Islam. Every clan covets its tradition of Arabian descent, and many Somalis belong to one or another of the Sufi dervish orders. Muhammad Ahmed bin Abdalla Hassan, the "Mad Mullah," was able to use the Salihiya as the ideological base of his twenty-one-year jihad (1899–1920) against Ethiopian and European rule. Attempting to assert the leadership of all Somalis, he imposed on his followers a ban against the use of clan names. There has been, further, the influence of the religious settlements (*jamiyah*) in southern Somalia, which strip their communicants of their clan robes, whether Sab or Samaale. Thus the Mullah, the jamiyah, and the educated sheiks expanded the thought patterns of the Somalis whom they influenced. In this way and to this extent, Islam was a forerunner of the modern political movement which has sought, above all, to eliminate tribalism. But the total effect has been limited; the Mullah himself ultimately had to fall back on his clansmen, the Daarood, for support against the Ishaaq.[4]

the basis of my data, only the Tunni, the Matan, the Ghelidle, the Elai, the Eile, the Leisan, and the Hadama of the Sab, and the Galgial and the Hauadle have dia-paying groups numbering more than 5,000 male voting members.

[4] The best treatise on Islam in Somalia is E. Cerulli, "Note sul movimento Musulmano nella Somalia," *Rivista degli Studi Orientali*, X (1923). See also J. S. Trimingham, *Islam in Ethiopia* (London: Oxford University Press, 1952), and Lewis,

The impact of the West did not significantly alter the traditional Somali social and political structure. Italian administration was essentially confined to the central zone of Somalia until 1925–1927, when control was extended to the Daarood in the Lower Giuba and in northern Somalia. The administration of the territory was carried out by a few hundred Italian administrative and technical personnel, and education was confined to the school for the sons of chiefs and to a few Catholic elementary schools. Contacts with the West were intensified with the fascist occupation of Ethiopia in 1935–1941; about 60,000 Italian troops were stationed in Somalia, 30,000 Somalis were engaged as askaris, and another 10,000 were employed as laborers. By encouraging the traditional Somali disdain for the Amharic Coptic Christians, and by establishing Greater Somalia, which included the Ogaden region of Ethiopia and Somalia, the fascist government unwittingly nourished the growth of Somali nationalism. Increased urbanization, with its accompanying social ills, so aroused Somali political consciousness that by 1939 the Italian administrator began to express concern over the modernist tendencies of townsmen, the unemployed, and some ex-servicemen.[5]

The British administration of Somalia (1941–1950) advanced Somali nationalism more positively by lifting the fascist ban on political activities, supporting progressive social and political movements, and encouraging secular education. British proposals of a united Somalia under British trusteeship gave continuity to the Greater Somalia concept. On the negative side, Britain's use of Kenyan, Ghanaian, and Nigerian troops in the territory, and her frugal economic policy, provoked resentment. Inadvertently, Britain's tolerance of local Italian political parties—Neo-Fascists, Socialists, Actionists, Christian Democrats, and Communists—contributed to the urbanized Somali's political sophistication.[6] Finally, the possibility of self-government, which Italy's defeat raised, accelerated

---

"Sufism in Somaliland." On Muhammad Ahmed bin Abdalla Hassan, consult D. J. Jardine, *The Mad Mullah of Somaliland* (London: H. Jenkins, 1923); F. S. Caroselli, *Ferro e fuoco in Somalia: Venti anni di lotta contro il Mullah e i Dervisci* (Rome: Sind. Arte Grafiche, 1931); and E. Cerulli, "Muhammad B. ʿAbd Allah Hassan al-Mahdi," *Encyclopedia of Islam*, III (Leiden: E. J. Brill, 1936), 667–668.

[5] For some indication of the character of Italian administration before World War II, see F. S. Caroselli, *Relazione del Governatore per l'anno 1939–1940* (Mogadiscio: Stamparia della Colonia, 1941); G. Corni, *Somalia Italiana*, II (Milano: Editoriale Arte e Storia, 1937); G. de Martino, *La Somalia nei tre anni del mio Governo* (Rome: Tipografia Camera dei Deputati, 1912); *Gli annali dell' Africa Italiana*, Ministero dell' Africa Italiana (Rome: Casa Editrice A. Mondadori, 1938–1942); C. Riveri, *Relazione sulla Somalia Italiana* (Rome: Ministero delle Colonie, Ufficio Studi, 1922).

[6] Published material on the British administration of Somalia is lacking. A. Bulotta, *La Somalia Sotto Due Bandiere* (Milano: Garzanti, 1949), is biased on the Italian side, and Lord Rennel of Rodd, *British Military Administration of Occupied Territories in Africa during the Years 1941–1947* (London: H.M.S.O., 1948), is sketchy.

political activities in the territory. The period of British rule helped prepare the way for changes that were effected in the decade 1950–1960,
under Italian trusteeship.

Neither the Italian nor the British administration seriously altered
the economic and social bases of Somali traditional society. The economy
lacked differentiation and specialism. Economic change had been confined primarily to a few coastal cities and to the area along the two rivers
in Somalia, where cash crops had been developed and several small
industries had emerged. The occupational structure of the population
(see table 3) has been an obstacle to modernization. Labor unions, a

TABLE 3

OCCUPATIONAL STRUCTURE OF THE SOMALI REPUBLIC
(In percentages)

Occupation	Somalia	Somaliland
Nomadic pastoralists	42.9	80.0
Seminomadic farmers	28.1	10.0
Cultivators	19.0	5.0
Fishermen and sailors	1.0	1.0
Merchants	3.2	0.5
Artisans	1.0	0.5
Miscellaneous	4.8	4.0

SOURCE: *Rapport du Gouvernement Italien à l'Assemblée Générale
des Nations Uniés sur l'Administration de Tutelle de la Somalie* (Rome:
Istituto poligrafico dello Stato, 1953), p. 346; and materials from the
Somaliland Protectorate.

recent development, did not significantly contribute to the nationalist
movement, and the most important commercial activities were carried on
by Arabs, Indians, and Italians.

The political changes brought about by the two wars occurred mainly
in the towns, where the traditional system of political and social organization had been somewhat weakened. The towns operate as centers of nationalist propaganda; from them new ideas radiate out into the interior,
carried by mobile pastoralists who stop to trade or to break the rhythm
of their nomadic movements. But townsmen are bound by traditional
interclan politics, as social relations are almost exclusively channeled
through agnatic lineage associations. By no means has urbanization been
so intense as in West Africa. Of fifty-one municipalities (forty-five in
Somalia, six in Somaliland), only nine have stable populations between
5,000 and 10,000, and only three, between 20,000 and 30,000. Mogadiscio,

the single cosmopolitan city, has about 95,000 inhabitants.[7] As these towns are scattered over a 1,300-mile-long area, and as there is no adequate transportation and communication network, the scale of interrelations is low.

POLITICAL PARTIES BEFORE TRUSTEESHIP

The organization of modern political parties in Somalia began with the establishment of the Somali Youth League (SYL) in May, 1943, known then as the Somali Youth Club. Initially it confined its membership to young men between the ages of fifteen and thirty in order to exclude from the party "reactionary elders who did not understand modern requirements," but in March, 1947, a new party statute extended the age limit to sixty. The aims of the party included eradication of "all harmful prejudices and ill feeling between tribes, rers, and *tariqa's*"; education of the youth in "modern ideas of civilization"; adoption of a Somali-invented script, Osmania, for writing the Somali language; and establishment of "workers' unions" on the Italian agricultural concessions. The two most important objectives of the party were (1) the establishment of a Greater Somalia which would unite all Somalis in the horn of Africa, and (2) the elimination of clanism. Party principles were matched with practical activities; the SYL held literacy classes in English and Arabic in all major towns, established social welfare centers, and set up farm and commercial organizations to advance Somali trade and agriculture.

In the first phase of party development (1943–1947), leadership was provided by moderate young men such as Sheik Abdulcadir Sheik Sakawa, the nephew of a famous religious leader, and Yassin Haji Ali, the son of a noble Daarood chief. Both held the presidency of the party. After May, 1947, the party's leadership was more militant; Haji Muhammad Hussein, a member of the Rer Hamar, a small Mogadiscian group uninvolved in traditional interclan conflicts, was president, and Abdullahi Issa, an Averghedir Hawiye, was secretary-general. The core of the party was made up of small merchants and traders, artisans, the literate elements,[8] and a few educated religious leaders.[9] Many of the party leaders,

---

[7] Most of the towns have seasonal floating populations. The over-all increase in the population of towns was about 20 per cent between 1938 and 1958. Compare the data in *Africa Orientale Italiana* (1938) with those in *Rapport du Gouvernement Italien à l'Assemblée Générale des Nations Unies sur l'Administration de Tutelle de la Somalie* (Rome: Istituto poligrafico dello Stato, 1953) (hereafter cited as *Rapport*). Population figures given in this paper should be regarded as conservative estimates. The Somali government claims that the total population of the Republic is 4 million.

[8] The term "educated" or "literate" refers to Somalis who had had some elementary school education or who had had koranic and Arabic training beyond that

such as Aden Abdullah Osman and Sheik Ali Giumale, had been employed by the Italian colonial administration; the latter had won the Croce di Guerra in the Italo-Ethiopian campaign. The Daarood dominated the party numerically, but the Hawiye clans (Averghedir and Hauadle) were also important. There were some key educated Sab members, such as Abdulcadir Muhammad Aden, who later became secretary-general of the main opposition party.

Although the party's statement on economic change and its religious orientation belied any Marxian influence, the SYL organizationally bore a resemblance to the Communist Party. It adopted a red flag with a crescent and a three-leaf clover, strikingly similar to the hammer and sickle. Ultimate power was vested in the party congress, composed largely of local committee secretaries, but invariably it was the Central Committee that made the crucial decisions. In 1949 the party was strengthened by the creation of *horsed*'s, action squads of ten men each established in party branches to act as the avant-garde of party propaganda and to take security measures on behalf of the party whenever it opened new sections, especially in antagonistic areas like the Sab-dominated Upper Giuba. The financial resources of the party were derived from monthly dues, but Somali residents in Aden, Liverpool, and Cardiff also contributed. When Abdullahi Issa appeared at the United Nations as the SYL representative, he was sponsored by Somali seamen and expatriates in Manhattan.

The British administration gave the SYL invaluable assistance. Between 1946 and 1948 there was a broad area of agreement between party and government. The SYL's goal of a Greater Somalia coincided with Ernest Bevin's plan for a British trusteeship over the area. British officers actively supported the party's educational program and its initiative in establishing social centers. It was particularly during 1947, before the Council of Foreign Ministers' Four-Power Commission of Investigation for the Former Italian Colonies arrived to solicit Somali desiderata, that British personnel took a positive hand in widening the scope and the organization of the party. When the party established branches in the

---

provided by the "koranic bush schools." It is estimated that during the fascist period (1922–1941) about 7,000 Somalis received some elementary education. There were no Somalis at that time, as far as I am aware, who had received intermediate or secondary school secular education (see A. Castagno, "Somali Republic" and "French Somaliland," in Helen Kitchen, ed., *The Educated African: A Country-by-Country Survey of Educational Development in Africa* [New York: Praeger, 1962], for an analysis of educational policies in Somalia, British Somaliland, and French Somaliland).

⁹ There is a distinction between educated religious leaders, a few of whom attended Al Azhar University, and illiterate religious preachers (*wadad*'s). The former constitute a small minority and are found in the main towns; the latter are wandering mullahs who follow the nomads in the interior.

Upper Giuba, the administration supported it in its conflicts with the Sab, who viewed the SYL as a Daarood organization. The administration also favored the employment of SYL members in the civil service and the gendarmery. The party's identification with government was so close that by 1948 an SYL party card was practically a prerequisite to government employment.

British relations with the SYL did not preclude the administration from becoming involved with clan considerations. The administration found it expedient to bolster the Daarood elements of the party, particularly because British hopes for a trusteeship required that the Daarood, who constitute the largest Somali group in the horn, be given a role of primacy. In addition, the 1946 anti-British riots, which the British interpreted as being Hawiye in origin and Italian-inspired, caused the administration to favor the employment of Daarood party members. The "moderate" Hawiye wing of the party, although it opposed the return of Italy as the administering power, was not so Italophobic as were Daarood members. In any event, by November, 1947, the Central Committee decided not to ask for a British trusteeship, but, rather, for a trusteeship under the four major powers. Thereafter, SYL-British relations seemed to deteriorate, and in 1948 Britain returned the Ogaden to Ethiopia and banned the SYL in Kenya.

Although the British were biased toward the SYL during these years, they did not obstruct the emergence of opposing political parties. The SYL's unequivocal position on the elimination of clanism alienated a number of traditional leaders in all clans, and its Daarood complexion evoked considerable anxiety among the Sab and some Hawiye groups. Prominent among the anti-SYL parties was the Hisbia Digil Mirifle (HDM), organized by the Sab in March, 1947, in order to "strengthen the brotherhood of the Digil and Mirifle (Rahanweyn) peoples" and to defend their interests. The organization of the HDM put the traditional Sab-Samaale cleavage on the modern political party level. On the other hand, inter-Samaale enmity was expressed through the organization of a number of Hawiye-dominated parties, such as the Abgal Youth Association, which sought to unite the numerically important Abgal clans. Other Hawiye formed the Somali African Union (SAU) with the ostensible aim of "uniting all Africans." The Hidaiet al Islam Shidle e Mobilen was organized by the Negroid Shidle cultivators and their Hawiye associates, the Mobilen, to advance their agricultural interests. The Bimal, the largest Dir group in Somalia, supported the Bimal Union; and northern Daarood chiefs, apprehensive of the SYL, rallied behind their party, the Somali Progressive League (SPL). There was, undoubtedly, some complicity between the anti-SYL parties and the large Italian community in Somalia, but the basic reasons for their formation stemmed from clan issues and the fear of SYL radicalism. The leaders of all these parties were, essentially, traditional chiefs, although each party had a sprinkling of educated young men. The organizational aspects of the parties were heavily influenced by the SYL party statute.

As a means of consolidating their forces at the time of the investigation by the Four-Power Commission, the anti-SYL parties formed a coalition called the Somalia Conference. In its twenty-three-point program, the conference advocated a thirty-year Italian trusteeship and a gradual approach to modernization, in contrast with the SYL's anti-Italian policy and its demands for rapid detribalization and independence in a decade. In terms of ethnic composition, the conference represented an uneasy association between the Sab of the HDM and a number of party-organized Hawiye groups which were antagonistic to the Daarood and the Averghedir clan of the Hawiye, which made up the bulk of the SYL membership. The Sab in particular were hostile to the SYL and regarded the party as a modern version of the traditional attempts of the Daarood to "invade our territory." [10] The pro-Italian position of the Somalia Conference was subordinate to the traditional factors; it performed the temporary function of welding together traditionally opposing genealogical associations.

The conference was an abortive attempt of ill-organized political parties to secure a modified Somali *gaashaanbuur-ta,* that is, an *ad hoc* coalition which the contracting parties, having some kinship ties, join for purposes of common defense. But as the conference lacked the basic quality of the gaashaanbuur—an agnatic framework—it functioned only as a liaison unit, and was continuously harassed by schisms. Neither the Sab-dominated HDM nor the Daarood-dominated SPL felt comfortable in the same organization. The conference also lacked the organizational ability, the tactical versatility, and the militancy of the SYL, as well as the favor of the British administration. Ideologically, its statements on nationalist goals were diluted by its pro-Italian stand. The issues of Greater Somalia, modernization, and rapid self-government had been preëmpted by the SYL. The conference claimed a membership of 180,000, and the SYL, 98,000; but party enrollment was probably no more than 30,000 for the SYL and 20,000 for the conference.

TRUSTEESHIP ADMINISTRATION, 1950–1960

The First Stage, 1950–1956

The transfer of authority from the British to the Italian trusteeship

---

[10] See "Report on Somaliland," Four-Power Commission of Investigation for the Former Italian Colonies (mimeographed; 2 vols.; London, 1948), for the conclusions of the commission and for the views expressed by representatives of various Somali traditional, political, and economic interests.

administration[11] in April, 1950, proceeded smoothly despite the SYL's sporadic anti-Italian demonstrations in 1948–1950.[12] The Italian administration predicated its policy on the assumption that the development of political parties through free elections was indispensable to the establishment of an independent and democratic state. But between 1950 and 1954, before the first municipal election, the trustee power leaned toward the more conservative and tradition-focused parties. This was reflected in the threefold increase in the stipends of traditional leaders and in the dominance of traditional leaders and non-SYL party members in the Territorial Council. There was considerable attrition between the SYL and the government, and clashes between the two occurred in the main towns, particularly in Daarood areas. The Daarood especially felt the impact of Italy's return. Daarood chiefs in Mogadiscio insisted that they would return north to "our own territory" (Migiurtinia) if the administration did not reverse its "anti-Daarood" policy.

In large part, Daarood antagonism was conditioned by the administration's policies of equal treatment of all ethnic groups and equality of employment, which signified a reversal of the pro-Daarood policy of the British. An Anglo-Italian agreement required Italy to retain personnel engaged by the British administration. This she did scrupulously, but in her employment policies she favored the Hawiye. Within the SYL itself, the moderate Hawiye wing, led by Aden Abdullah Osman, vice-president of the Territorial Council and one of the leading personalities of the party, took a more compromising attitude than was generally found among SYL members, and was largely responsible for establishing a *rapprochement* with the administration in 1953–1954.

One major effect of Italy's return was the proliferation of political parties. Opportunists who could gain a following jumped on the pro-Italian band wagon. Others viewed political parties as the only tangible means of supporting clan interests. Thus, by March, 1954, when the first municipal election based on direct male suffrage was held, there

---

[11] For a brief comprehensive survey of the political, social, and economic policies of the trusteeship administration, see A. Castagno, *Somalia,* Carnegie Endowment for International Peace, International Conciliation, no. 522 (March, 1959), 348–386. A detailed economic analysis is provided in Mark Karp, *The Economics of Trusteeship in Somalia* (Boston: Boston University Press, 1960). There is a plethora of UN documents relating to the trust territory of Somalia. The most important for the political scientist are the annual reports of the UN Advisory Council (1950–51 to 1959–60), the triennial reports of the UN Visiting Mission (1951, 1954, 1957), and the official records of the General Assembly and the Trusteeship Council. See also the annual reports of the administration (*Rapport*), 1950–1959.

[12] The most serious incident between Italians and Somalis in Somalia's history occurred on January 11, 1948; during the SYL anti-Italian demonstrations fifteen Somalis and fifty-two Italians were killed. The Somalis were SYL members or pro-Italian Somalis of the Abgal clan (*Somalia Courier,* Jan. 12–17, 1948). The results of the official inquiry were never published.

526 *Somali Republic*

were twenty-one political parties, as against eight in 1950. Some parties took on national appellations, whereas others frankly acknowledged their clan identification. But whatever the party label, there were dominant

TABLE 4

NUMBER OF VILLAGES WITH BRANCHES OF, AND DOMINANT
CLAN AFFILIATIONS OF, PARTIES IN SOMALIA (1950–1954)

Party	Number of villages[a]	Dominant clan affiliation[b]
INTERCLAN		
National		
Somali Youth League	34	Daarood, Hawiye
Somali Progessive League	12	Osman Mahmud (Daarood)
Somali African Union	22	Murosada, Averghedir Aer (Hawiye)
Somali National Union	7	Galgial, Hauadle (Hawiye)
Regional		
Benadir Youth Union	5	Rer Hamar, Rer Merca (Mogadiscio and Merca)
Local		
Somali National League[c]	1	Bimal (Dir), Marehan (Daarood)
Hidaiet al Islam Shidle e Mobilen	3	Shidle (Negroid), Mobilen (Hawiye)
CLAN OR TRIBAL		
Regional		
Afgoi-Audegle Group	2	Digil
Hisbia Digil Mirifle	15	Digil, Rahanweyn
Local		
Abgalia	1	Abgal (Hawiye)
Abgal Youth Association	1	Abgal (Hawiye)
Ancora	1	Bagiuni
Bagiuni Fichirini Youth	1	Bagiuni
Dir Youth Association	1	Dir
Giam Giamogia	1	Gosha (Negroid)
Murosada Bloc	1	Murosada (Hawiye)
Leopardo	1	Negroid
Palma	1	Negroid
Six Shidle	1	Shidle (Negroid)
Somali Democratic Union	1	[d]
Somali Patriotic Union	1	Dir

[a] The number of villages in which the parties had branches are estimates derived from the *Corriere della Somalia*, 1950–1954, and the reports of regional commissioners, not from party claims.

[b] My categorization differs from that of I. M. Lewis, "Modern Political Movements in Somaliland," *Africa*, XXVIII (July–Oct., 1958). Lewis does an excellent job of drawing the relationship between traditional ethnic groups and modern parties, but I regard his categories as too broad and his depiction of the vacillating pattern of affiliations and cleavages as too general.

[c] Not to be confused with the Somali National League in Somaliland.

[d] Data lacking.

patterns of agnatic affiliation within all political parties, as the breakdown in table 4 illustrates.

Despite the factiousness of Somali politics, the SYL and the HDM emerged from the 1954 municipal election with significant strength. The electoral results confirmed the superior position of the SYL; it gained 48 per cent of the 37,697 votes cast, and 141 of 281 municipal council seats. The HDM won 57 seats in fifteen municipalities, mainly among the Digil and the Mirifle, and a few among the Rer Baraawa of Brava, a Swahili-speaking group of mixed Asian and African origin. The SAU and the SPL, both organized on a national level since 1950, were regarded by some authorities as the two interclan parties most capable of competing with the SYL, but they won only 28 and 22 seats, respectively, all but 2 of them from Samaale areas. The Benadir Youth Union, formed in 1951 as a political party from the social group, the Hamar Youth Club, and representing the interests of the Rer Hamar and the Rer Merca, won only 5 seats, although it polled the fourth-largest number of votes cast. More revealing of the SYL's strength and its national character was its ability to obtain seats in all but one of the thirty-five municipalities; it won an absolute majority of councilors in fifteen municipalities, compared with five for the HDM and one for the SPL. Furthermore, the SYL penetrated the Sab area and gained one-sixth of the Rahanweyn and Digil votes.

An analysis of the voting data in terms of the clan structure of the municipalities illustrates the relationship between political parties and agnatic affiliations. Although the cohesiveness of the HDM began to show incipient signs of weakening, the party was still entrenched in the Sab area. Its leaders campaigned on grounds of the Sab-Samaale cleavage and repeatedly referred to the dangers of domination by the north, should the SYL succeed. The HDM's antagonism toward the SYL was reinforced by clashes between the Galgial clan (Hawiye) and the Rahanweyn and between the Rahanweyn and the Marehan (Daarood). Rahanweyn-Digil chiefs, demanding that the administration prevent further migratory incursions by the Samaale, resolved "to defend our sons and our land, by arms if necessary." The HDM and traditionalists made vigorous efforts, which sometimes led to violence, to prevent the establishment of new SYL branches in the Sab area, and launched sporadic attacks on Hawiye settlements in the Upper Giuba. It was in this atmosphere that one of the major leaders of the HDM, Usted Osman Muhammad Hussein, an Aden-educated teacher, was assassinated.

The anti-SYL Samaale-dominated parties optimistically believed they could exploit the fissiparous nature of the Samaale, particularly of the clans in the northern Migiurtinia and Mudugh provinces. In some areas the SPL and the SAU operated independently; in others they tacitly agreed that one or the other alone should oppose the SYL; and in still others each sought to win over the other's following. The SPL hoped to cut into the SYL's strength by nourishing the grievances held by the Osman Mahmud and Marehan clans against other Daarood affiliates, especially the Omar Mahmud. The SAU attempted to draw from Hawiye clans, particularly the Averghedir Soleiman, the Abgal, and the Murosada, all of whom had disputes with the Averghedir Saad. It also sought to take advantage of inter-Daarood conflicts. The Somali National Union banked on attracting adherents from the Hauadle clan of the Hawiye, which was engaged in periodic conflicts with the Marehan (Daarood). The Abgal had their own political parties, and their town, Itala, was the only municipality in which the SYL did not put up candidates. Most of the leaders of the non-SYL Samaale parties were discontented SYL members who were unable to attain significant power positions in the SYL and who used ethnic grievances to bolster their own political ambitions; they were often aided by Italian personnel who disagreed with the official policy of neutralism.

Despite its desire to extirpate clanism, the SYL was compelled to rely on traditional leaders and to employ agnatic cleavages wherever and whenever they could enhance the party's strength. In the Samaale areas, where the SYL won 90 per cent of its council seats, it had to hold the line against the challenge posed by the conservative and pro-Italian Samaale parties. It therefore became involved in traditional Samaale politics. Among Rahanweyn and Digil townsmen, the SYL appeared as the avant-garde of independence and nationalism, but its success in penetrating the Upper Giuba was also owing to its ability to gain the support of the large Samaale contingents residing in juxtaposition to the Sab, as in Lugh Ferrandi and Bardera. It successfully appealed to Samaale groups which were living as *harifa* (*sheegat* or clients) of the Sab, and similarly made inroads into the clusters of Sab harifa of Sab hosts. The harifa groups were persuaded to agitate for their own chiefs and for land rights denied them by the client relationship.[13]

These activities did not deter the SYL from functioning as the main nationalizing agent. In this regard, the HDM suffered from serious disadvantages. Whereas the SYL could organize among the Sab, the HDM, because of its tribal goals and the traditional Samaale disdain for the Sab, was unable to operate beyond the Sab ethnic boundaries. The scope of HDM activities was even restricted in the Upper Giuba, where some Sab traditional leaders viewed the more modernist HDM members with suspicion. Administration attempts to secure HDM representation at im-

---

[13] The sheegat system has now been outlawed. The majority of client relationships existed in the Upper Giuba in the Sab area; others were found in the Lower Giuba among the Daarood. Several important Sab political leaders in the SYL ranks were members of clans that were held as harifa. The harifa were only slightly inferior to the hosts.

portant Sab assemblies dealing with traditional issues were often blocked by the chiefs, whereas in the Samaale areas, traditional disputes were often settled by SYL conciliation committees. Religion also tended to favor the SYL; the better-educated sheiks could more easily identify themselves with the nationalist goals of the SYL than with the tribalistic pro-Italian orientation of the HDM. Although Italy returned to Somalia as a democratic power, there was no mistaking her non-Muslim garb. Non-Somali Arabic journals and radio broadcasts did not hide their pro-SYL predilections, and the mosques often became centers for SYL propaganda.

In several respects the 1954 election was a major turning point in Somali political development. The anti-Italian campaign of the SYL tended to gloss over conflicting clan ideologies, and Pan-Somali propaganda was assisted by intermittent disturbances along the Somali-Ethiopian frontier. Ultimately the SYL compelled every important party, including the HDM, to admit the need to alter the Somali traditional system and to adopt nationalist goals in their programs. Most important, the election lessened the animosity between the SYL and the administration, although anti-Italianism remained an important SYL propaganda weapon for several years. Before the election the administration would not admit the SYL's superior strength, but Italian district commissioners who kept a close watch on political party operations during the campaign proved conclusively that the SYL was the only party with the potentiality for national leadership. Thus, from 1954 to the end of the trusteeship period, there existed an SYL-administration concordance, despite attempts by the more radical wing of the party, mainly Daarood elements, and anti-SYL Italian personnel to disturb the relatively amicable relationship.

In the period between the municipal election and the first general election in February, 1956, there was a realignment of parties. Six of the Samaale parties, which won a total of 8,980 votes and 69 council seats in the 1954 election, formed the Somali Democratic Party (SDP) with Muhammad Sheik Osman, an educated Averghedir Aer chief and the former head of the African Union, as its leader. Osman's earlier pro-Italian and anti-SYL activities had provoked an attempt on his life at the height of the Italian-SYL friction in 1952. The SDP advocated gradual abolishment of the traditional social system, a unitary republican form of government with a decentralized administration, and Greater Somalia. The HDM was invited to participate in the coalition, and its refusal to do so made the SDP a Samaale party, although it organized a few branches in the Sab region. Two other Samaale parties were formed: the Marehan Union and the Somali Hawiye Youth Union. The former was established by Marehan livestock middlemen and traditional leaders in the trans-Giuba area in protest against the administration's refusal to grant them a monopoly over livestock trade and as an expression of their separateness from other Daarood clans.[14] The Hawiye Youth was aimed at the Hawiye in Mogadiscio, but it was mainly Abgal in composition. It was founded by Muhammad Boracco, who broke with the SYL when it refused to let him run as a candidate in the capital.[15] Other non-Samaale parties appeared for the election: the Six Shidle (formed in 1954), a splinter of the Hidaiet al Islam Shidle e Mobilen; the Bagiuni Fichirini Youth, comprising exclusively the Swahili-speaking racially mixed Baguini of the southern coast; and the Afgoi-Audegle Group, a Digil party of cultivators in the towns of Afgoi and Audegle.

The 1956 election, the last to be held under direct Italian supervision, was to determine the composition of the first all-Somali government. Direct elections in the municipalities and indirect elections in the rural areas were both based on universal male suffrage. In the rural elections, representatives designated by 613 shirs (agnatic units) voted with municipality residents, casting as many votes as they had received in the shir elections. There was no method by which the accuracy of the shir elections could be checked, nor would the northern Daarood permit scrutiny of the numerical composition of their clans.[16] It was expected that the representatives would cast their votes in accordance with the express wishes of their subclans; although this did not always occur, the votes were uncontested.

The SYL won a decisive electoral victory, gaining 43 of the 60 Somali seats;[17] the HDM won 13. The Somali Democratic Party was able to muster only 3 seats among the Samaale. The Marehan Union's single candidate won over his SYL competitor, but the Hawiye Youth's candidate, Muhammad Boracco, was unable to defeat his opponent, Abdullahi Issa, the key figure in the SYL. Issa's victory over Boracco was significant because Boracco had campaigned exclusively on clan grounds; the Abgal had supported Issa. In the Upper Giuba, the SYL made small

---

[14] Agnatically, the Marehan constitute one of the two main branches of the Daarood clan family. In the nineteenth century the Marehan split into two groups, one of them moving south into the trans-Giuba area. During the Italian colonial administration the northern group sided with the Italians in putting down a revolt of the southern Marehan. Their vigorous sense of independence has not changed significantly.

[15] The clan breakdown in Mogadiscio is as follows (1950 statistics): Hawiye, 27,100 (21,600 Abgal, 3,500 Averghedir, 2,000 Murosada); Rer Hamar, 10,800; Arabs, 12,000; Daarood, 2,900; Mirifle, 1,700; Digil, 4,500; Shekal, 1,200; and others, 5,000.

[16] Voting records of the 650-odd shir elections (some were disqualified) may be found in various issues of the *Corriere della Somalia*, Nov., 1955–Jan., 1956.

[17] There were 70 seats, 10 of which were allotted to the European and Asian communities. Asian and European deputies did not take part in debates on purely Somali issues; in fact, very few of them attended the sessions.

inroads, securing about one-fifth of the Sab votes. A number of Sab *shir*
representatives, who had pledged their ballots to the HDM, switched
their votes to SYL candidates. The largest group to do so was the
Ghelidle, whose chief in Baidoa cast the 8,005 votes of his group for the
SYL; the chief and the religious leaders of the Ghelidle were historically
chosen from the Samaale Dir clan family. The SYL was beginning to
break down the homogeneity of Sab voting behavior by taking advantage
of the class distinctions among the Sab.[18] In addition, a few HDM party
leaders with modernist tendencies were drifting toward the SYL. The
president of the HDM, Abdi Nur Muhammad, elected on the HDM
ticket, shortly thereafter joined the SYL. The Sab were bitter about these
desertions. An attempt was made to assassinate the Ghelidle chief, and,
when the Somali government imposed *shamba* (farm) taxes on the Sab,
it was greeted with violence.[19]

Among the anti-SYL parties, only the HDM, relatively, had cohesion
and a large following. The Somali Democratic Party obtained 80,000
votes, but these were spread thinly over fifteen of the thirty Samaale
electoral districts. The Benadir Youth proved to be a weak regional
party, although for the first time it penetrated the Sab area, where it
exploited several fissions among the Rahanweyn and the Digil. The
Hawiye Youth, the Six Shidle, the Afgoi-Audegle Group, and the Bagiuni
Youth together polled only 7,263 votes. It was evident that clan parties
could not produce sufficient votes to capture seats in the Legislative
Assembly; the Marehan Union was the single exception, and even its
leaders transferred their allegiance to the SYL, although somewhat
reluctantly. After the election the Hawiye Youth was absorbed into a
new party, the Liberal Party of Somali Youth, with Boracco again as
the leader. The Six Shidle and the Afgoi-Audegle Group went over to
the HDM. Except for the Bagiuni Youth, which was outside the Somali
genealogical orbit, and the HDM, parties organized along strictly clan
lines no longer made an appearance in Somali elections. The magnitude
of the SYL victory put a brake on political party proliferation.

The Issa Governments, 1956–1960

The trusteeship administration devolved the control of domestic
policy upon the Somalis in May, 1956, but retained its veto power as
well as its jurisdiction over military and foreign affairs until June, 1960.
Abdullahi Issa was appointed by the Italian administrator to form the

---

[18] In general, those Sab whose origin can be traced to noble Samaale elements
are in the upper stratum, and others are in the lower stratum.
[19] Italy devised shamba taxes in the 1920's and again in 1952, but they were
never implemented. The burden thus fell on the Somali government. The British
military administration was similarly confronted with hostility when it sought to
implement policies of direct taxation.

first all-Somali government. The relationships among agnatic affiliations, political parties, and government influenced the policy of Issa and the SYL. Aden Abdullah Osman, president of the SYL, advocated a multi-party cabinet so that other parties could gain experience in executive responsibility, but the party congress voted down the proposal because it felt that to bring in HDM members would imply an acceptance of tribalism. In the Legislative Assembly, the Samaale Marehan Union and the SDP affiliated with the SYL government, and the HDM took the mantle of the opposition. The first government thus bore the imprint of the traditional Sab-Samaale cleavage.

The ethnic-group composition of the government showed the extent to which the Samaale dominated important positions, with the Hawiye asserting primacy. Prime Minister Abdullahi Issa, an Averghedir (Hawiye), chose three Hawiye (two Averghedir and one Hauadle), one Dir, and two Daarood (both Osman Mahmud) for his cabinet; Abdirizak Haji Hussein, an Omar Mahmud (Daarood) and ex-president of the SYL, was given the presidency of the Somali Credit Institute. The Abgal were passed over, although later, upon their protest, a secretarial post was created for one of their more prominent party members. The Legislative Assembly (composed of twenty Hawiye, twenty Daarood, and twenty Sab), elected President Osman of the SYL, a Hawiye from a numerically unimportant clan, as its president. The Samaale also dominated by as much as 80 per cent the civil service, the police, and Somali enrollment in the School of Politics, the Higher Institute of Law and Economics, and the University of Rome, whose graduates later constituted the core of the new middle class.[20] The large majority of administrative and police officials, as in the days of the British occupation, were members of the SYL; many of those who were not, shifted their allegiance to the party after the elections.

Thus the SYL, when assuming the leadership of the nation, seemed to have a centralized monolithic control over all facets of Somali political life. The HDM was too small to offer serious opposition; obstructions came instead from inter-Samaale controversies. Samaale cleavages, previously expressed exclusively through the establishment of new political groups, such as the Marehan Union and the Liberal Party, took on serious proportions within the party and the government. This was only natural, for the main issues that had provided a basis for coöperation—gaining control over the government and anti-Italianism—were lost when the SYL-dominated Somali government assumed responsibility.

[20] Both Somalis and Europeans have stressed that this situation derives not from any discriminatory policy but rather from the fact that the nomadic Somali is "more adept and more intelligent." Nomadic Somalis are regarded as making better soldiers than sedentary Somalis.

Strain was first placed on the government by repeated allegations that the Hawiye members of the cabinet discriminated against the Daarood in their appointments. Sheik Ali Giumale (Hauadle, Hawiye), the minister of social affairs, and Muhammad Abdi Nur (Dir), the minister of general affairs, held the most lucrative patronage positions; the former, particularly, was accused of nepotism. Concurrently, there was a rift between Daarood and Hawiye ministers over the issue of sending a delegation to Addis Ababa to negotiate the Somali-Ethiopian boundary dispute. The Daarood, whose coclansmen make up the vast majority of Somalis in the Ethiopian Ogaden region, have always taken a more spirited anti-Ethiopian position than other groups. Haji Musa Bogar, who in 1950 had led the protest against the anti-Daarood policy of the Italian administration, was slated to be on the delegation but refused to take part, as did his colleague Salad Abdi, the minister of finance. At the same time a conflict broke out in the south between the Omar Mahmud (Daarood) and their clients the Averghedir (Hawiye), which had all the intensity of the traditional Omar Mahmud–Averghedir dispute in the northern Mudugh. These events culminated in the government crisis of December, 1957, when Bogar and Salad Abdi threatened resignation.

In the Legislative Assembly, the SYL Daarood deputies sought to destroy parliamentary confidence in the government by defeating a financial measure. The votes of the HDM opposition and the SYL Daarood deputies would have been more than sufficient. But a major shift occurred within the established Sab-Samaale cleavage in modern politics. Abdulcadir Muhammad Aden, leader of the HDM opposition and a former member of the SYL Central Committee (1944–1950), consolidated the Sab deputies behind the Prime Minister and his Hawiye colleagues. The shift resulted, not from a Hawiye effort to establish an alliance with the Sab, but rather from the HDM's fear of Daarood attempts at hegemony. The Sab-Daarood cleavage had always been deeper than the Sab-Hawiye cleavage. The government survived its first major challenge, and Hawiye leadership of the SYL was sustained when the Central Committee, with a majority of Hawiye and Sab, supported Issa. The Italian administrator succeeded in persuading Daarood cabinet members to remain in the government.

The inter-Samaale attrition within the SYL spilled over into the Fifteenth Party Congress of March-May, 1958. The main issues concerned the activities of Muhammad Hussein, who had been elected president of the SYL in November, 1957. After serving as party president from 1947 to 1952, Hussein spent five years in Cairo, where he occasionally made anti-Western broadcasts. His reëlection as president of the SYL was attributed to the lingering pro-Egyptian sentiment evoked by the Suez crisis and to the party's attempt to mollify the effects of the assassination by a Somali of the highly respected Egyptian ambassador. These two developments made it undesirable for the SYL to elect Hussein's main contender for the presidency, the pro-Western Aden Abdullah Osman. Hussein returned to Somalia in the midst of the Daarood-Hawiye crisis, hoping to forge an alliance that would put him in absolute control of the party mechanism. His aim was to bring about an abrupt termination of Italian rule and, with Egyptian support, to secure the presidency of an independent Somali republic. But his precipitous acts and his vitriolic anti-Western speeches alienated the majority of the party congress and the Central Committee. Because his anti–Italian administration statements, which also tried to discredit the Issa government, were without party approval, he was expelled from the SYL on grounds that he impaired the unity of the party, showed dictatorial tendencies, and had acted contrary to the party statute. In June the party congress elected Aden Abdullah president by a bare majority of 44 to 42 votes. Abdullah's chief opponent was Mohamud Ahamed Muhammad Aden, the Abgal (Hawiye) secretary of the cabinet who complained that his position carried no power; in the party presidential election he received the full support of Daarood members.

Shortly after his expulsion, Muhammad Hussein formed the Greater Somalia League (GSL). He negotiated with Daarood leaders, particularly the Omar Mahmud, an important clan (frequently in competition with the Osman Mahmud) which had not been given significant representation in the cabinet, and at the same time he hoped to capitalize on Abgal disenchantment with the SYL. The GSL Central Committee was a balance of representatives from Rer Hamar, Hussein's ethnic group, Daarood, and Hawiye. The only other major change in the party system before the 1958 municipal election was the formation of the Liberal Party. The HDM, now changing its name to Hisbia Destour Mustaquil Somali (Somali Independent Constitutional Party), went through a phase of vigorous reorganization and recruitment, particularly among the Negroid groups and the Rer Baraawa of the ancient coastal city of Brava. It did not try to establish party branches in Samaale areas.

The October, 1958, municipal campaign differed sharply from previous campaigns in that the SYL, not the Italian administration, was on trial for the conduct of government. Leaders of the HDM, noting that their party had "saved" the government in the 1957 crisis, demanded an equitable distribution of police and administrative positions and of scholarships. The party called for a federal system of government based on regional autonomy. The GSL confined its campaign to the main municipalities and Daarood towns. Hussein demanded more effective measures to attain a Greater Somalia, advocated a pro-Egyptian policy, and concentrated his attacks on the "pro-Italian" SYL government "which sought to deliver Somalia to the Italian and American imperialists." The Liberal Party took a still different position, campaigning on a platform of "gradual detribalization" and "friendship with all nations," including Ethiopia. Both HDM and Liberal Party leaders visited Addis Ababa just before the elections. The Somali Democratic Party was split beyond repair, and most of its members joined the SYL or the Liberal Party. The SYL was on the defensive, but it did not engage in a demagogic campaign; it pointed to the problems that Somalia faced and stressed the need to maintain cordial relations with the Italian administration. It denounced the advocacy of federalism as high treason and called on all parties to divest themselves of clan concepts and join the SYL in a national pact.

In the election, the first in which women were granted suffrage,[21] the SYL again received an impressive majority. The party mechanism, which showed some signs of vulnerability at the height of the GSL campaign, remained intact. Local secretaries were able to hold the line in the Samaale areas after the Daarood members of both the cabinet and the Assembly moved into the districts to support the party platform. Many of them had earlier remonstrated against Issa and had voted against Hussein's expulsion, but they now coalesced behind the party when it seemed to be threatened by the GSL.

The SYL won 416 seats out of 663 in forty-five municipalities, compared with 175 for the HDM in twenty-one municipalities. Voting took place in only twenty-seven centers, and the SYL was unopposed in eighteen, all of them Samaale. The GSL gained 36 seats in nine municipalities where it ran candidates, and the Liberal Party came through with 27 councilors, mostly Abgal, in eight municipalities. The GSL won the majority of its seats in Daarood towns, whose Daarood deputies took a strong anti-Issa position. But more significant was the size of the HDM vote. Not only did the HDM increase its strength, but it gained the majority formerly held by the SYL in Merca, Bardera, and Lugh Ferrandi. The over-all voting trend seemed to be away from the SYL, as the data in table 5 indicate. The new trend was considered ominous by the SYL hierarchy, which felt it incumbent on the party to produce a substantial majority in the forthcoming March, 1959, general election.

The general election was of paramount importance, as the term of office for Assembly members was established at five years, that is, four years beyond the date of independence. The electoral law provided that ninety seats should be allocated on the basis of population estimates, rather than of a census, and that no voting should take place in electoral

---

[21] Women's committees were established in all political parties at an early date. Political parties in Somaliland, however, had been more reluctant to give women a role in politics.

TABLE 5

PARTY STRENGTH IN THE ELECTIONS OF 1954, 1956, AND 1958 IN SOMALIA
(In percentages[a] of total vote)

Party	1954	1956	1958
SYL	48.0	54.3	51.0
HDM	22.0	26.0	28.5
Benadir Youth	6.1	3.5	1.9
SAU	6.9		
Liberal			8.2
GSL			7.6
SDP		13.2	
Others	9.4	3.0	2.8

[a] As no votes were recorded in the election of councilors in eighteen municipalities where the SYL was unopposed, percentages were calculated on the basis of previous voting behavior and the general increase of votes in other areas.

districts where only one list of candidates was presented. The opposition parties, as well as the UN Advisory Council in Mogadiscio, took strong issue with these provisions; the Italian administration officially maintained a discreet "hands-off" policy, though some high officials were disposed toward the five-year term. With considerable indignation, opposition parties insisted that an assembly elected during the trusteeship period could not legitimately be regarded as representative of the independent state. But the Assembly confirmed the law in a secret ballot by a vote of 32 to 20, with some of the HDM deputies voting for the legislation.[22]

The interim between the municipal and the general elections (October, 1958, to March, 1959) was one of the most difficult periods in Somali political history. In November, 1958, a crisis was precipitated at Merca between opposition party leaders and the public authorities over ethnic issues. In the following month tension mounted, and the Legislative Assembly, noting the Ghanaian precedent, granted emergency powers to the government. The Assembly also passed a resolution remonstrating against foreign intervention. It was alleged that foreign consulates, particularly those of Egypt and Ethiopia, were employing financial and other means to influence the outcome of the election. Disorderly and violent conduct led to the incarceration of several hundred members of the GSL and the Somali National Union (SNU), formerly the Benadir Youth. At the same time the government closed GSL and SNU party

[22] The general election was slated for 1958, but the Legislative Assembly, on a motion presented by the HDM opposition leader, Abdulcadir Muhammad Aden, voted 50 to 2 to postpone it until the following year. Assemblymen of all parties were reluctant to hold new elections.

branches in the Benadir region. The link between the SNU and the GSL derived not only from Hussein's ethnic affiliation with Rer Hamar, but also from the inability of the SNU merchants of Mogadiscio to forgive the SYL government for having tripled taxes on retail licenses.

The GSL and the SNU formed an alliance with other opposition parties to boycott the election. They complained that the government was using its power to restrict the presentation of lists of candidates and to limit the travel of opposition leaders. Muhammad Hussein was arrested while campaigning in the Migiurtinia.[23] The opposition parties demanded that the UN supervise the elections, but the most the government would agree to was a brief postponement. On election eve the nineteen Liberal Party candidates and seven of the forty-seven HDM candidates disavowed the alliance and ran for office. But even had there been no tampering with the preëlectoral machinery, it is doubtful that any of the parties could have competed with the SYL on a national basis. The GSL in particular was unable to make any inroads on SYL strength; all its candidates were relatively unknown, although originally the party had hoped to draw them from among important SYL members. Had Hussein developed a more effective strategy, and had some of the SYL Daarood candidates proved bold enough to follow their inclinations, the GSL might have emerged as an important opposition party.

What the SYL wanted most from the election was a unanimous confirmation of its role as the forger of Somali nationalism and independence; nation, party, and government were one, and the electorate could acknowledge this unity by giving the party an overwhelming victory. But more was at stake in the election. Foreign interference in Somali politics could be eliminated once and for all if SYL strength proved formidable enough to make it inexpedient for consulates to exploit the party system and traditional leaders. All techniques were employed to secure that comfortable margin of electoral victory. District commissioners, prefects, and local secretaries functioned as a highly coördinated propagandizing machine. The swift and efficient operation of the police in curbing violence in Mogadiscio had its effect in the interior. In addition, after the municipal election, there had been a number of shifts in party allegiance. In Dinsor and Baidoa, two HDM strongholds, important traditional, HDM, and religious leaders went over to the SYL. The almost mass shift from the HDM derived from government inducements and from the conviction held by many Rahanweyn and Digil leaders that by supporting the SYL they could increase the weight of the Sab

---

[23] An interesting footnote to Somali politics was revealed when a Communist senator from Rome went to Mogadiscio to support Muhammad Hussein; the defense counsel chosen by Hussein was a prominent ex-fascist attorney who had supported anti-SYL parties during the British occupation.

in government, strengthen the Hawiye wing of the SYL, and, concomitantly, weaken the Daarood segment. The SNU, the HDM and the GSL in Brava, the Liberal Party in Itala, the GSL in Bosaso, the Liberal Party in Bulo Burti, the SNU in Merca, and others were absorbed by the SYL. Where shifts did not occur, the parties were divided into anti-League and pro-League factions. As conversions were made, former opponents acclaimed the SYL as the only genuinely national party and denounced other parties as clanistic.

The election was a foregone conclusion. The SYL piled up the largest majority it had ever received: 237,134 votes against 40,857 for the HDM and 35,769 for the Liberal Party. The total number of SYL votes did not include those from nineteen Samaale and Sab electoral districts where the party was unopposed. It was without competition in Baidoa and Dinsor; in all other Sab districts, which had formerly voted heavily for the HDM, its majority was better than two to one. Of the seven HDM candidates who ignored their party's ban on participation in the election, five were elected. The Liberal Party won 2 seats, and the SYL won 83. Shortly after the election, the two Liberal Party deputies, including the party's president, and one HDM deputy joined the SYL ranks.

Although the SYL had won a commanding majority, the formation of the government was not an easy task. Some Daarood members of the Central Committee and of the new Assembly preferred Aden Abdullah Osman as premier because he seemed less Hawiye-oriented than did Abdullahi Issa, but they were unable to surmount the majority that Issa had constructed in the Hawiye-Sab ranks, in the Central Committee, in the party congress, and in the legislature. Before forming the new government, Issa firmly advised the committee that although the SYL had dedicated itself to the elimination of clanism, the only choice available was to compose a government based on a "balance of ethnic groups," that is, to give a fair share to each of the three main clan families. The "one-third doctrine" had its *raison d'être* in political reality: the Assembly consisted of 33 Daarood, 30 Hawiye, and 27 Sab. In the committee, Abdirizak Haji Hussein and Nur Hasci, vice-president of the party, both Daarood, assailed the doctrine. Furthermore, Osman insisted that only the appointment of a modernist Daarood as prime minister could alleviate party tensions and ruptures. The party supported Issa by a slim majority.[24]

The Prime Minister's one-third doctrine implied more than a fair share for each group. Issa sought a counterpoise that would maximize Hawiye-Daarood, that is, inter-Samaale, coöperation; should this coöper-

---

[24] The SYL party congress in its session of May 22, 1959, supported Abdullahi Issa against his main opponent, Osman, by a vote of 68 to 52.

ation fall short, the Hawiye would always be in a position to count on support from the Rahanweyn and the Digil. To realize this objective necessitated not only a Hawiye-Daarood *rapprochement* on the one hand, and a Hawiye-Sab agreement on the other, but also a balancing of the numerically important clans of each group within the government. The cabinet was divided as follows: four Hawiye, one Dir, three Daarood, and one Sab. Two of the five undersecretarial posts went to the Sab. In the Assembly, Aden Abdullah Osman (Hawiye) was elected president, and Abdulcadir Muhammad Aden, rewarded for presenting an HDM list at the election, was elected vice-president, as was Haji Bascir Ismail (Daarood).[25] The increased Sab representation in government gave the group more political importance than it had ever had before. This position derived from the Sab's ability to operate as a lever within inter-Samaale SYL politics.

The Issa balance of power did not placate all the Daarood or the Abgal clan of the Hawiye. Abdirizak Haji Hussein (Omar Mahmud) complained before the UN Trusteeship Council that clan balance formalized clanism in politics and was "incompatible with the political evolution of Somalia and fatal to its unity." Thirteen deputies, all Daarood and Abgal, signed the complaint. At the same time Haji Musa Bogar, the Daarood minister of the interior whose wife had joined the GSL, resigned his post, ostensibly on grounds that the Prime Minister refused to permit the reopening of GSL and SNU headquarters. In the Assembly, Abdirashid Ali Shermarke, of an important chiefly Daarood clan and one of the first Somalis to receive a doctorate from the University of Rome, submitted a motion demanding termination of the trusteeship by December, 1959. This motion went counter to the government's policy, and Shermarke, Abdirizak Haji Hussein, and Nur Hasci were expelled by the SYL Central Committee, but were permitted to return after partial recantation.

There were still other forms of disenchantment. Daarood deputies, vociferously challenging Ethiopia's "provocative acts of aggression" along the frontier, demanded that the government take definite action on the Greater Somalia issue. SYL branches in the Daarood areas complained about the Central Committee's deviation from the party's detribalization principles, and noted that, as the committee was composed in part of government officials, it could not act independently. But it was not only the SYL Daarood wing that took issue with government. Coinciding with Abdirizak's protestations before the UN, a large number of Daarood

[25] The vote was 76 for Aden Abdullah for president, and 46 and 39, respectively, for Abdulcadir Muhammad Aden and Haji Bascir Ismail for the two vice-presidencies. This result suggests Osman's national appeal, the extraparty Hawiye-Sab coalition behind Abdulcadir, and the Abgal-Daarood coalition behind Ismail. The Legislative Assembly approved the government (Aug. 2, 1959) by a vote of 67 to 10.

and Marehan chiefs issued a manifesto denouncing the government and demanding new elections. The manifesto was reminiscent of the 1950 complaint to the UN that the Italian administration was discriminating against the Daarood. But, significantly, Marehan and Daarood deputies and merchants on this occasion publicly rebuked the chiefs. It is of some historical and contemporary interest that Musa Bogar's signature appeared first on the 1950 complaint, that he threatened to resign from the cabinet in 1957, that he did resign in 1959, and that the Daarood-Marehan manifesto received strong support from Bogar's clan, the clan that had offered considerable resistance to the Italian conquest of Migiurtinia in 1925–1927.

There were, therefore, two forms of Daarood protest: one was modernist, embodying the Greater Somalia and tribal-balance issues; the other was traditional, reflecting Daarood resentment against Hawiye dominance in government. The latter stemmed from the historical Hawiye-Daarood enmity, but it was linked with the former because the Daarood numerically dominate the Ogaden region in Ethiopia. These conflicting forces within the party did not, however, destroy party unity, a unity that was enhanced by the proximity of full self-government. Nonetheless, before independence, it was clear that Issa's popularity was waning. Furthermore, the unification of Somaliland with Somalia on July 1, 1960, necessitated the establishment of a new equilibrium in government, for the thirty-three elected members of Somaliland's Legislative Council automatically became deputies of the National Assembly of the independent Somali Republic.

Development of Somaliland Parties

One of the most striking differences between the political development of Somalia and that of Somaliland lies in the lack of maturation of political parties in the latter.[26] Britain did not permit political party representation in the town, district, or protectorate advisory councils, or in the Legislative Council, until 1959. Representation was based pri-

---

[26] A. Castagno, "Observations on the Political Development of the Somaliland Protectorate" (unpublished MS, 1958). There are no secondary sources treating the administrative and political history of Somaliland. The following are useful: A. Hamilton, *Somaliland* (London: Hutchinson, 1911); J. A. Hunt, *A General Survey of the Somaliland Protectorate, 1944–1950* (London: Crown Agents for the Colonies, 1951); Jardine, *op. cit.;* and A. C. A. Wright, "The Inter-Action of Various Systems of Law and Custom in British Somaliland and Their Relation with Social Life," *Journal of the East African Natural History Society,* XVII (1943), 66–102.

The important official publications are *War Somali Sidihi* and its successor, the *Somaliland News;* the *Debates* of the Legislative Council (1957–1960) and of the Protectorate Advisory Council (1946–1958); the Colonial Office biennial reports on the Somaliland Protectorate (1950–1951 to 1958–1959); and the 1958–1959 reports of the Commission of Enquiry on Representational Reform and the Commission on the Somalisation of the Civil Service.

marily on clan lines. An adequate electoral machinery was not established until 1959, and the franchise was extremely limited before 1960. The protectorate administration also proscribed the participation of Somali government employees in politics, with the consequence that the few educated Somalis in the protectorate would not enter the partisan realm of politics for fear of disqualifying themselves in public administration, the only significant area of employment. Members of the Somali Officials' Union, persons employed by the government, constituted a politically mature group, but they made no substantial contribution to the development of political parties.

The administration's insistence on clan rather than party representation[27] deprived the parties of the main techniques and institutions with which to appeal for broader support. But the over-all political development in Somaliland lagged sharply behind that in Somalia for these additional reasons: nomadism is a more dominant activity and nomadic movements are more widely dispersed in Somaliland, and there are no cash crops or secondary industries; there was no real expansion in the school system until after 1956, and higher education was not seriously undertaken until 1958; there was little contact with foreigners, who numbered only 300; the Legislative Council was established at a late date (1957); Somalization did not begin in earnest until after 1958; and local government was limited to six towns, compared with forty-five in Somalia. A final important factor was that Somaliland did not come under the influence of the United Nations, which encouraged progressive political parties, rapid Somalization, and a broad scholarship program in Somalia.

Before World War II the protectorate had only a skeleton administration, with a maximum staff of thirty-five British officers and no established secular schools. The Italian conquest in 1940–1941, a highly progressive British military administration during the war, the return of the Somaliland battalion from Burma, and the breaking of Muslim resistance to Western education all helped to provide a new basis for political development. Until the war British policy had been conditioned by the costly and enervating mullah uprisings (1899–1920) and by the inability of the administration to curb the feuds that wracked the countryside. Any innovations in administration would have required a heavy expenditure which the Colonial Office was not prepared to meet, given the economic and political insignificance of Somaliland in the total complex of the Empire.

By 1951 there were two political parties: the Somali National League

---

[27] The Protectorate Advisory Council, established in 1946, was composed of eight Ishaaq, four Daarood, and two Dir. In addition, there were three merchants, three religious leaders, one Indian, and one Arab.

(SNL) and the Somali Youth League (SYL). The former had its strongest adherents among the Ishaaq clan family, and the latter, among the Daarood, although both sought to organize on a national basis. The SNL was a ramified continuation of the Nadi Ateyat al Rahman, formed in 1935 as a social organization, and the Somali National Society which grew out of the Nadi in 1947. The party had the advantage of the government's favor, particularly during the administration of Governor Gerald Reece (1951–1953). Reece, as provincial commissioner of the Somali-inhabited Northern Province in Kenya, had been largely responsible for banning the SYL in 1948, and, as governor of Somaliland, he viewed the SYL as Communist-influenced. The SNL leadership was composed of merchants, traditional leaders, former government employees, and modernist sheiks who sought to check the "potential extremism" of the SYL. Initially the SNL advocated the incorporation of Somaliland in the Commonwealth, whereas the SYL made no move in this direction. The SYL leadership, looking singularly unrevolutionary and somnolent, was made up in the main of tradesmen and merchants. Although it had the same aims, it did not receive the active support of the SYL in Somalia, probably because a close link between the two would have introduced into the politics of Somalia the historical inter-Daarood animosity between the Dulbahante of Somaliland and the Migiurtinia Daarood (which produced almost annual clashes).

Other political groups were formed after 1955 under the impetus of the November, 1954, Anglo-Ethiopian agreement, which transferred the Somali-inhabited pasture lands of the Haud and Reserved Area to Ethiopia.[28] The transfer was viewed by most Somalis as a betrayal of the protectorate treaties that Britain had signed with traditional leaders in 1884–1886. The National United Front (NUF) was organized by traditional and religious leaders, some of whom were refugees from the Ogaden, and by a number of educated Somalis, prominent among whom was Michael Mariano, the Aden-educated Christian Somali who had in 1948 aided the SYL in Mogadiscio in presenting its case before the Four-Power Commission. The NUF was established to function as a liaison between the SYL, the SNL, the Somali Officials' Union, the Somali Old Boys' Association, and the Somali Islamic Association of Aden, on the one hand, and traditional and religious leaders on the other, to coördinate efforts to effect the return of the Haud and Reserved Area. The NUF program, reflecting the position of the political parties, came out strongly for the elimination of *herr*, the interclan treaties of alliance, war, arbitration, and peace, which had long been regarded by religious and political leaders as contrary to koranic principles and which "gave substance to the divide-and-rule policy" of the administration. The program

---

[28] The agreement implemented the 1897 Anglo-Ethiopian Convention.

also advocated a Greater Somalia. To a much greater extent than in Somalia, the clans depend on access to the Ethiopian-controlled pasture lands for survival, with approximately half of the population spending about six months of the year in the Haud and Reserved Area.

The NUF sent missions to the UN and to the British Parliament to press for an adjudication of the boundary question by the International Court, a legal impossibility in view of the Anglo-Ethiopian agreements. Funds for the NUF poured in from all sections of the territory, but the bulk came from the clans that had been most adversely affected by the transfer of the pasture lands. By 1957 the financial sources dried up, as the NUF had failed to accomplish its main goal, and the political influence of the liaison unit waned rapidly. Yet no other organization in Somaliland had done so much as the NUF to gain sympathetic and active support from members of Parliament and from the British press.

The most significant turning point in the growth of political parties came in May, 1957. The SNL District Committee of Burao, a town that lies at the crossroads of the routes leading to the Haud and Reserved Area, took the initiative in demanding immediate independence. It denounced the pro-Commonwealth stand, which was stressed by all parties except the SYL. In particular, Michael Mariano and the traditional leaders in Hargeisa, the capital, were singled out as "British collaborators," as they seemed to be coöperating with the administration on a high level. The Burao members gained the support of other SNL district committees, and Sheik Omar Askar, educated in Cairo, assumed the leadership of a recast, more militant, and effectively pro-Cairo party. In the main towns of Hargeisa, Berbera, and Burao, Cairo-educated young men (the majority having intermediate schooling) asserted their domination over the district committees, the backbone of the party. In 1958 a new party constitution was ratified on the annual mourning day, which commemorates the loss of the Haud and Reserved Area. All during the year, anti-British plays and folk songs were presented in the principal towns. SNL members in the United Arab Republic, where Somaliland Somalis far outnumber those from other Somali regions, regularly broadcast anti-Western propaganda. Several hundred scholarships were assigned by Cairo to the SNL to distribute among the Somali youth. "National schools," subsidized by the UAR, were set up by the party in the three main centers. By November, 1958, the SNL was monopolizing the issues of "independence now" and "unification with Somalia."

The leaders of the liaison NUF who were unassociated with political parties established the NUF as a political party in March, 1959, but it could not divest itself of the proadministration label which the SNL had attached to its leaders, including Michael Mariano. Mariano, because of his religion, was given the vice-presidency of the party rather than the presidency, which went to Sheik Abdulrahman Kariyeh, a religious leader, but Mariano remained the party's dominant personality. Another new party, the United Somali Party (USP), was formed in 1959 at the Daarood center of Las Anod; its leaders were important chiefs. Ali Gerad Jama, the university-educated son of the Gerad (chief) Jama Farah (who went into voluntary exile in Mogadiscio from 1952 to 1958 as a result of his conflict with the British administration), provided the main drive behind the party.

The first general election to be held in the territory took place in March, 1959, but it was too limited in scope to provide an index of party strength. First of all, representation in the Legislative Council was still based on occupational and clan, rather than party, identification. The SNL boycotted the election on the ground that the administration had "rigged" it against the parties. Muhammad Haji Ibrahim Egal, SNL secretary-general in Berbera and university-educated son of an important merchant, was, however, elected as a representative of the mercantile interests and became the party's forceful spokesman in Legco. The first real political trial came in the February, 1960, general election, which was based on universal male suffrage.

Before the election the USP and the SNL agreed to support each other's candidates where it was prudent to do so, and to amalgamate in the Legislative Council should they win the election. On the other hand, the NUF linked forces with the SYL of Somaliland, which could not stand by itself and had nowhere else to go. The chief differences in the party platforms were that the SNL assumed advanced progressive positions on political and social reform, whereas the NUF and the SYL, only in order to present a program opposite to the SNL's, assumed the traditional and conservative position. Ninety per cent of the membership of all parties came from centers of district administration: Berbera, Hargeisa, Borama, Burao, Las Anod, and Erigavo. In the election the SNL swept the polls, winning 20 of the 33 seats, in most instances with large majorities, and losing only one of the seats that it contested. The USP secured 12 seats. Although the NUF gained 24.6 per cent of the votes, it won only 1 seat, and this by Mariano. The SYL failed to get a single seat and polled less than 5,000 votes, almost all from the Warsangeli clan of the Daarood in the Borama district.

In the main, all political parties received their support from the kinship groups that identified themselves with the parties. Unlike Somalia, Somaliland had no parties organized along single-clan lines. The Mahlia, organized by the Habr Awal (Iise Muuse) of Somaliland, an Ishaaq clan, with the aim of promoting Iise Muuse interests, was short-lived (1952–1954). That there are no such parties has been ascribed to a weak modern political consciousness in Somaliland, but it is more ap-

propriate to attribute their absence to a lack of the diverse political opportunities found in Somalia in 1943–1956. This does not imply that
agnatic associations are weaker than in Somalia; they are, on the contrary,
more pervading. The February, 1960, election revealed the clan-party
identifications shown in table 6. The SNL and the NUF are essentially

TABLE 6

CLAN-PARTY IDENTIFICATIONS AS SHOWN IN THE FEBRUARY, 1960,
ELECTION IN SOMALILAND

Party	Per cent of votes	Dominant clan association	Per cent of population
Somali National League	52.2	Ishaaq	
		Habr Yunis	20.1
		Habr Awal (Iise Muuse)	4.5
		Eidegalla	6.0
		Arap	3.0
National United Front	24.8	Ishaaq	
		Habr Toljaala	15.6
		Habr Awal (Saad Muuse)	15.6
United Somali Party	16.4	Daarood	
		Dulbahante	15.6
		Warsangeli	3.5
		Dir	
		Gadabursi	7.5
		Iise	8.6
Somali Youth League	5.7	Daarood	

Ishaaq parties, and the SYL is almost exclusively Daarood, although its
Daarood following was lost to the USP, which had in its ranks an important chief of the Dulbahante.[29] The USP undertook to assuage the
historical Gadabursi-Iise cleavage, and was able to form a Daarood-Dir
combination. The persistent conflict between the Daarood and the Ishaaq,
as intense as the Hawiye-Daarood enmity in northern Somalia, was expressed by their association with separate political parties.

---

[29] The political history of the Dulbahante illustrates the vacillating nature of
Somali politics, and shows how political relations are affected by local considerations.
Gerad Jama, a traditional chief of the Bah Arasama Dulbahante, with authority over
the most numerous of Dulbahante subclans, the Farah Gerad, supported the SYL as
a protest against the government's local authority system, which had the effect of
reducing his powers. The government-appointed local authorities at this juncture
joined the SNL en masse, as did competitive Dulbahante of the Ain. In 1958 Gerad
Jama agreed to coöperate with the British in local administration. He left the SYL
and later joined the USP. His son, Ali Gerad Jama, was elected to the Legislative
Council and was later appointed to Shermarke's cabinet.

Within the Ishaaq clan family, the Habr Yunis and the Habr Toljaala belong to different political organizations because of their long-standing mutual animosity, which in 1955–1956 took a heavy toll of lives. The Eidegalla and the Arap, despite their intermittent disputes, are genealogically close to the Habr Yunis and are classified with them under the generic name, Habr Gerhajis. The only significant division in the clan category occurs within the Habr Awal, between the Iise Muuse and the Saad Muuse. The traditional basis of enmity was exacerbated when the Saad Muuse of the Hargeisa district preëmpted the most important government positions from the Iise Muuse of the Berbera district after the center of transportation and governmental operations had been shifted from Berbera to Hargeisa. Similarly, the SNL derived the core of its strength from the Habr Yunis of Burao, many of whom were displaced in government employment by the Saad Muuse and the Habr Toljaala when the government moved numerous activities from Burao to Hargeisa. The SNL electoral alliance with the USP was essentially directed against the NUF and its Habr Awal (Saad Muuse) and Habr Toljaala components. This was not incompatible with traditional relationships; when interclan struggles straddle the maximal lineage, they sometimes take the shape of competition between the Dulbahante and the Habr Toljaala, with the former relying on the subclans of the Habr Yunis for assistance.

GOVERNMENT AND POLITICS, 1960–1963

When Somaliland joined with Somalia to form the Somali Republic, the SYL of Somalia and the SNL and the USP of Somaliland agreed to act jointly on all matters affecting the unification of the two territories, and a coalition cabinet was made up of SYL, SNL, and USP members. The NUF and the SYL of Somaliland were largely ignored, the latter having proved to be quite ineffectual. The question was whether or not a united government could be formed from the complex crosscurrents of agnatic ideologies and politics. The problem became more complicated when several of Somalia's opposition parties initiated anti-Somaliland demonstrations in Mogadiscio during the negotiations over the formation of the union. In addition, Somaliland had been remote from the process of politicization which had taken place in Somalia among the Sab and the Samaale. There was the further problem of integrating within a common pattern two different systems of law, finance, administration, and education.[30]

The formula for establishing a new government was again found

---

[30] By the fall of 1963 some progress toward integration had been made; legislation was passed integrating the civil service, regularizing the judiciary, and imposing a common currency.

in clan balance, the establishment of an equilibrium of the major ethnic groups, including those of Somaliland, in the central government. Aden Abdullah Osman was elected almost unanimously by the National Assembly to serve as provisional president of the Republic until the July, 1961, National Assembly presidential election. In the decade of trusteeship, he had emerged as the most respected statesman in Somalia; he was the astute arbitrator who could reach beyond partisan politics to reconcile conflicting factions. Although a Hawiye, Osman represented a small clan which rarely entered the politics of the inter-Hawiye cleavages. As president of the SYL in 1954, 1955, and 1958, he did more than any other individual to establish amicable relations with the trusteeship administration and to curb extremism.

When Abdullahi Issa failed to get sufficient support to form a cabinet, Abdirashid Ali Shermarke, whom Osman had advanced as a candidate for the premiership in 1959, was appointed premier. Somaliland was accommodated in the government by the appointment of two Daarood and two Ishaaq: Abdi Hassan Boni (USP, Dulbahante) as vice-premier; Ali Gerad Jama (USP, Dulbahante), son of an influential chief, as minister of education; Muhammad Haji Ibrahim Egal (Habr Awal, Iise Muuse), former secretary-general of the SNL, as minister of defense; and Ahmed Haji Duale (SNL, Habr Yunis) as minister of agriculture. Two Sab, Abdulcadir Muhammad Aden, former secretary-general of the HDM, and Muhammad Abdi Nur, former president of the HDM, were given the ministries of Finance and of Public Works and Communications, respectively. Among the Hawiye, Abdullahi Issa took the important Ministry of Foreign Affairs; Sheik Ali Giumale (Hauadle) became minister of health and labor; Ali Muhammad Hirave (Abgal), minister of information; and Mohamud Ahamed Muhammad Aden (Abgal), minister of justice. The Daarood were represented by the Premier, by Interior Minister Abdirizak Haji Hussein (Omar Mahmud), General Affairs Minister Osman Mohamud Ibrahim (Osman Mahmud), and Sheik Abdullah Mohamud (Marehan). Undersecretarial posts were similarly distributed according to the balancing formula. Four ministers had some university education, compared with none in 1959. In August, 1961, a cabinet, reduced to twelve members, was formed, but few changes in personnel were made and the ethnic balance was approximately the same.

The first few years of independence amply illustrated that equilibrium in government was not easy to maintain; in two years the government faced two major crises. The first occurred in July, 1961, when Sheik Ali Giumale sought to gain the presidency from Aden Abdullah Osman. The latter, after three ballots, squeaked through by a vote of 61 to 59 deputies. Giumale received his support from the Hawiye members, who accused Osman of abandoning his own ethnic group, the Hawiye, and from the Ishaaq composition, which felt that Somaliland's (or the Ishaaq's) interests were being subordinated to those of Somalia. The President again called on Shermarke to form a new cabinet, which he succeeded in doing only after six weeks of political manipulation and compromise. Had there been further delay, Osman was prepared to run the government through the bureaucracy, the police, and the army. Another crisis was provoked in April, 1962, several months after the President dismissed Sheik Ali Giumale from the cabinet. The Ishaaq and Hawiye members came close to obtaining a vote of no confidence in the government. Two factors saved Shermarke: the mounting acrimony between Ethiopia and the Republic, to which the Premier responded vigorously, and the support Shermarke gained from the Upper Giuba region.

In both crises the coalescence of the Sab behind the Daarood signaled a major shift in the balancing process. The Abgal, although long classi-fied with the Hawiye, voted with the Daarood, some of them, such as the Warsangeli and the Harti Abgal, underlining the fact that their clans bore Daarood names.[31] If there had been any doubt about it in the past, it became clear in 1962 that the modern requirements of political expedience could override historical cleavages. Unlike the Sab-Daarood concordance in government, the Hawiye-Ishaaq alignment was not in-compatible from the viewpoint of the traditional bases of premodern Somali politics. The almost annual clashes between the northern Daarood and the Ishaaq were as intense as were those between the northern Daarood and the Hawiye.

The alignment of ethnic groups, as conditioned by independence, was revealed on a national scale in the June, 1961, constitutional ref-erendum. The percentage for the constitution was much higher in Somalia than in Somaliland, and the groups most in favor were the Sab, the Abgal, and the Daarood. The only area in Somalia where a vote was registered against the constitution (62 per cent) was the dominantly Hawiye-populated Hiran province.[32] In his opposition to the constitution, or rather to the government, Giumale received the support of his Hauadle clan, a numerous and cohesive Hawiye group.[33] In Somaliland the

---

[31] See Colucci, *op. cit.*, pp. 116–117. It will be remembered that the Abgal have always tried to maintain a separate identity, as they did in the various Abgal political parties.

[32] The national vote was 1,756,216 for and 183,000 against the constitution. In Somaliland it was 54,270 for and 49,706 against; in Somalia, 1,701,946 for and 133,294 against. But these figures are not accurate, as the numbers noted for Somalia far exceed the estimate of Somalia's total population.

[33] The Hauadle inhabit a relatively fixed area around Belet Uen. Although popu-larly classified as Hawiye, they are members of the Pre-Hawiye. According to some

Warsangeli and Dulbahante clans (Daarood) of the SYL and the USP
overwhelmingly supported the constitution. The NUF (Ishaaq) and
a large number of the SNL (Ishaaq), flouting the recommendations of
the SNL parliamentary members, rejected the constitution.

The opposition to the constitution, which was by no means numerically or quantitatively significant, was based not on disagreement
with procedural or substantive aspects of the document, but rather on
the disgruntlement of political leaders who had failed to gain tangible
political rewards. In particular, SNL local party leaders were using the
traditional Ishaaq-Daarood cleavage to promote modern political ambitions and ideological objectives. This apparent dichotomy was quite
consistent with the character of Somali politics, as was the almost complete acquiescence in the constitution by all those who had opposed it
after it had been confirmed on a national basis.

Independence was bound to introduce some changes in the party
system. The most important came within the ranks of the Greater Somalia
League and of the Somaliland parties. In its November, 1960, party
congress, the GSL split into two factions when Haji Muhammad Hussein,
after his return from Peiping, advocated a socialist state and a pro-
Communist foreign policy. One faction of the party, like the SYL in
1958, accused Hussein of dictatorial tendencies and of administrative irregularities; it insisted that the party program must remain nationalistic,
democratic, and Islamic. Hussein's sudden ideological switch merely
comported with political needs. In April, 1962, he was able to use the
remnants of a party seriously debilitated by schisms to help forge a new
opposition party, the Somali Democratic Union (SDU), which, as it
turned out, was composed mainly of unemployed townsmen. He found
ready allies among the discontented local leaders of the SNU and the
USP of Somaliland. The new party program called for more rapid
modernization, for nationalization of foreign firms, and for a pronounced
shift to the left in domestic and foreign policies.

The fate of the GSL and of the Somaliland parties demonstrates a
typical phenomenon that recurs in Somali politics: the factious and fissionable character of the traditional political system may rub off on the
modern party system. In December, 1960, the SNL and the USP amalgamated in a united SNL-USP party. The parliamentary SNL-USP
members were relatively satisfied with their governmental positions, and
would express dissatisfaction only within the framework of the ethnic
balance, but local party leaders who remained unrewarded were vociferous in their opposition to the government and to the SNL-USP
deputies who, it was felt, were abandoning the ideological goals of the

anthropologists, four main ethnic units make up the Pre-Hawiye: Aurmale, Hauadle,
Gherra, and Hober.

party and the interests of Somaliland. Schisms occurred in each of the main towns (particularly Hargeisa, Burao, and Berbera) except Mogadiscio, where the local branch remained completely loyal to the party. By the fall of 1962 the SDU had stripped the SNL segment of the SNL-USP of much of its following.

In the struggle between the remaining members of the SNL-USP and the SDU over party sites and funds, the government arbitrarily intervened on behalf of the SNL-USP. In the process, the USP segment was split into three sections, one being totally depoliticized, one switching to the SDU, and the last one remaining as the emasculated USP section of the SNL-USP, not specifically knowing what its direction was to be. The NUF suffered a somewhat similar fate, though the splits were not nearly so devastating. After the party changed its name to the Somali Progressive National League (SPNL), it lost some of its adherents to the SNL-USP and to the SDU. There was little agreement within the party on what program should be adopted. Michael Mariano's moderate position was scorned by a number of his followers, who subsequently behaved more like members of the SDU than like members of the SPNL. For all practical purposes, the real strength of the SNL-USP and of the SPNL lay in those members who held parliamentary or administrative posts. Financially, they were supported by merchants and traders who, unlike the unskilled and partially educated elements who were suffering from severe unemployment, were experiencing a sudden burst of prosperity. The SDU reputedly derived its financial support from Soviet bloc countries.[34] Its leadership, however, had neither the ability nor the quality to maintain effective opposition. Haji Muhammad Hussein was relegated to the vice-presidency, while the secretary-generalship and the presidency went to former local party leaders in Somaliland.

A large number of SNL-USP leaders in the administration believed that, with independence, the functions of their parties had come to an end. The same sentiment was not so overt among their SYL counterparts, but in the several years since independence it has become clear that administrative responsibilities and political realism have cooled the ideological fervor and the organizational enthusiasm of the party branches. The party's best men have been absorbed into the three branches of government, the largest realm of lucrative employment in the Somali Republic. Few favors have been passed out to ward politicians, especially to those of mediocre ability. Admonishments to reinvigorate the party, particularly by Interior Minister Abdirizak Haji Hussein, who is viewed

---

[34] As of July, 1963, there were approximately forty Chinese Communists and fifty Soviet Union Communists in the Somali Republic. The latter seemed to be more actively and more effectively concerned in social and economic development programs than the former.

by some intellectuals as the most progressive and the least tribal-minded member of the government, have not been lacking, but unless the SDU (or some other party) emerges as an important challenge, it is doubtful that the vigor that the SYL displayed during the trusteeship period can be resuscitated.

Of the two governing parties, the SYL and the SNL-USP, the former remains overwhelmingly predominant in politics and government. Its party congress, made up of some 120 delegates (largely parliamentary members, local branch secretaries, and the Mogadiscio Central Committee), still influences policies, but the government tends to rely more and more on parliamentary members and on the bureaucracy for its decisions.[35] In any event, there never has been a clear distinction between government and party, for the interlocking relationship was laid down during the British military administration, when the most important Somali positions in the police and the administration were monopolized by the SYL. Currently, the SYL is able to secure considerable acquiescence through its control of rewards and patronage: import licenses, foreign exchange permits, allocation of cultivable land, positions in the administration, overseas assignments, and so forth.

The party-government relationship has had the effect of mollifying the opposition as well; as the Somalis have learned, the least bloody way to behead political opposition is to bestow political plums. Nonetheless, opposition parties do exist, and new parties are formed from time to time. After 1960 the Liberal Party, many branches of which fused with the SYL in the 1959 election, revitalized its organization, but did not succeed in curbing intermittent splits. The Somali Fichirini Youth (formerly the Bagiuni Youth), the only clan-tribal party besides the HDM to survive independence, has a "pact of friendship" with the SYL, but has become largely inactive. The National African Union, the Somali Socialist Party, the Somali Popular Party, and the Somali Republican Party were all formed in Mogadiscio in the period 1959–1961, but none has had any influence on national or local politics. Many of those who defected from the HDM to the SYL in 1959 returned shortly after independence, but as the HDM's former leaders, such as Muhammad Abdi Nur and Abdulcadir Muhammad Aden, have been accommodated in the government, the party lacks leadership and is frequently confronted with schisms. Despite the absence of effective leadership, however, the HDM remains the second most numerous and cohesive party in the land; its cohesion stems from the relative solidarity of the Rahanweyn-Digil ethnic groups.

---

[35] Although local secretaries are consulted, and bear some influence on government and on the Central Committee, their powers are limited by the fact that they, as well as the local committees, are subject to election every six months.

The main function of the opposition parties, with the possible exception of the SDU, is not to oppose the government's policies or to inform the electorate on what they regard as the objective needs of modern government, but rather to secure compensation for the leaders of the opposition and for the ethnic groups that support them. Ethnic issues are frequently manipulated to serve this end. This does not imply that opposition and criticism do not exist or that the government is not responsive to criticism. On the contrary, government reacts sensitively to criticism whether it emanates from opposition parties, from traditional or religious leaders, from parliamentary members, or from within the SYL. The all-pervading pride of the Somalis in their democratic system (often cited as a bold contrast to the "totalitarianism" of the Ethiopian imperial system), the highly democratic character of the indigenous political system, the ethnic balancing process, and the extreme individualism that is ingrained with nomadism, all militate against an arbitrary government. The government will respond to criticism insofar as it is economically feasible to do so, and insofar as this response does not seriously disrupt the pattern of rewards and privileges.

This description of the Somali political system has touched briefly upon the aims and the principles of the political parties. The treatment was necessarily brief because, outside the SYL, few parties have clearly spelled out and consistently subscribed to political programs. The aims of the SYL remain essentially what they were in 1947: unification of all the Somali-inhabited territories of northeast Africa (including French Somaliland, the Northern Frontier District of Kenya, and the Ogaden region of Ethiopia); detribalization; educational, social, and economic development (now along the lines of a modified African socialism); and the adoption of a national Somali script.[36] Eventually all political parties, even the HDM, subscribed to these goals in one form or another. In a society where modern economic differentiations and specialism are so limited, the nontraditional issues that divide political groups are bound to be few. Debate occurs over the means and the pace of implementing the goals rather than over the goals themselves. Furthermore, where prestige, wealth, and power are obtainable almost exclusively in government areas, ideological issues tend to be subordinated to political expedience.

In only one important aspect of foreign policy has the government significantly departed from the policies pursued during the trusteeship period; it has moved away from a "neutralism inclined toward the West"

---

[36] Originally the SYL advocated the adoption of the Osmania script, but when opposition arose on the ground that it is a Daarood script, the party merely came out for a "national" script. In 1962 a parliamentary commission issued a report on the language question in which it implied a favorable disposition toward the adoption of a Latin script. On the language question see Castagno, "Somali Republic" and "French Somaliland," in Kitchen, *op. cit.*

to a more "positive" neutralism. Considerable pressure to alter the direction of foreign policy was put on the government by second-generation nationalists, by Haji Muhammad Hussein, and by the Somaliland parties, which tended to be more pro-Cairo and anti-West than the Somalia parties. These factors, along with protestations against American military aid to Ethiopia, made it expedient for Shermarke to accept the Soviet bloc's offer of a $52 million credit in May, 1961—the largest per capita credit assigned by the Soviet bloc to an African nation. But if two years of implementing the Soviet aid agreements and of the Somali state's voting in the United Nations is any indication of future policy, it cannot be assumed that the SYL will maintain a pro-Soviet stance unless a substantial *quid pro quo*, such as Soviet support for Greater Somalia, is secured.

The shift toward center was also a consequence of redefining foreign policy goals in the context of the new ethnic balance. When the Hawiye dominated the party and the government, they strongly inclined toward Italy because the trusteeship administration seemed to favor the Hawiye elements in the establishment of the first Somali government in 1956. Psychologically and politically, independence required a detachment from the dominance of Italian economic policy. The move away from Italy had implications for domestic policy. Eventually the new government circumscribed the activities of several Italian companies and threatened them with nationalization.[37] It is therefore not unreasonable to assume that Italian economic interests in Somalia might have supported the Hawiye elements in their struggle for power during the two crises. In any event, the Somali Republic was certain to apply the principle of balance in her foreign relations as she applied it domestically, and, having applied it with maximum sagacity, she has been able to maximize aid from both East and West.

Greater Somalia remains the cardinal objective of the SYL, the SNL-USP, and the SDU. This objective has cornered the activities of the government in the past few years, and has helped to shape policies toward other states. The need to win support from other African states on the Greater Somalia issue has pushed the Somali Republic into a position somewhere between the Monrovia and the Casablanca powers on the subject of Pan-Africanism,[38] although sentiment among the intellectuals leans toward Sékou Touré's views on domestic and interna-

---

[37] The two companies concerned, SAIS (the sugar monopoly) and Vincenzo (producer of electricity), are most inefficient. Both have equipment that dates back to the 1920's. Electricity rates in Mogadiscio are the highest in the world.

[38] The Somali state received tacit and lukewarm support at Cairo in January, 1958, and at Tunis in January, 1960, for her resolutions condemning "all" (i.e., including Ethiopian) forms of colonialism in the horn of Africa. Parenthetically, Ethiopia's increased involvement in Pan-Africanism is partly owing to her need to respond to the Somali initiative.

tional policies.[39] The government has also pressed for the formation of and for Somalia's admission to a future East African federation.

The SYL, and other political parties, are hopeful that admission into an East African federation will eventually lead to an accommodation of the Somali claims to the dominantly Somali-inhabited area of the Northern Frontier District (NFD) of Kenya, despite the clear opposition of both the Kenya African Democratic Union and the Kenya African National Union to the modification of Kenya's boundaries. The Northern Province People's Progressive Party (NPPPP) and the Northern Frontier Democratic Party (NFDP),[40] and the Somali government, despite its vigorous efforts, has consistently failed to persuade Great Britain that the area should be ceded to the Somali Republic. The Kenyan Northern Frontier District Commission, created in 1962 to appraise opinion in the NFD, found the Somalis almost unanimous in wanting a self-governing status within the Somali state.[41] Given the conclusions of the commission and the administrative history of the NFD, the Somalis regard an East African federation as a means by which Kenya could take steps toward meeting Somali desires. The SYL is also optimistic that it might eventually secure French Somaliland through negotiations with France. At some future date the Somali government may bring the issue of the Ogaden Somalis in Ethiopia before the General Assembly of the United Nations, with the aim of obtaining a plebiscite in the Ogaden.[42]

Failure to achieve any of the three goals in the Greater Somalia objective may injure the position of the SYL and widen the support of opposition parties, particularly as the SYL cannot count on major accomplishments in the field of social and economic development in the immediate future. This is one reason that foreign policy issues and the role of foreign powers in the horn of Africa exert a major conditioning force on Somali domestic politics, both traditional and modern.

Criticisms of domestic policies have emanated from various sources, but nobody has sought to organize them under one oppositional banner. They are best articulated by second-generation nationalists who received, and are now receiving, higher education abroad, but who did not par-

---

[39] Most Somali politicians and intellectuals look upon Kwame Nkrumah as dictatorial and excessively ambitious. In the spring of 1962 the Ghanaian ambassador to Mogadiscio was impelled to withdraw on the ground that Ghana was interfering in Somali domestic affairs.

[40] The NPPPP has a larger following that the NFDP. The Somali Independent Union is confined to Nairobi and does not seem to be politically active.

[41] *Report of the Northern Frontier District Commission*, Kenya, Cmnd. 1900 (1962). It is interesting to find that ethnic groups classified as "half-Somali" and non-Somali Muslim groups, such as the Muslim Boran, supported the Somali view.

[42] The recent liberal interpretation of Article 2, Section 7, of the UN Charter makes such a view quite plausible, as does the General Assembly's action on the West Irianian issue. For a recent discussion on Greater Somalia developments, see A. A. Castagno, "The Somali Republic in Transition," *Africa Report,* VII (Dec., 1962), 8–10.

ticipate in Somali politics before 1960. These criticisms concentrate on the practice of ethnic balance, which is equated with corruption, nepotism, and tribalism. In particular, issue has been taken with the government's failure to deal effectively with clanism; to modernize the tax structure; to speed up development in the social and economic spheres; and to diversify agriculture in such a way as to break the dependence on Italian trade and on the Italian banana and sugar concessions. In Somaliland, criticism centers on the government's lack of response to the problems and the needs of the northern territory and on the "all-pervading inefficiency" of the Italian procedures of administration, finance, and justice. But few of those who render rational critiques of the government would think of identifying themselves with the HDM, which is tribal, or with the SDU, which is regarded as lacking leadership and as irresponsible.

CONCLUSION

Given the manner in which Somali politics has evolved during the past two decades, and excluding the possibility of any major economic progress, we may assume that there will be few immediate changes in the role of lineage associations and cleavages in the political system. The strength of traditional clanship ties has been revealed in each of the elections and in the formation of each of the Somali governments. It was Abdullahi Issa, one of the main forgers of Somali independence, who took the initial steps in altering the traditional social system by granting suffrage to women, by modifying the system of collective responsibility for homicide, by reducing the powers of the cadis over criminal jurisdiction, by abolishing the sheegat system, and by attempting, in the face of considerable opposition, to reduce the Somali language to a Latin script. Yet it was he who introduced the concept of clan balance. Shermarke and Minister of the Interior Abdirizak Haji Hussein denounced the concept at some political risk, but once at the helm of government, they found that it comported with reality. They have, however, taken strong measures to eliminate other Somali traditions regarded as repugnant to a modern society. Even Haji Muhammad Hussein, who helped to spearhead the nationalist movement and whose Rer Hamar identification immunized him against involvement in the traditional pattern of agnatic cleavages, ultimately had to employ those cleavages in his own political strategy, as had the Mad Mullah, Muhammad Ahmed bin Abdalla Hassan, the first modern Somali political leader to issue the call for detribalization.

Despite the relatively large number of educated Somalis who will return from foreign universities in the next few years, politics will continue, to a large degree, to be founded on the system of clan alliances and alignments within the political parties as they operate in the context of modern government, unless the present structure of government is altered along more authoritarian lines. The basic pattern of lineage rivalry and association may change as conditions require, as it has in the shift from the dominant Hawiye-Daarood combination to a Hawiye-Sab *rapprochement* and to a Daarood-Sab-Abgal concordance. Rer, subclan, clan, and clan-family alignments will move with the vagaries of political expedience and ideology, but they will most probably do so within the broad, if erratic, framework set down by the pattern described in this paper.

A government that must depend on the balancing of multifarious kinship groups might be called upon to appease so many conflicting interests that it could govern only precariously in the haunting fear of instability, particularly where the kinship cleavages seem to be constantly shifting, waning, and waxing with the opportunities arising from new political conditions. Yet, as the Issa and Shermarke governments illustrate, the process of accommodating clan balance, although it may delay the attainment of objective national goals, has not altogether impeded the resolution of critical national and international problems. That it has been possible to establish a government over a quasi-acephalous society, which has not experienced the disciplinary aspects of a hierarchical structure based on territorial concepts, is owing, to a large extent, to the development of modern political parties which have accommodated the traditional cleavages. Within the parties the cleavages have found outlets through competition for national power and influence.

Political continuity and stability in both government and parties will hinge on the ability of political leaders to compromise competing clan claims, to balance competitive forces, and to reconcile conflicting modernist and traditionalist objectives. This process of balancing and compromising is not new to the Somalis; in the traditional Somali political system, the ability to arbitrate and compromise is often rewarded with chieftaincy, just as in modern politics it was Aden Abdullah Osman who gained the presidency of the Republic. But to work effectively, clan balance must take into account the claims of all major clan groups. It must maximize participation in the decision-making process and it must dispense patronage and economic, political, and social privileges in proportion to the strength of the political leaders as manifested in the support they are able to secure from their agnatic associates. Effective clan balance may prove to be the formula that will harmoniously blend the traditional and modern political systems, and it may also prove to be the main guarantee against the hegemony of any one clan family and against authoritarian one-man rule.

But ethnic balance also carries with it major disadvantages. Recruitment for top administrative positions is often based on ethnic association rather than on merit. The decision-making process becomes cumbersome when the implications of every decision must be weighed in the context of multifarious ethnic considerations. Popular fronts, such as that attempted by the National United Front in 1955, and cohesive oppositional movements rapidly crumble away under the strains characteristic of a fissionable society. But, above all, ethnic balance impedes the development of effective national leadership, whether in the dominant parties or within the opposition. As soon as a leader gains national stature and prominence, his clan affiliation is exploited by his competitors, within and outside his political party, in order to reduce his appeal. Whatever national confidence he may have gained may be transformed into widespread mistrust based on ethnic provincialism. This is one basic reason—the extreme individualism of the Somali is another—that the pendulum of leadership in the SYL does not remain steady and that there are no "national heroes" in the Somali nationalist movement comparable to Kwame Nkrumah in Ghana or Sékou Touré in Guinea. Even the present attempt to build up Muhammad Ahmed bin Abdalla Hassan as the founder of modern Somali nationalism has met only limited success among intellectuals and political leaders.[43]

One consequence of the tenuousness of political leadership is that it induces in the politician a short-range view of politics. Once victory is gained, a deputy must "deliver the goods" to his ethnic group and at the same time give attention to his own future security, mainly in the business realm. The concept of public service to the nation must necessarily be restricted when national recognition of that service is rarely, if ever, forthcoming. But even those who have served the nation selflessly and with devotion do not find it prudent to use the various media of communication to seek national support for their policies. Ethnic balance and its concomitant consequence of restricting the radius of appeal of statesmen and politicians find their origin in the relative slowness of the process of social mobilization.[44]

Finally, after some three years of independence, ethnic balance has not fully overcome the obstacles of unifying all elements of the Northern and Southern regions. On the administrative, legal, and financial levels, considerable progress on integration has been made. Economically,

---

[43] This failure does not preclude the possibility that Muhammad will eventually be regarded as a preëminent national hero by all groups. The call for strong national leadership by intellectuals and by bards and singers is particularly compelling. The latter are most influential in conveying political views on the preintellection level through indigenous folk songs, which proved quite effective in the independence movement. The folkways record, "The Freedom Songs of the Somali Republic" (FD 5443), is a useful compilation of folk songs dealing with independence, strong leaders, and patriotism.

[44] See Karl Deutsch, "Social Mobilization and Political Development," *American Political Science Review*, LV (Sept., 1961), 493–514. It should be noted, however, that Deutsch does not explore the variety of indigenous forms which may be employed to facilitate the process of social mobilization.

traders and entrepreneurs are helping to consolidate the Republic by expanding commerce and transportation between north and south. The national police, under the effective and brilliant leadership of General Muhammad Abshir, and the army, under General Daud Abdulle, have been integrated. Both units have taken the initiative in operating as nationalizing agents, particularly by adopting a Somali written language based on the Latin script. Politicians, however, have not gone so far. Since independence there has been a considerable turnover of ministers from Somaliland in the cabinet. Contending claims over the degree of contribution made to the nation's political development, over important government assignments, and over the allocation of funds for economic and social development have tended to revitalize the north-south division. But this situation may be remedied as time whittles away at the colonial background and as political experience increasingly buttresses the national structure.

I do not seek to establish that the Somali nation is incapable of producing strong national leaders of the tone and temper of a Gandhi or a Roosevelt. Nor do I say that Somali leadership has been mediocre in comparison with that of other nations. On the contrary, given the economic basis of the Somali society, only the ultimate in political sagacity could have produced independence and avoided serious internal disturbances once independence was obtained. I only wish to suggest that the waxing and waning of political leadership will continue to characterize the Somali political system so long as ethnic considerations remain all-pervading in government and politics, and so long as the present government and party procedures permit ethnic considerations to exercise their maximum influence.

Although I have stressed the persistence of agnatic cleavages and their relationship to modern political parties, I am not arguing that the centrifugal forces of Somali politics will predominate over all other factors. For, despite their lineage divisions, Somalis possess a proud sense of identity as a race, separate and distinct from all foreigners, African, Asian, or European. Important national integrating factors are Islam, as manifested in the Wahabism that characterizes some of the present leaders; Somali-Ethiopian hostility, frequently fired by boundary conflicts; and the dream of Greater Somalia. In their efforts to temper clanism and to reduce its impact on over-all national goals, the Somalis have a distinct advantage in their possession of a common language, culture, and religion, for the Somali Republic is perhaps the most homogeneous state in Africa south of the Sahara in these three elements. Insofar as the system has that foundation of communality, it is even possible to conjecture that with time the segmentary character of the social system may prove to be an advantage rather than a liability in the process of politicizing and nationalizing the state.

APPENDIX TABLE

RESULTS OF ELECTIONS IN SOMALIA AND SOMALILAND

SOMALIA[a]

Party	Municipal, 1954		General, 1956		Municipal, 1958[b]		General, 1959[b]	
	Votes	Seats	Votes	Seats	Votes	Seats	Votes	Seats
Somali Youth League	17,982	141	333,820	43	39,178	416	237,134	83
Hisbia Destour Mustaquil Somali[e]	8,198	57	159,967	13	38,214	175	40,857	5
Somali National Union[d]	2,273	5	21,630		6,322	6		
Greater Somalia League					10,125	36		
Liberal Party of Somali Youth					11,004	27	35,769	2
Somali Bagiuni Fichirini[e]			426		341	3		
Somali Democratic Party			80,866	3				
Marehan Union			11,358	1				
Afgoi-Audegle Group			3,441					
Somali Hawiye Youth Union			1,846					
Six Shidle	954	8	1,550					
Somali African Union	2,584	28						
Somali Progressive League	1,681	22						
Somali National Un'on[f]	1,137	9						
Palma	415	3						
Somali Progressive Union	1,759	4						
Abgal Youth Association	351							
Ancora	125	1						
Murosada	124							
Leopardo	24							
Abgalia	47	3						
Democratic Somali Union	43							
Total	37,697	281	614,904	60	105,184	663	313,760	90

SOMALILAND

Party	General, February, 1960	
	Votes	Seats
Somali National League	42,395	20
United Somali Party	13,350	12
National United Front	20,249	1
Somali Youth League	4,626	
Independent	746	
Total	81,366	33

[a] The number of votes required to elect a municipal council member varies; fewer votes are needed for election to councils in smaller communities.

[b] The votes for the SYL and the HDM in the 1958 and 1959 elections do not include votes cast in districts where there were unopposed lists.

[c] Formerly the Hisbia Digil Mirifle.

[d] Formerly the Benadir Youth Union.

[e] Formerly the Bagiuni Fichirini Youth.

[f] Not to be confused with the Somali National Union which before 1959 was called the Benadir Youth Union.

SOURCES: *Corriere della Somalia* (Mogadiscio), April 23, 1954; Nov. 10, 1958; March 30, 1959; *Le Prime Elezioni politiche in Somalia*, Italian Trusteeship Administration (Mogadiscio, 1956), p. 226; *Somaliland News* (Hargeisa), Feb. 22, 1960.

15. CONGO (LEOPOLDVILLE)

By René Lemarchand

The sudden proliferation of political movements and associations which attended the Congo's accession to independence is undoubtedly one of the most striking and perplexing features of its recent evolution. Although many of these so-called "parties" had only an ephemeral existence, and did not develop much beyond the embryonic stage, their sheer number and permutations provide a measure of the difficulties involved in the creation of a national consensus out of a multiplicity of ethnic and sectional particularisms.

Behind the fragmented pattern of modern associational development in the Congo lies the precolonial past. It has shaped and continues to influence the group loyalties and the political perspectives and behavior of most Congolese. Within the boundaries of the Congo, the largest country in Tropical Africa, there is a multitude of ethnic groups of varying size whose traditions of cultural distinctiveness and intergroup conflict are at the root of many of the contemporary sharp antagonisms. To understand the feelings of mutual hostility which permeate intergroup relations between, say, Tshokwe and Lunda, Baluba and Bayeke, Bayaka and Bakongo, it is necessary to move backward in time to the precolonial era, to the days of Nkongolo, Mwata Yamvo, and Msiri, whose memory is still very much alive in the minds of their descendants. Likewise, the political objectives, the leadership, and the organization of Congolese parties must be viewed against the background of the ethnic diversity of traditional Congolese societies.

The essentially static character of Belgian colonial policy is a second major background consideration. Given the absence of meaningful procedures and institutions for popular participation in governmental and administrative processes at the central Congo-wide level, the problem of political unification at levels above the tribe or "nationality group" has been rendered all the more difficult. In several aspects, however, the uneven operation of commercialization and industrialization processes, coupled with the uneven geographical distribution of economic resources and opportunities, has provided new focuses of political involvement among otherwise unrelated tribes. What has emerged in such instances has been a distinctive regional consciousness, superseding ethnic loyalties, which has set important limits to the field of operation and the

560

ultimate objectives of certain political groups. This phenomenon is nowhere better illustrated than in the Katanga, where, in the process of
adjusting to modernity, certain tribes have acquired a group consciousness of their own, coextensive with and limited to the boundaries of the
province.

These two major sources of fragmentation—one inherent in the traditional society, and the other in the socioeconomic environment of the
Congo—have combined to produce a host of tensions and polarities
which, to this very day, impede the development of a secular, stable
system of authority.

BACKGROUND TO CONGOLESE POLITICAL AWAKENING

As elsewhere in Africa, the emergence of Congolese nationalism
(here understood as a reaction to and a protest against alien domination)
is the end product of the impact of the social and economic forces that
are linked with the "colonial situation." Whereas in the former territories
of French and British West Africa, the thrust of nationalist activity manifested itself early in the post–World War II period, the Congo remained
relatively free of overt manifestations of political agitation until as late
as 1956. Among the several factors that help to explain the delayed appearance of Congolese political groups, at least three deserve mention.
One is the reluctance of the Belgian government to define the objectives
of its colonial policy in other than the vaguest terms. The essence of
Belgium's "civilizing mission" was usually formulated in terms of hu-
manitarian ideals, for the most part identified with hackneyed slogans
about the moral and material well-being of the Africans. Beyond this,
however, no effort was made to give a precise content to the goals of
Belgian rule. It was not until January, 1959, that the metropolitan government, realizing the explosive potentialities of the situation, formally announced its "firm intention" to "lead the Congolese populations forward
toward independence in prosperity and peace." [1] Meanwhile, however,
this uncertainty regarding the ultimate goals of Belgian policy had deprived the Congolese of the psychological stimulus and the organizational
impulse derived elsewhere from the expectation of constitutional changes
and independence.

An important element in the attitude of Belgian officials was the
presumably genuine conviction that the Congolese were not ready, and
indeed would not be ready for a long time, for self-government. The
rationale underlying this conviction was that a certain level of economic
and social development was a *sine qua non* for effective democratic government; until that level was reached, all attempts at democratization

---

[1] Cited in Ruth Slade, *The Belgian Congo: Some Recent Changes* (London:
Oxford University Press, 1960), p. 50.

would fail. Whether or not the argument reflected the true beliefs of Belgian officialdom is beside the point. What must be noted here, however, is that it permeated all Belgian assumptions and policies and thereby contributed directly to the climate of political apathy and presumed political stability which made the Congo a model colony in the eyes of numerous Western observers.

Another inhibiting factor was the major assumption underlying Belgian educational policy in the Congo until well after World War II. The Belgians believed that primary education and training limited to a few technical skills were the most appropriate form of education for Africans in the light of Belgium's gradualist goals. This does not mean that there were no Congolese with postprimary education before 1956. There were in fact several hundred, but they were almost exclusively concentrated in the African Catholic clergy, an apolitical social category. Yet the absorption of African intellectuals into the Church did not mean that they were necessarily indifferent to the appeals of nationalism; indeed, a large proportion of Congolese leaders abandoned the priesthood to engage in nationalist activities. By and large, however, the priesthood served for a time to absorb the interests and the energies of many potential nationalists, and to foster an attitude of passive and faithful acquiescence toward the colonial order.[2]

The most effective instrument for ensuring political quietism was undoubtedly the rigorous censorship and surveillance exercised by the colonial authorities over all media and forms of public expression. It was not until August, 1959, that the Belgian government finally consented to grant wider freedom of expression. Even then, what appeared at first glance to be a major step toward the inauguration of a more permissive political climate was largely nullified by the role that the administration continued to play behind the scenes. These legal controls were not always applied with the same rigor throughout the Congo. Depending on the attitude of the district commissioners toward Africans, or on the parties to which they belonged, meetings were held in some places which would not have been tolerated elsewhere. Thus by January, 1959, a number of political groups had been constituted and recognized by the administration, even though some of them could conceivably be regarded as subversive.

While these restrictive policies and practices were helping to delay the political awakening in the Congo, other influences were spurring the growth of nationalist sentiment and activity. One that has often been overlooked is the part played by Christian missionaries in reviving and

---

[2] For a fuller discussion of the Belgian record in the field of education see Bernard Fall, "Education in the Republic of the Congo," *Journal of Negro Education*, XXX (Summer, 1961), 266–276.

rehabilitating certain aspects of African culture, either through the publication of ethnographic and historical works pertaining to the customs and history of specific ethnic groups, or simply as a result of the personal sympathy shown by some members of the clergy toward these groups. Insofar as they did communicate to the Africans a sense of pride in their culture, and a conviction that their culture was as worthy of recognition as that of the Belgians, Christian missionaries, in effect, gave the Congolese elites a justification for their fight against Belgian colonialism. But in so doing they also gave an ethnic direction and focus to nationalist assertions. An example in point is Father Joseph Van Wing, whose writings had a significant impact upon the development of a sense of cultural nationalism among the Bakongo, the major ethnic group in the lower Congo.

Another factor that must be taken into account was the attitude toward Africans of white settlers in the Congo. Despite notable differences in character, distribution, and strength of settler interests, the *colon*'s image of himself in relation to the African was almost invariably colored by his display of racial and cultural superiority. The insistence upon white supremacy by the settlers contributed in no small way to the bitterness and hostility of the Congolese toward Belgian rule, and to the rise of the racialist component in African nationalist sentiment. But in contrast with most other multiracial territories, where common African opposition to the presence of European settlers served to weaken particularisms, in the Congo the contrary was true. Regional differences in the numerical importance and the economic status of the *colonat* affected the political options of African leaders in radically different ways. The separatism of Katanga Province, for example, is directly related to the fact that the white-settler oligarchy in that province was by far the most powerful in the Congo in terms both of numbers and of economic potential. Indeed, the political history of the Katanga since independence cannot be fully understood without taking into consideration the part played by the European community in making the idea of secession politically meaningful and economically attractive.

A third element in the background of Congolese nationalism is the impact of metropolitan influences. This is most strikingly illuminated by two issues: (1) the question of state subsidies to nonconfessional schools (*écoles officielles laïques*) for Africans, and (2) the use of languages in schools and court proceedings. After 1954 each of these issues became the focal point of a bitter controversy between the clerical Right and the anticlerical Left in Belgium.[3] But the divisive implications of these issues were by no means restricted to the metropolitan arena. In the Congo the

---

[3] Thomas Hodgkin, "Battle of Schools in the Congo," *West Africa*, Jan. 28, 1956, p. 79.

question scolaire caused a deep rift between the clergy and the colonial administration, thereby destroying the monolithic unity that had existed between the Church and the Establishment since Belgian rule had commenced. Similarly, the *question linguistique,* reflecting the historic schism between Flemings and Walloons in Belgium, was also intruded into the Congo. These internal strains and rivalries in Belgium, which were inevitably projected into the Congo, had a corrosive impact upon African attitudes, helping to further the development of African nationalist activity. It revealed to the Congolese that they were not ruled by a strong united foreign people, but by a small weak country of bickering groups, each morally challenging the actual or potential domination by the other. This metropolitan spectacle not only dramatized for the Congolese the competitive struggle for power within a political arena, but also forcefully impressed upon them the idea that aggrieved groups had the right to seek relief through political action. The ethical and moral arguments used by the Flemings in support of their right to self-determination within the Belgian community were easily related to the situation of alien domination in the Congo.

In addition to these background factors, a number of special circumstances and events helped to crystallize nationalist sentiment in organizational form. Historically, perhaps the most significant of these was the publication in February, 1956, of A. A. J. Van Bilsen's "Thirty-Year Plan for the Political Emancipation of Belgian Africa." [4] Despite its gradualist overtones, the Van Bilsen proposal did not go unnoticed among the *évolués*[5] of Leopoldville; indeed, only a few months later a group of African journalists decided to use it as a basis for a nationalist manifesto. The latter, an epoch-making document in Congolese history, appeared in the July, 1956, issue of the newspaper *Conscience Africaine.* In it, for the first time in the history of Belgian colonization, a group of Congolese explicitly stated their desire to see the Congo become a "great nation in the center of the African continent." [6]

In retrospect, the manifesto of *Conscience Africaine* was a relatively mild statement of nationalist objectives. Although "total political emancipation" was specifically mentioned as the only acceptable alternative to colonial rule, the authors of the manifesto envisaged it as progressive

---

[4] The text of the Van Bilsen plan will be found in *Dossiers de l'Action Sociale Catholique* (Feb., 1956), pp. 83–111.

[5] In the Congo the term "évolué" referred to a class of Africans who had achieved literacy and showed certain other evidences of Westernization. As used here, however, the term does not necessarily imply disaffiliation from traditional membership groups.

[6] For the English version of the manifesto, see Alan P. Merriam, *Congo: Background of Conflict* (Evanston: Northwestern University Press, 1961), pp. 321–329.

emancipation extending over a period of thirty years. Feeling that so cautious and gradualist an approach fell far short of their expectations, a group of Bakongo of Leopoldville, on August 24, 1956, issued a violent and devastating critique of the ideas set forth in the manifesto. Speaking for the Association pour le Maintien, l'Unité, et l'Expansion de la Langue Kikongo (Abako), a Bakongo cultural association, the authors of the countermanifesto stated: "Rather than postponing emancipation for another thirty years, we should be granted self-government today." [7] From then on the Abako, under the leadership of Joseph Kasavubu, placed itself in the forefront of the struggle for independence. Van Bilsen's thirty-year plan for independence thus brought into sharp focus the issue around which nationalist sentiment first crystallized.

Another precipitant of overt nationalist activity was the constitutional reform introduced in 1957 (the so-called "Statut des Villes"), which made it possible for the African population of Leopoldville, Elisabethville, and Jadotville to elect their own municipal councilors and *bourgmestres*. Although extension of the franchise to Africans did not sanction the right of Africans to organize political groups, the municipal election of December, 1957, was in fact the occasion for such groups to come into being. Belgian restrictions on the formation of political parties, however, explain in part why the elections were contested on a tribal basis and through the medium of ethnic or regional associations.[8]

A third factor has been the influence of political developments in other African territories. Although some Congolese had long been aware of the significance of postwar constitutional reforms in French and British West Africa, it was not clear until 1958 what this development really meant. In the summer of that year General de Gaulle visited Brazzaville, and his speech of August 24, confirming his intention to give French overseas territories the choice between immediate independence and membership in the French Community, had a profound psychological impact on the African population of Leopoldville. Two days later a group of évolués presented Léon Pétillon, then minister to the Congo, with a petition denouncing the "anachronistic political regime of the Congo" and demanding that a date be set for "complete independence." And it was only a matter of weeks before they decided to follow up these demands with concrete organizational moves. In point of fact, among the

---

[7] *Ibid.*, p. 333.

[8] Technically, municipal councilors and bourgmestres were to be appointed by the administration after "consultation." Except for Jadotville, however, where the African bourgmestre was chosen by the administration, appointments were everywhere made on the basis of the poll. For fuller information on the electoral procedure, see C. A. G. Wallis, "The Administration of Towns in the Belgian Congo," *Journal of African Administration*, X (April, 1958), 97 ff.

signatories of this petition were a number of persons who later became associated with the Mouvement National Congolais, including Patrice Lumumba, Joseph Ileo, and Cyrille Adoula. Then, in December, 1958, the All-African People's Conference, a nongovernmental association of political parties, met in Accra. Aside from the publicity given the resolutions adopted by the conference, the presence of three Congolese delegates—Lumumba, Gaston Diomi, and Joseph Ngalula—decidedly heightened nationalist pressures for self-government.

There followed a new burst of nationalist activity among the Africans of Leopoldville, culminating in rioting and bloodshed during the early days of January, 1959. These disturbances, however, were only a prelude to further violence, first in Leverville, among the workers of the Huileries du Congo Belge, then in Luluabourg, Matadi, and Stanleyville. Although these demonstrations were not always manifestations of anti-colonial sentiment, the Congolese nationalist leaders claimed that they were, in order to fortify their position in pressing their demands upon the Belgian government. At the same time, as each party sought not only to emulate but to surpass the claims of its rivals, the rather bold promises for reform in the government's declaration of January, 1959, lost their appeal for the African masses. By November, when Minister Auguste de Schrijver announced before the Congo Press Association of Leopoldville that a "grand conference" would be held in January, 1960, for the purpose of elaborating the future political structures of the Congo, few nationalists were willing to settle for less than immediate independence.

Commenting in 1955 on Belgium's tendency to "concentrate on economic and social developments, to the exclusion of any provision for participating in political activity," Kenneth Robinson observed that "there are dangers in too long a delay in establishing a basis for some form of political participation, since too long a delay means that when at last the pressure cannot be withstood, a big jump has to be made overnight." [9] And that is precisely what happened, although few observers at the time seemed to share such misgivings; once the "big jump" had been made, the Congolese were suddenly faced with the fact of independence before they had had an opportunity to test their political aptitudes. More important, perhaps, the sudden withdrawal at the same time of Belgian authority destroyed the unifying urge which only a struggle for independence could sustain. In a sense, therefore, it was the absence of transition between colonial rule and self-rule which made most Congolese parties ethnically centered, structurally underdeveloped, and ideologically barren.

---

[9] Kenneth Robinson, "Colonial Issues and Policies with Special Reference to Tropical Africa," *Annals of the American Academy of Political and Social Science,* 298 (March, 1955), 92.

GENESIS OF CONGOLESE POLITICAL GROUPS

As a form of protest against colonialism, political parties must be distinguished at the outset from earlier syncretistic or protonationalist movements, such as those initiated by African "prophets" to assert their independence from European churches. As formal organizations, they must also be distinguished from tribal and kinship associations, *clubs d'évolués,* friendly societies, alumni associations, and similar voluntary groupings. Whereas nativistic and messianic movements lacked most of the structural characteristics of political parties, voluntary associations tended to operate more like pressure groups seeking to influence the administration within the framework of established institutions. Once these preliminary distinctions are made, however, one must recognize that Congolese parties, like parties elsewhere in Africa, are very closely related to these earlier manifestations of group activity.

Influence of Messianic Movements

The earliest and most widespread forms of colonial protest in the Congo were independent African churches and prophet movements. Kimbanguism, the best known of such movements, was founded in 1921 by Simon Kimbangu, a former catechist of Bakongo origins. Although its manifest objective was the creation of an African church, it was in fact a far more deep-seated and broadly based movement of protest against European domination. In the minds of many of his followers, Kimbangu was the "elect" who would expel the whites and become the ruler of Africa; for others, he was the heir apparent to the throne of the old Kongo Kingdom. This peculiar mixture of traditionalism, nationalism, and anti-white elements explains the extraordinary success that Kimbanguism enjoyed among the African population.

Another major movement was the Watch Tower Movement, or Kitawala, which seems to have been introduced into the Congo in 1923, when a group of propagandists from Nyasaland attempted to set up local branches in the southern part of the Katanga. Beginning in the 1930's, the movement underwent a rapid expansion, recruiting adherents in Elisabethville, Kipushi, Jadotville, and Albertville, and in many rural areas of the Katanga. In Elisabethville alone it claimed more than a thousand members by 1932, and in subsequent years the sect made rapid headway in Orientale, Kivu, and Equateur provinces. Like that of Kimbanguism, the appeal of Kitawala lay in its xenophobic orientation and its vehement opposition to all imported religions. Unlike Kimbanguism, however, which was primarily a Bakongo phenomenon, Kitawala was relatively free of tribal bias, as evidenced by its rapid expansion through the whole eastern region of the Congo.[10]

---

[10] For fuller information on Kimbanguism, see P. Raymaekers, "L'Eglise de Jésus-

Just as there are variations in the character and the doctrinal orientation of these movements, so they have exercised a variable difference on the growth of nationalist parties. The precedent of resistance, and the climate of social and political unrest the movements created, were conducive to the birth of more explicitly political nationalist protest groups. Indeed, the recurrent waves of messianic agitation which have swept over the Lower Congo help to explain why nationalist activities first appeared in that area. Similarly, the extraordinarily rapid expansion of nationalist movements in Orientale and Kivu provinces is partly attributable to the heritage of protest created by movements of a chiliastic or nativistic character.

The early movements have suggested to subsequent generations of nationalists ways and means of furthering their immediate political goals. The usual approach was to espouse the grievances, rather than the doctrinal convictions, of sect members. The Abako, for example, without in any way identifying its political objectives with Kimbanguist doctrines, indirectly sought the support of Kimbanguists by paying homage to their prophet. This may explain why some Kimbanguists in turn looked upon Kasavubu as the reincarnation of Simon Kimbangu. In any event, this phenomenon provides a partial explanation for the rapid rise to prominence of a party like the Abako.[11]

Finally, these movements have sometimes contributed to the cultural revival attendant upon the emergence of some political groups. For example, the efforts made by the Kimbanguists to adapt their doctrine to the context of the traditional Bakongo culture have probably encouraged the rise of cultural nationalism among the Bakongo. This factor, however, is only one among many that have stimulated cultural revivalism among the Africans. Equally important was the part played by cultural associations in strengthening the traditional loyalties of certain groups.

Growth of Voluntary Associations

Whereas nativistic and messianic movements tended to provide an outlet for the emotional strains and stresses produced by the colonial

---

Christ sur Terre par le prophète Simon Kimbangu," *Zaïre*, XIII, no. 7 (1959), 680–698; cf. E. Andersson, *Messianic Popular Movements in the Lower Congo*, trans. Donald Burton *et al.* (London: Kegan Paul, 1958). On the development of Kitawala in the Congo, see "Kitawala," *Bulletin des Juridictions Indigènes et du Droit Coutumier Congolais* (1943–44), pp. 231 ff.

[11] Certain movements of a messianic character were instigated for secular purposes. In the Kasai, for example, Sébastien Kapongo is reported to have launched a Mau Mau sect in order to enlarge the membership of the Association Lulua-Frères. Kapongo was described in a Sûreté report as "the promoter, initiator, and high priest of a sect that he calls Mau Mau." "The number of devotees," notes the same report, "is extremely high, and the movement has gained a strong foothold in the Demba territory" ("Note relative à l'Association Lulua-Frères," Luluabourg, 1954, unpublished document).

situation, voluntary associations were the principal medium through which Africans sought to adjust themselves to the disintegrative influences of urban life. Like many of the political parties that evolved from them, these associations frequently served as substitutes for structures found in the traditional society, and thus offered their members an opportunity to recapture the sense of belonging and intimacy which once characterized individual relations within the tribe.

In its most generic sense, the term "voluntary association" covers many different types of institutionalized groupings, such as tribal and regional associations, alumni societies, and clubs d'évolués, all of which performed a social, cultural, recreational, or educative function for their members. Although some of these associations can be traced back to the early 1930's, if not earlier, most of them came into being after the war as a result of the massive influx of rural Africans into urban areas. Thus, by 1956 there were as many as 137 associations in Leopoldville alone, including 85 tribal associations, 27 cultural groups, 18 alumni societies, and 7 professional associations.[12]

Of these voluntary groupings, tribal associations were not only the most numerous but by far the most dynamic. Although usually organized and directed by Westernized elements, their main objective was to preserve and strengthen the loyalty of their members to their group of origin.[13] In Leopoldville, for example, the Abako had as its declared objective the "unification, preservation, and expansion of the Kikongo language," but it also served as a mutual-aid society, providing jobs for the unemployed, hospitalization for the sick, financial assistance for the destitute, scholarships for qualified students, and so on. Although not nearly so active as the Abako, the Association des Bangala (Liboke Lya Bangala) performed somewhat similar functions for the so-called Bangala of Leopoldville.[14] Comprising a diversity of ethnic components, it never acquired the same degree of cohesion as the Abako, and for this reason it may well be regarded as a regional association.

The *associations de ressortissants* were the main type of regional association in Leopoldville. Most notable among them were the Fédéra-

---

[12] *La Voix du Congolais* (Leopoldville), no. 88 (July, 1953), 470.

[13] For a good description of the functional aspects of tribal and regional association in Elisabethville, see F. Grevisse, "Activités sociales des Indigènes dans le Centre Coutumier d'Elisabethville," *Bulletin de l'Association des Anciens Etudiants de l'Institut Universitaire des Territoires d'Outre-Mer,* no. 10 (1950), 7 ff.

[14] "In its widest meaning," writes Herman Burssens, "[the term] Bangala includes about half of the total population of the Congo-Ubangui and the Tshuapa Districts, viz. also many people who for a major part belong to the Sudanese tribes of Ubangui or the Ngombe group" ("The So-called Bangala and a Few Problems of Art-Historical and Ethnographical Order," *Kongo-Overzee,* XX, no. 3 [1954], 221). In Leopoldville, however, the term "Bangala" was used principally to designate the members of tribes other than the Bakongo who lived and worked in the city.

tion Kwango-Kwiloise and the Fédération Kasaïenne, whose members were recruited exclusively from expatriate elements of the tribes located in the Kwango-Kwilu area and Kasai Province, respectively. Although membership in these groups was determined by regional criteria, their internal organization was based entirely on tribal affiliations. The Fédération Kasaïenne, for example, included in its membership some thirty different *associations primaires* based on kinship and tribal ties. On the whole, therefore, these associations were not so much the expression of residential affiliations as of aggregated tribal loyalties.

A third major type of association was the club d'évolués, whose membership was restricted to Westernized elements somewhat loosely referred to as "detribalized." Its over-all objectives, as described in the statutes of the Association des Evolués de Stanleyville, were to "create an atmosphere of understanding and solidarity among its members, to organize their leisure according to their level of education, and to improve their intellectual, social, moral, and physical lives." [15] In other words, here there is the same diffuseness of objectives which characterized tribal and regional associations, but with the major difference that the principal motive for joining a club d'évolués was to transcend the pale of tribal and ethnic loyalties and seek reintegration through a broader ordering of human relationships.

Other associations were organized to perform specialized functions for their members. Because of its limited potentialities, however, this form of activity aroused little enthusiasm among the Congolese masses. By 1956, for example, Congolese trade unions claimed a total membership of 8,829, or less than 1 per cent of the estimated labor force at the time.[16] In fact, rather than the trade unions per se it was their satellite organizations—*amicales, cercles,* study groups, and so on—which became the main nuclei of political activity.

Many of these associations proved to be short-lived, but others developed into powerful pressure organizations. By agitating in favor of economic concessions, sponsoring motions to local advisory councils, and "advising" the administration on the choice of customary chiefs, they performed a variety of important functions, while at the same time serving as informal training grounds for future political leaders. Indeed, in such arenas men like Lumumba, Kasavubu, Jean Bolikango, and many others learned the basic skills of the practicing politician.

Moreover, just as they differed in their objectives and orientations, these associations have conditioned the outlook and behavior of Congolese leaders in different ways. Because tribal and ethnic associations

---

[15] *La Voix du Congolais,* no. 65 (Aug., 1951), 466.
[16] *Rapport sur l'Administration de la colonie en 1956* (Brussels, 1957), p. 100.

emphasized the pervasiveness of cultural affinities, their leaders were naturally inclined to organize ethnic parties once they had the opportunity to do so. In contrast, nontribal associations have usually furnished the leadership cadres of broadly based, panterritorial parties. Among the more prominent leaders who served their apprenticeship in a club d'évolués were Patrice Lumumba, at one time chairman of the Association des Evolués de Stanleyville; Jean-Chrysostome Weregemere, president of the Cercle des Evolués de Costermansville (now Bukavu); and Cléophas Kamitatu, once a leading personality in the Cercle des Evolués de Kikwit.

Finally, to the extent that some of these associations were identified with metropolitan parties and interest groups, they were occasionally used by Africans to enlist the support of Belgian politicians against the administration. And, at a later stage, many Congolese leaders used these "connections" to strengthen their position vis-à-vis their competitors. Although these links were usually established for reasons of expediency, they sometimes led to active organizational collaboration between Congolese leaders and metropolitan interest groups.

In any event, whether these associations simply politicized themselves by attaching party labels to their names, as the Abako did, or served as building blocks for the development of broadly based parties, as the Association des Bangala did, their formative influence cannot be overlooked. Not only did they shape the political perspectives and orientation of Congolese leaders, but they also provided the basic organizational matrix from which most Congolese parties evolved.

DISPERSION OF POLITICAL FORCES

A rather widespread stereotype among outside observers is that the history of Congolese political parties may be reduced to a sequence of tribal and ethnic antagonisms steadily increasing in intensity and widening in scope. Although such antagonisms are certainly the most conspicuous feature of the Congolese scene, they are not the only form in which political conflicts have found expression. Intergroup tensions have also led to the emergence of parties that became vehicles for and symbols of regional loyalties, a phenomenon somewhat loosely referred to as "regionalism." Indeed, the essence of Congolese politics is the continuing opposition between the powerful centrifugal forces of ethnicity and regionalism on the one hand, and the still very weak forces of national integration on the other.

The scope of this chapter does not permit a detailed examination of the origins and the development of all Congolese parties. The discussion will be limited to the main developmental trends in the growth of party activities in the period preceding independence.

Emergence of Ethnic Nationalism

Although intergroup rivalries were widespread throughout the Congo long before the introduction of electoral processes, they were markedly heightened by the municipal elections of December, 1957. In both Leopoldville and Elisabethville political parties were organized on the basis of ethnic or regional loyalties, and existing tribal and regional associations became highly politicized. In Leopoldville, where the Abako swept eight of the ten posts of bourgmestre, the Bangala reacted by organizing the Fédération des Bangala, a party based exclusively, like the association from which it originated, on the presumed solidarity of the Bangala of Leopoldville. Similarly, in Elisabethville the victory scored by Kasaian immigrants of Baluba origin prompted the leaders of several associations of tribes indigenous to the Katanga to form a coalition called the Confédération des Associations Tribales du Katanga, better known as Conakat. With the extension of the Statut des Villes to other towns in 1958, a somewhat similar situation developed between the Lulua and Baluba tribes of Luluabourg (Kasai). There the Association Lulua-Frères—a tribal organization aggregating the interests of the Lulua—won a decisive victory over the Baluba. As elsewhere in the Congo, this tribal challenge was met with a tribal response; in the early part of 1959 the leaders of several kinship associations of Luluabourg founded the Mouvement Solidaire Muluba (MSM), which attracted the overwhelming majority of the Baluba of Luluabourg.[17]

Meanwhile, the government's declaration of January, 1959, announcing substantial constitutional reforms, gave a fresh impetus to party activity. As the prospects of independence finally entered their vision, certain leaders sought to consolidate their bases of support through the amalgamation of tribally heterogeneous groups within the same party organization. Their efforts, however, were inevitably frustrated by a near-universal tendency on the part of the Congolese elites to use their tribal bases as steppingstones to positions of leadership.

The effect of the twin processes of consolidation and fragmentation on the growth of Congolese parties is perhaps best illustrated by the different leadership positions assumed by the Bangala leader, Jean Bolikango, in the early phase of his political career. First he was the leader of the Fédération des Bangala. Then, early in 1958, he tried to organize a broadly based, interethnic political party (the Interfédérale) which would incorporate several tribal and regional associations of Leopoldville: the Fédération des Bangala, the Fédération Kwango-Kwiloise, the Fédération Kasaïenne, the Fédération des Basonge, the Fédération des Bateke,

---

[17] For an excellent case study of the Luluabourg elections, see A. Kalanda, "A propos du Régime communal au Congo: La consultation de Luluabourg," *Mouvement Communal*, no. 332 (Sept., 1959), 418–427.

and other similar groups. No sooner had the party been constituted, however, than it commenced to disintegrate under the centrifugal pressures of its ethnic and regional organizational components. In March, 1958, the Association des Batetela and the Association des Basonge bolted the party to form, respectively, the Fédération des Batetela (Fedebate) and the Parti de l'Unité Basonge. Then, in April, 1959, the leaders of the Fédération Kwango-Kwiloise formally announced their intention to withdraw from the party on the ground that "they disapproved of the procedure through which they had become affiliated with the Interfédérale." [18] Ultimately, the Fédération Kwango-Kwiloise itself split up into three contending groups: (1) the Parti Solidaire Africain (PSA), which drew its support from a number of small tribal entities of the Kwilu region (Bambala, Bapende, Babunda, Lampuku, etc.); (2) the Union Kwangolaise pour l'Indépendance et la Liberté, which rallied the support of the Bayaka of the Kwango; and (3) the Alliance des Bayanzi (Abazi), identified with the Bayanzi people of the Kwango. Finally, faced with these defections, Bolikango was forced to return to his own group of origin for his political support. This led to the creation of the Front d'Unité Bangala, whose strength was largely restricted to Leopoldville.

These organizational manifestations of centrifugal tendencies were in part the result of the extreme competition precipitated and exacerbated by the approach of independence. The prospect of self-government led many Congolese politicians to appeal to their own people in order to find a secure political base and thereby maximize their electoral chances. Yet in part the gravitational pull of ethnicity was a manifestation of deeper aspirations. It was evidence of a genuine desire on the part of some Congolese leaders to inculcate respect for and pride in the cultural, linguistic, and historical heritage of the group they claimed to represent.

The Abako demonstrates, perhaps better than any other party, the pervasive influence of traditional culture and institutions on the growth of Congolese parties. From the very beginning of its existence the Abako sought to provide a common cultural focus for the loyalties and the aspirations of its members. Once transformed into a political party, however, it represented far more than a mere attempt at cultural revival. From then on its ultimate political objective was the erection of an autonomous Bakongo state coterminous with the boundaries of the old Kongo Kingdom, which meant that the Bakongo peoples—presently divided among Angola, the Congo, and the former French Moyen-Congo—would eventually become reintegrated within a single territorial unit. This, at least, was the ideal implicit in the succinct formula coined by one Abakiste: "L'Abako c'est l'union rétablie." [19]

---

[18] *Courrier d'Afrique*, April 7, 1959.
[19] *Salut du Peuple par l'Abako* (Leopoldville, n.d.), p. 9.

A corollary Abako objective, according to the party leaders, was the revival of certain sociopolitical institutions—above all, the kinship system —of the traditional Bakongo society. Just as authority was traditionally structured around the clan (*kanda*), so membership in a clan was regarded by the Abako as the only badge of citizenship among the Bakongo.[20] Equally striking was the emphasis placed on the principle of kingship, which served both to underwrite the authority of the party leader, Kasavubu, and to define his role in the future Bakongo polity. Indeed, that Kasavubu was consciously recognized as a modern version of the king (*ntotila*) is clearly evidenced by the numerous litanies devoted by the official organ of the party, *Kongo Dieto*, to "King Kasa's tenacity, courage, wisdom, calm, intelligence, and comprehension," virtues that were traditionally identified with the king's personality.

The use of traditional symbols of authority also encouraged the Bakongo masses to appreciate the values of traditional society. The ubiquitous display of the *kodia*, which is both the emblem of the party and a symbol of ancestral virtues, is an illustration. At the same time, however, the magico-religious properties attributed to the kodia tended to reflect the spirit of messianism which so strongly characterized the predispositions of the Bakongo masses during the colonial period.[21] This combination of secular and magico-religious features is in itself indicative of the highly complex, syncretistic nature of the Bakongo nationalist movement.

Yet, despite its emphasis on traditionalism, the Abako was not fundamentally opposed to all forms of innovation. Like most pantribal movements, it represented a curious blend of traditional and modernist strains, a coalescence of the old and the new. This kind of eclecticism was clearly brought out by members of the Central Committee: "L'Abakisme est une tendence nationaliste qui cherche à grouper des personnes ayant une même origine, une même histoire, et des traditions, des coutumes communes, patrimoine des ancêtres, *aux fins de sauvegarder la culture africaine et de l'améliorer.*" [22] In other words, the ideal of the Abako was to adapt the cultural heritage of the Bakongo to the requirements of the modern nation-state system, while at the same time retaining the fundamental institutions of indigenous social life.

This ideal found its clearest expression in a draft constitution, issued by the Abako in June, 1959, for a projected state to be called the Republic of Central Kongo. According to this document, the province of

---

[20] See *Kongo Dieto*, Nov. 14, 1959.

[21] For fuller information on this particular aspect of the Bakongo nationalist movement, see my article, "The Bases of Nationalism among the Bakongo," *Africa*, XXXI (Oct., 1961), 344–354.

[22] *Statuts de la République du Congo Central* (Leopoldville, 1960), p. 1 (italics added).

Leopoldville was to be organized into an autonomous "democratic and social republic." Its "national" territory was to be divided into five provinces, roughly coinciding with the existing districts, and each province was to be divided into territories and communes.[23] Executive authority was to be vested in the hands of a popularly elected president, who would be assisted by a bicameral legislature elected by universal suffrage. In other words, the "Kongolese nation" was here envisaged as a sovereign state, operating under its own constitution and according to its own laws.

Actually, the brand of separatism advocated by the Abako leaders may not have been so extreme as the foregoing document suggests. According to Van Bilsen, "the Abako did not seek to secede à la Tschombe, but to obtain the constitution of a Bakongo province. . . . Messrs. Diomi, Yumbu and others were by no means separatists."[24] Whether the leadership of the Abako was at the time committed to secession or to provincial autonomy is open to question. But there can be little doubt that the feelings and the expectations of the Bakongo masses were in complete harmony with the separatist ideas expressed by the Abako.

A variety of factors have combined to give the Bakongo nationalist movement its distinctive cohesion, as well as its petulance and aggressiveness. The very size of the Bakongo "culture cluster," the centralized character of its precolonial institutions, and the contiguity of the Bakongo traditional habitat have all contributed to foster a strong sense of pantribal allegiance among the Bakongo peoples. This type of ethnic nationalism, however, is also found, albeit in a more diluted form, among certain other groups which did not necessarily share all these characteristics (e.g., the Baluba, the Mongo, and the Bayaka). What must be stressed here is that the persistence of ethnic loyalties among the present and emergent generations of Congolese politicians has provided one of the most enduring and cohesive bases for the organization of political groups.

Panterritorial Nationalism: The Mouvement National Congolais

Of the several political groups that aimed at the creation of a single national movement, the Mouvement National Congolais (MNC) was by far the most significant. Its origins may be traced back to November, 1956, when, shortly after publication of the manifesto of *Conscience Africaine*, its authors announced the creation of a national movement to "lead the Congolese toward the consciousness of their national unity and

---

[23] The text of the draft constitution of the Republic of Central Kongo may be found in *Abako: 1950–1960* (Brussels: Centre de Recherche et d'Information Socio-Politiques [CRISP], 1962), pp. 315–340.

[24] Personal communication.

responsibilities, to pursue the emancipation of their country, and to make the Congolese nation a living reality based on the equality of races, mutual respect, and justice." [25] At first, and contrary to what might have been expected, this announcement stirred little enthusiasm among the African population. In Leopoldville, where the rivalry between Bakongo and Bangala had already come into focus, the appeal of the new movement was limited to a small group of African literati identified, for the most part, with the Catholic Church. And where ethnic polarities were not so acute its fame was largely overshadowed by that of the Abako, justly considered after 1956, for reasons previously noted, as the only really militant nationalist organization.

It was not until the fall of 1958 that the MNC began to gather momentum. In October, on the occasion of the visit of the *groupe de travail* appointed by the Belgian government for the purpose of "conducting an inquiry into the aspirations of the inhabitants of the Congo," a group of Congolese of Leopoldville formally announced the creation of a new MNC. Although the maintenance of national unity was still the paramount objective, the terms on which independence was to be granted had become characteristically less compromising. Furthermore, its membership was no longer confined to a mere handful of intellectuals but included a substantial number of dedicated nationalists, drawn largely from trade-union organizations. Finally, its leadership had changed hands. With the arrival in Leopoldville of Patrice Lumumba, the MNC was converted into a tightly knit, militant nationalist organization, in many respects similar to those fashioned by Kwame Nkrumah, Sékou Touré, and Julius Nyerere to wrest independence from the colonial powers.

As the organizational development and the ideology of the MNC are largely reflections of Lumumba's efforts and personality, it may be of some value to consider how he visualized his role as a national leader. Probably the most salient feature of Lumumba's personality was his profound aversion to all forms of particularism, and above all ethnic particularism. On April 13, 1958, in a speech to the Fédération des Batetela, Lumumba urged its members to "liquidate all ethnic antagonisms and [to seek] the *rapprochement* of all, regardless of origin, class, or fortune." [26] Citing Jacques Maritain's statement that "the common good is the basis of authority," he insisted that it was the duty of all the Batetela "to promote the union of all, . . . to reject all forms of reactionary nationalism, and opt instead for an intelligent nationalism which is nothing

[25] *Conscience Africaine*, Nov., 1956.

[26] "Conférence donnée le 13 Avril 1958 aux membres de la Fédération des Batetela par Monsieur Lumumba, Conseiller Permanent" (mimeographed; Leopoldville, n.d.).

but the love of one's country." It was the pursuit of this same objective —the creation of "a new, organized, integrated society," to use Lumumba's own words—which, a few months later, led him to join the MNC.

But Lumumba's dedication to a single national, supratribal movement did not imply rejection of the values of African culture. As conscious as he was of the need to transcend the purview of ethnic particularisms, he also realized that the future could not, and should not, be separated from the past, and that the new political order could not be entirely divorced from the context of African culture. More specifically, what Lumumba sought to achieve was "the transformation of the typically African cultures of the past into a new, Neo-African culture, drawing its inspiration from the old principles, and retaining the distinctive genius [*le génie propre*] of the African peoples." [27] As he explained, "we do not want these ancestral traditions to remain fixed in their archaic mold, but on the other hand we do not want a slavish copy of European civilization. What we want is to improve and perfect our own culture by adding to it certain elements of European civilization." We find here an echo of some well-known Pan-African themes, in particular an insistence on the uniqueness of African culture and a conviction that the political institutions of independent Africa must be adapted to the context of African traditions.

Another highly relevant aspect of Lumumba's personality was the charismatic quality of his messianic fervor and the flamboyant radicalism that characterized his leadership. As the MNC leader he had an extraordinary appeal among certain segments of the African population. Indeed, his great success as a national leader was due not so much to his organizing genius and his adeptness at tactical maneuverings, vital as these qualities were, as it was to the image he created of himself as a messiahlike leader. These were critical elements in the mobilization of the support of a large segment of the Congolese population by the MNC.

On the other hand, as a consequence of his efforts to play the role of a demiurge, Lumumba tended increasingly to arrogate to himself unfettered control over the affairs of the party, thereby antagonizing many of his followers. There was a major split in the leadership of the party in July, 1959, when Joseph Ileo, Cyrille Adoula, and Joseph Ngalula decided to organize a separate wing. This became known as the MNC-Kalonji, although Albert Kalonji was not directly involved in the crisis of July, 1959. His subsequent endorsement of a federal formula was the symptom, rather than the cause, of more fundamental differences within the leadership of the party. At the root of the controversy between the

---

[27] *Ibid.*

two groups lay two basically divergent conceptions of the process of decision making within the party: Lumumba's adamant insistence upon the need for a highly centralized party organization, and the equally emphatic belief by the dissident wing in a more flexible, collegial, and democratic pattern.

The effect of this rift on subsequent developments was profound. It not only deprived the party of some of its ablest elements, but it also substantially limited its potential territorial spread. In the Katanga, where a provincial branch of the MNC had already been established, the conflict divided the party into hardly reconcilable factions. In the Equateur the MNC underwent similar convulsions. And in the Kasai Lumumba's party lost the support of almost the entire Baluba population. These defections underline the close ties of ethnic solidarity which linked the leadership of the Leopoldville organization to that of its provincial branches. In fact, the split was to bring renewed intensity to the competitive struggle among certain ethnic groups. For example, Kalonji's commitment to the "moderate" views of Ileo and Ngalula did not prevent him from seeking the support of his own people, the Baluba of the Kasai. And as the Kalonji wing of the MNC came to identify itself with the cause of the Baluba, the Lumumba wing responded by throwing its weight behind the Lulua, thereby aggravating a tribal feud that had already assumed explosive force.

From then on the strategy of the MNC revealed a striking lack of consistency with its professed objectives. For example, at the Lodja Congress (March 9–12, 1960) Lumumba did not hesitate to capitalize on his ethnic origins to win over the support of the Batetela-Bakusu populations of the Congo. Although one of the declared objectives of the congress was to "minimize and if at all possible to destroy tribal tendencies," its immediate goals were to awaken a sense of group consciousness among the delegates; to make them aware of the social, economic, and educational needs of the Batetela-Bakusu people; and to relate these to the political goals of the MNC.[28] In effect, then, by bringing closer together a group of culturally related tribes, the MNC leader became the unwitting inspirer of tribalism, the very evil that he so loudly condemned.

In fact, a major weakness of the MNC was that a substantial segment of its following, notably in the Kasai, joined it for ethnic reasons, or for tactical convenience, or both. Another weakness was its heavy dependence upon Lumumba's own charismatic personality. That Lumumba's "heroic" leadership was no substitute for a national conscience was clearly demonstrated by the internal dissensions that wrecked the party once its leader had disappeared from the political scene.

---

[28] See *Le Congrès de Lodja* (Lodja, n.d.), p. 12.

Regional Separatism: The Katanga Secession

The separatist nationalism that ultimately led to the secession of Katanga Province evolved from a highly complex and rapidly changing situation which, at the outset, involved two major sources of disunity: (1) the presence of a politically conscious, anti-integration settler community, and (2) a relatively high concentration of Kasaian immigrants in the main urban centers of the province. Although these communities have affected the balance of forces in the Katanga in different ways and through different means, their respective roles cannot be understood independently from each other.

From the early days of Belgian colonial rule, the settlers of the Katanga displayed a distinctive brand of parochialism, characterized by a conspicuous distaste for all measures or institutions that smacked of centralization. In their efforts to gain a degree of provincial autonomy they relentlessly emphasized the imperative need to transform the Katanga into an autonomous entity enjoying dominion status under white supremacy; this goal, they said, was not only desirable from the standpoint of administrative efficiency, but indispensable to the establishment of mutually satisfactory relations between whites and blacks.

As long as the metropolitan government remained in full control of the situation, these efforts were ineffectual. But once challenged for supremacy by the burgeoning forces of African nationalism, the white-settler oligarchy of the Katanga opted for an independent course of action, and in May, 1958, organized the Union Katangaise. This party, as the name suggests, aimed at the constitution of a "genuine and multiracial Katangese community." [29] In the following weeks this theme gained widespread support, not only among the white settlers, but also among a substantial segment of the native population of the Katanga.

To understand how this identity of interest came about, we must refer to the social and political consequences of the distinctive pattern of economic development in the Katanga. Broadly speaking, the bases of Katangese separatism among Africans were the economic grievances of certain indigenous tribes of the Katanga toward immigrants from the Kasai, mostly Baluba in origin. As the immigrants were the main beneficiaries of the economic and job opportunities available in the province, their presence aroused widespread anti-Baluba feelings among urban Africans who regarded themselves as genuine Katangese. After the elections of December, 1957, the latter became increasingly resentful of the dominance of the immigrant Kasaian middle classes in the municipal

---

[29] For a discussion of settler politics in the Katanga, see my article, "The Limits of Self-Determination: The Case of the Katanga Secession," *American Political Science Review*, LVI (June, 1962), 404–416.

councils of Elisabethville. It was the decision to resist the inroads of these alien tribes that led the indigenous Katangese, in November, 1958, to organize the Conakat. Under the leadership of Godefroid Munongo and Moise Tshombe, the Conakat soon asserted itself as the stanchest advocate of provincial autonomy.

Despite subsequent evidence to the contrary, the attitude of Conakat leaders toward the white settlers was anything but accommodating. At one point they openly criticized the provincial authorities for allowing "an ever-increasing number" of Kasaian elements to reside in the province, calling attention to the "flagrant injustices" committed by the administration.[30] At the same time they vehemently denied that they had any separatist leanings, and insisted that their only wish was to terminate the role of "second-class citizens" hitherto played by the Katangese. This claim, however, was seriously open to question after May, 1959, when the Conakat suddenly decided to enter into an alliance with the Union Katangaise.

A number of circumstantial factors confirmed the impression that the alliance was little more than a marriage of reason. Indeed, after the government's declaration of January, 1959, few Europeans could reasonably expect the Katanga to become a bastion of white supremacy, at least in the form that was initially contemplated. Furthermore, the resolutions adopted at the first congress of Congolese parties, held in Luluabourg in April, 1959, made it quite plain that the Katanga would in all likelihood enjoy even less autonomy under a centralist Congolese government than it ever did before independence. For the so-called "genuine Katangese," on the other hand, the dominant position assumed by the MNC during the congress carried ominous implications. It conjured up the threat not only of "alien domination," but of Baluba domination, because at the time the top leadership of the MNC consisted essentially of Baluba elements. In brief, the alliance could not fail to benefit both sides even though some Katangese Africans viewed it as nothing short of an act of treason on the part of the Conakat leaders.

Actually, the alliance caused an increasing polarization of sentiment, not only between the Conakat and its political rivals but also within the party itself. This culminated in the defection in November, 1959, of one of the Conakat's most important constituent groups, the Association des Baluba du Katanga (Balubakat), led by Jason Sendwe. Like many other Katangese, Sendwe opposed the merger of the Conakat with the Union Katangaise because the latter's leadership was entirely made up of individuals whose reputation as "white supremacists" was already firmly established. Moreover, the campaign of ever-increasing invective launched by the Conakat against the Baluba of Kasai ultimately

---

[30] See *Etoile-Nyota*, Jan. 8, 1959.

provoked resentment among the Baluba of the Katanga. Although there are substantial cultural differences between the two Baluba groups, and although some Katangese Baluba shared the general Katangese economic grievances against the Kasai immigrants, they could not remain indifferent to the mounting anti-Baluba activities of the Conakat. At any rate, the withdrawal of the Balubakat sharply altered the balance of political forces in the Katanga. For one thing, it narrowed the potential territorial spread of the Conakat, whose influence was thereby limited to the southern districts of the province. Second, after the formation of the Cartel Katangais in November, 1959, which included in its membership the Tshokwe of the Katanga and the Baluba of both Kasai and Katanga provinces, the main lines of cleavage were no longer drawn between genuine Katangese and immigrants, but between Baluba and Tshokwe on the one hand, and the remaining tribes on the other.[31] Finally, it precipitated new identifications between metropolitan or colonial interest groups and Congolese parties.

Long before this crisis occurred, however, close personal contacts had been established between certain African leaders in the Katanga and Belgians associated with the anticlerical Left, especially with the Belgian Socialist Party (PSB) and the Belgian Liberal Party (PLB). Whether they served as functionaries in the provincial administration, as social workers in one of the *foyers sociaux* of Elisabethville, or as administrators at the Université Officielle, these Belgians had all been appointed to their positions under the Liberal ministry of Auguste Buisseret (1954–1958). Before the mid-1950's the influence of the Belgian Left on the attitude of the Katanga leaders was not nearly so conspicuous or so effective as that of the colonat.[32] After the break between the Conakat and the Balubakat, the rivalry between the Conakat and the Cartel Katangais and the influences of resident Europeans of both Right and Left on African politics assumed significant proportions. Those of the Left supported the Cartel Katangais, some of them assuming the role of *conseiller technique* or acting as intermediaries between certain metropolitan pressure groups and the Katanga. The Conakat, on the other hand, could count on the active support of the colonat as well as on the financial backing of such powerful corporate interests as the Union Minière du Haut Katanga (UMHK) and the Société Générale de

---

[31] The Cartel Katangais included, besides the Balubakat, the Association des Tshokwe du Congo, de l'Angola et de la Rhodesie, led by Ambroise Muhunga, and the Fédération Kasaïenne, led by Isaac Kalonji and representing the interests of the Baluba of the Kasai residing in the Katanga.

[32] It was presumably to counteract the influence of Socialist pressure groups and personalities that late in 1957 a Belgian lawyer, Antoine Rubbens, launched the Union Congolaise, a party in which "Congolese nationalism and Christian Social doctrines were intermingled with Socialist ideas" (see A. Rubbens, "Political Awakening in the Belgian Congo," *Civilisations*, X, no. 1 [1960], 66).

582 Congo (Leopoldville)

Belgique (SGB).[33] Moreover, the Conakat, unlike its rival, enjoyed the organizational collaboration and the technical assistance of the provincial administration. It was through these various linkages and connections that the Conakat derived the moral, financial, and logistic support that made the secession of the province both attractive and feasible.

In sum, external influences intruding upon the Katangese scene aggravated the situation of nonintegration created by ethnic and sectional antagonisms. Because the competition among parties provided an outlet for the expression of personal and ideological rivalries between European conservatives and liberals, or clericals and anticlericals, the Katangese leaders have been led to adopt far more intransigent stands on concrete issues than they might otherwise have done. Second, the financial and material support given to Katangese separatists via the colonat and European expatriate enterprises enhanced their position out of all proportion to their actual degree of popular support. For these reasons Katangese separatism is as much a product of Belgian pressure-group politics as an expression of basic incompatibility among the several indigenous African groups of the Katanga.

ORGANIZATION OF CONGOLESE PARTIES

Before we turn to an examination of the structure of Congolese political groups, at least two important caveats must be entered. First, comparison of the rather amorphous, unstructured, and short-lived Congolese parties with the older and more fully developed parties in many other African territories, in terms of structural regularities, is of somewhat questionable value. Moreover, many Congolese parties, at one time or another, underwent a radical structural transformation, either because of internal dissensions, or simply because their leaders felt the need to build a more effective or a different type of organization. Therefore, any attempt at classification must necessarily be tentative.

Types of Congolese Parties

The uniqueness of Congolese parties, in their multiplicity and their structural properties, does not mean that they do not have certain features in common with political parties elsewhere in Africa. Thomas Hodgkin's classic distinction between "mass" parties and "elite" or "patron" parties is applicable to at least some of the Congolese parties, even if these distinguishing marks are found only in embryonic form.[34] However different

---

[33] The Conakat, however, was not the only party that benefited from the campaign funds made available by the SGB. Commenting upon the financial aid extended to Congolese parties by "Belgian institutions with important moral and material stakes in the Katanga," Jules Gérard-Libois notes that "the paradox lies in the fact that the Belgian source remained the same" and that "only the channels were different" (*Etudes Congolaises*, no. 1 [March, 1961], 38).

[34] See Thomas Hodgkin, *African Political Parties* (Penguin Books, 1961), p. 69.

in goals and orientation, parties like the MNC, the PSA, the Centre de Regroupement Africain (Cerea), and the Abako all tended to take on the characteristics of popular movements approximating mass parties in structural properties. On the other hand, the Parti du Régent Abraham Lwanwa de Ngweshe (Reco) and the Alliance Rurale Progressiste (ARP) in Kivu Province, the Parti Travailliste in Leopoldville Province, and the Parti Traditionaliste and the Mouvement de l'Evolution Rurale pour le Congo (Mederco) in Equateur Province were little more than conclaves of local notabilities, and consequently never had a strong grass-roots appeal for the African masses. Even the Parti National du Progrès (PNP), which at one time established branch organizations in several provinces, was neither national in scope nor progressive in character, but consisted rather of dispersed clusters of factional interests based on ethnic and sectional ties.

Yet Congolese parties differed markedly from one another, and those that were nationwide differed from province to province, in the extent to which they could fit into either one of Hodgkin's two categories. For example, no group achieved so much structural cohesiveness and internal discipline as the Abako; and the MNC-Lumumba, though more like a mass party in Orientale Province than either the Cerea or the PSA, in Leopoldville Province could hardly be described in those terms. Some parties were both mass and elite, depending on their field of operation. In some urban areas of the Katanga, for example, the Conakat functioned as a mass party, but in the countryside, where its influence depended largely on the support of customary chiefs, it assumed the character of an elite party.

In the Congo, the claim to authority of mass-party leaders tended to be legitimated through charisma. This does not mean that all of them possessed the same type of charisma. Some, like Kasavubu, had a charismatic appeal only within a particular ethnic group (the Bakongo) whereas Lumumba was able to claim a Congo-wide charismatic legitimacy. In elite parties, however, claims to authority stemmed from the acceptance of traditional norms, that is, from "piety for what actually, allegedly or presumably has always existed." [35] The PNP leaders, for example, repeatedly emphasized their devotion to ancestral patterns of authority, and bitterly criticized any departure from these time-honored customs. As one of them pointed out in November, 1959: "Naguère au village quand il fallait prendre une décision lourde de conséquence, on écoutait le chef et les notables, et puis les villageois venaient lui donner raison ou évoquer d'autres arguments. Aujourd'hui nous constatons que

---

[35] See H. Gerth and G. W. Mills, eds., *From Max Weber: Essays in Sociology* (London: Oxford University Press, 1946), p. 79.

certains de nos frères ont oublié le leçon de leur jeunesse." [36] According to this view authority is legitimized by the fact that it has always been so, and will continue to remain so in the future social order.

Another significant difference between the Congo versions of elite and mass parties concerns the social origins of their respective leaders. As might be expected of individuals who placed so high a premium on tradition, the leaders of elite parties were usually recruited among customary or appointed chiefs—*chefs de secteur, chefs de territoire,* and so on—or from the membership of advisory councils. Of twenty-four Congolese who served on the Conseil de Gouvernement from 1957 to 1959, nine became identified with elite parties. Among them, Antoine Lopes, Sylvestre Mundingay, and André Edindali became vice-presidents of the PNP; André Anekonzapa became the founder and self-appointed leader of the Mederco; and Abraham Lwanwa founded a prosettler party, the Reco, in the Kivu.[37]

In contrast, the leaders of Congolese mass parties were usually recruited from discontented elements who felt that they had something to gain and nothing to lose from the termination of colonial rule. Clerks employed in the *secteur privé* constituted one important social category from which they were drawn. Among the more prominent leaders who came from this class were Patrice Lumumba; Albert Kalonji; Isaac Kalonji, founder of the Fédération Kasaïenne (Fedeka); Sylvain Kama, founder of the PSA; and Anicet Kashamura, secretary-general of the Cerea. Unencumbered by the restrictions placed on government clerks, they became involved in nationalist activities at a much earlier date than did African employees of the colonial administration, who were reluctant to join the nationalist crusade lest they lose their jobs.[38] By April, 1959, however, twenty-one *agents de la quatrième catégorie*[39] had applied for a *mise en disponibilité* and resigned their positions. Among them were Justin Bomboko, founder of the Union Mongo (Unimo); Sébastien Kini, founder of the short-lived Parti Démocratique Congolais (PDC); and several others who reached prominent positions in the MNC-Lumumba.[40]

---

[36] *Mbandaka* (Coquilhatville), Nov. 14, 1959.

[37] See *L'Echo du Kivu,* March 22, 1960.

[38] Evaluating the effect of these restrictions on the growth of political parties in Equateur Province, one Congolese journalist observed: "L'inexistence de partis ou de mouvements politiques est due au fait que la majorité des intellectuels de Coquilhatville oeuvrent dans l'administration. Or il ressort que ceux-ci, de par leur fonction d'agents de l'administration, se voient frustrés une fois reconnues leurs activités politiques; ils deviennent les souffre-douleurs, les boucs émissaires du service, traqués par tous les moyens mis à la disposition des chefs de service" (*Cuvette Centrale* [Coquilhatville], May 15, 1959).

[39] In official Belgian terminology, this category included *commis principaux* and *rédacteurs* employed in the colonial bureaucracy. Until the Statut Unique was enacted in January, 1959, this was the highest position to which a Congolese could aspire.

[40] *La Voix du Congolais,* Supplement (April, 1959).

Medical assistants constituted a third group from which mass parties recruited some of their cadres. Because of their training they were expected to play a variety of roles which predisposed them to seek positions of leadership; because of their low wages and perquisites they felt the effects of racial discrimination more acutely than any other group. Moreover, their exposure to a broad education in liberal arts made them particularly receptive to the appeal of nationalism. Two of the most able members of the provisional Executive Committee set up by the MNC in 1958, Gaston Diomi and Martin Ngwete, had been employed as medical assistants. A final category is that of former seminarians who, for one reason or another, abandoned the priesthood to join the nationalists. Seven of the ten members of the PSA's Central Committee had at one time attended a seminary. Edmond Nzeza-Landu, founder of the Abako, is a product of the Seminary of Mayidi, and its chairman, Kasavubu, spent three years at the Seminary of Kabwe. Despite their different social backgrounds, these leaders all shared a common urge to bring about a radical transformation in the *status quo.*

Elite and mass parties also differed in the degree to which rank-and-file members submitted to party directives. Unlike elite parties, which tended to be rather loosely organized and comparatively undisciplined, mass parties did not hesitate to root out deviationist elements. Just how effective some of them actually were in maintaining party discipline is indicated by the percentage of members who voted or failed to vote in the communal elections of December, 1959. In predominantly Bakongo areas the overwhelming majority of the African population, in conformity with directives issued by the Abako, abstained from voting. In Matadi, for instance, 98.27 per cent of the qualified voters stayed away from the polls, and in some villages, such as Luozi, Songololo, and Madimba, the figure reached 100 per cent.[41] The same rigorous discipline was shown by the MNC-Lumumba in Orientale Province, where its last-minute decision to participate in the elections was carefully heeded by the rank and file. In the Kasai, however, the boycott advocated by the Kalonji wing of the MNC was not uniformly observed. In Luluabourg, for example, where the MNC-Kalonji polled twice as many votes as its nearest opponent (the Union Congolaise), the electoral participation of the Baluba was just as high as that of the Lulua. Like the Balubakat in the Katanga and the Lulua-Frères in the Kasai, the MNC-Kalonji never managed to instill in its members a strong sense of party discipline, not so much because its organization was deficient or its communication system inadequate, but mainly because its leadership was unable to cope with ethnic tensions. The organizational laxity of the PNP, the Parti de l'Unité Nationale (Puna), the ARP, the Rassemblement Démocratique du Lac, Kwango et

---

[41] *Courrier Africain* (published by CRISP), Jan. 22, 1960, p. 7.

Kwilu (RDLK), the Abazi, and similar elite parties stemmed from their comparatively weak articulation and loose structuring.

The foregoing survey suggests that the general contours of Congolese parties are best delineated by reference to the sources of authority and the social origins of their leadership, as well as by the degree of commitment of their members. At one end of the scale are parties like the Abako, the MNC, the Cerea, and the PSA, which tended in the direction of tightly knit mass organizations; at the opposite extreme, parties like the ARP, the Reco, and the PNP resembled electoral machines functioning at the beck and call of local personalities whose prestige and influence depended on their accommodation to the established order. A middle category, represented by the Conakat, the MNC-Kalonji, and the Lulua-Frères, assumed the character of mass parties in urban areas and of elite parties in the countryside. As we shall see, these differences suggest corresponding variations in the distribution of power within the party hierarchy.

Internal Party Organization

Few parties succeeded in developing a strong internal organizational structure. Except for the Abako, no Congolese parties effectively penetrated the rural areas until the elections of December, 1959. The usual form of organizational structure at the local level was cellular, with sections and subsections reaching down from the urban communes to *chefferies* and villages. Most of the units were organized on the basis of existing administrative subdivisions. In the Lower Congo, for example, the Abako set up local sections, known as *cellules-mères* after 1959, in each *secteur,* and by November, 1959, regional sections, designated alternatively as *sections régionales, sections territoriales,* or *fédérations,* were added in each territory for purposes of coördination.[42] In the towns, the *sections communales* functioned as the primary units. National parties, or parties that aspired to build a national organization, also established intermediary links in the provincial capitals in the form of provincial branches, each one directed by a *comité provincial.*

At the central level, despite wide variations in formal organization, Congolese parties tended to fall into two distinctive categories. One, consisting of mass parties, featured a central committee or a political bureau, a small nucleus of party officials to whom all other functional bodies and field units were subordinated. The central position in this body was occupied by the president who, in theory at least, enjoyed full control over the affairs of the party. The other, comprising elite parties, permitted greater flexibility in decision-making processes, usually through the use of a collegial device. After the MNC split in July, 1959, as a safe-

---

[42] *Ibid.*

guard against the recurrence of similar crises, the presidency of the MNC-Kalonji was assumed by a collegial body composed of the heads of the party's functional committees. Instead of using the collegial plan, some parties, in an effort to satisfy the aspirations of different ethnic groups, adopted a system of rotation. In the Interfédérale, for example, the presidency was to be held alternatively for one-year terms by each of the presidents of the tribal associations incorporated into the party. Another formula was to create as many positions as could reasonably be filled by prospective candidates. For instance, the Central Committee of the PNP included, in addition to a national president, three national vice-presidents and eighteen counselors, three from each province. In short, although procedures differed from one party to another, a common characteristic of elite parties was loose structuring of the central organization.

In contrast, the hallmark of mass-party organizations was the centralization of directing organs. A striking feature of the Abako was the broad authority conferred upon its Central Committee and its president. The committee exercised full control over all the functional committees (*secrétariats*) attached to the party, and enjoyed the exclusive right to call a meeting of the national congress, to determine the number of fédérations and their jurisdiction, and to suspend or dissolve a *comité fédéral*. Its membership included the president of the party and ten members who qualified for the office by "militating for at least three years on behalf of the party." The key position, however, was held by the president, whose powers were officially defined as follows: "The president controls the activity of the party and its subordinate organs. He orients his policy in accordance with the motions adopted at the party congress. He decides on all matters that have been submitted to the Political Bureau. He watches over the life of the party." [43] As a party congress rarely met, Kasavubu, as president of the Central Committee, clearly enjoyed a dominant position in the party hierarchy.

The leadership structure of the MNC-Lumumba was equally illustrative of the centralizing tendencies of mass parties. Its highest executive organ was the National Central Committee, composed of the national president, the national vice-president, and six provincial presidents. According to Article 12 of the party statutes, "the National Central Committee is the principal organ of the movement. It ensures its proper functioning and decides on all questions of general interest related to the activities of the party." Even more significant, however, was the power vested in the National Bureau, a four-man directorate consisting of the national president, a secretary-general, a deputy secretary-general, and a treasurer. Besides acting as the official representative of the party, the National Bureau was given exclusive responsibility to determine the

---

[43] *Abako: 1950–1960,* p. 334.

"party line." As stipulated by the party statutes, a "local or provincial committee may not decide on matters of national concern without consulting the National Bureau." Compliance with central directives was ensured by the obligation imposed upon all party members and organizations "to observe party discipline and carry out the decisions taken by the directing organs of the MNC." In short, the National Bureau was really a "party within a party." Operating under the direct patronage of Lumumba, this select group of party faithful was the core agency from which all important directives emanated.

In formal organization, then, mass parties were like strongly centralized "machines," enforcing a rigorous discipline from the top of the hierarchy down to the basic units. This view, however, bears only a distant relationship to the facts of party life. The outstanding characteristic of all Congolese parties, whether mass or elite, was decentralization of the organization. Most local and provincial officials retained a substantial power of initiative, especially where constituency organizations were spread over several provinces. But even in a party like the Abako, regional presidents in practice enjoyed a wide measure of autonomy. This concentration of power in the hands of a few party officials frequently led to friction; on some occasions the president of a local section did not hesitate to go over the head of the *comité régional* to present his case to the Central Committee in Leopoldville.

On the other hand, at the central level ultimate control over party affairs was frequently exercised by a dominant personality. This personalization of power is perhaps best illustrated by the role played by Lumumba in managing the affairs of the MNC. Not only did he control virtually all aspects and phases of policy making within the party, but in so doing he paid relatively little attention to formal procedures. Decisions involving day-to-day questions of policy, like the appointment of party officials, the selection of candidates for election, and other less important matters, depended in the last resort on the will of the MNC leader. Similarly, Kasavubu's personality overshadowed all other offices in the hierarchy of the Abako. But, whereas Lumumba consciously sought to impose his will on his following, Kasavubu, like de Gaulle, looked upon himself as a "guide," insisting also that his real mission was to consummate the will of his people: "J'estime que ma mission est de réaliser la volonté de mon peuple." [44] On some occasions, however, the Abako leader did not hesitate to make unilateral decisions, as when he suddenly left the Brussels Round Table in protest against the refusal of the delegates to consider the issue of a provisional government.

In the PSA this concentration of authority was perhaps less apparent, yet important decisions were ordinarily subject to the approval of a duum-

[44] *La Libre Belgique,* Jan. 21, 1960.

virate composed of Antoine Gizenga, national president of the PSA, and Cléophas Kamitatu, a provincial president. Both were equally popular among certain segments of the Kwilu populations, Gizenga among the Bapende and Kamitatu among the Bambala. Although a semblance of unity was maintained, differences of personality and character between the two leaders, and their different interpretations of their functions, produced serious tensions at the top level of the party hierarchy. In time, Gizenga became identified with the more radical, militant wing of the party, and Kamitatu, with the more moderate. But neither faction achieved dominance within the party, at least not until independence.

If leadership was highly personalized, internal dissensions were likely to arise between the top leaders and those who opposed excessive centralization. The vice-president of the Abako, Daniel Kanza, bitterly criticized Kasavubu for his dictatorial attitude at the Brussels Round Table and, in particular, for his failure to consult the other members of the Abako delegation. The controversy led to Kanza's expulsion from the party on February 1, 1960, and on March 4 he announced the formation of a dissident wing, which became known as the Abako-Kanza. On March 24 the MNC-Lumumba experienced a similar crisis when its national vice-president, Victor Nendaka, publicly accused Lumumba of extreme left-wing tendencies; later he resigned his post in order to set up his own moderate wing, the MNC-Nendaka. In April, 1960, the secretary-general of the Cerea, Jean-Chrysostome Weregemere, openly dissociated himself from the leadership of the party and proceeded to organize a separate wing, the Cerea-Weregemere. Taking his cue from Nendaka, Weregemere accused the president and the vice-president of the Cerea of Communist leanings, pointing out that they had chosen as technical adviser a leading figure in the Belgian Communist Party (Jean Terfve), and had taken it upon themselves to visit Prague without consulting the other members of the Central Committee.[45] In each instance the split seems to have resulted from not only a clash of personalities, but also from a fundamental opposition to the overconcentration of authority in the hands of certain leaders.

Another source of tension was the presence of dominant tribal groupings in party leadership. It was precisely to avoid the charge of having unduly weighted the leadership of the Abako in favor of the Bantandu that Nzeza-Landu invited a Mayumbe, Kasavubu, to join the Central Committee of the association. Nevertheless, the fact that six of the ten members of the committee were of Bantandu extraction aroused the suspicion of other Bakongo subgroups. Far more dangerous, potentially, was the overrepresentation of a particular tribe or of groups of tribes in

---

[45] See Weregemere's letter to Provincial Governor E. Borlée in *L'Essor du Congo,* April 13, 1960.

the directing organs of a party that otherwise claimed to be tribally heterogeneous. One factor contributing to the secession of the Bayaka from the PSA was their virtual exclusion from the Central Committee. Although the vice-presidency of the party was once entrusted to a Bayaka, Pierre Mazikata, almost all the members of the committee belonged to the tribes of the Kwilu—Bambala, Bapende, Babunda, Lampuku, and Badjinga.[46] Late in 1959, anxious to find a way out of this situation, a group of Bayaka under the leadership of André Petipeti organized the Union Kwangolaise pour l'Indépendance et la Liberté, better known as the Luka. For the same motive, a few weeks later, the Bayanzi withdrew their support from the PSA and set up the Alliance des Bayanzi. Equally noteworthy, though not leading to major defections, was the predominant position held by the Bashi tribes in the leadership of the Cerea, of the Ngombe in the Puna, and of the Lunda in the Conakat.

Decision-making processes within Congolese parties were also affected by the sporadic involvement of European elements in party activities. Until the Brussels Round Table, their influence was usually felt only in the presence of technical advisers. One notable exception, however, was the Conakat. From the very beginning of its collaboration with the Union Katangaise, it abdicated a large measure of its autonomy to European settlers. At first this seemed amply compensated for by the material help that the Conakat could reasonably expect from settler interests. European tutelage became increasingly burdensome, however, and the Conakat leaders decided to regain their freedom of action. On March 10, 1960, Tshombe declared before the party's Central Committee: "Ces Messieurs [the colons] ont récolté beaucoup d'argent au nom de la Conakat. ... Ils se sont fait propriétaires de notre argent. ... La rupture doit être nette, et même brusque." [47] Tshombe's proposal was vigorously countered by Evariste Kimba. Cautioning against the possible disastrous consequences of a sharp break with the settlers, Kimba observed: "Si on se séparait des colons brusquement, ils pourraient être une arme destructive pour la Conakat. ... Il ne faut pas que la rupture avec les colons soit une bombe atomique [*sic*] pour la Conakat. ... La rupture doit être progressive et justifiée." [48]

By the end of April, 1960, the Conakat had successfully disengaged itself from the hold of the colonat. In a communiqué published in the newspaper *Conakat* on April 30, 1960, the Union Katangaise declared: "In response to the wishes of different political leaders, our association has decided to restrict its activities to the study of economic questions

[46] José Lobeya, "Notice sur le PSA," Commissariat à l'Information, Leopoldville, June 11, 1960 (mimeographed).

[47] "Procès-verbal du Comité Exécutif de la Conakat," March 10, 1960 (unpublished document).

[48] *Ibid.*

and the defense of the professional interests of independent workers." Despite this announcement, prominent settlers like J. Humblé, G. Thyssens, and A. Belina continued to exercise considerable influence upon the leadership of the Conakat.

Meanwhile, at the Round Table, a number of influential metropolitan personalities engaged in "brokerage activities" between Belgian vested interests and Congolese politicians. Insofar as they succeeded in providing financial assistance for otherwise insignificant groups, they decisively altered the balance of forces among parties. Here an examination of the different sources of financial support available to political parties is in order.

In the Congo, as elsewhere in Africa, the collection of membership dues, together with the sale of party cards, was a major source of income. It was particularly useful to the more extremist groups, not only because they claimed a mass membership, but also because the party card often served as a safe-conduct for both blacks and whites who otherwise would never have become party members. An accurate assessment of the proceeds from the sale of party cards is, however, well-nigh impossible, as their price varied markedly from one region to the next, and from one client to another. For example, Abako cards were sold for 30 Belgian francs in the Mayumbe area, and for twice as much in the Madimba territory.[49] The Abako also received significant sums from coöperative organizations such as the Cooperative Cobakwa, whose director, Edmond Nzeza-Landu, had founded the party. Finally, in some areas, particularly in the Lower Congo and the Kwilu district, party officials sometimes acted as tax collectors, adding the taxpayers' contributions to party funds in defiance of the administration. Shortly before the general elections, PSA officials canvassed the Kwilu district to collect what they called *l'impôt de l'indépendance,* consisting of the *centimes additionnels* destined for the *caisses de chefferies.* This money-raising technique was also employed by the Cerea in some parts of the Kivu, and by the MNC-Lumumba in the Orientale.

Equally important was the financial backing given to political parties by business groups and settler interests. The main beneficiaries of these funds, though by no means the only ones, were the PNP, derisively referred to by its opponents as *le parti des nègres payés,* and the Conakat. Just how much financial help the Conakat received from European settlers is difficult to say, but there can be little doubt that their contribution was substantial. On January 20, 1960, Bonaventure Makonga, speaking on behalf of the Conakat, flatly told the spokesmen of the colonat, Thyssens, Humblé, and J. Onckelynckx: "Il faut que ces Messieurs nous donnent de l'argent—5 millions de francs [$100,000] ou plus,

---

[49] *Courrier Africain,* April 22, 1960, p. 5.

Congo (Leopoldville)

pour activer notre propagande à l'intérieur ... car les intérêts que nous défendons sont les intérêts du Katanga, sans distinction de race ou de couleur." [50] Even more substantial were the contributions of the UMHK to the campaign funds of the Conakat. A rough indication of the amount the company gave to Katangese political groups is found in its annual report for 1960, which stated that "exceptional expenditures . . . incurred through the political events in the Congo in July, 1960, composed mainly of expenses of evacuating members of our personnel and their families, expenses for their return to the Katanga, and various allowances," amounted to $2.5 million. Yet, "since mining-company personnel were evacuated almost exclusively by road (a distance of less than 200 miles) and most of them were back at work within three or four days, it is obvious that the entire $2.5 million could not possibly have been spent for this purpose." [51]

Finally, one of the most valuable sources of financial support enjoyed by the MNC-Lumumba, and to a lesser extent by the PSA, the Cerea, and the Parti du Peuple, were subsidies from Moscow, Prague, and such "neutralist" states as Ghana, Guinea, and Egypt. The sum of 140 million Belgian francs, cited by Pierre Houart, may sound like a gross overestimation of the aid received by the MNC-Lumumba from Communist states and Belgian fellow travelers, but the campaign machinery utilized by the party in Orientale Province testifies to the fact that their contribution was far from negligible.[52] This should not, however, be regarded as a sign of doctrinal affinity between Lumumba's party, or Lumumba himself, and international communism.

In general, however, the comparatively loose internal structuring of Congolese parties, and the personalized character of their leadership, served to enhance the influence of metropolitan and foreign pressure groups and personalities. For example, the names of A. A. J. Van Bilsen, Arthur Doucy, Serge Michel, and Madame Blouin became associated, at one time or another, with the Abako, the Balubakat, the MNC-Lumumba, and the PSA, respectively. The exact role played by these personalities will probably never be known, but undoubtedly such "connections," insofar as they became identified with particular ideological undercurrents, have significantly added to intergroup tensions.

Associated Organizations

Most parties have functioned in conjunction with one or several other groups such as youth associations, women's organizations, and syndi-

---

[50] "Procès-verbal du Comité Exécutif de la Conakat," Jan. 20, 1960.

[51] Smith Hempstone, *Rebels, Mercenaries, and Dividends* (New York: Praeger, 1962), p. 98.

[52] P. Houart, *La Pénétration communiste au Congo* (Brussels: Centre de Documentation International, 1961), p. 12.

cates, identified with particular social categories. Some of these, like the Front Patriotique de la Jeunesse, founded in May, 1960, to "provide Congolese youth with a civic and patriotic formation," [53] or the Mouvement des Femmes Nationalistes Congolaises, founded in February, 1960, to "promote the political education of Congolese women and assist the men in their struggle for the liberation of the Congolese people," [54] did not attach themselves to any particular party. Others, like the Jeunesse Banunu Bobangi, the Jeunesse Lukunga, and the Fédération des Jeunes Budja, addressed themselves to specific tribal groupings regardless of their political affinities. Beginning in 1960, however, there was a general tendency for parties to extend and solidify their bases of support by forging associational links with special-interest groups. Sometimes this goal was achieved by incorporating the membership of preëxisting associations into the party structure. As early as 1955, for example, the Abako had established close connections with a number of mutual-aid societies, youth organizations, and sports associations, such as the Mutuelle du Mayumbe, the Aurore Jeunesse Ngidienne, and the Association Sportive Beerschoot. Likewise, the consumers' coöperative of Kikwit became organically linked to the PSA. More often, however, these specialized bodies were created within the parties themselves. They were deliberately organized by the party leadership to mobilize a wide array of potential supporters.

The MNC-Lumumba was the only party that attempted to set up an affiliate labor organization. Early in 1960 it created the Union Nationale des Travailleurs Congolais (UNTC), which affiliated with the World Federation of Trade Unions (WFTU) and the Conakry-based Union Générale des Travailleurs d'Afrique Noire (UGTAN). The UNTC was led by Antoine Tshimanga, spokesman for the pro-Lumumba youth group, Alliance de la Jeunesse Congolaise.[55] Despite these efforts, however, the linkage between organized labor and the MNC-Lumumba remained extremely tenuous, not only because the UNTC was established at a relatively late date, but also because the field of trade-union activity had already been preëmpted by the Union des Travailleurs Congolais (UTC) and the Fédération Générale des Travailleurs Congolais (FGTC), identified respectively with Christian Democratic and Socialist tendencies.

Most parties tried to create youth organizations. In March, 1960, the Leopoldville branch of the MNC-Lumumba announced that the Jeunesse du Mouvement National Congolais (JMNC) had been formed for the purpose of "mobilizing and regrouping the young into a vast national movement, providing the young with a civic and patriotic formation,

---

[53] *Courrier d'Afrique*, May 6, 1960.
[54] *Ibid.*, Feb. 19, 1960.
[55] Houart, *op. cit.*, pp. 13–14.

creating and organizing cultural and artistic sections, and providing its members with scholarships." [56] On May 13 the Leopoldville section of the JMNC merged with the Jeunesse Atetela and the Jeunesse Lulua-Frères to form the Confédération des Jeunes Congolais (also known as the Alliance de la Jeunesse Congolaise), led by the late Emmanuel Nzouzi.[57] Meanwhile, the MNC-Kalonji organized the Mouvement National des Jeunesses Congolaises (MNJC), the Abako organized the Jeunesse Abako (Jabako), the PSA organized the Jeunesse PSA (JPSA), and so forth.

In Leopoldville, as in most other urban centers, these groups were associated with their parent parties through horizontal links at the communal level, but they nevertheless formed distinct organizational entities. For example, the Jabako, though operating in close liaison with the Abako, came under the control of a separate leadership structure and printed its own newspaper (*Vigilance*), and its members usually wore a distinctive uniform. And, as elsewhere in Africa, this organizational autonomy frequently expressed itself through independent action.

Sometimes a youth organization like the JMNC was given a free hand by the parent party to "verify and control" activities at the local level.[58] But when such groups did not enjoy freedom of action, they simply took the initiative in formulating demands intended to support or criticize the parent organizations. For example, when Daniel Kanza was expelled from the Abako, the spokesmen of the Jabako gave their full support to the decision of the Central Committee; at the same time, however, they urged the committee to remove Kanza from the *collège exécutif provincial*: "Kanza revoqué par le très honorable Comité Central de l'Abako ne peut en aucun cas occuper le siège important qui vient de lui être attribué par l'administration colonialiste." [59] A few weeks later, on April 12, the Jabako unilaterally rejected the nomination of a certain Ndebo Mantezolo to the *collège exécutif territorial* on the ground that he lacked the support of the local population.[60] In short, although youth organizations undoubtedly played a significant role in indoctrinating the young and converting them into party activists, they usually operated as semi-independent pressure groups.

The relationships between youth organizations and political parties underwent a radical change in the weeks following independence. The Jabako suddenly transformed itself from a semiautonomous pressure group into an organ of criticism directed against the party's parliamentary representatives. In a motion issued early in August, 1960, the Kintambo section of the Jabako bitterly attacked the *élus nationaux* for their failure to fulfill their promise to establish the independent and

---

[56] *Courrier d'Afrique*, March 11, 1960.
[57] *Ibid.*, May 13, 1960.
[58] *Ibid.*
[59] *Ibid.*, March 17, 1960.
[60] *Ibid.*, April 12, 1960.

sovereign Kongo State. Threatening to destroy the Abako unless the promise was kept, the leaders of the Jabako bluntly declared: "Cet état souverain, nous l'attendons, ou bien nous serons obligés de saccager l'Abako, les biens, les dirigeants aussi et les élus enfin." [61]

Similarly, the youth organization of the MNC-Kalonji continually pressed for the division of the Kasai into two separate provinces. In July, 1960, in a motion to the president of the Senate, Joseph Ileo, the MNJC stated: "Pour nous une solution équitable n'est autre que la division du Kasaï en deux provinces, comme l'a exprimé la lettre que le Mouvement Solidaire Muluba a adressé au Premier Ministre." [62] In Orientale Province, JMNC opposition to the élus led its spokesmen to adopt a firm stand in favor of a dictatorial regime. In an article entitled "Vive la Dictature pour mettre fin au sabotage," Yvon Thompson Yakusu wrote in August, 1960: "En notre qualité de membres fanatiques de la JMNC, et au nom de tous les jeunes nationalistes soucieux de l'avenir de notre beau pays ... nous réclamons la dictature." [63] In the Katanga, the Jeunesse Baluba-kat asserted its complete independence from party leadership, and soon transformed itself into a terroristic, nativistic organization, inaugurating a reign of terror in many parts of the northern districts of the province.

On the whole, Congolese developments confirm the observation of Thomas Hodgkin that "youth organizations have shown a fairly consistent tendency to independent action and radicalism," to the point where they eventually supplanted the parent parties.[64] That this tendency was even more apparent in the Congo than elsewhere in Africa is itself indicative of the organizational weakness of Congolese parties. Although it was the natural tendency for youth groups to become potential centers of opposition once independence had become a reality, the parent parties made no effort to control them. The parties simply lacked the means and the opportunity to do so.

This again stresses the dominant characteristic of Congolese parties —their highly rudimentary, underdeveloped organizational apparatus. With one or two exceptions, they resembled jerry-built organizations rather than effective political organisms, a fact that reflects the recency of their development as much as their natural handicaps, such as the size of the Congolese territory and the absence of adequate communication facilities. Under the circumstances, it is hardly surprising that so few Congolese leaders managed to extend the influence of their organizations beyond the confines of the major towns. Nor is it surprising, in view of their structural weakness and limited geographical extension, that so few parties survived the turmoil that followed independence.

[61] *La Voix du Peuple*, Aug. 4, 1960.
[62] *Ibid.*, July 27, 1960.
[63] *Uhuru* (Stanleyville), Aug. 28, 1960.
[64] Hodgkin, *African Political Parties*, p. 122.

CONCLUSIONS

In the spectrum of African political groups, Congolese parties present a number of distinguishing characteristics. First, the competitiveness of the Congolese party system has virtually no parallel in other African territories except perhaps for the Sudan before the military coup of November, 1958. Second, because almost all Congolese parties sprang into being under the pressure of ethnic and sectional rivalries, they tended to reflect the cultural, linguistic, or historical affinities that existed before the imposition of Belgian rule, as did the Abako, or a common opposition to the actual or potential threat of tribal domination, as did the Interfédérale and, in a qualified sense, the Conakat. Third, except for the Abako, Congolese parties were primarily confined to urban areas. Their organizational structure in the countryside was thus never so strong or so extensive as that of political groups in other African territories. Fourth, most Congolese parties suffered at one time or another from factional divisions. Although these sometimes stemmed from honest differences of opinion over questions of leadership and organization, others were tangible manifestations of a struggle for power and influence among Congolese leaders. Whatever the cause, personal rivalries like those between Patrice Lumumba and Joseph Ileo, Jason Sendwe and Moise Tshombe, and Jean-Chrysostome Weregemere and Anicet Kashamura have directly encouraged the growth of competing political factions.

This pattern of political development illuminates the infinite difficulties faced by the central government of the Republic of the Congo in its continuing struggle against ethnic and regional separatism. Whereas in other African territories the integrative structure of a dominant mass party held ethnic and regional particularisms in check, in the Congo political parties institutionalized, and hence reinforced, intergroup conflicts. Under the circumstances, a resurrection of party activities would probably serve merely to perpetuate and harden centrifugal tendencies. It seems clear, in any event, that the long-term solution to the Congo's political problems will not be found in the lingering structures of an amorphous, tribally oriented party system. The civil service and the army are now the two major vehicles of social change, with the former already playing a dominant role in the process of national integration. As one observer recently stated: "What matters, in the short run, is whether the administration can develop the national outlook and innovating capacity which parties have inspired elsewhere in Africa. This seems to be the most the Congo can hope for until new political roots can be established." [65]

<hr>

[65] Crawford Young, "Congo Political Parties Revisited," *Africa Report,* VIII (Jan., 1963), 20.

16. NIGERIA

By Richard L. Sklar
and C. S. Whitaker, Jr.

INTRODUCTION

The Federal Republic of Nigeria comprises some 35 million people in
three principal political units, the Northern, Eastern, and Western regions. Government in each region is patterned after the Westminster parliamentary model, including a bicameral legislature and an executive
council (cabinet) headed by a premier. There are three major political
parties, each in control of a regional government. The Northern Region
alone contains 54 per cent of the Nigerian population, and the Northern
Peoples' Congress (NPC), which controls the regional government, held
a plurality of 45.5 per cent of the seats in the federal House of Representatives when Nigeria attained independence on October 1, 1960. The
government of the federation is formed by a coalition of the NPC and
the second-largest party in the House of Representatives, the National
Convention of Nigerian Citizens (NCNC; formerly the National Council
of Nigeria and the Cameroons), under the leadership of an NPC prime
minister. The NCNC also controls the government of the Eastern Region,
and shares power in the Western Region; it operates in the north through
an ally, the Northern Elements' Progressive Union (NEPU). The federal
opposition is provided by the Action Group of Nigeria (AG), which also
controls the government of the Western Region and forms the official
opposition in both the Northern and Eastern regions. (For recent changes
in Nigeria's political configuration, see postscript.)

It has been observed that each of the three regions has a dual cultural make-up: a preponderant majority of culturally related tribes speaking the same language, and a heterogeneous group of cultural-linguistic
minorities.[1] The three major cultural groups—the Hausa-Fulani in the
north, the Ibo people in the east, and the Yoruba people in the west—
have divergent histories and traditions, including dissimilar traditions of
political organization. Diversity among and within the regions is reinforced by religious heterogeneity and variations in levels of Western education, standards of living, and degrees of modernization. This pattern of
social and cultural pluralism has helped shape the character of the major
political parties and has stimulated intense party competition.

It is important to observe further that the underlying conditions of

---

[1] K. M. Buchanan and J. C. Pugh, *Land and People in Nigeria* (London: University of London Press, 1955), p. 94.

political development in the two southern regions have differed substantially from those obtaining in the north. Succinctly, political parties in the Eastern and Western regions of southern Nigeria were introduced into an atmosphere of pervasive social and economic change. By contrast, political parties in the Northern Region have emerged in an environment characterized by a relatively high degree of social, economic, and political continuity. Traditional norms of behavior and institutions affect politics to some degree in all the regions, as will be seen. But the decisive contrast between basic structural change in the south and basic structural continuity in the north governs the analysis of political parties presented in this paper.

Origins of the NCNC and the Action Group

In 1923 a restricted number of taxpayers in the seacoast colony of Lagos were given the right to elect three representatives to the Nigerian Legislative Council. This innovation induced the "father of Nigerian nationalism," Herbert Macaulay, civil engineer, surveyor, and journalist, to organize the Nigerian National Democratic Party. Under his guidance the party espoused the cause of African freedom; indeed, its president, barrister Joseph Egerton-Shyngle, was a founder of the interterritorial National Congress of British West Africa at Accra in 1920. In practice, however, the energies of the Democratic Party were expended on parochial issues of local politics in Lagos, and the party came to be regarded by the nationalistic youth of prewar Nigeria as a mere electoral machine lacking serious ideological direction.

In 1938 the elective seats of Lagos in the Legislative Council were captured by a new party, the Nigerian Youth Movement, led by a self-conscious ethnosocial elite of Yoruba-speaking heritage, prominently represented in the professional and entrepreneurial spheres of Lagos society. Most members of this elite were Western-educated, Christian, and first- or second-generation settlers in the town. In contrast, the indigenous Yoruba-speaking masses of Lagos were overwhelmingly Muslim and strongly committed to traditional values. Traditional leaders won the loyalty of the vast majority of Lagos indigenes for the Democratic Party. In Lagos, the Nigerian Youth Movement derived its popular support from a nonindigenous working class of both Yoruba and non-Yoruba descent. Ibo-speaking people from the Eastern Region formed the largest single non-Yoruba cultural group. Their allegiance to the Youth Movement was inspired by their most prominent compatriot, Nnamdi Azikiwe, editor and publisher of a nationalistic daily newspaper, the *West African Pilot*.

In 1941 Azikiwe broke with the Youth Movement,[2] carrying with

---

[2] James S. Coleman, *Nigeria: Background to Nationalism* (Berkeley and Los Angeles: University of California Press, 1958), pp. 227–228.

him the support of many nonindigenous Yorubas in addition to the Ibo settlers of Lagos. In 1944 the Nigerian Union of Students, whose members were nationalistic youths of diverse ethnic origins, persuaded Azikiwe to join with Herbert Macaulay in the formation of a national front, which became the National Council of Nigeria and the Cameroons. Although all existing nationalistic associations, including tribal unions, trade unions, professional groups, and political parties, were invited to join, the Nigerian Youth Movement resolved to remain aloof. Soon the nationalist initiative passed from the Youth Movement to the more aggressive and more broadly representative NCNC.

Within a year of its inauguration, the NCNC embarked upon a campaign to compel the revision of a postwar constitution which was repudiated by nationalists for its failure to provide democratic representation and responsible government. Leaders of the NCNC toured Nigeria, enlisting support for a delegation of protest to the Colonial Office in London. Early in the tour Herbert Macaulay died; subsequently Azikiwe succeeded to the presidency of the NCNC, and led the delegation to London.

Thereafter the militancy of the NCNC was overtaken by an official colonial policy of constitutional reform. As frustrations over constitutional advance were temporarily assuaged, debilitating tribal antagonisms were injected into the political conflict between Azikiwe and his opponents in Lagos. A desire to revive the nationalistic vigor of the NCNC led youthful militants to launch a new organization devoted to "positive action," which they called the Zikist Movement.[3] The strategies of civil disobedience advocated by the Zikists, however, were incompatible with the political tactics favored by Azikiwe, after whom the movement was named. With irony Zikists reflected, some of them in prison, that Azikiwe, whose teaching on the redemption of Africa had inspired Zikism, refused to abet their revolutionary exploits. Azikiwe, like other mass party leaders in Nigeria, seized the opportunity to win political power through a system of party competition engendered by the introduction of electoral reforms.

The Constitution of 1951 provided for indirect elections to three regional houses of assembly, each of which was empowered to choose from among its membership a stipulated number to the central House of Representatives. Lagos was placed under the jurisdiction of the Western Region, enabling Azikiwe's opponents to offset his strength in Lagos by mobilizing support among the Yoruba peasantry in rural areas of that region. To organize the peasantry, it was necessary for the educated elite to enlist the coöperation of the Yoruba chiefs. The key instrument of

---

[3] On the theory of Zikism, as formulated by its originator, see A. A. Nwafor Orizu, *Without Bitterness* (New York: Creative Age Press, 1944).

collaboration was a cultural organization, inaugurated in 1948, called the Egbe Omo Oduduwa ("Society of the Descendants of Oduduwa," the mythical progenitor and culture hero of the Yoruba people).

The principal political objectives of the Egbe were to bring together the new elites of Yoruba nationality and to educate the Yoruba chiefs in the ways of democracy. But the Egbe's membership was sufficiently conservative to be thought incapable of formulating the kind of political program desired by its more energetic and radical wing.[4] Under the leadership of a young barrister, Obafemi Awolowo, the vanguard of the Egbe organized a new political party, the Action Group. Encouraged by the Action Group, prominent settlers in Lagos and Ibadan returned to their home villages and towns, presented themselves to the chiefs, and entered the electoral contest for the Western House of Assembly. All five seats in Lagos were won by NCNC candidates, including one by Azikiwe, but the Action Group won an over-all majority in the Western Region, entitling Awolowo to head the regional government. Meanwhile, in the Eastern Region, an NCNC government was formed by political lieutenants of Azikiwe, who was himself included in the Western House of Assembly as an unofficial leader of the opposition.

The Action Group and the NCNC since 1951

Few developments have been so conducive to the rise of a national party system in Nigeria as the transformation of the Action Group from a Western Regional organization based mainly on the Yoruba people to a transregional party of multicultural composition. This development was fostered mainly by the radical wing of the party, which has consistently taken a federationist position in Nigerian constitutional controversies. In the early 1950's the federationists had to contend with the opinions of those who favored maximum regional autonomy, among whom conservative businessmen were conspicuous. The evolution of Action Group organization reflects the resolution of this conflict. Shortly after the formation of the first AG government in the Western Region, radical elements pressed successfully to enforce the authority of the Central Executive Committee over the party's parliamentary council. In 1953 a radical member of the Executive Committee, in pursuance of a resolution adopted by the preceding annual conference of the party, filed a motion in the central House of Representatives calling for national self-government in three years, without consulting the parliamentary council. The Action Group as a party supported the motion, despite the reluctance of its conservative wing. But the northern representatives, who occupied 50 per cent of the seats in the House, rejected the motion. The

---

[4] See Obafemi Awolowo, *Awo: The Autobiography of Chief Obafemi Awolowo* (London: Cambridge University Press, 1960), pp. 217, 220–221.

result was a constitutional crisis and a temporary alliance between the Action Group and its rival, the NCNC.

An ensuing all-party conference in London (1953) reconstituted the essentially unitary government of Nigeria as a genuine federation, vesting residual powers in the regions. Furthermore, it was decided that national independence would be achieved through preparatory stages of regional self-government. At the Action Group annual conference of 1953, federationists consolidated their control of the party organization, thereby diminishing the influence of an irregular clique that had previously provided greater leverage for business elements in Lagos. Thereafter the party launched its program of expansion into the other regions.

The emergence of the Action Group as a mass organization, with an enlarged territorial scope, required the establishment of a highly centralized and efficient secretariat to facilitate control by the leadership. At the same time Chief Awolowo developed a method of arriving at policies through extensive deliberation and wide consultation. After 1955 leaders and influential supporters of the party, including chiefs, businessmen, and local notables, gathered regularly on an informal basis at Awolowo's home in Ikenne to air opinions and project long-term strategies. A concrete manifestation of the party's collegial method of leadership was the decision in 1957 of its Executive Council to participate in a national government over the objection of Awolowo, who felt that collaboration with the NPC and the NCNC at the federal level would undermine the Action Group's posture of opposition in the north and the east. In 1959, in accordance with party policy, Awolowo resigned his premiership in the Western Regional government to contest the federal election. Subsequently he became the leader of the opposition in the federal House of Representatives, and Chief Samuel L. Akintola, deputy leader of the party, succeeded to the premiership of the Western Region.

Whereas the Action Group evolved from a narrowly based party into a mass organization, the NCNC, beginning with the election of 1951, has undergone a transformation from a national front of affiliated groups into a political party in the stricter sense.[5] After that election the Pan-Nigerian NCNC was strained internally by resistance to the efforts of its president, Azikiwe, to assert the authority of the national organization over independent-minded NCNC ministers in the eastern and central governments. Ultimately the ministers were expelled from the party for insubordination, and the Eastern House of Assembly, in a state of virtual paralysis, was dissolved.

Azikiwe's assumption of the premiership of a reconstituted Eastern

---

[5] The evolution of congress-type associations into political parties for electoral and parliamentary purposes is the major theme of Thomas Hodgkin's chapter, "Parties and Congresses," in his seminal work, *Nationalism in Colonial Africa* (London: Frederick Muller, 1956), pp. 139–168.

Regional government in 1954 was of great consequence for the organization of the party. After the Constitutional Conference of 1953, it was obvious that the leaders of the Action Group and the Northern Peoples' Congress would become the first premiers of the Western and Northern regions, respectively. But antiregionalism was a cardinal tenet of NCNC policy. The party's stanch advocates of unitary government, in particular, were anxious that its national president, Azikiwe, not take office in a region where he would preside over the affairs of his own cultural nationality, the Ibo-speaking people. Yet political power under the new constitution inhered mainly in the regional governments, and no provision had been made for a federal prime minister. It was therefore argued that Azikiwe should have equal status with his counterparts and assume direction of the only government subject to the NCNC's control. These considerations prevailed, and the political center of gravity in the NCNC shifted to the east, while central direction of the party organization as a whole lapsed seriously. As central control waned, the party came to rely increasingly on a system of regional working committees. In the Western Region, the system, making maximum use of zonal leaders, countenanced extreme local autonomy and failed to provide effective coördination. In the Eastern Region, conflicts over local issues became commonplace.

In 1956–1957 the party experienced an epic crisis which stemmed from the investment and deposit of public funds in the African Continental Bank, a private institution which Azikiwe had acquired in 1944 to finance his nationalistic press. In keeping with settled policies of the party, public funds were injected into the bank to enable it to extend credit to African businessmen. But Azikiwe's opponents objected strenuously to the fact that his was the main private interest in the bank at the time of investment, an issue of some complexity which cannot be explored here. The Secretary of State for the Colonies appointed a tribunal of inquiry, some of whose findings were unfavorable to the eastern Premier. The NCNC, however, viewed the case as a conflict between indigenous and foreign banking. On that issue the eastern government resigned, and successfully sought its vindication at the polls.

The events of this tumultuous period sowed seeds of discord and provoked expressions of discontent with NCNC management in high party circles. At the annual convention of 1957, Azikiwe declared that drastic reforms were required to restore discipline in the party. He obtained the right to appoint the national officers of the party subject to the approval of the annual convention; this marked a return to the cabinet system of party management which had been abandoned in 1951. Eight months of further intraparty turmoil ensued in the Eastern and Western regions, culminating in the emergence of a reform committee in June, 1958, which demanded the resignation of Azikiwe as NCNC president and premier of the Eastern Region. But Azikiwe was upheld by the majority of the National Executive Committee and by the people of the Eastern Region, the latter through public rallies, voluntary associations, and local councils. Radical members of the party regarded the outcome of the crisis as a stroke for centralization and a substantial setback for the conservative, *arriviste,* and business-minded social elite.

In 1959 Azikiwe, like Awolowo, contested and won election to the federal House of Representatives. Upon the formation of the NPC-NCNC coalition government under Alhaji Sir Abubakar Tafawa Balewa, the federal prime minister, Azikiwe surrendered his seat and became president of the Nigerian Senate. Subsequently he resigned the presidency of the NCNC in order to accept appointment as the governor-general of Nigeria, the nominal head of state. His colleague of many years' standing, Dr. Michael I. Okpara, the new premier of the Eastern Region, was elected to the presidency of the party. When, in 1961, the people of the Southern Cameroons Trust Territory chose to terminate their association with Nigeria and to join the neighboring Cameroun Republic, the NCNC was renamed the National Convention of Nigerian Citizens.

Both the NCNC and the Action Group were born of circumstances that unite patriotic men and women irrespective of their social status or ideological conviction. Each party is rooted in a primary region where many of the administrative and economic spoils of office are distributed among members and supporters. Social and ideological intraparty cleavages inevitably result. By and large, the vested interests in Nigeria are attached to regional power. The leveling spirit is antiregionalist, and criticisms directed against the federal government imply that it is the instrument of predominately regionalistic, hence monied, interests.[6] Predictably, these criticisms were echoed by the federal opposition. By 1962 the Action Group had developed a flagrantly split personality. As an opposition party in the federal parliament, it championed the radical point of view in debates on domestic and foreign policy; as a government party in the Western Region, it was identified with indulgence toward the social and political *status quo.*

An irreparable breach occurred when the Federal Executive Council of the party, under the leadership of Awolowo, requested Akintola to resign his premiership of the Western Region. Akintola resisted, but the governor of the Western Region was persuaded to take action against him which, however, was ultimately held unconstitutional by the federal Supreme Court. He dismissed the Premier, designating as his replacement Alhaji D. S. Adegbenro, a supporter of Awolowo. There ensued a disturb-

---

[6] Scathing criticisms of this kind have been voiced by the Nigerian Trades Union Congress, the recently organized Nigerian Youth Congress, and the small Dynamic Party, in addition to radical elements associated with the major political parties and their allies.

ance on the floor of the Western House of Assembly. The federal government reacted swiftly; a state of emergency was declared in the west and a federal administrator was appointed to govern the region pending new elections. Meanwhile a federal commission of inquiry undertook an investigation of the post-1954 administrative and financial practices of the regional government.

The Action Group's plight in 1962 was reminiscent of previous crises in the development of the NCNC. It will be recalled that in 1953 the NCNC was rent by the refusal of its eastern parliamentary leadership to accept central party direction. Nine years later a clash between Awolowo and his successor as premier of the West, Akintola, cast a shadow over the Action Group's future as a major political party. In 1956 the president of the NCNC had been compelled by his political opponents and the British Colonial Secretary to bear a searching examination of his personal (but politically significant) financial relationships. Ultimately, Azikiwe's cause was sustained by popular belief in his devotion to Nigerian freedom and his sagacity in pursuit of that goal. Similarly, Awolowo's best hope in the hour of his ordeal was the prospect that public opinion might identify his cause with another momentous issue— social justice.

Origins of the NPC and the NEPU

Nationalistic political consciousness in the Northern Region of Nigeria received its first organized expression with the inauguration in 1939 of the College Old Boys' Association at Kaduna. These graduates of Kaduna College, the only existing secondary school in the north, and its predecessor, the Katsina Teachers Training College, were in some ways the social equivalents of the elite groups that formed the early parties of Lagos and their successors. Like the Western-educated southern elites, the College Old Boys were destined to assert claims of leadership based on their command of skills relevant to a political economy in the process of modernization.

In 1939, however, the situation in the north was unfavorable to the appearance of political parties. The elective principle had not been introduced and the Northern Provinces were not yet represented in the Nigerian Legislative Council. Equally inhibiting was the authoritarian political tradition of the Hausa-Fulani emirates, traditional units of government which survive today and encompass roughly two-thirds of the northern population. These vigorous states had been deliberately preserved by the colonial government, in keeping with its doctrine that African political development should proceed, *sui generis,* from indigenous tradition. Any political activity on the part of educated and consciously "enlightened" young men based on nontraditional principles was bound to be viewed suspiciously by British officials and emirs alike. The College Old Boys, nearly all of them employees either of the colonial government or of native administrations under control of the emirs, faced hostility from both quarters. Within two years of its inauguration, the association was moribund.

It is pertinent to note that Kaduna College and its predecessors had been established by the British primarily for purposes of educating the traditional ruling class of the emirates. In terms of social background, therefore, most of the old boys were members of the traditional as well as of the "modern" elite; indeed, even today these two elites mostly coincide in the northern emirates. Although there were radicals in this group, the majority of them sought only limited reform which would accommodate their special talents without undermining the position of the traditional ruling stratum as a whole. This conservative impulse characterized all the later northern political organizations which traced their ancestry to the association.

After the demise of the College Old Boys' Association, its objectives were pursued by former members in discussion groups established in various northern towns. The groups that displayed prudence and moderation were tolerated by the native authorities and the British, who nevertheless watched their activities closely. Groups that fell under the influence of radical northerners fared less well. The Zaria Friendly Society, for example, was disbanded when its founder, the noted nationalist figure and koranic scholar, Sa'adu Zungur, used its platform to attack the system of native administration. Similarly, official recognition was withdrawn from the Bauchi Discussion Circle when the salaries of the British resident and the emir were discussed in the presence of both. Later, other ostensibly nonpolitical organizations served as centers of political deliberation. For example, the first convention of the Northern Teachers' Association, founded in 1948, was devoted more to matters of politics than to strictly occupational concerns.

The continuing ferment among the "old boys" elite, evidenced by the recurrent appearance of these quasi-political groups, crystallized in the fall of 1948. Dr. R. A. B. Dikko, then the only government medical officer of northern origin, and Mallam D. A. Rafih, an official of the Nigerian Railways, both called meetings of interested individuals at their homes on September 28, in Zaria and Kaduna, respectively, with the intention of forming a new region-wide political organization in the north. Each was apparently unaware of the other's effort, and two separate groups were organized. The one at Kaduna, inaugurated on October 3, adopted the name Jam'iyyar Mutanen Arewa A Yau (Association of Northern People of Today), and the Zaria group assumed the name Jam'iyyar Jaman Arewa (whose nonliteral English name was Northern Nigerian

Congress). At a second meeting in Zaria, the two organizations merged into the Jam'iyyar Mutanen Arewa (now rendered in English as the Northern Peoples' Congress). Key individuals throughout the north were recruited to set up local branches. Surviving discussion groups at Sokoto, Kano, and Bauchi were among the organizations transformed into local affiliates of the Northern Peoples' Congress.

At this time the NPC described itself as a "social and cultural organization," a guise it was considered prudent to adopt because nearly all its members were government or native authority employees for whom political activity was proscribed or discouraged. But the pursuit of progressive political reforms was implicit in the NPC's declaration of intention: *yakin jahilci, lalaci, da zalunci* (to war against ignorance, idleness, and oppression) in the north.

A small group of progressive-minded young men in Kano were less cautious. In February, 1947, they organized the Northern Elements' Progressive Association (NEPA) for the avowed purpose of defending the public interest before the authorities. It is noteworthy that the founders of the NEPA, although educated, were in the second rank of official employment (mostly clerks), or were similarly engaged by private commercial firms. A son of the Emir of Kano was a secret member, but none of the others enjoyed high traditional status. Old boys were scarce among their number, and a few members came from outside the geographical area of the emirate system. Moreover, whereas the NPC restricted its membership to people of northern origin and had as one of its objects "to prevent southern domination," the NEPA, encouraged by Azikiwe and other southern nationalists, worked closely with local adherents of the NCNC. Details of organization and program were also treated secretively, but its chosen Arabic motto did not hide the NEPA's boldness (*man lam yakhful laha, yakhafu kulla sha'in / man yakhful lah kullu, sha'in yakhafahu,* roughly translated as "He who does not fear God fears everybody, but he who fears God is to be feared by some"). The innuendo was not mistaken by the authorities; important NEPA members were abruptly dismissed from their posts in Kano, and the organization folded.

The first overt and viable political party in the north, the Northern Elements' Progressive Union (NEPU), was founded in Kano on August 8, 1950, by eight young people, mostly Hausa commoners. The name was suggested by one of the party's early members who thought the implied affinity with the NEPA was justified by the revolutionary ideology that inspired the new group. The Declaration of Principles issued in October, 1950, bluntly proclaimed the existence of "a class struggle, between the members of that vicious circle of the Native Administrations on the one hand and the ordinary *'Talakawa'* commoners on the other," and announced the NEPU's dedication to the "emancipation of the *Talakawa* from domination by these privileged few" through "reform of the present autocratic political institutions." The president of a Kano organization called the Taron Masu Zumunta (Friendly Society), Mallam Abba Maikwaru, was elected president of the NEPU, and he brought members of the former group with him into the new party. Several prominent members of the NEPU simultaneously belonged to the NPC, holding that the latter's formal nonpolitical status justified dual membership.

The showdown between the radical and conservative elements in the northern political awakening came at the Jos convention of the NPC in December, 1950, which proscribed dual membership in the NEPU and the NPC and insisted upon the elimination of radical elements from the NPC executive. NEPU adherents within the Kano delegation countered with a proposal to convert the NPC into a political party. The rejection of this proposal marked the final break between the two factions. Soon thereafter, Mallam Aminu Kano, a young teacher in Sokoto, resigned his position, returned to Kano, and joined the NEPU. A strongly worded statement left no doubt that he considered his new role to be militant leadership of a radical political movement.[7] In April, 1951, he was elected vice-president of the party, and early in 1953 he was elevated to the presidency.

The NPC and the NEPU since 1951

Electoral regulations under the 1951 Constitution provided for a series of indirect "tier" elections to the Northern House of Assembly, extending from village and ward units up to the final stage of provincial colleges. Native authorities were given the right "to inject" into the final electoral college 10 per cent of the number reaching that stage through the series of protracted elections at lower levels. This compromise marriage between democratic representation and traditional authority was to produce curious, but significant, results.

At the primary and intermediate stages of the elections in Kano City, Jos, Kaduna, Maiduguri, and Kabba, victories were registered for candidates standing on the platform of the NEPU. In an editorial, the editor of the *Nigerian Citizen,* who was also an officer of the NPC, raised the alarm that this revolutionary party might actually capture control of the

---

[7] "I resigned because I fanatically share the view that the Native Administrations, as they stand today, coupled with their too trumpeted 'fine tradition' are woefully hopeless in solving our urgent educational, social, economic, political and even religious problems. . . .

"I am prepared to be called by any name. Call me a dreamer or call me a revolutionary, call me a crusader or anything you will. I have seen a light on the far horizon and I intend to march into its full circle either alone, or with anyone who cares to go with me" (Aminu Kano, "My Resignation," *Daily Comet,* Nov. 20, 1950, pp. 1, 4).

Northern House of Assembly.[8] Hastily, certain Executive Committee members met and decided to convert the NPC into a political party as of October 1, 1951. They declared the new status of the party in a published announcement which suggested the party's intention to act as a progressive but moderate counterweight to the NEPU. This step was taken too late to permit the party, as such, to present candidates. But the device of 10 per cent "injection," plus the susceptibility of the electoral college arrangement to outside manipulation, allowed the native authorities to rally their supporters in the final stage. No NEPU candidates survived the provincial colleges; rather, candidates identified with native authorities were elected to all parliamentary seats in all but a few provinces, notwithstanding the fact that many of them had lost to NEPU opponents in earlier phases of the election. Subsequently, the overwhelming majority of elected members in the Northern House of Assembly declared for the NPC.[9]

These events ultimately transformed the structure of the NPC. When it declared its new status as a formal political party, the government invoked a standing order proscribing participation in politics by civil servants (some of whom had been radical or reform-minded members of the NPC). This action compelled civil servants to resign from the party, whereas no such restriction was placed on native authority officials. The net result was that a rump, composed essentially of native authority officials and a few wealthy, self-employed merchant-traders, was left in control of the party. In the newly elected House of Assembly, the same group predominated.

It has previously been intimated that almost all the high officials and most of the other employees of the native administrations were either well born or patrician by virtue of a close connection (by marriage or clientage) with hereditary rulers, and that they tended to be fundamentally sympathetic to the traditional social and political order, even if they sought to modify it. Thus the stage was now set for a subtle but emphatic shift in the locus of party power, from a congress of moderate progressives primarily concerned with reform to a parliamentary caucus equally interested in the defense of traditional authority and in traditional definitions of prestige. The impending new balance between traditionalists and modernists was personified in 1951 by the belated but dramatic entry into the party of two men: Alhaji Ahmadu, Sardauna of Sokoto and direct

[8] *Nigerian Citizen*, Oct. 25, 1951, p. 6. The intervention of the *Citizen* and of the vernacular newspaper *Gaskiya Ta Fi Kwabo* against the NEPU was bitterly resented by the party. Both papers were nominally independent, being controlled by a corporation set up by the government.

[9] Thus the new Northern House of Assembly was not originally organized on a party basis, nor were ministers so appointed. The House remained in this state until the government acknowledged control by the NPC in December, 1953.

descendant of the founder of the Fulani empire, who eventually became president of the NPC and premier of the Northern Region, and Abubakar Tafawa Balewa, a lowborn but highly successful modern schoolteacher, now first vice-president of the NPC and prime minister of the federation.

Once the new balance was struck, it tended to be self-perpetuating. Some native authority officials now occupied a dual role as local administrative subaltern in a traditional bureaucracy and politician in a modern elective parliament. Given the political influence of emirs and other traditional notables on the one hand, and their command of the local native bureaucracies on the other, these roles became interdependent. Consequently, one of the rewards for loyalty and service to one's superior in the context of the local administrative bureaucracy was the support of that superior in one's candidacy for elective office. Conversely, one's adherence to the cause of traditional institutions in the context of this new regional legislative body enhanced one's security and prospects for advancement within the local bureaucracy. And it follows, quite obviously, that disloyalty in either context was punishable in the other.

The altered direction of the NPC was reflected in organizational developments. To facilitate the assertion of authority by the parliamentary over the extraparliamentary party, the central secretariat was moved to Kaduna (the northern capital), where it could more easily be controlled by government ministers. At the local level of organization, the party machinery became fused with the administrative apparatus of the traditional native authorities. Successive constitutional reforms after 1951 required the NPC to contest ever more democratically organized elections; the last two (in 1959 and 1961) used the methods of adult male suffrage, direct voting, and secret balloting. Yet the ideological charter of the party, its organizational structure, and the social composition of its leadership have all remained remarkably intact.

The development of a competitive party system had an important, if less readily visible, impact on the NEPU. The party realized after its experience in the 1951 elections that it faced the task of nurturing a revolutionary movement in soil saturated by well-entrenched traditional institutions. It seemed unlikely that a largely peasant population, less than 15 per cent of whom are literate and most of whom are wed to traditional assumptions and expectations regarding traditional authority, would immediately respond to expressions of democratic radicalism. Thus it is not surprising that the NEPU's electoral successes have been largely confined to towns. The NEPU's response to these obstacles to the development of a radical mass political party has entailed two significant steps. First, in 1954 the party concluded an alliance with the NCNC which has provided, especially in the 1959 elections, organizational and financial support. (Alliance with a southern party was also consistent with the

NEPU's advocacy of unitary government for Nigeria.) Second, it has attempted in the key area of the Hausa-Fulani state system to translate the party's appeal into terms comprehensible to the peasantry through traditional history, values, and susceptibilities.

The NEPU, particularly as it operates in the key emirates of Sokoto, Kano, Katsina, and Zaria, has sought to interpret the meaning of Western-inspired ideas of democracy and egalitarianism in terms of the historic, traditional conflict of interest between the majority of conquered indigenous people of the emirates (the *Habe,* a Fulani word for the original, non-Fulani inhabitants of the emirates) and their overlords (the Fulani), and through the classic social division between the *sarakuna* (ruling class) and the *talakawa* (commoner class). By astutely making use of traditional themes, the NEPU has served as a focus of political and social protest, and has acted as a gadfly to the NPC. By retaining a high degree of organizational centralization and discipline, the NEPU has tried to ensure that the invocation of traditional tensions and sentiments for electoral purposes does not interfere unduly with the party's primary purpose of articulating a program of social and political modernization. Independent organizational support from the NCNC has helped the NEPU to exercise control in these delicate circumstances, while the alliance between the two parties has also given the NEPU a far more significant role in national politics than its electoral strength alone would have provided.

The United Middle Belt Congress

In the decade 1950–1960, a third major northern political party emerged in the southern half of the Northern Region—known variously as the "Middle Belt," the "riverain provinces," or the "lower north"—an area inhabited by multifarious ethnic groups whose numbers total about one-third of the region's population. Together, these numerous groups of the lower north also constitute a cultural and social minority vis-à-vis the peoples of the Hausa-Fulani states system of the "upper north" in that they are predominately non-Muslim (i.e., animist and Christian) and natively non–Hausa-speaking peoples; most of them have histories and traditions that favor small-scale or highly decentralized, parademocratic forms of political organization. The devolution of constitutional power to regional units stimulated the rise of a political movement to secure for the northern minorities a separate state or region in which they would not be numerically or culturally dominated by the majority people of the upper north.

Middle Belt separatism took organizational form in 1945 when a former Catholic seminary student, Patrick Dokotri, founded the Birom Progressive Union which espoused the idea of a Middle Belt state. A few prominent Christian leaders, including Dokotri, later organized the Northern Non-Muslim League, but in 1950 changed its name to Middle Zone League (MZL) in order to emphasize the goal of a separate region and to disclaim any intention of fostering religio-political conflict. After 1953 the movement was seriously hampered from within by ethnic particularism, inconsistency and division among its leadership over fundamentals of tactics, and organizational factionalism. Briefly, one group composed primarily of the originators of the MZL has tended to favor coöperation with the NPC, hoping thereby ultimately to change the NPC's declared policy of "one North, one people, regardless of rank, tribe, or religion." Other leaders have preferred outright opposition to the NPC and alliance with southern nationalist parties. Each faction has relied on different ethnic groups for its organizational base. Conflict between the two positions has been reflected in splintering, amalgamation, and resplintering of various wings of the movement. A breakaway organization called the Middle Belt Peoples' Party was formed after the MZL negotiated an alliance with the NPC. The two groups came together again in 1955 under the name United Middle Belt Congress (UMBC), but split into two factions within a year. Temporary unity was again achieved in 1956 when all factions decided to break the connection with the NPC, but dissension arose once more when a majority segment of the party ratified an alliance with the Action Group in 1958 over the strong objections of certain leaders (some of whom, including former leaders of the Middle Belt Peoples' Party, subsequently joined the NPC).

The Middle Belt State movement has suffered in that the majority of the peoples of the lower north seemed not to see in separatism a solution to minority problems. Rather, they have regarded accommodation to, or even assimilation with, the forces represented by the NPC as offering more security and better opportunity, an attitude deliberately encouraged by the northern government. Yet the electoral strength of the movement for a time increased steadily, owing to the persistent and deep-seated apprehensions of certain important groups (e.g., the populous Tiv of Benue Province). In 1959 members of the United Middle Belt Congress, under the presidency of J. S. Tarka of Tiv Division, contested the federal election as official Action Group candidates, and won in twenty-six constituencies in the lower north. Thus the Action Group became the largest opposition party in the Northern Region. By 1959 the UMBC, like separatist movements in the Eastern Region, was functioning as an integral part of the Action Group. Between 1959 and 1961 the strength of the Action Group in the Middle Belt sharply declined, and the party won in only nine northern constituencies, mostly in Tivland, in the 1961 regional election. The resulting distribution of power was attributable to the magnetic attraction evidently being exerted on traditionally alien minorities by governmental power in the hands of the Hausa-Fulani majority, and to the tenacity of the historically independent-minded Tiv people in the face of this attraction. In 1963 the UMBC broke away from the Action Group and combined with the NEPU (renamed the Nigerian Elements' Progressive Union) to form a new opposition alliance, the Northern Progressive Front.

PATTERNS OF LEADERSHIP

Social Background

Tables 1 and 3 present comparatively the factors of social background for the principal leaders of the major parties. It is seen that the

TABLE 1

ETHNIC DISTRIBUTION OF MAJOR PARTY LEADERS, NIGERIA
(In percentages)

Party	Ibo	Other eastern groups	Yoruba	Other western groups	Northern groups	Cameroonians, non-Nigerians, and unknown
NCNC[a]	49.3	9.9	26.7	5.6	2.8	5.6
Action Group[b]	4.5	15.2	68.2	7.6	3.0	1.5

Party	Fulani	Habe	Nupe	Kanuri	Yoruba	Other northern groups	Unknown
NPC[c]	32.4	18.9	9.4	6.8	6.8	16.2	9.4
NEPU[d]	14.0	67.1	4.6	3.1	0.0	7.1	3.2

[a] Data have been tabulated for seventy-one officials of the NCNC, including forty-five members of the National Executive Committee, members of the Eastern Working and Western Working committees, and ministers in the eastern and federal governments (1958).

[b] Data have been tabulated for sixty-six members of the Federal Executive Council of the Action Group, including federal officers, regional representatives, ministers in the western and federal governments, and Western Regional officials (1958).

[c] Data have been tabulated for seventy-four members of the National Executive Committee of the NPC (1958).

[d] Data have been tabulated for sixty-four members of the National Executive Committee of the NEPU (1959).

top leadership groups of all parties reflect their primary ethnic foundations. The largest single ethnic group in the NPC is Fulani, although the extreme ethnic heterogeneity of the Northern Region, including emirate areas, is reflected in the composition of the party leadership. NEPU leadership is overwhelmingly Habe, although some Fulani and others are represented. Despite the widespread expansion of the Action Group into minority areas of the Eastern and Northern regions, the ethnic core of its leadership is essentially Yoruba.[10] The NCNC seems to be the most cosmopolitan party, at least with respect to the ethnic groups of southern Nigeria, an impression corroborated by the fact that seven of the ten NCNC federal ministers in October, 1960, were non-Ibo, and four of them were Yoruba.

The religious affiliation of leaders is a factor of some political consequence in all parties (see table 2). Prior to the 1957 elections Catholic leaders were known to have felt that their church interests were underrepresented in the eastern government. Unlike the Eastern Region, where few Muslims are found, the Western Region has almost equal numbers

TABLE 2

RELIGIOUS DISTRIBUTION OF MAJOR PARTY LEADERS, NIGERIA
(In percentages)

Party	Christian	Muslim	Unknown
NCNC[a]	91.5	8.5	0.0
Action Group[b]	75.6	7.5	18.2[e]
NPC[c]	12.2	86.5	1.3
NEPU[d]	6.2	90.6	3.2

[a] See note *a*, table 1.
[b] See note *b*, table 1.
[c] See note *c*, table 1.
[d] See note *d*, table 1.
[e] All but one member of this group were northern residents of Yoruba, Ibo, or Idoma ethnic origin, who were probably Christians.

of Muslim and Christian adherents in its Yoruba areas; yet the overwhelming majority of Action Group leaders have been Christian. (This trend is largely owing to the historic connections among Christian penetration, Western education, and nationalist political activity.) Muslim predominance in the NPC and the NEPU stems not only from the numerical preponderance of Muslims in the Northern Region, but also from the parties' close relationship to the emirate system. All parties have taken steps to correct these politically exploitable imbalances: after 1957 the

---

[10] Table 1 does not reveal the concentrated effort, beginning in 1958, to recruit non-Yoruba northerners into the Action Group, at least three of whom were then members of the federal Executive Council. On the other hand, this tabulation omits some of the most important Action Group leaders of Yoruba nationality who were not members of the executive, and includes some non-Yoruba members of comparatively minor importance.

NCNC cabinet had a substantially larger Catholic component; the Action Group leadership has endeavored to attract more Muslim colleagues; and the NPC has recruited leaders from among Christians in the lower north.

James S. Coleman's tabulations on the educational background of Nigerian parliamentarians from 1952 to 1957 show the differential impact of Western education on party leadership in the Northern Region and in the south. Thus, about two-thirds of the eastern and western members of the House of Representatives and of the regional Houses of Assembly had received secondary education, and about one-third had been educated at the university level. In contrast, only 49 per cent of the northern members of the House of Representatives had been educated up to the secondary level, and only 8 per cent of them had reached the university level. In the Northern House of Assembly, the secondary level had been attained by only 17 per cent, and the university level, by 2 per cent.[11] It is estimated that the average level of Western education attained by members of the NEPU Executive Committee is about three to four grades lower than that of their NPC counterparts.

Table 3 clearly indicates that elite occupational groups constitute

TABLE 3

OCCUPATIONAL DISTRIBUTION OF MAJOR PARTY LEADERS, NIGERIA
(In percentages)

Party	Professionals (law, medicine, and the learned professions)	Educators	Businessmen (finance and entrepreneurship)	Business managers, retired senior civil servants, and administrative functionaries of the northern native authorities
NCNC[a]	26.8	19.7	28.2	5.6
Action Group[b]	33.3	18.2	21.2	1.5
NPC[c]	1.4	6.7	25.7	63.5
NEPU[d]	3.1	3.1	17.2	20.3

[a] See note *a*, table 1.
[b] See note *b*, table 1. Data unavailable for 3 per cent of the total.
[c] See note *c*, table 1.
[d] See note *d*, table 1. Data unavailable for 7.9 per cent of the total.

the core of leadership in Nigerian political parties. Leaders were drawn by the three major parties from the professional, educational, business, managerial, senior civil service, and native administration categories as follows: NCNC, 80.3 per cent; Action Group, 74.2 per cent; and NPC,

---

[11] Coleman, *op. cit.*, pp. 378–383. These figures do not imply graduation. In 1959 there were no university graduates either in the Northern House of Assembly, or among members of the federal House of Representatives from that region.

97.3 per cent.[12] Very small percentages of the categories of petty trade, crafts, shopkeeping, laboring, and farming advance to leadership. Only the NEPU draws its leaders substantially from these latter groups.

Leadership Status and Recruitment

Ralph Linton's analytical distinction between ascribed and achieved status[13] is relevant to patterns of party leadership in Nigeria. The difference between ascribed and achieved status is roughly that between the relative importance attached to "who you are" as against "what you can do." Socially achieved leadership status is the rule in the Action Group and the NCNC. Socially ascribed leadership status is the dominant pattern in the NPC (we refer, of course, to significant tendencies; leadership status is never exclusively ascribed or achieved, and this is true of Nigerian political parties). The achievement orientation of traditional cultures in southern Nigeria has doubtless contributed to the prevalence of this quality in party leadership patterns in the Eastern and Western regions. The Ibo people, for example, are noted for their valuation of individual achievement and "receptivity to change."[14] Among the more hierarchical Yoruba, merit or achievement has always been one of the important avenues to a chieftaincy title, as it is today.[15] Furthermore, the processes of commercialization, modern urbanization, and Western education have generated a new rising class, whose members have also imparted to southern society the achievement-oriented values of their social and occupational roles.

The major types of leaders in the Action Group and the NCNC may be characterized as "organizational intelligentsia," "cosmopolitan celebrities," "communal heroes," and "traditional notables," roughly in that

[12] This result is confirmed by tabulation of the occupational backgrounds of party leaders at the local level in 1958. Of 228 leaders of the NCNC in eight urban areas of the Eastern and Western regions, 54.9 per cent belong to these categories, as do 68.3 per cent of 202 Action Group leaders in Lagos and twelve other townships or local areas. (The figure for the Action Group corrects the false impression given by the figures in table 3, that NCNC rather than Action Group leadership is more elitist in composition.) Of 195 members of provincial and divisional executive committees of the NPC in eight major emirates, 85.6 per cent belong to the occupational elite category.

[13] *The Study of Man* (New York: D. Appleton-Century, 1936), p. 115.

[14] S. Ottenberg, "Ibo Receptivity to Change," in W. R. Bascom and M. J. Herskovits, eds., *Continuity and Change in African Cultures* (Chicago: University of Chicago Press, 1958), pp. 130–143.

[15] "It is the prerogative of the *Oba* [king], in consultation with his Chiefs, to confer a chieftaincy title on any citizen who in his judgment possesses the necessary qualities. The candidate for a chieftaincy title must be an outstanding person in the community, possessing good character and integrity, and fairly well-to-do. . . . The appointment of educated, enlightened, well-to-do or prominent young persons as Chiefs is a modern innovation, and it is an eloquent proof of the importance attached to western education and culture in present-day Yoruba society" (Awolowo, *op. cit.*, p. 8).

order of importance. The most numerous and most important group of leaders, the organizational intelligentsia, are typically educators, professionals, and businessmen who enjoy high social position and have devoted their talents and lent their prestige to the service of a nationalist party. Cosmopolitan celebrities are popular lawyers and businessmen whose charismatic qualities appeal to the electorates of multitribal urban communities. The communal hero combines assets of ascription and achievement; he personifies the political values of a homogeneous cultural subgroup in an area of traditional habituation, and provides the crucial link between traditionalists who resist change at the local level and radicals who foster change at the national level. In each of these instances the personality type and the requirements of leadership mutually reinforce the social importance attached to performance. Skillful and successful men are sought after by a political party, which is itself a broad channel of upward mobility. Indeed, service to the party alone has sometimes been responsible for the enhanced social position enjoyed by party leaders.[16] Finally, the traditional notable represents the incidence of ascription on leadership in southern Nigeria. Normally, in that area, the traditional heads of customary hierarchies are not party members, but they frequently consent to be identified as patrons. The degree of influence wielded by men of this category in southern Nigeria is limited by the extensive political control that government parties in the east and the west exercise over traditional institutions.

The ascriptive nature of traditional northern emirate leadership is basically a function of the rule that the highest traditional office, emirship, is available only to those eligible by birth to seek it, whereas all other offices and titles are awarded primarily on the basis of kinship, marriage, hereditary vassalage, or clientage (personal allegiance) to the emir. Furthermore, in Hausa society the "system of occupational status . . . is almost wholly ascriptive in its orientation since its units are closed descent groups between which all movement is disapproved";[17] however, clientage and to some degree marriage have always provided possible channels of

<hr>

[16] In 1960 there were about 650 legislators in the four parliaments of Nigeria at stipends of £800 per annum, about 55 junior ministers (parliamentary secretaries) at stipends of £1,500 on the average, and about 75 senior ministers at £3,000. For a few of them, such as barristers whose private practices net more than £3,000 per annum, ministerial service has involved a financial sacrifice, but for the vast majority of ministers and legislators, politics has been enormously rewarding in terms of status and income. Indeed, this has been an underlying cause of intraparty conflict. Since 1955 the NCNC Youth Association has agitated for the reduction of ministerial, legislative, and administrative salaries in order to narrow the income gap between the privileged political class and the poor. In 1957 the average per capita income for Nigeria as a whole was estimated at £25–£29.

[17] M. G. Smith, "The Hausa System of Social Status," *Africa*, XXIX (July, 1959), 251.

upward mobility. Furthermore, royal slaves were frequently utilized in certain official capacities, were awarded special titles, and were therefore considered to be part of the ruling class.

The impact of traditional status patterns of NPC leadership is best observed in the Northern House of Assembly, where 94 of 131 legislators elected in 1959 from constituencies located in emirates were NPC members. Almost one-fourth of this group (24 per cent) were sons of incumbent or former emirs. If the measure of kinship is extended to include more distant relatives (brothers, grandsons, nephews, first cousins), more than one-third (37 per cent) of such seats in the House were held by the blood kin of ruling emirs. Of the remaining NPC members in this category, 6 per cent were men married into ruling houses, 7 per cent were identified as *fadawa* (sing. *bafada;* an emir's courtiers or servants, who are invariably in a relationship of clientage), and 17 per cent were members of hereditarily titled families; other titled nobles and high officials accounted for another 11 per cent. Four seats were held by persons who were not then prominent but whose fathers were high traditional officials; the father of one was a native court judge. Altogether, 87 per cent of the NPC members from emirates belonged to the traditional ruling class, and half of the remaining number were lower-rank employees of native authorities.

It is significant, however, that, although persons with unmistakably high ascriptive credentials dominate the top party ranks, some of those in such positions apparently do not fit this description. Traditional emirate rules excluded even wealthy merchant-traders (*attajirai*) from holding political title and office, yet a northern minister who was also regional president of the party, and fifteen others in this occupational category, were NPC members of the Northern House of Assembly in 1959.[18] Persuaded by the traditional elite to enter politics after the introduction of popular elections, attajirai are usually Habe talakawa who are in command of considerable financial resources; these attributes have made them valuable allies of the aristocratic party chiefs in the competition for mass political support. As allies, the attajirai offer an additional advantage in that the persistence of a relatively low cultural evaluation of their status, and their own well-ingrained habits of deference, tend to prevent them from appearing or acting as rivals of the aristocracy, even in modern politics. Those attajirai who themselves might entertain such thoughts are probably deterred by the consideration that nowadays the more lucrative business opportunities require public support (trading licenses, investments, loans, etc.). Thus the NPC has become increasingly more

---

[18] Six of these, however, belong by origin to the sarakuna class, having taken up commerce after losing administrative office.

sensitive to the interests of entrepreneurs, but it has not converted entrepreneurial assets into the political power they might represent in a society
where tradition is less pervasive.

A few leaders at the very top also come from a background of relatively low traditional status. Prime Minister Balewa's father was a slave,
as was the father of the incumbent NPC federal Minister of Mines and
Power;[19] the northern Minister of Finance is the son of a koranic *mallam*
and bafada to a Nupe nobleman. These three leaders especially, who
have risen primarily through educational attainment and demonstrated
ability, represent the incidence of achievement criteria in NPC leadership recruitment. As we have noted, however, their rise is not completely foreign to traditional preconceptions. Paradoxically, the relative
flexibility of traditional rules of leadership recruitment has facilitated the
survival of the traditional aristocracy by permitting assimilation of modern political talent. That this flexibility is not without limits, however, is
suggested by the assertion of conservative northerners that a person of
Balewa's traditional status is far more acceptable as prime minister than
he would be as premier of the Northern Region (which constitutes a
position of direct formal authority over the emirs).

Northern leadership ascription is fostered by active relationships
between individuals in the two spheres of party and native administration. Native administration officials, who leave their posts to take up
ministerial appointments, do not resign, but rather are designated as being
"on leave without pay." Several prominent government ministers are also
the most influential members of their respective emirs' councils. Ministerial office is often the steppingstone to advancement in the traditional
hierarchy; in eight years no less than six ministers or junior ministers
resigned their posts (one since the attainment of regional self-government) to take up office in their emirates. This is also a measure of the
attraction that traditional administrative office continues to hold. These
relationships reflect a process of mutual coöptation of traditional and
modern party elites, a mode of recruitment which contrasts markedly
with the leadership recruitment patterns of southern parties.

NEPU leadership reflects the party's ideological objective of a radical
democracy in which the ordinary talakawa have a fair share. By any
measure—occupation, education, or traditional status—the majority of
NEPU leaders at national and local levels are drawn from the lower strata

---

[19] Although legal slavery was abolished in northern Nigeria in 1900, the social
designation of slave (*bawa;* pl. *bavi*) persisted, and the son of a slave (*dimajo* or
bacucane; pls., *dimajai, cucunawa*) continues today to be so identified in terms of
traditional society. See M. G. Smith, *Government in Zazzau, 1800–1950* (London:
Oxford University Press, 1960), pp. 253, 254 ff., and "Slavery and Emancipation in
Two Societies (Jamaica and Zaria)," *Social and Economic Studies* (published by the
Institute for Social and Economic Research, Mona, Jamaica), III, no. 4 (1954).

of society. Many salaried clerks and technical workers employed in native administrations, and other educated individuals, covertly sympathize with the NEPU's program, but are inhibited from assuming leadership roles by considerations of career. Few NEPU leaders have aristocratic origins.

The presence of certain wellborn individuals among NEPU leaders is significant, however. The life president-general, Mallam Aminu Kano, is himself a member of an eminent Fulani family of traditional Kano jurists; the patron of the party is a descendant of the royal family of Sokoto; and the secretary general is a member of one of the ruling dynasties of the Bida Emirate. Leaders such as Aminu Kano typify the patrician radical whose ideological convictions lead to identification with the common people, but whose high ascriptive status proves advantageous in mobilizing radical political action in ascription-conscious societies. Other leaders of this status, found more often in local NEPU branches, are products of chronic friction within the aristocracy. They are men who have lost their positions and have become disaffected, either because certain administrative offenses they have committed were exposed or because they have fallen victim to the intense competition that is waged among the eligible for traditional title and office, or because of both, as the dynamics of traditional politics often relate the two causes. For the disaffected, the NEPU represents an alternative channel of political activity and a chance to recoup influence and position. Because formerly powerful officials usually retain some following, the party sometimes gains additional support through being associated with them. This situation was epitomized by the candidacy under the NEPU banner in the 1959 elections of two deposed emirs, the ex-Emir of Dikwa and the ex-Lamido of Adamawa. Although the amount of support that the NEPU picks up in this manner may easily be exaggerated (e.g., the ex-emirs were not elected), this strand in the NEPU leadership is not inconsequential.

PARTY MEMBERS AND SUPPORTERS

The major Nigerian political parties are comprehensive membership groups. Any Nigerian may be a member of the Action Group or the NCNC, and any person of northern origin is eligible for membership in the NPC and the NEPU. During the final decade of colonial rule, millions of Nigerians were drawn by the major political parties into the main stream of national politics; more than 7 million persons voted in the general elections of December, 1959.

It is a common observation that political parties in Nigeria and elsewhere in Africa rely strongly upon communal participation, that is, political alignment on the basis of ethnic or religious affinity. If defined to mean only religious and ethnic ties, however, the concept of communalism provides inadequate insights into Nigerian party politics. Maurice Duverger's analysis of the quality or nature of participation, based on Ferdinand Tönnies' classic distinction between *Gemeinschaft* (community) and *Gesellschaft* (society), is more suggestive.[20] Pure Gemeinschaft relationships are natural, spontaneous, and involuntary—for example, as Duverger suggests, the attachment of an individual to his family, village, country, or race. For purposes of the present discussion, party alignment on a Gemeinschaft or communal basis means that members and supporters conceive of their party as an extension of a social order into which they have been born and to which they attribute spiritual or mystical significance. Gesellschaft, or associational participation, means purposeful alignment on the basis of a perceived interest.

By so restricting these concepts, it becomes apparent that ethnic affinity is not a sufficient condition of communal participation. For example, settlers in a new urban area of Nigeria may support a political party largely for ethnic or tribal reasons, but commitment to a party in a new town does not have the intensely emotional quality that attaches to identification with a social order to which moral excellence is attributed. On the contrary, membership or support may also be contingent on the position of the party on issues of social conflict, endemic to the class structure of a commercial town, which affect settlers' interests. Once individuals no longer perceive the social order as sacred and inviolable, ethnic affinity does not produce communal participation in the Gemeinschaft sense.

Communal participation became important with the introduction of popular elections in 1951, which obliged nationalist leaders to enlist the support of the peasantry. Party leaders quickly perceived that customary institutions and associations based on cultural solidarity could be employed to supplement and sustain local organizations that were deficient in membership and laggard in performance. The first political party to utilize customary institutions and traditional authorities for the purpose of systematic organization of the peasantry was the Action Group in western Nigeria. As previously noted, a Yoruba cultural organization called the Egbe Omo Oduduwa was of invaluable assistance to the Action Group's program of mass organization. By and large, the Yoruba traditional chiefs resigned themselves to the era of democratic government, and hoped that in return the dignity of chieftaincy would be preserved in the new order. The alignment of these chiefs with the Yoruba-speaking intelligentsia of the Action Group was essentially associational in nature,

[20] Maurice Duverger, *Political Parties*, trans. Barbara and Robert North (New York: John Wiley & Sons, 1954), pp. 124–132; Ferdinand Tonnies, *Fundamental Concepts of Sociology* [*Gemeinschaft und Gesellschaft*], translated and supplemented by Charles P. Loomis (New York: American Book Company, 1940).

but through the role of the chiefs the Action Group at the local level was widely endowed with the aura of traditional sanction.

A key feature of party politics in southern Nigeria is that parties frequently rely on mass participation of a communal nature in local areas of traditional habitation, although the commitment of party leaders who belong to a rising class is associational in character. Usually the integrated community will accept the political leadership of its emergent class. On occasion, however, the people of traditional communities have rebelled against such leadership. At Ibadan, capital of the Western Region, the indigenous community repudiated the leadership of rising-class elements who declared for the Action Group. One explanation is that the Ibadan Yoruba identified the Action Group with the interests of their traditional rivals, the Ijebu Yoruba. Their antipathy to the Action Group was aggravated by the presence in Ibadan of many Ijebu settlers who pressed for democratic representation in the local government council and for the right of settlers to acquire urban land on a freehold basis. Most of the Ibadan indigenes do not share the Pan-Yoruba and nontraditional perspectives of the settlers. In 1954 they rallied to a communal party called in Yoruba the Mabolaje. (*Mabolaje* means "[Do] not reduce the dignity of chiefs.") Its founder, the late Alhaji Adegoke Adelabu, a leader of the NCNC, was the prototype of the communal hero as party leader.

The Ibadan experience suggests that stimulating communal participation may entail encouraging values that are inimical to modernization, but it also suggests that if secular leadership is in control, the device is likely to result in less reactionary political activity than might otherwise occur. In matters of local administration, Adelabu of Ibadan often acquiesced in the narrow views of traditional chiefs and their followers, but he gained their loyalty to a political party that pursued secular and modernistic goals on the wider national scene.

The impact of rivalry between Ijebu and Ibadan Yoruba on party competition in the Western Region also suggests that subcultural segmentation within ethnic nationalities may constitute a problem for political parties that rely on communal appeals. In eastern Nigeria, where vast numbers of rural Ibo people are attached to the NCNC by virtue of sentiments largely communal in nature, communal reactions erupted within the party in 1957 among the indigenous people (the Udi Ibo) in the area of Enugu, the capital city. Many Udi Ibo partisans were also laborers in the Enugu coal mines, and their object was to wrest control of the local NCNC and the local government council from cosmopolitan Ibo settlers under the leadership of businessmen, professionals, and other rising-class elements. The Ibadan and Enugu conflicts also illustrate the point that in the transitional environment of southern Nigeria, forces of community and class are constantly interacting within and between the political parties in a highly complex and not always predictable fashion.

In the emirate areas of northern Nigeria, participation on the basis of traditional affinities is not synonymous with communal participation, in that social stratification is rooted in antiquity and is not primarily the consequence of recent Western contact or of socioeconomic change. The associational principle is inherent in the distinction the Hausa-Fulani make between sarakuna and talakawa. The purview of northern political parties, however, is not exclusively traditional, nor are they precluded from enlisting support by asserting communal values.

By and large, the active membership of the NPC comprises a coalition of interests, including hereditary rulers, traditional notables, elements with a higher modern education, the *ma'aikata* or native administration clerical and technical workers, and well-to-do merchant-traders. This coalition is definitely structured, with traditionalists in the upper echelons of the hierarchy. Clearly the NPC could not have remained dominant in an era of democratic elections if its support had been limited to a coalition of minority interests. The requisite mass support has been enlisted through appeals that make use of both associational and communal principles of participation on the one hand, and of both traditional and modern sentiments on the other. Associational principles bind individuals who seek patronage in the modern form of opportunities for remunerative employment, for profitable enterprise, and for special services, which have opened up because of the postwar emphasis on economic development; both the government and the native administrations are in a position to dispense such patronage. At the same time, NPC supporters include many people who have simply remained within the nexus of the traditional institution of clientage or personal allegiance to members of the traditional ruling hierarchy. Until very recently, this relationship represented not only the main channel of upward mobility to and within the traditional hierarchy; it also, for the talakawa, constituted virtually the only political means of protecting themselves against the possibility of ill-treatment at the hands of other individual members of the local, traditional bureaucracies. In effect, these clients have transferred their dependence on persons—their allegiance to individual traditional patrons—to the modern party of their patrons.

Given the potentially divisive class structure of Hausa society, however, the logic of strictly associational principles of participation is a sword of Damocles to the *status quo*, a situation of which the traditional ruling class, as others, is well aware. Hence, if the NPC is to succeed in preserving the traditional order in the upper north, as it clearly desires to do, the party must emphasize principles of solidarity; it must stress the basically integrative forces within the traditional community.

In the emirates virtually the only such force is Islam. Thus, in its approach to the masses, the party constantly asserts the bonds of the community of the faithful, and benefits from the strictures in Islamic doctrine against schism. Inasmuch as the NPC is identified with fostering traditional authority, and as traditional authority is religiously sanctioned, party, faith, and community may be convincingly portrayed as one. That the NEPU's alliance with the NCNC within the Northern Region embodies an allegiance incompatible with fidelity to Islam is a corollary of the doctrine of communal unity, which the NPC has relentlessly and effectively propagated (notwithstanding its coalition with the NCNC in the federal government).

The active NEPU members are largely those who are least enthralled by hierarchical relationships and assumptions, notably petty traders, artisans, and youths of the towns. Petty traders and artisans are less dependent for their livelihood on the good will of eminent personages than are either peasants or attajirai; moreover, they commonly have special grievances in connection with taxation. In large urban centers like Zaria and Kano, initials or insignia openly proclaiming NEPU affiliation may be seen on the outer walls or doors of certain houses, which are usually found to belong to members of this socioeconomic segment. Similarly, the numerous *gardawa* (itinerant pupils engaged in memorizing the Koran) are by definition unattached to settled social hierarchies, and the NEPU has been able to draw many of them into its fold. In general, youths of the towns have not entered into the normally adult relationships of clientage. Indeed, many of them have migrated to towns precisely in order to escape the inevitable toil, discipline, and subservience of peasant life. In the towns they are exposed to cosmopolitan influences and attractions, and are able to subsist by working intermittently for wages. That such youths are relatively liberated from normal social bonds is implied in the Hausa epithet with which the more "substantial" members of the community deride them: *yan iska* (literally, "sons of the wind").

But these urban activists are not numerous enough to provide sufficient electoral support; in fact, many of the youths concerned are below voting age. In rural areas the associational appeal of the NEPU derives from its efforts on behalf of peasants who complain of maladministration and corruption. Paradoxically, however, the NEPU's efforts to articulate such grievances—by making them public, by petitioning government administrative officers for alleviation, or by prompting litigation—are often considered by the peasants to be less effective than traditional antidotes.

As the NEPU's avowed intention is to do away with the traditional system in the emirates, to invoke the unity of the existing community would obviously be incongruous if not self-defeating. Yet the NEPU, too, makes a communal appeal. It has sought mass support by trying to evoke the special identity and solidarity of the Habe vis-à-vis their conquerors, the Fulani. In conjuring up glories of the past, of a social and political order without the overlordship of the Fulani, the NEPU is invoking what might be called vestigial communalism—a sense of an antecedent and morally preëminent community underneath and beyond the existing one. Wherever this sense has always been strong, notably in the predominately Habe sections of Kano City, the NEPU has enjoyed substantial support in all elections between 1951 and 1961. Alternatively, but in like vein, the NEPU is careful to emphasize what it proclaims to have been the authentic ideals of the jihad (a righteous war for the purification of Islamic faith and practice) which helped to put the Fulani rulers in power, with the imputation that these ideals have been betrayed by those who succeeded the founding fathers of the Fulani empire. Although the NEPU evidently has not succeeded in rallying the bulk of the peasantry around such communal values, the values help to explain the size of the party's peasant following.

PARTY STRUCTURE AND ORGANIZATION

Primary Elements: Local Levels

The National Convention of Nigerian Citizens and the Action Group are "direct," individual membership parties, based on branches formed at various levels of local government, normally at the level of local or district council. NCNC branches in the Eastern Region are usually formed in local government areas; they are coördinated by executive committees at the regional constituency level. Some branches of the NCNC in the Western Region are, in effect, organizational units of communal participation; parochial names symbolize their unique local origins: for example, the Otu Edo (Edo Community) of Benin and the Egbe Oyo Parapo (Oyo People's Party). Although membership in these tribal parties is restricted to the indigenous population of Benin and Oyo, respectively, the parties are the major components of integrated local NCNC branches which include settler elements as well.

The Action Group prescribes the formation of branches at the level of local government electoral wards. Heretofore, Action Group branches in the Western Region, like those of the NCNC in the Eastern Region, have been coördinated by conferences and executive bodies at the level of the division, formerly the basic unit of colonial administration. Several divisions coincide with the traditional jurisdictions of paramount chiefs, and the eclipse of divisional organizations by new units of coördination

at the level of the constituency for the regional House of Assembly reflects the decline of traditional authority in local party affairs.

NPC local party branches invariably coincide with units of local
government and administration. Moreover, the importance of a party
branch in village, ward, rural district, town, division, or province cor-
responds roughly to the importance of the parallel administrative level.
Traditional-administrative authority and party leadership tend to be exercised by the same personnel, especially in rural districts. Of sixty-eight
rural district branches surveyed in 1959, sixty had a party chairman
who was also the district head (traditional subchief of an emirate).

In conformity with the party's close relationship with the emirate
system, NPC party authority is highly decentralized. The key decision-
making unit is normally located at the level of the division, except, significantly, when the divisional unit does not correspond to the unit of
traditional habitation; thus, in divisions that include more than one traditional emirate, all important party matters affecting the latter (nominations, finance, etc.) are within the jurisdiction of the lower branch,
corresponding to the emirate rather than to the division. This arrangement indicates that NPC organization reflects and acknowledges the
traditional status of emirates as virtually autonomous states.

One of the inestimable advantages offered to the NPC by the fusion
of party with local administrative authority was stated in an early memorandum on party organization: "The party must make every effort to
have one member at least in every village of fair size in the region. This
is possible if the party can win the hearts of village and district scribes
[clerks], schoolteachers, and native authority employees whose work concerns touring, for example, agricultural, veterinary, medical, and forest
mallams. The services of such officers to the party are most important." [21]
Indeed, at the local level, the relationship between the party machinery
and the administrative apparatus of the traditional emirate unit may best
be described as symbiotic. The party acts in defense of traditional authority, and traditional authority sustains the party.

Significantly, the most important local NEPU units do not coincide
with the division or the emirate, but are at the rural district, town, or
provincial level; those at the provincial level, especially the annual provincial conferences, are the most important. Also in contrast with the
NPC, the NEPU organization is highly centralized, and a direct chain of
command links the local branches to one another and to the central party.

Primary Elements: Federal and Regional Levels

National Convention of Nigerian Citizens.—Supreme authority in the
NCNC is vested in its national convention, held annually and for special

---

[21] "Sake Tsarin Jami'iyyan Mutanen Arewa," NPC Secretariat, Dec. 13, 1953.

purposes. Nine annual and four special conventions were held in the twelve-year span from 1948 through 1959. The right of representation is extended to every regional constituency and to units of the principal ancillary organizations—the Women's Association and the Zikist Movement; to all parliamentary members; and to members of the National Executive Committee. The conventions of the NCNC are well known for the freewheeling spontaneity of their proceedings. To cite an illustration, the motion empowering the national president to appoint the national officers, adopted by the Aba convention of 1957, was moved from the convention floor as an alternative to more drastic measures proposed by Nnamdi Azikiwe. Currently, all national officers (with the exception of the national organizer, who is a full-time employee of the party), including the national president and the national secretary, are subject to annual reëlection by the national convention. In addition to the national officers, who compose the Central Working Committee, the national convention elects forty-four other members to the National Executive Committee, with due regard for the representation of geographical areas and groups that have been active in the nationalist movement. The Executive Committee meets semiannually and as required; some of its famous meetings have been, in effect, "little conventions," distinguished by a presidential address, the presence of many observers, and an air of controversy. Under Azikiwe, the effective powers of the committee were sometimes delegated to a small group called the Strategic Committee, which included the Central Working Committee.

Regional agencies of the National Executive Committee, created in 1951, were dissolved in 1953 in order to remedy autonomistic tendencies. After adoption of the federal constitution for Nigeria in 1954 and Azikiwe's assumption of the eastern premiership, regional working committees were restored under regional conferences, with safeguards to ensure the supremacy of the national organization. These safeguards proved faulty, and after the crisis at the Aba convention of 1957, central control was extended by introducing centralized budgets and by appointing a national organizer to be responsible for the conduct of all elections. These innovations have decisively tipped the balance in favor of the central organization.

Like that of the British Labour Party, the nonparliamentary origin of the NCNC has created a "problem of extra-parliamentary control," [22] which gave rise to the eastern government crisis of 1953.[23] An ensuing revision of the party's constitution affirmed the subordination of all parliamentary wings to central party organs, in particular to the Central

[22] R. T. McKenzie, *British Political Parties* (New York: St. Martin's Press, 1955), p. 385.
[23] See p. 601.

Working Committee, the National Executive Committee, and the national convention. It is stipulated, however, that the deposition of a parliamentary leader requires action by the parliamentary party concerned.

Action Group.—Supreme authority in the Action Group, which has made a virtue of organizational efficiency, is vested in its annual federal congress, comprising two representatives of every federal constituency, all federal parliamentary members, all regional ministers or members of the regional shadow cabinets, two representatives of the party in the Lagos Town Council, and all members of the Federal Executive Council. Prior to independence, congresses of the Action Group were significant for the promulgation and exposition, rather than the formulation, of party policies. The principal decision-making unit is the Federal Executive Council, a large body composed of all officers of the party, all ministers or shadow-cabinet members in all the governments of Nigeria, and twelve members elected annually by each regional conference. The powers of the council, which meets quarterly, are delegated to the Working Committee, which directs the administrative and financial affairs of the party at both federal and regional levels. All officers of the Action Group are elected annually.[24]

Until 1957 the Action Group was virtually governed by its Western Regional organization. Concomitant with the expansion of the party into the east and the north on a grand scale, centralization of authority has been affirmed by constitutional provisions which designate the federal president as the principal officer of each region's executive committee, and stipulate that the chairman of each regional conference shall be a federal officer, subject to election by the federal congress. In 1959 zonal organizations were established in accordance with the party's ideas on the creation of new states. Two zonal executives were organized in the east and five in the north, composed of representatives elected by divisional and provincial conferences, respectively.

Although the origins of the Action Group are extraparliamentary, the primary object of the party founders was the attainment of power under a colonial constitution leading to self-government. It is only since independence that radical nonparliamentarians have asserted their views vigorously within Action Group councils, creating a potential for conflict between parliamentary and organizational elements. The party constitution provides for the election of regional parliamentary leaders by joint meetings of the regional parliamentary council and the executive com-

---

[24] An exception was the office of "Father of the Party," abolished in 1963. It was personal to Dr. Akinola Maja, a medical practitioner, who was formerly president of the Nigerian Youth Movement (1944–1951), chairman of the all-party National Emergency Committee (1949–1950), chairman of the Board of Directors of the National Bank of Nigeria, and president of the Egbe Omo Oduduwa.

mittee of the regional conference concerned. Provision is made also for a high degree of coördination among the several legislative wings.

Obafemi Awolowo, federal president of the Action Group, is also styled "Leader of the Party"; he is elected to the latter office by a joint meeting of all parliamentary councils, both regional and federal. The leader and the deputy leader hold office for life. Although there is no constitutional provision for deposition of the leader or the deputy leader by the joint parliamentary councils, it is thought inconceivable that either one would remain in office should he fail to be reëlected as leader of the legislative house to which he belongs, to win a vote of confidence by a parliamentary council, or to be elected to a regular party office. During the crisis of 1962 it was established that the federal Executive Council may direct the removal of a parliamentary leader.

Northern Peoples' Congress.—Under the constitution of the NPC, the annual convention of the party theoretically enjoys "absolute power to decide major policies." Originally adopted in 1948, the constitution seldom provides a guide to current practices and arrangements. No ordinary annual conventions were convoked in 1951, 1953, 1957, 1959, or 1960, although emergency conventions were held in July, 1952, and in September, 1957. The constitution also provides for the annual election of party officers; however, in 1955, the year after Alhaji Ahmadu, the Sardauna of Sokoto, assumed the presidency, the convention voted to "freeze" the slate of officers selected then for five years. As it happened, these years coincided with the crucial period during which terms for the transfer of colonial power to the federal and the NPC regional governments were negotiated. The culmination of a process by which the parliamentary party achieved ascendancy over the extraparliamentary convention seemed to have been reached in 1959, when all the parliamentary members of the party met at Kaduna to propose and adopt the party's electoral manifesto, which no other party body formally considered before its publication.

It is reported that on no occasion since 1951 has the platform been outvoted on issues discussed in the convention; indeed, existing records suggest that voting has rarely been a part of convention proceedings. This remarkable control of the rank-and-file membership by the parliamentary party has never been legislated, but seems rather to reflect the hierarchical relationships and expectations vis-à-vis authority which prevail in the dominant sector of northern society.

Day-to-day party business at the central level is conducted by a body called the National Working Committee, which in practice consists of an *ad hoc* group of advisers called in from time to time to consult with the president-general or with officers acting in his behalf, and commonly includes other ministers, prominent nonparliamentary members of the Executive Committee, and a few top-ranking secretariat officials.

Party policy discussion has centered in the parliamentary caucuses of the federal and regional legislatures. The principle of decentralization carries over to the organization of the parliamentary party. In meetings held at the Premier's House in Kaduna during sessions of the Northern House of Assembly, two delegates from each province often "represent" the other members of the House from their area. A minister from each province serves as a permanent chairman of his delegation. In contrast with proceedings at annual conventions, the atmosphere of parliamentary party meetings is said to be one of free give-and-take. Discipline is invoked on motions of importance to the government, but the principle of decentralization is honored in the right of a representative to assert the views and the interests of his locality. The relative uniformity in social status of the parliamentary group (compared with the composition of open conventions) facilitates the process of reciprocal exchange and debate. During the last decade harmony prevailed between the federal and regional NPC parliamentary bodies. In 1960, however, the federal government, led by Alhaji Sir Abubakar Tafawa Balewa, the prime minister and first vice-president of the NPC, declared its willingness to accept a loan from Israel even though the NPC-controlled regional House of Assembly passed a resolution voicing its opposition to the proposal.

Northern Elements' Progressive Union.—In the NEPU, supreme authority at the central party level is vested in an annual conference (which has never failed to meet), attended by branch representatives and representatives of local youth and women's sections. Formerly, the president-general was elected annually, but at the Jos convention of January, 1959, Aminu Kano was elevated to the position of life president. Four party officers are selected by the life president, and the others are chosen by a committee consisting of one representative from each of the twelve northern provinces plus Kano City, over which the life president presides. The life president also submits a list of candidates for membership on the National Executive Committee to the annual conference for its approval. A great deal of party business is in practice conducted by subcommittees, the most important of which are those of elections and finance, of which Aminu Kano is chairman. Local branches are instructed through paid provincial organizers to adhere to policies arrived at by the National Executive Committee.

Until 1960, dissension within the party was rare, probably owing in part to the powerful position occupied by Aminu Kano. The only notable instance of a conflict between the extraparliamentary party and a parliamentarian on a matter of policy was resolved by expulsion of the parliamentarian. A further indication of the degree of centralization and control exercised by the national party was the selection of several candidates to contest the 1959 federal election in constituencies of which they were neither natives nor residents, a risk rarely assumed by other Nigerian parties. In 1960 a minor NEPU breakaway organization was formed, ostensibly over the issue of the NEPU's participation, through its continuing alliance with the NCNC, in the federal coalition government dominated by its archfoe, the NPC. After Aminu Kano (who reportedly had refused a ministerial post in 1959) assumed the post of government whip, he became the target of accusations on the part of this new group that the NEPU was being "sold out."

Ancillary Elements

The NCNC constitution has always provided for the organization of auxiliary groups, such as the Women's Association, the Youth Association, and the Zikist National Vanguard. These groups are forbidden to present candidates for election, and their local branches are required to accept the guidance of local party executives. The branches of the auxiliaries are represented at national conventions of the party, and their central executives are represented on the National Executive Committee. Both the Youth Association and the Zikist National Vanguard sought to preserve the heritage of the militant Zikist Movement.[25] The Vanguard was formed in November, 1955, after conservative leaders of the NCNC had tried to render the radical Youth Association ineffectual by the imposition of a twenty-five-year age limit on its membership. Youth leaders disregarded the ban, which was repealed in 1957, but the Vanguard refused to relinquish its identity until 1961, when it merged into the Zikist Movement. Other organizations affiliated with the NCNC include numerous ethnic group associations and minor local parties, such as the Ilorin Araromi Congress in the north and the Nigerian Commoners' Liberal Party in the west.

Ancillary elements are less important in the Action Group. Women's organizations are active at local and regional levels, but youth groups are localized in order to preclude insubordinate movements, and an eighteen-year age limit is strictly enforced. Ethnic group associations are related on a *de facto* basis to certain local branches, although the Action Group constitution does not provide for their membership. In the Northern Region, parties affiliated with the Action Group include the United Middle Belt Congress, the Bornu Youth Movement, the Ilorin Talaka

---

[25] See p. 599. The Zikist Movement was declared an unlawful society by the colonial government in 1950. It was succeeded by the Freedom Movement and other sectarian radical groups before the NCNC Youth Association was organized in 1952.

Parapo (Commoners' Party), and the Habe-Fulani People's Party of southwestern Bauchi.

Two important ancillary bodies of the Northern Peoples' Congress are the Youth Association and, notwithstanding the fact that the NPC opposes female suffrage, the Women's Section, which renders service to the party by attracting the enfranchised males. The Ex-Servicemen's Association, two student societies, two trade unions (one of which is the influential Northern Mineworkers' Union of Jos), a business association (the Northern Transport Owners' Union of Zaria), and ten tribal unions in the Middle Belt are listed as affiliates of the national organization. In 1953 a group identified with the NPC, called the Yam Mahaukata ("sons of madmen"), sprang up in Kano City after the courts failed to punish NEPU supporters for acts of verbal abuse against traditional authorities. Until declared illegal by the government, the Yam Mahaukata terrorized local members of the NEPU. This auxiliary was succeeded by the now-defunct Alheri Youth Association.

A major offshoot of the NEPU, the Askianist Movement, existed from 1951 to about 1955, when it collapsed after irregularities in the management of its funds had disillusioned its followers. The group took its name from the famous Muhammad Askia who usurped the throne of the medieval western Sudanic Songhai empire, initiated a period renowned for its cultural and religious renaissance, and eventually conquered the Hausa states ("Askia" was a title meaning "usurper").[26] To a group of young Habe adherents of the NEPU, Muhammad Askia seemed a perfect symbol for projection of the party's program and its leader, Aminu Kano (occasionally, Aminu Kano was referred to by the Askianists as "Muhammad Aminu," and the organization as the "Northern Askianist–Aminiyya Movement"). The Askianist Movement was an intriguing example of the NEPU's efforts to penetrate the peasantry through consciousness of and pride in a pre-Fulani political order.

In 1956 the NEPU established a youth wing, the Reshen Samarin Sawaba (Freedom Youth Wing), to succeed the Askianist Movement, and the Women's Wing. In response to the NPC's Yam Mahaukata, the NEPU organized the Positive Action Wing (PAW), which disappeared when its rival did. In Kano City, strong-arm associates of the NPC and the NEPU are presently known as the Yan Akusa and the Yan Kwaria because of their helmetlike hats made of wood and calabash, respectively.

Several currently functioning NEPU ancillaries with Arabic names are associated with Islam and with Muslim education. These include Zaharal Haq ("truth is revealed"—the revelation is the NEPU's interpre-

---

[26] See S. J. Hogben, *The Muhammedan Emirates of Northern Nigeria* (London: Oxford University Press, 1930), pp. 48–52.

tation of Islam as being opposed to political authoritarianism), Tab'iunal Haq ("the masses will rule those now ruling"), and Nujumu Zaman ("start of the day"). The NEPU realizes full well that to succeed it must counter the contention that the party's doctrines are not in conformity with Islam; therefore much importance is attached to these groups, whose emphasis is on religious training with the NEPU's own political slant.

Party Finance

The main regular sources of revenue for the major parties may be tabulated as follows:

1) Enrollment fees (1 shilling for the NCNC-NEPU and the Action Group; 2 shillings, 6 pence for the NPC), monthly dues (6 pence for the NCNC-NEPU; 1 shilling for the Action Group and the NPC), and affiliation fees of 1 guinea from local branches and member unions of the NCNC; Nigeria-wide organizations which affiliate with the national headquarters of the NCNC are required to pay 5 guineas. In 1958 the NCNC initiated a central registry of members who contributed 1 pound each to the national treasury.

2) The sale of party constitutions, literature, emblems, flags, and so forth.

3) Income from public lectures and social events. (The Action Group Palm Tree Clubs were organized to derive funds from the social activities of members, as were NEPU and, later, NPC dances.)

4) Levies on the salaries of parliamentarians and members of statutory boards and corporations. These levies are the main "fixed" source of party revenue, notwithstanding the difficulties frequently attendant upon their collection. The NCNC levies 10 per cent of the salaries of ministers, parliamentary secretaries, ordinary parliamentarians, and political appointees to public boards and corporations. The Action Group and the NPC impose a 10 per cent levy on parliamentary emoluments and on the salaries of those who hold patronage positions, but the Action Group exempts ministerial salaries on the ground that these are professional rather than political stipends. Ministers and junior ministers in both parties, however, are expected to defray a substantial portion of the expenses of their constituency or divisional organizations.

5) Donations by supporters. This is a variable source. It has been most lucrative for the Action Group which, it has been noted, was the offspring of a union of the intelligentsia and the commercial "middle class" of western Nigeria, possibly the most affluent and most numerous African business group in Tropical Africa. All parties enjoy loan facilities provided by allied banking institutions, as indicated in the next section.[27]

---

[27] Party records indicate that in 1958–59 only the Action Group enjoyed a buoy-

RELATIONSHIPS

Traditional Authorities

In most Ibo areas of the Eastern Region, chieftaincy, as a political factor, is relatively insignificant. Yet the regional House of Chiefs was established in 1959 in response to demands from minority ethnic groups, among whom the political role of chieftaincy is greater than among the Ibo. These demands were supported by an influential lobby in Iboland, called the Eastern Region Chiefs' Conference. Most of the inaugural members of the Eastern House of Chiefs were NCNC supporters.

From 1952 to 1959 the Western House of Chiefs was a coördinate chamber of the regional parliament; its assent was required for the enactment of regional legislation, which never met with obstruction in the chiefs' chamber. Its political complexion is evident in the fact that in 1958 only one of the fifty-four members was identified as a supporter of the opposition party. Traditional members of local government councils normally vote with Action Group elected members, and often ensure the party's ability to organize and control these councils. On occasion, as at Benin in 1958, Action Group strength in closely divided councils has been reinforced by timely "injections" of traditional members upon the recommendation of a head chief. It has been observed that a great many of the "recognized chiefs" (a legal term) in the Western Region are so-called "honorary chiefs" rather than traditional rulers. All told there are more than 1,500 recognized chiefs, constituting a pressure group of the first importance which has a motivation of its own despite the mechanisms of regional government control.

At the local level in both eastern and western Nigeria, party leaders are obliged to weigh the opinions of the leaders of age groups, secret societies, and title societies, which continue to exert political influence in most rural communities.[28]

Although northern emirs are not technically members of political parties, previous observations have indicated the close ties existing between them and the NPC. At times emirs perform important informal party roles (e.g., in connection with party nominations and the NPC sub-

---

ant financial condition; the party budgeted an unrivaled sum—in excess of £290,000 —for its operations in all parts of Nigeria. NCNC accounts were then in deficit, and NPC revenues were close to the relatively negligible figure of £15,000. It is reported that the Action Group alone spent a sum in excess of £1 million on the federal election campaign of 1959.

[28] Dr. Eme O. Awa has observed that as yet "no rational effort" has been made in the Eastern or the Western Region to reconcile these important "elements of traditional authority" with the structure of local government ("Local Government Problems in a Developing Community (Nigeria)," paper read at the International Conference on Representative Government and National Progress, University College, Ibadan, March 16–23, 1959, pp. 8–9).

committee on self-government). The three most powerful emirs (of Sokoto, Kano, and Katsina) are regional ministers without portfolio, and as such they are inevitably associated with party policies. Unlike the upper houses in the federal and the other regional legislatures today, the Northern House of Chiefs has concurrent powers with the lower house, including power over appropriations. In practice, the intimate relationships between traditional and elective leadership tend to obviate friction, but they also help to give traditional authority a degree of political influence in modern political institutions probably unique in emergent Africa.

Administrative-Governmental Groups

Each of the three major parties has its system of patronage by means of which governmental and administrative structures are exploited for partisan advantage. A clear case of partisan exploitation of a public corporation is the Eastern Nigeria Information Service, publisher of the *Eastern Outlook,* which is, in effect, an NCNC party organ. Similarly, the Gaskiya Corporation of the Northern Regional government publishes weekly newspapers, in both Hausa and English, which tend to reflect the policies of the Northern Peoples' Congress.

The major instrumentalities of commercial patronage are the regional marketing boards and the regional development corporations. The marketing boards appoint qualified firms and individuals as their licensed buying agents. Although licenses are issued on the basis of commercial criteria, political good will is a latent asset which seldom is spurned.[29] In like manner, fledgling firms that need government loans are well advised to cultivate political good will.

Marketing board funds provide investment and loan capital for the regional statutory corporations, which frequently undertake agricultural and industrial projects in partnership with private interests. In 1962 a federal commission of inquiry into the financial practices of the Western Regional government disclosed that the Western Marketing Board had made loans in excess of £6 million to a private company, owned in its entirety by four leading members of the Action Group. Most of this money seems to have been channeled into the coffers of the party.

Commercial contracts are awarded by the several governments and their statutory corporations. All governments utilize tendering procedures which are strictly monitored by civil servants, but ministers, junior ministers, or other politically reliable administrators participate. In the north, the economic power of native administrations (the largest of which, at

---

[29] In 1958 the Eastern Region Marketing Board refused to reappoint as soybean buying agent a previously licensed firm headed by the leading financial backer of the Democratic Party of Nigeria and the Cameroons, formed in opposition to Azikiwe by ex-members of the NCNC.

Kano, budgeted for a revenue of £1.5 million in 1959) is wielded comparably, if on a more modest scale.

Finally, it is a fairly unexceptionable fact that government party supporters in all regions predominate in local government services, in the membership of local loans boards, and in customary or native courts.

Economic Interest Groups

Politically, the most important relationships in this category involve Nigerian banking institutions. Marketing board funds, channeled into Nigerian banks, have enabled the banks to extend credit to Nigerian businessmen, notably to licensed buying agents.[30] In 1955 the Eastern Regional government acquired 87.7 per cent of the stock of the African Continental Bank by virtue of a £750,000 investment; it has since become sole owner, acquiring the shares held by companies related to the *West African Pilot* and the Zik Group of newspapers, a chain founded by Azikiwe before he began his career in government. In 1959 the managing director of the bank was also the managing director of the newspapers, editor in chief of the *West African Pilot,* and national auditor of the NCNC; the general manager of the *West African Pilot* was the national secretary of the NCNC. Neither the *Pilot* nor the several local newspapers of the Zik Group are subject to formal party control. But they are devoted to the party's cause, and, as with the party itself, a state of indebtedness to the African Continental Bank has been normal.

In 1955 the Western Regional Marketing Board invested £1 million in nonparticipating shares of the National Bank of Nigeria, the oldest existing African private bank with the largest volume of business. (This bank was nationalized by the Western Regional government in 1961.) Obafemi Awolowo has described the relationship between the National Bank and the Action Group as "pure and simple, one between banker and customer." It may be added that this particular customer—that is, the party—is chiefly responsible for the bank's recent growth and for its expanding capacity to meet the financial requirements of a rising entrepreneurial class. Formerly the bank was the major shareholder of the Amalgamated Press of Nigeria, publisher of the former *Daily Service* and of a chain of local newspapers which support the Action Group. In 1960 the Amalgamated Press inaugurated a new daily newspaper in partnership with a Canadian firm. The managing director of the Amalgamated Press is the federal publicity secretary of the Action Group. In 1959 two smaller private banks, under the direction of Action Group members, were also supported by that party and by the Western Regional

---

[30] W. T. Newlyn and D. C. Rowan, *Money and Banking in British Colonial Africa* (Oxford: Clarendon Press, 1954), p. 217 n. 1; *The Economic Development of Nigeria,* International Bank for Reconstruction and Development (Baltimore: Johns Hopkins University Press, 1955), pp. 158–159.

government. In 1960 the Northern Peoples' Congress acquired a financial ally in the Bank of the North, inaugurated with the participation of the Northern Regional government.

In all regions the principal business associations tend to support the regional government party. In several urban areas of southern Nigeria, notably in Lagos, organized market women participate actively in party affairs. Trade unions, as a rule, are relatively independent of formal party relationships, owing partly to the disaffection of radical unionists from the major political parties and partly to tactical considerations of collective bargaining.[31]

Ethnic and Religious Interest Groups

The relationships of certain ethnic-group associations to particular political parties have created an exaggerated impression of the purely ethnic impact on party policies. In fact, the two best-known and most highly politicized nationality associations are rising-class movements among the Ibo- and Yoruba-speaking peoples, respectively.

The Ibo Federal Union, which later evolved into the Ibo State Union, was inaugurated by politically conscious representatives of the Ibo intelligentsia. Azikiwe served as president of the union from 1948 to 1952, when he declined to accept reëlection in the face of political criticisms stemming from his association with a "tribal" movement. During the eastern government crisis of 1953, the leadership of the union was divided. Largely as a result of that cleavage, the political elite withdrew from union office. But the Ibo State Union remains a sensitive index of Ibo public opinion, and Ibo ministers of state frequently attend meetings of its executive as coöpted members or observers.

In theory, the Egbe Omo Oduduwa is nonpartisan; in practice, its relationship to the Action Group, as described by an officer of both associations at an Egbe general assembly, is that of wine to water. In certain rural areas of Yorubaland, the two associations are virtually identical. For a decade the Egbe has served the Action Group in many ways, not the least of which is the settlement of disputes among Yoruba personalities (particularly chiefs) before disagreements become politically disruptive.

Other nationality associations, such as the Ibibio State Union and the Edo National Union, are less highly politicized than the Ibo and Yoruba

---

[31] Since 1951 the representation of organized labor in the NCNC National Executive Committee has been relatively minor and confined primarily to the conservative wing of labor leadership. Practicing trade-unionists were never prominent among the leaders of the Action Group, although several trade-union leaders are understood to have Action Group sympathies, and radical intellectuals with trade-union connections are numbered in the Action Group fold. Oddly, the leading example of a trade union in alignment with a major political party is provided by the Northern Mineworkers' Union, a virtual instrumentality of the Northern Peoples' Congress, the least socialistic or laboristic of the major parties.

associations; they encompass informal groups which support both major southern parties. Exceptions include the quasi-political Urhobo Renascent Convention and the Warri People's Party of Delta Province, which may be classified as adjuncts of the NCNC, and the Tiv Progressive Union of Benue Province in the lower north, which supports the Action Group. At local levels, many branches of the NCNC and the Action Group are intimately related to ethnic-group associations of the subnationality type.[32] In the upper Northern Region, ethnic-group associations play a comparatively minor role in politics. Their absence among the Hausa-Fulani may be attributed to alternative bonds of religion and to the multi-tribal span of the traditional Fulani empire.

A few of the associations based on religious affinity are closely related to major parties. In 1957, leaders of the Action Group in the Western Region formed the United Muslim Council to counter the influence of the National Muslim League (later the National Emancipation League, an ally of the Northern Peoples' Congress). From time to time, leaders of Islamic congregations in southwestern Nigeria have been highly partisan to one party or another, particularly in Lagos and Ibadan. Interdenominational conflict in the Eastern Region over the issue of public support for parochial schools has ranged the Eastern Nigeria Catholic Council against the Convention of Protestant Citizens, although both associations are subject to dominant NCNC influence. In the Northern Region, leaders of the separatist United Middle Belt Congress are typically members of Christian mission congregations.

In northern Nigeria, the Muslim mallams (here meaning specifically teachers or learned men), as the main interpreters of religious doctrine to the masses, wield enormous influence. Probably the largest number of and certainly the most influential mallams identify and are identified with the NPC. They tend to be extremely conservative, if not reactionary, in their outlook on the modern world.[33] To propagate its "religious" dicta, the NPC must cultivate the mallams, whose counsel usually reinforces the predilections of its more tradition-minded members and supporters.

In contrast with the role of the mallams, the religio-political tendencies of the Tijaniyya *turuq* (Arabic; pl., *tariqa*), or mystic brotherhood,

---

[32] For example, in 1958 the effective power system of the Port Harcourt NCNC extended to ethnic-group associations affiliated with the Port Harcourt Ibo Union. Among those to which members of the executive committees of the NCNC branch and Youth Association belonged were the Nnewi Patriotic Union, the Orlu Divisional Union, the Orlu Youth League, the Oguta Union, the Owerri Divisional Union, the Mbasi Clan Union, the Bende Divisional Union, the Ikwerri Development Union, the Okogwe Union, and the Abiriba Improvement Union.

[33] The NPC's policy of "no entangling alliances with southern parties," and the NPC government's inclusion of certain religious transgressions in the definition of criminal offenses under the Northern Penal Code, are areas in which the mallams have undoubtedly wielded great influence.

tend to link it to the NEPU. Probably the majority of Tijaniyya adherents in northern Nigeria vote for the NPC and are politically quiescent. What may be called a "left wing" of the Tijaniyya in northern Nigeria—the Yan Wazifa[34]—is, however, a radical influence in both religion and politics. Religiously the Tijaniyya, and especially the Yan Wazifa, are reformist, puritanical, missionary-minded groups; they rival the Khadiriyya—the other major turuq in northern Nigeria—which is identified with the ruling house of Sokoto.

It has been suggested that in northern Nigeria the Tijaniyya stands politically in relation to the Khadiriyya and orthodox Islam as a nonconformist sect stands to an established church. Where the head of an emirate follows the Khadiriyya, but the Tijaniyya is strong, as in Sokoto, the latter is regarded as a threat to existing authority and is treated accordingly. More orthodox Tijani emirs look on the Yan Wazifa in much the same way. Such hostility merely intensifies friction between the traditional ruling class and members of the Tijaniyya, the majority of whom are Habe commoners. The net result is a natural alliance between this turuq and the NEPU in certain parts of the upper north.[35]

GOALS AND VALUES

The salient goals and values of the major Nigerian parties are reflected in their respective attitudes in three broad areas of public policy: the political system, socioeconomic development, and foreign policy.

The Political System

The nature of the union.—During the period of constitutional development leading to national self-government, each party was associated with a distinctive attitude on the subject of a desirable constitutional framework for Nigeria. The NCNC preferred unitary government, and the Action Group and the NPC advocated federalism, with the NPC usually insisting on wide powers for regional units. The reservation of certain powers to the regions under the constitution has been crucial to the NPC's control of the extent and the pace of change in the quasi-feudal system of the upper north. It has also helped to diminish the persistent fear of the northern elites that an independent Nigeria, embarked on a course of modernization, might elevate the more highly Western-educated southern elites to a position of dominance over the entire coun-

---

[34] The term means those who practice the litany of Wazifa. For this and other doctrinal and practitional aspects of the Tijaniyya, see J. Spencer Trimingham, *Islam in West Africa* (Oxford: Clarendon Press, 1959), pp. 99–100.

[35] The NEPU member of the preceding Northern House of Assembly for the constituency of Kaura Namoda (in eastern Sokoto) is an avid Tijani adherent, and in this and other parts of the upper north (e.g., southern Katsina, Argungu, northern Adamawa) membership in the two organizations tends to be reciprocal.

try. Because the NPC has the largest stake in keeping certain powers (particularly, those affecting chieftaincy affairs, local government, the public service, and the judiciary) within the purview of regional governments, the party's "states' rights" attitude is likely to persist. The Action Group insists that federalism is necessary to protect cultural-group interests. This principle has led the party to advocate the creation of three new states or regions out of the existing regions in order to accommodate cultural diversity, a program that would inescapably entail a redress of the present constitutional balance in favor of a stronger central government.[36] The Action Group's apparent willingness to countenance an enlarged role for central institutions was also implicit in its proposal in 1959 that the federal government assume responsibility for achieving national minimum standards in education, welfare, and economic development. Since 1953 the NCNC has accepted the idea of a federal structure. It is fair to say, however, that the NCNC supports federalism as a necessary rule of order under present conditions, and not from the conviction that permanent and serious limitations on the powers of the central government are intrinsically desirable.

Democracy versus authoritarianism.—All major political parties in Nigeria have proclaimed their dedication in principle to democracy. Doubtless some practices of each party could be cited as inconsistent with current Western formulations of that ideal; but that democracy is recognized by all parties as an organizing principle, and acknowledged as a standard of public responsibility, cannot be doubted on the evidence of policies, statements, and manifestoes covering more than a decade of political activity. It is noteworthy that the Action Group and the NCNC-NEPU insisted that a comprehensive declaration of fundamental rights (based largely on the Universal Declaration of Human Rights) be inserted into the Nigerian Constitution. The NPC also publicly endorses the goal of democracy, and has accepted the introduction of every major formal institution characteristic of modern parliamentary governments, save female suffrage. The NPC, however, is also committed to upholding traditional political institutions, particularly in the upper north, including theocratic authority, of which the party has at times seemed to regard itself as an instrument.[37] It is therefore evident that the NPC both tacitly

---

[36] In 1961 the federal parliament, with the approval of all parties, passed a resolution providing for the creation of a Mid-West state out of the Western Region only. In the view of the Action Group this step would strengthen its demands for the creation of a Calabar-Ogoja-Rivers state in the east and a Middle Belt state in the north. But the Action Group opposed legislation implementing the Mid-West State Resolution of 1962 because it disagreed with the inclusion of certain areas.

[37] During the debate on the 1959 Northern Penal Code Bill in the Northern House of Assembly, the northern premier is quoted as having stated: "As long as [my] party, the NPC, is in power in the Region, it . . . [will] not legalize what God has forbidden" (*Daily Times*, Sept. 3, 1959, p. 3).

and explicitly acknowledges the claims of ideals and allegiances that are essentially antagonistic to those of democracy, and that its proclaimed attitudes alone embody a dualism of basic political values.

Prior to independence a shade of difference was discernible between the Action Group and the NCNC-NEPU in their respective tendencies to identify the essence of democracy as equality of opportunity on the one hand, and as substantive social equality on the other. Since independence the Action Group has edged painfully but surely away from liberal democracy to democratic socialism, whereas the NCNC has become increasingly vague on doctrinal matters. Probably the view that democratic values would be better served in Nigeria under a one-party system has wider currency within the NCNC. A former NCNC leader of the opposition (in the Western Region) has argued this point on the grounds that party competition is not a prerequisite to the right to disagree, that it increases the potentiality of communal conflict, that it precludes full utilization of available talent, and that in the present Nigerian environment party rivalries lead to arbitrary acts of government against individuals.[38] But Awolowo, who is an ardent exponent of the competitive party system, argues that the defense of one-party systems in Africa by non-African commentators shows a patronizing lack of confidence in the ability of Africans to operate democratic forms of government.[39]

Socioeconomic Development

Traditionalism versus modernity.—The NCNC and the Action Group, especially the latter, take a certain pride in the traditional institution of chieftaincy, which stands as a symbol of an authentic, indigenous political culture surviving in dignity beneath the weight of adopted institutions. Such pride in traditional forms is indulged, however, only to a degree deemed compatible with the attainment of the paramount goal of social and economic modernization; and, on balance, it would seem that both parties' approach to the institution of chieftaincy has been guided primarily by regard for its instrumental rather than its inherent value.[40] Only the NPC seems to look upon the preservation of traditional institu-

---

[38] See Dennis Osadebay, "Next? Nigeria Needs a One Party System," *ibid.*, Nov. 18, 1960, p. 5. Osadebay, a well-known libertarian, formerly served as national legal adviser to the NCNC. He succeeded Azikiwe as president of the Nigerian Senate and became premier of the Mid-West Region in 1964.

[39] *Op. cit.*, pp. 302–304.

[40] Awa, *op. cit.*, has suggested that the recent "resurgence" of chieftaincy in the Eastern Region—the establishment of the Eastern House of Chiefs and provision for traditional representation on local government councils—is attributable in large part to the appeal of examples set in the west and the north, where partisan chiefs have enhanced the electoral strength of the ruling parties. A celebrated instance of a southern party's limited tolerance of chieftaincy was the deposition in the mid-1950's of one of the most important traditional rulers in the Western Region—the Alafin of Oyo—by the Action Group government because of his opposition to party policies and his alleged culpability for the instigation of political violence.

tions and values as a significant part of its substantive goals. Although economic development and expansion of welfare services are also major NPC goals, the expression of these aspirations is seldom unaccompanied by references to claims of tradition. Thanks in part to the viability, thus far, of the emirate system, NPC leaders have not felt called upon to reconcile or to establish priorities among fundamental objectives; indeed, a fair conclusion to be drawn from various utterances would be that they anticipate the party's continued ability, at least in the larger emirates, to achieve substantial economic progress within the bounds of a largely traditional order, or at least under the auspices of the traditional ruling class.[41]

Approaches to development.—Both the NCNC-NEPU and the Action Group profess socialistic articles of belief, and leading members of both admit to an avowed socialist or Marxist persuasion. The basic orientation of the NPC is avowedly nonsocialistic. For several reasons, however, all parties have nondoctrinaire attitudes toward concrete problems of development. In the first place, all parties, anxious to attract private foreign capital to the regions under their respective control, have disavowed any intention to nationalize existing foreign enterprise, and expatriate firms are increasingly responsive to the demand that Nigerian personnel be trained for their technical and managerial positions. Second, regardless of doctrinal propensities, all parties support private enterprise by indigenous Nigerians; indeed, Nigerian entrepreneurial success commands widespread admiration as a manifestation of African development. Third, the nationalistic outlook of the Nigerian business elite induces it to support measures by the state which will promote development and ensure indigenous control over natural resources. Thus, all parties, in practice, pursue "mixed" programs which allow for both private and public participation, and they tend to evaluate programs by the results achieved rather than by the conformity of the measures adopted to ideological prescription. For all parties nationalism is a creed that is far more compelling than the dogmas of either socialism or capitalism.

Foreign Policy

All parties support Nigerian membership in the Commonwealth of Nations and the close relationship of Nigeria to the United Kingdom. All

---

[41] E.g., the northern premier, in a speech given at Sokoto on March 15, 1959, when the region achieved self-government, said: "When we survey all the phenomenal changes that have occurred in our recent history we are gratified with an important factor in our way of life, that quality of the Northern peoples—an ability to absorb, adapt, or renovate new ideas without completely discarding [our] social inheritance, even despite the attractions of glittering alien systems. In so doing we are proud to follow the old Hausa saying, 'It is better to repair than to build afresh.' I am told that this belief has helped other nations to greatness and I have a firm conviction that, God willing, it will do so for us."

of them have expressed their determination to work for the abolition of racial and colonial oppression throughout Africa. Both the Action Group and the NCNC-NEPU alliance are pledged to support the formation of a West African federal union and to initiate preliminary steps to that end in the sphere of economic coöperation and cultural interchange. Until 1961 the Action Group was reluctant to accept Pan-Africanism as an operative program, mainly on the ground of an objection to its recent connections with the Pan-Arab movement. In contrast, Pan-Africanism has always been a canon of NCNC doctrine.[42] The Northern Peoples' Congress is highly cautious in its approach to all forms of interterritorial organization, but it is amenable to cultural and functional coöperation among African states.

In world affairs, all parties support the United Nations and oppose both the involvement of Nigeria in non-African military blocs and the penetration of Africa by non-African military powers. Since independence, the nonalignment policy which Azikiwe enunciated in the election campaign of 1959 seems to have gained wide acceptance, although it should be noted that the Prime Minister's studied avoidance of the term "neutralism" may stem from the fact that the NPC, in 1959, officially repudiated that policy.

Table 4 briefly summarizes the attitudes of the parties on major political issues at the time of independence, before the leftward trend of the Action Group became conspicuous. A glance up and down the columns suggests that it would at that time have been reasonable to range Nigerian parties along a conventional ideological spectrum from left to right. Thus, the various combinations of attitudes with regard to the political system, modernization, and foreign policy justify the conclusion that the NCNC occupies a left-wing position, the NPC the right-wing position, and the Action Group a center position.

On the other hand, it is essential to observe that overt agreements and differences on goals and values fail to account either for the intensity of party competition in Nigeria or for the present basis of party alignments within and among the regions. It is indicative that after the federal elections of 1959 all possible combinations (NPC-NCNC, NPC-AG, NCNC-AG) of partners were considered by party leaders before a coalition was finally formed. Table 4 makes clear the great extent to which

---

[42] "Pan-Africanism is a desirable philosophy and a long term objective. It is a philosophy for black peoples and peoples of African descent to unite and find their common destiny. As a philosophy, it is anticommunistic or ought to be so; but as an objective of policy, it is a clarion call made by Africans themselves for the liberation of all African peoples, racial equality and racial tolerance—the most passionate and yet the most constitutional appeal made in the history of modern nationalism" (policy paper of the National Council of Nigeria and the Cameroons on foreign policy, *Daily Times,* Oct. 23, 1959).

TABLE 4

ATTITUDES OF NIGERIAN PARTIES ON MAJOR ISSUES

Subject	*NPC*	*NCNC–NEPU*	*Action Group (and allies)*
POLITICAL SYSTEM			
Ideal	Limited democracy	Egalitarian democracy	Liberal democracy (post-independence shift toward egalitarian democracy)
Nature of the Nigerian union	Retention of present federal structure; residual powers to remain with regions	"A quasi-federal Constitution with residual powers in the center . . . providing for no less than eight autonomous states"[1]	Modification of structure by creation of new states (beginning with Mid-West, Middle Belt, and C–O–R states); residual powers to remain with regions
SOCIAL AND ECONOMIC DEVELOPMENT			
Program	Industrialization, mechanization of agriculture, social and welfare services	Industrialization, mechanization of agriculture, social and welfare services	Industrialization, mechanization of agriculture, social and welfare services
Priority	Social and welfare services	Social and welfare services	Social and welfare services
Emphasis in relation to other goals	To degree consistent with political ideal and traditional values	Primary	Primary
Indigenous agency	Mixed public and private enterprise	Mixed public and private enterprise	Mixed public and private enterprise
Private foreign capital	Guarantees and inducements; no nationalization of existing enterprises	Guarantees and inducements; no nationalization of existing enterprises	Guarantees and inducements; no nationalization of existing enterprises
Sources of technical and financial assistance	Primary reliance on Western sources; division on acceptability of Israel	All sources acceptable	All sources acceptable
TRADITIONAL VALUES			
Traditionalism versus modernity	Strong emphasis on continuity of traditional values	Preoccupation with modernity; only slight emphasis on traditional forms	Preoccupation with modernity; some emphasis on traditional forms
FOREIGN POLICY			
Alignment versus neutralism	Pro-Western; formal nonalignment	Neutralism	Nonalignment; pro-Western orientation (postindependence shift to neutralism)
Pan-Africanism	West African union premature; functional cooperation preferred	Early union of West Africa	Eventual union of West Africa (postindependence shift to early union of West Africa)
United Arab Republic	Positive	Positive	Negative

[1] From the program and manifesto of the NCNC–NEPU alliance for the federal election of 1959.

all parties agree on issues of social and economic development; and it also reveals that the NPC disagrees more often with both southern parties (and their allies) than the southern parties disagree with each other. Furthermore, the table suggests that of the two southern parties, the NPC was more frequently or more closely in accord with the Action

Group, although the NCNC and the NPC are partners in the present federal coalition government. These seeming anomalies support a conclusion that at present forces other than party ideologies and programs generate the competitive system of political parties in Nigeria.

THE PATTERN OF POLITICAL ACTION

The key to the pattern of political party competition lies rather in the social and cultural pluralism of the Nigerian environment, and in the way in which political parties manipulate, exploit, and are affected by the social tensions that inevitably inhere in such an environment. Communal and class conflicts have been identified previously as the most general forms of social tension, and these, indeed, may be related to the broad pattern of party politics in Nigeria.

Communal tensions are the most obvious social factor affecting the distribution of party strength in Nigeria. Every major party is to some degree vulnerable to particularistic ethnic or religious sensibilities which its rivals exploit for purposes of electoral support. It is no accident that opposition political parties in all three regions are frequently built on a foundation of communal participation, a source of political support that is most rewarding in the minority areas of all regions. Table 5 lists selected examples of areas where parties rely on communal factors for a margin of political advantage. (Tables 5–7 are intended to be illustrative rather than exhaustive.) Table 6 cites instances in which the internal cohesion of the parties is reduced by factional tendencies attributable to communal tensions, although the party is dominant in that area.

In all regions, as we have noted, the vast majority of emergent- or traditional-class elements are drawn by their interests into the fold of the regional government party, where the rewards of administrative and commercial patronage are distributed. Significantly, this has seriously weakened all the "separate state" movements, inspired by sentiments primarily communal in nature. Indeed, all parties woo the cultural minorities within their domains by extending more than proportionate opportunities for political, economic, and educational advancement to the elites of minority groups. Instances in which political support is built primarily on a foundation of class allegiance are given in table 7, as well as a few examples of cleavages between traditional communities and emergent-class elements in nonminority areas; prominent business and professional men almost invariably adhere to the government party, despite the hostility of local public opinion.

In general, communal and class appeals represent alternative bases of political party action in given localities. Probably the most common form of political competition between political parties is class versus communal group, where one party represents class interests and the other in-

Table 5

Selected Communal Bases of Party Support
in Situations of Interparty Competition

Party	Eastern Region	Western Region and Lagos	Northern Region
Action Group	Most sections of the Ibibio people Efik people in Calabar Division Aro people of Enyong Division	Most sections of the Yoruba-speaking people Itsekeri people in Warri Urban District Okpe-Urhobo people in Western Urhobo District and in Sapele Urban District	Bornu people of Bornu Division Chamba people of Adamawa Division All peoples of Numan Division (except the Kanakuru) Birom people of Jos Division Tiv people of Tiv Division Arago people of Lafia Division Jarawa and Sayawa people of Bauchi Division Ekiti, Igbolo, and Igbomina Yoruba people of Ilorin Division
NCNC–NEPU alliance	All sections of the Ibo-speaking people Annang people in Ikot Ekpene Division Qua people in Calabar Division	Illa District (Yoruba)[1] Ilesha Urban District[1] (Yoruba) Oyo Yoruba of Modakeke[1] ward, Ife District Most Edo- and Ibo-speaking peoples of the midwest Urhobo settlers in Warri Urban District and Hausa Hausa and Ibo settlers in Lagos and Ibadan	Ngizim and Karekare people of Fika Division Kilba people of Adamawa Division Gwari people of Minna Division Strong Tijaniyya (Yan Wazifa) adherents of the eastern part of Sokoto, the southern part of Katsina, Adamawa, and Bauchi divisions
Northern Peoples' Congress	Ijaw people of Brass Division who support the Niger Delta Congress–NPC alliance	Ibadan Yoruba (Mabolaje Grand Alliance, an affiliate of the NCNC until 1959) A minority of the Yoruba Muslims who support the National Emancipation League–NPC alliance	Peoples of the Hausa-Fulani state system and the Bornu Emirate Igala people of Igala Division Idoma people of Idoma Division

[1] Traditionally, the Illa, Ilesha, and Oyo Yoruba subgroups are all rivals of the Ife Yoruba.

vokes communal sentiments against a coalition of interests. Class conflict (i.e., social class versus social class) is chiefly manifested in the new urban areas of southern Nigeria and the lower north, where incipient class structures are distinguishable, and in the upper north, where the phenomenon of social stratification antedates modern social and political history, and where ideological rivalries are expressed largely in traditional terms.

TABLE 6

SELECTED SITUATIONS OF INTRAPARTY FACTIONALISM ATTRIBUTABLE
TO COMMUNAL TENSIONS IN AREAS OF PARTY DOMINANCE

Party	Eastern Region	Western Region	Northern Region
Action Group		Epe Yoruba of Lagos origin versus Epe Yoruba of Ijebu origin in Epe Division of Colony Province Idanre Yoruba versus Akure Yoruba in Ondo Province (land dispute) Ondo Yoruba versus Ile-Oluji Yoruba in Ondo Province	
NCNC–NEPU alliance	Onitsha Ibo indigenes versus non-Onitsha Ibo settlers in Onitsha Urban District Udi-Nsukka-Awgu Ibo indigenes versus nonindigenous Ibo settlers in Enugu Municipality Ngwa Ibo indigenes versus non-Ngwa Ibo settlers in Aba Urban District Ikwerri Ibo indigenes versus non-Ikwerri Ibo settlers in Mile 2 Diobu, Port Harcourt Province "Onitsha Ibo" settlers versus "Owerri Ibo" settlers in Port Harcourt Municipality Aro Ibo solidarity as factional element in Iboland Catholic-Protestant rivalry in Onitsha Urban District and elsewhere in Iboland		
Northern Peoples' Congress			Christian-Muslim rivalry in Igala and Igbirra divisions

Many situations of political conflict seem, at first sight, to be concerned exclusively with ethnic tensions, but on closer investigation they turn out to be the result of an intermixture of communal tensions with developments that accompany a process of secularization. A common political conflict is that between the sons of the soil or the natives of an area and the strangers who settle in burgeoning towns for the sake of more rewarding occupations. A second form of conflict in new urban areas

647   *Nigeria*

TABLE 7

SELECTED CLASS BASES OF PARTY SUPPORT IN
SITUATIONS OF INTERPARTY COMPETITION

Party	Eastern Region	Western Region	Northern Region
Action Group		Most elements of the new and rising class in all sections, including areas of opposition strength, such as Oyo, Ibadan, Ilesha, and Benin	Yoruba people of the "metropolitan districts" of Ilorin Division Bornu commoners of Bornu Division
NCNC–NEPU alliance	Most elements of the new, emergent class in all sections Nonindigenous working-class elements in most urban areas, as in Calabar Urban District, where the indigenous people tend to support the Action Group	Nonindigenous working-class elements in most urban areas and in Lagos	Habe commoners of the Hausa-Fulani state system
Northern Peoples' Congress			Elites of the Middle Belt peoples (Tiv, Birom, Igbirra, Yoruba, etc.) Traditional ruling class of the Hausa-Fulani state system

involves two or more nonindigenous groups of settlers, neither of which represents a traditionally cohesive community. Many of the manual and clerical workers in the principal cosmopolitan centers of Nigeria are Ibo settlers from the Eastern Region; they hail from districts where the NCNC is supported mainly on ethnic grounds. But, as a majority of all manual and clerical workers probably support the NCNC, both ethnic and class motivations are involved, inextricably, in the allegiance of these Ibo workers to the NCNC. Perhaps the most important point to be noted about the pattern of political party action in Nigeria is that, typically, communal and class tensions combine to produce particular situations of interparty competition and intraparty factionalism, and that of all the possible forms and permutations of social tension, simple communal conflict (i.e., traditional community versus traditional community) is the least frequently encountered and is politically the least consequential.

CONCLUSION

A few concluding observations may be pertinent for the study of political parties in an African setting. One observation concerns the current use of the term "tribalism" in the analysis of political dynamics in

Africa. As far as Nigerian political parties are concerned, tribalism would seem to be a grossly inadequate if not a seriously misleading conceptual tool. The term almost invariably conjures up a picture of political behavior based essentially on ethnic factors, a picture that hardly does justice to the complexity of the factors that determine the behavior of Nigerian political parties. More seriously, the concept of tribalism fails to reveal the particular impact the ethnic factor may have on various local political situations in Nigeria. Ethnic solidarity or friction, for instance, is sometimes an aspect of communalism in its more deeply psychological Gemeinschaft sense, implying identification of a political party with a sacred social order, normally in the form of a response to the violation of that order—a phenomenon that ethnic sentiments alone are insufficient to produce. On the other hand, ethnic solidarity or friction in Nigeria, as in other (African and non-African) countries, may reflect and may even be produced by socioeconomic class solidarity or tension, which is devoid of that a-rational, spontaneous, mystic dimension of political behavior to which the concept of communalism suggested here refers. By failing to distinguish these different types of political reaction, both of which may involve ethnic factors, the term "tribalism" fails to explain or even to identify significant aspects of the bases and the strategies of Nigerian political parties.

We have previously observed, and it is worth reiterating, that communal and class factors in conjunction typically create areas of political tension and vulnerability in Nigeria, and that these factors together govern the strategies of the major parties. In varying degrees, all parties capitalize on their chieftaincy assets, socialize their financial institutions, liberalize credit for their business-minded supporters, and activate the sympathies of peasant communities. Although the parties offer some choice in terms of ideological programs, policies and strategies are shaped to a large extent by the imperatives of electoral contests, and these are seldom decided on ideological issues. It is significant that communalism seems to have become more important as a political factor in Nigerian politics since the introduction of elections based on mass suffrage under the 1951 Constitution. To this extent, the course of party development lends support to the view that exacerbation of communal tensions results from the functioning of democratic competitive party systems in the type of pre-industrial environment presently characteristic of most African countries.

A final, related observation is that the political form of the democratic political party seems able to sustain vastly different types of political regimes. In southern Nigeria the political party has served as an instrument of the political ascendancy of new elites produced by the complementary processes of Western education, urbanization, and commercial development, whereas in northern Nigeria the political party has served equally well as the instrument of an *ancien régime* that has controlled and limited the political thrust of the "new men." The role of the political party in Nigeria has been determined, it would seem, less by the nature of the norms and the rules that formally govern the institution than by the nature of the underlying social and economic conditions in which the institution operates.

POSTSCRIPT

The context of the analysis above is the period before 1962; certain prominent features of the Nigerian political scene have changed since then, evidently without loss of its essential elements. The NCNC now forms the government in the Mid-West, the new fourth region of the federation. Predictably, the emergence of a fourth region reinforced sentiment in favor of the creation of others elsewhere, most notably in the so-called C-O-R area of the Eastern Region.

On October 1, 1963, the federation assumed the new status of a republic, with an indirectly elected president as head of state instead of a governor-general, who had been nominally the representative of the British sovereign. The new office, like the old, is occupied by Sir Nnamdi Azikiwe, and is hardly less ceremonial in character. The transition to republican status was accompanied by abolition of the Judicial Service Commission (in which some had placed trust as an instrument of judicial independence) and the Privy Council (which before had rather anomalously represented a last legal resort beyond the Supreme Court); otherwise the move as such seemed devoid of any significant implications for party politics. It is noteworthy, however, that an all-party conference convened by the Prime Minister in the summer of 1963, ostensibly to discuss constitutional modifications, considered and ultimately rejected (amidst impassioned defenses of libertarian principles in the Nigerian press) a proposal to introduce a preventive detention act, which presumably would have permitted imprisonment of persons suspected of "subversive" activities, as in Ghana. Several prominent leaders, including the Prime Minister, afterward spoke out in favor of "national" or all-party governments in the regions as well as at the federation level, thus far without avail. Such proposals clearly stemmed, in part at least, from weariness with the strains and limits imposed on the effort aiming at national social and economic regeneration by a competitive party system, operating in an atmosphere of massive communal susceptibilities.

Intense political controversy surrounded the new official census, initially undertaken in 1962. It was widely rumored that the first count yielded a majority in the southern regions, with obviously profound implications for the balance of power between the northern-based NPC and the other parties. (The new finding, had it been accepted, would have necessitated the redistribution of constituencies.) The federal government, made up of a coalition dominated by the NPC, promply ordered a recount, which eventually placed the population of Nigeria at the surprisingly high figure of nearly 56 million (ninth largest in the world) and reaffirmed the north's predominant position.[43] Thus the NPC's prospects of retaining its present decisive power in national affairs are reaffirmed. The outcome was a bitter pill for the NPC's federal coalition partner, the NCNC, whose president, it is significant to note, immediately revived (in an address to his party's annual convention held just after the announcement of the final tabulation) the party's former advocacy of a federation consisting of a larger number of drastically reduced units, along the lines of the colonial administrative provinces.[44] These developments reflect the persistence of the crucial north-south cleavage.

The most apparently far-reaching changes occurred in the wake of the political crisis which, starting in 1962, swept the Western Region. (The initial circumstances are briefly recounted above.) The Action Group's embarrassment in connection with the investigation of its financial negotiations was overshadowed in September, 1962, by the far graver indictment that certain party leaders, including Chief Awolowo himself, were engaged in a plot forcibly to overthrow the Nigerian government. (The complexity of the issues arising out of the prolonged ensuing trial precludes discussion of them here.) Finally, in August, 1963, a number of convictions for treasonable felony were handed down; Awolowo's sentence was ten years in prison. In the meantime, the Akintola faction of the Action Group had emerged as a full-fledged breakaway party—the United Peoples' Party—and assumed power in the west, with Akintola as premier, through a coalition with some elements of the former NCNC opposition. Evidently the trial soon further disrupted the Action Group ranks; in March, 1964, S. L. Akintola announced the formation under his leadership of a new party which incorporated some highly influential ex-leaders of both the Action Group and the NCNC. Significantly, the new party borrowed its name from an illustrious predecessor—Herbert Macaulay's Nigerian National Democratic Party[45]—and its familiar symbol (a hand) from a more recent political entity—the Mabolaje of Ibadan.[46] The coming federal election of 1964 will test the

---

[43] The margin of the north's majority is now somewhat reduced. The total population of 55,653,821 is distributed as follows: Northern Region, 29,777,986; Eastern Region, 12,388,646; Western Region, 10,278,500; Mid-West Region, 2,533,337; and the federal capital, Lagos, 675,352. These figures are preliminary, but only minor changes are anticipated in the forthcoming official publication.

[44] *West Africa,* Feb. 29, 1964, p. 231.

[45] See p. 598.
[46] See p. 62.

new NNDP's now-uncertain popular foundations. If the party's choice of name and symbol may be assumed to indicate the nature of its intended political strategy, this election is certain to offer a new context in which the forces of class interests and communalism suffuse the institutions of democratic government in Nigeria.

APPENDIX TABLE

RESULTS OF NIGERIAN ELECTIONS, 1951–1960

Election and party	Vote[a]	Per cent of total vote[a]	Seats
EASTERN REGIONAL ELECTION, 1951			
NCNC			65
United National Party			4
WESTERN REGIONAL ELECTION, 1951			
Action Group			45
NCNC			30–35[b]
NORTHERN REGIONAL ELECTION, 1951			
NPC			64[c]
EASTERN REGIONAL ELECTION, 1953			
NCNC			72
National Independence Party			9
United National Party			3
FEDERAL ELECTION, EASTERN REGION, 1954			
NCNC			32
United National Independence Party			4
Action Group			3
Independents			3
FEDERAL ELECTION, WESTERN REGION, 1954			
NCNC			23
Action Group			18
Commoners' Liberal Party			1
FEDERAL ELECTION, NORTHERN REGION, 1954			
NPC			79
Middle Zone League (allied with NPC)			2
Idoma State Union (allied with NPC)			2
Igbirra Tribal Union (allied with NPC)			1
Middle Belt Peoples' Party			1
Action Group			1
Independents			4
FEDERAL ELECTION, SOUTHERN CAMEROONS, 1954			
Kamerun National Congress			5
Kamerun People's Party			
FEDERAL ELECTION, LAGOS, 1954			
NCNC			1
Action Group			1
WESTERN REGIONAL ELECTION, 1956			
Action Group	623,826	48.3	48
NCNC	584,556	45.3	32
Nigerian Commoners' Party	5,133	0.4	
Nigerian People's Party	3,029	0.2	
Dynamic Party	4,841	0.4	
Nigerian Commoners' Liberal Party	5,401	0.4	
Independents	64,388	5.0	

APPENDIX TABLE — *Continued*

Election and party	Vote[a]	Per cent of total vote[a]	Seats
NORTHERN REGIONAL ELECTION, 1956			
NPC			100
Independents allied with NPC			7
Rival wings of United Middle Belt Congress			11
NEPU–Bornu Youth Movement alliance			9
Action Group and Ilorin alliance			4
EASTERN REGIONAL ELECTION, 1957			
NCNC		63.26	64
Action Group		10.75	13
United National Independence Party		6.32	5
Independents		19.67	2
FEDERAL ELECTION, 1959			
Total			
NPC	2,027,194	28.2	134
NCNC–NEPU alliance	2,592,629	36.1	89
Action Group	1,986,839	27.6	73
Others	578,893	8.1	16
East			
NCNC–NEPU alliance	1,246,984	64.6	58
Action Group	445,144	23.1	14
Small parties and independents	237,626	12.3	1
Niger Delta Congress (NPC ally)			1
West			
Action Group	933,680	49.5	33
NCNC–NEPU alliance	758,462	40.2	21
NPC	32,960	1.7	
Small parties and independents	162,107	8.6	8
Mabolaje of Ibadan			7
Independents			1
North			
NPC	1,994,045	61.2	134
Action Group	559,878	17.2	25
NCNC–NEPU alliance	525,575	16.1	8
Small parties and independents	179,022	5.5	7
Igbirra Tribal Union (NPC ally)			1
Independents (declared for NPC)			6
Lagos			
NCNC–NEPU alliance	61,608	55.9	2
Action Group	48,137	43.8	1
NPC	189	0.2	
Small parties and independents	138	0.1	
WESTERN REGIONAL ELECTION, 1960			
Action Group		53.6[d]	79
NCNC–NEPU alliance		36.2	33
Mabolaje of Ibadan (NPC ally)		10.1	10

654   *Nigeria*

Election and party	Vote[a]	Per cent of total vote[a]	Seats
NORTHERN REGIONAL ELECTION, 1961			
NPC		69.2	160
Action Group		14.6	9
NCNC–NEPU alliance		14.2	1
Others		1.8	
EASTERN REGIONAL ELECTION, 1961			
NCNC	901,887	58.0[c]	106
Action Group	240,075	14.4	15
Dynamic Party	68,007	4.4	5
Independents	344,451	22.2[e]	20
MID-WESTERN REGIONAL ELECTION, 1964			
NCNC			53
Midwest Democratic Front (NPC ally)			11
Others			

[a] Blanks indicate that data are not available. Percentage calculations are based partly on J. P. Mackintosh, "Electoral Trends and the Tendency to a One-Party System in Nigeria," *Journal of Commonwealth Political Studies*, I (Nov., 1962), 194–210.

[b] Exact number not known.

[c] As of November 18, 1953.

[d] Percentage figures for the last three elections here tabulated, based on Mackintosh, *op. cit.*, seem to reflect minor changes in party alignment since we made our original calculations.

[e] Most of the independents were NCNC members who campaigned against party orders. If they are regarded as NCNC candidates, the NCNC won 80.2 per cent of the total vote.

CONCLUSIONS

In this symposium we have had two objectives. One has been to identify and to illuminate the variant manifestations of the general tendency toward the establishment and consolidation of one-party-dominant political systems in the new states of Tropical Africa. The second objective has been to examine, in the light of this general trend, as well as of the character of other political groups in contemporary Africa, the different dimensions of the problem of integration confronted by the builders of new states. Drawing upon the many insights and the large body of empirical evidence in the papers in this symposium, we will suggest in this concluding essay certain generalizations regarding the political group structure of independent Africa, and the ways in which it impedes or facilitates the process of nation building.

We turn first to the question of why there has been a tendency for one-party-dominant regimes to be established in all but a few of Tropical Africa's new states. As the seven studies in Part I have shown, there is no simple single answer to this question. Among the many explanations suggested by these and other studies, however, several seem to be particularly in point: (1) the situation party leaders confronted at independence; (2) supportive or predisposing elements in traditional African society; (3) various aspects of the colonial legacy; and (4) the political culture of the new African elite. We do not suggest that this list is exhaustive, nor that these explanations are universally applicable. Indeed, despite the universality of the phenomenon, in each country the process of one-party evolution reflects the operation of a distinctive mix of considerations, most of which, in one way or another, fall under the above four headings.

When their countries achieved independence, African leaders confronted a situation that was not only conducive to the consolidation of one-party dominance, but also made strong government attractive, if not necessary. They inherited the plenitude of autocratic power possessed by the departing colonial government, with few institutionalized restraints upon its exercise. Divisive and separatist tendencies, unchecked by any countervailing sense of national loyalty, threatened the geographic integrity and the internal security of the state, and even the authority of government itself. Political opposition groups tended to be suspect either because they were closely identified with the former colonial power, because they were based upon tribal, ethnic, or regional sentiment, or because they were linked with hostile regimes or movements in neighboring

655

states. The leaders also faced the enormous task of modernization which, if not tackled vigorously and successfully, could convert the revolution of rising expectations, which had helped catapult them to power, into a counterrevolution of rising frustrations, which would most certainly ensure their demise. These and other aspects of the postcolonial period are now commonplace. The point here is that they created a situation favorable to the growth of one-party-dominant systems.

Two particularly significant aspects of the immediate postcolonial situation are (1) the heavy functional load thrown upon the new polity the state builders are seeking to stabilize and legitimate, and (2) the fact that, initially at least, the party is, or is rationalized as being, the most visible, immediately available, national organization for the performance of many, if not most, of the functions involved. Some of the main ingredients in what we may call the "functional load" of the polity in a new state, and the implications for dominant-party performance, are set forth in table 1.

As full and effective performance of all these functions constitutes a staggering burden for even the most highly developed political systems, we must at the outset make clear what we mean by "function" and "functional load" in this particular analysis. We do not mean that if any of these functions are only intermittently or inefficiently performed, or not performed at all, the new states will inevitably disintegrate or their economies stagnate, although such a development is not impossible. African societies are admittedly undergoing profound transformation, and their governing parties are heavily burdened with a multitude of complex problems. Yet these societies have considerable resilience. Large segments of the population are not yet exclusively dependent upon central government or the modern sector. In their interstices, the rich pluralism and the persisting family pattern, there are still important dimensions of functional performance. Thus, although the crises and the burdens confronted by governing parties are very real, we believe that chaos is neither imminent nor inevitable.

A second qualification regarding the concept of function is that its use in the present context does not mean that the single party is considered to be a structural requisite in new African political systems, or even that it necessarily is the most effective or desirable structure. Simply for analytical purposes, we consider it useful to postulate the existence of certain minimal political functions which are performed in all polities, although with varying degrees of explicitness and emphasis, and with wide structural variation. It is possible that a competitive party system in a new state could be the structural arrangement producing the most effective functional performance, as well as the most rapid modernization. We are seeking an explanation for, not a justification of, the single-party

TABLE 1

THE FUNCTIONAL LOAD OF THE POLITY IN A NEW AFRICAN STATE

Function	Character of functional load
Interest articulation and aggregation	Unaggregable character of most interests, and nonexistence, weakness, or ethnicity of interest associations, dispose governing party unilaterally to identify and to determine interest satisfactions in terms of its concept of national interest as well as the state of public opinion.
Political recruitment	Monopoly over political arena and hostility to alternative structures or channels of recruitment dispose governing party to develop, routinize, and regulate recruitment processes within all authoritative and nonauthoritative structures in society.
Political socialization	Widespread persistence and pervasiveness of parochial ties dispose party to perform dual function of (1) facilitating the extinction of old psychological commitments to subcultures viewed as terminal communities, and (2) politically socializing both present and upcoming adult citizenry into (i.e., inculcating respect for and loyalty to) new national political culture, new authority structures, and new bases of legitimacy.
Political communication	Absence or weakness of mass communication media and underdevelopment and discontinuities in communication network increase need for governing party to develop a penetrative communication process both within the party structure and between party and population, as well as to ensure high informational output regarding government plans and programs and expected commitments from population.
National integration	Ethnic, regional, and other parochialisms, not transcended or contained by sense of national community or by habituation to national institutions, and the elite-mass gap dispose party to serve as the main instrument, singly, or through auxiliary instrumentalities it controls, for both territorial and political integration.

trend; and it is a fact that in the *immediate* postcolonial period in many African states the dominant party seemed to be the national institution most capable of performing a variety of political functions.[1]

[1] The list of functions in table 1 is drawn partly from those used in Gabriel A. Almond and James S. Coleman, eds., *The Politics of the Developing Areas* (Princeton:

The magnitude of the functional load a particular governing party may carry is only partly the result of the character of the particular mélange of peoples out of which it seeks to make a nation, and for which it must stabilize a polity and develop an economy. It is also a result of the compulsiveness and the determination with which the dominant party desires to achieve modernizing objectives. The load is manifestly heavier in revolutionary-centralizing one-party-dominant states whose leaders seek simultaneously to extinguish the *corps intermédiaires* between the central government and the individual; to assimilate the structures of party, government, and all functional associations into one vast monolithic unity; to plan and direct the total economy; to launch a vigorous foreign policy; and to reduce the dependence of their countries upon the external world.

Traditional Africa has exerted a variable influence upon the emergence of systems in which one party is dominant. In most instances it has played an obstructive role, as evidenced by the fact that traditionalism in all its forms and manifestations has been one of the principal targets of leaders in most one-party states of the revolutionary-centralizing persuasion. Yet, in several contexts, particularly in Sierra Leone, the Cameroun, and northern Nigeria, traditional factors have strongly supported the pragmatic-pluralistic pattern of one-party development. In all three instances the traditional authority systems, preserved and adapted as they were during the colonial period, provided an organizational infrastructure which modern territorial parties favorable to the traditionalists could use to penetrate and control the rural areas. Given the inexorable erosion of chiefly power, and of traditional symbols and sanctions, the tenure of the parties that have depended upon such power remains very much an open question. The presumption is that their days are numbered. Much will depend upon their skill in consolidating their authoritative position, in immobilizing the opposition, in developing their

Princeton University Press, 1960), pp. 26–58. The functions so listed are meant to be only illustrative. Neither the number nor the formulation of the functions of the polity is immutable; they are no more than *ad hoc* heuristic devices. Dominant parties, for example, may also contribute to the performance of a variety of authoritative functions, such as the making and application of rules and the mobilization and allocation of resources, as well as constitutive and legitimating functions of formal institutions of government.

The long and continuing debate over the use of the concept of function in the social sciences has tended to stigmatize the concept with an inherent conservative or teleological bias, leading frequently to the charge that purportedly neutral explanation is a mask for moral justification or rationalization. For a recent contribution to this polemic see Irving Louis Horowitz, "Sociology and Politics: The Myth of Functionalism Revisited," *Journal of Politics,* XXV (May, 1963), 248–264. The fact is that both functionalists and critics of functionalism do not always carefully distinguish among the mathematical, biological, and ordinary usages of the term, thereby confusing normative and existential considerations.

organizational structure, and in finding new social bases for support. Very much in point is the perpetuative power acquired by the
Northern Peoples' Congress in Nigeria through its vigorous action against
powerful traditional rulers who have been corrupt, its absorption of most
of the leaders of the dissident Middle Belt groups, and its development
of an organizational structure independent of the traditional systems.

The relevance of traditional authority structures in the development
of one-party-dominant systems, whether they were supportive or obstructive, is a function of two factors: (1) their inherent strength, resilience,
and adaptability, and (2) the character of the colonial legacy, that is,
whether they were protected and supported, or neglected and ignored,
during the colonial period. In most British areas they were protected,
and, where possible, were made units of local government, in accordance
with the principle of indirect rule. Although in some French territories
they were shown some deference (for example, the chiefs of northern
Togo and the Cameroun, and the Marabouts in Senegal), French policy
in general accelerated the demise of the traditional order. This difference
in the colonial legacy helps to explain why national integration and the
consolidation of one-party rule have been comparatively easier in former
French territories than in those previously under British administration.

Closely related to the foregoing is the influence of the highly centralized, even quasi-military, systems of colonial administration upon
African political perspectives and attitudes. Modern colonialism in Africa
everywhere tended toward bureaucratic authoritarianism, even though
it was paternalistic in motivation. Although colonial powers endeavored
to establish democratic parliamentary government in the period preceding the grant of independence to their African territories, the fact
remains that the exposure to pluralistic democracy was relatively brief,
and that the present generation of Africans—whether party elites or the
masses—were subjected during most of their lives to an authoritarian
political order. However different the political socialization patterns of
their respective traditional societies may have been—and these varied
from virtually pure egalitarianism to sheer autocracy—it is believed that
in most instances the really determinative factor in the orientation of the
present party elites to the political order has been their exposure to
bureaucratic centralism during the colonial period. In a sense, one-party
rule and "national party" government are simply postcolonial terms for
the same phenomenon. In the realm of government and administration in
Africa, there is far more continuity than innovation.

A third element in the colonial legacy facilitating one-party development has been the so-called "aura of legitimacy" with which many of the
governing parties were endowed at the time of independence. As the
papers on Guinea and Mali have shown, parties such as the Parti Démo-

cratique de Guinée (PDG) and the Union Soudanaise established themselves in the public image, through ceaseless nationalist agitation before independence, as the true carriers of the African revolution. Even such parties as the Parti Démocratique de la Côte d'Ivoire (PDCI) and the Convention People's Party (CPP) in Ghana, which actively collaborated with the colonial governments during a protracted period of diarchy (1950 to 1960 for the PDCI, and 1951 to 1957 for the CPP), were able to perpetuate and to capitalize on a popular belief that they were also the parties of revolution. During a brief period in the late 1940's, each of these parties was more militantly nationalist than its competitors. Like the National Convention of Nigerian Citizens (NCNC), they were thereby endowed with the special mantle of grace. Once the CPP had won a majority, it was able to consolidate its power in the Ghanaian political system with the protection, support, and collaboration of the British government; at the same time it was vigorously denouncing imperialism and demanding "Self-Government Now!" Thus the critical element in the legitimating power of revolutionary imagery is not necessarily ceaseless struggle and uncompromising resistance until the final full surrender of imperial power—although leaders and supporters in the PDG and the Union Soudanaise continue to be fortified by their memories of sacrifice and martyrdom—but the establishment by a party of a favorable image in the public mind at that point in time when the imperial power seriously launched the protracted process of disengagement and withdrawal. Strengthened by an early revolutionary popularity which chastened and indulgent colonial powers allowed to be kept alive, protected from the opposition by the full support of the imperial government, and progressively endowed with real power enabling it to consolidate its position of primacy within the state, the governing party in many new states entered the era of independence not only with its aura of legitimacy virtually untarnished, but also with decisive control over the authoritative structures of government.

The consolidation of a party's position of primacy was frequently facilitated in the crucial phase of terminal colonialism by electoral systems based upon the single-member constituency, or the single-list principle, as well as by parliamentary forms of government based upon the sovereignty of the majority. The operation of these factors, both singly and in combination, tended in practice to give relatively unfettered control to a victorious party, although it may have won no more than a plurality of the popular vote or only a bare majority of the total constituencies. The Ghana essay, among others, vividly illuminates this phenomenon. In more developed countries such a system is rationalized and defended in terms of its capacity to produce strong leadership and effective government. Given the highly fragmented and unintegrated character of most new African states, and the consequent need for strong and effective government, the argument in favor of such a majoritarian system is logically even more persuasive. Yet there is a difference: in more highly developed countries there are structural and psychological restraints upon the arbitrary use of the relatively unlimited governmental power enjoyed by a party commanding a parliamentary majority. All aspects of this interesting and important issue obviously cannot be discussed here; suffice it to note that electoral and other institutional innovations in the terminal colonial period disproportionately favored the majority party, and that these were, in some instances, strongly determinative factors in the process of consolidation and maximization of its perpetuative power.

Imperial countries were not only the source of electoral systems and parliamentary models; party organization in Africa also reflected the strong influence of Socialist and Communist parties. In Senegal, as Foltz has observed, the formal structures of the three older parties were similar, resulting "as much from the continued influence of a common European Marxist tradition as from a common response to Senegalese conditions." Hodgkin and Morgenthau have noted the special significance of the Groupes d'Etudes Communistes. The strength and the pervasiveness of these various influences upon party organization were the result not only of the special efforts made by European parties of the Left to give support and guidance to African parties on organization, strategy, and tactics, but also of a determined effort by African leaders to secure advice and assistance in the development of a revolutionary organization. Even had left-wing European parties been indifferent or uncoöperative, African leaders would still probably have borrowed heavily from them because the monolithic and penetrative character of those parties was manifestly appropriate to the creation of an independent power base from which to launch their assault upon the colonial regime. Thus, whether European parties of the Left deliberately influenced African political groups, as the French Socialist Party (SFIO) did in Senegal, or were deliberately emulated, as President Kwame Nkrumah claims was true in the initial organization of the CPP, they were a not irrelevant part of the total colonial legacy.

These aspects of traditional society and of the colonial experience undoubtedly facilitated the development of one-party-dominant systems, but they are not full explanations. They become meaningful only when situational factors are favorable, and only when one-party predispositions are present among governing party elites.

The political culture of the new African elites has probably been the decisive factor in the general trend toward the one-party polity, although the contributions of traditional society and colonialism and the "ripe situation" were essential preconditions. By elite political culture, we refer to attitudes, beliefs, values, orientation toward authority, and self-images of the leaders of new states regarding their political roles and capacities.[2] This culture reflects the socializing influences both of traditional society and of the colonial period, as well as the postcolonial perceptions and evaluations of the elite, and their estimate as to what should, and realistically could, be done to realize elite objectives. Although there are numerous exceptions and qualifications to any generalization about African political phenomena, there are at least three rather common elements in the political culture of African party leaders: elitism, statism, and nationalism. These are all interrelated and mutually reinforcing, and each is supportive of one or another aspect of the one-party syndrome.

The elitism of African political leaders is manifested in many ways: through their perception and definition of their own roles in the political system; through the suggestion that in a population mainly illiterate the "educated" have a special claim to leadership, either because of superior enlightenment or because of a greater capacity to handle the complex affairs of a modern state; and through the "elect" pretensions and the paternalism which frequently creep into their references to their "people." It is not an ascriptive, aristocratic, or closed elitism; indeed, the political culture is saturated with achievement norms, ultrapopulistic slogans, and egalitarian assumptions. Nor is it an arrogant, condescending elitism crudely flaunted before the people. On the contrary, political leaders are fortified in their elitist proclivities by the deference accorded them by the masses. Elitism has, however, clearly furthered the one-party tendency, because it carries the implicit presumption that the governing group possesses a monopoly of wisdom and legitimacy. It follows, therefore, that in their view an opposition group recruited from the nonelite is incompetent and illegitimate and that one recruited from the same social strata as the elite is either frivolous and irrelevant, or dangerously subversive because its members seek only power.

The statism in the African elite political culture reflects three facts: (1) the present generation of Africans has been politically socialized within the framework of a society whose private sector was extremely undeveloped, and consequently the state was dominant in all modern sectors of the society (e.g., the economy, the educational system, public works and utilities) and was as well the main employer, the source of all amenities, and the initiator and manager of most aspects of social and economic development—in a word, it was "socialist"; (2) the leaders inherited this system from the colonial powers, and by default it must serve them as the instrument for rapid modernization; and (3) Marxism has

---

[2] The term "political culture" is here used essentially as it is in Gabriel Almond and Sidney Verba, *The Civic Culture* (Princeton: Princeton University Press, 1963).

strongly influenced a substantial segment of the present generation of Africans, partly because of the appeal of the Leninist interpretation of modern imperialism, and partly because of the courting and indoctrination of Africans by European parties of the Left. Yet none of the governments of the new African states are totalitarian; indeed, large segments of their populations only partially or intermittently participate in the modern sectors. This fact, coupled with the extreme weakness of the authoritative governmental structures, makes African one-party-dominant systems a species of the larger genus of movement-regime.[3] A statist society is essentially a bureaucratic society; and, the more bureaucratic a society, the more difficult, if not illogical, it is to envisage a competitive political process, because of the normative and structural incompatibilities of the two systems.[4] It is in this sense that statism in contemporary Africa has supported the one-party tendency.

The African elite political culture is "nationalist" in that party leaders in African one-party-dominant states have been basically committed to "national unity" as the supreme value and goal. They either condemn or reluctantly tolerate (under firm central control) tribalism, ethnicity, regional autonomy, and other manifestations of subnational sentiment. They are also nationalist in that they rule out all forms of political opposition which threaten, actually or symbolically, the integrity of the nation they are seeking to build. Throughout Africa, political opposition has tended to be stigmatized by its link with external or subnational forces or influences. As a consequence, opposition is regarded as anti-nationalist, and therefore illegal in spirit, if not by statute. Yet this particular strand in elite political culture is not simply suppressive; it also reflects a widely held belief among African leaders that what is needed at this stage is a national party, a *parti unifié*, or, indeed, no party at all. Here it is pertinent to recall George Washington's opposition to political parties during the first decade of America's independence as the first "new nation." A penetrating analysis of the obstacles to party development in the early postcolonial period in the United States points out that,

For men like Washington or Hamilton, . . . [doubts about the wisdom of parties] were concentrated around the question of the legitimacy of an opposition party. A man of forceful presence, a balancing and unifying force in politics, and the supreme hero of the Revolutionary War, Washington was convinced that once the new national government had been put in his hands, it was up to him and his chosen aids to manage it. Filled with determination to join the struggling states into a great and powerful nation, a far-seeing leader

---

[3] Robert C. Tucker, "Towards a Comparative Politics of Movement-Regimes," *American Political Science Review,* LV (June, 1961), 281–289.

[4] Cf. Joseph A. Schumpeter, *Capitalism, Socialism and Democracy* (New York: Harper and Brothers, 1950), pp. 205–209.

of determined purpose, Hamilton also was impatient with criticism, intolerant of democratic demands or the very idea of opposition.[5]

Yet, despite the historical similarity, there is a striking difference between postcolonial parties in the United States and postcolonial parties in the new African states. In the United States, parties as we know them today had yet to be created. In the new African states, however, parties existed as organized associations before national independence; moreover, constitutional norms, procedures, and institutions presumed their existence as sources for the recruitment of national political leadership. Thus, although the leaders of all new states have tended to be hostile toward political opposition in the interest of national unity, the problems they have confronted have been markedly different. The problem of Washington and Hamilton was to prevent the emergence of parties, whereas the problem of Kwame Nkrumah and Modibo Keita, and most of their contemporaries, has been to consolidate the primacy of one party over all others. It is this process of consolidation of one-party dominance with which we are primarily concerned here.

The papers on different countries in this symposium have revealed the speed and ease with which one-party consolidation has occurred in the new African states. In the Cameroun, for example, Le Vine has shown how the governing Union Camerounaise rapidly transformed itself—admittedly with the help of the French, but also against the ever-present challenge of one of Africa's major guerrilla forces—from a northern regional party holding only 50 per cent of the seats in the legislature in 1960 to a national party commanding unquestioned political predominance in 1963. In many other African countries not discussed herein, the trend has been similar. The generality of the trend underscores not only the generic quality of the background factors noted earlier, but also the enormous power over persons and things which the governing party in a new African state commands. Without such control, the process of consolidating one-party dominance could not have been carried out with such rapidity and relative absence of resistance.

The process of consolidation has encompassed four types of activity. One is the explicit actions taken by ruling party elites to convert, neutralize, or eliminate overt political opposition, actions so persuasive that they also deterred the later manifestation of opposition by dissident elements. Second, ruling party elites, in their effort to achieve structural unity, have "nationalized" all nonparty associations and made them either integral parts or adjuncts of the national party. A third set of measures includes those postcolonial constitutional and electoral innovations designed to strengthen unitary one-party rule. Fourth, party leaders have

---

[5] William Nisbet Chambers, *Political Parties in a New Nation: The American Experience, 1776–1809* (New York: Oxford University Press, 1963), p. 5.

set forth a body of ideas—a political theory if you will—defending, ra-
tionalizing, or affirming the virtues of a one-party system. These elements
in the consolidation process—opposition conversion or neutralization, associational integration, constitutional innovation, and ideological rationalization—will be briefly examined in the following sections.

A wide variety of consolidation techniques have been available to
governing party elites both in neutralizing existing opposition and in preventing the emergence of potential opposition. These techniques fall
roughly into two categories: rewarding those who support, or at least do
not resist, the governing party, and punishing those who oppose it. Rewards include patronage, educational opportunities, developmental
amenities, and preferential treatment in the award of government contracts and licenses. Punishments include deprivation of the foregoing
rewards, of course, and, more directly, range from harassment by local
chiefs, police, and courts to physical incarceration or deportation. None
of the techniques are peculiarly African. Many are time-honored stratagems used with varying degrees of crudeness or subtlety by governing
parties everywhere. Others, such as deportation, or physical restriction
and punishment, are part of the colonial legacy, and therefore represent
continuity in the governmental treatment of opposition rather than postcolonial African innovations.

The selective use of patronage to assimilate or control political opposition, or to enlist the support of potentially dissident elements, has
been an extremely powerful weapon. It has extraordinary importance in
the new African states because of the strongly statist character of their
societies. Because government is deeply involved in all aspects of the
modern sector of the economy, because it is the chief employer of labor
and the only source of capital grants for modern amenities, and because
it is the sole channel through which massive inputs of foreign assistance
enter the society, African ruling parties are able to pursue with remarkable effectiveness the old Latin-American custom of *continuismo*. Foltz
has shown how the leadership of the Union Progressiste Sénégalaise has
used government employment and public funds as the "standard means
of rewarding the faithful and enticing dissidents into the fold." Liebenow
points out that "the Whig leadership [in Liberia] has, for more than
eighty years, relied upon patronage as its principal weapon in keeping the
party faithful in line and in undermining the opposition by wooing away
its qualified leadership." With continuing expansion in public works and
economic development programs, and the corollary insignificance of the
private sector in providing employment and career opportunities, government patronage will remain a subtle and effective means of perpetuating
the power of the present ruling party elites, provided, of course, their
parties remain united.

The preferential awarding of government scholarships for higher education has been, and will continue to be, an enormously effective instrument of one-party consolidation. Very few African parents are financially able to give their children the higher and professional education necessary for their advancement in the new African societies. Although during the terminal colonial period government sought to minimize political manipulation of scholarship programs, since independence party elites have used these programs as a source of patronage as well as a means of controlling entry into the elite ranks. The implications of this are clear. An African parent or guardian will be very careful not to jeopardize the educational opportunities of his dependents. By accepting government largess he will be forced into a position either of political passivity or of dutiful support of the dominant party. As long as higher education provides the most rapid and direct access to high status, as it tends to do in contemporary Africa, the dominant party's power of self-perpetuation through allocation of educational opportunities is greatly enhanced.

The selective areal allocation of public funds and grants for modern amenities (piped water, electricity, hospitals, schools, etc.) and for the development of the country's infrastructure (communications, energy, roads, transportation facilities, etc.) has also been an important instrument of consolidation. In many new states the phenomenon known as the "vanishing opposition" is in large measure explained by the strong pressures placed upon opposition leaders by their constituents to join the governing party and share in this preferential treatment. It is a phenomenon manifested in a variety of contexts. Immediately after elections there is frequently a massive shift of elected members of a defeated party, or of independents, to the government party, under the time-honored rationale, "If you can't beat them, join them." This propensity is strengthened by the sense of futility engendered by the conviction that the party in power is impregnable.

Groups, as well as individuals, have abandoned the role of opposition, for the same reasons and in response to the same pressures discussed above. Among French-speaking African states voluntary mergers and fusions of political parties have been widespread, usually taking the form of assimilation of all parties into the dominant party. Between 1952 and 1957 the governing PDCI in the Ivory Coast absorbed all significant opposition parties; in Guinea, immediately after independence was achieved in 1958, the last of the opposition groups voluntarily merged with the dominant PDG; and in 1959 the Parti Soudanais Progressiste, the leading opposition party in the former French Soudan, was absorbed into the Union Soudanaise. The spirit of merger or integration has stemmed partly from the manifest advantages of a comprehensive "national front" (usually expressed in French as a *parti unifié*) in tackling the problems of independence and modernization. For opposition groups that were being absorbed, the impulse to merge was in part a response to the known wishes, or the determination, of the dominant party that opposition cease. But it also reflected the desire of opposition leaders that their groups not be excluded from all the benefits accruing from participation in the government. This issue was for some time at the heart of the argument among the leaders of the principal opposition party in Nigeria: Would not abandonment of the role of opposition contribute to the unity of the country and, at the same time, help the people of the Western Region, who have been denied access to federal patronage and amenities?

Although the dominant ruling parties in Africa's new states have preferred to use the more subtle techniques of neutralizing overt political opposition, they have also been prepared to take restrictive or punitive actions. Threats designed to create a climate of fear and to ensure conformity have occasionally been employed. Preventive detention acts, censorship and control over the press, limitations upon public demonstrations and public criticisms of the regime, and other means have been used to maintain "law and order" and to ensure control over oppositional behavior. In general, highly visible punishments such as imprisonment or deportation have been meted out only as a last resort. Punishment has been used as much to impress latent or potential opposition with the consequences of overt dissent as to inflict retribution for the act of opposition.

The second major category of activity in the uniparty consolidation process is the effort by ruling party elites to draw in all forms of existing associations. The intensity, the comprehensiveness, and the determination with which this objective has been pursued have varied considerably. In Mali, as Hodgkin and Morgenthau have shown, the Union Soudanaise has systematically sought the total integration of all associations, including those formed by the important groups of youth and women. In the Ivory Coast, leaders have been less compulsively centralizing in their approach; associations such as the Syndicat des Chefs Coutumiers have not been structurally integrated into the PDCI, although they have been deferential to its primacy. Despite these variations, however, the general trend has been toward the creation of single nationwide interest associations closely linked to the dominant party. These and other aspects of the process of nationalization of nonparty associations and groups have been treated in detail by Wallerstein in his essay; it is sufficient to note here that this process is one of several methods used to consolidate oneparty dominance.

The third type of consolidation activity comprises electoral and constitutional changes instituted by leaders of dominant parties in order to strengthen the legal position, if not to establish the constitutional pre-eminence, of their parties. One of the most common and effective inno-vations has been the single-list electoral system by which all members of a national legislature are elected on a single slate covering the entire country. In the many French-speaking states where this system has been used, the victorious party has won all the seats in the legislature. A second development has been the progressive strengthening of the execu-tive power. This has been particularly marked in French-speaking states and in Ghana and Tanganyika, and certainly represents a general trend. The French-speaking states modeled their constitutions on that of the Fifth French Republic, which clearly provided for the undisputed pre-eminence of the executive power. In Ghana, President Nkrumah's pro-gram of centralization and solidarity has been reflected in constitutional changes introduced since the achievement of independence in 1957. For example, the constitution of July 1, 1960, fused the functions of president and prime minister into a single, powerful executive endowed with full legal control over all structures of authority in the state. This constitu-tional ratification of the *de facto* consolidation of unitary power unques-tionably enhanced the legal position of the CPP in the Ghanaian political system. The final step in the consolidation process, as Apter has shown, was the January, 1964, referendum formally making Ghana a one-party state. Similarly, the Tanganyika African National Union has used con-stitutional means to bolster its position, and the tendency is visible in most other new states where one party has undisputed control.

Fourth, in order to consolidate uniparty systems, African party lead-ers have put forward a theoretical defense, a rationale, for the new type of polity. Their speeches and writings on this topic reflect a fairly com-mon stock of ideas, although eclectically drawn from many sources and experiences. Collectively these ideas constitute a rather amorphous and unsystematic, but nonetheless extremely illuminating, African political theory. This loose mélange of ideas, which we will call the theory of uni-partyism, is a mixture of defensive explanations and categorical postu-lations. In it one finds the ever-present and irrepressible sentiment of anticolonialism, a frequently romanticized African traditionalism, and a buoyant progressivism. Like most political ideologies, it serves primarily to rationalize and legitimate a particular political state of affairs, which in this instance is postcolonial unipartyism.

A key element in the theory of unipartyism is that the staggering problem of nation building and modernization requires a central and unitary organization of power within the state, and that Africa's parties are the only structures available for this purpose. Nkrumah has described the situation as "almost analogous to a state of war and national emer-gency which is always met in the older established countries by the formation of coalition or national governments." Multiparty systems are regarded as forms of "institutionalized factionalism" which not only divide the national will and dissipate national energies, but also threaten internal stability. Thus, *raison d'état* is the primary and most obvious rationale for unipartyism.

Another common theme is that a uniparty form of government is not only rooted in, but is a modern expression of, certain aspects of traditional political culture. It is argued that traditional African culture was communal in character, and that the individual had no identity apart from his group. Decisions were made only after unanimity had been achieved through institutionalized "talking it out" in a "village palaver"; because such decisions embodied the collective will, the idea of a permanently organized opposition was not only alien, but intolerable. It does not follow that traditional societies were autocratic; on the contrary, there were, it is argued, constitutional checks upon the arbitrary exercise of political authority, as well as direct popular involvement in decision making. Nkrumah, a leading spokesman for African unipartyism, has declared, for example, that Ghanaian society is by "form and tradition fundamentally democratic in character."

The theory also connotes the absence of sharp differentiation into classes, either in traditional or in contemporary African societies. Because most African leaders lean heavily upon Marxian theory, including the assumption that parties are solely a reflection of class interests, it is argued that the lack of class differentiation in Africa renders competing parties unnecessary. In traditional African societies, it is reasoned, the transcendent influence of highly diffuse communal and familial rights and duties prevented or retarded differentiation into distinct classes. President Julius Nyerere of Tanganyika, in expounding the communal basis of African socialism, adopts essentially this position:

In traditional African society *everybody* was a worker. There was no other way of earning a living for the community. Even the Elder, who appeared to be enjoying himself without doing any work and for whom everybody else appeared to be working, had, in fact, worked hard all his younger days. The wealth he now appeared to possess was not *his*, personally; it was only "his" as the Elder of the group which had produced it. He was its guardian. The wealth itself gave him neither power nor prestige.[6]

---

[6] Julius Nyerere, *Ujama: The Basis of African Socialism* (Dar es Salaam, 1962). This argument is fairly common among uniparty spokesmen. Sékou Touré, for example, has claimed that traditional African society is essentially "communaucratique." For these and similar arguments see Rupert Emerson, *Political Modernization: The Single-Party System,* University of Denver Monograph Series in World Affairs, No. 1 (Denver, 1964), pp. 26 ff. For a debate between two anthropologists on the traditional basis for unipartyism, see Robert F. Gray, "Political Parties in New

In modern African societies, uniparty theorists assert that class differentiation has not yet occurred on a significant scale; accordingly, there are no capitalist or proletarian classes, and hence no social bases for competing parties. As Hodgkin and Morgenthau have noted in their Mali study, the crux of Madeira Keita's position is that "there is no objective social basis for interparty conflict in a system such as that of modern Mali."

A more affirmative theme in the theory of unipartyism, not entirely congruent with the foregoing, is that the highly differentiated (i.e., pluralistic and heterogeneous) character of the social base of the new states manifestly makes a one-party structure the best form of governmental organization. It is both an integrative and a stabilizing structure which can fuse the diverse groups together into a new sense of community in order that they may realize their common potentialities. It provides an organizational means for conflict resolution, as well as for representation of all interests in society. In short, the structure of the single party, with its network of branches and allied functional associations, is seen as the most appropriate and effective "African" way of organizing society and governing a state. Indeed, the party and the state are one.

Sensitive to, but defiant of, the fact that their behavior as a governing class is being watched closely and is being judged by democratic norms of the West, African uniparty theorists place special emphasis upon the essentially democratic character of African one-party politics. The leaders of the TANU, for example, have declared that one-party democracy under a strong president is not only more appropriate to African conditions, but more readily understood by Africans. The repeated and overwhelming TANU majorities in Western-style democratic elections clearly demonstrate, it is claimed, that Tanganyikans neither require nor desire more than one party. Intraparty democracy is all that is required, and this they believe is assured in African uniparty systems. A variant of this theme is found in Nyerere's assertion that "where there is *one* party—provided it is identified with the nation as a whole—the foundations of democracy can be firmer, and the people can have more

---

African Nations," *Comparative Studies in Society and History*, V (July, 1963), 449–461, and Lucy Mair's comments thereon, pp. 462–465.

The proposition that traditional African society was essentially egalitarian cannot be uncritically rejected as political romanticism. Lloyd Fallers has argued, for example, that one of the distinctive features of traditional African society, even in the larger kingdoms, was a rather pervasive egalitarianism. Tendencies toward crystallization of rigid horizontal strata were checked by a fairly common pattern of kinship and family structure (exogamous unilineal descent groups) and by the "absence of literary religious traditions, which might have provided the basis for more clearly differentiated elite subcultures" ("Equality, Modernity and Democracy in the New States," in Clifford Geertz, ed., *Old Societies and New States* [New York: Free Press of Glencoe, 1963], p. 180).

opportunity to exercise a real choice, than where you have two or more parties." [7] Other statements reflect the persistent effort made to establish the fact that African one-party polities are functionally democratic, even though structurally they do not conform to the classical Western model. Nkrumah has declaimed that "we in Africa will evolve forms of government rather different from the traditional Western pattern but not less democratic in their protection of the individual and his inalienable rights." [8] In the same vein, Tom Mboya of Kenya argues that the "countries of Africa emerging from political subjection are entitled to modify, to suit their own needs, the institutions of democracy as developed in the West. *No one has the right to cavil at this so long as all citizens—irrespective of their social, tribal or religious affiliations—are treated alike.*" [9] Here one finds that interesting mixture of defensiveness and assertiveness employed by African leaders to interpret and justify postcolonial political institutions in terms of the external standards by which they feel they are being judged, while at the same time affirming their right to develop political forms that are distinctively African.

Although the foregoing aspects of the process of one-party consolidation represent a general tendency in all new states, there are significant differences in the emphasis given them by those states oriented toward the revolutionary-centralizing pattern, on the one hand, and states leaning toward the pragmatic-pluralistic type on the other. The differences are both structural and psychological. Structurally, the revolutionary-centralizing uniparty regimes seek to absorb and control all forms of associational life in the country; psychologically, they endeavor to create a climate of full and continuous involvement and commitment on the part of the population regarding party-state goals. In contrast, pragmatic-pluralistic regimes are structurally far less pervasive and all-embracing, for they tolerate considerable associational and traditional pluralism (providing it does not threaten the integrity of the party or the tenure of the governing elite); psychologically, they are far less demanding.

These contrasting orientations are very real; nevertheless, various factors and forces operate to narrow the differences between them. The realities of African conditions—ethnic and regional disunities, serious shortages of trained high-level manpower, limited financial resources, and a variety of other incapacitating circumstances—have exerted a powerfully sobering and temporizing influence upon leaders of the compulsive revolutionary-centralizing persuasion. The almost insuperable ob-

---

[7] Quoted approvingly in Tom Mboya, "The Party System and Democracy in Africa," *Foreign Affairs*, XLI (July, 1963), 655.

[8] Kwame Nkrumah, *I Speak of Freedom: A Statement of African Ideology* (New York: Praeger, 1961), p. 58.

[9] Mboya, *op. cit.*, p. 658. Italics added.

stacles they have confronted since independence have compelled them to be more pragmatic and pluralistic in practice, even though they may persist in their declamatory revolutionary-centralizing position. Similarly, the regimes in the pragmatic-pluralistic uniparty states have been rather firmly urged by younger and more militant elements to adopt a more revolutionary and centralizing position with respect to such issues as obstructive traditionalism, accelerated Africanization, and vigorous pursuit of African socialism.

These two countervailing forces—the deterrents to and the limited capabilities for the establishment of a totalitarian state, balanced against the presence of a frustrated younger generation driven to consummate the "African Revolution"—are among the critical determinants of the future development of African polities. And further evolution there will be. The one-party syndrome described in this symposium does not necessarily represent the end of the line in the political evolution of the new African states. Indeed, the triumph of one-party rule, the emergence of the dominant party as the political center of gravity immediately after independence, may prove to be no more than a transitional phenomenon.

In addition to other factors already mentioned, at least three generic features of the postcolonial situation could affect, if not determine, future patterns of political change in African one-party states: (1) the ideological and structural vulnerability of the single party under the radically altered circumstances created by independence; (2) the strain toward primacy and autonomy of the formal institutions of government; and (3) changes in the social structure brought about by the modernization processes launched or accelerated by independent statehood. These three factors are obviously interrelated. Their impact upon the course of change will be highly variable. Yet in all new states, in one way or another, they will introduce stresses and tensions that will continually challenge the primacy, unity, and omnipotence of the single party.

We have seen that certain aspects of the immediate postcolonial situation facilitate the consolidation of one-party dominance. Other aspects, however, render the governing party highly vulnerable to popular disenchantment and unmask its inherent weaknesses. Most obviously, the attainment of independence means the abrupt loss of the party's main *raison d'être*, indeed, the loss of its ideology. "Defending a revolution," as Foltz puts it, "is always a less exciting and onerous task than making it"; moreover, secondary goals—for example, external ventures in support of the liberation of the African continent or Pan-African unity, the elimination of residual colonial influences and of continued unbalanced dependence upon the former metropolitan country (neocolonialism), or the pursuit of some purely internal goal such as economic development —neither generate the emotional commitment nor provide the mobilizing power which characterized the drive toward national independence.[10] There is no ideological substitute of equal integrating and purposive force, and a single party without an ideology is critically handicapped.

Independence also means shifts in the forms and goals of political action: the shift from vilification and agitation against government to its support and defense; the shift from mobilization and maximization of grievances to their containment, sublimation, or projection onto some new internal or external enemy; the shift from the stimulation of exaggerated hopes to the inculcation of duty, sacrifice, and postponed rewards; and the shift from the image of the party as an instrument of liberation to its role of coercion, repression, and self-aggrandizement and enrichment of the elite. In short, independence may become the watershed at which the revolution of rising expectations becomes the revolution of rising frustrations, and the single party has the glory and the stigma of being, respectively, the vanguard of both.[11]

Governing single parties are vulnerable not only because of the psychological deflation produced by independence, but also because many of them, at the outset, were organizationally weak and faction-ridden, and lacked a mass base. The harsh realities of the immediate postcolonial period have made this increasingly clear. Nationalist rhetoric, the romantic predisposition of most persons to believe that an oppressed people struggling for freedom and modernity must have a single-minded purpose, and the high visibility of those few parties possessing a strong national organization and a mass base (for example, the PDG in Guinea,

---

[10] William J. Foltz, "Building the Newest Nations: Short-Run Strategies and Long-Run Problems," in Karl W. Deutsch and William J. Foltz, *Nation-Building* (New York: Atherton Press, 1963), p. 122. For three other highly perceptive essays on the changing role of the party in new African states see Pierre de Briey, "Notes on a Conference: The Institutions of the New States," *Civilisations,* XIII, no. 3 (1963), 227–249; Immanuel Wallerstein, "Political Parties in Post-Independence Africa: Recruitment and Participation," and Rupert Emerson, "Political Parties and National Integration in Tropical Africa" (papers presented at the Conference on Political Parties and Political Development held at Frascati, Italy, Jan. 6–9, 1964, under the auspices of the Committee on Comparative Politics of the Social Science Research Council). Both these essays will be published in a forthcoming volume edited by Joseph La Palombara and Myron Weiner, to be entitled *Political Parties and Political Development.*

[11] Tucker has noted that this dual role is a generic phenomenon of nationalist revolutionary movement-regimes, which "show a definite tendency to spend their revolutionary force rather early. In some cases this happens soon after the achievement of the original revolutionary goals and prior to the completion of the revolutionizing of the old society. In other words, the nationalist movement-regime is peculiarly the prey of the phenomenon of 'extinction' " (*op. cit.,* pp. 286–287). A study group of INCIDI put the idea in these terms: "Independence . . . usually brought disillusionment. . . . The narrowed horizons of the nationalist struggle after independence and the difficulty of implementing the promises and hopes of the leaders have led to a certain estrangement of the masses. In the period following independence a large part of the population has broken away from the leaders, ignored the new institutions and sunk into almost complete apathy" (de Briey, *op. cit.,* p. 237).

the Union Soudanaise in Mali, and the TANU in Tanganyika)—all these elements combined to create the belief among most persons that the single party was one of monolithic unity and widespread popular commitment.[12] The reality is often very different, as the studies on several countries in this symposium have demonstrated. The single party, with few exceptions, has been the end product of a succession of amalgamations in which preëxisting pluralism and competition were not necessarily extinguished, but merely subsumed under a more inclusive organizational label. In effect, competing parties within an emergent state often became competing factions within a one-party state.

Governing single parties in new states were further weakened immediately after independence by the diversion of key party personnel to other activities. As Foltz points out, "Talents that once were available for the crucial work of party organization may now be preoccupied with running a ministry or government bureau. . . . Unless new sources of loyal organizational and administrative talents can be found immediately, the party's organization—and, therefore, the major link between the regime and the masses—is likely to be weakened." [13] The effect of this leadership mobility upon party continuity or survival was frequently demonstrated during the preindependence agitational period, when the transfer to other activities of only a few central party figures bore devastating results, partly because of the highly personalistic—frequently charismatic—quality of revolutionary leadership, and partly because of the small size of leadership cadres. In any event, both the attractions and the requirements of high bureaucratic office have brought a rather marked shift from emphasis on party roles to emphasis on new governmental roles.

The factors that weaken the single party at the very moment it is establishing its supremacy are also affected by the increased prominence of formal bureaucratic structures. The major element in the colonial legacy to the governing party elite in a new African state has been a centralized administrative system. Indeed, colonial rule in Africa was bureaucratic authoritarianism—the "administrative state"—in its purest form. This "machinery of government" has been indispensable to the party elite in maintaining governmental continuity during the transfer of power, as well as in consolidating its hold over the country. Preindepend-

---

[12] Rupert Emerson points out, as a characteristic element in the nationalist rhetoric of one-party apologists, the tendency to assert that the single party is an expression of an existent national unity, while at the same time arguing for it as an essential instrument to achieve national solidarity (*op. cit.*, pp. 24–25).

[13] Foltz, *op. cit.*, pp. 123–124. Also see Wallerstein (*op. cit.*, p. 8), who notes that a party official's governmental responsibilities increasingly diminish the amount of time available for party work. Also, once the single party has consolidated its position, there seems to be less need for party activity, a psychological consideration of no little significance.

ence hostility toward the government as a structure of "alien imperialist domination" and as a haven of antinationalist "Uncle Toms" tended to be quickly dissipated after independence, for a centralized administrative system was manifestly necessary to a modern state. Party control of that system, coupled with accelerated Africanization of all positions, progressively endowed the public service with legitimacy and made it a truly national structure. Operating simultaneously, other factors—the organizational and administrative requisites of accelerated modernization, the weakness of the private sector and the statist orientation of the new elites, and the patronage pressures upon party leaders for jobs for loyal party members—have everywhere led to a vast postindependence expansion in the public service.

The acceptance, legitimation, and expansion of the bureaucracy should be a source of strength, rather than of weakness, to the governing party. Yet the classic theory of bureaucracy, as well as actual developments on the African scene, suggests that formal structures of government tend to assert their autonomy, indeed, their primacy. Carl Beck has summarized this theory as follows:

The establishment of a legal-rational system is the end product of the process of modernization. As society becomes rationalized, a specialization of roles takes place. Specialization of roles requires the development of formal rules and a hierarchical structure for the enforcement of these rules and the settlement of conflicts. *These pressures cluster together to dictate a bureaucratization of society with an increased power position for members of the formal bureaucracy.* As this occurs, the nonrational (ideological) components of the political milieu tend to be dissipated. The political style tends to become pragmatic.[14]

Foltz argues that a trend of this sort in the new African states is both likely and already discernible. Moreover, if modernization is given priority by party elites, the new managerial and technical elites required to carry it out are bound to become ever more powerful and assertive, as happened in Senegal.[15]

Modernization not only requires and begets new managerial and technical elites; it also brings about fundamental changes in the social structure and unleashes a host of politically destabilizing forces.[16] These

---

[14] Carl Beck, "Bureaucracy and Political Development in Eastern Europe," in Joseph La Palombara, ed., *Bureaucracy and Political Development* (Princeton: Princeton University Press, 1963), p. 270 (italics added). Beck states the theory simply to refute its relevance to Eastern European experience since World War II.

[15] *Op. cit.*, pp. 124 ff.

[16] These are reviewed in Mancur Olson, Jr., "Rapid Growth as a Destabilizing Force," *Journal of Economic History*, XXIII (Dec., 1963), 529–552; Ronald G. Ridker, "Discontent and Economic Growth," *Economic Development and Cultural Change*, XI (Oct., 1962), 1–15; James C. Davis, "Toward a Theory of Revolution," *American Sociological Review*, XXVII (Feb., 1962), 5–19; and Bert F. Hoselitz and Myron Weiner, "Economic Development and Political Stability in India," *Dissent*, VIII (Spring, 1961), 172–179.

are both short- and long-run forces, and all pose a threat to the stability and the survival of a ruling single party, or of any other type of regime.[17] In the contemporary African scene the most immediately visible, potentially dysfunctional, demographic categories produced by the modernization process are the unemployed primary-school leavers and the frustrated second-generation university students. The former constitute an anomic potential available for exploitation by rival leadership; and the latter are presumptively disposed to assert such leadership.[18] In the long run, modernization means ever-greater differentiation and functional specialization, heightened demands and claims upon government, and a pluralization of the social bases of new centers of power and influence.

In the light of the inherent weaknesses and the vulnerability of a one-party regime, the increasing strength and the strain toward primacy of the bureaucracy in developing societies, and the destabilizing consequences of the modernization process itself, what are the likely patterns of future development of the single or dominant party in the new states of Africa? There are many possibilities, including the final emergence of a stable competitive party system. Because the latter possibility seems somewhat remote at this stage, we will focus upon two tendencies more clearly discernible within the one-party syndrome: the drift toward a "no-party state," and the consolidation of a "party-state."

The no-party state would reflect the culmination of what Wallerstein has called the trend toward inanition, that is, the progressive decline of the party as the center of power and decision making. This outcome would represent a victory for the first two of the three major generic trends discussed above. The most extreme development possible in this direction would be the emergence of a purely administrative state (not unlike the preindependence colonial situation), with the party being kept alive by the governing elite for purely symbolic, ceremonial, legitimating, and community development purposes. In addition to the factors previously mentioned, two others could contribute to this trend. One is the tendency in all African one-party regimes for one dominant personality finally to emerge in states where unitary leadership was not ini-

---

[17] It should be stressed that the implications of many of the changes discussed here are not peculiar to one-party regimes but would challenge or threaten any type of government. It is theoretically possible that a one-party regime can cope with them more effectively, under certain circumstances, than could alternative institutional forms.

[18] On the primary-school leaver problem, see Archibald Callaway, "Unemployment among School Leavers," *Journal of Modern African Studies,* I (Sept., 1963), 351–372. Also see Philip J. Foster, "Secondary Schooling and Social Mobility in a West African Nation," *Sociology of Education,* XXXVII (Winter, 1963), 150–171, and J. P. N'Diaye, *Enquête sur les Etudiants noirs en France* (Paris: Editions Réalités Africaines, 1962), pp. 223–239.

tially established. The other is the already discernible potentiality of the new military elites.

The broad tendency in all movement-regimes (and most African mass single parties fall into this category), Tucker argues, "is oligarchical rule by the top leadership of the ruling party under the over-all direction of a dominant personality." [19] In some instances there is a further tendency toward "fuehrerism," that is, a tendency for the dominant personality to emancipate himself from the control of the party oligarchy and to subordinate the party to the state, with the latter, as personified in the leader, displacing the party as the supreme symbol. In this process the party is eclipsed and downgraded; it becomes only one of several instrumentalities employed by the leader.[20] The eclipse of the governing party in this manner is only a potentiality in Africa's one-party states, but it is one way in which there could be a movement toward an administrative state.

The potential role of the military in the future political life of Africa's new states has already been vividly demonstrated. Military rule in the Sudan, as well as the use of armed groups at crisis points in the Congo, Togo, and Senegal, is an illustration. The capture of political power in Zanzibar by an armed band of hastily recruited malcontents, and the serious challenge presented by army "strikes" throughout East Africa in early 1964, are even more dramatic evidence of the enormous advantage possessed by even the smallest armed group, especially in the circumstances of extreme institutional fragility and organizational weakness. The monolithic governing party (TANU) of Tanganyika, East Africa's most self-conscious one-party state, was helpless in the face of a few hundred disgruntled soldiers striking for higher pay and accelerated promotions. That the military has not been even more prominent in Africa's political evolution may be attributed partly to the fact that most new states commenced their existence about 1960 either without an army or with only an embryonic one, and partly to the fact that in countries (Sudan excepted) where the military did intervene, its leaders sought relief of specific grievances rather than political power.[21]

---

[19] *Op. cit.*, pp. 288–289.

[20] Merle Fainsod has pointed out that under Stalin the party "declined in vitality, and its apparatus became simply one of several channels through which he communicated his commands," whereas Khrushchev "has poured new life into the party and lifted its apparatus to a central position in his structure of direction and control" ("Bureaucracy and Modernization: The Russian and Soviet Case," in La Palombara, *op. cit.*, p. 258).

[21] See James S. Coleman and Belmont Brice, Jr., "The Role of the Military in Sub-Saharan Africa," in John J. Johnson, ed., *The Role of the Military in Underdeveloped Countries* (Princeton: Princeton University Press, 1962), pp. 359–406; William Gutteridge, *Armed Forces in the New States* (London: Oxford University Press, 1962); and *Africa Report,* VIII (Jan., 1964), 4–21.

The foregoing situation has presented African leaders in single-party states with an extraordinary opportunity to create a military establishment, almost from scratch, along lines that might guarantee the continued supremacy of the party and the loyalty of the new military elites. Such loyalty, however, could be only transitional. The army, like all institutional groups, tends to develop and to assert considerable autonomy. Although the Sudan is atypical in many respects, its experience has shown that the authoritarian rule of the military, in conjunction with a civilian bureaucracy, is not necessarily an ephemeral arrangement; indeed, it may be a substitute for party government. It may be the "no-party" administrative state par excellence.

A second possible pattern of future party development is the "party-state," a fully developed one-party state in which the dominant party remains supreme in the face of generic forces tending to weaken it. Structurally there would be effective fusion of party and government hierarchies at all levels. Neither the party nor the state would "wither away." This form of polity, the immediate goal of all revolutionary-centralizing parties, has been most closely approximated where the party, such as the PDG in Guinea, has had the opportunity (the mass exodus of French civil servants in 1958) and the determination (as reflected in a strong ideological compulsion) to build, *ab initio,* parallel party-state hierarchies fused at all levels through dual office holding.[22] Those recruited into the two hierarchies came from the same social strata and had the same political orientation. The incomplete fusion in Ghana, on the other hand, reveals the failure to move from a one-party-dominant state to a party-state, despite the rhetorical claim that "the CPP is Ghana and Ghana is the CPP."

The creation of an isolative rather than a fused relationship between the bureaucracy and the party in Ghana stems from a number of factors, including earlier educational development, and, consequently, greater Africanization of the public services during the terminal colonial period; the development of a national university, insulated for more than a decade from party penetration or manipulation, which produced a substantial number of new entrants into the state administrative hierarchies; and a protracted period of diarchy (roughly 1952–1957) during which merit criteria and a neutral public service commission, and not party membership or loyalty, determined recruitment to bureaucratic office. During this same period the CPP recruited most of its activists from entirely different social strata. The consequences of this isolative pattern

---

[22] Fusion of party-state structures has also occurred in the Northern Region of Nigeria, where the hierarchy of the dominant party (NPC) has been fused with a preëxisting indigenous administrative hierarchy. In this respect, however, northern Nigeria is *sui generis* in contemporary Africa.

are tension and conflict between the bureaucracy and the party, illuminated by David Apter in the postscript to his essay. One might anticipate a similar development if a revolutionary-centralizing party were to emerge and attempt to establish a party-state in a country where there had been differential recruitment to the dominant party, the bureaucracy, and the military.

What is the likely fate of the one-party states of the pragmatic-pluralistic pattern? Many will probably move in the direction of variant forms of the no-party state, for the reasons already discussed. Others, however, losing their revolutionary momentum, drifting toward bureaucratic stagnation, and spawning new militant leadership groups determined to complete the revolution, could be catapulted in the opposite direction toward the party-state.

What is the survival capacity of the party-state type of regime? Can it survive the assertiveness of new bureaucratic and technical elites, and the pluralization and social restructuring consequent upon modernization? Experience in the Soviet Union and in Eastern European bloc countries, one-party states that serve as the prototype of the revolutionary-centralizing states, does not support the assumption that increased bureaucratization of a modernizing society necessarily produces extraparty managerial and technological elites who inevitably establish their primacy.[23] Nor does their experience support the proposition that the emergence of new functional groups as a result of industrialization necessarily pluralizes authority or creates a constitutional system of regularized competition among factions and parties.[24] Once these experiences are noted, however, there remains the question of their relevance for the contemporary African scene. It is most unlikely, as Apter has argued, that African one-party states will enter an industrial phase in the predictable future.[25] Not having to confront the destabilizing pluralism created by industrialization, the capacity of the single dominant party to survive should presumably be enhanced. On the other hand, it does confront all the other challenges of state formation and nation building previously discussed. Moreover, none of the African single parties have yet approxi-

---

[23] Beck (*op. cit.*, pp. 296–298) notes that the new managerial class that has emerged in the Eastern European countries is represented in the key administrative and political hierarchies of the state, that the political systems have been successful in "absorbing these changes without creating a bureaucratized administrative system," and that, in any event, there is little evidence to support the view that members of the new class "must be a different type of political man than those now in power."

[24] "Nor should one be unduly beguiled by that special variety of technological determinism which assumes that those who possess important technical skills in a society inevitably transmute these skills into political power. There is no iron law which prevents dictators from presiding over the destinies of highly industrialized societies" (Fainsod, *op. cit.*, pp. 262–263).

[25] David Apter, "Political Religion in the New Nations," in Geertz, *op. cit.*

mated the degree of monolithic unity and ideological cohesion characteristic of their Eastern bloc prototypes. In short, at this stage of Africa's development we must be extremely cautious in calculating future probabilities on the basis of experience elsewhere.

Survival of the one-party regime will be primarily determined by the extent to which the parties concerned can overcome the inherent weaknesses they suffer in the postcolonial situation. Wallerstein has argued that success here will depend partly on the explicitness of party ideology, and partly on the degree to which they mobilize and train middle-level party cadres to replace those absorbed by bureaucratic and other structures of the new state.[26] It will also be determined by the effectiveness with which they perform certain crucial political functions. The single party can continue to play a critical role in the processes of political socialization, political communication, and national integration.[27] To the extent that it preserves a measure of its aura of legitimacy, the party can also continue to facilitate the legitimation of the formal institutions and processes of government. Insofar as dynamic and revolutionary pressures within the party continue to be the main stimulus for accelerated modernization, the party can infuse the bureaucracy with a sense of national purpose, thereby helping to overcome propensities toward conservatism and routinization. The party can also be an effective extrabureaucratic instrumentality in the hands of governing elites for mobilizing human resources throughout the society in the task of national development. Indeed, all these functions, and probably others, can be performed by the single party in an African one-party state. But it is not preordained that they must do so, or that other structures or institutional arrangements, which are even more effective, and certainly more democratic, will not emerge in time.

As previously noted, our second major concern in this symposium has been to examine the role of parties in the resolution or the aggravation of the problem of national integration. For analytical purposes we have drawn a distinction between those situations of vertical discontinuity found in Africa's historic oligarchic states, and those situations where the problem of national integration has arisen as a result of the effort to expand the scale of political organization through political union or to develop large-scale federations. In the introduction we noted that the problem of vertical integration is an outgrowth of the massive impact of

---

[26] *Op. cit.*, p. 16.

[27] These functions must be performed by the national party in most one-party states, irrespective of their ideological orientation. See Clement Henry Moore, "The Neo-Destour Party of Tunisia: Structure for Democracy," *World Politics*, XIV (April, 1962), 461–482; L. Vincent Padgett, "Mexico's One-Party System: A Re-evaluation," *American Political Science Review*, LI (Dec., 1957), 995–1008; and Beck, *op. cit.*, p. 281.

the egalitarian forces and influences of modernity upon societies dominated by culturally distinct oligarchies. Against the backdrop of the contrasting case studies of Liberia and Zanzibar, we will endeavor here to examine in more general terms the problem of vertical malintegration in contemporary Africa.

In the process of political restratification in oligarchic situations where a historically dominant resident minority is confronted by egalitarian political demands from a culturally distinct and historically dominated majority, at least four challenge-response patterns may be identified:

Pattern I: Oligarchic Perpetuation—Separate Development.—A challenged dominant oligarchy attempts to perpetuate itself by force and by the "separate development"—politically, economically, culturally, and socially—of the oligarchy and the dominated groups as closed political communities in a permanent superordinate-subordinate relationship. The Republic of South Africa represents this pattern in its purest form. Powerful elements in the dominant oligarchies of Kenya and Northern Rhodesia were of this persuasion until externally enforced political restratification made their position untenable. The overwhelming majority among the dominant racial oligarchy of Southern Rhodesia would prefer this pattern, because Pattern II, where they currently stand, is no longer tenable, and Patterns III and IV are intolerable to them.

Pattern II: Oligarchic Perpetuation—Token Assimilation.—An oligarchy attempts to perpetuate its dominance through declamatory and legally sanctioned assimilation, but there is only token *de facto* absorption into the oligarchy of selected elements from the dominated majority. Representative of this pattern under colonialism are former French Africa, former Belgian Congo for a brief period, and contemporary Portuguese Africa. Liberia and Ethiopia, Southern Rhodesia, and the now-defunct Federation of Rhodesia and Nyasaland should also be included. The maintenance of this pattern by the oligarchy depends upon widespread political quietism among the mass, and deferential emulation of, and a striving to be identified with and assimilated into, the culture of the oligarchy among the more active elements in the dominated majority.

Pattern III: Progressive Political Restratification.—The dominant oligarchy has been persuaded or compelled, usually by superior external pressure or control, to accept the goal of its own ultimate extinction as a culturally distinct ruling group through gradual but progressive expansion of the franchise, and ever-widening access to all authoritative roles by nonoligarchic elements of the population. There is declamatory, legal, and *de facto* assimilation, all directed toward the creation of a political community in which racial or cultural origin is irrelevant to the political process. This was the pattern sought by Britain, commencing in the early 1950's, for those of its territories where a racially or culturally distinct oligarchy was actually or presumptively entrenched in the political system (e.g., the Federation of Rhodesia and Nyasaland, Kenya, Tanganyika, and Zanzibar). The governing oligarchies in the Northern Region of Nigeria (Hausa-Fulani), Liberia (Americo-Liberian), and Ethiopia (Amharas) also have moved, and are continuing to move, albeit very slowly and haltingly, toward this pattern.

Pattern IV: Revolutionary Political Restratification.—A status reversal between the oligarchy and the dominated majority occurs more or less abruptly as a result of the external imposition (i.e., by a colonial power) of a new constitution or universal suffrage, or by revolution. The former process occurred most spectacularly in the former Tutsi oligarchy in Rwanda during the terminal stages of Belgian rule; it has taken place successively in Tanganyika and in Nyasaland; and it has now been consolidated in Kenya and Northern Rhodesia. A complete status reversal did not occur in Zanzibar until after independence, and then by revolution, for the interesting reasons discussed in Lofchie's essay.

The pattern of oligarchic-mass relationships prevalent in any particular country, including the sequence and the rate of movement from one of the foregoing patterns to another, has been a function of at least three factors: (1) the presence or absence of control over the country by a colonial power, and the character of such control; (2) the make-up of the oligarchy and its mode of domination; and (3) the nature of the dominated majority. In Africa, colonial rule has been the most decisive factor affecting the process of political restratification. Ethiopia and Liberia, Africa's two historic oligarchies which escaped protracted colonial rule, vividly reveal the remarkable perpetuative power of a culturally differentiated oligarchy having relatively unfettered control over the population. Developments in the Republic of South Africa and Southern Rhodesia underscore the consequences of an early British colonial policy of surrendering effective political control to a resident white-settler oligarchy in dependencies inhabited by colored non-Western peoples. By contrast, Kenya, Tanganyika, Nyasaland and Northern Rhodesia, and Sierra Leone and Uganda, under British rule, the Congo under Belgian rule, and Algeria under French rule, demonstrate the way in which a colonial power has been able either to prevent the consolidation of oligarchic rule by alien settlers or to dismantle such rule where it was in the process of being established. In Zanzibar, Britain provided the constitutional framework for a change in the relationship between the historically dominant Arab oligarchy and the subordinate Afro-Shirazi majority, although, as Lofchie has shown, this "setting the stage" for political restratification did not prove decisive. In general, except for Portuguese Africa and earlier British policy in southern Africa, the role of colonialism has been either to facilitate or to impose—

albeit in response to strong nationalist pressures and demands—processes of political restratification in most of Africa's oligarchic states.

The make-up and the size of the oligarchy are also critically important factors, not only because they affect the ability of a colonial power to enforce restratification, but also because they affect the ability of the oligarchy to find another way of relieving the tensions inherent in a society deeply divided. Of great significance are the capacity and the predisposition of the oligarchy to assimilate elements of the nonoligarchy, not only politically, but economically and culturally as well. Gross physical and cultural differences between the dominant oligarchy and the dominated mass (e.g., Anglo-Dutch vs. Bantu, or Batutsi vs. Bahutu) seriously weaken the predisposition for, and perhaps render impossible, assimilation by the oligarchy. In this respect, at least, the Amharas in Ethiopia, the Americo-Liberians in Liberia, the settled Fulani in northern Nigeria, and even the Arabs of Pemba have demonstrated an assimilative capacity. A second variable is the size of the dominant oligarchy in proportion to the total population, which profoundly affects the psychology of both dominant and dominated groups. If the oligarchic community is large (as in South Africa, Southern Rhodesia, Algeria, and Ethiopia), its determination to perpetuate itself, and its confidence that it can do so, are greatly strengthened. If it comprises only a small fraction of the population, its position is extremely vulnerable, both to the dictates of a colonial power and to the egalitarian or nationalist demands of the dominated majority.

The character of the dominated majority is also an important determinant of the development pattern of elite-mass relationships in oligarchic states. Here the important variables are the degree of cultural homogeneity and unity (including capacity for united political action) among the elements making up the nonoligarchy; their assimilability (psychologically, culturally, and politically) into the culture of the dominant oligarchy; and the extent to which they have been affected by the leveling ideas of nationalism and equality, have become involved in modernizing processes, and are "socially mobilized," to use Karl Deutsch's happy phrase. In Ethiopia and Liberia the groups making up the dominated majority are not united; politically relevant elements drawn from those groups have proved to be highly assimilable; and thus far the masses have participated very little in modern processes. In Africa's European-settler oligarchies, the sharpness of the physical and cultural differentiation between oligarchy and mass has forged a sense of unity among an otherwise highly pluralistic and heterogeneous African majority. Moreover, owing to the modernizing influence of a substantial European population, significant numbers of persons have become "socially mobilized" through wage labor, urbanization, and commercialization of the economy. Indeed, except for Portuguese Africa, a marked degree of social mobilization is characteristic of all the territories of formerly colonial Africa. Thus, even though colonial rule did not bring about the institutionalization of democracy, it was unquestionably the vehicle for widespread dissemination of the idea of equality and the spirit of populism, both of which are hostile to the perpetuation of entrenched oligarchy.

The different combinations and patterns of interaction among the foregoing variables account for the differences not only in mode and tempo of political restratification in Africa's oligarchic regimes, but also in the character of the political groups that have participated in the process. These groups fall into three rather obvious categories: (1) those organized within the dominated majority for the purpose of articulating and advancing its interests vis-à-vis the oligarchy; (2) those organized by the dominant oligarchy to protect and preserve its interests; and (3) those based upon the principle of political assimilation, whose ultimate objective is the creation of a homogeneous political community. (It should be noted that certain oligarchic systems, such as those in Portuguese Africa, Ethiopia, and Liberia, are not involved here because the absence of freedom of association has prevented competing political groups from emerging.) The cleavage between oligarchy and nonoligarchy transcends religious, tribal, or sectional divisions, for example, as a basis for the definition of political issues and the organization of political life.

Among dominated majority communities political groups characteristically emerged first to articulate, and to seek relief from, specific grievances created by the policies either of the colonial government, or of the oligarchic regime supported by colonialism. Subsequently, more programmatic, territory-wide political organizations evolved, but most of them were initially assimilationist in their political orientation; they seldom asked for more than social and political equality. But, stimulated by progress toward self-government elsewhere in Africa, and frustrated by the gradualism of, or the resistance to any significant change on the part of, the dominant racial oligarchies, leaders of these organizations were driven to redefine their political goal as self-determination based on the principles of universal suffrage and majority rule. Realization of such a goal would mean nothing less than a complete reversal in the political status of the oligarchy, a prospect that exhilarated the leaders of the dominated group but terrified the oligarchy. Where an oligarchy has obstructed either rapid and meaningful assimilation or a basic transformation in power relationships, as in South Africa, Southern Rhodesia, Portuguese Africa, early postwar Kenya, and preindependence Rwanda, African political groups became, or threaten to become, instruments of violence. The same potentiality exists in both Liberia and Ethiopia. Where progressive political restratification has been realizable within the predictable future, and assured by the continued presence of a colonial power committed to it, political groups have confined their political action within the boundaries of the evolving constitutional order (as in Tanganyika, post-1960 Kenya, Nyasaland, and Northern Rhodesia).

Political groups organized by dominant oligarchies have taken several forms, each reflecting the interests and goals of the oligarchy within a particular historical or situational context. The True Whig Party has been, as was the ZNP in Zanzibar before the January, 1964, revolution, an organization designed to consolidate and perpetuate the political supremacy of the Americo-Liberian oligarchy and the Arab oligarchy in Liberia and Zanzibar, respectively. The Zanzibar revolution dramatizes the difference in effectiveness. The True Whig Party was able to establish itself very early as the exclusive structure for recruitment into and participation in the political life of Liberia, not only because it consolidated a political monopoly before the peoples of the hinterland majority became politically conscious, but also because there was no colonial or other external presence to guarantee freedom of association to such peoples. In Liberia, therefore, the party of the oligarchy has been able to enforce political assimilation. In contrast, British rule in Zanzibar made it possible for, and in fact encouraged, the dominated communities to organize their own separate political associations to challenge Arab supremacy. These contrasting examples once again underscore the importance of the colonial factor.

The colonial presence, however, has not always been unambiguous in its effect upon processes of political restratification. Indeed, one of the ironic aspects of British rule in Africa has been its tacit or explicit support of oligarchies (indigenous oligarchies being supported by the policy of indirect rule and the principle of native self-government, and European-settler oligarchies being supported by the time-honored extension of local self-government accorded to "kith and kin" overseas), concurrent with the dissemination of the ideals of democracy which assured a dominated majority the freedom to organize and agitate for a democratic (i.e., nonoligarchic) society. Again, in territories that were presumptively or potentially white racial oligarchies until the "winds of change" forced a status reversal, British policy fostered the growth of communal political groups. During the early prenationalist, preparty phase of British rule in such territories, official policy encouraged, or at least tolerated, communal (i.e., racial and tribal) modes of petition, representation, and association. Thus, long before either the oligarchy or the mass faced the problem of domination of one group by the other in a postcolonial independent society, communal groups had already been formed for the purpose of articulating grievances or of representing communal interests. The preëxistence of such communal associations, reflecting, as they did, the division of the society into oligarchy and nonoligarchic elements, contributed significantly to later politicization along communal lines, once the conquest of political power had become the goal. Once competitive politics got under way on a communal basis, the process of schizmogenesis[28] led inexorably to a polarized situation in which the solidarity of both the oligarchy and the nonoligarchic elements was vastly increased.

Confronted with these consequences of the contradictions in its African policies, the British sought amelioration through the positive encouragement of multiracial associations of an economic, social, and political character. During a brief transitional period in the evolution of several of the racially pluralistic societies, there was a faint hope that the multiracial associations could prevent the polarization of political activity along communal lines and provide the organizational basis for the progressive transfer of power to a genuinely multiracial political community. Subsequent events very quickly proved the futility of artificially and externally induced multiracialism. African nationalists regarded it as nothing more than a formula for perpetuating the dominance of the oligarchy. In any event, except for a small minority of Africans who had in varying degrees been assimilated by the oligarchy, or who continued to maintain deferential attitudes toward it, the vision of uniracial African self-government was irresistible. As a consequence, throughout the plural societies of British Africa, multiracial political groups have invariably yielded to African nationalist movements, the carriers of the ideals of equality and democracy.

Political malintegration in Africa's "plural societies" results from the existence of a culturally, and usually racially, distinct minority exercising either actual or presumptive dominance over the mass of the population. Although the dominated majority is culturally heterogeneous, the peoples concerned are, as an aggregate, rather sharply differentiated from the dominant minority. In focusing on this dimension of discontinuity, we do not intend to ignore a second form of vertical malintegration, that of oligarchic rule, found in most new states of Africa. We refer here to the elite-mass gap—the gap between the modernizing political elite and the traditional mass—which is generic to the Afro-Asian world. Edward Shils has described and analyzed this phenomenon with perceptive ac-

---

[28] The concept of "schizmogenesis" was introduced by Gregory Bateson to refer to the "process of differentiation of the norms of individual behaviour resulting from cumulative interaction between individuals," in his *Naven* (2d ed.; Stanford: Stanford University Press, 1958), p. 175. For his discussion of how the process of differentiation tends toward increase of ethological contrast and hostility in situations of intergroup cultural contact, see pp. 184 ff.

curacy, and Leonard Binder argues that it is the core of the issue of national integration in these states.[29] There can be little question of its generality or of its importance; however, it is a form of malintegration in the new polities which national parties have served to ameliorate rather than aggravate. National parties of the revolutionary-centralizing tendency have been ultrapopulist, and their leaders, as the papers on Mali and Guinea have shown, have zealously sought to bridge the gap between the modernizing elite and the traditional mass. Even parties of the pragmatic-pluralistic type have been committed to democratic goals and to modernizing objectives which require popular involvement. Few parties have been explicitly elitist. In short, the political associations in African states not encumbered with entrenched oligarchies have striven to transcend and to eliminate the elite-mass gap. In historic or racial oligarchies, political parties have tended to divide and isolate the two groups from each other. This differential orientation of political groups is a basic distinction between the two kinds of oligarchies, and it is one that should be stressed.

The second major problem confronted in the process of national integration, which we have here termed the problem of "territorial" integration, stems from the persistence—indeed, the paramountcy—of "primordial" attachments or ties;[30] that is, individuals identify themselves much more strongly with historic groups defined in terms of kinship, religion, language, or culture than with the civil order of the new states. This phenomenon is not peculiarly African; indeed, as Geertz has shown, it is "literally pandemic" to all the new states of the Afro-Asian world, "as the countless references to 'dual' or 'plural' or 'multiple' societies, to 'mosaic' or 'composite' social structures, to 'states' that are not 'nations' and 'nations' that are not 'states,' to 'tribalism,' 'parochialism,' and 'communalism,' as well as to pannational movements of various sorts demonstrate."[31] In Tropical Africa the term "tribalism" has been used most frequently, and in many instances erroneously, to refer to this very common phenomenon. Such gross oversimplification in part reflects the widespread currency of the false notion that the only form of social organization or primordial tie in Africa was and is tribal in character. It is also, in part, an accurate indication that in Africa, compared with other major world areas, primordial ethnic links (some of them genuinely tribal,

[29] Edward Shils, *Political Development in the New States* (The Hague: Mouton, 1962), pp. 30 ff.; Leonard Binder, "National Integration and Political Development" (unpublished manuscript).
[30] Edward Shils, "Primordial, Personal, Sacred and Civil Ties," *British Journal of Sociology*, VIII (June, 1957), 130–145; Clifford Geertz, "The Integrative Revolution: Primordial Sentiments and Civil Politics in the New States," in Geertz, *op. cit.*, pp. 105 ff.
[31] Geertz, "The Integrative Revolution," p. 106.

but most of them linguistic-cultural) have been in fact more prominent than religious or regional ties, although the latter have not been absent.

The relevance of primordial ties in the politics of Tropical Africa—whether the reference group concerned transcends interstate boundaries (for example, the Somali described by Castagno or the Bakongo discussed by Lemarchand) or constitutes only a part of the population of a new state—is determined by a number of complex factors. These include, among other things, the mode (direct or indirect) and the duration of colonial rule; the incidence (even or uneven, intermittent or continuous) and the impact (heavy or superficial) of modern integrative influences; the comparative size, cohesiveness, and compatibility of the diverse groups bunched together within the boundaries of a new state; and the stability or the fragility of central nationwide institutions. Because of the variable combinations and interactions of these factors, there are marked differences in the political significance of primordial ties. This variability is vividly illuminated by the contrast between Senegal, where, according to Foltz, ethnicity has had little relevance, and the Congo, where politics have been based almost exclusively upon ethnic and tribal sentiments. Thus, in addition to recognizing that "tribalism" in politics, as a manifestation of primordial sentiment, is a generic phenomenon found in varying forms in all new societies, we must also emphasize the highly variable occurrence of this phenomenon within Africa itself.

The difference between the two types of malintegration—one created by historic oligarchies and the other resulting from the persistence of tribal, ethnic, and sectional parochialisms—is that the malintegrated elements of the population in the oligarchies are in a superordinate-subordinate relationship, and the dominant group is a culturally alien minority. In both situations, of course, the task of nation building is to make "from many one." The crux of the difference, therefore, is the definition of the aggregate to which there is a primordial attachment. As we have seen, in oligarchic situations there tends to be an inevitable polarization-schizmogenesis, in which the linguistic, tribal, or ethnic parochialism among the dominated majority is, for the time, submerged in or attenuated by a wider sense of being an "oppressed" community. In the second situation the essence of the problem is not the dismantling of an established oligarchy, but the welding together of a mélange of peoples of widely varying primordial attachments into a new and larger "terminal community." The problem may be acutely aggravated by fears among some of the constituent groups that in the process of creating the new civil order a particular minority ethnic group may emerge as dominant in the larger whole (as, for example, the Ewe in Togo, the Baoule in the Ivory Coast, the Ibo in Nigeria, etc.); this problem is still rather different from that of bringing about political restratification in an already entrenched oligarchy.

The effect of primordial attachments upon the emergence and the development of political groups in Tropical Africa has been examined rather fully in Wallerstein's essay, and is further illuminated in several of the studies on different countries. Our only purpose here is to review briefly and to highlight two sets of circumstances under which primordial sentiments and ties have tended to become obstructive in the nation-building process in contemporary Africa. Almost everywhere, the transfer of power from a colonial regime to a locally based regime has intensified the parochial or tribal basis of already existing groups, or has activated latent parochialisms and led to the formation and proliferation of new communalistic political associations. Just as the vision of self-government tended to polarize and to intensify communal sentiment and political activity between the dominant minority and the dominated majority in oligarchic situations, so the prospect of a transfer of imperial power to a local power elite has generated fears and ambitions among competing elements in the plural societies of the new states in the process of birth. Lemarchand's essay on Congolese parties vividly illuminates the way in which the sudden vision of a fundamental transformation in the power structure of a prospective new state creates a climate of instability and unpredictability, in which there is a heightened consciousness of primordial ties and a resultant frenzied attempt, through political organization, to maximize the relative position of one's primordial group in the new and uncertain civil order. This process of primordial fragmentation is most dramatically revealed in the rapid proliferation of political parties immediately before independence in the Congo, not only because of the failure of the Belgians to create even the semblance of a national Congolese civic order, but also because of the precipitate Belgian decision to transfer power to the Congolese in a sharply truncated transitional period. It has been, however, a phenomenon common to many new states in Africa, and in Asia as well.[32]

A proliferation of political groups in the terminal stages of colonial rule has tended to jeopardize, in the immediate postcolonial period, the unity and the integrity of the new state. Indeed, the terminal colonial legacy of heightened politicization and associational fragmentation has been one of the chief arguments advanced in support of a one-party regime. Concern over this problem is reflected in the many statements of

---

[32] *Ibid.*, pp. 124 ff. Geertz adds that even "in those new states where such discontent has not progressed to the point of open dissidence, there has almost universally arisen around the developing struggle for governmental power as such a broad penumbra of primordial strife" (p. 124).

African leaders identifying "tribalism" as one of the major evils confronting Africa's new states. It also helps to explain the firm, indeed frequently ruthless, repressive action taken by ruling elites regarding any tribal or regional manifestation of separatism, as well as the specific outlawing of tribal or regional parties by several governments. The point here is not that the removal of authoritarian colonial rule precipitated a return to a tribal and parochial past—as Afrophobes would like to believe—but, rather, that the radical shift from one authority system to another inevitably created a highly fluid and unstable situation in which latent parochialisms and primordial sentiments were easily activated and inflamed. It is the awesome task of the ruling elites of the new states not only to establish their legitimacy and consolidate their power, but also to stabilize both the physical and juridical boundaries of the new system, routinize the political process, and minimize or extinguish the wildly speculative atmosphere generated by the uncertainties of the transfer of power.

A second set of special circumstances tends to intensify primordial sentiments and attachments. When primordial loyalty coincides with, and is therefore enormously fortified by, other interests of an economic, social, or class character, the resulting combination is powerful, and virtually indestructible. Throughout Africa, certain tribal, linguistic, or ethnic groups are in a more advantageous competitive position than others. This favored position may be the result of one or more different factors: greater adaptive capacity of the traditional culture; earlier and more intensive exposure to modernity (education, commercialization, urbanization, accumulated wealth, and so forth), and the resultant competitive advantage of the individual in the quest for status and influence in the new order; more natural resources or greater economic potential of the area; and preferred treatment during the colonial period. Several such groups have been identified in some of the studies in this symposium. Sklar and Whitaker, for example, have noted the coincidence between ethnicity and rising-class status in the two large nationality associations (Ibo State Union and Egbe Omo Oduduwa) which have played so crucial a role in Nigerian political development. Again, Le Vine has pointed up the way in which socioeconomic conditions have reinforced ethnicity among the Bassa and the Bamileké, and account for their particular dominance in the Union des Populations du Cameroun. Reciprocal reinforcement of primordial ties, economic interest or condition, and relative status are similarly found among the Baganda of Uganda, the Baoule of the Ivory Coast, the Ashanti in Ghana, the Wachagga in Tanganyika, to mention but a few of the more striking illustrations.

It has been argued that the massive social and economic developments now under way in most new states will progressively reduce the disruptive potential of tribal or regional separatism. The expansion of the wage-earning and commercialized sectors of the economy, more extensive social mobility, and the emergence of a more national-minded generation of leaders are among the changes envisaged. Coupled with these hopefully ameliorative and integrative developments in the economy and the social structure are the explicit measures being taken by governing elites to inculcate a wider national outlook through the educational system, to "level up" the less developed and heretofore disadvantaged areas through centrally controlled resource allocation, to adhere scrupulously to merit criteria in recruitment to the public service, and, in general, to work toward the realization of equality of access to and participation in the new civic order without reference to primordial attachments. The governing elites in the revolutionary-centralizing one-party states have been markedly vigorous and self-conscious in striving for these objectives. In all states, moreover, there are at work historic processes which elsewhere have been integrative and are associated with modern civic orders. Still, the lesson of history is that these major transformations in loyalties and attachments are complex and long-term phenomena. Just as the accidental juxtaposition of particular groups or influences, or the uncontrollable differential in the rate of development of particular areas or collectivities, has activated or inflamed primordial sentiments in the recent past, so it is likely that some unanticipated set of circumstances in the future will trigger similar manifestations and activity.

In all but a few of Africa's new states the primary structure—in most instances the only structure—for coping with the myriad parochial and ethnic pressures is the national political party, the single or dominant party currently governing the state. Indeed, the existence of such pressures bulks large in the rationalization of one-party regimes. Containment, accommodation, neutralization, and suppression are the strategies these dominant parties have employed, with varying degrees of success. Experience elsewhere, as well as the manifest tenacity of these forces throughout Tropical Africa, suggests that Africa's primordial ties can be neither easily nor rapidly extinguished; and they certainly cannot be ignored. Zolberg's description of the experience of the PDCI in the Ivory Coast is an excellent example. After repeated abortive efforts to terminate dependence upon tribal associations or ethnic units as the nuclei for party committees, the party leaders reluctantly decided that such action would have to be postponed "until people learned to live together regardless of tribe." This has been and remains the crux of the problem of national integration in contemporary Tropical Africa. If we accept Arnold Toynbee's notion of "tribe" as reflecting the inherently parochial nature of man everywhere, we are in the presence of a problem that is both universal and timeless in human affairs.

SELECT BIBLIOGRAPHY

This bibliography is not meant to be an exhaustive list of all literature on political groups in Tropical Africa; rather it is a selective compilation of the more readily available and representative sources. It does not include, for example, the ever-expanding massive quantities of party literature and political ephemera, partly because of their quantity, but also because of their general unavailability. One is dependent here upon the private collections of scholars who have done research in the field, and upon the important, but still not comprehensive, archives in such specialized collections as the Hoover Library at Stanford University. Nor does this list include the large number of important government documents, such as the reports of commissions of inquiry and of British royal commissions, or of elections. Here again one must rely upon the more detailed studies included herein for the appropriate citations. Finally, we have not listed the growing number of general works (ethnographic, historical, and so forth) on the individual territories covered in this symposium, nor the more general theoretical works on the various problems of integration. As it is the list is very long, and those interested in greater depth should consult the footnotes to each paper, and the specialized studies cited both there and in this bibliography.

BOOKS AND DISSERTATIONS

Amon d'Aby, F. J. *La Côte d'Ivoire dans la cité africaine*. Paris: Larose, 1951.

Andersson, E. *Messianic Popular Movements in the Lower Congo*. Trans. Donald Burton *et al*. London: Kegan Paul, 1958.

Ansprenger, Franz. *Politik im Schwarzen Afrika*. Cologne and Opladen: Westdeutscher Verlag, 1961.

Apter, David E. *Ghana in Transition*. New York: Atheneum, 1963.

——. *The Political Kingdom in Uganda: A Study in Bureaucratic Nationalism*. Princeton: Princeton University Press, 1961.

Artigue, P. *Qui sont les leaders Congolais?* Brussels: Editions Europe-Afrique, 1960.

Awolowo, O. *Awo: The Autobiography of Chief Obafemi Awolowo*. London: Cambridge University Press, 1960.

Balandier, Georges. *Sociologie actuelle de l'Afrique noire*. Paris: Presses Universitaires de France, 1955.

Bennett, George, and Carl G. Rosberg. *The Kenyatta Election: Kenya 1960–1961*. London: Oxford University Press, 1961.

Blanchet, A. W. *L'Itinéraire des Partis Africains depuis Bamako*. Paris: Plon, 1958.

Brockway, A. Fenner. *African Socialism*. London: Bodley Head, 1963.

Buell, Raymond L. *The Native Problem in Africa*. New York: Macmillan, 1928. 2 vols.

Carey, A. T. *Colonial Students: A Study of the Social Adaptation of Colonial Students in London*. London: Secker and Warburg, 1956.

692

Carter, Gwendolen, ed. *African One-Party States*. Ithaca: Cornell University Press, 1962.

Carter, Gwendolen, and W. O. Brown. *Transition in Africa: Studies in Political Adaptation*. African Research Studies, no. 1. Boston: Boston University Press, 1958.

Coleman, James S. *Nigeria: Background to Nationalism*. Berkeley and Los Angeles: University of California Press, 1958.

Congo 1959. Documents belges et africains. Brussels: Centre de Recherche et d'Information Socio-Politiques, 1960.

Crowder, Michael. *Senegal: A Study in French Assimilation Policy*. London: Oxford University Press, 1962.

Decraene, Philippe. *Le Panafricanisme*. Paris: Presses Universitaires de France, 1959.

The Development of a Middle Class in Tropical and Sub-Tropical Countries. Institut International des Civilisations Différentes, 29th session, London, 1955. Brussels, 1956. Especially the reports by Assane Seck, Marcel Soret, and Georges Balandier.

Dia, Mamadou. *The African Nations and World Solidarity*. New York: Praeger, 1961.

Diop, Cheikh Anta. *Les Fondements culturels, techniques, et industriels d'un futur état fédéral d'Afrique Noire*. Paris: Présence Africaine, 1960.

Diop, Majhemout. *Contribution à l'Etude des problèmes politiques en Afrique Noire*. Paris: Présence Africaine, 1959.

Du Bois, Victor D. "The Independence Movement in Guinea: A Study in African Nationalism." Unpublished Ph.D. dissertation. Princeton University, 1962.

Dugué, Gil. *Vers les Etats-Unis d'Afrique*. [Dakar]: Lettres Africaines, 1960.

Emerson, R. *From Empire to Nation: The Rise of Self-Assertion of Asian and African People*. Cambridge: Harvard University Press, 1960.

———. *Political Modernization: The Single-Party System*. University of Denver Monograph Series in World Affairs, No. 1. Denver, 1964.

Epstein, Arnold Leonard. *Politics in an Urban African Community*. Manchester: Manchester University Press, 1958.

Fawzi, Saad Ed Din. *The Labour Movement in the Sudan, 1946–1955*. London: Oxford University Press, 1957.

Friedland, William H. "Institutional Change: A Study of Trade Union Development in Tanganyika." Unpublished Ph.D. dissertation. University of California, Berkeley, 1963.

Gardinier, David. *Cameroun: United Nations Challenge to French Policy*. London: Oxford University Press, 1963.

Gigon, Fernand. *Guinée: Etat-Pilote*. Paris: Plon, 1959.

Historical Survey of the Origins and Growth of Mau Mau. Cmnd. 1030 (Corfield Report). London: H.M.S.O., 1960.

Hodgkin, Thomas. *African Political Parties*. Penguin Books, 1961.

———. *Nationalism in Colonial Africa*. London: Frederick Muller, 1956.

Kimble, David. *A Political History of Ghana: The Rise of Gold Coast Nationalism, 1850–1928*. Oxford: Clarendon Press, 1963.

Kitchen, Helen A., ed. *The Press in Africa.* Washington: Ruth Sloan Associates, 1956.

Legum, Colin. *Pan-Africanism: A Short Political Guide.* New York: Praeger, 1962.

Lemarchand, René. "Political Awakening in the Former Belgian Congo." Unpublished Ph.D. dissertation. University of California, Los Angeles, 1963.

Le Vine, Victor T. *The Cameroun: From Mandate to Independence.* Berkeley and Los Angeles: University of California Press, 1964.

Ly, Abdoulaye. *Les Masses africaines et l'actuelle Condition humaine.* Paris: Présence Africaine, 1956.

Mackenzie, W. J. M., and Kenneth Robinson, eds. *Five Elections in Africa.* Oxford: Clarendon Press, 1960.

Le Mali continue . . . République du Mali, Congrès Extraordinaire de l'USRDA, Sept. 22, 1960.

Le Mali en marche. Edition du Secrétariat d'Etat à l'Information, République du Mali, 1962.

Low, D. A. *Political Parties in Uganda, 1949–1962.* London: Athlone Press, 1962.

Milcent, Ernest. *L'A.O.F. entre en scène.* Paris: Edition du Témoignage Chrétien, 1958.

Millen, Bruce H. *The Political Role of Labor in Developing Countries.* Washington: Brookings Institution, 1963.

Morgenthau, Ruth Schachter. *Political Parties in French-speaking West Africa.* Oxford: Clarendon Press, 1964.

N'Diaye, J. P. *Enquête sur les Etudiants noirs en France.* Realités Africaines. Paris: Picard, 1962.

Nkrumah, K. *The Autobiography of Kwame Nkrumah.* Edinburgh: Nelson, 1957.

Padmore, George. *Africa: Britain's Third Empire.* London: Dobson, 1949.

———. *The Gold Coast Revolution.* London: Dobson, 1953.

———. *Pan-Africanism or Communism?* London: Dobson, 1956.

Pan-Africanism Reconsidered. American Society of African Culture. Berkeley and Los Angeles: University of California Press, 1962.

Porter, Arthur T. *Creoledom.* London: Oxford University Press, 1963.

Post, K. W. J. *The Nigerian Federal Election of 1959.* London: Oxford University Press, 1963.

Rawcliffe, D. H. *The Struggle for Kenya.* London: Gollancz, 1954.

Le RDA dans la lutte anti-impérialiste. Rassemblement Démocratique Africain. Paris, 1948.

Richards, Audrey. *East African Chiefs.* New York: Praeger, 1960.

Rothchild, Donald. *Toward Unity in Africa.* Washington, D.C.: Public Affairs Press, 1960.

Segal, Ronald. *Political Africa: A Who's Who of Personalities and Parties.* New York: Praeger, 1961.

Senghor, Léopold. *Congrès Constitutif du P.F.A.: Rapport sur la doctrine et le programme du parti.* Paris: Présence Africaine, 1959.

————. *La Nation et la voie africaine du socialisme.* Paris: Présence Africaine, 1961.

Sklar, Richard. "Nigerian Political Parties." Unpublished Ph.D. dissertation. Princeton University, 1961.

Smith, T. E. *Elections in Developing Countries.* New York: St. Martin's Press, 1960.

Suret-Canale, Jean. *Afrique noire.* Paris: Editions Sociales, 1958.

Taylor, J. Clagett. *The Political Development of Tanganyika.* Stanford: Stanford University Press, 1963.

Thompson, Virginia, and Richard Adloff. *The Emerging States of French Equatorial Africa.* Stanford: Stanford University Press, 1960.

————. *French West Africa.* Stanford: Stanford University Press, [1958?].

Touré, Sékou. *L'Action politique du Parti Démocratique de Guinée pour l'émancipation africaine.* Conakry, 1958. "Territoire de la Guinée" at head of title. The author considers this to be Volume I of his collected works, although it is not so designated on the title page.

————. *L'Action politique du Parti Démocratique de Guinée pour l'émancipation africaine.* Vol. II. [Conakry, 1959?]

————. *L'Action politique du Parti Démocratique de Guinée pour l'émancipation africaine.* Vol. III. Conakry, [1960]. "République de Guinée" at head of title. This volume has been reprinted, except for some twenty pages, as *La Guinée et l'émancipation africaine.* Paris: Présence Africaine, 1959.

————. *La Lutte du Parti Démocratique de Guinée pour l'émancipation africaine.* Vol. IV. 2d ed. Conakry, [1960?]. "République de Guinée" at head of title.

————. *Planification.* Vol. V of *L'Action politique du Parti Démocratique de Guinée pour l'émancipation africaine.* Conakry, 1961.

————. *L'Action politique du Parti Démocratique de Guinée pour l'émancipation africaine.* Vol. VI. Conakry, 1961.

————. *L'Expérience guinéenne et l'Unité africaine.* Paris: Présence Africaine, 1959. Incorporates Vols. I and II of *L'Action politique du Parti Démocratique de Guinée pour l'émancipation africaine.*

————. *Report on Policy and Doctrine.* General Congress of the Union Générale des Travailleurs d'Afrique Noire, held at Conakry. Paris: Présence Africaine, 1959.

————. *Textes des Interviews accordées aux représentants de la presse.* Conakry, 1959.

————. *Toward Full Re-Africanisation: Policy and Principles of the Guinea Democratic Party.* English text. Paris: Présence Africaine, 1959.

Touval, Saadia. *Somali Nationalism: International Politics and the Drive for Unity in the Horn of Africa.* Cambridge: Harvard University Press, 1963.

Van Reyn, Paul. *Le Congo politique: Les partis et les élections.* Collection Carrefours Africains, no. 1. Brussels: Editions Europe-Afrique, 1960.

Wallerstein, I. *Africa: The Politics of Independence.* New York: Vintage Books, 1961.

Welbourn, Frederick B. *East African Rebels: A Study of Some Independent Churches.* London: Student Christian Movement Press, 1961.

What Are the Problems of Parliamentary Government in West Africa? London: Hansard Society, 1958.

Zolberg, Aristide R. *One-Party Government in the Ivory Coast.* Princeton: Princeton University Press, 1964.

ARTICLES AND PAMPHLETS

"African Elites," *International Social Science Bulletin,* VIII, no. 3 (1956), 413–498.

"African Nationalism," *African Affairs,* XLIV (July, 1950), 224–228.

Africa Report (special issue on African socialism), VIII (May, 1963). Contains summary of Dakar Colloquium on African Socialism, and excerpts of statements by African leaders.

Akpan, N. U. "Chieftaincy in Eastern Nigeria," *Journal of African Administration,* IX (July, 1957), 120–124.

———. "Senior Chiefs in Africa Look to the Future," *ibid.,* pp. 124–129.

Albert, Ethel M. "Socio-Political Organization and Receptivity to Change: Some Differences between Ruanda and Urundi," *Southwestern Journal of Anthropology,* XVI (Spring, 1960), 46–74.

Alexandre, Pierre. "Marxism and African Cultural Traditions," *Survey,* no. 43 (Aug., 1962), 65–78.

Aloba, Abiodun. "Tribal Unions in Party Politics," *West Africa,* July 10, 1954, p. 637.

Amandou Fall, Lt.-Col. "La Jeunesse d'A.O.F. devant le problème des cadres," *Tropiques,* 55th year (Dec., 1957), 50–56.

Andrade, Mario de. "Angolese Nationalism," *Présence Africaine* (English ed.), vol. 14/15 (Third Quarter, 1962), 7–23.

Andrain, Charles. "The Pan-African Movement," *Phylon,* XXIII (First Quarter, 1962), 5–17.

Apter, David. "Political Religion in the New Nations," in Clifford Geertz, ed., *Old Societies and New States* (New York: Free Press of Glencoe, 1963), pp. 57–104.

———. "The Role of Traditionalism in the Political Modernization of Ghana and Uganda," *World Politics,* XIII (Oct., 1960), 45–68.

———. "Some Reflections on the Role of a Political Opposition in New Nations," *Comparative Studies in Society and History,* IV (1962), 154–168.

———. "Stratification and Emerging Political Parties in Underdeveloped Areas," in David Apter and H. Eckstein, *Comparative Politics* (New York: Free Press of Glencoe, 1963).

Apter, David E., and Carl G. Rosberg, Jr. "Nationalism and Models of Political Change in Africa," in *The Political Economy of Contemporary Africa,* Symposia Studies Series 1, National Institute of Social and Behavioral Science, George Washington University, 1959.

Austin, Dennis. *The Convention People's Party in Ghana.* London University Institute of Commonwealth Studies seminar paper, 1958.

697   *Select Bibliography*

————. "Elections in an African Rural Area (Ghana)," *Africa,* XXXI (Jan., 1961), 1–18.

————. *Parties and Tradition in Ghana.* London University Institute of Commonwealth Studies seminar paper, 1959.

————. "People and Constitution in Sierra Leone," *West Africa,* Sept. 20, 27, Oct. 4, 11, 1962.

————. "The Working Committee of the United Gold Coast Convention," *Journal of African History,* II, no. 2 (1961), 273–298.

Austin, Dennis, and William Tordoff. "Voting in an African Town," *Political Studies,* VIII (June, 1960), 130–146.

Awa, E. O. "Federal Elections in Nigeria, 1959," *Indian Journal of Political Science,* XXI (April-June, 1960), 101–113.

Azikiwe, Nnamdi. *The Development of Political Parties in Nigeria.* London: Office of the Commissioner in the U.K. for Eastern Nigeria, 1957.

Balandier, Georges. "Contribution à l'étude des nationalismes en Afrique noire," *Zaïre,* VIII (April, 1954), 379–389.

————. "Messianismes et nationalismes en Afrique noire," *Cahiers Internationaux de Sociologie,* XIV (1953), 41–65.

————. "Les Mythes politiques de colonisation et de décolonisation en Afrique," *ibid.,* XXXIII (1962), 85–96.

————. "Remarques sur les Regroupements politiques africains," *Revue Française de Science Politique,* X (Dec., 1960), 844–849.

Banton, M. P. "Tribal Headmen in Freetown," *Journal of African Administration,* VI (July, 1954), 140–144.

Barnes, J. A. "African Separatist Churches," *Rhodes-Livingstone Journal,* IX (1950), 26–30.

Beattie, J. M. H. "Checks on the Abuse of Political Power in Some African States," *Sociologus,* IX, no. 2 (1959), 97–115.

————. "L'Evolution politique du Congo belge et les autorités indigènes," *Problèmes d'Afrique Centrale,* XIII, no. 1 (1959), 3–77.

Bédos, G., and A. Dajamet. "Le Rassemblement Démocratique Africain," in *L'Evolution politique de l'Afrique Noire,* Association Française de Science Politique, Table Ronde, March, 1959 (Paris, 1959).

Bembe, Luc. "Elections au Congo belge," *Présence Africaine,* n.s., no. 17 (Dec., 1957–Jan., 1958), 115–117.

Bennett, George. "The Development of Political Organisations in Kenya," *Political Studies,* V (June, 1957), 113–130.

————. "The Gold Coast General Election of 1954," *Parliamentary Affairs,* VII (Autumn, 1954), 430–439.

Berg, Elliott. "French West Africa," in Walter Galenson, ed., *Labor and Economic Development* (New York: John Wiley & Sons, 1959).

Bernard, Charles. "Un Parti politique africain: Le Parti Démocratique de Guinée," *Revue Française de Science Politique,* XII (June, 1962), 312–359.

Biebuyck, Daniel, and Mary Douglas. *Congo Tribes and Parties.* London: Royal Anthropological Institute, 1961.

Bird, O. M. "Administrative Problems of Elections in Developing Countries," *Journal of African Administration,* IX (Oct., 1957), 167–173.

Blanchet, A. "Les Nationalismes africains frustrés d'une révolution?" *Preuves,* no. 112 (June, 1960), 40–47.

Bonnafe, P., and M. Cartry. "Les Idéologies politiques des pays en voie de développement," *Revue Française de Science Politique,* XII (June, 1962), 417–425.

Bowen, Walter. *Colonial Trade Unions.* Fabian Research Series, no. 167. London, 1954.

Boyd, Robert. "Characteristics of Candidates for Election in a Country Approaching Independence: The Case of Uganda," *Midwest Journal of Political Science,* VII (Feb., 1963), 1–27.

Bretton, Henry L. "Current Political Thought and Practice in Ghana," *American Political Science Review,* LII (March, 1958), 46–63.

[Brian, Willis.] *Le Problème des chefferies en Afrique Noire française.* France. Direction de la Documentation. Notes et Etudes Documentaires, no. 2508. Feb. 10, 1959.

Brockway, Fenner. "Rapport sur le Syndicalisme en Afrique Noire," *Présence Africaine,* no. 13 (1952), 359–367.

Burke, F. "The New Role of the Chief in Uganda," *Journal of African Administration,* X (July, 1958), 153–160.

Bustin, Edouard. "Les Partis politiques africains," *Etudes Congolaises,* no. 7 (Aug.-Sept., 1962), 1–80.

Campbell, Jane. "Multiracialism and Politics in Zanzibar," *Political Science Quarterly,* LXXVII (March, 1962), 72–87.

Castagno, A. A., Jr., *Somalia.* Carnegie Endowment for International Peace, International Conciliation, no. 522 (March, 1959).

Charles, Bernard. "Un Parti politique africain: Le Parti Démocratique de Guinée," *Revue Française de Science Politique,* XII (June, 1962), 312–359.

Charles, V. "Les 'Colonial Students' d'Afrique en Grande-Bretagne," *Zaïre,* V (Dec., 1951), 1059–1066.

Chidzero, B. T. G. "African Nationalism in East and Central Africa," *International Affairs,* XXXVI (Oct., 1960), 464–475.

Coleman, James S. "The Character and Viability of African Political Systems," in *The United States and Africa* (rev. ed.; New York: American Assembly, 1963).

———. "Current Political Movements in Africa," *Annals of the American Academy of Political and Social Science,* 298 (March, 1955), 95–108.

———. "The Emergence of African Political Parties," in C. Grove Haines, ed., *Africa Today* (Baltimore: Johns Hopkins Press, 1955), pp. 225–255.

———. "Nationalism in Tropical Africa," *American Political Science Review,* XLVIII (June, 1954), 404–426.

———. "The Politics of Sub-Saharan Africa," in Gabriel A. Almond and James S. Coleman, eds., *The Politics of the Developing Areas* (Princeton: Princeton University Press, 1960), chap. 3.

———. "The Problem of Political Integration in Emergent Africa," *Western Political Quarterly*, VIII (March, 1955), 44–58.

———. *Togoland*. Carnegie Endowment for International Peace, International Conciliation, no. 509 (Sept., 1956).

Coleman, James S., and Belmont Brice. "The Role of the Military in Sub-Saharan Africa," in John J. Johnson, ed., *The Role of the Military in Underdeveloped Countries* (Princeton: Princeton University Press, 1962), pp. 359–405.

Comhaire, Jean. "Sociétés secrètes et Mouvements prophétiques au Congo Belge," *Africa*, XXV (Jan., 1955), 54–59.

"Le Congrès R.D.A. de Bamako et l'évolution constitutionnelle de la République française," *Nouvelle Revue Française d'Outre-Mer*, n.s., XLIX (Nov., 1957), 517–564.

Cornevin, Robert. "Evolution des Chefferies traditionelles en Afrique Noire d'expression française," *Recueil Penant* (April-May, 1961), pp. 235–250; (June-Aug., 1961), 379–388; (Sept.-Oct., 1961), 539–556.

Crowley, Daniel J. "Politics and Tribalism in the Katanga," *Western Political Quarterly*, XVI (March, 1963), 68–78.

Davidson, R. B. "Trade Union Organisation in the Gold Coast," *West Africa*, Oct. 6, 13, 1951.

———. "Trade Unions and Politics in the Gold Coast," *ibid.*, Aug. 18, 25, 1951.

Decraene, Philippe. "L'Evolution des Partis politiques en Afrique au sud du Sahara," *Civilisations*, XII, no. 2 (1962), 196–210.

———. "The Origins of Congo Nationalism," *West Africa*, Jan. 24, 31, 1959.

———. "Pan-Africanisme et grand puissances," *Politique Etrangère*, 24th year, no. 4 (1959), 408–421.

Dembour, J., and J. Putzeys. "Les Elections législatives au Congo et les Collèges exécutifs et consultatifs," *Journal des Tribunaux d'Outre-Mer* (1960).

Demt, M. J. "Elections in Northern Nigeria," *Journal of Local Administration Overseas*, I (Oct., 1962), 213–224.

Drake, St. Clair. "Traditional Authority and Social Action in Former British West Africa," *Human Organization*, XIX (Fall, 1960), 150–158.

Dresse, Robert. "Etudiants d'Outre-Mer en Angleterre," *Eglise Vivante*, IV (1952), 390–404.

Drew, Walter H. "How Socialist Are African Economies?" *Africa Report*, VIII (May, 1963).

Dupire, M. *Planteurs autochtones et étrangers en Basse Côte d'Ivoire orientale.* Etudes Eburnéennes, no. 8 (1960).

Dupuis, J. "Un Problème de minorité: Les nomades dans L'Etat Soudanais," *Afrique et Asie* (Second Quarter, 1960), pp. 19–44.

Emerson, Rupert. "Nationalism and Political Development," *Journal of Politics*, XXII (Feb., 1960), 3–28.

———. "Pan-Africanism," *International Organization*, XVI (Spring, 1962), 275–290.

Entin, L. "Political Parties of West Africa," *Mirovaya Ekonomika i Mezhdunaro-dyne Otnosheniya*, II (1961), 135–138.

"Les Etudiants noirs parlent . . . ," *Présence Africaine*, no. 14 (1953). Includes: A. Franklin, "Le Paternalisme contre l'Etudiant africain"; Assane Seck, "Problème de Modernisation de l'Ouest Africain"; David Diop, "Etudiant africain devant le Fait colonial"; Ab Wade, "Afrique Noire et Union Française"; and Majhemout Diop, "L'unique Issue: l'Indépendance totale."

Fallers, Lloyd. "Equality and Modernity in the New States," in Clifford Geertz, ed., *Old Societies and New States* (New York: Free Press of Glencoe, 1963).

——. "Ideology and Culture in Uganda Nationalism," *American Anthropologist*, LXIII (Aug., 1961), 677–686.

——. "The Predicament of the Modern African Chief," *ibid.*, LVII (April, 1955), 290–305.

Fischer, Georges. "Quelques Aspects de la doctrine politique guinéenne," *Civilisations*, IX, no. 4 (1959), 457–478.

——. "Trade Unions and Decolonisation," *Présence Africaine* (English ed.), vol. 6/7 (1961), 121–169.

Fleury, R. "Les Partis politiques en A.O.F. (1945–58)," *Marchés Tropicaux du Monde*, Aug. 30, Sept. 6, 13, 20, 27, 1958.

"La Formation politique des indigènes congolais," *Problèmes d'Afrique Centrale*, IV (Second Quarter, 1951), 132–135.

Friedland, William H. "African Trade Unions: From Bush to Copperbelt," *Information* (International Research Office on the Social Implications of Technical Change), Oct. 22, 1959, pp. 1–6.

——. "Four Sociological Trends in African Socialism," *Africa Report*, VIII (May, 1963).

——. "The Institutionalization of Labor Protest in Tanganyika and Some Resultant Problems," *Sociologus*, XI, no. 2 (1961), 132–147.

Gardiner, R. K., "Relationship between Political Parties and the Government in West Africa," in *What Are the Problems of Parliamentary Government in West Africa?* (London: Hansard Society, 1958), pp. 79–83.

Gardinier, David E. "The Movement to Reunify the Cameroons." Mimeographed. 1960.

Gareau, Frederick H. "Bloc Politics in West Africa," *Orbis*, V (Winter, 1962), 470–488.

Garigue, Philip. "Changing Political Leadership in West Africa," *Africa*, XXIV (July, 1954), 220–232.

Geertz, Clifford. "The Integrative Revolution: Primordial Sentiments and Civil Politics in the New States," in Clifford Geertz, ed., *Old Societies and New States* (New York: Free Press of Glencoe, 1963).

——. "The West African Students' Union," *ibid.*, XXIII (Jan., 1953), 55–69.

Genevray, J. *Eléments d'une Monographie d'une division administrative liberienne*. Dakar: IFAN, 1952.

George, John B. "How Stable Is Tanganyika?" *Africa Report*, VIII (March, 1963), 3–9.

Giro, G. "Note sul Sindacalismo Africano," *Civitas* (April-May, 1962).

Gluckman, Max. "Tribalism in Modern British Central Africa," *Cahiers d'Etudes Africaines,* no. 1 (Jan., 1960), 55–70.

Goldthorpe, J. E. "An African Elite," *British Journal of Sociology,* VI (March, 1955), 31–47.

Gosnell, Harold F. "The 1958 Elections in the Sudan," *Middle East Journal,* XII (Fall, 1958), 409–417.

Gray, Robert F. "Political Parties in New African Nations: An Anthropological Viewpoint," *Comparative Studies in Society and History,* V (July, 1963), 449–461.

Griffiths, James. "The Role of Trade Unions in the Colonies," *West Africa,* Dec. 8, 15, 1951.

———. "The Trade Unions: A Growth of Membership in the Colonies," *Times British Colonies Review,* no. 7 (Autumn, 1952), p. 12.

Grubbe, P. "Kongo—Eine Afrikanische Grossmacht?" *Aussenpolitik* (June, 1960).

———. "Die Stimme Afrikas," *ibid.* (Sept., 1958).

Grundy, Kenneth W. "Marxism-Leninism and African Underdevelopment: The Mali Approach," *International Journal,* XVII (Summer, 1962), 300–304.

Guillemin, Philippe. "Les Elus d'Afrique Noire à l'Assemblée Nationale sous la Quatrième République," *Revue Française de Science Politique,* VIII (Dec., 1958), 861–877.

———. "La Structure des premiers Gouvernements locaux en Afrique Noire," *ibid.,* IX (Sept., 1959), 667–685.

Gyasi-Twum, K. "Minorities Pose Threat to West African Unity," *Africa Special Report,* IV (Aug., 1959), 13–14.

———. "West Africa's Prospects for Democratic Rule," *ibid.,* IV (June, 1959).

Hailey, Lord. "Nationalism in Africa," *Journal of the African Society,* XXXVI (April, 1937), 134–147.

Hamon, L. "Introduction à l'Etude des partis politiques de l'Afrique Française," *Revue Juridique et Politique d'Outre-Mer,* XIII (April-June, 1959), 149–196.

———. "Le Parti Démocratique de Guinée d'avant l'indépendance à 1960," *ibid.,* XV (July-Sept., 1961), 354–368.

Hampaté Bâ, Amadou. "Des Elites," *Afrique en Marche,* I (Jan., 1957), 10–11; (Feb., 1957), 10–11.

Hapgood, David. "Unions in Search of Their Roles," *Africa Today* (June, 1962), pp. 7–8.

Hepple, Alex. "African Trade Unions and the New Powers," *Africa South,* I (July-Sept., 1957), 21–34.

Hertefelt, Marcel d'. "Les Elections communales et le consensus politique au Rwanda," *Zaïre,* XIV, no. 5–6 (1960), 403–438.

———. "Stratification sociale et Structure politique," *Revue Nouvelle,* XXXI (May 15, 1960), 449–462.

Hess, Mahlon M. "Political Systems and African Church Polity," *Practical Anthropology,* IV, no. 5 (1957), 170–184.

Heyerm, Sarjit S. "The Asian in Kenya," *Africa South in Exile*, V (Jan.-March, 1961), 77–84.

Hinden, R. "Africa and Democracy," in *Encounter*, no. 8 (London, 1962).

Hodgkin, Thomas. "Background to Nigerian Nationalism," *West Africa*, Aug. 4, 11, 18, Sept. 1, 8, 15, 1951.

——. "Islam and National Movements in West Africa," *Journal of African History*, III, no. 2 (1962), 323–327.

——. "Islam and Politics in West Africa," *West Africa*, Sept. 15-Nov. 10, 1956.

——. "A Note on the Language of African Nationalism," in *African Affairs*, no. 1, St. Antony's Papers, no. 10 (London: Chatto and Windus, 1961).

——. "A Note on West African Political Parties," in *What Are the Problems of Parliamentary Government in West Africa?* (London: Hansard Society, 1958), pp. 51–62.

Hodgkin, Thomas, and Ruth Schachter. *French-speaking West Africa in Transition.* Carnegie Endowment for International Peace, International Conciliation, no. 528 (May, 1960).

Holas, B. "La *Goumbé*: Une association de jeunesse musulmane en basse Côte d'Ivoire," *Kongo-Overzee*, XIX, no. 2/3 (1953), 116–131.

Holt, P. M. "Sudanese Nationalism and Self-Determination," *Middle East Journal*, X (Summer, 1956), 239–247.

Houphouet-Boigny, F. "Rapport sur l'Avenir de la Communauté présenté au Congrès Extraordinaire du R.D.A.," *Afrique Nouvelle* (Dakar), Sept. 11, 1959.

Husband, J. I. "Wage-fixing and the Role of Workers' and Employers' Unions in Collective Bargaining in Kenya," *Bulletin of the Inter-African Labour Institute*, VI (Nov., 1955), 27–38.

Jahoda, Gustav. "Nationality Preferences and National Stereotypes in Ghana before Independence," *Journal of Social Psychology*, L (Nov., 1959), 165–174.

——. "The Social Background of a West African Student Population (Gold Coast University College)," *British Journal of Sociology*, V (Dec., 1954), 355–365; VI (March, 1955), 71–79.

Jennings, Sir Ivor. "Is a Party System Possible in Africa?" *Listener*, Feb. 16, 1961.

Kartun, D. "The National Movement in Africa," *International Affairs* (Moscow) (June, 1956), pp. 75–82.

Katsman, V. Ya., and P. I. Kupriyanov. "On the Status and the Role of Leaders in African Society," *Sovetskaya Etnografiya* (1962). (Article is in Russian.)

Keita, Fodeba. "La Suppression de la chefferie," *France Outre-Mer*, XXXV, no. 341, pp. 23–25.

Keita, Madeira. "Le Parti unique en Afrique," *Présence Africaine*, n.s., no. 30 (Feb.-March, 1960), 3–24.

Khaly, Nene. "La Loi-Cadre et les élections territoriales en Afrique Noire," *ibid.*, no. 13 (April-May, 1957), 126–132.

Khazanov, A. M. "The Anticolonial Movement in Somalia under the Leadership of Muhammad bin Abdullah," *Problemy Vostokovedeniya*, no. 2 (1960), 113–123.

Kiano, Gikonyo. "The Pan-African Freedom Movement of East and Central Africa," *Africa Today* (Sept., 1959), pp. 11–14.

Kilson, Martin. "The Analysis of African Nationalism," *World Politics*, X (April, 1958), 484–497.

———. "Authoritarian and Single-Party Tendencies in African Politics," *ibid.*, XV (Jan., 1963), 262–294.

———. "Land and Politics in Kenya: An Analysis of African Politics in a Plural Society," *Western Political Quarterly*, X (Sept., 1957), 559–581.

———. "Land and the Kikuyu: A Study of the Relationship between Land and Kikuyu Political Movements," *Journal of History*, XL (April, 1955), 103–153.

———. "Nationalism and Social Classes in British West Africa," *Journal of Politics*, XX (May, 1958), 368–387.

———. "The Rise of Nationalist Organizations and Parties in British West Africa," in *Africa Seen by American Negroes* (Paris: Présence Africaine, 1958), pp. 35–69.

———. "Sierra Leone Politics," *West Africa*, June 18, 25, July 2, 9, 1960.

———. "Social Forces in West African Political Development," *Journal of Human Relations*, VIII (Spring and Summer, 1960), 576–598.

"Le Kimbanguisme," *Courrier Hebdomadaire* (Centre de Recherche et d'Information Socio-Politiques), Jan. 29, 1960, pp. 16–17.

Kirby, D. "Ballots in the Bush: A Case Study in Local Elections in the Bo District of Sierra Leone," *Journal of African Administration*, IX (Oct., 1957), 174–182.

Kraft, L. "Pan-Africanism: Political, Economic, Strategic, and Scientific," *International Affairs*, XXIV (April, 1948), 218–228.

Lamberton, J. "Les Bamileké dans le Cameroun d'Aujourd'hui," *Revue de Défense Nationale* (March, 1960).

Lang, Nicolas. "Les Partis politiques au Congo belge," *Le Flambeau*, XLII (Jan.-Feb., 1959), 70–80.

Laqueur, W. Z. "Communism and Nationalism in Tropical Africa," *Foreign Affairs*, XXXIX (July, 1961), 610–621.

Le Grip, A. "Aspects actuels de l'Islam en A.O.F.," *Afrique et Asie*, XXIV, no. 4 (1953), 6–20; XXV, no. 3 (1954), 42–61.

Lemarchand, René. "Bases of Nationalism among the Bakongo," *Africa*, XXXI (Oct., 1961), 344–354.

———. "L'Influence des Systèmes traditionnels sur l'évolution politique du Rwanda et du Burundi," *Revue de l'Institut de Sociologie* (1962), pp. 333–357.

———. "The Limits of Self-Determination: The Case of the Katanga Secession," *American Political Science Review*, LVI (June, 1962), 404–416.

Leriche, A. "Notes sur les Classes sociales et sur quelques tribus de Mauritanie," *Bulletin de l'Institut Française d'Afrique Noire*, Series B, XVII (Jan.-April, 1955), 173–203.

Lewis, I. M. "Modern Political Movements in Somaliland," *Africa*, XXVIII (July, 1958), 244–261; (Oct., 1958), 344–363.

———. "Pan-Africanism and Pan-Somalism," *Journal of Modern African Studies*, I (June, 1963), 147–161.

————. "Problems in the Development of Modern Leadership and Loyalties in British Somaliland Protectorate and U.N. Trusteeship Territory of Somalia," *Civilisations,* X, no. 1 (1960), 49–60.

Leys, Colin. "Tanganyika: The Realities of Independence," *International Journal,* XVII (Summer, 1962), 251–268.

Lichtblau, George E. "The Communist Labor Offensive in Former Colonial Countries," *Industrial and Labor Relations Review,* XV (April, 1962), 376–401.

Liebenow, J. Gus. "Responses to Planned Political Change in a Tanganyika Tribal Group," *American Political Science Review,* L (June, 1956), 442–461.

Little, Kenneth. "The African Elite in British West Africa," in A. W. Lind, ed., *Race Relations in World Perspective* (Honolulu: University of Hawaii Press, 1955), chap. xii.

————. "The Organisation of Voluntary Associations in West Africa," *Civilisations,* IX, no. 3 (1959), 283–300.

————. "The Role of Voluntary Associations in West African Urbanization," *American Anthropologist,* LIX (Aug., 1957), 579–596.

Lloyd, P. C. "Action Group and Local Government," *West Africa,* Nov. 7, 14, 1953, pp. 1039, 1065.

————. "Cocoa, Politics and the Yoruba Middle Class," *ibid.,* Jan. 17, 1953, p. 39.

————. "The Development of Political Parties in Western Nigeria," *American Political Science Review,* XLIX (Sept., 1955), 693–707.

————. "Kings, Chiefs and Local Government," *West Africa,* Jan. 31, Feb. 7, 1953.

————. "Some Comments on the Elections in Nigeria," *Journal of African Administration,* IV (July, 1952), 82–92.

Lodge, George C. "Labor's Role in Newly Developing Countries," *Foreign Affairs,* XXXVII (July, 1959), 660–671.

Lofchie, Michael. "Party Conflict in Zanzibar," *Journal of Modern African Studies,* I (June, 1963), 185–207.

Loveridge, A. J. "The Present Position of the Temne Chiefs of Sierra Leone," *Journal of African Administration,* IX (July, 1957), 115–120.

Low, D. A. *Political Parties in Uganda, 1949–1962.* University of London, Institute of Commonwealth Studies. London: Athlone Press, 1962.

Lowenkopf, Martin. "Tanganyika Achieves Responsible Government," *Parliamentary Affairs,* XIV (Spring, 1960), 244–257.

Mackintosh, J. P. "Electoral Trends and the Tendency to a One Party System in Nigeria," *Journal of Commonwealth Political Studies,* I (Nov., 1962), 194–210.

Mair, Lucy P. "African Chiefs Today," *Africa,* XXVIII (July, 1958), 195–205.

————. "Independent Religious Movements in Three Continents," *Comparative Studies in Society and History,* I (Jan., 1959), 113–135.

————. *The Nyasaland Elections of 1961.* University of London, Institute of Commonwealth Studies. London: Athlone Press, 1962.

Marie-Andrée du Sacre Coeur. "L'Activité politique de la Femme en Afrique

Noire," *Revue Juridique et Politique de l'Union Française,* VIII (Oct., 1954), 476–491.

Marvick, Dwaine. "Higher Education in the Development of Future West African Leaders," in James S. Coleman, ed., *Education and Political Development* (Princeton: Princeton University Press, in press).

Mboya, Tom J. "The Party System and Democracy in Africa," *Foreign Affairs,* XLI (July, 1963), 650–658.

————. "Trade Unionism in Kenya," *Africa South,* I (Jan.-March, 1957), 77–86.

Mercier, Paul. "Evolution of Senegalese Elites," *International Social Science Bulletin,* VIII, no. 3 (1956), 441–451.

————. "Le Groupement européen de Dakar," *Cahiers Internationaux de Sociologie,* XIX (July-Dec., 1955), 130–146.

————. "Le Parti unique à la Poursuite de la démocratie," *Preuves,* no. 101 (July, 1949).

————. "Political Life in the Urban Centers of Senegal," *PROD Translations,* III (June, 1960), 3–20.

————. "Remarques sur la Signification du 'Tribalisme' actuel en Afrique Noire," *Cahiers Internationaux de Sociologie,* XXXI (July-Dec., 1961), 61–80.

————. "La Vie politique dans les centres urbains du Sénégal," *ibid.,* XXVII (1959), 55–84.

Merle, Marcel. "Les Relations extérieures de la Côte d'Ivoire," *Revue Française de Science Politique,* IX (Sept., 1959), 686–706.

Middleton, John. "The Role of Chiefs and Headmen among the Lubara of West Nile District, Uganda," *Journal of African Administration,* VIII (Jan., 1956), 32–38.

————. "Society and Politics in Zanzibar," *Civilisations,* XII, no. 3 (1962), 375–383.

Milcent, E. "Evolution des Partis en Afrique Noire," *Revue de l'Action Populaire,* no. 139 (June, 1960), 707–718.

Mitchell, John P. *Changing Liberia: A Challenge to the Christian.* Report of the United Christian Fellowship Conference of Liberia, Switzerland, 1959.

Mondet, L. "La Formation professionelle en Afrique française," *Union Française et Parlement,* XCI (Feb., 1958), 24–27.

Moore, C. H. "The National Party: A Tentative Model," in *Public Policy* (Cambridge: Harvard University Press, 1960).

Morgenthau, Ruth Schachter. "African Socialism: Declaration of Ideological Independence," *Africa Report,* VIII (May, 1963).

Morris, Stephen. "Indians in East Africa," *British Journal of Sociology,* VII (Sept., 1956), 194–211.

Mortimer, Molly, and Marjorie Nicholson. "Nationalism in the Cameroons," *Venture,* V (March, 1953), 4–5; (April, 1953), 6–7.

Morton-Williams, P. "A Discussion of the Theory of Elites in a West African (Yoruba) Context," in "Proceedings of the Fourth Annual Conference of the West African Institute of Social and Economic Research" [held in March, 1955] (mimeographed; University College, Ibadan, 1956).

Mwanjisi, W. B. K. "Tanganyika African National Union," *Africa Today* (Dec., 1961), pp. 10–11.

"La Naissance des Classes moyennes congolaises: Travailleurs indépendants à Léopoldville," *La Revue Congolaise du Bâtiment et de l'Industrie,* IV (Feb., 1956), 1–4.

Naville, Pierre. "Note sur le Syndicalisme en Afrique Noire," *Présence Africaine,* no. 13 (1952), 359–367.

"New Trade Unionism in Ghana," *West Africa,* Jan. 17, 24, 1959.

Ngubane, Jordan K. "African Political Movements," *Africa South,* I (Oct.-Dec., 1956), 70–78.

Nicol, Davidson. "Politics, Nationalism and Universities in Africa," *African Affairs,* LXII (Jan., 1963), 20–27.

Nkrumah, Kwame. "La Naissance de mon Parti et son programme d'action positive," *Présence Africaine,* n.s., no. 12 (Feb.-March, 1957), 11–26.

Nyerere, Julius. "The Future of African Nationalism," *Tribune,* May 27, 1960.

———. "One Party Government," contribution to a seminar on "The Concept of Democracy in Africa," *Spearhead* (Dar es Salaam), I (Nov., 1961), 7–9.

———. "One Party System," *ibid.,* II (Jan., 1963), 1, 12–23.

———. "The Relationship between the Civil Service, Political Parties and Members of the Legislative Council," *Journal of African Administration,* XIII (April, 1961).

———. "The Task Ahead of Our African Trade Unions," *Labour* (Ghana) (June, 1961).

———. "Will Democracy Work in Africa?" *Africa Special Report,* V (Feb., 1960), 3–4.

Obi, C. *The Dynamic Party.* Ibadan, 1954.

Oloko, Tunde. "Religion and Politics in Nigeria," *West Africa,* Feb. 2, 9, 1957.

Oluwasanmi, H. A. "Nigerian Students' Role in Their Society," *World University Service Bulletin,* XXI (Winter, 1960), 1, 5–6.

Onipede, F. Oladipo. "African Nationalism," *Dissent,* III, no. 3 (1956), 276–285.

Orlova, A. S. "The Place and the Function of Traditional Authorities in African Society in the Past and Today," *Sovetskaya Etnografiya* (1960), 92–106.

Osadebay, Dennis. "Evolution of Democracy: Solution to Embody African Chiefs in Modern Constitution," *West African Review,* XX (March, 1949), 734–738.

Ottenberg, S. "Improvement Associations among the Afikpo Ibo," *Africa,* XXV (Jan., 1955), 1–28.

Padmore, George. "Pan-Africanism and Ghana," *United Asia* (Feb., 1957).

Parker, Mary. "Municipal Government and the Growth of African Political Institutions in the Urban Areas of Kenya," *Zaïre,* III (June, 1949), 649–662.

Parrinder, Geoffrey. "Indigenous Churches in Nigeria," *West African Review,* XXXI (Sept., 1960), 87–93.

"Les Partis politiques en Afrique Noire et Madagascar," *Chroniques de la Communauté* (Dec., 1959), pp. 20–26.

Pauvert, Jean-Claude. "L'Evolution politique des Ewé," *Cahiers d'Etudes Africaines*, no. 2 (May, 1960), 161–192.

Penney, J. C. "Notes on the Election in the Protectorate of Zanzibar, 1957," *Journal of African Administration*, X (July, 1958), 144–152.

Popplewell, G. D. "Chiefs and Politics," *Corona*, IX (Dec., 1957), 448–450.

Porter, A. T. "The Social Background of Political Decision Makers in Sierra Leone," *Sierra Leone Studies*, XIII (June, 1960), 1–13.

Pratt, R. C. "Nationalism in Uganda," *Political Studies*, IX (June, 1961), 157–178.

———. "Tribalism and Nationalism in Uganda," *Oversea Quarterly*, II (Sept., 1960), 78–80.

Prescott, B. P. "The Nigerian Election and the Minorities," *West Africa*, Feb. 20, 1960, p. 207.

Prescott, J. R. V. "Les Régions politiques des Camerouns anglo-français," *Annales de Géographie*, no. 367 (May-June, 1959), 263–267.

Pribytkovskii, L. "A Study of the Labour Movement in Nigeria, 1945–1949," *Problemy Vostokovedeniya* (1960), pp. 84–93.

Price, J. H. "The Muslim Vote in the Accra Constituencies," in "Proceedings of the Fourth Annual Conference of the West African Institute of Social and Economic Research" [held in March, 1955] (mimeographed; University College, Ibadan, 1956).

———. "The Role of Islam in Gold Coast Politics," in "Proceedings of the Third Annual Conference of the West African Institute of Social and Economic Research" [held in March, 1954] (mimeographed; University College, Ibadan, 1956).

"Le Problème de la Chefferie coutumière," *Chroniques d'Outre-Mer*, 31 (Jan., 1957), 13–14.

"Le Problème du Peuple Ewé," *Bulletin des Nations Unies*, VIII (March 15, 1950), 247–249.

Ranger, Terence. "The Malawi Party," *Africa Special Report*, V (Aug., 1960).

Richards, Audrey I. "Tribal Groups in Kenya," *Times British Colonies Review*, no. 29 (1958), 21–22.

Riddell, J. "Trade Unionism in Africa as a Factor in Nation Building," *Civilisations*, XII, no. 1 (1962), 27–45.

Ritzenthaler, R. "Anlu: Women's Uprising in the British Cameroons," *Zaïre*, XIV, no. 5–6 (1960), 481–504.

Robinson, Kenneth. "Political Development in French West Africa," in Calvin W. Stillman, ed., *Africa in the Modern World* (Chicago: University of Chicago Press, 1959), pp. 140–181.

Robinson, Kwasi. "Background to Gold Coast Nationalism," *West Africa*, July 8, 15, 22, 29, Aug. 5, 12, 19, 26, Sept. 2, 1950.

Rosberg, Carl G., Jr. "Democracy and the New African States," in *African Affairs*, no. 2, St. Antony's Papers, no. 15 (London: Chatto and Windus, 1963).

Rosberg, Carl G., Jr., with Aaron Segal. *An East African Federation.* Carnegie Endowment for International Peace, International Conciliation, no. 543 (May, 1963).

Rotberg, Robert. "The Political Outlook in Zanzibar," *Africa Report*, VI (Oct., 1961).

———. "The Rise of African Nationalism: The Case of East and Central Africa," *World Politics*, XV (Oct., 1962), 75–90.

Rothchild, Donald. "The Politics of African Separatism," *Journal of International Affairs*, XV, no. 1 (1961), 18–28.

Schachter, Ruth. "Single Party Systems in West Africa," *American Political Science Review*, LV (June, 1961), 294–307.

Schwartz, Walter. "Varieties of African Nationalism," *Commentary*, XXXII (July, 1961), 27–35.

Scott, D. J. R. "Elections in Sierra Leone, 1957," *West Africa*, April 27, May 4, 25, 1957.

Senghor, Léopold. *African Socialism*. New York: American Society for African Culture, 1959.

———. "Les Elites de l'Union Française au service de leurs peuples," *Marchés Coloniaux du Monde*, X (Feb. 27, 1954), 573–575.

———. "Le Voie africaine du Socialisme," in *Séminaire organisé à l'occasion du Congrès de l'Union Nationale de la Jeunesse du Mali*, Parti de la Fédération Africaine (Dakar, 1960).

———. "What is Negritude?" *West Africa*, Nov. 4, 1961, p. 1211.

"Senior Chiefs in Uganda Look to the Future," *Journal of African Administration*, IX (July, 1957), 124–129.

Seurin, Jean-Louis. "Elites sociales et Partis politiques d'A.O.F.," *Annales Africaines* (1958), pp. 123–157.

Shepperson, George. "Ethiopianism and African Nationalism," *Phylon*, XIV (First Quarter, 1953), 9–18.

———. "External Factors in the Development of African Nationalism, with Particular Reference to British Central Africa," *ibid.*, XXII (Third Quarter, 1961), 207–225.

Shils, Edward. "The Intellectuals in the Political Development of the New States," *World Politics*, XII (April, 1960), 329–368.

Sisulu, W. M. "The Development of African Nationalism," *India Quarterly* (July-Sept., 1954).

Smythe, Hugh. "The Nigerian Elite," *Sociology and Social Research*, XLIV (Sept.-Oct., 1959), 42–45.

Sofer, Cyril. "Working Groups in a Plural Society," *Industrial and Labor Relations Review*, VIII (Oct., 1954), 68–78.

Sutton, Francis. "Authority and Authoritarianism in the New Africa," *Journal of International Affairs*, XV, no. 1 (1961), 7–17.

Sydon, Diallo. "Développement du Syndicalisme chrétien en Afrique," *Dossiers de l'Action Sociale Catholique* (April, 1959), pp. 330–334.

———. "Le Syndicalisme africain en marche," *Les Missions Catholiques*, n.s., no. 58–59 (Jan.-Feb., 1957), 14–21.

Tiryakian, Edward. "African Political Development," *World Politics*, XIV (July, 1962), 700–712.

Torres, José Arsenio. "The Political Ideology of Guided Democracy," *Review of Politics*, XXV (Jan., 1963), 34–63.

Touré, Sékou. "Le Leader politique considéré comme le représentant d'une culture," *Présence Africaine,* n.s., no. 24–25 (Feb.-May, 1959), 104–115.

Vansina, J. "Miko mi Yool: Une Association Religieuse Kuba," *Aequatoria,* XXII (1959), 7–20.

Van Wing, Joseph, "Les Mouvements messianiques populaires dans le Bas-Congo," *Zaïre,* XIV, no. 2–3 (1960), 225–237.

Vignaud, M. "Les Elections de janvier 1956 en Côte d'Ivoire," *Revue Française de Science Politique,* VI (July-Sept., 1956), 570–582.

Von der Mehden, Fred R. "Party Development in Newly Independent States," *Social Science,* XXXIV (June, 1959), 139–143.

Wallerstein, Immanuel. "Ethnicity and National Integration in West Africa," *Cahiers d'Etudes Africaines,* no. 3 (Oct., 1960), 129–139.

———. "How Seven States Were Born in Former French West Africa," *Africa Report,* VI (March, 1961).

———. "The Political Ideology of the P.D.G.," *Présence Africaine* (English ed.), vol. 12 (First Quarter, 1962), 30–41.

Whiteley, W. H. "The Changing Position of Swahili in East Africa," *Africa,* XXVI (Oct., 1956), 343–353.

———. "Language and Politics in East Africa," *Tanganyika Notes,* 47/48 (June-Sept., 1957), 159–173.

Williams, R. W. "Trade Unions in Africa," *African Affairs,* LIV (Oct., 1955), 267–279.

Young, M. Crawford. "Congo Political Parties Revisited," *Africa Report,* VIII (Jan., 1963), 14–20.

Zolberg, Aristide R. "Effets de la structure d'un parti politique sur l'integration nationale," *Cahiers d'Etudes Africaines,* no. 3 (Oct., 1960), 140–149.

———. "Mass Parties and National Integration: The Case of the Ivory Coast," *Journal of Politics,* XXV (Feb., 1963), 36–48.

———. "One-Party Systems and Government for the People," *Africa Today* (May, 1962).

———. "Politics in the Ivory Coast," *West Africa,* July 30, Aug. 6, 29, 1960, pp. 847, 883, 939.

INDEX

ABBREVIATIONS USED IN INDEX

AATUF	All-African Trade Union Federation
Abako	Association pour le Maintien, l'Unité, et l'Expansion de la Langue Kikongo
AG	Action Group
AMU	African Mineworkers' Union
ANC	African National Congress
AOF	Afrique Occidentale Française (French West Africa)
APC	All People's Congress
ARP	Alliance Rurale Progressiste
ARPS	Aborigines' Rights Protection Society
ASP	Afro-Shirazi Party
BAG	Bloc Africain de Guinée
Balubakat	Association des Baluba du Katanga
BDS	Bloc Démocratique Sénégalais
BMS	Bloc des Masses Sénégalaises
BPS	Bloc Populaire Sénégalais
Cerea	Centre de Regroupement Africain
CFU	Cameroons Federal Union
CGKT	Confédération Générale Kamerunaise du Travail
CGT	Confédération Générale du Travail
CGTA	Confédération Générale des Travailleurs Africains
CMUN	Courant Mouvement d'Union Nationale
CNF	Cameroons National Federation
Conakat	Confédération des Associations Tribales du Katanga
CPNC	Cameroon People's National Convention
CPP	Convention People's Party
CYO	Committee on Youth Organization
DSG	Démocratie Socialiste de Guinée
Esocam	Evolution Sociale Camerounaise
FPTU	Federation of Progressive Trade Unions
FPUP	Front Populaire pour l'Unité et la Paix
FRTU	Federation of Revolutionary Trade Unions
GCP	Ghana Congress Party
GSL	Greater Somalia League
HDM	Hisbia Digil Mirifle
ICFTU	International Confederation of Free Trade Unions
IOM	Indépendants d'Outre-Mer
IPP	Independent Progressive Party
Jabako	Jeunesse Abako
JMNC	Jeunesse du Mouvement National Congolais
JRDA	Jeunesse Rassemblement Démocratique Africain
JRDACI	Jeunesse RDA de la Côte d'Ivoire
JUS-RDA	Jeunesse de l'Union Soudanaise–RDA

INDEX

AATUF, 298, 308

Abako, 335, 565, 583, 587, 588, 594; and separatism, 573, 574–575; and traditionalism, 573–575; Abako-Kanza, 589

Abdalla Hassan, Muhammad Ahmed bin, 518, 555, 557

Abdi Nur, Muhammad, 533, 547, 551

Achieved status: Nigeria, 614, 615–619 *passim*

Achimota College, 263, 267, 297n

Action Démocratique et Sociale, 186, 188

Adamafio, Tawia, 279n, 302, 308, 311

Adelabu, Adegoke, 621

Aden, Abdulcadir Muhammad, 522, 533, 539, 547, 551

Aden, Mohamud Ahamed Muhammad, 534, 547

Adjei, Ako, 276, 279n, 308, 311

Adoula, Cyrille, 566, 577

Afgoi-Audegle Group, 530, 531

Africanization, 119, 178, 377

African personality, concept of, 307, 310, 439

African Railway Workers' Union, 355, 371

African socialism, 52, 177, 310, 669

African unity, 212, 213, 257, 504. *See also* Pan-Africanism

AG, 390–391, 597, 600, 611; and traditional rulers, 391, 392–397, 633; as mass organization, 600–601, 603–604; and regionalism, 603; leaders, 615–616; members and supporters, 620–621; structure, 624–625; power distribution, 627–628; auxiliary organizations, 630–631; goals 638–641

Agnatic cleavages, 517–518, 526, 527–528, 555–557, 558

Ahidjo, Ahmadou, 133, 142, 144, 147, 153, 168; on one-party state, 132, 136, 146; and traditional rulers, 152; on African socialism, 177

Ahmadu Shehu, 223, 226

Akintola, Samuel L., 391n, 601, 650

Alafin of Oyo, 640n

Alex-Hamah, John, 309

Alien groups: Senegal, 49–50; Sierra Leone, 117; Liberia, 472–473

All-African People's Congress: first, 116, 122, 566; second, 116–117

Americo-Liberian oligarchy, 449, 452, 474, 682

Amicale Gilbert Vieillard, 186, 334

Amponsah, R. R., 279, 284

AMU, 353–355, 356

ANC (Northern Rhodesia), 334, 353–355

Animation rurale, 53–54

AOF, 17, 71, 217n, 323, 357–358; *sujets*, 18, 229; *citoyens*, 229

APC, 92, 105, 114–115; external relationships, 93, 116, 117

Appiah, Joe, 275, 284

Arab Association, 483–484, 485

Arab minority (Zanzibar), 482–483

ARP, 583, 585

ARPS, 261, 263, 265, 267, 332

Asantehene, 277, 279, 404, 406, 409

Asante Youth Association, 271, 273, 277

Ascribed status: Liberia, 456; Nigeria, 615–619 *passim*

Ashanti, 262n, 277, 288–289; Confederacy, 266n, 281, 404

Askar, Omar, 543

Askianist Movement, 631

ASP, 487, 489, 503, 508, 509; organization, 502–503; factions, 503; and African unity, 504; leaders, 504; supporters, 505–506

Assalé, Charles, 134, 139, 142, 145, 159

Association des Ancien Elèves de Terrasson de Fougères, 229, 327

Association Lulua-Frères, 568n, 572

Aujoulat, Louis, 139, 155, 164

Authoritarianism, 121

Auxiliary organizations: Senegal, 45–47; Ivory Coast, 79; Ghana, 293–299, 300, 302; Liberia, 465–466; Zanzibar, 499, 500, 505; Congo, 592–595; Nigeria, 626, 630–632. *See also* Party organization

Awolowo, Obafemi, 390–391, 600, 601, 628, 635, 650; on chieftaincy, 382–383, 391; and students, 430–431

719   *Index*

Conakry
  Congress: MSA (1957), 24, 191; RDA (1955), 194
  Convention: UGTAN (1959), 360n
  Meeting: RDA (1958), 195
Conférence des Fédéralistes (1958), 26, 241
Congo, 677, 688; nationalist manifesto, 564, 575; disturbances (1959), 566; Luluabourg congress, 580; Round Table talks on, 591; and primordial ties, 689
Congress of Free Trade Unions (Ghana), 351
Conseil de l'Entente, 87–88
Constituencies, 88, 275, 286
Constitutional progressives (Ghana), 265, 267–268, 281–284
Constitutional reforms, 565; and political parties, 3; and traditional rulers, 96, 102. *See also* Loi-Cadre of 1956
Convention Africaine, 25; Dakar congress (1957), 24, 194
Coöperatives, 323; Senegal, 51, 54; Mali, 254–255; Ghana, 294–295, 298: Liberia, 470
Cornut-Gentille, Bernard, 189
Cotonou
  Congress: PRA (1958), 25
  Meeting: labor organizations (1956), 194
Coulibaly, Ouezzin, 71, 229
Coussey Commission, 271, 272, 408
CPNC, 135, 162, 163, 170, 184
CPP, 121, 271–302 *passim*, 660; members, 104, 273; and government, 259–260; as party of solidarity, 262; and factionalism, 262, 308–310; supporters, 271–273, 281; leaders, 273; and voluntary associations, 273; organization, 273–274, 299, 300–303; and elections, 274, 286, 288–289, 292; and youth groups, 274, 296–297; and chiefs, 274–275, 279; and trade-union movement, 294, 295, 297–298, 348, 349–351, 371; and coöperative movement, 294–295; and women's organizations, 296, 298–299; ideological organizations, 296–297; Study Groups, 297, 304; external relations, 308; positive-action campaign, 348
Crabbe, Kofi, 279n, 308
Creoles, 90, 100–101
Cudjoe, Hannah, 273, 299
Cults: of personality, 302, 467–468; religious, 329–334
Cultural associations, 229–230

Cummings-John, Constance, 115
CYO, 271, 273

Daarood, 513, 515, 540; and Hawiye, 517
Dahomey, 26, 241
Dakar
  Conférence des Fédéralistes Africains (1959), 242
  Congress: Convention Africaine (1957), 24, 194
Dakar-Niger railway, 242
Danquah, J. B., 267, 268, 271, 272, 275–276, 288, 292, 409; on self-government, 276; chiefly kinship of, 277; biography of, 282n
Danquah, Martin Appiah, 295n, 298
D'Arboussier, Gabriel, 232
Davies-Bright, William O., 481
Decolonization, 337, 338
De Gaulle, Charles, 194–195, 240, 565
Democratic centralism: Senegal, 42; Ivory Coast, 73, 80; Cameroun, 169; Guinea, 200, 202, 206–208
Democratic institutions: Senegal, 55–58; Ivory Coast, 87; Sierra Leone, 120; Cameroun, 177, 178, 181; students on, 439–440; Somali Republic, 552; Nigeria, 639–640
Denise, Auguste, 76, 82; on economic development, 84–85
Depression, 263, 267
DeShield, McKinley, 462–463n, 463
Development plan: Senegal, 53, 54, 58–59, 63; Guinea, 213; Mali, 254–255; Ghana, 312
Dia, Mamadou, 20, 38, 39, 52, 242; in Dec., 1962, crisis, 16n, 63; on labor leaders, 44n; on economic development, 52–53
Diagne, Blaise, 17, 18
Diallo, Abdoulaye, 239, 303, 357, 365
Diallo, Saifoulaye, 206
Diallo, Yacine, 186, 189
Dia-paying groups (Somali Republic), 512, 517
Diarchy: Ivory Coast, 70–72; Ghana, 678
Diarra, Idrissa, 250, 251; on democratic centralism, 246
Dibonge, Jobea K., 148, 149
Dicko, Hamadoun, 232, 234, 242n
Dikko, A. R. B., 605
Diola, 30
Diop, Abdou Rahmane, 35
Diop, Anta, 35
Diop, Majhemout, 57
Diop, Samba, 35
Diouf, Galandou, 18